China in Crisis VOLUME 2

China in Crisis VOLUME 2

China's Policies
in Asia
and America's
Alternatives

Edited by Tang Tsou
With a Foreword by Charles U. Daly

SBN: 226-81519-6 (clothbound); 226-81521-8 (paperbound)
Library of Congress Catalog Card Number 68-20981

The University of Chicago Press, Chicago 60637
The University of Chicago Press, Ltd., London

Foreword

China's role in world affairs has occupied scholar and official alike, but information, and the analysis of that information, have been sparse. One useful course of action in this situation is to bring together scholars concerned with China and individuals engaged in policy-making roles to promote the exchange of ideas and to give new impetus and direction to research.

The China project of The University of Chicago Center for Policy Study began in March 1966 with a series of seminars, public lectures, and less formal meetings held on the average of once a month. These sessions were supported by the New World Foundation. The meetings exposed students, faculty, and guests to experts on China's legal system, international trade, nuclear capability, foreign policy, internal policy, Sino-American diplomatic contacts, and United States military and foreign policy.

The series culminated in February 1967 with two five-day conferences supported by the University. The first was devoted to "China's Heritage and the Communist Political System." Its proceedings were published by The University of Chicago Press as the first volume in this series.

The present volume contains most of the original papers and comments discussed at the second conference, "China, the United States, and Asia." The planning of this conference was undertaken principally by the editor of this volume, Tang Tsou, professor of political science at The University of Chicago and a fellow of the Center. Professor Tsou, author of, among other works, *America's Failure in China: 1941–50,* also played a vital role in the planning of the first conference and in the editing of that volume. He included in the first volume some of the papers discussed at the second conference, since they were more concerned with continuity and change in China's political development than with matters of foreign policy.

This volume begins with Richard Lowenthal's assessment of Peking's

V

foreign policy in terms of China as a dissatisfied power. He examines Peking's setbacks within the framework of the conflict between ideology and national interests. Uri Ra'anan then documents the differing stances on foreign policy adopted by the contenders for power in China. Norton Ginsburg analyzes Peking's "concentric" view of the world. Hans Morgenthau reviews United States policy in Asia, while Robert Scalapino focuses on the "Two Chinas" dilemma. Morton H. Halperin discusses the impact of nuclear weapons on Mao's thesis of "people's war." Frank Armbruster deals with China's capability to launch conventional offensive actions and its ability to defend itself from invasion. The discussion turns to specific areas of policy in Asia with Harold Hinton's review of China's role in the Vietnam war and Donald Zagoria's assessment of the debate in Peking over strategy. Roger Hilsman deals with American response to the "people's war" and specifically with the two approaches to Vietnam which have divided the American people and government. Davis Bobrow views the adaptability of "liberation wars" in other countries and the American capability to deal with them. David Mozingo and Ruth McVey discuss Indonesian affairs: the former deals with China's role in Indonesia and the latter with the relationship between Indonesian Communism and Peking. Wayne Wilcox discusses China's diplomatic opportunities in South Asia, and A. M. Halpern examines Sino-Japanese relations.

It is our hope that the analyses presented here will lead to greater understanding of China at many levels. In an effort to increase public understanding of the issues, the Center has published a series of special papers selected from the monthly sessions and has made tapes available to radio stations. A one-day seminar was held in San Francisco following the cumulative conferences and, with the support of the Johnson Foundation of Racine, a two-day conference was convened in Chicago for editorial writers.

On behalf of the fellows of the Center, I thank all the participants, my assistant, Jonathan Kleinbard, and Chung-chi Wen, Peter Sharfman, and David Adams, graduate students at the University who helped assemble this material for publication.

CHARLES U. DALY
Director, Center for Policy Study
Vice-President,
The University of Chicago

Contents

Maps and Tables

Maps

Tables

Richard Lowenthal

1

Communist China's Foreign Policy

Motivations of a Dissatisfied Power

Communist China is today the greatest dissatisfied power in the world and therefore a major factor of international instability. This dissatisfaction is due to a combination of different causes. It is rooted both in China's national situation and history and in the ideological needs arising from the present internal problems and the historical experience of its Communist leadership.

The national situation of the Chinese People's Republic (CPR) is characterized by a striking disproportion between its power potential and the actual influence and recognition enjoyed by it on the world scene. The CPR is conscious of the fact that the size of its population and the extent of its resources make it a potential world power second to none, and even over-conscious of the actual growth of its strength and of the rapidity with which it hopes to approach the realization of this potential. Yet despite the concentration of large parts of its national energies in the military field and the spectacular advances in nuclear technology, the CPR is still unable to ensure its security by the strength of its deterrent power, is still surrounded by hostile military bases, and is still suffering from a considerable degree of diplomatic isolation. China today has atomic bombs but no allies; it is widely feared by its neighbors but has no secure sphere of influence; its possibly dangerous intentions are discussed by all, yet it is not consulted on world affairs.

The discontent arising from this disproportion is intensified by the national memory of the humiliations suffered by China at the hands of foreign powers during the century that preceded the creation of the CPR. Thus China sees itself as a former semi-colony that has at last emancipated itself from foreign tutelage and exploitation after

1

long and bitter struggles, but is still denied its rightful place in the world by the oppressors of yesterday.

The effects of China's national situation and of the national memories of the Chinese people converge with the ideological needs and the historical experience of the Chinese Communist leaders. The dictatorship of Mao Tse-tung and his supporters, like every dictatorship of a totalitarian party, finds part of the legitimation of its rule in proclaiming an irreconcilable conflict between the aims of its revolution and the aims of every non-Communist, and indeed of every non-Maoist, power: it does not pursue the limited objective of gaining a recognized place within the given international system, but the unlimited objective of overthrowing that system as a whole. The ideological need to maintain that sense of irreconcilable conflict has been made more acute by the tremendous internal problems attending the present difficult stage in China's process of industrialization: the failure of the attempt at domestic relaxation undertaken by the regime in 1956–57, when a safety-valve was opened for intellectual criticism and for the expression of "contradictions among the people," has convinced Mao and his supporters that the necessary sacrifices can only be imposed on the Chinese people in a climate of the "besieged fortress," that is, by representing every opposition to their policies as counter-revolutionary and by proclaiming the unceasing struggle against domestic counter-revolution as a sector of a world-wide front in a single irreconcilable conflict, in which all the advanced industrial nations are in the enemy camp.

In engaging in this struggle against vastly superior forces, the Chinese Communist leaders are fortified by the experience of their own road to power, which led them to victory after decades of civil war against numerically stronger and better equipped armies and in which they were repeatedly threatened with annihilation. This experience has imbued them with a belief in the fundamental instability of the power of their enemies and in the crucial role of armed violence in overthrowing it. On the analogy of their internal struggle for power, Mao and his followers thus regard their external enemies as both irreconcilable and unstable, and violence as the highroad for reaping the fruits of that instability.[1]

[1] For this interpretation of the impact of the experience of the Chinese Communists' long struggle for power on their present thinking, see Tang Tsou and Morton Halperin, "Mao Tse-tung's Revolutionary Strategy and Peking's International Behavior," in *American Political Science Review*, March, 1965. Also Richard Lowenthal, "Soviet and Chinese Communist World Views," in Donald W. Treadgold, ed., *Soviet and Chinese Communism: Similarities and Differences* (Seattle: University of Washington Press, 1967).

At the same time, this experience has not encouraged an adventurous neglect of the actual relations of forces in the day-to-day tactical conduct of the conflict. The Chinese Communists are convinced that if only they do not renounce their unlimited aims and do not confuse temporary compromises with an end to the conflict, they can afford to protract the struggle over as long a period as may be necessary and to engage in acute clashes with the enemy only when and where conditions favor them. This combination of tactical realism with strategic voluntarism enables them to maintain a posture of the utmost militancy without losing their ability to weigh the risks of particular actions.

From the above analysis of the motivations of Communist China's foreign policy, it follows that the Western discussion of whether that policy should be seen as aggressive or defensive must remain inconclusive because it is laden with semantic ambiguities. In practice, Peking's foreign policy is labeled as defensive by those who regard the ending of the disproportion between the power potential and the actual international influence of the CPR as desirable or legitimate, and as aggressive by those who wish to oppose such an adjustment. What can be said definitely is that Chinese Communist foreign policy is *not* defensive in the specific sense that the achievement of some identifiable list of limited objectives would automatically turn the CPR into a satisfied power; the importance of the ideological factor ties the regime to the pursuit of unlimited aims by irreconcilable conflict. But neither is Peking's policy aggressive in the specific sense that Communist China would, like Nazi Germany in its time, *act* on the belief in the inevitability of world war, would even view it as desirable, and would be willing to stake its existence—as a nation and as a regime—on a gamble for world power, regardless of the relation of forces at the given moment. Hence Chinese foreign policy, though pursuing unlimited aims and cultivating international tension for its own sake, has so far consistently avoided a major, direct physical challenge to either of the superpowers—be it to the Americans in Taiwan or Vietnam or to the Soviets along the disputed portions of the border.

Peking's Short-Term Objectives

Orientation to the pursuit of unlimited long-term aims does not prevent the Chinese Communist leaders from concentrating on limited objectives in their short-term practice. Most of these priority objectives are determined, as in the case of other powers, by their view of their immediate national interests; others serve the purpose of building up

Chinese ideological authority among Communist and national revolutionary movements abroad for the future.

1. Among the national objectives, the preservation and completion of national unity and of independence from any kind of foreign tutelage come first. This includes notably the recovery of Taiwan and the permanent removal of any form of subordination to Soviet "guidance." It is perfectly conceivable that the present form of acute ideological conflict with the Soviet Union may one day be succeeded by a *modus vivendi* based on a more pragmatic attitude which would permit both sides to combine cooperation in some areas with opposition in others. But it is inconceivable that any future Chinese Communist leadership would accept a return to the principle of a bloc with the Soviet Union in world affairs, based on a common ideology, as this would imply some degree of acceptance of Moscow's leading role.

2. Full international independence, in the Chinese view, necessarily includes freedom of action in the fields of economic relations and of armaments. The former means that in the interest of Chinese development, the channels of trade with the outside world, and with the advanced industrial countries in particular, must be kept open whatever the state of political tension. While advocating the cutting of economic ties with the capitalist countries throughout the underdeveloped world, the Chinese do not practice it themselves; on the contrary, they feel that their internal control is strong enough to afford an expansion of their trade with more advanced countries and even to seek credits from them. Their efforts in this field are primarily concentrated on the countries of the so-called "second intermediate zone," that is, Japan, Western Europe, and the advanced countries of the British Commonwealth; but there is no reason to assume that Peking would refuse a future revival of trade with the Soviets or the United States, if one of those powers was willing to aid China's economic development on its own terms.

3. In the field of armaments, China is determined on the untrammeled development of her growth potential as a military power. Hence Peking will not agree to any limitation of armaments, at least not until such time as effective equality with the superpowers in destructive capacity would be attained, so that China's security from attack would then be assured by its own strength.

4. Closely linked to the general objectives of national unity, independence and freedom of action are China's immediate *regional* objectives, among which the removal of the threatening military presence of the United States from the neighboring areas of Southeast and East

Asia comes first. This applies most urgently to the American presence on Taiwan, which is regarded as part of China's national territory, on portions of the Asian mainland adjoining China (Vietnam, Thailand, South Korea), and in the waters off China's shores; beyond that, it applies also to the American island bases, from Japan to the Philippines.

5. The negative objective of removing the United States from China's neighborhood is supplemented by the positive objective of establishing a secure sphere of Chinese influence, first of all in Southeast Asia, and of excluding all rival influences—Soviet, Indian, and British, as well as American—from that region. This does not necessarily imply the establishment of Communist regimes throughout that region at an early stage: the Chinese leaders seem well aware of the weakness of Communist movements in most of that area, except for Vietnam, and regard the creation of non-Communist client states of the Cambodian type as easier, less risky, and more urgent. This interpretation is suggested by the course of Chinese policy towards Burma (up to July, 1967), Nepal, and Pakistan, as well as Cambodia; even in fostering the abortive military coup of September 30, 1965, in Indonesia, the Chinese seem to have aimed not at the replacement of Sukarno by a Communist regime, but merely at strengthening the Communist and pro-Chinese influence within it by eliminating the military leaders opposed to that influence.

6. Another major national objective, in the medium-term if not in the short-term perspective, is the achievement of the world-wide recognition of China as a power without which no serious international problem can be solved. It seems unlikely, however, that Peking is envisaging this in the form of its belated acceptance as a permanent member of the United Nations Security Council; more probably it is thinking of playing its role in a series of international conferences on specific questions—somewhat on the precedent of the Geneva conference of 1954—once it feels strong enough to hope for satisfactory results.

7. Turning finally to the short-term objectives flowing from China's world-wide ideological pretensions, we may define them as the establishment of an image of China as the one major stronghold of uncompromising revolutionary struggle against the imperialist world order, and the creation of reliable cadres for the preparation of a Chinese-oriented revolutionary International throughout the world. What is intended here is the staking of a claim to China's uniqueness as a revolutionary power radically different from the "revisionist" Soviet Union—a uniqueness on which the claim to world-wide ideologi-

cal leadership can then be based; it is this foundation, not the actual direction of Communist revolutions or even the immediate creation of effective mass parties, that is regarded as urgent and feasible at the present time.

Changing Strategies

It may be assumed that most if not all of the above objectives have been in the minds of the Chinese leaders from the foundation of the Chinese People's Republic. Yet the strategies followed in seeking to achieve them have varied in response not only to changes in the international constellation, but to the growth of Chinese power and to the ideological needs generated by the internal development of the regime. It may even be asserted that the two last-named factors have been the decisive influences on Chinese Communist strategy, at times preventing any adjustment to changes in the behavior of the outside world.

Communist China first appeared on the world scene as a part of the Soviet bloc, determined to lean to one side in world affairs; this posture corresponded to a situation in which the unity of the "socialist camp" under Soviet leadership appeared to the Chinese leaders as a condition for the consolidation and growth of their power. The long duration of the initial negotiations for the Soviet-Chinese alliance, the privileged position in Manchuria on which Stalin insisted, and the combination of military sacrifices and indebtedness to the Soviets in which the Chinese got involved as a result of the Soviet-inspired Korean War leave little doubt that the Chinese had considerable reason for dissatisfaction with their treatment at Soviet hands even in Stalin's time; however, they did not then feel strong enough to show their dissatisfaction in public.

The gradual consolidation of the CPR combined with the temporary instability in the Soviet leadership after Stalin's death to enable Peking to press successfully for formal equality and greater material recognition of its interests by Moscow, as shown by the revision of the Sino-Soviet treaty of alliance in October 1954. Subsequently, the blow inflicted on Soviet ideological authority by Khrushchev's de-Stalinization was perceived by the Chinese leaders both as a danger to the cohesion of the bloc and as an opportunity to enhance their own political and ideological role within it. They evidently began to conceive the idea that their one-sided dependence on Soviet material support in the economic, military, and diplomatic fields could now be compensated by an inverse dependence of the Soviet giant on Chinese ideological support; and during the 1956–57 crisis they worked for maintaining the unity of the bloc on the basis of increased autonomy for all its members but also of general recognition of the leadership of the Soviet Union in foreign policy and basic doctrine—a leadership they hoped to influence decisively.

This hope was disappointed in the course of 1958–59 by the Soviet refusal to aid Chinese economic development to the extent expected, to respect Chinese prestige in the Middle-East crisis of the summer of 1958, to take risks on behalf of Chinese interests in the Quemoy crisis, to aid China's development of nuclear weapons, and to back China in the dispute with India in 1959, as well as by Khrushchev's efforts to develop a dialogue with the United States. As a result, the Chinese began to see Soviet foreign policy as an obstacle to the further growth of their own power, and to supplement pressure within the alliance by the gradual elaboration of an alternative diplomatic and ideological line—a line which burst into the open in their public challenge to Soviet leadership of the bloc and of the world Communist movement in 1960.

Despite the formal compromise reached in the Communist world conference at the end of that year, subsequent Chinese behavior showed the intention to maintain that challenge and to engage in a long-term factional rivalry for leadership with the Soviets. But the conflict became generalized and more important to Peking than the remnant of cooperation only when the second de-Stalinization and the adoption of a new party program at the Twenty-second Congress of the CPSU convinced Mao and his followers that the Soviet Union was embarking on a "revisionist" course of internal development—the liquidation of the class struggle at home—the example of which could endanger the internal stability of the Chinese Communist regime no less seriously than Soviet foreign policy endangered its national interests.

From then on Chinese policy developed rapidly towards an open political and ideological break with the Soviet Union, a break which was consummated in the charges of betrayal that followed the Soviet's retreat from Cuba and particularly their signing of the test-ban treaty. Thereafter, the struggle for leadership *within* a divided bloc and movement was clearly replaced by the open proclamation of Peking as an *independent* factor of world politics and the center of a *new* worldwide movement.

By the time of Khrushchev's fall, a point had been reached where China's internal need to expose the "capitalist degeneration" of the Soviet system had become more important to Mao than any material advantages that might have been gained from an ideological truce. Chinese strategy towards the Soviet Union is now primarily geared to its ideological exposure by an uncompromising rejection of any joint conferences or any form of cooperation, even on behalf of Vietnam.

Chinese policies towards the new states of Asia and Africa have undergone repeated major changes under the influence of the same main factors. At first the Chinese were slow—though less slow than the Soviets under Stalin—to recognize the effective political independence of the new states and started from a position of doctrinaire hostility towards all of them, including the support of armed Communist uprisings against their governments. But with the consolidation of their own internal position, the Chinese were able to grasp the diplomatic opportunity offered by the rise of neutralist states in Asia and Africa and to respond to the need to avoid an encirclement by anti-Communist alliances. The "Bandung strategy," seeking a united front of the Communist powers and the ex-colonial neutrals under the slogans of anti-imperialism and peaceful coexistence, considerably improved China's diplomatic position during the period of 1954–58.

From 1959 onward, however, the pressures of China's internal troubles, particularly in Tibet, of regional competition for influence against India, and of ideological rivalry with the Soviets for the support of revolutionary movements in the Third World have combined to cause Peking to abandon that strategy. Ever since then, China has continued full, undoctrinaire support only for Afro-Asian governments and movements that are either involved in active conflict with the imperialists, as were the Algerian FLN and Indonesia in the later years, or willing to accept the status of Chinese client states, like Nepal and until recently Cambodia; but it has adopted an attitude of bitter hostility, not only towards the pro-Western states, but towards strong independent neutrals not engaged in conflict with the West, like India or at times Egypt.

Out of this distinction there have developed in recent years one general and one regional strategy. The general strategy was an effort to induce a majority of the Afro-Asian governments to accept China as the champion of their common cause and to commit themselves to a policy that would be both anti-American and anti-Soviet—a policy that was to find expression in the second Bandung conference, actively promoted by China in 1964–65. The regional strategy worked toward creation of a militant anti-Western axis in South and Southeast Asia, based on cooperation with the governments of Indonesia, Pakistan,

Cambodia, and possibly Burma and Nepal, as well as with the Vietnamese Communists, and directed against India and Malaysia as much as against the West. Both strategies were clearly aimed at the eventual creation of a "counter-United Nations," based on the "new emerging forces" of the Third World, which was to have started from the regional bloc and to have expanded by means of its influence within the larger Afro-Asian group.

Throughout all phases, Chinese policy vis-à-vis the Western powers has distinguished sharply between policies towards the main enemy, the United States, and towards the states of the "second intermediate zone." China has never hesitated to support militant anticolonial movements against the latter—as against France in Indochina and Algeria, Britain in Malaya, or Holland in Indonesia—even while seeking to maintain normal trade relations and, if possible, a minimum of diplomatic relations with them at the same time. But it has always seen the United States not only as the leader of the imperialist camp, but as the irreconcilable national enemy—the one-time backer of its opponents in the civil war, the "interventionist" whose forces took countless Chinese lives in Korea, and the power whose presence prevents China from recovering Taiwan. Chinese policy towards the United States has been consistent, however, both in maintaining a spirit of confrontation in unremitting hostility, and in avoiding a direct challenge to all-out war. The technique of issuing "serious warnings" to the United States, combined with the preservation of a minimum of diplomatic contact in Prague or Warsaw, expresses both aspects of that policy. Chinese efforts, at an earlier stage, to commit the Soviets to a similarly uncompromising attitude and, more recently, to involve as many Afro-Asian states as possible in conflicts with the United States, must also be seen largely as strategies for weakening the main enemy, America, and diverting and dispersing its strength. In addition, Chinese support for "revolutionary wars of liberation" today has its principal strategic function in this context.

Based on the experience of the Chinese Communists' own rise to power, support of partisan warfare in the colonial, semi-colonial, and ex-colonial areas of Asia was viewed as one of China's most promising international weapons in the early years of the CPR, before the importance and the possibility of obtaining diplomatic support from nonrevolutionary, uncommitted governments of ex-colonial countries had been perceived. After 1958–59, disappointment with the Soviets and rivalry with India converged with Peking's domestic ideological needs to cause it to give increasing emphasis to this specific revolutionary activity throughout the Third World—in Africa and Latin America no less than in Asia. The model of the Chinese Communists' "People's War" against Japan is now invoked to recommend the most varied types of armed insurrection in "the countryside of the world," ranging from broadly based mass movements, as in Algeria and Vietnam, to tribal uprisings, as in Cameroon, the former Belgian Congo, or Ruanda, and to the activities of small bands of isolated (and often imported) terrorists, as in Venezuela and Bolivia.[2] The only strategic criterion is that these movements must serve to undermine the stability of governments that are allied or friendly to the United States, including independent neutrals not willing to engage in conflict with them; they must never be directed against governments involved in conflict with the West or willing, in the case of Asian neighbors, to accept Chinese tutelage. This exception applies regardless of the social and ideological character of such governments, even to the authoritarian regimes of pro-Chinese traditional rulers. *A fortiori,* there can be no "people's war" against pro-Chinese "progressive" governments: it is precisely because the abortive Indonesian *coup* of September 30, 1965, was *not* directed against Sukarno's government that it was prepared as a purely technical operation, without the slightest attempt at mobilizing the large Communist following for a popular uprising.

The strategic concept underlying the Chinese propaganda of "people's wars," then, is to obtain a maximum of dispersal and attrition of American strength with a minimum commitment of China's own power and without ever risking a direct military clash between Chinese and American forces. It is not a strategy for an all-out offensive to force an expansion 'of Chinese-dominated territory, but for making the American presence in the region bordering China increasingly costly while seeking to cause an increasing drain on American power in other regions of the world at the same time. Nor is it a strategy for generally

---

[2] The slogan of encircling the industrialized "world cities" by the uprising of the "countryside of the world," on the analogy of Chinese domestic experience, was first formulated by the late leader of the Indonesian Communist Party, D. N. Aidit, in a speech printed as a pamphlet in English under the title *Set Afire the "Banteng" Spirit! Ever Forward, No Retreat!* (Peking: Foreign Languages Press, 1964). It was quoted approvingly by the former Chinese Politburo member P'eng Chen at the Djakarta celebration on the 45th anniversary of the foundation of the Indonesian party (*Peking Review,* June 11, 1965)—before being taken over by his successful rival, Lin Piao, in his much-quoted speech at the 20th anniversary celebration of China's victory over Japan ("Long Live the Victory of the People's War," *Peking Review,* Sept. 3, 1965).

attempting the creation of Chinese-type Communist regimes at the present stage: the Chinese leaders consider that many of the under-developed nations among whom they promote revolutionary uprisings are only at a level of consciousness corresponding to China's Taiping insurrection of more than a century ago and lack the experience and the cadres necessary for a Communist victory—but that this does not make them less effective in weakening China's main enemy.

As stated above, the creation of such cadres that would be dedicated and consistent revolutionaries trained in the Maoist version of Marx-ism-Leninism and oriented to the Chinese model is Peking's short-term objective in the ideological field. Both Peking's intransigent rejection of any form of cooperation with the Soviet "revisionists" and its insist-ence on supporting so-called "people's wars" in various parts of the world, regardless of the ideological level of the movement or of its chances of mass support, must therefore also be seen as strategies di-rected to this purpose: the recruiting and training of cadres for a new and truly revolutionary International under Peking's leadership. The adoption of armed struggle as the criterion of an authentic revolution-ary movement, rooted in the history of the Chinese Communists' own struggle for power, and the dogmatic assertion that the Soviet leader-ship is on the road to capitalist restoration and committed to coopera-tion with the United States imperialists, hence opposed to the libera-tion of the exploited peoples and unacceptable as a partner in aiding their struggle, are both intended to establish the uniqueness of Com-munist China as the only stronghold of revolutionary movements and the only fountainhead of a consistent revolutionary doctrine. On the organizational level, this has led Peking to the rejection of any joint international conferences with the Soviets, to efforts to make all Com-munist parties that sympathize with Peking's views cut any party rela-tions with Moscow, to the encouragement of splits and the creation of new Peking-oriented parties wherever Peking's supporters are in a minority (not only in the Third World, but also in the advanced Western countries, and even underground in some countries of the Soviet bloc), and to the initiation of training schools for cadres from some African countries in which no Communist parties exist.

Achievements and Failures

If we compare Chinese achievements during the past eighteen years with the presumed priority objectives listed above, we are forced to the conclusion that the results have been extremely uneven. The CPR has certainly been successful in consolidating the unity of the national territory except for Taiwan, at least if we leave out of account the as yet uncertain effects of the crisis of the regime provoked by Mao's Cultural Revolution. It has established beyond any possible doubt its complete independence from Soviet aid and Soviet ideological guidance at the price of considerable economic setbacks and of losing the certainty of protection by the Soviet deterrent against military attack. It has increased its trade with the advanced capitalist countries, except for the United States, and has even obtained credits from them; and it will be able to keep these channels open in the future, so long as it avoids destroying its export capacity by domestic upheavals or paralyzing the functioning of Hong Kong by anti-colonial campaigns. It has made great strides in developing nuclear weapons of its own without submitting to any kind of international agreement on the limitation or control of armaments, and it has good prospects of further remarkable advances in arms technology so long as it continues to give the present priority to that sector of science and industry and to grant the specialists in this field immunity from political interference.

On the other hand, Communist China has made no progress whatever in removing the hostile American bases from its neighborhood; on the contrary, it is today faced with a major increase in the American presence on the Asian continent, which combines with the state of tension along the Soviet frontier to create a situation perceived by Peking as approaching military encirclement by hostile powers. China's regional influence in Southeast Asia, which in earlier years was growing remarkably, though without ever amounting to the creation of a secure and exclusive power sphere, has declined dramatically in recent years. The disproportion between China's strength and its voice in world affairs has become greater rather than smaller. Even China's ideological influence among foreign Communist parties and revolutionary nationalist movements abroad appears much more limited today than five years ago; and the extent of progress in the training of reliable Maoist cadres in other countries, while admittedly difficult to judge, must seem at least doubtful.

A survey of the causes of these important setbacks and partial failures suggests that they have not only, and perhaps not even mainly, been due to the determined resistance of Peking's enemies, but to a growing extent also to the contradiction between the ideologically inspired strategies adopted by the Chinese leaders since 1958 and the realities of the international scene.

The Chinese policy of seeking a united front with the uncommitted states of Asia and Africa against the imperialists in general, and of actively fomenting conflicts between individual new states and the Western powers, was in principle well designed to serve Chinese interests, and indeed did so for a time. But the Chinese initiative to make the tenth anniversary of the Bandung conference, at which that policy had been inaugurated, the occasion for a second Bandung was linked with an attempt to assert Chinese leadership over the new states by turning the conference into an anti-American demonstration and, at the same time, by excluding the Soviet Union from participation. This amounted to an effort to get a majority of non-Communist governments to commit themselves to a policy that would be both anti-American and anti-Soviet, hence to renounce development aid from both the Western and Soviet blocs—an effort that was clearly beyond China's strength. Its obvious lack of realism suggested that ideological concepts about the anti-imperialist solidarity of the underdeveloped countries had blinded the Chinese leaders to the plainly visible interests of the countries and governments concerned. After vainly resisting the first postponement of the conference in June 1965, the Chinese themselves had to take the initiative for the second and final adjournment when it became obvious that they would be unable to control its decisions. The defeat they had thus to acknowledge was aggravated by the fact that their revolutionary propaganda had unintentionally created the impression that Peking intended to foment revolutions against some of the very same Afro-Asian governments which it was seeking to line up against Washington and Moscow.

The attempt to create a regional anti-Western axis as the nucleus of a counter-United Nations in Southeast Asia has suffered even more serious setbacks in recent years. Close cooperation with Sukarno's Indonesia was to have been the core of that axis, and it appeared to have made striking progress as Sukarno successively committed himself to the rejection of neutralism, the confrontation with Malaysia, opposition to the United Nations, and support for the Chinese plans for a second Bandung. Yet as he moved further and further along Peking's line at the expense of the economic viability of his country, the balance between the Communist and anti-Communist elements previously backing his government became increasingly precarious; and a clash became inevitable. Presumably without wishing to impose Communist rule on Indonesia at the present stage, Peking was thus in part responsible for pushing Sukarno into the untenable position which ended with the failure of the pro-Communist coup, the massacre of Peking's staunchest supporters, and the creation of an anti-Communist government that within a few months returned to the U.N., liquidated the confrontation, and turned to bitter hostility towards Communist China.

Also in 1965, the ineffectiveness of Peking's attempt to back Pakistan against India by the threat of opening a second front led to another setback of an importance second only to that of the Indonesian disaster. When Peking was deterred from carrying out its threats—presumably by both American and Soviet warnings—Pakistan was forced to seek Soviet mediation without Chinese participation. Though the Tashkent Conference brought no solution to the Indian-Pakistani conflict, it did bring a defeat for China. More recently, attempts to export the Cultural Revolution have led to diplomatic conflicts with Burma and Cambodia as well; and despite the settlement of the latter by Chinese concessions, the net result is that at the time of writing, hardly anything remains of the "regional axis."

Nor has the encouragement of wars of national liberation been more successful in fostering the achievement of China's objectives. As we have suggested, Peking's direct national interest in these wars is to tie down American forces in widely dispersed areas where they do not threaten Chinese security. Yet on one side, no serious "people's war" has erupted in regions far from China's shores since Algerian independence was finally achieved in 1962; none of the recent tribal uprisings in Africa and none of the guerrilla actions started by Castro's supporters in Latin America have reached a level where they could constitute a drain on American strength. On the other hand, Peking appears to have encouraged the Vietnamese Communists to renew a major insurrection in the South in 1959–60, at least partly in order to win the competition against the Soviets for their allegiance; and later the Chinese leaders have presented Vietnam as a test case for the invincible force of their type of "people's war." As the United States administration, taking the ideology at its face value, has chosen to accept the challenge, this has led to a vastly increased commitment of American forces in Vietnam and Thailand, hence in China's immediate neighborhood.

Finally, the policy of demonstrating China's uniqueness as a revolutionary power and of influencing the international movement by rejecting all cooperation with the Soviet "traitors" appeared easy so long as it required only a rejection of Khrushchev's invitation to an international conference of Communist parties at which China's ideological "deviations" were to be condemned. It became much more difficult when Khrushchev's successors suggested, from November 1964 onwards, an end to active Sino-Soviet polemics, with each side maintaining its different ideological viewpoint, and a resumption of cooperation in support of the Vietnamese Communists, and even more difficult when, in the face of American bombing, the Soviets resumed active arms deliveries to Vietnam and, at the same time, postponed the international party conference. Acceptance of the Soviet offer in these circumstances would have been perfectly compatible with Chinese independence and dignity. Its rejection by Mao Tse-tung, due to the ideological need to use the specter of Soviet revisionism at home and to the ideological desire to continue unmasking Soviet "treachery" abroad, had the effect of increasingly isolating not the Soviet but the Chinese Communists in the international movement: such formerly pro-Chinese parties as the Korean and Japanese Communists have criticized the Chinese attitude as have the Cuban Communists, and the Vietnamese Communists themselves have expressed their disagreement by paying equal public tribute to Soviet and Chinese aid. As the consequences of the Chinese refusal of all offers of a united front were reinforced by the negative impression caused by the Cultural Revolution, even the left-wing Communist party established in India with Chinese support felt the need to emphasize its independence from Peking; and after the physical destruction of the Indonesian party, this left only the Albanians and a number of splinter groups firmly committed to Chinese guidance.

Alternatives and Prospects

The growth of the potential danger to Chinese security as a result of the escalation of the war in Vietnam and of the increased American presence in Southeast Asia, as well as the severity of the setbacks to Chinese influence in Indonesia, Pakistan, and throughout Southeast Asia, in the Afro-Asian and in the international Communist movement have, of course, been perceived by the Chinese leaders. The cumulation of some of the most dramatic of those setbacks in 1965 is even likely to have aggravated the conflicts that already existed within that leadership, and thus to have contributed to the open outbreak of the internal crisis of the regime in the following year. That crisis, in turn, by bringing about a further increase in Peking's ideological fervor and a period of even more exclusive preoccupation with domestic "struggles," has temporarily prevented the leaders from making a realistic analysis of the setbacks and drawing conclusions in the direction of a new change of strategy. The paroxysm of the purge has meant a temporary paralysis of foreign policy.

Assuming, however, that the CPR will somehow survive the crisis and that one or another faction will be able to consolidate its hold on all or at least the essential part of its territory, the victorious faction will sooner or later have to acknowledge the basic lesson of the period of self-isolation, that with the present relation of forces, it is self-defeating for China to pursue a policy of equally acute antagonism towards both superpowers. Logically, this would leave Peking with three possible alternative strategies.

The first alternative would consist of seeking a measure of accommodation with the Soviets sufficient to regain Soviet backing against the United States, even while maintaining China's diplomatic and doctrinal independence from Moscow. Such a strategy would not require a return to world-wide ideological solidarity with the Soviet Union but only an attitude of pragmatic flexibility under which Peking could at one and the same time cooperate with the Soviet Union in Vietnam and oppose it in India. The Soviets, in accordance with their earlier offers, would probably be willing to accept Chinese cooperation on those terms, because it would meet their tendency to adjourn the major conflict with China in order to give priority to a renewal of pressure on the West. The development of China's power potential would be accelerated by such a policy of partial cooperation with Russia, and Peking would thus become a more real danger to the West.

In terms of the attitudes of the outside world, this would seem to be the most realistic of the options that are logically open to Peking; yet it is not open in practice to Mao Tse-tung and his faction, who, for domestic reasons, are committed to doctrinaire hostility to the Soviet Union as representing the danger of "capitalist degeneration" they are fighting at home. The choice of this alternative thus presupposes the internal defeat of Mao and his faction; indeed, as other contributions to this volume suggest, there is evidence that some of Mao's opponents have been charged precisely with the crime of favoring conditional acceptance of the Soviet offers of a united front.

The second logically conceivable alternative would be the exact opposite—to seek a temporary détente with the United States in order to concentrate on the conflict with the Soviet Union. This option would be more in tune with Mao's present preoccupations than the first, but it would meet formidable difficulties both on the ideological and the realistic side. Ideologically, such a course would still be extremely hard to swallow for the bulk of the Chinese or pro-Chinese Communists; its adoption would thus presuppose the complete and unchallenged victory of the Maoists at home and would even then carry the risk of further setbacks in the international competition with the Soviets. Realistically, the terms for such a détente with the United States would be almost impossible to define, both because of the objectively acute and serious character of the conflict of interests opposing both powers over Taiwan, Vietnam, and Thailand, and because a possible American partner for such a policy is not at present visible.

To speak more concretely, a Chinese-American détente will at least require the establishment of a kind of neutral zone in Southeast Asia; but it would be very late in the day for China to accept a settlement in which such a zone would comprise a non-Communist South Vietnam guaranteed by both sides, and there is little prospect that the present United States administration would accept the establishment of a neutral zone, requiring American withdrawal from South Vietnam and Thailand, under any other conditions. A Chinese-American détente on terms that any conceivable Chinese leadership could afford to accept and could impose on its Vietnamese allies thus does not, barring a major change in American policy, appear as a realistic option.

The third conceivable alternative would be a bold attempt to achieve a temporary improvement of relations with both superpowers at once. Because Soviet policy towards China, as we have seen, is at present more flexible than American policy, this could in practice only take the form of agreeing with the Soviets on a joint approach to the United States for the reduction of war-like tensions in Southeast Asia; in that sense, the third alternative would be a variant of the first rather than of the second. It follows that this is not an option open to Mao and his faction, because China would in this case both have to accept the Soviets as partners and to accept their method of seeking compromises with the United States, which Mao has unceasingly denounced for the last eight years. But a Chinese leadership not committed to Maoist ideological extremism could use this approach to combine joint Sino-Soviet pressure on the Americans with offers of a settlement; if such offers were not accepted by the United States as a basis for negotiations, they would at least have the effect both of improving China's influence among the neutral states of Southeast Asia and in the Third World generally, and of strengthening China's case in the continuing argument with the Soviets about the right way of dealing with the United States.

Given the present policy of the United States, the conclusion emerging from our analysis would appear to be that Communist China has only the choice of continuing the present foreign policy of self-isolation under Maoist leadership or of seeking, after a change of leadership, to improve her relations with the Soviet Union in order to confront the United States with the alternatives of accepting a compromise amounting to retreat or of isolating itself in its turn. The pressures of China's international position, like the needs of China's economic development and the effects of the crisis of the regime brought about by Mao's Cultural Revolution, are thus likely to militate against a long continuation of the Maoist course.

Comments by Roderick MacFarquhar

As always, I find myself in substantial agreement with much of what Professor Lowenthal has written. My principal dissent is with his conclusion that the basic lesson of China's period of "self-isolation" is that "with the present relation of forces, it is self-defeating for China to pursue a policy of equally acute antagonism toward both the superpowers." In reaching this conclusion, Professor Lowenthal points out that American power in Asia, which the Chinese would like eradicated, has in fact increased; that Chinese influence in Southeast Asia has diminished; that Chinese influence among foreign Communist parties and revolutionary nationalist movements has shrunk. True enough, but this does not mean the Chinese must mend their ways if they are to do better.

In the first place, I do not believe the Chinese have to assign themselves as much blame for the worst setbacks as Professor Lowenthal apparently thinks. He says, for instance, that Peking appears to have encouraged the Vietnamese Communists to renew a major insurrection in the south in 1959–60 which has led to an increased American commitment on China's borders. But P. J. Honey indicates that the decision to start guerrilla operations was taken in Hanoi, and for domestic reasons.[1] Furthermore, it has been argued that the American decision to intervene in strength in Vietnam was the result of the Vietnamese Communists forcing the pace and that the Chinese disapproved of their

[1] *Communism in North Vietnam* (Cambridge, Mass.: MIT Press, 1963), pp. 66–68.

tactics. And even if the Chinese were responsible in some measure for the presence of half a million American soldiers in South Vietnam, if the final outcome is an American withdrawal and a gradual Vietnamese Communist takeover, Peking would clearly be quite satisfied.

Again, take Indonesia. Professor Lowenthal phrases himself carefully ("Presumably without wishing to impose Communist rule on Indonesia at the present stage, Peking was thus in part responsible for pushing Sukarno into the untenable position which ended with the failure of the pro-Communist coup . . ."), but clearly implies an activist Peking policy ending in disaster. It is my impression that most specialists on Indonesia do not attribute a really significant role to China in the *Gestapu* incident, but stress rather the importance of autonomous, indigenous factors.

In short, I believe that in these and a number of other cases, the Chinese leadership can legitimately hold that their cause has suffered from other people's blundering or from misfortunes rather than from the pursuit of incorrect policies by Peking.

But there is a second and more fundamental reason why the Chinese leadership should not conclude that their present policy of equally acute antagonism towards both superpowers is self-defeating. Any modification of that policy—for instance, in the direction of one of Professor Lowenthal's three suggested alternatives—would inevitably lead to the erosion of China's determination to achieve what Professor Lowenthal calls her "unlimited objective of overthrowing [the international] system as a whole." To Mao's lifelong hatred of imperialism is now added his obsessional fear of the degeneration of Communism; to compromise with either the chief imperialist or the chief revisionist power would represent not just a tactical retreat but an abandonment of the Maoist vision of a truly Communist world in the interests of more limited national objectives. In other words, the policy of hostility towards both superpowers may undermine some short-term objectives, but in the long term it will not be self-defeating because it is in fact the only policy that could lead to the attainment of the ultimate Maoist vision. The policy may entail a long and frustrating vigil under siege conditions—revolution in one country, and only cultural revolution at that—but as Professor Lowenthal indicates, the Chinese Communists' experience in the civil war gives them an innate self-confidence for the long haul. Professor Lowenthal realizes that a Maoist faction would find it virtually impossible to embrace any of his three alternatives; he has not pointed out that if a non-, anti-, or post-Maoist faction were to embrace one of those alternatives, it would entail a radical alteration in the catalogue of Chinese objectives which he has listed.

My other comments are more in the nature of glosses, and I will only mention the more important one. I think Professor Lowenthal under-rates Peking's current interest in getting into the United Nations. I would agree that a major Chinese aim is to sit down at important international conferences, the acknowledged equal of Russia and America; indeed, I would argue that Peking sees her nuclear armory more as an entry ticket to such conferences than as protection against possible attack. But Peking realizes that much diplomatic business is transacted at the United Nations and would certainly want to be there in order to rouse the Third World and prevent the passage of nonrevolutionary resolutions on, for instance, Middle East crises. I believe, too, that the record indicates that the Chinese toyed only briefly with Sukarno's NEFO United Nations project, realizing its limited appeal and its basic instability if Sukarno were to play a large role in promoting it.

There are one or two points I would like to make also about changes in Chinese policy. Professor Lowenthal argues that it was the failure of the Hundred Flowers that led Mao and his supporters to decide on the necessity of the besieged fortress atmosphere to induce the requisite sacrifices from the people. This analysis overlooks the significant domestic relaxation that attended the collapse of the Great Leap Forward in the early sixties. Indeed it appears to have been the dissent that emerged during this latter period—dissent no longer among "bourgeois intellectuals" but, far more dangerous, among party officials—coupled with developments in the Soviet Union, that convinced Mao of the urgency of staging a "cultural revolution."

Of course, Professor Lowenthal is obviously right in pointing to the Hundred Flowers fiasco as the event which led Mao to initiate that first phase of domestic upheaval. Yet, strangely, he does not stress the importance of the fiasco in altering China's *immediate* foreign policy objectives, perhaps because he believes that China has been consistent in its unremitting hostility towards the United States. It seems to me, however, that the collapse of the Hundred Flowers policy helped Mao to decide to liquidate a policy of exploring the possibilities of the "peaceful liberation" of Taiwan via détente with the United States and compromise with Chiang Kai-shek. Chou En-lai, it will be remembered, initiated the ambassadorial talks with the United States in 1955. Although the United States was still denounced, the tone was less shrill. Chou let it be known that the Communists were ready to cooperate again with the Nationalists, hinting that an honorable position would be found for Chiang in Peking. By 1957 it was becoming clear that the policy was not paying off. Dulles was more concerned about building up SEATO. The Nationalists did not even respond to the "We're all Chinese together" propaganda that Peking issued during anti-American riots in Taiwan. But the coup de grâce was given to the policy when Mao decided he had to squash the "bourgeois intellectuals"; once that happened, no one in Taiwan was going to believe Communist protestations that a new era of good feelings was possible. Most of Chiang's civilian supporters were precisely the kind of people who were denounced in the anti-bourgeois rightist campaign that followed the Hundred Flowers period.

A final word on Chinese "aggressiveness." Professor Lowenthal differentiates between China and Nazi Germany on the grounds that China would not gamble for world power "regardless of the relation of forces at the given moment." This suggests that Professor Lowenthal believes that though the men in Peking are more careful than the Nazis, given appropriate military strength they might use it in the pursuit of their unlimited ideological aims. Clearly, Mao does not shrink from the use of force, but I subscribe to the view that where he has used it—Korea, the Indian border—he has done so for defensive reasons. The essential Maoist strategy, as laid down in Lin Piao's article on people's war, states that the achievement of Peking's unlimited ideological goal—a Maoist world—is to come via indigenous revolutions, on the Chinese pattern, throughout the Third World. This plan does not call for Chinese military intervention; indeed it precludes it, because the Maoist line is that native revolutionaries should always be able to go it alone successfully. If China ever has to intervene, for instance, in Vietnam after an appeal for help from Hanoi, it would mean the Maoist strategy had failed. In short, I do not think the Maoist texts indicate "aggressiveness" in the conventional use of that term. Furthermore, those texts do not express a belief in the inevitability of *world* war, but only war. The Chinese attitude on world war is that it is not inevitable, but that if the imperialists were to "impose" it, then Communism would emerge triumphant.

Uri Ra'anan

2

Peking's Foreign Policy "Debate," 1965–1966

Introduction

This paper attempts to establish whether a detailed textual analysis of documents concerning Peking's political strategy can produce significant clues about the policies advocated by various Chinese factions in 1965–66, the period immediately preceding the climax of the Great Cultural Revolution. Scholars have been understandably hesitant to indulge in so speculative an exercise, since very little could be known outside China of the real nature of personal relationships at Mao's "court"; it was also felt, correctly, that foreign affairs do not normally occupy first place on Peking's order of priorities. Nevertheless, prolonged immersion in Chinese policy documents can enable the analyst to come up with significant, if tantalizingly fragmentary, evidence, indicating that the present conflicts among Chinese leaders, whatever their deeper ideological and personal causes, are at least not totally unrelated to serious differences between various groups on vital questions of Peking's international strategy. Needless to say, within the complex of China's internal arguments on global policy, the future of Peking's tangled triangular relationship with Moscow and Washington has been the central problem at issue. Obviously, this question cannot be separated from related matters, such as the running debate over the posture to be adopted by China's armed forces, the problem of Peking's policy towards Vietnam, China's relationship with the "minor" Western powers and with Afro-Asian regimes, as well as economic and other domestic issues, including the ideological and personal conflicts of the last two years.

From early 1965 onward, Peking was confronted with a situation which required a comprehensive policy decision, determining China's future global posture. For a number of reasons, the Peking leadership was unable to reach a clear-cut decision at that time; instead, a policy

23

"debate," held in characteristically esoteric language, broke into print. Of course, this is not an unknown phenomenon among Communist elites during periods in which a temporary balance of power among competing groups prevents the imposition of a single point of view. More surprising is the lengthy duration of the debate; it erupted early in February of 1965 and continued for that entire year, with last echoes still to be heard as late as the summer of 1966.

In a major convulsion, such as China is experiencing now, which determines the political and, probably, the personal survival of the various leaders, their consistency in matters of policy cannot be taken for granted. The history of the last half century is full of instances in which the victorious faction appropriated the ideological slogans of the vanquished, once the originators of these slogans were safely out of the way. Moreover, alignments on global questions, during the last few years, were apparently *not* identical with the domestic divisions which observers have inferred from Red Guard "big-character posters" and from the more esoteric press attacks against the opponents of the "Mao-Lin" faction. This may be one of the typical cases in which a leader embarked on a purge has lumped together his various adversaries in one category, although, in fact, they belong to very different schools of thought. Since Peking's factional alignments over external, domestic, and personal issues apparently have not coincided, it is also possible that kaleidoscopic realignments occurred from one showdown to the next; thus, political reality may have been far too complex to warrant the usual simplistic presentations.

The present paper is concerned only with the problem of factional differences over international and strategic questions; it does not attempt to provide an all-embracing framework into which overlapping patterns of alignment on domestic and personal issues can be fitted neatly and consistently.

As for methodology, the present analysis has concentrated upon certain highlights of the "debate," during which a specific aspect of the global situation was treated by two or more Chinese leaders in clearly contrasting terms (in many instances on the same day and on consecutive pages of the same journal). In most cases, by simply juxtaposing the relevant paragraphs from two different statements dealing with the same question, it is possible to see immediately that significant words and phrases used by one leader were omitted or altered by another. In view of the great importance attached to the precise wording of operative sentences throughout the Communist world (as the polemics of the Sino-Soviet conflict testify so clearly), and in view of the particular Chinese penchant for esoteric communication (exemplified by the controversy concerning the historical play "Hai Jui Dismissed From Office"), there can be little serious doubt about the significant implications of such textual differences. Moreover, allowing for the exigencies of a changing situation, the views advocated by the various political personalities were, in most cases, quite consistent throughout the period. In other words, whatever direction Peking's general line may have been taking, the words of one leader will generally be found to have deviated some 20 degrees east, and those of another about 20 degrees west. This is unlikely to have been mere coincidence.

Needless to say, textual analysis is still far from being an exact science. Not all statements couched in Aesopian language refer to events in the public domain, some alluding to developments which are not known from other sources and cannot readily be identified. Moreover, Chinese speakers, in discussing foreign affairs, are addressing several audiences at once: their domestic opponents, the general public at home, potential allies abroad, and the world at large. It is not always possible to distinguish arguments aimed at one audience from messages intended for another. Nevertheless, with all due reservation, textual analysis can and usually does add significantly to the insight which the observer of Communist affairs can bring to bear; hopefully, China is no exception to this rule.

The evidence examined here suggests the existence of at least four groups, as far as their views on international issues were concerned. These appear to have coalesced into two major factions that divided over such vital issues as China's future military posture and the build-up of its armed forces, the options available in Vietnam and, above all, whether the United States or the USSR was to be treated as the main enemy in the immediate future.

Within the army, two groups of officers fought out a bitter and protracted battle. The "professional" faction, led by Chief of Staff Lo Jui-ch'ing, argued that an early military confrontation with the main forces of the United States was highly probable. Thus it was necessary to create a modern, sophisticated, relatively small and highly mobile army, equipped and trained with Soviet assistance. Moreover, Chinese forces would have to rely upon the Soviet nuclear deterrent to keep the battle on reasonably equal and non-catastrophic terms. Therefore, at least a conditional and limited reconciliation between Peking and Moscow was required.

While the professionals admitted that the Soviet political leadership had not always treated China well, they insisted that in the event of conflict with the enemy, "reliable" people in Moscow, headed by the Red Army, would certainly overrule the "Khrushchev revisionists." Specifically in relation to Vietnam, the professionals maintained that guerrilla tactics were not the final answer to all problems, and that "unity of action" between Moscow and Peking would enable both countries to give more meaningful aid to North Vietnam's main-line forces. They apparently favored a positive Chinese response to Moscow's request for airfields in southern China which could be used to provide Soviet air cover for Hanoi.

Ranged against Lo and his professionals was another military group, consisting of "political" or "guerrilla" officers and headed by Defense Minister Lin Piao. Lin's faction strongly resented the insinuations of Chief of Staff Lo that the defense ministry had taken inadequate steps to prepare the armed forces for all eventualities. The guerrillas ruled out any reconciliation with the Soviet Union, on the grounds that "unity of action" would give the Russians dangerous control over China's military and political moves.

They also insisted that it was unnecessary because early war with the West was highly improbable. If Peking only encouraged other people to wage guerrilla struggles against the West, and if China itself refrained from all forms of direct involvement, there would be no reason for a confrontation with the United States. Even in the unlikely event that such a clash did occur, it would be sufficient to mobilize China's masses gradually, while withdrawing into the interior. Eventually, the invader would be submerged by China's millions employing their traditional guerrilla methods.

If the Lin strategy were followed in Asia, Africa, or Latin America, the United States would certainly not use nuclear weapons to cope with essentially domestic struggles in other parts of the world, so that the existence of a Soviet nuclear deterrent would hardly be relevant. The guerrilla group went on to stress that, at this particular stage, it was the "modern revisionists" in Moscow who were the immediate enemy, not the West. The Soviet Union was a hostile and treacherous neighbor, who would inevitably stab China in the back if it were to become involved in a battle with the West.

In addition, unlike the "imperialists," the "modern revisionists" were attempting to interfere in China's domestic problems and had ways of influencing the local scene. "Khrushchev's successors" must be fought "to the end"; that was the only way to clear the decks for a later struggle against imperialism. In fact, this meant that the fight against the United States would be relegated to a much lower place on China's agenda—a matter to be taken up at some unknown distant date when "victory" had been won over the Soviets.

These arguments between the rival military factions were reflected in similar conflicts among the top civilian cadres. The main leaders of the entrenched Chinese Communist Party (CCP) bureaucracy, especially Liu Shao-ch'i (Mao's heir presumptive before Lin Piao's elevation to the position of Mao's "closest comrade"), and CCP General Secretary Teng Hsiao-p'ing, urged a limited and conditional rapprochement with the Soviet Union, primarily for economic and political, rather than military, reasons. On one occasion in 1965, Teng made it clear that the early modernization of China's economy was intimately linked with the problem of aid from the more advanced Communist countries.

The Liu-Teng group appears to have realized, however, that its policy package could be sold in Peking only if it were wrapped up as a plan for militant action by both China and the USSR to rescue a "fraternal" country (Vietnam). Otherwise, a rapprochement with Moscow might look suspiciously like an act of Chinese surrender, and no faction in Peking could afford to create such an impression.

This led the Liu-Teng group to support Chief of Staff Lo and his professionals in advocating a favorable response to Soviet proposals for "unity of action" in Vietnam. The Liu-Teng group repeatedly used terms implying a larger degree of military and political commitment in Vietnam than other Chinese factions were prepared to risk. Liu and Teng also backed reunification of North and South Vietnam, an issue on which other Chinese leaders remained strikingly ambivalent.

In the top party bureaucracy, only one personality appeared to oppose the Liu-Teng-Lo line—the number two man in the secretariat and head of the CCP's Peking apparatus, P'eng Chen. During the first half of 1965, P'eng seemed to be advocating a limited, tacit arrangement between China and the United States. He remained violently opposed to Moscow and was actually singled out personally in the Russian press as the man in China who had been most consistently anti-Soviet ever since the 1940's.[1]

P'eng bitterly denounced the very concept of "unity of action" with Moscow and warned that, since the Soviets were totally unreliable and the West was enormously strong, China should do its utmost to avoid any military confrontation with the West. Anticipating the arguments advanced later in Lin Piao's name, he advised China to let other

[1] See, for instance, *Kommunist,* no. 7, May, 1964.

peoples fight guerrilla campaigns against the West without becoming involved itself.

There are some indications that at one stage of the Peking debate on strategy, P'eng Chen actually joined forces with Lin Piao's guerrilla faction. He may even have been instrumental in drawing up the guerrillas' joint policy platform, which subsequently became famous in the form of Lin Piao's article, "Long Live the Victory of People's War."

Mao himself apparently decided to back this alliance between the army guerrillas and P'eng Chen[2] whose arguments closely resembled the party chief's own strategic concepts and reflected his personal bitterness against the Soviet leaders. In any case, late in the fall of 1965 the guerrillas and their allies were able to decapitate the army's professional group by purging Chief of Staff Lo. Once this was achieved P'eng became dispensable. Some months later (apparently for personal and domestic reasons), Mao had P'eng Chen purged.

Until recently, some observers have assumed that the prominent victims of China's upheaval necessarily belonged to the same faction, simply because the term "revisionist" was indiscriminately hurled at all of them. But on foreign policy matters, at any rate, Peking's Mayor P'eng Chen and Chief of Staff Lo Jui-ch'ing belonged to diametrically opposed groups.[3] P'eng favored an ultracautious line toward the West, while Lo advocated militant "unity of action" with Moscow and mili-

[2] If this assumption is correct, then the alignment in the late summer of 1965 would have repeated the history of Yenan, during 1942, when, after the "rectification" campaign, Mao became president of the party school and his vice-presidents were Lin Piao and P'eng Chen.

[3] The author is aware that Red Guard literature has persistently linked the names of P'eng Chen and Lo Jui-ch'ing as having "plotted" together in February, 1966. This may be as unfounded as were Stalin's fantastic charges of an "unholy conspiracy" between the right (Bukharinite) and left (Trotskyite) opposition groups. Even if true, it would apply only to the period when Lo was already in disfavor and P'eng was becoming alarmed at the blasts emanating from Mao, then in Shanghai, against members of P'eng's Peking faction. Danger can produce strange bedfellows. However, there can be little doubt (as will be seen) that, until the fall of 1965 at least, Lo and P'eng were on *opposite* sides, at any rate with regard to global strategy. Moreover, P'eng Chen's Peking faction is known to have disseminated material praising the former defense minister, P'eng Te-huai; consequently, they had good reason for disliking Lo, a hatchetman from the security forces whose appointment as chief of staff was clearly intended to promote the purge of the P'eng Te-huai group in the army. The fact that Lo afterward appropriated some of the slogans of the ousted defense minister, probably in order to win over the "professional" elements among the People's Liberation Army (PLA) officers, would not have endeared him to P'eng Te-huai's friends in Peking.

tary preparation for an early confrontation with the West. It should be remembered that the term "revisionist" is broad and elastic, covering many sins: It can refer either to a man who is less than militant on international issues or to one who advocates friendship with Moscow, and the two need not necessarily coincide.

These considerations and, indeed, the whole Peking debate on foreign policy and strategy, are highly relevant for any analysis of the present and future global effects of China's internal strife. It is, of course, perfectly true that policy platforms, which are tactically useful in rallying various groups when power is being contested, need not necessarily be implemented by the victorious faction once the struggle is over. It is equally erroneous, however, to assume that such platforms can give us no clue whatever to the attitudes governing the political thinking of those who advocate them. The most scientific approach would be to regard the Chinese debate as an interesting indication of the attitudes of individual Chinese leaders toward international issues.

The author is very conscious of the fact that the issues of international strategy discussed here were most probably not among the immediate and primary issues of China's present convulsions. He does not believe that one can or should find a solution to the conundrum of China's upheaval by means of an analysis devoted to international questions only. Indeed, this is not the purpose of the present exercise. The evidence examined in the following pages is merely intended to bring out the fact that an overt Chinese "debate" on foreign policy and military affairs did take place—in traditional "coded" terminology— and that some particular views may be identified with certain individuals and groups.

"The Debate"

At the beginning of February, 1965, and during the months thereafter, Peking was confronted with the need for an early decision on several vitally important problems; a number of central issues had arisen almost simultaneously, thus complicating the general situation. Only a few weeks previously, Mao Tse-tung had committed himself to the view that the United States had become more or less resigned to defeat in Vietnam and would shortly draw the consequences; he envisaged the withdrawal of American troops within a year or two, at the most.[4] Now, his plans and prophecies were confounded, and the United States bombardment of North Vietnam left little doubt that America's commit-

[4] Edgar Snow, "Interview with Mao," *New Republic,* February 27, 1965.

ment to a stand in Vietnam had been reinforced rather than liquidated. The most important question was what, if anything, China could or ought to do under the circumstances.

This problem was intimately linked with the whole issue of Sino-Soviet relations, not only because of the obvious military implications of any new Chinese commitment in Vietnam, but also for the simple reason that Soviet Premier Alexei Kosygin was visiting the Far East at this very time. He came to Peking both before and after his famous Hanoi visit, and the issue of possible joint Sino-Soviet action to aid North Vietnam was probably broached for the first time during Kosygin's conversation with Chinese leaders.

Even if the Vietnamese crisis had not become acute at this time and Kosygin had stayed away, it would have been imperative for Peking to come to some final decision on future relations with the USSR. Some three and a half months had passed since Khrushchev's overthrow and the Sino-Soviet dispute remained in an unnatural state of suspense (although not of abeyance). The Chinese had been inclined, at first, to treat Khrushchev's ouster as a victory for their cause; Chou En-lai's visit to Moscow, shortly after Khrushchev's removal, soon disabused them of the idea that the Russians might now be inclined to reach an agreement on terms which could be acceptable to Peking. The Russians were willing, indeed eager, to drop the polemics between the two countries, without, however, consenting to a fundamental settlement on the questions of political strategy which had agitated Peking ever since 1957. Moreover, Khrushchev's successors were not willing to abandon his attempts to re-create some form of international Communist authority, at least by way of a gathering of representative Communist parties; this plan was naturally suspect in Peking's eyes since it savored of earlier Russian efforts to restore worldwide Communist discipline under Moscow's aegis. An international Communist meeting in Moscow was scheduled for March, 1965, and it was quite obvious that Peking would have to reach a final decision whether to escalate the more overt manifestations of the Sino-Soviet dispute to a new climax or to strive for some acceptable compromise.

Clearly this question could not be dissociated from the problem of what to do in Vietnam. The Russians almost immediately raised the question of Chinese transit facilities for Soviet military supplies to Hanoi; some time early in the spring, the Russians came with the additional proposal that China should consent to an air corridor, as well as airfields in southern China, for Soviet planes and for Soviet military personnel.[5] This was presumably suggested as an effective way of providing an air cover for Hanoi, which might operate from a "safe" base area. One can only speculate whether the Russians seriously expected the Chinese to agree to such alienation of their territory, or whether this was simply a maneuver to insure a Chinese refusal, thus enabling the Russians to appear as Vietnam's only sincere friends. In any case, it is quite likely that some such suggestion was already broached during Kosygin's visit, even if a detailed proposal was only submitted later on.

The options confronting Mao were limited, and the situation was both complex and dangerous from the Chinese point of view. It was conceivable that Peking might decide on an open collision course with the United States and prepare for full-scale armed intervention in Vietnam, along Korean lines. However, such a decision made very little sense unless Peking insured that the Soviet nuclear shield was extended over China itself, and that sophisticated Soviet military equipment was given to China. What might be needed in Vietnam was not, of course, Chinese military manpower—at least not in terms of masses of ill-equipped and indifferently trained foot soldiers—since the North Vietnamese were not noticeably short of infantry at that time or eager to welcome a massive influx of PLA units. Chinese intervention could be helpful only if the North Vietnamese main forces were to be assisted to launch full-scale, mobile offensive warfare, i.e., an overt, massive invasion of the south, accompanied by a direct onslaught upon United States bases. In that case, an efficient tactical air cover, modern armor, and other sophisticated weapons would be needed, as well as more mechanized and armored units than Hanoi possessed. Thus, China's military power could be effective only if she first staged a reconciliation with the Soviet Union, and made the necessary preparations to turn her army into an efficient instrument of modern warfare, useful not merely for smothering an enemy invader in masses of ill-equipped men, but to carry on a sophisticated, mobile campaign in areas outside China's borders.

Another option for Peking was, of course, to conclude that a conflict close to China's borders was altogether undesirable and that, since reconciliation with Moscow might have to be bought at the high price of permitting Soviet military personnel to operate from Chinese soil, it was preferable to reach a tacit arrangement over Vietnam with the United States. Once that conflict started to die away, the Russians would be unable to resort to an embarrassing propaganda weapon by

[5] Column by Edward Crankshaw, *Observer*, November 14, 1965.

which to pressure China. After all, if an agreement could be reached accepting the partition of Korea, there was no a priori reason why a similar arrangement in Vietnam should prove totally incompatible with Chinese interests.

A third possibility was to do neither. It was conceivable that Peking might decide not to intervene in Vietnam to any really meaningful extent, not to stage a reconciliation with the Soviet Union and not to reach a tacit arrangement with the United States, but simply to do her utmost to encourage this and other guerrilla wars, taking good care, at the same time, to refrain from all actions which might cause China herself to become involved.

A fourth option, theoretically, was to permit enough of a rapprochement with Moscow to warrant the resumption of major Soviet economic and technical aid, so that China might at long last proceed with its third five-year plan and repair the ravages of the Great Leap Forward. In that case, it would, of course, also be necessary to insure conditions of relative tranquillity and safety along China's frontiers, so as to prevent serious diversions from the country's economic build-up. This aim could be achieved either by means of an arrangement with the United States or, at least, through abstention from direct provocation of the United States and through a rapprochement with "secondary" Western powers, such as France and, possibly, Britain, West Germany, and Japan. If the first or fourth options were adopted, China would need—or, at least, be in a position to take—the necessary measures for the creation of a relatively small, modern, professional, highly trained, and equipped army. If the second or third options were adopted, China would neither need, nor be able to take this course, and would probably proceed to plan and operate in terms of a "people's army," suitable primarily for a "people's war."

It is clear, therefore, that the decision Peking had to make in the first half of 1965 was of far-reaching consequence, not only with regard to China's foreign policy and her whole ideological posture, but also domestically, as far as the nature of her military forces and of her economic framework was concerned.

This, then, was the background for Peking's foreign policy "debate." It is only possible to surmise just why this argument broke into the open. Mao's personal prestige must have suffered considerably when it turned out that he had miscalculated completely and that the United States, so far from accepting defeat in Vietnam, was taking operative steps to deepen its commitment in that area. It is also possible that, as a consequence, Mao felt uncertain himself and hesitated to reach a final decision, letting his entourage argue it out. In any case, it cannot be ruled out that, at this time, as during various periods since 1958, Mao was by no means in complete and sole control of the handling of China's affairs—especially in view of his striking misjudgments and failures; consequently, the balance of forces around him may well have been such that not one single opinion—or group—could achieve supremacy to the extent of suppressing rival views.

Whatever may be the correct explanation, during the second week of February, 1965, the opening shots were fired in this "debate." The two extreme opposites in this argument were, for several months, represented by P'eng Chen, Politbureau and secretariat member, as well as head of the CCP's Peking committee, who was considered by many observers to be very much in the running as one of Mao's potential "successors," and, on the other side, by Lo Jui-ch'ing, PLA chief of staff and former minister of security. This fact, in itself, raises many questions, since the two men were to be among the most prominent purge victims of the earlier stages of the Cultural Revolution, and it was subsequently assumed by many that they must belong to the same grouping. It appears from the arguments on foreign policy and on military affairs, that the very opposite was the case and that the "Main-line Faction" had, in fact, purged men from both extremes of the spectrum (perhaps after first using one to help in removing the other).

A third opinion, during the initial stage of the "debate," was expressed by Liu Ning-i, head of China's trade unions, a man who has been generally regarded during China's present upheaval as a typical representative of the entrenched "cadres" of the CCP, headed by CCP Vice-Chairman Liu Shao-ch'i (Liu Ning-i's predecessor in the trade union organization) and by CCP General Secretary Teng Hsiao-p'ing.[6] The differences between the opinions expressed by Liu Ning-i, P'eng Chen, and Lo Jui-ch'ing were sharp; what is equally significant, the basic premises laid down by each of the three were clearly developed and expanded as the months went by, in the case of P'eng and Lo by these two men themselves and in the case of Liu Ning-i by the persons who apparently were his associates, Liu Shao-ch'i and Teng Hsiao-p'ing. Later in the year, as will be seen, P'eng adapted his views to those of a new-found ally, Lin Piao, while Lo Jui-ch'ing's platform was brought closer to that of Liu Ning-i, Teng Hsiao-p'ing, and Liu Shao-ch'i.

P'eng Chen's view initially seems to have been that a major confrontation with the United States both could and should be prevented.

---

[6] Although, from Mao's point of view, Liu Ning-i must appear as a very dubious personality, Liu has been adroit enough, so far, to survive politically.

His definition of the aid to be given to Vietnam was highly limited and full of reservations, while his attitude towards any possible rapprochement with the Soviet Union was completely negative. In this particular context it is very significant to see how P'eng Chen and Liu Ning-i respectively treated an important definition by Mao Tse-tung, which seems to have been used as a kind of banner, behind which to rally various factions. Several Chinese leaders (including Mao himself) freely "adapted" this particular quotation to their own views, as the "debate" proceeded.

In his message to Panamanian revolutionaries in 1964, Mao had said:

> The people of the countries in the Socialist camp should unite, the people of the countries in Asia, Africa and Latin America should unite, the people of all continents should unite, all peace-loving countries and all countries subjected to U.S. aggression, control, interference and bullying should unite, and should form the broadest united front to oppose the U.S. imperialist policies of aggression and of war and to safeguard world peace.[7]

At a Peking mass rally, on February the 10th, in support of Vietnam, P'eng Chen and Liu Ning-i both spoke. The first misquoted Mao in the most significant fashion.

> We, the peoples of the Socialist camp, the oppressed nations and peoples, as well as all the peace-loving countries and people *must persevere in unremitting struggles in order to secure and safeguard peace.*[8]

P'eng Chen omitted all of Mao's original reference to the countries in the socialist camp *uniting,* as well as Mao's original request that an accommodation should be sought with the "secondary" Western powers (France, Western Germany, and possibly Japan) against the United States.[9] Instead of "uniting" with the other countries of the Com-

---

[7] Mao Tse-tung, *Statement Expressing the Chinese People's Firm Support for the Panamanian People's Just Patriotic Struggle* (Peking: Foreign Languages Press, 1964), p. 3.

[8] *Peking Review,* February 12, 1965, p. 11. [Italics are the author's.]

[9] Premier Chou En-lai had explained quite clearly in his policy address to the first session of the Third National Peoples Congress, seven weeks earlier, that Mao's reference to countries which the United States was "controlling and bullying" meant America's allies, among whom he particularly pointed to France (New China News Agency [hereafter cited as NCNA], Peking, December 30, 1964; also reported in *Peking Review,* January 1, 1965, pp. 16–20).

munist bloc, including the USSR, as Mao had still offered to do in 1964, as well as with the Western allies of the United States, in order to create a worldwide anti-American front, P'eng Chen clearly hinted that an accommodation with the "main enemy," i.e., the United States, was feasible. Mao's statement had said that the united front ought to be created in order "to oppose the United States imperialist policies of aggression and of war." P'eng Chen completely omitted this phrase and went straight to the end of Mao's quote, which, moreover, he enlarged and embellished beyond recognition. Mao had added, almost as an afterthought, that in addition to opposing the United States, such a united front would also "safeguard world peace." These three little words were turned by P'eng Chen into the emphatic phrase "must persevere in unremitting struggles in order to secure and safeguard peace."[10]

It is most revealing to contrast this approach with Liu Ning-i's treatment of the identical quotation on the very same occasion. Liu said:

> . . . the peoples of the Socialist camp unite, the peoples of Africa, Asia and Latin America unite, all the peace-loving countries and peoples of the world unite, to *support the Vietnamese people* in their just struggle against United States aggression and wage a resolute struggle to *smash thoroughly* the United States imperialist scheme of extending the war in Indochina and to safeguard world peace.[11]

Liu Ning-i was distorting Mao's original statement in one direction, as much as P'eng Chen had done in the opposite direction. Mao had only said that the Communist camp *should* unite; Liu intimated that this was already in the process of happening, by simply saying, in the present tense, "unite." Moreover, he specifically stated that this rally of the bloc was occurring around the issue of aid to Vietnam and in a joint attempt to grapple with United States power.

Equally striking were the differences between P'eng and Liu over the type and amount of aid to be given to Vietnam. P'eng simply promised "concrete action" to help Vietnam, while Liu stated that it was the unshakable internationalist duty of every Socialist country to give Vietnam "all necessary support and assistance in terms of concrete action," explaining that this meant "whatever is within their power." Liu Ning-i asserted "we are ready," while P'eng Chen merely said the

[10] See *supra* note 8.

[11] *Peking Review*, February 12, 1965, pp. 12–13. [Italics are the author's.]

Chinese people would "intensify their efforts and *increase their pre-paredness* on all fronts." Clearly, therefore, P'eng Chen did not regard China as being "ready." Moreover, while Liu stated that China should do whatever was within its power to give firm support to the Vietnam-ese people (i.e., South as well as North Vietnamese) in their "just struggle against United States aggression and in defense of their mother-land," P'eng Chen said that China would increase her preparedness so as to support Vietnam's fight (presumably North Vietnam's) against the U.S. imperialist war of aggression and "to repulse their war provoca-tions." Clearly P'eng was implying that China should give some very limited help, after adequate preparation, to North Vietnam, just suffi-cient to deter the United States from approaching too closely to China's frontier. He made it quite clear that China's help was likely to be limited to one single field, when he said that Peking would "by no means stand idly by with regard to United States imperialist outrageous *bombing and strafing.*" Liu had not limited his promise of aid in this way but had given a general commitment that China would not "stand by idly" without helping the Vietnamese.[12]

Chief of Staff Lo Jui-ch'ing had spoken two days earlier at a recep-tion in the Korean embassy in Peking, at which he had advocated a line which, while far closer to the views of Liu than those of P'eng, went considerably beyond the line of the former in militancy. Like Liu, Lo promised support for the struggle of the Vietnamese *people* (i.e, in both North and South) but employed a term implying a still greater degree of commitment, "our utmost"; moreover, he stressed that China "abso-lutely will not stand idly by before the U.S. imperialist action of ex-tending the war to the DVR" while Liu had said only that China "will definitely not stand by idly *without lending a helping hand.*" It seems therefore that Liu was merely advocating a serious amount of aid, while Lo was hinting at intervention. Lo clarified this point when he said "the Korean people and their armed forces were the *first* to wage a *head-on* struggle against the United States aggressive forces after the Second World War, and made them suffer a most serious defeat." He clearly seemed to be hinting that a full-scale overt North Vietnamese invasion of the south, on the Korean model, was feasible and desirable and would have full Chinese military backing, as in Korea. Moreover, he seemed to be hinting that, as in Korea, such action could be shielded from the more catastrophic forms of United States retaliation, if the bloc was united and the USSR adopted a deterrent posture. Thus, Lo

[12] *Ibid.*, pp. 11, 12, and 13. [Italics are the author's.]

kept referring to the Communist bloc as an entity which he apparently still regarded as being in full existence. He specifically emphasized the part played by Korea in holding the "eastern outpost of the Socialist camp."[13]

It is of some interest that two editorials in *Jen-min Jih-pao* (People's Daily) which appeared at that time were, on the whole, fairly close to the spirit of P'eng Chen's words. They appeared to constitute the opening of a subtle and indirect dialogue with the United States, in an almost pleading tone. In one case, the newspaper seemed to be trying to persuade the United States that, in Vietnam "you are really overexerting yourself," and in another case that "choosing Indochina or Southeast Asia as the theater of war is extremely unfavorable to Washington." The paper left considerable doubt whether an extension of the Vietnamese conflict would *automatically* bring in China. "If United States imperialism persists in spreading the flames of war *and forces a war on us,* then we shall have no other choice but to be resolved to take it on to the end." This extremely lukewarm and highly conditional sentence stands in obvious contrast to Lo's threat that China "absolutely will not stand by idly before the United States imperialist action of extending the war."[14]

Official Chinese government statements of the time were a shade stronger than the two *Jen-min jih-pao* editorials, although still reasonably cautious. For instance, a statement of February 13, 1965, said China had "long been prepared and knows how to aid" Vietnam, i.e., that Chinese action would presumably take the form only of additional assistance.[15] Chinese government releases left little doubt that whoever prepared them was far less favorably inclined towards reconciliation with the USSR than the forces behind Liu Ning-i. A government statement of February 9 mentioned the Socialist countries only in the context of preaching that they had the "unshirkable international obligation" of assisting Vietnam, the implication being that someone was trying to shirk this duty. Unlike Liu, the statement did not say that "the peoples of the Socialist camp unite," but simply called "upon the peace-loving countries and people of the world to

[13] *Ibid.,* p. 10 and *Survey of China Mainland Press* (hereafter cited as *SCMP*), Hong Kong, No. 3396, February 12, 1965, pp. 24–25. [Italics are the author's.]

[14] "U.S. Aggressors Must Be Punished," and "The Johnson Administration's Gangster Talk," *Jen-min jih-pao* [People's Daily], February 9, 1965, and *ibid.,* February 10, 1965; also *Peking Review,* February 12, 1965, pp. 17–20.

[15] *Peking Review,* February 19, 1965, pp. 5–6.

unite,"[16] a deliberately ambiguous phrase which contained no overt commitment of "unity of action" with Moscow, as Liu Ning-i's speech had done.[17]

There are some indications, therefore, that, by the second week of February, the persons responsible for Chinese government statements felt that unity of action with Moscow was no longer seriously on the agenda. Whoever these persons were, they would appear to have opposed the line advocated by Liu Ning-i (and by Teng Hsiao-p'ing, who insisted on Mao's original formulations even a year later, when the whole concept of a "Socialist camp" had already been dropped), as well as by Lo Jui-ch'ing. It would be sheer speculation to attribute the official statements to specific personalities; by a process of elimination, however, one might assume that these releases, which opposed the line of Liu Ning-i, Liu Shao-ch'i (as will be seen subsequently), Teng Hsiao-p'ing, and Lo Jui-ch'ing, but which also differed somewhat from P'eng Chen's concepts, were compromises, possibly emanating from Premier Chou En-lai, and meeting with Mao's approval.

It may be assumed that Mao himself, after the frictions of Kosygin's second visit to Peking, lent his support to the forces opposed to any rapprochement with the USSR. There is considerable evidence that P'eng Chen was prominent among these anti-Soviet forces.

After the February "debate," Chinese relations with the Soviet Union deteriorated rapidly, as the Russians went ahead with their international gathering of Communist parties in March and as Chinese students at the same time clashed with Soviet mounted police in Moscow. In spite of these developments, however, and in the face of growing United States commitments of troops to Vietnam, the policy "debate" in China continued and escalated.

Early in April, an article by a close personal associate of Chinese Defense Minister Lin Piao, Li Tso-p'eng,[18] was prominently reproduced in the Chinese press. Li Tso-p'eng had published a lengthy analysis in *Hung-ch'i* (Red Flag) some three and a half months earlier, which had re-emphasized the contemporary significance of Mao's work on

[16] *Peking Review*, February 12, 1965, pp. 6–7.

[17] As will be seen subsequently, six months later the atmosphere between Moscow and Peking had already deteriorated so much that even the assertion "all peace-loving countries are becoming united" had become a slogan with pro-Soviet rather than neutral overtones.

[18] Who shared Lin's career both in China's northeastern and south-central regions.

the strategy and tactics of "people's war." The article insisted that only by using cautious guerrilla tactics and by avoiding confrontation with a superior force could a weak country succeed; "acting counter to [this thesis] we shall lose." The article pointed out that the West "may still be powerful for a certain period, may still enjoy a temporary military advantage. The revolutionary people must take the enemy seriously, be *prudent*." China needed to

> prepare fully for every battle and not to fight any battle unprepared or without assurance of victory; we are opposed to counting on a lucky chance; we are opposed to taking the enemy lightly and *advancing in a reckless way;* we strive to make certain that we will win every engagement we fight, otherwise *we avoid battle*. The enemy can only be annihilated bit by bit . . . this is called a piecemeal solution.

The article attacked "some people" who thought that because China was willing to stand up to a powerful enemy over a prolonged period ("strategically pit one against ten"), this necessarily meant that China should already risk an outright battle with that enemy now. To this, the author replied,

> Concentrating a superior force to destroy the enemy forces one by one is the most effective way of fighting to change the situation in which *the enemy is strong while we are weak*.

The article quoted ten major principles of operation of which the first and most imporant two were,

> 1. attack dispersed isolated enemy forces first; attack concentrated strong enemy forces later; 2. take small and medium cities and extensive rural areas first; take big cities later.[19]

The reappearance of this piece clearly constituted a broadside at the forces, apparently headed by Chief of Staff Lo Jui-ch'ing, which had become convinced of the inevitability of a "head-on" confrontation with the enemy now. Li's article preached the ideology of guerrilla struggles and of caution. Since by this time Moscow had made its proposal that Peking should permit Soviet military personnel to take over air bases in southern China so as to provide air cover for North Vietnam, it seems likely that the prominent reprinting of this article

[19] Li Tso-p'eng, "Strategically Pitting One against Ten, Tactically Pitting Ten against One," *Hung-ch'i* [Red Flag], December 22, 1964; also *Peking Review,* April 9, 1965, pp. 12–17. [Italics are the author's.]

was also intended to warn those military and party "cadres" who favored negotiations with the Russians on this subject. Clearly there was no point in making such a dangerous concession to the USSR if an outright confrontation with the United States was to be avoided now and if the correct way of fighting "imperialism" was to wage a long drawn-out guerrilla struggle, rather than full-scale battles between opposing main forces.

Two weeks after the reappearance of the Li Tso-p'eng article, these arguments found some political reflection in simultaneous but different messages on the Bandung anniversary delivered by CCP General Secretary Teng Hsiao-p'ing (acting premier while Chou En-lai was abroad) and by P'eng Chen. Whereas P'eng very cautiously said that China supported the Vietnamese "in their fight," Teng said that China supported them in "their great struggles to defend the northern part of their country, liberate the southern part, safeguard national independence and *reunify* their fatherland."[20] (It is interesting that, at this time and later, most official Chinese pronouncements quoted *Vietnamese* leaders as desiring these objectives, but refrained from saying that China was supporting these aims or, to be precise, that Peking was supporting reunification. Thus Chou En-lai, in his farewell address from Djakarta, a week later, said that "the United States must stop its aggression against Vietnam, and United States forces must withdraw from South Vietnam," without so much as mentioning the word "reunification."[21])

There were striking differences between the degree of Chinese commitment in Vietnam implied by Teng's words and the implications of P'eng's speech. The former said, *"No matter what happens* and no matter what cost is involved, we will resolutely perform our internationalist duty."* P'eng cautiously stated "We will go a *step forward* in supporting them *according to their needs.* The Chinese people will spare no sacrifice. . . ."[22]

It is thus apparent that a public—if carefully coded—"debate" had been proceeding for at least three months when, early in May, the argument received more detailed and overt expression. The formal occasion was the anniversary of victory against Germany in World War II. On that occasion, some previously separate strands of arguments concerning military posture, Vietnam, relations with the United

[20] *Peking Review,* April 23, 1965, pp. 10–14.

[21] *Peking Review,* April 30, 1965, pp. 6–8.

[22] See supra note 20. [Italics are the author's.]

States and the USSR were woven together. Chief of Staff Lo Jui-ch'ing delivered a detailed and programmatic address, which appeared simultaneously with a summation of the opposite case, published in the form of an editorial in *Jen-min jih-pao*. While the earlier "debates" passed almost unnoticed in the West, the public disputation of May 8–9 did arouse some attention, although not all of the material published on that occasion has received full interpretation.

To start with, it must be recalled that Lo Jui-ch'ing was speaking after the appearance and reappearance of Li Tso-p'eng's article which had praised guerrilla warfare and had intimated that the enemy was stronger than China and that caution would, therefore, have to be practiced. There is little doubt that Lo Jui-ch'ing was actually challenging this statement. His first point was that Li Tso-p'eng and the people behind him were entirely wrong in assuming that the West was still so "powerful" and enjoyed so much of a "military advantage," that China had to "avoid battle," or, indeed, that "avoiding battle" at a time when "the enemy is strong while we are weak," as Li had suggested, was the appropriate policy.

Lo Jui-ch'ing argued, in effect, that the United States was more bellicose even than Hitler's Germany and that it meant to make war in any case, so that evasive tactics would not work; at the same time, the United States forces were actually weaker than Hitler's army and need not be regarded with such awe. "United States imperialism is playing a role more ferocious than that of Hitler. . . . [It] is . . . the main source of war and aggression in our times and the sworn enemy of the people of the world. . . . [It] is preparing to impose another world war on the people. . . . U.S. imperialism means war." Yet "its army has frequently been defeated . . . it is an army of pampered soldiers far inferior to Hitler's fascist army."[23]

Jen-min jih-pao took strong issue with these assertions and it is highly significant that its attack upon Lo's thesis wove together the arguments voiced earlier by two separate elements—the "political" group in the PLA, which was calling for guerrilla strategy, and P'eng Chen who appeared to be advocating a tacit understanding with the United States. *Jen-min jih-pao* nowhere subscribed to the view that the United States meant to initiate world war. Where Lo had said that the United States was the main *source* of aggression and war, *Jen-min jih-pao* said that it was the "main *force* of aggression and war." The first thesis im-

[23] Lo Jui-ch'ing, "Commemorate the Victory over German Fascism! Carry the Struggle against U.S. Imperialism through to the End!" *Hung-ch'i*, no. 5, 1965; also *Peking Review*, May 14, 1965, pp. 7–15.

plies that the United States is causing and planning a war, whereas the second merely states the obvious, namely, that in a conflict, the United States would be the main military force encountered. *Jen-min jih-pao* immediately went on to make the point that peace "can be effectively preserved" provided one waged "resolute struggles against imperialism"; various victories won against the West in guerrilla struggles had already "punctured the arrogance of the United States" (i.e., had diminished the willingness of the United States to proceed to extremes) and therefore "were all effective in defending world peace." The peoples had the power to "prevent another world war."

Jen-min jih-pao then said quite overtly that, providing "the basic interests of the people are not violated, it is perfectly permissible and *even necessary to conduct negotiations with the imperialists and to reach certain agreements* with them on certain occasions." As examples of such occasions, the article quoted not only the Korean armistice and the two Geneva agreements but the Soviet-German pact, i.e., an agreement between a Communist country and the "main enemy."[24]

Lo Jui-ch'ing took sharp issue with this thesis; he stressed that Hitler had attacked the Soviet Union "less than two years after he had concluded a non-aggression treaty with it" and that, moreover, the "United States is actually many times more insidious and deadly than Hitler." Obviously therefore, one could not really risk such an arrangement with the main enemy. Lo Jui-ch'ing then added "whoever wants to insure his own safety by making concessions to the aggressor and by satisfying his greed *at the expense of other peoples' interests*" would only harm himself.[25] *Jen-min jih-pao* had stated that such an agreement was possible if "the basic interests of the people" were not violated. Clearly, *Jen-min jih-pao* meant the national interest of the Chinese people, whereas Lo Jui-ch'ing's case was that, even if the national interest called for such an arrangement, this would be impermissible if it harmed the interests of "other peoples," i.e., the Vietnamese. Lo left little doubt just what he had in mind: "supporting others means supporting oneself and, therefore, no one has the right to assume the airs of a benefactor or liberator." The touchstone of a true revolutionary was "whether or not a country which has won victory dares to serve as a base area for the world revolution." Of course, this could also apply to the Russians; however, in this context one must recall

24 *Jen-min jih-pao,* May 9, 1965; also *Peking Review,* May 14, 1965, pp. 15–22. [Italics are the author's.]

25 [Italics are the author's.]

that Moscow had asked Peking to "serve as a base area" by granting the use of air fields in southern China to Soviet military personnel in order to extend an air cover over North Vietnam. Lo appeared to be urging his government to accept this request in spite of the risks involved. He specifically stated that support for Vietnam was essential "whether or not United States imperialism bombs our country."

Jen-min jih-pao, on the other hand, simply said that it was the bounden international duty of all revolutionary forces "to support and aid" Vietnam, with no implication whatever that China should risk being drawn into a conflict in so doing.

Chief of Staff Lo then proceeded to take direct issue with his opponents. "Some people may say: after all, United States imperialism has the atom bomb and therefore it is more powerful than Hitler." Clearly, Lo was insinuating that his opponents were advocating caution and, perhaps, retreat, because of their fear of United States nuclear power. In reply, he mentioned Mao's famous thesis that the bomb is a "paper tiger," but immediately indicated that he did not think very much of such amateurish chatter. "What is more [i.e., presumably what is more to the point than Mao's thesis], the United States monopoly of the atom bomb was *broken many years ago.*"[26] In other words, what mattered was the fact that the United States could be deterred by the *Soviet* nuclear shield; the country which had broken the monopoly "many years ago" was, of course, the USSR and not China.

Jen-min jih-pao, on the other hand, stated that Mao's theory had been entirely borne out by the fact that the United States "despite its possession of nuclear weapons" was not able to prevent a series of revolutionary and guerrilla struggles. In other words, while Lo wanted to rely on the Soviet nuclear deterrent, his opponents pointed out that China did not need the Russians, provided she limited herself to indirect support of Asian guerrilla struggles, since, in *such* situations, the United States had never yet employed nuclear weapons.

Lo made it perfectly clear that his opponents, because of their theories, had neglected essential military preparations; this could hardly be anything less than an accusation against the Minister of Defense, Lin Piao. Lo emphasized that it was essential to

> strengthen national defenses and make adequate preparations against imperialist wars of aggression. It makes a world of difference whether or not one is prepared once a war breaks out . . . preparations must be made not only against any small-scale war-

[26] [Italics are the author's.]

fare but also against any medium or large-scale warfare that imperialism may launch. These preparations must envisage the use by the imperialists of nuclear weapons. . . .

Moreover, he attacked those who preached

passive defense . . . a spurious kind of defense . . . the only real defense is active defense . . . for the purpose of . . . taking the offensive.

His opponents made the point that nothing so drastic was necessary: *Jen-min jih-pao* stressed that, by the method of "people's war," an invading enemy could gradually be inundated by the masses, without need for radical early preparatory measures. "The people will *gradually* grow stronger . . . *gradually* change the balance of forces." Two days earlier, *Jen-min jih-pao* had published another editorial which, in the forms of a dialogue with the enemy, appeared to be debating Lo Jui-ch'ing: "You may seize cities while I occupy the countryside . . . you rely on modern weapons and I wage guerrilla war everywhere."[27]

Lo insistently demanded unity of action with the Soviet Union. "The Socialist countries and all revolutionary people" must make effective preparations against the eventuality that imperialism "may suddenly impose a war on us." However, this could be done only provided "we are good at *uniting the Socialist camp* and the people's anti-imperialist forces in all countries as well as at making use of the contradictions within the imperialist camp." The article concluded with an emotional peroration "we . . . express our full confidence in the great Soviet people and the great Soviet army . . . we are deeply confident that we will be united on the basis of Marxist-Leninism and . . . will fight shoulder to shoulder against our common enemy."[28]

The article in *Jen-min jih-pao* not only failed to include such passages, but specifically attacked "the successors to Khrushchev" as well as "unity against the enemy" which was described as "nothing but a swindle." It pointedly reversed the order of priorities by saying "we must thoroughly expose the true face of Khrushchev revisionism, eliminate its influence and carry the struggle against it *through to the end,* in order to promote the revolutionary struggles. . . ." In other words, first China must battle against Soviet power and influence, and then she can tackle other issues. In its peroration, *Jen-min jih-pao* strongly recalled

[27] *Jen-min jih-pao,* May 7, 1965; also *Peking Review,* May 14, 1965, pp. 23–24. [Italics are the author's.]

[28] See supra note 23. [Italics are the author's.]

P'eng Chen's words on February the 10th: "the possibility of averting a world war has enormously increased. Through their common struggle the revolutionary countries and peace-loving people [no mention of the Socialist camp] can frustrate the U.S. imperialist plans for aggression and war."[29] The fact that *Jen-min jih-pao* in its sharp reply to Lo Jui-ching was drawing heavily not only upon the arguments advanced by the "political" faction in the PLA, represented by Lin Piao's associate Li Tso-p'eng, but also upon the views of P'eng Chen, received further confirmation in a programmatic speech P'eng delivered two weeks later in Indonesia.

Speaking in Djakarta on May 25, P'eng strongly took issue with Lo's thesis that the United States Army was militarily inferior to Hitler's. He stated that the United States was, in fact, tremendously powerful, both militarily and economically. "It has made use of its economic strength, which was inflated during the war, to build up an *unprecedented* and *colossal* war machine." (If United States might is "unprecedented," clearly the United States must be stronger than any other power, including the USSR.) He went on to say that the United States was thus "strong in appearance"; if it was possible to call the United States weak in essence, this meant simply that its "ambition far surpasses Hitler's," but that "the disparity between strength and ambition" was "greater" than in the case of Germany. P'eng was clearly taking issue with Lo's point that the United States Army, being "pampered," was "far inferior" to Hitler's forces, by saying that the United States was vulnerable only in so far as the disparity between its strength and its global aspirations surpassed the gap which had separated the power and the essentially European ambitions of Nazi Germany.

P'eng went on to explain that, in view of "the dispersion of its forces," piecemeal tactics could be adopted against the United States. Clearly this was in support of the guerrilla theories proposed by Li Tso-p'eng. P'eng sharply attacked "exponents of the theory that weapons, and in particular nuclear weapons, decide everything." In reply to Lo's assertions that urgent military preparations were required, he stressed that revolutionary forces "are invariably weak to begin with, but . . . they always keep on growing, developing from small and weak to large and strong forces." P'eng re-emphasized the point made in *Jen-min jih-pao* on May 9, that, in combatting "people's war," the United States had always refrained from employing nuclear weapons; P'eng stressed that the United States "has expended thousands of mil-

---

[29] See supra note 24. [Italics are the author's.]

lions of United States dollars, sent in tens of thousands of troops and employed new weapons of all kinds, except nuclear weapons." Obviously, therefore, as long as China merely encouraged guerrilla activities beyond her frontiers and refrained from a direct clash with the United States, she would not be exposed to a nuclear threat and had no cause whatever to rely on the Soviet nuclear deterrent.

P'eng delivered one of the sharpest Chinese attacks upon the Soviet leadership ever heard up to that time. Specifically attacking "Khrushchev's successors," he delivered a diatribe against the very thought of "unity of action" with the USSR against the West. He actually stated that the leadership of the Soviet Union was inferior—"really cannot be compared"—to "the anti-imperialist and revolutionary representatives of the *national bourgeoisie* in Asia, Africa, and Latin America, nor even with the anti-imperialist and patriotic representatives of *royal families and the nobility*."[30] In other words, kings, noblemen, and capitalists are preferable to Russian Communists! This assertion caused Soviet representatives to protest violently to the leadership of the Indonesian Communist Party before whom P'eng Chen was speaking.

It was on this occasion that P'eng Chen presented a most detailed and clearly defined program for transferring the center of the global struggle to the Third World; P'eng quoted a statement by the Indonesian Communist Party (PKI) leader Aidit, who had stressed "on a world scale, Asia, Africa, and Latin America are the village of the world, while Europe and North America are the town of the world. If the world revolution is to be victorious, there is no other way than . . . to give prominence to the revolutions in Asia, Africa, and Latin America."[31] (This theme has, of course, been wrongly attributed, since September, 1965, to the inventiveness of Lin Piao, who was, in fact, quoting it at third hand.) P'eng's Djakarta address contained another phrase which was almost literally incorporated into Lin Piao's famous article. The United States in Vietnam was compared to "a buffalo rushing into a fiery maze [which] will certainly be burned to death."[32] This unusual image was incorporated into Lin Piao's *Long Live Victory in People's*

[30] [Italics are the author's.]

[31] For the origin of this concept, see Tang Tsou, "Mao Tse-tung and Peaceful Coexistence," *Orbis,* 8, no. 1 (Spring, 1964): 42. Professor Tsou points out that the phrase first appeared in the Resolution of the Second Plenum of the PKI's Central Committee and was subsequently reprinted by the Chinese. P'eng Chen seems to have been the first Chinese leader to incorporate this image into his political program.

[32] *Peking Review,* June 11, 1965, pp. 10–20.

War, five months later, which said "United States imperialism like a mad bull dashing from place to place, will finally be burned to ashes."[33]

P'eng Chen's speech, in fact, already contained the essence of Lin Piao's Third World strategy, shorn only of its lengthy references to China's history which would hardly have been appropriate in a speech before an Indonesian audience. There were some differences, of course. Unlike Lin Piao's article, P'eng Chen in Djakarta did not specifically state that revolutionaries in Afro-Asia would have to rely entirely upon themselves and should not depend upon outside aid, even from China. On the other hand, he made no promises whatsoever that China *would* help, even his reference to Vietnam being completely devoid of such commitments. He made it pretty clear that the United States was to be engaged by the Vietnamese alone. Another difference in emphasis stemmed from P'eng Chen's characteristic insistence that world peace could and would be saved. P'eng praised the policy line adopted, so he said, by the CCP and the PKI which "persists in opposing imperialism, resolutely supports the revolutionary struggles of the oppressed peoples and nations and *defends world peace. . . .* Only by following this line is it possible to puncture the arrogance of the United States imperialist aggressor, *thwart its plans for aggression and war* and thereby both promote the people's revolution of all countries and *win world peace.*"[34] (Lo Jui-ch'ing, it will be recalled, had insisted that "United States imperialism means war," i.e., that United States war plans most probably could not be thwarted, at least not by China alone.)

In his address, P'eng used a phrase which became something of a rallying cry for opponents of reconciliation with Moscow, namely that the USSR was "selling out the German Democratic Republic."

The previously-used slogan, concerning the need for union of the "peoples of the Socialist camp," disappeared entirely in P'eng's speech; instead he emphasized a different concept: "Socialist countries which *persevere in the Marxist-Leninist line,*" which definitely excluded Communist countries of the revisionist persuasion. In another sentence, he spoke of "the Socialist countries *which uphold Marxism-Leninism.*" Mao's original 1964 call for a broad united front, including all the countries of the Communist bloc, the Third World, and other anti-American forces was now pared down by P'eng to the narrow definition "unite with all the forces *that can be* united." P'eng explained that this slogan

[33] Lin Piao, "Long Live the Victory of People's War," *Jen-min jih-pao*, September 2, 1965; also *Peking Review*, September 3, 1965, pp. 9–30.

[34] [Italics are the author's.]

at present, means unity of the international proletariat and the *revolutionary* people of all countries . . . [it] is a slogan which draws a clear-cut line of demarcation between enemies and friends . . . the unity of the international communist movement can be achieved only on the basis . . . of opposition to modern revisionism.

He made it perfectly clear that the struggle against the Soviets was now a precondition for any struggle against imperialism, i.e., it had taken first place on China's agenda.

For the victory of the struggle against imperialism . . . we must resolutely go on exposing the true features of Khrushchev's revisionism and carry the struggle against it through *to the end*.[35]

He summed up the new platform in his peroration "boldly advance in the fight against imperialism, reaction, and modern revisionism."[36] This phrase is highly significant when compared with a revelation two weeks later in an authoritative ideological statement (published, as is customary in such cases, both in *Hung-ch'i* and *Jen-min jih-pao*) which pointed out that the original "general line" proposed by the CCP in 1963 could be summed up as "oppose imperialism and reaction in all countries . . . *consolidate and expand the Socialism camp. . . .*" *Hung-ch'i* explained that the new line adopted by the CCP now was "carry forward to the end the struggle against imperialism and reaction *headed by the United States,* carry forward to the end the struggle against Khrushchev's revisionism. . . ."[37] What is most interesting is the one major dissimilarity between the new CCP line defined by *Hung-ch'i* and the slogan used by P'eng Chen. Both dropped the reference to "consolidating" the Communist bloc, which had been part of the 1963 line, and both added modern "revisionism" to the evils which had to be fought; P'eng Chen, like *Hung-ch'i,* demanded, in one part of his speech, that the struggle against modern revisionism be carried through "to the end." However, *Hung-ch'i* stated "carry forward to the end the struggle against imperialism and reaction *headed by the United States . . . ,*"[38] while P'eng Chen's slogan said "boldly advance in the fight against imperialism, reaction . . ."; in other words, he did *not* ask

---

35 [Italics are the author's.]

36 See supra note 32.

37 *Peking Review,* June 18, 1965, pp. 5–10. [Italics are the author's.]

38 [Italics are the author's.]

for a struggle "to the end" against imperialism, and he dropped specific mention of the United States as the main imperialist power to be fought.

Thus, there are clear indications of one continuous line, linking P'eng Chen's February 10 speech, the *Jen-min jih-pao* editorial of May 9 and P'eng Chen's speech of May 25; all of these include unusual signs of a conciliatory, or at least a realistic attitude toward the United States and of a strong belief that conflict can and will be averted, and all are strongly opposed to "unity of action" with Moscow.

It seems quite likely, therefore, that the *Jen-min jih-pao* editorial of May 9, 1965, which entered the lists against Chief of Staff Lo Jui-ch'ing and his concept of militant "unity of action" with Moscow against Washington, was inspired, perhaps even written, by P'eng Chen or his subordinates.

Another concept which was underlined by P'eng and which subsequently became an important feature in the statements of the more anti-Soviet factions in Peking, was praise for the allegedly increasing activities of the revolutionary masses in "Western Europe, North America, and Oceania." The implication was obvious: China did not want to rely upon the deterrent power of the Soviet nuclear shield; she hoped that United States nuclear power would never be brought to bear, provided anti-Western actions were confined to guerrilla situations in the Third World, without major Chinese participation, and provided public campaigns in the West could inhibit any possible United States decision to employ nuclear weapons. (This is reminiscent of some aspects of Stalin's policy around late 1948–early 1949, when Russia was just becoming a nuclear power.) As local guerrilla forces failed to achieve victory against the United States, Peking seems to have placed increasing emphasis upon the hope that action by the "masses," in "Western Europe, North America, and Oceania," might somehow weaken the staying power of Western counter-insurgency efforts.

P'eng Chen, in his Djakarta address, left no doubt that he was continuing the "debate" against certain opposing groups in Peking, when he said "some have asked" whether China had not "established very good united front relations with many non-Marxist-Leninists and non-Communists?" "Why," P'eng quoted these anonymous forces as asking, could China not "enter into united action with the modern revisionists?"[39] It is perfectly true that this question must have been asked by

[39] See supra, note 32.

many Asian Communists, as well as by P'eng's opponents in Peking, but, in the light of the evidence concerning the ongoing "debate" in the Chinese capital, it seems hard to believe that P'eng did not have his domestic adversaries in mind.

The day before P'eng spoke in Djakarta, there had been an indication from Peking that his main opponents in the "debate," the PLA "professionals," headed by Lo Jui-ch'ing, were being attacked within their own fortress by the "political" bosses of the PLA, headed by Lin Piao, and that P'eng, therefore, would now have a powerful ally. On May 24, 1965, all formal ranks and insignia in the PLA were abolished, reverting to the pre-1955 situation. [It was in 1955 that, five months after his appointment, the new minister of defense and spokesman of the "professionals," P'eng Te-huai, had introduced the new rank system as a step towards creating a modern, efficient and professional army. His successor and opponent, Lin Piao, was clearly attempting to revert to the guerrilla traditions of the revolutionary period.]

To offset this development, Lo Jui-ch'ing and his "professionals" seem to have attempted to recruit support for their attitude among top "cadres" of the Communist party's entrenched bureaucracy, who, for reasons of their own, apparently feared that the dispute with the USSR was getting out of hand and welcomed some modicum of "united action" with Moscow.

A very interesting indication of the way in which these top party "cadres" were thinking appeared on July 30, 1965, in a speech by CCP General Secretary Teng Hsiao-p'ing, to the Ninth Congress of the Rumanian Communist Party. In flat contradiction to P'eng Chen's Djakarta speech, Teng said "In our common struggle against imperialism *headed by the United States* . . . the Chinese people will *always* march forward *hand in hand* . . . with *the fraternal peoples of the Socialist camp* and with the oppressed peoples and nations throughout the world." This was a clear indication of support for the "unity of action" theme against the United States.

Teng made no bones about the reasons for this attitude. "The Chinese people are determined to build their country into a powerful Socialist state with modern agriculture, *modern industry, modern national defense,* and modern science and technology in *not too long an historical period.*" In direct reference to this economic and defense program, he said "we are by no means isolated in our struggle. We have constant *international support* and encouragement from Rumania and *other fraternal countries.*" The very use of this phrase leaves little doubt that Teng, in complete contradiction to all Chinese complaints concerning Soviet and East European aid programs, was actually indicating his gratitude and his desire for renewal of such Soviet assistance. "Fraternal" countries means Communist countries, and, since Rumania was already mentioned separately, what other Communist "countries" (in the plural) could there be, which had actually given "support" to China's economy, except the USSR, Czechoslovakia, etc.? While P'eng had explained that, at the present stage, "unity of action" meant simply "unity of the international proletariat and the revolutionary people . . . ," Teng said that in order "to fight against the United States imperialist policies of aggression and war . . . the people of all continents are becoming united, all *peace-loving countries* are becoming united. . . ." No one in Peking, at that time, had yet suggested that the USSR should be ejected from the category of "peace-loving" countries, even though Moscow was accused of being, in fact, an accomplice of the United States. Consequently, Teng's phrase clearly does not exclude the USSR from the ranks of the forces which "are becoming united," while P'eng, in Djakarta, had most sharply ruled out any "unity" with Moscow.[40]

Moreover, Teng obviously still regarded a possible reunion of the bloc as a reasonably practical proposition; he implied that, provided certain Chinese positions were accepted (of which he specifically named only the 1957 and 1960 Moscow statements, which were unobjectionable from the Soviet viewpoint, while, at the same time, he also vaguely invoked "theoretical positions of Marxism-Leninism"), it might still be "possible to speak of genuine unity of the international Communist movement and of the Socialist camp."

Even more interesting was Teng's declaration that the CCP would "continue firmly to combat modern revisionism, the main danger of the international Communist movement, and at the same time *firmly to* combat modern dogmatism."[41] In its emphasis, this statement differs remarkably from the slogans used at that time both in the CCP and even in those "fraternal" Asian parties that were presumably a little less one-sided than the Chinese in the struggle between "revisionism" and "dogmatism." Thus, *Jen-min jih-pao* in a November 7, 1965, editorial stated "The international proletariat must wage a struggle against modern revisionism and modern dogmatism . . . in particular it must wage an *uncompromising* struggle against *modern revisionism,*

[40] [Italics are the author's.]

[41] Teng Hsiao-p'ing, speech delivered to the 9th Congress of the Rumanian CP, July 20, 1965, *Peking Review,* July 30, 1965, pp. 8–10.

which is the main danger. . . ."[42] In other words, *Jen-min jih-pao* demanded an "uncompromising struggle" against "modern revisionism" and merely a "struggle" against "modern dogmatism," whereas Teng demanded a "firm" struggle against *both* "modern revisionism" and "modern dogmatism." Even the PKI and the Japanese Communist Party (JCP) were not quite so "neutral" in the struggle between "modern revisionism" and "modern dogmatism" as was Teng.[43] Thus Aidit, in Djakarta on May 23, 1965, stated that "revolutionary offensives" should be launched against "modern revisionism," while against "modern dogmatism" Communists should merely "continue our fight."[44] The JCP leader Miyamoto, in March, 1966, when his party was already shifting towards somewhat more neutral ground in the contest between "revisionism" and "dogmatism," still stated: "It is essential to *oppose* modern revisionism, the main danger in the present . . . while *guarding* against dogmatism and sectarianism."[45] Even so, P'eng Chen, who was on the stage with Miyamoto, apparently still did not consider Miyamoto's emphasis sufficiently "anti-revisionist," and therefore emphasized that "our two parties *resolutely* oppose modern revisionism, the main danger in the international Communist movement."[46] (Miyamoto had merely said revisionism was the main danger in the *present* international Communist movement.) As compared with his emphatic stress on the fight against modern revisionism, P'eng merely added "we also oppose modern dogmatism."[47]

[42] *Jen-min jih-pao*, November 7, 1965; also *Peking Review*, November 12, 1965, pp. 8–9. [Italics are the author's.]

[43] The fact that Teng was addressing the Rumanian Communist Party, which was drifting towards neutralism in the Sino-Soviet dispute, did not entitle him to make a major change in a slogan of such ideological significance. As will be seen, P'eng Chen was *not* willing to make such concessions to an equally important party, the JCP.

[44] *Peking Review*, June 4, 1965, pp. 8–12.

[45] *SCMP*, Hong Kong, No. 3668, March 30, 1966, pp. 33–36. [Italics are the author's.]

[46] *Ibid.*, pp. 30–33.

[47] In the light of these facts, it is not possible to concur with the prevalent view that P'eng Chen's speech on that occasion somehow constituted an "unprecedented" Chinese condemnation of modern dogmatism and, consequently, should be regarded as an indication that P'eng Chen had adopted a more "revisionist" attitude. In fact, formal condemnation of "modern dogmatism" was normal practice both for the CCP and for its Asian allies, as has been shown; P'eng Chen's condemnation of "modern dogmatism" was infinitely *weaker* than his attack on "modern revisionism," whereas Teng, nine months

If the assumption is correct that the search for "unity of action" with Moscow was bringing together top party cadres under Teng and Liu and military "professionals," led by Lo Jui-ch'ing, this might explain Lo's audacity in the late summer of 1965. He continued with the bold advocacy of his platform in spite of clear indications that he faced growing opposition from the "guerrilla" (or "political") group in the PLA, from P'eng Chen, and probably from Mao himself. On August 1, 1965, Lo Jui-ch'ing delivered an address on the thirty-eighth anniversary of the founding of the PLA, in which he again harped on the Korean precedent (i.e., a conflict in which Chinese main forces had engaged the United States Army in open battle). Moreover, he seemed to poke fun at Mao's famous adage that the atom bomb was a "paper tiger" and that the really effective weapon was the "spiritual atom bomb" of the revolutionary masses. Lo said "We are materialists . . . who will continue to master the material atom bomb." . . . "with the spiritual atom bomb *plus our own material bomb,* we have *greater* confidence. . . ."[48]

The "political" group in the PLA seems to have retaliated immediately; early in August, Ho Lung, a veteran of the civil war period and, apparently, an antagonist of Lo Jui-ch'ing, prominently published an article on "The Democratic Tradition of the Chinese PLA" which attacked an anonymous person who considered himself an "overlord" and a "number one authority"; there is little doubt that these epithets were intended for Lo Jui-ch'ing and not for Lin Piao[49] since the article went on to refer to people who had their "heads crammed full with foreign doctrines." Addressing the "overlord" himself, apparently, Ho Lung said that the imperialists do not fear "your modern techniques."[50]

To rub in the lesson still more, *Hung-ch'i,* on August 21, reprinted

---

earlier, had been *neutral* between these two forces and P'eng Chen's Japanese guests in 1966 were infinitely more guarded in their condemnation of "modern revisionism" than was P'eng Chen. In fact, P'eng Chen, in March, 1966, i.e., at the bitter end of his career, was just as fiercely anti-revisionist as he had been in 1965 and during the previous years.

[48] *Peking Review,* August 6, 1965, p. 5. [Italics are the author's.]

[49] Although he seems to have shared the views of the "guerrilla" faction, Ho Lung had his personal differences with Lin Piao, to whom he was, apparently, not much more devoted than he was to Lo Jui-ch'ing (as the course of the Cultural Revolution has demonstrated).

[50] *Ibid.,* pp. 6–17.

Mao's "Problems of Strategy in Guerrilla War." The editorial introduction said very pointedly, "Many people . . . belittled the important
strategic role of guerrilla warfare and pinned their hope on regular
warfare alone, and particularly on the operations of the Kuomintang
[read Soviet] forces."[51] The editorial then added that guerrilla strategy
was of particular importance both for the Chinese people and for the
people of Afro-Asia and Latin America.

The "debate" was clearly working up to a climax, which was duly
reached on September 3, when the anniversary of victory in the war
against Japan was celebrated in Peking. On that occasion, the arguments both of the "guerrilla" protagonists in the PLA and of civilians,
such as P'eng Chen, who opposed reconciliation with or reliance upon
Moscow, were incorporated in the famous article "Long Live the Victory of People's War," which appeared under Lin Piao's signature. At
the same time, Lo Jui-ch'ing, in the presence of Liu Shao-ch'i, Teng
Hsiao-p'ing, and others, addressed a victory rally in Peking, in which he
referred to Lin Piao's article by name and then proceeded, without ado,
to tear its basic theses to shreds.

Lin's article had placed all the blame for present difficulties and
weaknesses on the Russians. "The . . . revisionists . . . demoralized . . .
revolutionary people everywhere . . . they have greatly encouraged U.S.
imperialism in its war adventures. . . . To win the struggle against
United States imperialism and carry people's wars to victory, the Marxist-Leninists must resolutely oppose Khrushchev revisionism." Thus,
like P'eng Chen, Lin Piao was placing the struggle against the Soviets
first in order of priorities.

Lin added that it was of "vital" importance to go back to Mao's
tenets of "people's war" because the United States and the Khrushchev
revisionists were "colluding" to "extinguish the revolutionary flames."
In other words, one could not rely on Soviet help in confronting the
United States since the Soviet Union was actively hostile, and therefore
one had to retreat and rely on guerrilla warfare.

In reply to this point, Lo used an argument which his allies, such as
Teng Hsiao-p'ing, were still to utilize long after Lo himself had been
purged. He said, "Of what avail can the help of a handful of Khrushchev revisionists be to the United States imperialists? . . . they are a
mere handful of people . . . and . . . cannot change the situation in
which the East wind is prevailing over the West wind." Lo was insinuating that Lin had used the excuse of Soviet treachery to cover his un-

[51] *Hung-ch'i*, August 21, 1965; also *Peking Review*, August 27, 1965, pp.
6–22.

willingness to risk confrontation with the West; Lo's answer was that, if China followed the call of revolutionary duty, the Soviet leadership would not be able to refuse its help to China, since the Soviet leaders were weak and would be overruled [presumably by the Red Army] if they misbehaved.

Lo left no doubt as to his pro-Soviet sympathies, in spite of his dutiful attacks on the "Khrushchev revisionists." At this late date, he reinvoked the concept of the Communist bloc as if it were still a reality. "But what is the situation today? The Socialist countries, whose population has grown from 200 million to more than one thousand million, form a powerful Socialist camp . . . the united front against United States imperialism today is much broader than the anti-fascist front in the past." To speak in this fashion, openly, of unity of action with Moscow, was an unprecedented challenge not only to Lin Piao or P'eng Chen but surely, at this stage, to Mao himself.

Lin Piao rejected Lo's whole concept of looking to the USSR for military assistance, invoking China's historic experience during the war, "the problem of military equipment was solved mainly by relying on the capture of arms from the enemy, though we did turn out some weapons too . . . foreign aid can only play a supplementary role." Lin indignantly attacked his opponent's platform: "certain people assert that China's victory in the war . . . was due entirely to foreign assistance. This [is an] absurd assertion. . . ."

Lin proceeded to trot out the typical arguments of the "guerrilla" group in the PLA, as well as making use of P'eng Chen's theories. Lin strongly questioned Lo's repeated assertion that the United States was weak and could be challenged with impunity. "United States imperialism is *stronger,* but also more vulnerable, than any imperialism of the past." Lin explained that, in fact, the United States was vulnerable only in so far as its resources could not match its tremendous ambitions. He said that once the masses were fully mobilized, which, he indicated, would be a lengthy process, "superiority *will* belong not to the United States but to the people. . . ."[52] Clearly, therefore, Lin thought that *superiority now did* belong to the United States.

In line with his earlier statement, of May, 1965, Lo Jui-ch'ing vigorously denied these assertions. Clearly addressing Lin, he asked "but is not United States imperialism the strongest of all the imperialist powers?" His reply was, "We say, militarily speaking, it has become *weaker* and *more helpless* . . . as compared with . . . fascist Germany,

[52] [Italics are the author's.]

Japan, and Italy." The latter, he said "enjoyed temporary military superiority and could boast of some 'impressive military successes.' " However, "United States imperialism is now suffering one defeat after another and its much vaunted 'naval and air superiority' *is* no longer of any avail."[53]

Lin, on the other hand, proceeded to outline his strategy on the assumption that United States power was very real indeed. Quoting Mao, he said "the enemy advances, we retreat . . . we should first attack dispersed or isolated enemy forces and only concentrated and strong enemy forces later." In battle it is essential to "concentrate an absolutely superior force (two, three, four and sometimes even five or six times the enemy's strength)." Addressing an imaginary enemy, he said, "When you want to fight us, we don't let you and you can't even find us . . . when we can't [win], we see to it that you don't wipe us out." It was the strategy of a cautious man, well aware of the inferiority of his forces. Continuing his imaginary dialogue with the enemy, Lin proceeded, in fact, to polemize with the "professional" group in the PLA:

> you fight in your way and we fight in ours; we fight when we can win and move away when we can't . . . in other words, you rely on modern weapons and we rely on highly conscious revolutionary people . . . *it is adventurism if one insists on fighting when one can't win.*[54]

This was a harsh warning to Lo.

Lin's gradualism was completely rejected by Lo, who once again insisted that the United States was intent on war: "the Johnson doctrine is neo-Hitlerism . . . *it means . . . war.*" As in May, Lo's prescription was immediate military preparations: "we must . . . strengthen our preparations . . . and give still more effective support to the Vietnamese."

Lin, in a passage which used almost as many epithets against the United States as Lo had employed, managed to avoid saying that the United States "means war." Each passage that mentioned such a possibility was preceded by the conjunction "if": "*if* they insist on following in the footsteps of the Japanese . . . *if* the United States imperialists should insist on launching a third world war. . . ."[55] In the only passage which was not conditional, Lin, in fact, implied that the United States

53 [Italics are the author's.]

54 [Italics are the author's.]   55 [Italics are the author's.]

was trying to avoid conflict: "United States imperialism [is] ... trying to extinguish ... people's war ... to prevent ... people's war."

In recalling that, during World War II, the CCP had been able to exploit the "contradiction" between non-Communist countries, Lin actually managed to recall the fact of United States aid to China at that time: "in *helping* China during that period, the United States imperialists. ..." As for nuclear power, Lin simply proposed avoiding major confrontations and relying on guerrilla tactics as the best way of bypassing that problem. He explained that, in waging "people's war," one could not succeed "without taking full account of the enemy tactically, and without examining the concrete conditions and without being *prudent*."[56] He bitterly recalled that certain revisionists (he was probably as much concerned with those in Peking as with those in Moscow) "assert that nuclear weapons and strategic rocket units are decisive ... and that a militia is just a heap of human flesh."

There seems to be little doubt that this, indeed, was precisely Lo Jui-ch'ing's view. The latter stressed that there was one item the United States possessed which he did take seriously, "the atom bomb." "But [the United States] nuclear monopoly has *long* been broken and its nuclear blackmail is growing less and less effective."[57] As was shown earlier, the country which had "long" broken the United States nuclear monopoly was, of course, the USSR and not China, and in Lo's view it was only by means of the Soviet nuclear deterrent that American nuclear power could be made "less effective."

Lin, on the other hand, insisted that neither the Soviet nuclear shield nor Soviet military aid was essential and that China should operate "independently even when all material aid from outside is cut off." Lin's panacea was that China should prudently refrain from tackling United States might and rely on various guerrilla movements in the Third World to tie down the United States forces, which he described as overly "dispersed." He did not devote a single word to Chinese military preparations and confined himself to saying that if the United States should wish to attack, which was a contingency he clearly considered remote, American troops would simply be "submerged" in China's millions. Lin made it perfectly clear that China would not become involved in any confrontation and that Asian guerrillas should not expect too much from Peking.

> Revolution or people's war in any country is the business of the **masses** in that country and should be carried out primarily by

[56] [Italics are the author's.]   [57] [Italics are the author's.]

their own efforts; there is no other way. . . . If one does not operate by one's own efforts . . . but leans wholly on foreign aid—*even though this be aid from socialist countries which persist in revolution*—no victory can be won, or be consolidated even if it is won.[58]

Since China was clearly one of the "socialist countries which persist in revolution," stern notice was served on Asian guerrilla forces not to expect Peking to become involved directly. Lo, on the other hand, went out of his way to demonstrate his opposition to Lin's isolationist view by saying "we must . . . give *still more effective support* to the Vietnamese and other peoples."[59]

One of the most significant differences between the two statements concerned the treatment of Mao Tse-tung's personality. Lin, wooing Mao, as always, by intense flattery, stated that Mao "has enriched and developed Marxism-Leninism." Lo took exception to such hyperbole and pointedly put both Lin and Mao in their place: "the great thought of Mao Tse-tung has developed and *become* richer. . . ." There is all the difference in the world between stating that Mao has enriched Marxism and saying that Maoism has *been* enriched! Nor was this a mere play upon words. Lin was trying to resort to Mao's authority in order to overawe his opponents; Lo, speaking in front of party bosses Liu Shao-ch'i and Teng Hsiao-p'ing, was downgrading Mao and appealing to the party bureaucracy: "taught by the Chinese Communist Party and Comrade Mao Tse-tung and *guided by the Party's correct Marxist-Leninist line* . . . long live the great, glorious and *correct* Chinese Communist Party, long live our great leader Chairman Mao Tse-tung." It will be noticed that, for Lo, "correct" guidance came only from the Party and not from Mao.[60]

The text of the September "debate" between Lin and Lo leaves very little doubt that a climax had, indeed, been reached in the overt confrontation between the various groups, with all the parties employing phrases which were now almost openly provocative and insulting. There are significant indications that a showdown must, in fact, have occurred almost immediately afterwards. A mere four weeks later, Foreign Minister Ch'en Yi gratuitously informed foreign and Chinese correspondents, "In China, too, there are revisionists and people who have illusions about United States imperialism. Some people are in the

[58] [Italics are the author's.]

[59] [Italics are the author's.]

[60] See supra note 33; also *Peking Review,* September 3, 1965, pp. 31–39. [Italics are the author's.]

process of remolding themselves, and some have not yet remolded themselves. But these elements play no role in the making of China's policies. . . ." For good measure, he added "some people say that the United States has not yet exhausted its strength. . . ."[61] In view of the evidence before us, it would hardly be fanciful to assume that the "revisionists" he referred to were, in fact, Lo Jui-ch'ing, Liu Shao-ch'i, Teng Hsiao-p'ing, and Liu Ning-i. It may be presumed that the last three, who were a little less overtly militant in their views and continued to appear in public during most of the following year, were the people "who are remolding themselves"; Lo Jui-ch'ing, who disappeared from view shortly thereafter, was probably the man who had "not yet remolded" himself. As for "people who have illusions about United States imperialism" and who "say that the United States has not yet exhausted its strength . . . ," P'eng Chen might well fit the first category. Moreover, P'eng certainly had expressed the opinions summed up in the second definition, but there, as we have seen, he was in good company, being joined by Lin Piao and the "guerrilla" faction of the PLA, all of whom subscribed to the view "that the United States has not yet exhausted its strength. . . ." Perhaps it was this fact, together with his usefulness in opposing Lo Jui-ch'ing and Lo's allies, Liu and Teng, which saved P'eng Chen for the time being.

Actually, P'eng was able to gain an official endorsement for himself a month later, when *Jen-min jih-pao,* in its editorial of November 10, 1965, singled out certain Chinese documents and statements which had been particularly vilified by the Soviets and which, therefore, were presumably to be regarded as scripture in China. The list printed read like an official inauguration of the new "in-group" which was beginning to dominate Peking:

> Premier *Chou En-lai*'s remarks on September 9 concerning the Indo-Pakistani conflict, Comrade *Lin Piao*'s article "Long Live the Victory of People's War," Comrade *P'eng Chen*'s speech to the Aliarcham Academy of Social Sciences in Indonesia [the May 25 speech], the statement of Vice-Premier and Foreign Minister *Ch'en Yi* at the press conference of Chinese and foreign newsmen. . . .

These, then, were the reliable anti-revisionists who had joined together in the struggle against Lo Jui-ch'ing and his patrons in the party bureaucracy. In other words, Chou and Ch'en, the leaders of the state

[61] *Peking Review,* October 8, 1965, pp. 7–14.

apparatus, who had been maneuvering between the competing groups, had finally come down on the side of Lin Piao, who, by this stage, must clearly have been able to demonstrate that he enjoyed Mao's backing. Judging by the list in *Jen-min jih-pao*, P'eng Chen was still well "in" at that stage, although there were ominous rumblings concerning the fact that he had been too incautious in voicing his accommodating views towards the West. There were also the first sinister sounds of attack from Shanghai, where Mao was staying, against P'eng's associates in the Peking CCP Committee.

The "victors" against Lo Jui-ch'ing paraded prominently at a very important conference of the General Political Department of the PLA, held in the middle of January, 1966. Lin Piao, whose name was constantly invoked, was represented by Hsiao Hua, the head of the PLA General Political Department. Lo Jui-ch'ing had already disappeared, and, instead of him, his former deputy Yang Ch'eng-wu spoke. The main speeches were delivered by Chou En-lai and by P'eng Chen, on behalf of the victorious "anti-revisionists." Of the group which had previously backed Lo, one single member was permitted to speak and that was Teng Hsiao-p'ing,[62] apparently as a reward for "remolding" himself, i.e., for abandoning Lo.

The question arises what precisely was the part played by Mao in the disputes of the period February, 1965–March, 1966. Needless to say, Mao's personal opinions are more enigmatic than those of his associates, since practically no document published in 1965 can be ascribed to him with certainty. The question must arise as to why he tolerated these "debates" at all. One may speculate as to the causes: as will be shown, Mao had misjudged the international situation fundamentally at the beginning of 1965. This miscalculation may have led to one of two results—either, on top of China's other failures, it undermined his prestige and authority to such an extent that he had to permit two or three other "flowers" to "bloom"; or Mao himself felt undecided with regard to China's next move and was willing to let others argue it out until he could make up his mind. Statements directly or indirectly attributed to him in the January–February period would make it quite possible to align him with either side. However, there can be little doubt that, by September, 1965, Mao was backing Lin Piao and that it was this development which was responsible for Lo's scarcely-veiled sneers at the Maoist contribution to Marxism. In any case, some months later (March, 1966), Mao certainly had become firmly committed to unyield-

[62] *Peking Review,* January 21, 1966, pp. 5–6.

ing opposition to "unity of action," as we now know from independent (Japanese Communist) sources (*Akahata,* January 24, 1967; see also *Asahi Evening News,* January 24, 1967).

The date when Mao placed his weight behind the views expressed by the two determinedly anti-Soviet groups is a matter of some significance, since it might conceivably throw a little light on the question of P'eng Chen's purge. As has been pointed out earlier, P'eng's and Lin Piao's views were fairly close in the summer and early fall of 1965; thus, it may not, perhaps, be too fanciful to think in terms of an alliance of these two groups which helped to remove the most overt spokesman of the opposite factions, Chief of Staff Lo Jui-ch'ing. Judging by all the evidence, Lo's removal was accomplished sometime in October–November, 1965. Almost immediately afterwards, attacks on P'eng's personal associates and subordinates began to emanate from Shanghai, where Mao is believed to have been at that time. At first sight, therefore, it might appear that Mao and Lin, having used P'eng's good offices to neutralize Lo Jui-ch'ing's supporters in the party "apparat," then proceeded to rid themselves of their erstwhile ally. This phenomenon would hardly be unprecedented in Communist or general history. However, such an interpretation would have to assume that Mao had come to back the views of Lin and P'eng prior to this period and had then turned on P'eng, while continuing to support Lin.

It may well be that Mao, planning a general attack on the entrenched party bureaucracy, had, in the late summer of 1965, not yet decided on whom to rely in such a struggle, and that Lin offered himself for this task, in return for Mao's support in the military-political "debate." Lin (as he had habitually done in internal PLA literature), invoked Mao's personality in his 1965–66 statements, to the point of idolatry. P'eng, on the other hand, had been more than sparing in his references to Mao and to Mao's works and had clearly aspired to the status of an independent political thinker.

These, of course, are merely a few overt, superficial hints concerning disputes of a personal and ideological nature, of which hardly anything is really known. In any case, it is not impossible that the price of Mao's support for Lin was the removal of P'eng, whose associates on the Peking CCP committee are now known to have needled Mao for years. (P'eng Chen's friends, as has been pointed out, resented Mao's treatment of the former Defense Minister, P'eng Te-huai, whom they supported in his opposition to Mao's agricultural policy.) The downfall of P'eng Chen's Peking group was due, therefore, to primarily domestic and personal considerations, *not* to differences over international policy.

In February, 1966, P'eng himself deeply offended Mao by sponsoring the so-called "February Outline Report," which Mao regarded as fundamentally incompatible with his view on how the Cultural Revolution should be handled.

Of course, it is also possible that, as the spring of 1966 approached, with Lo Jui-ch'ing out of the way and his backers in the party bureaucracy retreating, Mao may have felt that men who had shown weakness *towards the West* could now be safely purged without upsetting the internal balance, since the main prop of the *pro-Soviet* elements had been removed. P'eng Chen's last major public appearance occurred in connection with the visit to Peking of the JCP delegation, in March, 1966. As had already been shown (see note 47), P'eng's posture on that occasion was perfectly consistent with his earlier stand and he remained strongly "anti-revisionist" to the end, at least as far as his hostility towards "unity of action" with Moscow was concerned. The episode is, however, interesting from another aspect. "Big-character posters" in Peking have recently attacked Liu Shao-ch'i and Teng Hsiao-p'ing for having, in March, 1966, concocted a communiqué with the JCP delegation, which was unduly conciliatory to the Soviet "revisionists" and which, consequently, had to be suppressed through the personal intervention of Mao himself. The JCP leadership, while admitting that such an incident occurred, claims that it had nothing to do with Liu Shao-ch'i but took place during the second stage of the talks, when Liu and Teng had left and Chou En-lai had taken over the chairmanship of the Chinese team of negotiators.[63] It is not clear, therefore, whether only Liu and Teng opposed Mao's virulently anti-Soviet line in March, 1966, or whether they were briefly joined by Chou En-lai. In any case, it is significant that P'eng Chen, whose star was already setting and who was not permitted to chair the Chinese team during any stage of the talks, apparently found ways of indicating his disapproval of the Japanese delegation's lack of hostility towards Moscow. (See note 47.) As far as the Sino-Soviet dispute was concerned, therefore, P'eng's views were still closer to Mao's, even at this stage, than were the views of Liu, Teng, or even Chou.

If Chou En-lai revealed a lack of militancy towards Moscow during this episode, he also showed a lack of militancy towards Washington (at least by Chinese standards) a few weeks later, when he gave a very ambiguous interview about Sino-American relations. He defined four points which, he felt, summed up the relationship between the two

[63] "In Answer to the Red Guards' Unreasonable Denunciation," *Akahata*, Tokyo, January 24, 1967; also *Asahi Evening News*, Tokyo, January 24, 1967.

countries and actually managed to omit all mention of Vietnam. He flatly stated that China would "not take the initiative to provoke a war" and stressed the importance of "negotiations" between China and the United States over Taiwan. He spoke of the need for a withdrawal of United States armed forces from Taiwan and the Taiwan Strait but said nothing at all about handing the island over to Peking's rule. As for the withdrawal of American troops from Taiwan, he added that this subject "admits no concession whatsoever," since it was a question of principle; clearly, therefore, issues like Vietnam were not questions of "principle" for Peking and thus did "admit concession."[64]

Whatever may have happened during the talks with the Japanese CP, Chou En-lai had returned to orthodoxy by the end of April, as can be seen from his attitude towards Liu Shao-ch'i. Immediately after the purge of Lo Jui-ch'ing, Liu Shao-ch'i, and Teng Hsiao-p'ing appeared to be "remolding" themselves, i.e., retreating, but in the spring they made a determined last stand. Between April 28 and May 6, 1966, a number of gatherings took place in Peking and Shanghai, in honor of the visiting Albanian Communist Party delegation, during which Liu, Teng, and Chou all spoke. The last major confrontations of the 1965–66 policy "debate" occurred at this time. In welcoming the Albanians on April 28, Liu seems to have chosen this unlikely occasion to raise again the drooping banners of "modern revisionism"; the slogan he considered suitable for this particular occasion was "unite still more closely with the peoples of *all socialist countries* and the whole world." He then toasted "the great unity of the peoples of the *Socialist camp* and the whole world." In other words, he was openly calling for united action with the USSR, which, by any definition, was included among "all socialist countries." The Albanian representative, M. Shehu, who appears to have been quite upset, launched a diatribe against the Russians and their various friends, presumably in reply to Liu. "With sheer demagogy, the modern revisionists are clamoring for 'unity' within the Socialist camp"[65] (the very slogan Liu had just mouthed). Two days later, Shehu still seemed to be replying to Liu when he said about the Russians "*we* treat them as enemies, not as friends."[66] Moreover, in his speech Liu had committed the heresy of separating the fight against "imperialism" from the fight against "modern revisionism"; at this stage, most Chinese speeches were harping on the theme that the

[64] *Peking Review*, May 13, 1966, p. 5.

[65] *Peking Review*, May 6, 1966, pp. 8–12. [Italics are the author's.]

[66] *Ibid.*, pp. 13–21. [Italics are the author's.]

struggle against revisionism had to be carried through to the end *in order* to fight imperialism. Thus it was emphasized that the fight against Moscow was *first* on Peking's order of priority. Liu was deliberately ambiguous on this point and seemed to be implying that these two struggles could be carried out *simultaneously*, without necessarily being interconnected: *"while* opposing United States imperialism . . . Marxist-Leninists . . . must oppose Soviet modern revisionism."[67]

Apparently in answer to this proposition, Shehu said, two days later, "We will never separate the struggle against modern revisionism from the struggle against imperialism." Speaking on the same occasion, Chou En-lai also seemed to be taking issue with Liu *"only* by firmly opposing modern revisionism, with the CPSU leading group at its center, can the fight against United States imperialism be victorious." While Liu had said "hold still higher the banner of Marxism-Leninism and the banner of opposing United States imperialism and Soviet modern revisionism," Chou demanded "hold still higher the banner of Marxism-Leninism and carry *through to the end* the struggle against United States imperialism and against modern revisionism, centered around *the CPSU leading group*." Where Liu had toasted "the great unity of the *peoples of the Socialist camp* and the whole world," Chou toasted "the great unity of the people of the whole world."[68] The omission of the "unity of the peoples of the Socialist camp" by Chou En-lai could not have been more pointed. Clearly, therefore, by May, 1966, Chou En-lai had taken over P'eng Chen's old role of assisting Lin Piao and Mao in their struggle against those who called for some degree of "unity of action" with Moscow.

It was precisely at this time that the Chinese press printed a very unusual picture of the top Chinese leadership, seated next to Mao in discussion with the Albanians, which was clearly meant to indicate the make-up of the new alignment in Peking. The four Chinese leaders in the picture were Mao, Lin, Chou, and Teng, with Liu Shao-ch'i very pointedly excluded.[69] If, however, the Mao-Lin-Chou faction was under any illusion that it had managed to separate Teng from the rest of the "revisionist" group, it was to have its hopes dispelled. Before the Albanian delegation had managed to leave, Teng Hsiao-p'ing delivered a highly ambiguous address in which he revived Lo Jui-ch'ing's old argument that one should not overemphasize the importance of the

[67] See supra note 65. [Italics are the author's.]

[68] *Peking Review*, May 6, 1966, pp. 21–25. [Italics are the author's.]

[69] *Peking Review*, May 13, 1966, p. 8.

"modern revisionists," not to speak of fearing them. The obvious implication was that those who feared the "modern revisionists" and placed
the fight against them first on the agenda were putting things the
wrong way round. After dutifully paying lip-service to the standard
denigrations of the "Khrushchev revisionists," Teng suddenly and
most inappropriately quoted the full original text of Mao's 1964 message to the Panamanian revolutionaries, including the slogan "the
people of the countries in the Socialist camp should unite"; moreover,
he added emphatically "such is the united front we want to form." As
has been seen previously, Mao's original formulation was being abandoned (probably by Mao himself) as early as February, 1965, undoubtedly because the meeting with Kosygin had engendered intense
disappointment in Peking. By 1966, it was becoming increasingly hard
to find any references whatever to the "Socialist camp," which was now
something of a mythical entity. For Teng, at that late date, to dig up
this formulation and to endorse it, was as clear an indication of unre-
pentant "revisionism" as one could find, even if, a few sentences later,
he dutifully added that "the leading group of the CPSU naturally cannot be included" in the united front.[70]

The last flickers of the debate died away two months later, as the
Cultural Revolution was already approaching its climax. At a rally in
support of Vietnam, at the end of July, Liu Shao-ch'i stated "*all* the
anti-imperialist, revolutionary countries and peoples of the world
stand on the side of the Vietnamese people. *All* the actions they are
taking to support and aid the Vietnamese people are entirely just." He
did not say a single word against the Soviet leadership and it is interesting that the phrase "anti-imperialist countries" (or, at least, "anti-
imperialist forces") had been proposed four months earlier by the JCP
as a convenient device with which to include both the USSR and China
in a "unity of action" framework.[71] As we now know from Japanese
sources, this was one of the phrases to which Mao objected.[72] Thus,
even in July, 1966, Liu seemed to be saying that *all* the actions of all
those aiding Hanoi, including, apparently, even the Russians, were
just.[73] The other Chinese speakers at the gathering, T'ao Chu and Li

[70] *Ibid.*, pp. 16–19.

[71] *Peking Review,* July 29, 1966, pp. 9–10. [Italics are the author's.]

[72] See supra note 63.

[73] It is true that Liu added the adjective "revolutionary" after the words
"anti-imperialist," but then he went on to speak of "countries and peoples" so
that the meaning could conceivably be "anti-imperialist countries and revolu-

Hsüeh-feng, did not employ Liu's slogan, or anything remotely resembling it, and violently attacked the Soviet leadership.[74]

A mere two weeks later, the "packed" Eleventh Plenary Session of the Eighth Central Committee of the CCP took place in Peking and, in its communiqué on foreign relations, endorsed not only all measures already taken by the leadership but even "all actions *to be taken*" (at least with regard to Vietnam). Giving the ruling group a blank check for the future was an unprecedented action, even for a totalitarian state.[75] The great "debate" on international strategy had come to an end.

Conclusion

It would appear that, whatever the underlying causes of China's present turmoil, international and strategic issues played their part during the preceding period in providing rallying cries for the various groups. While it cannot be assumed that the policy platforms which proved tactically useful to different factions during the period of struggle would necessarily be implemented once victory is won, they do, at any rate, provide useful insight into the attitudes of individual Chinese leaders and groups toward international issues.

It is important to note that in 1965–66 the Mao-Lin faction consistently advocated an international and strategic approach that was far more cautious and restrained toward the West than the policy favored by the Liu-Teng-Lo alignment. It was Mao's "main-line faction" which demanded that the fight against the West be relegated to a much lower place on the agenda, and that China should first carry the struggle against the Soviets "to the end." It was the Mao-Lin group, too, that rejected out of hand all proposals for additional Chinese commitments in Vietnam—whether under the guise of "unity of action" or otherwise —and replaced the concrete plans for action with vague guerrilla concepts committing China to no particular measures at all.

It was Mao's opponents who asked for more militant action in Vietnam under the guise of limited reconciliation with Moscow, or for conditional reconciliation with Moscow under the guise of militant

---

tionary peoples." He may, of course, have been deliberately ambiguous; in any case, the fact that he was the only Chinese speaker to refrain from attacking Moscow speaks for itself.

[74] *Peking Review*, July 29, 1966, pp. 13–16.

[75] "Communiqué of the Eleventh Plenary Session of the Eighth Central Committee of the CCP, Adopted August 12, 1966," NCNA, Peking, August 13, 1966.

action in Vietnam. (In either case, the end result was likely to be the same.) With regard to the effects of the "unity of action" proposals, it should be noted that they entailed not merely increased Chinese commitments and risks, but also implied a certain escalation of involvements and risks on the part of the USSR.

This possibility was already implicit in the dangerous Soviet suggestion, made in the spring of 1965, that China lease airfields in the south to Soviet planes and personnel to provide air cover for Hanoi. True, the Russians expected a Chinese rejection that would enable them to give Hanoi proof of Peking's unreliability. Still, the Russians must have considered the chance, however slender, that the Chinese might accept their suggestion. And as the 1965–66 debate shows, some people in Peking did advocate a favorable response to Moscow. While China's acceptance would undoubtedly have increased the measure of Soviet control over Peking's military and political actions, it is clear that it would have escalated the dangers run by Moscow as well. After all, Soviet planes and personnel would have become directly involved in Vietnam. This is just one indication of the kind of risk the Soviet leaders felt was commensurate with the prize of reestablishing their influence and control over China.

Such considerations would be magnified several times over if Mao's opponents were victorious, thus opening before Moscow the broad and enticing vista of bringing a "reasonable" Chinese leadership back into the Socialist camp. For the Soviet leader who wins that particular prize can expect to achieve a prominent niche in Soviet history and, more important, a secure place at the helm of the Soviet ship of state. With this prospect in mind, Soviet leaders are likely to take many a risk. Temptation has strange effects on politicians. Khrushchev, having embarked on the path of seeking a rapprochement with the United States, was apparently prepared to endanger both that project and peace itself when confronted by sudden temptation in Cuba. His successors seem to be more cautious, but may not be immune to such infections.

In the light of all this, it is difficult to understand why a substantial segment of the Western media has jumped to the conclusion that one should hope for the victory of the anti-Mao forces in China. No doubt the very natural revulsion against the outrages committed by the Red Guards has a great deal to do with this tendency. But if Mao's opponents are the same men who advocated a rapprochement with the Soviet Union, and if such a rapprochement would both involve China in serious commitments against the West and entice the Soviet leaders onto risky paths they might not otherwise tread, why should that be welcomed by the West?

Some observers, though not denying the validity of these concerns, feel they are applicable only in the short run; in the long run, they contend, the fanaticism of Mao's followers presages ill for the world, while the pragmatism of his opponents is said to hold out hopes for more rational behavior. This reasoning begs many questions. To start with, some extrapolations may be made from the recent past to the immediate future, but there are really no reliable data on which to base predictions for decades to come. It is utterly pointless to try to envisage the situation many years after Mao has passed from the stage.

As for the immediate future, it is significant that the current actions and statements of the Mao-Lin faction are entirely consistent with the views it advocated during the 1965–66 debate; indeed, it is not unreasonable to assume that its 1965–66 platform does constitute a fairly reliable guide to its attitudes and policies. This being the case, it can be asserted with some assurance that the domestic fanaticism of Mao's associates has little or no bearing on their foreign policy—which, to say the least, is extremely cautious and isolationist rather than interventionist. (Peking's attitude of active hostility toward Moscow is an exception to this rule, largely because of Mao's justifiable feeling that the "modern revisionists" are attempting to influence China's *domestic* affairs; the imperialists, on the other hand, can be ignored because they have little effect on the local scene.)

The "pragmatism" of Mao's opponents, moreover, is a very questionable proposition altogether. The most "practical" leader in China is probably Premier Chou En-lai, who appears to be with Mao and not against him. Among Mao's more important opponents, Liu Shao-ch'i, at any rate, has given many indications throughout his life of being anything but a moderate. But of far greater significance is the fact that, as the 1965–66 debate shows, even if one were to equate pragmatism with plans for modernization, Mao's opponents always linked such proposals to calls for a limited reconciliation with Moscow.

A rapprochement with the USSR also was consistently advocated by Mao's foes as part of militant "unity of action" in Vietnam, which would have involved both Peking and Moscow in considerable risks of confrontation with the United States. So it would seem that it was the pragmatists and not the fanatics who were the larger menace to peace and to the West. And there is no reason to assume that precisely the same policy motivations would be ignored now if Mao's opponents were able to defeat him.

What we know from both the statements and the actions of the Mao group promises limited but real advantages for the West, while, on the basis of their earlier platform, Mao's opponents appear to be favoring policies which are anything but reassuring. The foes of Mao and Lin have, of course, have been largely silenced in recent months, but the solicitude displayed by the Soviets about their fate indicates that Moscow does not believe their policies would change if they were to be victorious.

It is sometimes objected that the victory of Mao's opponents, a consequent rapprochement with Moscow, and even Sino-Soviet "unity of action" in Vietnam would simply mean increased Soviet ability to moderate China's actions. That is an extraordinarily static view of history. The current international postures of China and the USSR are the products of many tactical, personal, propagandistic and other considerations pertaining to *present* conditions. It is barely ten years since Peking stood on the right wing of international communism, propagating the "Spirit of Bandung" and supporting Poland's Wladislaw Gomulka, and the Russians were the leftist hard-liners. There is no reason whatever to believe that in an entirely changed relationship, such as would prevail during a Sino-Soviet rapprochement after the victory of Mao's opponents, the international postures of both these countries would remain frozen and immobile.

Technological advances have made an open collision course between East and West a nightmare no leader will risk. But there is no evidence that this has really been a serious matter for argument in the Sino-Soviet dispute (on the contrary, it was precisely militant Peking which, correctly, tongue-lashed Khrushchev for irresponsibility and adventurism in unleasing the Cuban confrontation). Even Lo Jui-ch'ing never suggested that China should take the initiative in precipitating a showdown; he merely thought that the West was likely to do so and that, in order to prepare for such an eventuality, Peking should lean on Moscow and agree to "unity of action" in Vietnam. The matters at issue between Peking and Moscow were tactical; both repeatedly paid lip-service to the thought that war could, under certain circumstances, be prevented, but the Chinese claimed that the Soviet path was most calculated to encourage the other side to precipitate a showdown.

What was really at stake, of course, was China's resentment at the thought of the other two great powers discussing the fate of the rest of the world between them, alone and in secrecy. The CCP had excellent reasons, covering some forty years of bitter experience in its relations with the CPSU (under Stalin, Khrushchev, and Brezhnev), for knowing that Moscow could always think of urgent motives for subordinating the interests of the Chinese "comrades" to other considerations. As they have shown at the meetings in Warsaw (and as both Chou En-lai and Foreign Minister Chen Yi have repeatedly indicated), Mao's men have no objections whatever to sitting down alone with the United States—they simply don't want the Russians to do so.

It is as unhistorical and unscientific to consider the Chinese necessarily militant in international relations and the Russians determinedly reasonable as it would have been for seventeenth-century observers to assume that the Swedes are always warlike invaders and the Germans always innocent victims of their neighbors' aggressions. It is quite true that, in the purely bilateral field of United States–USSR relations (test ban, space, perhaps even arms limitations), there are excellent technological reasons for a continued Soviet-American dialogue, above all since the thermonuclear giants must constantly define and redefine the "rules of the game" to avoid fatal errors. History has shown, however, that the gravest dangers to peace arise not in the area of direct relations between the two superpowers, but in the field of multilateral relations, where third parties are involved.

It is exactly in this region (Cuba, the Third World, etc.) that the Soviets have shown an occasional and disturbing tendency to succumb to temptations, and it is here that the most dangerous situations have arisen. The prospect of redeeming China with the help of Mao's opponents belongs precisely to this realm; as I have already indicated, an opportunity of this kind could probably be exploited only within a militant framework such as "unity of action" in Vietnam, which might prove acceptable both to the Peking and Moscow elites. But situations like this have their own momentum. Surely, it would be preferable for Mao's victory to rule out such concepts altogether and to shield the Russians from such temptations.

What is the point of discussing these hypotheses anyway when the West cannot influence the situation in China? Actually it can, at least in a negative sense. There is some danger, slight but real, that the rooting for the victory of Mao's opponents in the Western press could be misread by Moscow as a green light for various forms of Soviet interference in China's affairs. Some Western reporters, for instance, have joyfully speculated how pleasant it might be if the Soviets found ways, during the present upheaval, of permanently neutralizing or disposing of the nuclear installations in China's far west. It is hard to imagine a more dangerous or counterproductive suggestion.

The same cold and rational balance of power concepts which require that China should not unduly extend its control and influence beyond its present frontiers, demand also that China should under no circumstances be dismembered—nor should a power hostile to the West be encouraged to intervene in China's internal affairs and to bring a dissident faction to power. A Chinese government owing its existence to Soviet manipulations or outright Soviet intervention would constitute a major upset in the existing power system. To some extent, this might be a more negative development than was the victory of Mao's forces in 1949.

Those who have watched the Soviet scene carefully since the CPSU plenum in mid-December, 1966 (which reached certain unreported conclusions on the Chinese situation), have seen some disturbing indications of itching fingers in Moscow. To be sure, the Russians have no intention of getting bogged down in any invasion of China, but if China were reduced to anarchy and civil war, a careful, limited Soviet action to assist a local Chinese force which asked for help somewhere in the border regions should by no means be considered unthinkable. A Western "atmosphere" which could be interpreted as encouragement by those elements in Moscow who harbor such thoughts and desires is highly undesirable.

A world where the West has the option of pursuing two separate and bilateral relationships, one with Moscow and one with Peking, and where Moscow and Peking are mutually antagonistic and, objectively, vying to outflank each other in maneuvering with the West, may prove to be reasonably balanced and safe from temptations. And this is far more likely to develop if Mao's men win. If his opponents gain the upper hand, even temporarily and locally, the Russians will be sorely tried by two temptations: to intervene, or to join in a militant Sino-Soviet "unity of action" agreement with an anti-Mao government, or both. Neither possible result of victory by Mao's foes can be viewed with equanimity by the West.

Norton Ginsburg

3

On the Chinese Perception
of a World Order

A careful observer must be struck by numerous apparent paradoxes and contradictions in China's recent foreign policy.[1] These contradictions relate, *inter alia,* to the differential attitudes displayed by the Chinese toward various Asian and other countries; to the contrast between China's pronouncements about "wars of national liberation" and her actions; to certain non-ideological bones of contention between China and the USSR; to vacillations and peculiarities of China's relations with Japan; to the intensity of her concern with internal affairs in Korea and Vietnam and her relatively lesser involvement with them in other neighboring countries; to pronouncements about wars without boundaries; to China's behavior toward India and Pakistan, among others.

To some extent the questions raised by these seeming contradictions may be answered in terms of China's limited military capabilities, despite her possession of the "bomb," to act beyond her territorial confines. There is widespread consensus that China's military establish-

The concept of an idealized "world order" in Chinese culture has been discussed by Theodore Herman in his "Group Values toward the National Space: The Case of China," *Geographical Review,* April, 1959, pp. 164 ff.; and later, even more persuasively, by John K. Fairbank in "China's World Order," *Encounter,* December, 1966, pp. 1–7, although this article was not available to the author at the time this paper was drafted. Nevertheless, he has a clear intellectual debt to Professor Fairbank. See also the discussion in O. E. Clubb, *Twentieth Century China* (New York: Columbia University Press, 1964), especially pp. 413 ff., and in K. T. Young, "The Working Paper," in L. M. Tondel, Jr., ed., *The Southeast Asia Crisis* (Dobbs Ferry: Oceana Publications, 1966), especially pp. 18 ff. and 27–28.

[1] In part, these contradictions may reflect lack of harmony between China's "ideological aspirations" and the perception of her national interests. See C. P. FitzGerald, "Chinese Foreign Policy," in Ruth Adams, ed., *Contemporary China* (New York: Pantheon, 1966), pp. 7 ff. See also his *The Chinese View of Their Place in the World* (London: Oxford University Press, 1964), pp. 68–72.

ment, though admittedly formidable on its home ground, becomes less formidable with distance from the Chinese ecumene. Even more significant are ideological considerations. It would be both rash and incorrect to propose that major decisions about China's foreign policy are not grounded in ideology for, of course, they are; but even the careful study of ideological considerations, of Maoist doctrine and practice as they resemble or differ from other Communist philosophy and practice, fails to account for many of the paradoxes in that foreign policy, and in general much uncertainty remains.

To help resolve that uncertainty there is need to inquire into the Chinese perception of what a world order *ought* to be like, and about the role China would play in such an order. Admittedly, such an attempt is likely to be more speculation than scholarly inquiry, but this does not mean it should not be undertaken, given the importance of the issues at stake. How, then, might the Chinese see themselves, as a state among states, as a nation among nations, as the oldest, largest, longest-lived of all the countries of the world?

The fact that the Chinese state has been so long-lived and has a history of unprecedented longevity documented in voluminous records surely is relevant to the problem. Communist China's leaders, though in ideological disagreement on certain issues, including many aspects of foreign policy, are all middle-aged or elderly men. All have been educated in large if varying degree within the intellectual and historical framework of traditional Chinese society; all are nationalist; most appear to have a singularly limited knowledge of much of the outer world;[2] all appear to be conscious of their historical heritage. It would be incredible if their percepts of an ideal world order were not strongly influenced by these circumstances, subconsciously or otherwise. This is not to say that Marxist ideology is not of overriding significance in understanding their political behavior. It simply allows for the fact that they are the brainwashers, not the brainwashed, and their intellectual roots lie deep within a cultural matrix different from, and not merely antecedent to, the one they are trying to build.

That there is a long history for China in which accomplishment looms large, as compared with other parts of the Communist world

[2] Chou En-lai, for example, would be an obvious exception. See H. L. Boorman, ed., *Biographical Dictionary of Republican China* (New York: Columbia University Press, 1967), pp. 392–93. Other exceptions are found among younger officials such as Hsiung Hsiang-hui, the former Chinese Chargé d'Affaires in London. See Donald W. Klein, "Men of the Moment (III)," *China Quarterly*, no. 26 (April–June, 1966), pp. 102–4.

such as Russia, is not irrelevant for other reasons, let alone as it bears on Sino-Soviet rivalry itself. The Chinese classics, historical records, scholarship, and literature, all record the glories of the Chinese state at a time when other contemporary states were either not yet born or were struggling to acquire some identity. These documentary materials continue to be reproduced and circulated or commented upon within China, especially those which bear upon the power of China as an empire among empires on the one hand, or upon the aggression of China's enemies when China was divided and weak, especially in modern times, on the other. There is widespread consensus that one of the strong appeals of the Peking regime is to the Chinese sense of nationhood (qualitatively at least different from nationalism elsewhere) and national destiny. It would be beyond reason to assume that in some fashion this destiny does not assume a geographical pattern in the minds of Chinese, whether leaders or followers.

Furthermore, in the course of Chinese history there appear the broad outlines of a traditional view of the world political order. Although difficult to document, there is widespread agreement that such a view exists. There is reference to it in the ancient Yü Kung.[3] The territorial patterning of China's polity for over two millennia lends credence to it. The earlier relations of the Empire with the West, the lofty disregard for Western philosophy and achievement, though with notable exceptions, the assumption of autarchy, the seeming confusion between trade and tribute, all support the existence of an ideal construct, whether or not it has accorded at all times with political reality.

The traditional view of the world order was Sinocentric. This assertion is not merely a truism arising from a naïve interpretation of the term *Chung-kuo* (Central State). Most national views of the world order are to a greater or lesser degree centered upon the state concerned. This provincial, or national, view is true of modern France and to some extent of the United States of America; and it has been true of Britain, Germany, and at times of other Western powers. To this extent, then, China is by no means unique, but it is unique in that China possessed this view long before the modern European state had come into existence. This means that it was held long before it was assumed that state power extended to delimited and demarcated boundaries and that all the territories of a given state were equally well-controlled and were of

[3] James Legge, trans., *The Texts of Confucianism, Part I, The Shu King* . . . (Oxford, 1879), p. 19. See also the summary in Herman, "Group Values toward the National Space," pp. 171–72.

equal political value. On the contrary, China's traditional view of her role in the world order did not place equal premium on all of her territory, and also placed different value on territories beyond her actual control.[4] In other words, some areas were more important than others. The localization of power and authority was greatest in a core area and tapered off in all directions, in some direct relation with distance and accessibility. Formal boundaries, with one partial exception, were of little moment.[5]

The spatial model that incorporates these conditions was composed of a series of overlapping, merging concentric zones; each associated in somewhat different ways with the core; each varying somewhat in their relations with the others as the power of the Chinese state waxed and waned. The notion of concentric zonation need not be regarded simply as formal and static. Just as Ernest Burgess' concentric zonal hypothesis of metropolitan organization in modern America reflected the processes of urbanization,[6] so did the traditional Chinese model of the world order reflect the kinesis of China's internal organization and the dynamics of her changing relations with territories in political relation with her.

The zonal model, then, had at the center of the system Zone I or *China Proper*, what commonly is identified as the Eighteen Provinces (*shih-pa sheng*), or what might be termed the hub of a Sinocentric universe; but even this assertion is too simple. China Proper itself could be divided into at least two types of areas: those over which control was virtually continuous from Han times to the present and those over which control was present but less effective. These might be called the "Core" (or cores) and the "Ecumene," respectively.[7]

[4] I am grateful for this idea to Mr. J. B. R. Whitney of Earlham College whose chapter on China's political geography in H. L. Boorman's forthcoming history of modern China has been drawn upon freely, but the idea also appears in various guises in a number of secondary sources.

[5] This does not mean, however, that the Chinese were not concerned about their peripheral territories and how they were controlled. As Philip Kuhn has pointed out in a personal communication, one could even argue that "the farther from the . . . center, the more elaborate the control mechanisms" developed and applied.

[6] E. W. Burgess, "The Growth of the City," in R. E. Park, E. W. Burgess, and R. D McKenzie, *The City* (Chicago: University of Chicago Press, 1925), pp. 47–62.

[7] For a variant cartographic definition of the "Core," based on estimates of population and cultivated land, see Herman, "Group Values toward the National Space," p. 178.

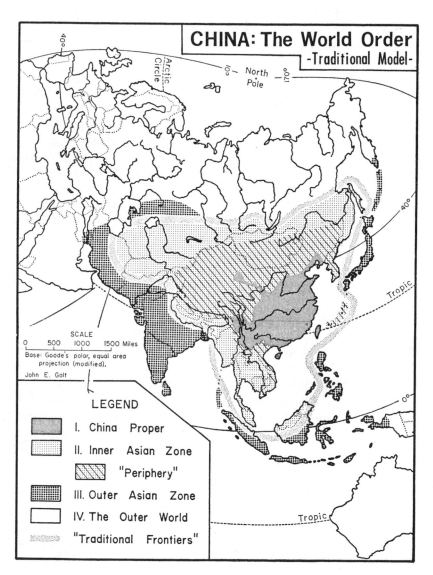

CHINA: The World Order
-Traditional Model-

SCALE
0   500   1000   1500 Miles

Base: Goode's polar, equal area
projection (modified).

John E. Galt

LEGEND

I. China Proper

II. Inner Asian Zone

"Periphery"

III. Outer Asian Zone

IV. The Outer World

"Traditional Frontiers"

MAP 1

Outside of China Proper lay an irregular concentric zone of territories over which China had exerted varying degrees of control or had
been in intimate relation, and which we might term the *Inner Zone*
(Zone II). As part of this Inner Zone and contiguous to the Eighteen
Provinces (to which must be added the so-called "Chinese Pale" in
Manchuria) were a number of extra-ecumenical areas over which China,
at least in Ch'ing times if not before, exerted nominal if not genuine
sovereignty and which included much of Manchuria, Mongolia, Chinese Turkestan, and both eastern Tibet and Tibet Proper. To these
could be added the sometime dependencies of strong Sinitic cultural
heritage—Korea and Annam. To this largely continuous but open ring
of territory we might apply the term, the "Periphery." In addition and
beyond these were various territories ranging from those actually held
under Chinese suzerainty for relatively long periods, such as the Trans-
Amur territories in eastern Siberia[8] or the eastern parts of Soviet
Middle Asia to those which were tribute-bearing or otherwise subordinate states, extending from Afghanistan to the Ryukyus.[9] Whatever
the particular relation of these territories to China, all were regarded
as, and to a large degree actually behaved as though they were, subordinate areas or "client" states.

Although no delimited boundaries girdled Zones I and II, Chinese
territorial claims during the Ming and especially the Ch'ing periods
suggest a north-south trending maritime frontier running through the
Sea of Japan and the Straits of Korea, through the Bashi Channel (between Taiwan and the Philippines), through the South China Sea but
incorporating most of British Borneo and the Sulu Archipelago, and
around the southern tip of the Malayan Peninsula until it recurved
northward through the Andaman Sea (Map 1). The frontier enveloped
all of mainland Southeast Asia and then recurved inland to include
Assam, the Himalayan Kingdoms, and much of Soviet Middle Asia—at
least the eastern portions of the contemporary six constituent republics

[8] These areas were not in fact part of China in terms of direct territorial
control prior to the Manchu period when they were "brought" to China by its
Manchu conquerors. See C. P. FitzGerald, "Chinese Expansion in Central
Asia," *Royal Central Asian Journal,* July–October, 1963, pp. 292–93.

[9] For a listing of areas which sent tribute embassies to the Ch'ing court, see
J. K. Fairbank and S. Y. Teng, *Ch'ing Administration,* Harvard-Yenching
Institute Studies, 19 (Cambridge: Harvard University Press, 1960): 193–98.
For references to tribute-bearing missions from Afghanistan, not noted by
Fairbank and Teng, see Dai Shen-yu, "China and Afghanistan," *China Quar-
terly,* January–March, 1966, pp. 213–15.

of the USSR there. Finally, to the north and northeast, it included all of Mongolia and the territories northward to the *taiga* in what is now the Soviet Union, and ran eastward to the Pacific, including Sakhalin Island.[10] Although the territories of Zone II were regarded in greater or lesser degree as "Chinese," they were held as being of lower value, except for certain commercial and strategic purposes, than those of Zone I.

Beyond Zone II lay an *Outer Asian Zone* (Zone III) composed of a number of territories, which was discontinuous and for the most part not contiguous to China, though parts of it lay very near to what was regarded as "Chinese" territory. All of this zone lay in Asia, and it ranged from Persia on the west through India, Indonesia, and most of the Philippines to, perhaps paradoxically, Japan on the east. With the partial exception of Japan, the states occupying these territories had never been in true tributary or client relationships with the Chinese Empire, but they were relatively well known to the Chinese and fell more in the category of *terrae cognitae* than otherwise. Indeed, the extent of Chinese trade and cultural relations with certain of these territories might suggest their more appropriate position in Zone II, of which more below.[11]

Beyond Zone III lay Zone IV. It is not inappropriate to suggest the name "The Great Beyond" for this *Foreign Zone,* which included only a small part of Asia (the eastern Mediterranean), but all of Europe, Africa, and the Americas. "All the Rest" would also not be an inappropriate nomenclature, since it was in Chinese eyes largely undifferentiated.

[10] These boundaries appear, with variations, in numerous atlases and reference works published in Republican China. See, for example, the middle-school atlas, *Hsien-tai pen-kuo ti-t'u* (Shanghai: World Geography Company, 1940), plate 45. A more refined presentation for the Ch'ing period appears in Albert Herrmann, *An Historical Atlas of China,* ed. Norton Ginsburg (Chicago: Aldine, 1966), plate 51.

[11] Fairbank, "China's World Order," pp. 1–4, also proposes four zones, but he restricts the second to "the closest and culturally-similar tributaries, Korea and Vietnam . . . and also the Liu-ch'iu Islands and in certain brief periods, Japan." This he calls the "Sinic Zone." The next he calls the Inner Asian Zone and composed of "the tributary tribes and states of the nomadic or semi-nomadic peoples of northern Manchuria, Mongolia, Eastern or Chinese Turkestan, and Tibet. . . ." Oddly, except for Vietnam, his scheme contains no specific zonal niche for Southeast Asia, but it apparently is included in his Outer Zone, "consisting of the 'outer barbarians' generally, at a further distance over land or sea."

In the traditional model, this concentric pattern reflected a political spatial system, a "space-polity" in short, within which China Proper might be likened to a sun and the areal constituents of Zones II and III to planets revolving about her, the whole blending off into other possible systems in the "Great Beyond," Zone IV. Over time, inventories of the members of this system would vary, however, as some most accessible would merge with the central sun as it flared across neighboring territories; others might be absorbed by *their* neighbors; still others might spin out of orbit; and yet others would become orbital (as in the case of European Russia during the early Mongol period) for limited periods of time. Nonetheless, these dynamics should not invalidate the basic premises or structure of the model.

For centuries upon centuries the perceived political spatial system remained Sinocentric, zonal, roughly concentric, without formal boundaries, characterized by a distance-intensity relationship between power and territorial control, almost exclusively Asian-oriented, and separated from the rest of the world by indifference or ignorance. Nowhere in those centuries of China's history for which the model appears to apply did China perceive of herself as a state of states, a neighbor among neighbors, a member of a family of nations.[12]

Although the model is geographically comprehensible as here proposed, certain constraints operated on it to make it geometrically asymmetrical and to distort its pattern, though such qualifications need not, again, diminish its utility. Concentricity was broken on the east by the sea and the offshore archipelagoes of eastern Asia to which, however, both maritime and trans-maritime Chinese claims were made. To the north, the Siberian *taiga* comes close enough to the Amur so that client states in the Trans-Amur territories were unlikely or short-lived; and even to the northwest the steppe and the northern forests which blended into it provided a distinctive ecological setting in marked contrast to those elsewhere and within which great nomad-controlled empires rose and fell. In the southwest, the Tibetan Highlands and the Himalayan ranges acted as formidable barriers to penetration and control and, in effect, greatly increased the effective distances from the Chinese Core and Ecumene (Zone I) to the southwestern frontiers. In the north, too, as Lattimore points out, is found the only clear expression of a boundary between China Proper and the rest of Asia, the

[12] Fairbank, "China's World Order," pp. 2–3, succinctly notes the lengths to which traditional China's foreign relations were distorted, so as to avoid implications of egalitarianism between China and other states.

Great Wall;[13] but even this extraordinary feature was less a political boundary in the modern sense than a somewhat arbitrary line marking an ecological transition from "sown" to steppe, across which Chinese and "barbarian" power has shifted from period to period.

In fact, the only direction in which the model operated with a minimum of such constraints (although they were there nonetheless) was the south, that is, along the frontier of expansion and "inclusion," to use Lattimore's term, leading toward and into Southeast Asia, in contrast with the frontier of "exclusion" in the north and northwest.[14] That the southerly frontier leads into Southeast Asia has relevance also to current events.

Finally, it should be understood that the various zones merged into one another and that their territorial composition varied from time to time. Thus, although Tibet has been included not only in Zone II, but also in that part of it functionally nearest China Proper, the so-called Periphery, in fact it did not clearly come within China's orbit until the Yüan, and for much of its later history, until the early eighteenth century, it would properly have fallen in the Outer Asian Zone (III). Conversely, Annam in its history has moved outward from Zone I to Zone II, and Japan, in Chinese eyes, apparently has fluctuated between Zones II and III.

Certain aspects of and problems in China's foreign policy become more nearly comprehensible, if one assumes that this spatial model still has relevance and that China's leaders perceive as one of the objectives of that policy a reconciliation of contemporary political geographical realities with the essence of that model. On the other hand, the course of history has resulted in certain substantial changes in the world map which make a return to the traditional spatial system impossible. Empires and dependencies have come and gone; the technological revolution in transportation and communications has resulted perforce in major shifts in the relations among areas; and the balance of power in Asia has been transformed not only because of these developments, but also because what Mackinder has called the "closed world" also has come into being.

It is not unreasonable to propose, therefore, that a current acceptable model of the "proper" world order, as perceived by China's leaders,

[13] Owen Lattimore, "Origins of the Great Wall of China," *Geographical Review*, October, 1937.

[14] Owen Lattimore, "The Frontier in History," *Studies in Frontier History* (The Hague: Mouton, 1962), p. 477.

would differ from the traditional model in some respects, though the principles of merger and fluctuation would continue to hold (Map 2). The Core and Ecumene of Zone I and most of the Periphery of Zone II would be regarded as inseparable, since they are joined as one to form the modern Chinese state. Zone II, as a zone of presumed or possible dependent or client states, would now include Korea, Mongolia, Vietnam, Laos, Cambodia, Thailand, Burma, the Himalayan States, and possibly Afghanistan,[15] as well as the northern irredentist territories which lie within the Soviet Union. Zone III would encompass the rest of Southeast Asia, Japan, and perhaps the countries of South Asia. Some of these territories border China itself, though generally removed from its ecumenical areas; others are more distant, but in some cases might be assumed to possess a more intimate relationship with China either on ethnic grounds, as in the case of Malaya, or by shared Sinitic cultural traditions, as in the case of Japan. Zone IV continues to be recognized, but now it falls logically into two parts: that which is developed, metropolitan, capitalistic or retrograde socialist, and presumably imperialistic; and that which is underdeveloped, "colonial," "rural," and unstable, as well as non-Asian.

China's relations with the countries and territories in these modified zones logically can be expected to differ, and indeed there is reason to believe that China's foreign policy varies with the roles prescribed for countries in them. This proposition may be illustrated with reference to some of the historical events that have led to differences between the "current" as contrasted with the "traditional" model. Two related hypotheses worth considering here as well propose that China's foreign policy reflects both an ambivalence between the two models and an attempt to adjust contemporary affairs to what the Chinese perceive as the "proper" ordering and distribution of power.

One of the crucial constraints on effecting a pattern based on the traditional model was the imposition of formal, delimited boundaries upon the Chinese state by foreign, chiefly European, powers, but also Japan.[16] The Chinese conception of a concentration of power in core

15 Dai lends support here by stating: "If China is to restore the glory of the Sui-T'ang period along the Silk Road . . . , it will be in the recognition of China's moral or political suzerainty, particularly along the Pamir-Himalayan fringes" ("China and Afghanistan," pp. 221). As a step toward establishing a détente with Afghanistan, China agreed to the demarcation of the short (75 km.) border between the two countries in March, 1964.

16 For a classification of these impositions, see Herman, "Group Values toward the National Space," pp. 175–76.

and ecumenical China, gradually tapering off into unbounded and fluctuating frontier zones, was confronted in the seventeenth century by Imperial Russia's drive to the Pacific and by the establishment in the nineteenth century of boundaries in the north and west, which marked the formal limits of Chinese power. Similar boundary impositions occurred, also in the nineteenth century, along China's southern frontiers, although, as is well known, not all the boundaries were delimited, let alone demarcated. In any case, there is little evidence to suggest that the Chinese, whether Imperial, Republican, or Communist, have accepted the modern notion of the delimited boundary as a formal limit of the power of the state,[17] although for special reasons referred to below, the Chinese have come to terms on boundary delimitations. *It follows, therefore, that a continuing problem in China's foreign policy will be border disputes, whatever other relations may exist between China and contiguous countries.*

As a corollary, the Chinese unwillingness to accept the boundary as an integral quality of the modern state must lead to disputes over territories which she regards as *terrae irredentae*.[18] For the most part such territories lie within the USSR, into which have been absorbed huge areas, up to 600,000 square miles, of northern and western forest, steppe, and desert, all of which at various periods formed part of Inner Zone II. The Mongolian People's Republic also falls into this category. To a remarkable degree, however, *terrae irredentae* in this sense are not part of the contemporary pattern in the southern and southeastern marchlands, where *direct* Chinese control either has never existed or was relatively long past. *It follows, therefore, that another continuing force in China's foreign policy would derive from attempts to restore Chinese hegemony not over Southeast Asia, but over those territories of Outer Mongolia and the Soviet Union which formerly were part of traditional Zone II.* So long as China and the USSR were wedded through ideological harmony, these pressures were thrust into the background.

[17] A special instance of this point is the Chinese espousal of the principle of *jus sanguinas* rather than that of *jus solis,* as shown in the Nationality Law of 1929.

[18] Shinkichi Eto correctly observes, however, that such claims and disputes need not mean "unlimited expansionism." See his "Some Underlying Principles of Peking's External Activities," *Japan's Future in Southeast Asia,* Symposium Series 2 (Kyoto: Center for Southeast Asian Studies, 1966), pp. 105 ff. For relevant maps other than those cited previously, see Clubb, *Twentieth Century China,* p. 415; and G. B. Cressey, *Land of the 500 Million* (New York: McGraw-Hill, 1955), p. 40.

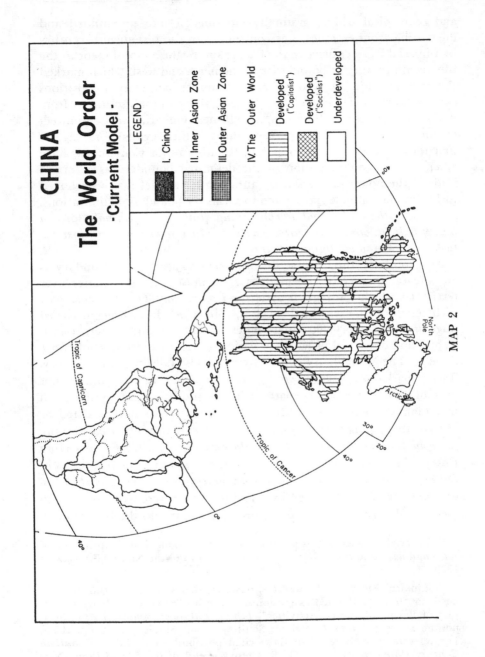

CHINA
The World Order
- Current Model -

LEGEND

I. China

II. Inner Asian Zone

III. Outer Asian Zone

IV. The Outer World

Developed ("Capitalist")

Developed ("Socialist")

Underdeveloped

Tropic of Capricorn

Tropic of Cancer

North Pole

Arctic

MAP 2

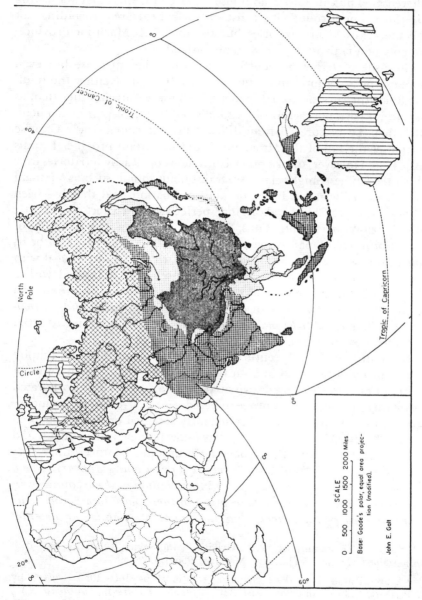

SCALE

0   500   1000   1500   2000 Miles

Base: Goode's polar, equal area projection (modified).

John E. Galt

MAP 2—Continued

85

Once harmony disappeared, they rose again to exacerbate ideological differences. Thus, in 1964 Mao himself spoke of China's not yet having "presented our account" for a list of Soviet-held areas including not only the Trans-Amur territories, but also the Soviet Maritime Province, the port of Vladivostok, and Sakhalin island.[19]

The issue of *terrae irredentae* appears in different guise but even more excruciating form in connection with Taiwan. Neither the traditional nor the current spatial model allows for a Taiwan other than as an integral part, not merely of a Chinese polity, but as part of ecumenical China. To be sure, Taiwan did not become convincingly Chinese until after the fall of the Ming, and it did not attain provincial status until 1886. However, unlike other contiguous or nearby territories over which the Chinese might claim suzerainty but do not, such as Vietnam and Korea, Taiwan has had only one incarnation, and that has been Chinese; the pre-Chinese aboriginal period was, in effect, prehistoric and therefore irrelevant. Thus, Taiwan, despite a half century of separation under Japan between 1895 and 1945, is perceived to be as much Chinese as is Hainan. It follows, then, that attempts to deal with Taiwan as an issue separate from China itself are confronted with a Chinese perception that blocks communication even before it can begin. *The restoration of Taiwan to China is an essential and particularly sensitive issue of China's foreign policy,* but it is strategic-spatial in nature, not ideological.

During the nineteenth century, as the power of the Chinese Empire waned, many of the areas in both the Inner and Outer Asian Zones of the traditional model were drawn out of China's orbit and incorporated in varying degrees into European-based empires, even as boundary agreements were proposed and reluctantly accepted or quietly ignored by the Chinese. Most of these areas have now become independent, and their relationships with China have been unstable or uncertain.[20] *One of the major objectives of China's recent foreign policy appears to be a clarification of these relationships and the aligning of these countries in accordance with the Chinese perception of their place in a Sinocentric, Asian-oriented power system; thus the policy of establishing détentes*

[19] For a fuller account see W. E. Griffith, "Sino-Soviet Relations 1964–65," *China Quarterly,* no. 25 (January–March), 1966, pp. 28–30.

[20] A useful analysis of these changing relationships since 1950 is given by V. P. Dutt, "China and Southeast Asia," *Japan's Future in Southeast Asia,* Symposium Series 2 (Kyoto: Center for Southeast Asian Studies, 1966), pp. 89–102, but his orientation is chiefly toward the relationship between ideology and policy.

with them wherever possible. Those which had been dependent or tribute-bearing states in the pre-modern period are expected to be both friendly and subordinate; those farther removed would be expected to be at least friendly. Of course, ideological intimacy would be welcomed, but it does not appear to be a prerequisite to the establishment of détentes, either for former tribute-bearing states of Zone II, such as Burma,[21] or of states in Zone III, such as Pakistan. As Richard Lowenthal has pointed out,[22] the issue is not whether these states follow China's ideological bent. Conditions of their entry into the system are not whether or not they are Communist, but whether they accept, or seem to accept, the Chinese conception of order. That concept involves, *inter alia,* no or minimal entangling alliances with non-Asian powers and the banning of foreign military forces.[23] In these terms, the presence of American troops in Thailand and Thailand's key role in SEATO present a particular embarrassment; but the terms of acceptance do not deny the possibility of a sub-dominant, non-Communist Thailand, free from these involvements and willing to suppress its own interests in *terrae irredentae,* some of which lie within China herself.

Even more difficult as a problem in foreign relations is Japan, which occupies a peculiarly equivocal position within the model political-geographic systems. On the one hand, Japan's partially Sinitic heritage is associated with mutual sentiments about the relations between the two countries, as A. M. Halpern has noted.[24]

On the other hand, Japan has always played an ambivalent role in China's foreign relations. Never occupied by the Chinese, it paid

[21] Thus, in 1960 China and Burma concluded a boundary agreement, not unfavorable to the Burmese, which might be regarded as a symbol of the costs the Chinese are willing to bear in order to draw Burma into the system, reconstitute Zone II, and prevent their "encirclement" by foreign, that is, United States power. Nevertheless, Peking's recent fulminations against the Ne Win government indicate extreme sensitivity to possible shifts in Burma's position vis-à-vis the Chinese and demonstrate China's willingness to exert strong pressure on the states of Zone II to prevent their "drift" away from dependency or subordination. For a succinct summary of the Sino-Burma rift, see John Badgely, "Burma's China Crisis: The Choices Ahead," *Asian Survey,* 7 (November, 1967): 753–61.

[22] In discussion at the China Conference, Chicago, February 8, 1967.

[23] See Rhoads Murphey, "China and the Dominoes," *Asian Survey,* September, 1966, p. 512.

[24] For a thoughtful appraisal of these views, see Sadako Ogata, "Japanese Attitudes toward China," *Asian Survey,* August, 1965, pp. 389–98, as well as A. M. Halpern's essay in this volume, chapter 15.

tribute to China only during a short period in the fifteenth and six-teenth centuries.[25] Later, it competed with China for control of certain territories in Zone II, such as Korea, and, what is more important, con-trolled Manchuria and Taiwan in Zone I and eventually large portions of the Core of China. Moreover, Japan has moved economically into the world of the developed nations and has become one of the world's leading industrial powers. *Ceteris paribus,* one would have anticipated China's making use of Japan's expertise in developing the Chinese economy, and the Japanese certainly have been willing. However, the Chinese have chosen, despite recent rapid increases in Sino-Japanese trade, more to ignore than to accept Japan, as also was the case during most of Ch'ing times. *Rooted in historical relationships, the Japanese enigma continues to be a crucial problem in China's foreign policy,* exacerbated by what appears to be a remarkable ignorance in China of the potency of the Japanese economy and the relevance of the Japanese socioeconomic revolution to the viability of the Chinese perception of the world order. Long regarded by the Chinese as a client state but never unambiguously one, Japan continues on her own increasingly non-Asiatic way. Nevertheless, there is some justification for regarding China's policies toward Japan as part of an attempt to bring Japan "back" into Zone III and indeed into greater involvement with Asia.[26]

Vietnam presents, in the short run, far more difficult problems to China, and their nature is illuminated by reference to the postulated Chinese scheme of things. Unlike Japan, but like Korea, Vietnam was for several centuries, until the tenth century, part of China's Periphery and even longer a client state in tributary relation to China. The tradi-tional spatial model suggests an involvement between China and Viet-nam, therefore, significantly greater than that between, say, China and Thailand or Burma. Ideally, then, one might expect an ambivalence in China's policies toward Vietnam, as between reabsorbing it into the traditional Periphery on the one hand and drawing it back into orbit as part of a contemporary Inner Zone of client states on the other. Here, as in the somewhat similar case of Korea, one would expect ideo-logical considerations to play a more significant role than elsewhere

[25] See Yi-tung Wang, *Official Relations between China and Japan, 1368–1549* (Cambridge: Harvard University Press, 1953), in which these relations are documented.

[26] Almost continually, China has expressed displeasure at Japan's ties with the United States and her failure to recognize the Peking government, but quasi-official relationships continue to exist.

among the contiguous territories, but these have come to be subordinated to an even greater problem.

The presence of American and other foreign troops in South Vietnam effectively prevents the reconstitution of continuous Zone II dominated by China and free from foreign involvement, and therefore the restoration of either the traditional or current hypothetical spatial orders. It means also the interjection of Russian influence in what the Chinese regarded as their appropriate sphere of influence (*shih-li fanwei*). From the Chinese point of view a unified, Communist, satellite Vietnam would be ideal, but, again, that view does not place an equal value on all territory, and it places some territorial objectives over others. It can be argued that reunification ranks low on the Chinese scale of values, whereas a dependent and ideologically intimate North Vietnam would rank higher; but highest of all would be a South Vietnam free of foreign troops which might become a threat to China itself, as escalation of the current war proceeds.

Under these circumstances, *the objectives of China's foreign policy might be attained, at least minimally, by a divided Vietnam in which the South need not be Communist but would be free from foreign troops and foreign interference in internal affairs.* Not only would the aspirations of the Democratic Republic of Vietnam toward a unified Communist state perpetuate a dangerous condition on the edge of ecumenical China, but they also would, if satisfied, create a potentially powerful element in the world Communist system, which might create further difficulties for China in her ideological conflict with the Soviet Union.

In this context one can begin to comprehend the agonies of irresolution which have wracked China's leaders with regard to the issue of more active and substantial support for North Vietnam and the Vietcong. A greater commitment means not only the dangerous extension of Chinese supply lines in mainland Southeast Asia, far more difficult of access than northern Korea for example, but also the even greater danger of American reprisals on the Chinese mainland. Failure to support means severe loss of face in Asia. Either might require abandonment of a China-oriented constellation of subordinate states in Asia.

Consideration of these issues suggests justification for the Chinese attitude toward wars of national liberation—encourage them everywhere but in those Asian areas in which Chinese domination is desired! Encourage them by words, money, and arms in the Near East, in Africa, in Latin America, but keep them far enough away from the Asiatic mainland so that foreign troops do not constitute a threat to China itself! It might be heretical, but consistent, to propose that the Chinese would not have encouraged a war of national liberation in Vietnam had one not, in effect, already been under way. When Lin Piao emphasizes the importance of adhering to the policy of "self-reliance" in fighting "people's wars," he recognizes both China's inability to participate directly and actively in them and her unwillingness to have responsibility for them on her doorstep. When Chen Yi speaks of "wars without boundaries," he serves notice that China does not necessarily recognize the system of territorial delimitation imposed on her.[27]

The underdeveloped, "rural" countries of the "Great Beyond," Zone IV, in contrast to the metropoles, provide superb milieus within which the ideologically hostile and physically threatening West might be distracted, diverted, and possibly weakened, even as China buys time for her internal economic development.[28] Such might well have been the policy adopted by China in late Ch'ing times had she had the technological and economic means to have done so, again with the objectives of distraction and diversion.

The metropoles, on the other hand, are little understood as compared with the poorer countries, and their motives, particularly those of the United States, barely comprehended. With a few exceptions, none of the senior Chinese leaders knows the United States firsthand. Their perception of the world order cannot explain the interests of the United States in Asia, except as a reflection of irrational aggression and the imperialistic ambitions associated with Admiral Mahan's views on Asia and the establishment of American power as far removed from the North American mainland as possible. Perhaps the Chinese understand Mahan, but they are apparently much less perceptive about the changes that have taken place in the United States since his death.

The purpose of this essay has been to suggest the need for considering alternative explanations to the ideological, in explaining, understanding, and forecasting Chinese behavior in the world political arena. Clearly that behavior is a function of four major ingredients: (1) ideo-

[27] Ideological considerations appear here as well, since "all (working) men are brothers," or are said to be, within the framework of Marxist philosophy, and national boundaries must not separate them. On the other hand, Chen Yi has also accused the United States, rather than China, of failing to respect boundaries. See *Peking Review*, October 8, 1965, p. 14.

[28] Charles Fisher would agree with this point as far as it goes, but would argue that the next step might be attempts at establishing hegemony over the Inner Zone countries. See his "The Chinese Threat to South-East Asia: Fact or Fiction," *Royal Central Asian Journal*, July–October, 1964, pp. 251–67.

logical considerations, vis-à-vis both the capitalist powers and the USSR; (2) domestic economic and other factors, including chance; (3) factors exogenous to China; and (4) strategic-political imagery and objectives, based in part on historical circumstances and tradition. For the most part the attention of analysts of China's foreign policy has been concentrated on the first and second of these and to some extent the third. The fourth has been relatively neglected. In approaching it, the models proposed should not be dismissed as mere exercises in spatial geometry. They relate to but are not identical with Professor Fairbank's exhortation to "look at the map" in seeking understanding of contemporary China. The important consideration is not symmetry or concentricity, but perception and imagery of the world as it ought to be, and the relations of these to the formulation of China's foreign policy. That partial concentricity and some symmetry may appear in that perception is a consequence of the processes that relate geography and history in contemporary China's polity and which feed back into the complex procedures by which China plays out her role in world affairs.

Hans J. Morgenthau

4

The United States and China

I   The Interests and Policies of China

China poses for the United States three fundamental issues, which can be separated for purposes of analysis but which in practice blend into each other. First, China is the most powerful nation on the mainland of Asia and potentially the most powerful nation in the world. Second, China has been for at least a millennium a great power of a peculiar kind in that her outlook upon, and relations with, the outside world have been different from those of other great powers. Third, China is today the fountainhead of the most virulent kind of Communism, proclaiming the inevitability of armed conflict and instigating and supporting Communist subversion throughout the world.

1.   China as a Great Power

As a great Asian power, China seeks to restore the position she occupied before she was reduced to a semi-colonial status in the middle of the nineteenth century. That goal has been proclaimed by the Chinese leaders, and the policies actually pursued by them with regard to the offshore islands and Taiwan, Korea, Vietnam, Burma, Cambodia, Tibet, and India conform to a consistent pattern: restoration of the territorial boundaries and of the influence the Chinese Empire possessed before its modern decline. These boundaries are likely to comprise Taiwan and the offshore islands, Outer Mongolia, and the Asian territories claimed by China and annexed by the Soviet Union during the nineteenth century. Physically, considering the distribution of power on the Asian mainland, China could go much farther—she could go virtually as far as she wanted to. But she has never done so in the past, and she is not likely to do so in the future. The reasons are to be found in the peculiar Chinese outlook upon the world.

According to Professor C. P. FitzGerald, "Rather more than a thousand years ago, the T'ang dynasty thus fixed the geographic limits in which the Chinese people were to live until modern times."[1] Instead of conquering neighboring states, which she could have conquered without undue risk, China has been traditionally satisfied with the establishment at her southern and southwestern borders of friendly governments, whose political identity was left intact and whose friendliness was assured and symbolized through tributary relationships of different kinds and degrees.

These subtle and indirect relationships are the result of the traditional Chinese conception of China as the center of the political universe, the only sovereign power worthy of the name, to which all other nations owe tribute. This extreme ethnocentrism goes hand in hand with contempt for, and ignorance of, the outside world, which from the Chinese point of view really does not need to be understood and dealt with on terms of equality with China. As the present relations between China, on the one hand, and Cambodia and Burma, on the other, can be regarded as a modern version of the tributary relations of old, so the present ignorance of the Chinese leaders of the outside world, their verbal assaults upon it, and their ineffective policies with regard to it can be understood as a modern version of China's traditional ethnocentrism.

2.   China as a Communist Power

The quandary which the United States faces in its relations with China is created by the addition to these traditional elements of Chinese foreign policy of a new and unprecedented one: the sponsorship of a militant world Communism. That quandary is similar to the one the United States dealt with successfully in the immediate aftermath of World War II when it had to distinguish between the great-power and world-communist aspirations of the Soviet Union. The Soviet Union modified and mitigated its world-revolutionary fervor when it began to realize, starting in the twenties, that the risks it ran for its own survival on behalf of world revolution were out of all proportion to the chances of achieving that revolution. It is at least possible, if not likely, that China will undergo a similar process of adapting world-revolutionary aims to political and military realities. The chances for such a development must exist, provided China has a rational government,

[1] C. P. FitzGerald, *The Chinese View of their Place in the World* (London: Oxford University Press, 1964), p. 19. Cf. also John G. Fairbank, *China, The People's Middle Kingdom and the U.S.A.* (Cambridge, Mass.: The Belknap Press of Harvard University Press, 1967), p. 8.

and they are enhanced by the nature of the foreign policies China has pursued in Asia since 1949.

These policies are characterized by two main interrelated qualities: caution and limitation to the traditional national objectives of China. These qualities stand in stark contrast to the militant rhetoric of the Chinese leaders, in which an ethnocentric disregard for the realities, and contempt for the interests, of the outside world manifest themselves.

Minister of National Defense Lin Piao's famous manifesto of September 3, 1965, provides a particularly impressive but by no means unique example of this ethnocentrism, which is intellectually absurd and politically impractical. Lin Piao tries to apply the lessons of the Communist revolution in China to the world scene. Just as the Communists conquered the countryside, isolating, surrounding, and finally conquering the cities, so, he suggests, the Communists will conquer the rural areas of the world and isolate and finally conquer the cities of the world, by which he means the capitalistic nations of the West. To consider these geopolitical metaphors as a program for political and military action as many people in the United States do, is to fail completely to understand their ethnocentric source. Lin Piao's manifesto is not the Chinese equivalent of *Mein Kampf,* for the simple reason that even a Chinese Hitler would be incapable of putting it into practice. Completely lacking in even the most elementary understanding of the outside world, it rather reminds one, if one needs a historic analogy, of the eccentricities of German geopolitics.

3.   The Future Policies of China

Provided China has a rational government, it can be expected that both the present and the coming generation of Chinese leaders will continue to learn from experience and to adapt their policies to the real world. Under the same proviso it is also quite possible that the coming generation will be less given to militant Marxist-Leninist rhetoric and to the instigation and support of subversion throughout the world. But it would be futile to expect that the new generation will be more accommodating than is the old one when it comes to the restoration of China's traditional domain in Asia. In this respect, Mao Tse-tung and Chiang Kai-shek see eye to eye, and so must Mao Tse-tung and his successor, whoever he may be. To mention only the most crucial issue where the traditional Chinese national interest is at stake, both Mao Tse-tung and Chiang Kai-shek consider Taiwan to be an integral part of China; they disagree only as to who shall rule China. Regardless of its ideological commitment, no patriotic government of China can be expected to give up the claim to Taiwan, and any Chinese government which believes itself to have the power will try to recover it. The issue of Taiwan has indeed proven to be the main stumbling block in the Warsaw negotiations between the United States and China, and it is bound to do so in the future. That it has proven to be no more than a stumbling block is due to China's temporary military weakness. Once China has realized its military potential, the issue of Taiwan, if it has not been settled in the meantime, will be the most likely *casus belli* between the United States and China.

One cannot rule out the possibility that the foreign policies of a powerful China, fully armed with nuclear weapons, will not be oriented towards the achievement of China's traditional national objectives but towards world conquest. The combination of traditional ethnocentrism with the ability to destroy the world might well call forth utterly irrational policies. However, while the possibility of such policies must be taken into account, their probability is small in view of the extreme caution Chinese foreign policy has shown thus far.

II   The Interests and Policies of the United States

1.   The Interests and Historic Policies of the United States

What are the interests of the United States with regard to China, and what are the policies most likely to serve those interests? The United States has two such interests: maintenance or, if need be, the restoration of a viable balance of power in Asia, and the maintenance of a world-wide balance of power.

Thus the United States has pursued in Asia the same basic interest it has tried to realize in Europe since the beginning of its history. For in both Europe and Asia the United States consistently opposed the power which threatened to make itself the master of the continent and in consequence place itself in a position to threaten the security of the United States from across the ocean.

As far as Europe is concerned, this interest has always existed even though it was not always recognized for what it was. Thus Jefferson would shift his sympathies from Napoleon to Great Britain and back again according to the fortunes of war, without being aware that he was acting in terms of the balance of power when he opposed the nation which seemed to be winning in any particular phase of the Napoleonic wars. When, during the Crimean War, American diplomacy took an active interest in preventing the ascendancy of any one power on the

European continent, it followed the rules of the balance of power without articulating them. The contrast between what this country was doing and what it thought it was doing has nowhere been more marked than in the European policies of Woodrow Wilson. The United States intervened in World War I in order to prevent a German hegemony over Europe, that is, on behalf of the European balance of power. Yet Wilson conceived of the purpose of American intervention not in terms of establishing a new balance of power favorable to American interests, but of making an end to the balance of power itself.

What from the beginning of the Republic to World War I remained largely implicit and was frequently concealed by a rhetoric which was either irrelevant or contradictory to the real issue has become perfectly obvious since World War II: United States concern for the balance of power is the rationale of its European policy. From the very outset of hostilities, while remaining legally neutral, this country took the side of Great Britain and France against Germany, the would-be hegemonial power, and took measures, such as lend-lease and the destroyer deal, which were incompatible with the status of a neutral. In the immediate aftermath of World War II, the United States perceived in the Soviet Union a new threat to the European balance of power and has ever since countered it by the policy of containment. The stationing, in virtual permanence, of American troops east of the Rhine has been a token of the determination to preserve the balance of power in Europe.

The active interest of the United States in Asia dates only from the turn of the century. Its first expression is the Open Door policy with regard to China. At the outset this policy had exclusively a commercial purpose: it sought to maintain freedom of competition for all interested parties in the semi-colonial exploitation of China. But very soon it took on a political and military connotation as well. For the United States recognized that any great power, European or Asian, which added the enormous power potential of China to its own would thereby make itself the master of its own continent, if not of the world. Thus the policy of the Open Door for China transformed itself organically into a policy of the balance of power for Asia, of which the independence of China was the cornerstone.

It is for this reason that the United States opposed from the very beginning Japan's attempts at creating an Asian empire, primarily at China's expense. That opposition started out ineffectually in the form of the Stimson Doctrine, that is, the refusal to recognize territorial changes effectuated by force. Yet from the late 1930's onward, ever more stringent actions implemented that verbal expression of this country's opposition until in the fall of 1941 it confronted Japan with the choice between giving up any further territorial expansion or going to war with the United States.

During and immediately after World War II, the United States tried to make China into a counterweight to Japan, thus restoring the Asian balance of power. In anticipation and furtherance of this development, the United States endowed China both legally and politically with the status of a great power. When the Communists defeated Chiang Kai-shek and took over China in 1949, they also destroyed the foundations of our Asian policy. Suddenly, China, instead of serving as a counterweight to a power inimical to the United States, became the ally of one of them. Japan, disarmed and occupied, could not serve as a counterweight to the emergent power of China. That function could be performed by only one power, the United States itself.

The policies through which the United States has implemented this function, it seems to me, have been decisively determined by the Chinese intervention in the Korean War. Before that intervention, the United States moved towards recognition of the Communist government of China and away from complete military and political identification with Chiang Kai-shek's regime on Taiwan. The policy which the United States then intended to pursue vis-à-vis China was clearly formulated in the famous and often misquoted speech which the then Secretary of State Dean Acheson gave at the National Press Club in Washington on January 12, 1950. That speech did not envisage a unilateral military commitment of the United States on the mainland of Asia. Acheson identified the island chain adjacent to the Asian mainland from Japan to the Philippines as the outer limits of America's military presence.

China's intervention in the Korean War radically transformed the Asian policies of the United States. The United States responded to that intervention with two policies: the policy of isolating China and the policy of peripheral military containment.

2.   The Policy of Isolating China

The policy of isolating China sought the downfall of the Communist government. It was intimately connected with the recognition of the Chiang Kai-shek government as the legitimate government of China and with the expectation of its return to the mainland. By maintaining close relations with the Chiang Kai-shek government and none with the Communist government, a policy in which the United States expected its allies to participate, this country tried to destroy the legitimacy of the Communist government. By interdicting all personal and commercial relations with mainland China, the United States expected to make it impossible for the Communist regime to govern. This policy has obviously failed. Chiang Kai-shek will not return to the mainland and his government survives only by virtue of the presence of the Seventh Fleet in the Strait of Taiwan. The Communist government of China enjoys diplomatic, cultural, and commercial relations with many nations, among which there are many allies of the United States, and it is the United States rather than Communist China which has been isolated in consequence of its policy of isolation. Insofar as China is isolated, as it is in the Communist world, that isolation is in good measure self-inflicted, and our policy of isolation has nothing to do with it.

Thus from the point of view of China, the American policy of isolation is no longer an important issue. Therefore, no favorable response can be expected from China if the United States should give up this policy. The real issue is not isolation but containment. This is the crucial point at which the traditional national interests of China and the policy of the United States clash. The slogan "containment without isolation" obscures that crucial issue. It is a formula for continuing the policy of peripheral military containment by making it appear that the abandonment of the policy of isolation portends a significant change in American policy. It tends to make the policy of peripheral military containment palatable by tying it to an apparently real and benevolent change in our China policy. It also carries a suggestion of condescension—"We are going to be nice to you from now on"—which is not likely to impress a China that is mindful of its humiliations, past and present.

Similar considerations apply to the proposal to end the isolation of China by engaging in trade with her. The existence and the volume of trade between the United States and China are irrelevant to the basic issues that divide the two nations. Furthermore, China looks at foreign trade not as a series of transactions undertaken for commercial gain, but as an instrument of national policy. To engage in indiscriminate trade with China, apart from an overall political settlement, is self-defeating; for such trade strengthens China politically and militarily without giving an equivalent political or military advantage to the other partner.

Finally, the seating of the Communist government as the representative of China in the United Nations is not likely to be successful if it is conceived merely as the liquidation of the policy of isolation and not also and primarily as a settlement of the issue of Taiwan. It is virtually inconceivable that a representative of the Communist government should set foot in the United Nations while a representative of the Chiang Kai-shek government is present; for the idea of "Two Chinas" is as repellent to Mao Tse-tung as it is to Chiang Kai-shek. If the General Assembly should vote that the representative of the Communist government replace the representative of the Chiang Kai-shek government, the latter would no longer be represented in the General Assembly but would still occupy the seat of China as a permanent member of the Security Council. It is here that the issue would be joined.

If the Security Council should decide to emulate the General Assembly and install the representative of the Communist government in the permanent seat of China—a decision the United States could prevent by vetoing it—the Chiang Kai-shek government would be deprived of any representation in the United Nations. In consequence, its claim to be the legitimate government of China would be destroyed, and its claim to be the legitimate government of Taiwan would be considerably impaired. Thus our policy of containing Communist China, which we could continue behind the military shield of the Seventh Fleet, would be politically undermined. For by weakening Chiang Kai-shek's claim, Communist China would have taken the first step towards achieving the recognition of its own. Thus it becomes obvious again that the real issue is not isolation but containment.

3.   The Policy of Peripheral Military Containment

The United States thought that the policy of military containment which worked so well against the Soviet Union in Europe would work equally well elsewhere, and so we applied it to the Middle East through the Baghdad Pact and to Asia through SEATO and have followed it in our policies vis-à-vis China. Yet what succeeded in Europe was bound to fail elsewhere. The reasons for that failure are twofold.

First, the threat that faced the nations of Western Europe in the aftermath of World War II was primarily military. It was the threat of the Red Army marching westward. Behind the line of military demarcation of 1945 which the policy of containment declared to be the westernmost limits of the Soviet empire, there was a highly developed civilization, only temporarily weak and able to maintain itself against the threat of Communist subversion.

The situation is different in the Middle East and Asia. The threat there is not primarily military but political in nature. Weak governments and societies provide opportunities for Communist subversion. Military containment is irrelevant to that threat and may even be counterproductive. Thus the Baghdad Pact did not protect Egypt from Soviet influence and SEATO has had no bearing on Chinese influence in Indonesia and Pakistan, to speak of Asia only.

China is, even in her present underdeveloped state, the dominant power in Asia. She is this by virtue of the quality and quantity of her population, her geographic position, her civilization, her past power remembered and her future power anticipated. Anybody who has traveled in Asia with his eyes and ears open must have been impressed by the enormous impact which the resurgence of China has made upon all kinds of men, regardless of class, political conviction, and national affiliation, from Japan to Pakistan.

The issue China poses is political and cultural predominance. The United States can no more contain Chinese influence in Asia by arming Thailand and fighting in South Vietnam than China could contain American influence in the Western Hemisphere by arming, say, Nicaragua and fighting in Lower California. If the United States is convinced that it cannot live with a China predominant on the mainland of Asia, then it must strike at the heart of Chinese power—that is, rather than try to contain the power of China by nibbling at the periphery of her empire, we must try to destroy that power itself. Thus there is logic on the side of that small group of Americans who are convinced that war between the United States and China is inevitable and that the earlier it comes the better will be the chances for the United States to win it.

Yet, while logic is on their side, practical judgment is against them. For while China is obviously no match for the United States in overall power, China is largely immune to the specific types of power in which the superiority of the United States consists—that is, nuclear, air, and naval power. Certainly, the United States has the power to destroy the nuclear installations and the major industrial and population centers of China, but this destruction would not defeat China; it would only set her development back. To be defeated, China has to be conquered.

Physical conquest would require the deployment of millions of American soldiers on the mainland of Asia. No American military leader has ever advocated a course of action so fraught with incalculable risks, so uncertain of outcome, requiring sacrifices so out of proportion to the interests at stake and the benefits to be expected. President Eisenhower declared on February 10th, 1954, that he "could conceive of no greater tragedy than for the United States to become involved in an all-out war in Indochina." General MacArthur, in the Congressional hearings concerning his dismissal and in personal conversation with

President Kennedy, emphatically warned against sending American foot soldiers to the Asian mainland to fight China.[2]

If we do not want to set ourselves goals which cannot be attained with the means we are willing to employ, we must learn to accommodate ourselves to the political and cultural predominance of China on the Asian mainland. It is instructive to note that those Asian nations which have done so—such as Burma and Cambodia—enjoy at least a measure of peace in the shadow of the Chinese giant. On the other hand, those Asian nations which have allowed themselves to be transformed into outposts of American military power—such as Laos in the late fifties, South Vietnam, and Thailand—have become the actual or prospective victims of Communist aggression and subversion. Thus it appears that peripheral military containment is counterproductive. Challenged at its periphery by American military power at its weakest —that is, by the proxy of client states—China or its proxies are able to respond with locally superior military and political power.

Thus, even if the Chinese threat were primarily of a military nature— and here is the second fallacy—peripheral military containment would be ineffective in the long run in view of China's local military superiority. By believing otherwise, the United States has fallen heir to a misconception of its containment of the Soviet Union and of the reasons for its success. The Soviet Union has not been contained by the armed forces this country has been able to put in the field locally in Europe. It has been contained by the near certainty that an attack upon these forces would be countered by the nuclear retaliation of the United States. If we are to assume that the Chinese armies stand, or one day will stand, poised to sweep over Asia, or that irrational Chinese leaders will try to conquer the world by threatening it with nuclear destruction, they will not be contained by the armed forces the United States or its allies can put into the field on the mainland of Asia. They will only be deterred by the near certainty that China as an organized society will be destroyed in the process of nuclear retaliation.

China is today protected from the full measure of American nuclear retaliation by her own technological backwardness; for she does not possess the number of industrial and population centers whose nuclear destruction would spell her defeat. It is for this reason that China is today more daring in words, and might well become more daring in action if her vital interests were sufficiently threatened, than would be justified in view of the overall distribution of power between the

[2] Arthur M. Schlesinger, *A Thousand Days* (Boston: Houghton Mifflin, 1965), p. 339.

United States and China. However, in the measure that China develops her nuclear capability, she also becomes vulnerable to nuclear retaliation; for once China has developed into a modern nation with a high technological capability, she will also have developed a large number of vital industrial and population centers and will then have become as vulnerable to nuclear attack as are the United States and the Soviet Union today. Assuming a modicum of rationality in the government which will then govern China, fear of nuclear retaliation must be assumed to have the same restraining influence upon Chinese policies as it has had upon the policies of the United States and the Soviet Union since the beginning of the nuclear age. Thus the nuclear arms race, at least as long as it is carried on among a few great powers, carries within itself its own corrective, however tenuous: nuclear power and nuclear vulnerability go hand in hand and so does the rational requirement of self-restraint.

4.   The World-Wide Containment of China

The peripheral military containment of China is, however, being justified not only in local terms but also, and to an ever greater extent, in world-wide terms. We are told that by containing China in South Vietnam we are containing her everywhere, and that by frustrating a "war of national liberation" in Southeast Asia, we frustrate all "wars of national liberation." This argument has the virtue of simplicity, but it is supported by no historic evidence. It brings to mind the statement which William Graham Sumner made at the beginning of the century: "The amount of superstition is not much changed, but it now attaches to politics, not to religion."

The so-called "domino theory" is indeed an echo of the Marxist dogma of historic inevitability which asserts that Communism will inevitably spread from country to country until in the end it will engulf the world. Nothing of the kind has actually happened. After World War II, the nations of Eastern Europe went Communist, but Finland to this day has not. After the collapse of French rule in Indochina in 1954, North Vietnam went Communist, but nobody else did. By 1960, half of Laos had gone Communist, but nobody else followed suit. For almost two decades, the fortunes of Communism in Indonesia have fluctuated according to local conditions, not according to what happened or did not happen elsewhere. Can anyone seriously maintain that the fortunes of the guerrilla wars in Guatemala, Colombia, or Venezuela will depend upon what happens or does not happen in South Vietnam? It stands to reason that the triumph or defeat of Communism in any particular country is not simply a by-product of what happens or does not happen in other countries. What will happen in Vietnam can at the very best be no more than one factor among many, and most certainly not the decisive one, that will influence developments in other countries.

III   A New China Policy for the United States

If this analysis of the interests the United States has in Asia, and of the policies it has pursued vis-à-vis China is correct, then it follows that we ought finally to overcome the trauma of the Chinese intervention in the Korean War and return to the principles Dean Acheson defined in his speech to the National Press Club referred to above. It is worthy of note that the policy proposals which Professor Edwin Reischauer has advanced since his resignation as ambassador to Japan appear to be inspired by the philosophy of that speech. If one applies that philosophy to the concrete issues with which the United States must come to terms in its relations with China, one arrives at the following five conclusions:

First, the policy of peripheral military containment ought to be gradually liquidated. This policy is not only irrelevant to the interests of the United States but actually runs counter to them.

Second, both the policy of isolating China and the policy of ending that isolation are essentially irrelevant to the issue at hand. One may aggravate, and the other ameliorate, the international climate; but they have no relevance, one way or the other, to the basic issue of containment.

Third, since the expansion of Chinese power and influence, threatening the Asian and world balance of power, proceeds by political rather than military means, it must be contained by political means. To that purpose, it is necessary to strengthen politically, socially, and economically the nations of Asia which are within China's reach, without exacting in return political and military alignments directed against China. We ought to pursue a similar policy with regard to the uncommitted nations outside Asia in which China in the recent past has attempted to gain a foothold.

Fourth, we ought to be clear in our minds that if the United States should continue the present policy of the peripheral military containment of China, we will find ourselves in all likelihood sooner or later at war with China. If we want to avoid such a war, we must change our policy. If we do not want to change our policy, we must be ready to go to war. That is to say, either we bring the means we are willing to employ into line with our objectives, or we cut down our objectives to the measure of the means we are willing to employ.

Fifth, the ultimate instrument for containing China is the same that has contained the Soviet Union: the retaliatory nuclear capability of the United States. It must be brought home to China, as it was brought home to the Soviet Union, that in the unlikely event that she should embark upon a policy of Asian or world conquest, she is bound to be at war with the United States.

Comments by Paul A. Varg

The heart of Professor Morgenthau's argument concerning present policy in Asia is no less impressive because we may question portions of his historical analysis. What is important in the case he presents is that China will by her sheer size, capacity, and achievement become the dominant power in Asia. The smaller nations on her borders will inevitably look to her. Therefore, "we must learn to accommodate ourselves to the political and cultural predominance of China on the Asian mainland." To seek to prevent this by military measures is, as Professor Morgenthau sees it, a tragic blunder. It would make sense to furnish technical assistance and economic aid so that the former colonial areas can solve their basic problems and become viable political and economic entities, but it does not make sense to shore up anachronistic regimes by military means.

Morgenthau is not impressed by the shift in policy toward China that has taken place since John Foster Dulles was secretary of state. Dulles sought to bring about a complete isolation of China and downfall of the Communist regime. Today, these aims have been replaced by the containment of China and at the same time an acceptance of the Communists' permanent control. Morgenthau readily acknowledges this significant transition but he has no more confidence in the new policy than he did in the old. Containment involves us in commitments and traps us into obligations where vital national interests are not at stake. He argues for a new approach whereby the United States escapes from meddling and faces squarely the only issue that is of legitimate concern, namely, any attempt by China to conquer Asia or any other part of the world. China should be made to understand when and if she crosses this line, it will involve her in an all-out war with the United States, including the use of nuclear weapons. Morgenthau considers such a course on the part of China unlikely.

Morgenthau's paper deals with the traditional ethnocentrism of China. He sees in present Chinese attitudes toward the outside world a continuum from the past. Some will question this simple interpretation. This writer would like to say that the present Chinese suspicion of the rest of the world is not identical with the traditional Chinese concept of the Middle Kingdom even though on the surface the similarity may be striking. The arrogance born of a sense of superiority over the barbarians is quite different from the distrust born out of one hundred years of humiliation in dealing with the arrogance of the white man. The depth of this Western arrogance, as seen by the Chinese, is not adequately explained by the policies of Western nations. More often it was the unhappy encounters that the Chinese had with Westerners in China in day-to-day experiences that left the deepest scars. What we confront today is not so much a Chinese feeling of supreme superiority but grim retaliation for insult. To this we must add that the Chinese, rightly or wrongly, continue to believe that Westerners do not really accept them as equals.

Morgenthau states that when a present day leader, for example, Minister of National Defense Lin Piao in his famous statement of September, 1965, engages in rhetoric about conquest of the world, his remarks must be interpreted in the light of traditional Chinese ethnocentrism. The rhetoric reveals an ignorance of the outside world and it should not be taken seriously. Is today's ethnocentrism based on ignorance to the degree that prevailed earlier? One is inclined to doubt it. The Chinese are well aware of the surging frustrations, hates, and aspirations of former colonial areas and propose to turn these to their own advantage.

There are questions to be raised about Morgenthau's central thesis although few would be inclined to disagree as to the importance of learning to live with a China enjoying a paramount position in Asia. For instance, one can wholly agree that it is most important to aid economic progress in each of the countries on China's periphery; but is not economic development to some degree dependent upon the security of these nations? Is it not likewise true that while there has been too great emphasis on military aid, the economic assistance programs have not been negligible? Moreover, I doubt that anyone really questions the vital importance of economic assistance.

It is one thing to dismiss the policy of containment as futile and befogging and quite another to liquidate it in practice. The policy has its basis in the many treaty commitments made in the 1950's. Professor Morgenthau was critical of many of these treaties at the time they were negotiated, particularly of SEATO, and many would agree with the position he then took, but the United States cannot readily escape from agreements even if they were unwise.

Taiwan, as Morgenthau correctly points out, is the chief obstacle to a settlement of the two problems of diplomatic recognition and China's admission to the United Nations. Both problems are desperately in need of solution. Yet, as is well known, neither Peking nor Taiwan will accept a two-China solution. Given this fact, the problems can only be solved if the United States writes off its mutual defense pact of 1954 with Taiwan and withdraws its fleet from the Formosa Strait. Professor Morgenthau does not explain how we can extricate ourselves. However, he does ask that we face the issue of Taiwan fully recognizing the price of the commitment when China achieves sufficient military strength to challenge us.

If we assume that a line can be drawn between the policies of containment and encirclement, there is room for further speculation. Containment of the Soviet Union did not mean intervention in the area already under Soviet control. Presumably, we may conclude that the same is true of China, and containment is therefore based upon the hope that attitudes in China will change as she confronts a situation which is not to her liking but is quite tolerable, certainly more so than war. The question then becomes one of whether containment is less likely to end in nuclear war than the withdrawal advocated by Morgenthau. The risks are not trivial in either case, and it would have been well to spell out these risks.

To raise these questions about the presentation is not to dismiss the importance of what Morgenthau has said. It is precisely the issues that he raises that must be faced and that are so worthy of debate.

Morgenthau's case need not rest on the several historical interpretations he employs. In fact his case is not strengthened by his use of history, for a number of his interpretations are open to serious question.

To assert that the basic policy of the United States in Europe has always been to maintain a balance of power and, more specifically, to fit the policy of Thomas Jefferson into this rubric, is to maintain what no historian of American diplomacy has found to be true. "Thus Jefferson would shift his sympathies from Napoleon to Great Britain and back again according to the fortunes of war . . . ," is a novel interpretation. Jefferson did shift, hoping to take advantage of the situation of the moment, but in so doing, rather than seeking a balance of power in Europe, he sought continental expansion or the protection of American maritime interests.

In his treatment of the entry of the United States into World War I, Professor Morgenthau sets forth once again that the major aim was to preserve the balance of power. This is too simple an explanation to jibe with the complexities. He is on firmer ground in stating that the United States' Far Eastern policy during the early decades of this century aimed at a balance of power in Asia; at least the historical evidence makes clear that this aim entered into the thinking of policy makers.

Professor Morgenthau states that the containment policy vis-à-vis the Soviet Union after World War II worked because the threat was military in nature and therefore military means were appropriate for countering it. The Chinese threat is not military, he explains, but political, and therefore it must be met with non-military measures. The Marshall Plan came into being because the threat arose in considerable part out of economic conditions, a fact that disputes his interpretation. As to China, and the appropriateness of military and naval containment, Professor Morgenthau certainly raises the key question. The strength of the regimes in the border states is more important to security than military alliances. It is likewise true that China has acted with restraint and caution. However, this caution is partly the product of the policies and the military strength of the United States.

Robert A. Scalapino

The Question of "Two Chinas"

In the aftermath of a major upheaval like World War II, certain new and intractable problems are inevitably born, problems defying solution yet representing major obstacles that block a healthy political evolution.

In Asia, Taiwan constitutes one such problem. No solution to the question of Taiwan is currently in sight, yet it is difficult to conceive of the status quo surviving into the distant, possibly even into the middle-range, future. In certain respects, the Taiwan problem is similar to that of other "divided states"; in other respects, it is significantly different. Unlike the cases of Germany and Korea, there are no compelling historical or cultural reasons for the unification of this island with mainland China. It is true, of course, that at various stages of history Taiwan came under Chinese control or influence and was claimed by China. But so did many other regions of Asia not properly a part of China today. For example, when the American government officially inquired of the Chinese in the late nineteenth century what regions came under their sovereignty, Korea, the Ryukyus, Taiwan, North Vietnam, and Nepal were all listed, along with other territories less precisely identified.

In general, however, Taiwan has had a different history, particularly in modern times. It is as yet unclear whether a region as vast, and in certain respects, as heterogeneous as mainland China can be successfully integrated, however authoritarian the system. China—and India as well —represent experiments in the political integration of continental-sized areas, comparable in certain respects with the problem of European integration, and with results that are far from clear at this point. Certainly there are no compelling cultural, geographic, or economic reasons why Taiwan is critical to the success of the stupendous task of Chinese nation-building. The fact that the great bulk of the island's population are ethnic Chinese is of no more significance than that

Nordics and Anglo-Saxons comprise dominant ethnic-cultural strains of northern and western Europe.

Taiwan represents a special problem because it is the symbol of a continuing "civil war," and because both the Chinese Communists and the Nationalists have viewed it as a pawn in a game where the stakes are much higher. At its roots, the problem of Taiwan rests upon psychological and political considerations involving the modern Chinese revolution, a revolution not yet finally determined with respect to course and scope. At the same time, however, it also involves the fate of some twelve million people, very few of whom are interested in being involved with the fate of the Chinese revolution. This central fact may provide the clue to the most appropriate method of approaching the issue.

Meanwhile, let us explore briefly the broad alternatives that are at least theoretically available. One would be to strive for, or place minimal obstacles in front of, the unification of Taiwan with mainland China. An alternative course of action would be to encourage, under some formula, the separation of Taiwan and China. A range of techniques from the use of a plebiscite to verify popular wishes to the development of policies involving full recognition are possible.

Are there broad alternatives other than an acknowledgment of Chinese sovereignty on the one hand or the acceptance of an independent Taiwan on the other? Perhaps a third course of action is the deliberate decision to leave the basic issue in an ambiguous status—to keep the options open pending further clarification of political trends in Asia generally and in China specifically. Such a policy, of course, can result from a conscious decision or it can be merely the product of inaction. In any case, current United States policy is perhaps best defined in those terms.

Let us now examine briefly the probable repercussions from each of these broad courses of actions. What political consequences would flow from an acceptance of Chinese sovereignty over Taiwan? Presumably, such a policy would not change the political realities dominating the scene. The Nationalists lost the civil war, but managed to retain the offshore islands of Quemoy and Matsu, and the Taiwan-Pescadores area. Despite the great turmoil currently under way in China, there is no present indication that the Nationalists as such will figure prominently in the political future of mainland China. Certainly, it would be unwise to build a policy upon that prospect.

Acknowledging that dramatic changes can always occur in a situation as fluid as that prevailing in mainland China today, the evidence still appears to support the following conclusions: first, the civil war between the Chinese Communist Party (CCP) and the Kuomintang (KMT) is over and will not be reopened. Ritualistic warfare—of value to both sides for political purposes—continues, to be sure. It is conceivable that if the present crisis were to be prolonged and to become more critical, a new regionalism might emerge on the mainland. Under such circumstances, the Nationalists might be able to interact effectively with certain regional forces. This is the only fashion, indeed, in which a Nationalist return to the mainland currently appears to be feasible.

It is important to emphasize the fact that KMT involvement in mainland politics on a significant level continues to be a very remote possibility. The bulk of the Nationalist armed forces are young men, most of them Taiwanese by birth and commitment. They can have only a limited interest in "return" to a region from which they never came, and one increasingly foreign to them in every respect. If a new civil war does develop in China, and the present indications are by no means clear with respect to this point, it is likely to center around new forces, not old ones.

What are the central arguments in favor of a policy that looks toward the unification of Taiwan with mainland China? First, China ultimately will be a major power, possibly *the* major power of Eastern Asia. If Taiwan is denied to China, it will always constitute *territory irredenta*, a cause of instability, and quite possibly conflict for the region as a whole. To acknowledge the residual sovereignty of China over this island, as has been done with respect to Okinawa in connection with Japan, would remove one major source of future conflict in Asia, it can be argued. Further, it would not be necessary to develop at this time any full solution to the issue. A number of alternative specific courses of action could be considered. The freezing of the status quo for twenty-five years would represent one possibility. Special autonomous status for the island (the "one and one-half Chinas" approach) would represent another. The acceptance of Chinese residual sovereignty, however, would point the broad path to be followed, and reduce the ambiguity now surrounding the issue.

Such an approach has its attractions. The commitment to Chinese sovereignty, providing there was no specification as to who or what constituted China, would accord with the strongly held views of both the Chinese Communists and Nationalists. It would also represent an accommodation to the force of Chinese nationalism without foreclosing (under certain approaches) the question of which Chinese political force was to inherit the nationalist mantle. One major source of potential conflict between the United States and China would be removed, or at least reduced.

On the other hand, any full and final acceptance of Chinese sovereignty over Taiwan at this point would almost certainly strengthen the case for ousting the Republic of China from the United Nations, and seating the People's Republic. If a policy is enunciated which strengthens the thesis that there is only one China and that China has the right to govern Taiwan, most nations can be expected to push strongly for the political and legal acceptance of Peking as the legitimate China. Only the ambiguous status of Taiwan at present, together with the fact that it has an operating *de facto* government, has protected the status quo.

Such a policy would also have uncertain, possibly adverse effects upon the internal politics of Taiwan. Certainly, the repercussions would be unfavorable among those Taiwanese who are committed to a new nationalism, and actively opposed to being placed under Chinese sovereignty. The Taiwan independence movement is weak and divided at present, but—with varying degrees of fervor attached—it does represent the sentiments of many of the "local people," as they are described in colloquial language. In part, the commitment to independence reflects the substantial cultural differences between Taiwanese and mainlanders; in part, it reflects the resentment of past abuses, and the general knowledge that mainland refugees continue to control political and military affairs, despite the fact that they number only two million out of the approximately twelve million residents of the island.

In all probability, a policy enunciating Chinese sovereignty would not produce political repercussions among the Taiwanese sufficiently strong to threaten immediate disorder or rebellion. There is no indication that dissidence can be expressed currently in an organized, effective fashion. It is likely, however, that a policy shift in this direction would provide the foundations for additional friction within the Taiwan scene. It might well deter the process of inter-community cooperation in Taiwan that is now proceeding on a slow and uncertain basis. It might well set afoot new and dangerous political movements, left and right. In sum, it is not the threat of a Taiwanese nationalist rebellion, but the more subtle problem of an action that would reduce, if not eliminate, the need for mainlander-Taiwanese cooperation and integration that currently exists, that argues strongly against this first course of action.

The major argument for acknowledging Chinese sovereignty over

Taiwan remains the thesis that only this act will make possible a broader accommodation with China—*one* China—at some point in the future.
No one can doubt that Taiwan has been a stumbling block of major
proportions to any improvement in American relations with Peking.
The Communists have ceaselessly repeated the thesis that the acceptance of Taiwan as an integral part of the People's Republic is a *sine
qua non* for any improvement in relations, indeed, for any serious discussion of other matters. Some would argue that a commitment by the
United States to defend Taiwan against the mainland Chinese will
ultimately lead to war. They insist that our choices are basically stark
ones—an accommodation to Chinese Communist nationalism on this
matter or armed conflict. Among those taking this view, moreover, not
a few would argue that Taiwan is not sufficiently important, either in
strategic or political terms, to warrant a massive struggle of the type
that would engulf Asia and possibly the world.

Such views, however, do not represent the sentiments of more than a
small minority of Americans at this time, and they can be challenged
at a number of points. For example, the thesis that our alternatives are
merely those of surrender or war is a dubious one if history, including
that of recent events in Europe, can serve as any guide. It was once
argued that on the issue of Germany, we would either have to accept
the Soviet position, especially the concept of a neutral, nonaligned,
pacifist Germany—or face a full-fledged conflict with the Soviet Union.
It was also firmly asserted that until this issue was resolved, there could
be no basic change in American-Soviet relations. We did not accept the
Soviet position on Germany, albeit, we also did not force the question
to the ultimate by providing West Germany with nuclear weapons. Nor
has the German issue been resolved. No one would deny, however, that
changes in the international environment, together with an evolution
within the two superpowers themselves, have provided a basis for significant alterations in Russo-American relations notwithstanding these
facts. The options available in international politics are far more subtle
than simplistic polar extremes.

It is also clear, of course, that a mere declaration accepting Chinese
residual sovereignty would not satisfy the Communists at this point
unless it were accompanied by specific policies or statements designed
to guarantee that Chinese Communist sovereignty had been underwritten. Otherwise, they might well see the move as a part of a broader
plot to restore the KMT to total control of China.

What is to be said of the second alternative, namely the development of policies leading to an independent Taiwan? In support of such a move, a number of impressive arguments can be mustered. Although hard evidence is scanty, there can be little doubt that independence would accord with the interests and the desires of a substantial number of Taiwanese. Quite apart from political considerations, it is inconceivable that any significant number of Taiwanese would voluntarily choose union with the mainland, whatever its political status. The reasons are economic as well as cultural. The standard of living for the average citizen of Taiwan will be far higher than that of the mainland Chinese for the long-range future. No matter what assurances might be given, any union or amalgamation with the mainland, especially under present conditions, would adversely affect every Taiwanese in economic terms.

If the concept of an independent Taiwan accords with popular sentiments and interests on the island, it also accords with the interests of non-Communist Asia. In this regard, there has been a major change within the past decade, although the public record does not reveal that change. Ten years ago, most of the newly independent states of East and South Asia—fiercely anticolonial and relatively unconcerned about ideological differences or the prospects of a powerful Communist China, and hazy concerning Taiwan's history—were fundamentally aligned with Peking on the Taiwan issue. Privately, at least, this is no longer the case insofar as the non-Communist states of Asia are concerned. It is extremely doubtful whether a single non-Communist Asian state would truly desire the incorporation of Taiwan into the mainland at present. As in the case of many other matters, not all states are prepared to vote or act publicly in accordance with their convictions on this issue at present. Nevertheless, an independent Taiwan would be in the interests of non-Communist Asian states and this fact is almost universally acknowledged.

Perhaps most importantly, however, an independent Taiwan exists, and has existed for nearly two decades now. Political myths cannot be allowed to obscure this very crucial fact. No one would seriously argue that the government of Taiwan is, in fact, the government of China. The Taiwan government has jurisdiction over some twelve million people. It has ruled with a greater measure of efficiency than most Asian governments in the course of the last decade, and with considerably more success in the economic field. To assert that it has had major economic assistance from the United States is true, but not definitive.

So have many states in which economic conditions are presently deplorable.

The problems of democracy in Taiwan place that nation in a status roughly comparable with a number of other non-Western societies that can be categorized neither as Western-style democracies nor as totalitarian states of the Communist or Fascist model. Certainly Taiwan is not to be compared with Communist China on matters like individual rights, freedom, and broad goals. At the moment, of course, the Communists face serious internal problems, with the top hierarchy badly split and conditions akin to anarchy prevailing in some regions. This may be temporary or it may continue for the indefinite future. Even if one were to ignore current conditions, however, the existence of an independent Taiwan is as demonstrable at this point as the existence of an independent China.

In every conceivable respect, moreover, the state of Taiwan has established its own identity, an identity as separate from that of mainland China as any other sovereign state despite its rule by a self-proclaimed exile government. Taiwanese political institutions are totally different, and they are continuing to evolve in a direction not only very different from Chinese Communist institutions, but also from those institutions of the Nationalists when they were in control of the mainland. The latter fact, moreover, will become increasingly significant with the passage of time. To put this important point succinctly, the way of life, the political values, and the institutional operations now characteristic of Taiwanese society are all basically separate from those of China, and the separation grows in a geometric ratio with each passing year. None of these facts is altered merely because the government in power on Taiwan proclaims itself Chinese, nor because at this stage, citizens outside the mainland refugee community have limited access to political office or political power.

One trend with respect to Taiwan is inescapable. As time passes, every aspect of life on the island will become increasingly "Taiwanized." Indeed, the progression of what can be called a Taiwan nation will be far more rapid from this point on than that of the Chinese nation on the mainland. In part, this is merely the product of size alone. The drama of modern China has not yet been played out, but it is certainly permissible to question whether a region so vast, encompassing so many millions of people is a suitable unit for the nation-building experiment. China may well achieve unification and progressively undergo modernization despite the enormous problems confronting it. There can be little question, however, that Taiwan's chances for success at this point are far more promising. The socioeconomic infrastructure for nationhood has already been laid in considerable measure. And any assertion that Taiwan is too small can easily be refuted. Its population of twelve million is greater than that of a majority of the present members of the United Nations. Its economic development and capacity for self-generating growth place it in the forefront of the emerging states.

To recognize the independence of Taiwan is not to approve of every aspect of the political situation there, any more than the recognition of Burma or Guinea connotes such approval. There are many reasons, however, to hope that the broad, evolutionary trends of the decade that lies ahead will be positive in political terms. Trends toward democracy, moreover, could be encouraged, were the framework of political evolution to be that of an independent Taiwan. Under such circumstances, all of the people of Taiwan would possess a heightened sense of community. Political legitimization could develop only through the broadening of the political base within Taiwan, and political power could be built only in this fashion. The process of political integration would thus be given powerful impetus.

The arguments against an independent Taiwan revolve primarily around two considerations, both of which have been noted. First, such a concept is unacceptable to any Chinese political faction, Communist or Nationalist, and might therefore lead to undesirable retaliatory measures. Would certain elements of the Nationalist community on Taiwan be prepared to reach secret agreements with the Communists turning the island over to Peking rather than accept Taiwanese independence? And would the Communists, when their military strength had reached formidable proportions, be prepared to challenge the new state? No doubt some risks exist in these respects, but it would be difficult to prove that these risks are overwhelming, or even likely, given current conditions.

Another consideration may be more serious. It can be argued that the possibilities of making an independent Taiwan "operational" in international politics are remote at this point. Approximately forty-eight states have indicated in the United Nations that they favor the admission of Communist China to that body, and almost all of these states have already recognized the People's Republic officially. Since the Communists have insisted that Taiwan must be considered a part of China if diplomatic relations with them are to be normalized, all or almost all of these states can be expected to resist formal recognition of an independent Taiwan under present circumstances, whatever private views some of them may hold. Some states, of course, do in fact have relations with both Communist China and Taiwan, notably Japan and West Germany, although in neither case are the relations with the Communists formal political ones.

Will the past be a certain indicator of the future? Is it possible that with the mainland facing multiple political problems, some of them likely to be of long-range character, that a number of states will entertain the notion of changes in their attitudes concerning Taiwan? Perhaps this is to introduce the third broad policy alternative noted at the outset, namely, the "let the dust settle" position. It can be argued that one cannot be certain at this point of the future status of the mainland either in terms of leadership or cohesion. Will the Maoists win or lose —both in the short and in the long range, and under what political aegis will the China of the future come? Is there to be one mainland regime or more? Will a degree of political disintegration occur sufficient to produce separate or quasi-autonomous political entities? Could a number of Chinas develop on the mainland, as was the case after the breakup of the Holy Roman Empire in Europe? And is it wise in the midst of these uncertainties to seek a determination of the Taiwan issue?

The evidence at present is certainly not sufficient to enable any prediction of multiple Chinas on the mainland, or even the defeat of Maoism, at least in the short run. It is quite possible, however, that the political picture on the mainland will continue to be an extremely complex one, even a chaotic one, for some time to come. Certainly, one finds it difficult to envisage the rapid, orderly reconstruction of a monolithic, efficient, centralized Communist Party in the aftermath of recent events, even if some of those events have been exaggerated or distorted. The thought of Mao still blankets most of the land, and his countenance shines down upon citizens everywhere from a myriad of billboards, posters, and publications. Mao may well win this battle. Yet Maoism seems doomed in the long run. "The spirit of Yenan" is in essence a form of primitivism which a developing China—Communist or not—must sooner or later cast off. And, on the other hand, if China were to be stagnant, a challenge would also have to be mounted.

Under these circumstances, an appealing argument can be advanced for "letting the dust settle." As is well known, it is always easier at any given moment to do nothing—or at least nothing dramatic—in the midst of complex, uncertain political circumstances. Troubled situations tend to reenforce caution with respect to policy alterations. There is another side to the coin, however, and a significant one. A change of policy, either on the part of the United States or a broader group of non-Communist states, could take place at this point under more advantageous conditions, psychologically and politically, than might otherwise be possible.

Consider the situation at present. No action could be interpreted as favoring—or attacking—a given Chinese faction or political group, since the future of all personalities, groups, and factions is so unclear. The current situation, indeed, would appear to permit an abstract, impersonal approach to the questions of China and Taiwan that could operate at a high level of rationality. For example, it is now impossible to charge that any policy adjustments were either in response to pressures from the Communists or from the Nationalists. Certainly, the former prospect may become a reality when and if a nuclear China develops that is capable of speaking with a unified, decisive voice. The risks of inaction relate to these considerations, to the possibility that now is an optimum time for the adjustment of policies and perspectives in the Asian area generally, and with respect to China specifically. Never have the psychological, political, and military factors been so favorable to the establishment of certain new postures and positions of the United States in Asia as they are at present.

Whatever course of action is elected, and whatever the future may hold, the issue of China poses in acute form certain critical questions for the policy maker and for the social scientist. Let us explore issues in the policy field first. Surely, we are now called upon to reexamine American practices with respect to recognition. No principle is so badly in need of reiteration as that principle which holds that recognition does not constitute approval, but signifies only the fact that a state exists having *de facto* control over its people and capable of exercising sovereign rights in the international scene. In specific terms, to be sure, it can be argued that China under the Communists gave no indication of being willing to live up to the minimal obligations implicit in recognition, namely, those responsibilities involved in an exchange of diplomatic representatives. But this question was largely untested when testing was possible.

The intertwining of issues relating to moral or political approval with those relating to recognition has not been advantageous to the American national interest. Nor have the substitutes for legal recognition been adequate. As is well known, we do recognize Communist China in certain senses. The regularly scheduled talks at Warsaw, the participation of China in the discussions on Laos, and a host of other events testify to this fact. But none of these contacts permits the kind of accountability enforced via legal recognition, and no need is more acute than to make all states—most particularly states like the People's Republic of China—fully accountable for their actions in the international scene.

A second complex of basic issues raised by the China problem is the supreme importance and difficulty of timing policies in a correct manner. Indeed, the timing of policies is scarcely less important than the substance of policies, and the two are related in a most intimate manner. Throughout the whole history of American relations with modern China, and especially during the period of the last three decades, the issue of timing has been badly handled. There were always logical explanations, sometimes extremely cogent ones. Often our opportunities to effect a change or bolster a position were fleeting ones. The periods of lull between storms grew progressively shorter at certain points in time. The entire momentum of world politics has speeded up, and this has added major new complications with respect to policy-making. Once again, a concrete illustration drawn from the China scene may be helpful. There was almost no time to readjust our China policy between the period when the Nationalist regime on the mainland collapsed and the onset of the Korean War. The next optimum period for some adjustment can be considered (roughly) 1955–58, just prior to the Great Leap. It has been argued here that another such period exists presently, a period of uncertain duration. This does not mean that policy adjustments now can—or should—be those that might have been contemplated in 1949, or 1955. It merely signifies the importance of discerning and being able to signal the time when opportunities for change arrive, and not losing the option to seize upon these opportunities if careful study indicates such a desirability.

One final consideration relating to policy might be the determination of the desirable American role in the modernization process, and in the broader effort to create the conditions of regional balance in Asia. No policy issues are more crucial to our own survival than these, and few if any are more complex. The lessons of failure and success as they relate to China and to Taiwan remain to be fully explored although some excellent pioneer work has been done. We are now confronting such questions as "high posture" versus "low posture" in Asia, unilateral versus multilateral approaches, and the socioeconomic, political, and military mix required in successful policies along with the even more basic question of involvement versus non-involvement. In the final analysis, none of these fundamental questions can be answered in an absolutistic, either-or fashion. The intricate components that must fashion policy, however, can only be properly weighed, mixed and applied as a fuller account is taken of the experiences derived from United States–China relations over the past several decades.

To the social scientist also, the problems of China and Taiwan offer extensive data for new conceptualizations. The phenomena of national communism in its current Chinese form bids fair to challenge some of the most deeply held theses about the operation of Marxism-Leninism in the twentieth century, and may ultimately force upon us a radically new typology of political systems. The relationship between geographic-cultural units and political systems, the concept of optimum and possible units for nation-building purposes provides another critical area of research that will be powerfully influenced by developments in both China and Taiwan. Indeed, the concept and character of Asian nationalism is itself badly in need of a more sophisticated treatment. Old myths and shibboleths abound in this field. Everyone asserts—and has asserted for at least twenty years—that we should interact with Asian nationalism, but what does that statement mean? Asian nationalism takes many forms, presents many fundamental paradoxes and conflicts, and currently represents a political phenomena highly elitist in most regions, scarcely in accord with popular conceptions of it.

These are but a few of the basic policy and theoretical considerations that make the issues of China and Taiwan of major importance. If predictability is to be built into social science on a broader scale, surely there is no region of the world where initial experimentation could be more valuable, were it to be successful, than with respect to China and Taiwan. Thus, the failures of the past in this respect should not inhibit us from pushing ahead by every conceivable means to discern and quantify, where possible, future likelihoods. Meanwhile, a choice between the three broad alternatives suggested here must be made, and it has been the burden of this paper to indicate that on balance, the acceptance of an independent Taiwan accords in reality with the interests of the people most immediately concerned, with the needs of the broader Asian context, and thus, with American national interest.

Comments by George E. Taylor

Professor Scalapino has discussed United States policy towards China with special reference to the problem of our relations with the Republic of China on Taiwan. He has provided us with an analysis of what he considers to be the three main courses of action open to the United States. One course is to accept China's residual sovereignty over Taiwan and to avoid putting obstacles in the way of the unification of Taiwan and Communist China; another is to encourage the separation of these two parts of historical China; a third is to leave the situation ambiguous, to keep the options open, as the United States appears to be doing at the present time. With his usual skill Professor Scalapino has identified the advantages and disadvantages of each of these courses of action and has effectively demolished all of them.

Somewhat surprisingly, he himself comes out in favor of preparing the way for an independent Taiwan and of taking steps at this time to make our intentions clear. Very persuasively, he argues that now is the time to do this because the face of Asia is changing, new regional balances are developing, and new concepts of political organization are in the making. For these reasons, he suggests, to work for the emergence of an independent Taiwan accords with reality (we cannot turn over the people of that country to Peking), with the interests of the people most concerned (the Taiwanese), with the needs of the broad Asian context (regional political and economic grouping including Japan), and with the national interest of the United States (to consolidate the situation and bring Communist China into the family of nations on terms acceptable to both Peking and Washington). It is a persuasive argument, closely reasoned, but it does not, in my view, take account of several important assets or allow for some serious consequences. It would in all probability lead to the same conclusion as the policy of deliberately permitting the unification of the two Chinas but with maximum humiliation to the United States.

Much of the argument for an independent Taiwan rests on the

121

assumption that there are no compelling reasons for its unification with the mainland, that neither history nor cultural affinity demands it. The unification of the mainland itself is presented as a condition which has not always been achieved in the past and may well not be achieved in the future. There is some point to the argument, perhaps, in the sense that nothing is permanent and there is no such thing as abstract justice, but the facts are that China has been a going concern for a good many centuries. Formosa was taken away from China in 1895, not from an independent Taiwanese regime. Manchuria, which did not even become Chinese in an ethnic sense until the twentieth century, was accepted by most of the world powers as part of the Chinese Republic when Japan set up the Manchukuo regime. When the central government of China grows weaker there is certainly a tendency towards what has been called regionalism but this regionalism is of a specific sort. Historically the centers of regional power have been autonomous but not sovereign parts of the empire or republic. The tendency is for the central authority to survive, however meager its functions, largely because the political, cultural, and economic environment puts serious obstacles in the way of regionalism in the sense of Balkanization into sovereign states. It is true that China had to accept an independent Korea and Vietnam but in both cases there had been a long history of successful resistance to Chinese rule, which there was not on Taiwan. Is there not also something illogical in suggesting that Taiwan does not belong, by history or cultural affinity, to China while allowing China's claims to Tibet to go by default? Unlike the Taiwanese, who came from the mainland and speak mainland dialects, the Tibetans are linguistically distinct, have had long periods of independence, and have gone out of their way in recent times to resist Chinese imperialism.

There is a certain relevance to Professor Scalapino's argument that a division of the ethnic Chinese among several states is not more significant than similar divisions of the Nordics and Anglo-Saxons but it is more likely to appeal to us, as a rationalization of a political decision, than to the Chinese. Professor Scalapino is on much firmer ground when he points out that the real significance of Taiwan is that it is a symbol of civil war and that the political problem has its roots in an unfinished revolution. Indeed, that is the root of the matter. On this every party agrees. But it is hard to follow the next step in the discussion, the claim that the Taiwanese are not interested in this civil war and the implication that they have in them the makings of a nation. Where is the evidence? There was an independence movement on

Taiwan against the Japanese and there are some Taiwanese intellectuals who continue this tradition, substituting the Kuomintang for the
former rulers, especially since the unfortunate behavior of Nationalist
troops on Taiwan after the war. But this is a very small movement, if it
can indeed be given that name. The Taiwanese people, as distinct from
their leaders, have had no more to say about the Communist takeover
than have the people on the mainland. Their leaders have come to
share in the political as well as the economic control of the island during the last ten years. As of today Taiwan is the most prosperous province of China and both leaders and people have less to be disaffected
about than do their compatriots on the mainland.

It is wiser, in my view, not to think of Taiwan as a unique phenomenon but rather as the main branch of the Chinese revolution, the only
part of the Chinese Republic which is in the main stream of modernization and which can count on the loyalty of the large numbers of
Chinese intellectuals who are now resident in the United States and
other countries. Recent surveys carried out by the National Science
Foundation show that a very high percentage of Chinese scientists
living in the United States are willing to return to Taiwan for shorter
or longer periods to assist in the processes of research and training in
their fields. Surely it is in the interest of the United States to keep alive
a China that is becoming integrated with the intellectual and economic life of the free world. No one now doubts the startling economic
and social progress made by the National government on Taiwan
although many do not see the vital connection between the social
change and the economic growth (a matter of dogma in discussion of
other developing countries), perhaps because the political stability is so
obvious. But there is bound to be a second echelon on Taiwan as on
the mainland and I would rate the chances of its favorable political
development much the higher.

Such a view is not a matter of faith. The economic growth of Taiwan
has not been brought about by tired old party hacks. It has been done
by modern-minded men of great ability and with an intimate knowledge of the rest of the world. Economic forces in this lively economy
will tend to demand efficient, clean, and flexible government. I am
suggesting not that the political appeal of the National Government is
certain to increase but that it might. It is one possibility that is usually
excluded from American calculations because of political prejudice
against Chiang Kai-shek. An objective social scientist, however, cannot
afford the luxury of such prejudice. To write off the National Government is to write off a good deal of United States investment, both mili-

tary and economic, in a modest success story in Asia. Here is a case study of how industrialization takes place successfully when democratic changes in the social relations of the agrarian sector are pushed through first. It stands out in vivid contrast to the incredible mistakes and failures on the mainland, mistakes which arise not from the normal fallibility of man but from the false dogmas and the world view of the Peking regime. I think that Professor Scalapino would agree that Taiwan is a going concern in which the United States has a political investment but he would see its future as part of an economic and political regional bloc, including Japan. This view naturally goes with the view that the civil war is over and that Taiwan must be politically defused, as it were, in order to make it easier to bring Peking into the family of nations.

On this we have an honest difference of opinion. It is my view that the option of an independent Taiwan is not a realistic one because it is unacceptable to those who are in power on Taiwan and those who are likely to come to power. Once it became clear that the United States was willing to let the National Government gradually dissolve into a new nation of Taiwan, thus presumably losing the legal identity of the Republic of China, there would be inevitable divisions in Taiwan as to what to do. Many would feel it necessary to come to terms with Peking. Peking would have a great advantage which it would press both in Taiwan and on the international scene. Once started on this slippery path, the United States would find it very difficult to keep a footing. Having retreated on the major issue and thus embittered its relations with the National Government, the United States would not find it easy to define what it is willing to defend. The moral basis of the National Government's rule is only partly the promise of a return to the mainland. It is mainly that both government and people represent the main stream of Chinese culture and institutions and this position is best preserved by preserving the legal identity of the Republic of China.

The only sound option for United States policy is to keep the options open. We do not know what is going to develop on Taiwan but we do know that change it must. Politically the change may be for the worse but it may be for the better. In this connection it is interesting that many of those who insist that there has been a change for the better in the behavior of the Soviet Union as a result of the civilizing influence of industrialization and affluence—a speculation of doubtful merit— find it convenient not to apply the same wishful thinking to Taiwan.

Compared with the mainland, Taiwan can boast of political stability and economic growth.

What about the mainland? What can we expect of the future? Not all American scholars, but certainly the majority, assumed until recently that the Communists were always in complete control of the mainland and would, by definition, succeed in their economic plans. There was much admiration for the supposed harmony of the Chinese Communist Party (CCP) when compared with that of the Soviet Union. Actually the domestic and international policies of Chairman Mao have been far from successful. They have resulted in economic chaos and international isolation. Now there is obvious political division within the party itself.

Communist China is not a great power today in any sense of the word except for the extent of its territory. Measured in terms of military capacity, per capita income or production, total volume of industrial and agricultural production, and technological levels, China has a long way to go. It is difficult to see how she can succeed and remain Communist. She may be able, as have the Russians, to build a modest power economy, a military, industrial complex, on the basis of subsistence for the mass of the population. But it is difficult to see how she can get into the first rank of industrial and military powers for a very long time to come. Nor is it to the interest of the United States that China should be strong and Communist. Our interest is merely that the regime, so long as it lasts, should observe its international obligations and assist in maintaining the peace. In the meantime it seems more than likely that there will be significant divisions within the CCP leadership and that the time may come when it might be possible for an alert Taiwan to play a role in bringing about a change on the mainland and thus a possible re-unification. Given the problems of China it is reasonable to proceed on the hypothesis that communism must either change or collapse and in either event there is a decisive role to be played by a modern, successful, politically astute, and flexible government on Taiwan. Better reasons than those advanced would be needed to justify a policy which would throw away existing assets on Taiwan and the possibility of much greater ones in the future.

Professor Scalapino's paper shows an acute awareness of the disadvantages to the United States of its commitments to Taiwan in view of the unfinished civil war and Peking's insistence on destroying the Republic of China before it will discuss the normalization of relations. If we left Taiwan to Peking's tender mercies, however, what difference would it really make? The fateful decision to lean to one side was taken at a time when Peking fully expected to capture Taiwan and we were quite prepared to see it happen. The question so often asked—why does the United States ignore the existence of China—can be turned around—why does Peking ignore the existence of the United States? An offer by Peking to exchange diplomatic representatives with Washington as a new state with a new name would be difficult to refuse. After all, the alliance with the Soviet Union was accepted in 1950 with considerable invasions of the sovereignty of the People's Republic, such as Soviet occupation of Port Arthur and other concessions. For that matter Peking has made claims to territories allegedly occupied by the Russians quite recently. Given the general pattern of behavior of Communist states, an agreement on our part to remove our presence from Taiwan and to give up our present treaty obligations would not of itself lead to the normalization of relations. Nor is it particularly useful to try to explain the behavior of Peking in terms of a century of humiliation and of traditional forces, such as ethnocentrism, because the argument collapses when we observe the behavior of the National Government, now on Taiwan but also run by ethnic Chinese who have the same historical legacy.

Surely there are advantages as well as disadvantages in our commitment to the Republic of China. Its very existence is a political challenge to Peking and therefore of enormous importance in the competition with the Communist powers whether the war is warm or cold. Surely it is an advantage to have a Chinese government which is successful in its economic and social policies at home, which keeps alive the traditions of Chinese civilization in conditions of growth and freedom, and which is a member of the United Nations in good standing. We have, in the contrast between Peking and Taiwan, a beautiful test case of two different ways of going about a revolution. The chances are that the longer the competition continues the greater will be the contrast between the two and that the contrast will be to our advantage.

To pursue the policy suggested in this paper does not mean that we should forever exclude Peking from the United Nations or refuse to establish diplomatic relations. But this should happen on our terms, not theirs. The People's Republic is a new state. By no stretch of the imagination can it be said to be the same China that took its seat in the Security Council in 1945. It can apply to the United Nations as a new state and should be admitted when that body becomes universal and all other states are admitted. Some form of diplomatic relationship can

also be worked out with the new state, not necessarily on the ambassadorial level, if Peking is interested. The advantage of such a posture on
the part of the United States is that it would keep its assets in the
Republic of China and protect its assurances and obligations to its
allies in Asia and the rest of the world.

Comments by Richard A. Falk

Professor Scalapino's main conclusion appears to be that there is no
obvious or immediate solution for the cluster of problems centering
upon the administration of Taiwan by the remnants of the Nationalist
government of China. His analysis of the various options is admirably
sensitive to the difficulties of each, difficulties that concern both the intrinsic merits of each option and the likelihood that interested parties
would have a converging response to any specific proposal. At the same
time, Professor Scalapino is aware that any stabilization of east Asian
politics presupposes an eventual resolution of the conflict created by
Peking and Taipei both claiming to be the legitimate government of a
China that includes Taiwan and the Pescadores. Finally, his emphasis
on the timing as well as the substance of a settlement strategy is most
welcome, especially his cautious optimism about the opportunities of
the present period of mainland turmoil when Western initiatives cannot possibly be viewed as buckling under Peking's aggressiveness.

There is a suggestion in Professor Scalapino's essay that any further
acknowledgment of Chinese sovereignty over Taiwan would strengthen
Peking's prospects of admission to the United Nations as China, carrying with it the possibility of ousting the Taiwan regime from the organization altogether. Underlying this speculation is the flawless reasoning that if there is to be only one political entity entitled to govern both
the mainland and Taiwan, then the Peking regime is far more entitled,
by almost any relevant measure of entitlement, than is the Taipei

regime to represent China in the United Nations. The tenability of preserving a situation in the United Nations that has long been superseded by Mao's victory on the mainland depends on the prospect of bargaining with Peking for an independent Taiwan with its own sovereign status. But such bargaining leverage, even if it exists, should not be confused with the desirability of maintaining the constitutional anomalies created by insisting that the government in Taipei is entitled to continue acting in the United Nations as the state of China.

I would argue that one of the major costs of the present policy of the United States toward China has been to inflict upon the United Nations the absurdity of having an unpopular government in an island inhabited by less than fourteen million people serve as the only permanent Asian member of the Security Council. For over 15 years Taiwan has not possessed a substantial claim to serve on the Security Council as compared even to that of India, Japan, and Indonesia, let alone to the government in charge of the destinies of the world's most populous society. Therefore, even aside from determining which Chinese elite is properly "China" for United Nations purposes, the perpetuation of Taipei as China obviously has meant that Asian participation in the Security Council has been of nominal proportions, reflecting more a stalemate in the cold war than any attempt at securing serious Asian representation. The fiction that the Taiwan regime can represent China in the United Nations could only command literal respect, even from its ideological partisans, so long as there existed an ongoing civil war in which it was a principal faction with a plausible prospect of victory. Once the civil struggle was effectively ended by the retreat from the mainland of the Nationalist forces in 1949, it has become increasingly unreal and manipulative to confer, at the expense of the United Nations, this juridical afterlife upon Chiang Kai-shek's claims to govern China. The rigidity of American insistence on such a fiction must also cast doubt, if only indirectly, on our capacities to exercise enlightened diplomatic leadership in the non-Communist world.

John Fairbank has dramatically emphasized the long tradition by which Chinese leaders manipulate "non-Chinese barbarians" by writing that "Contenders for power in traditional China found it essential to utilize the barbarians, for the latter were powerful fighters, though often naïve in politics and easily swayed by their feeling of pride or fear."[1] It would appear to some extent that the United States has been

[1] John K. Fairbank, "Formosa through China's Eyes," *New Republic*, October 13, 1958, p. 9.

manipulated by Chiang's diplomacy into a rigid and ill-conceived sub-servience to his goals, however much support for these goals has ceased to serve American or world community interests in the mid-1960's. A real cost of this manipulation is to prejudice the protection of legiti-mate United States interests, through this ritualistic adherence to an outmoded and over-generalized "China policy."[2] One legitimate United States concern is to protect Taiwan from mainland control. As Profes-sor Scalapino shows the consequence of mainland control, aside from its geo-political effects on Western interests, would be adverse to the inhabitants of Taiwan in economic, cultural, and political terms. Of course, the Chiang regime is itself a form of mainland control, the evil consequence of which culminated in a Nationalist crackdown of 1947 that included the commission of large-scale genocide against the Tai-wanese upper classes.[3] This form of mainland control is also epitomized by the internal administration of Taiwan that has prevailed since the Chinese took over the control of the island. Taiwan is treated as if it were one of China's thirty-five provinces and is accorded representation proportional to that status in the organs of the Taipei government. This domestic correlate of the claim that China is centered in Taipei rather than in Peking has the same reality-denying impact as the ac-ceptance of Taiwan's claim to be China has had within the United Na-tions setting. Support for Chiang's desperate myth should be sharply distinguished from the diplomatic support given to governments-in-exile during World War II or to rebel governments seeking to end Portugal's colonial administration of Angola and Mozambique. In both of these latter cases the diplomatic support is a symbol of serious in-tentions to give substance to the claim by sooner or later taking appro-priate action. In the Chinese setting there is now even in official Ameri-can thinking the admission, implicitly at least, that it is necessary to reconcile ourselves to Peking's claim to govern mainland China for the foreseeable future. Such an admission, however, needs to be followed up by an American repudiation of the claims of the Chinese counter-elite on Taipei to be "China."

Repudiating these claims would result in no necessary change in the bilateral relationship between the United States and mainland China, but it would pave the way for such a change as well as maximize, al-though not guarantee, the long-term prospects of a stable and inde-

[2] Cf. Denis Healey, "Formosa and the Western Alliance," *New Republic*, October 13, 1958, pp. 11–12.

[3] George H. Kerr, *Formosa Betrayed* (Boston: Houghton Mifflin, 1965).

pendent Taiwan emerging as a separate state with full sovereign status. This diplomatic initiative by the United States could appropriately include a refusal to implement the Cairo Declaration of 1943 and the Potsdam Declaration of 1945 in which the Allied Powers in World War II proclaimed their intention to transfer Taiwan from Japan to China. As Dennis Healy observed of these determinations—"It was in flagrant disregard for the rights of small nations that the Great Powers agreed to give Formosa to China at the end of World War II."[4] Taiwan had been ceded to Japan in the Treaty of Shimonoseki in 1895 as part of the peace settlement reached after the Chinese defeat in the Sino-Japanese War of 1894–95. Prior to that time Taiwan had been loosely associated with the Chinese empire, having been formally annexed in 1683 by the Ch'ing Dynasty. During this long period of Chinese affiliation, the island enjoyed considerable autonomy. The subsequent Japanese half-century of colonial rule resulted in industrializing Taiwan far above mainland levels and in providing the inhabitants with a high standard of living and a sense of cultural identity separate from that of the mainland. This sense of separation had been deepened by the further modernization of the country since 1945, achieved initially through large quantities of United States foreign aid but more recently by an impressive record of self-sustaining economic accomplishment. The consequence of a socioeconomic profile distinct from that of the mainland is to make it very doubtful whether a high proportion of the inhabitants of Taiwan, whether Taiwanese or Chinese, could benefit, or, for that matter, could have ever benefited, from incorporation in China. It seems plain, then, that the elimination of Japanese control over Formosa should not automatically have been followed by the substitution of Chinese control, and that the entire context has been unduly confused by the premature commitment during World War II to support Chinese claims. This first commitment then was adapted by the United States to take account of the emergence of a hostile government in Peking. The result was that instead of one ill-considered commitment, there evolved a second—namely, to maintain as legitimate the claims of Chiang to rule "China". even though his effective power was limited to the successful, but oppressive, occupation of Taiwan. The full impact of this entanglement of error has been to equate in American eyes the legitimate government of China with the Taiwan regime, that is, with a government that has maintained a symbolic but relative-

4 Healy, "Formosa and the Western Alliance," p. 11.

ly invulnerable zone of resistance after decisively losing a bitter and prolonged civil war to determine control of Chinese society.

The firmness of this kind of United States commitment, as distinct from an alternative commitment to preserve an independent Taiwan has, of course, an inflammatory impact on Peking. The retreat of Chiang repeats a seventeenth-century pattern in which the remnants of the Ming dynasty held out for twenty years against the victorious Manchus.[5] More significantly, perhaps, to help keep in being the defeated faction in a civil war as a rival claimant is to challenge the legitimacy of the victorious faction's claim, necessarily fragile in a post-revolutionary society, to exercise political authority. The inevitable result is to prolong a wartime psychology. To perpetuate the lost faction's claim entails a loss of diplomatic freedom in dealing with the victorious faction, making it more difficult to accord recognition to the victorious faction, and almost making it necessary to deny the new government normal governmental status in international diplomatic channels. Such a situation is especially true if, as in China, a long civil war is won by the insurgent faction that seeks to establish its new authority as the constituted government and to displace altogether whatever lingering attachment remains for the former incumbent regime.

The point, then, is that it is time that the United States govern its relationship with Taiwan in accordance with its specific interests. These interests suggest as minimum first steps a repudiation of the acknowledgment made during World War II of Chinese sovereignty over Taiwan and a dissociation from any claims by the Taipei regime to constitute China. A further step would be to withdraw support from the claims of Taipei to represent China in international organizations. Such a withdrawal of support would be consistent with continued United States opposition to the presence of the Peking regime in the United Nations and with a continued policy of diplomatic non-recognition. However, both admission and recognition policy could thereafter be handled by the United States on their intrinsic merits rather than being intertwined with the future of Taiwan. Furthermore, the United States commitment to protect Taiwan against military attack would rest on firmer legal and moral grounds if Taiwan were no longer

[5] John K. Fairbank, *China—The People's Middle Kingdom and the U.S.A.* (Cambridge: Harvard Press, 1967), pp. 69–70; cf. also on the general phenomenon of traditional cultural patterns reappearing in new guises Ann Ruth Willner, "The Neotraditional Accommodation to Political Independence," Research Monograph No. 26, Center of International Studies, Princeton University (1966).

treated as if it were part of China. This reorientation of American
policy would not even be interventionary in Taiwanese politics. The
Chiang regime could still insist on its China myth, although its fictive
character would grow apparent as soon as it lost American backing.
Chiang's posture only acquires a certain plausibility because it has been
endorsed by the United States.

What would be the cost to the United States of acting on the basis of
the foregoing analysis? It is, of course, difficult to anticipate consequences. The suggested separation of our China policy from our Taiwan policy is unlikely to have spectacular or immediate results. It is a
change of orientation so far as the Peking regime is concerned that cannot be calculated to generate a more conciliatory attitude in the short
run, especially as it would be interpreted as merely a new tactic to
prevent or delay mainland control over Taiwan and a provocative and
belated way for the United States to disengage itself from the cham-
pionship of Chiang's pretension to rule China. It is a provocative way
because it repudiates the one aspect of the American stance that Peking
agrees with, namely, the validity of Chinese claims to govern Taiwan.
It is a belated manner of disengagement because it appears to be the
only means of revising the United States relationship with the Chiang
regime that does not involve the Western loss of influence in Taiwan.

At the same time, Taipei could hardly find comfort in a unilateral
diplomatic initiative by the United States that involves both the rejection of Taipei's claim to represent China and China's claim to govern
Taiwan. John Fairbank has written very persuasively about the depth
and reality of Chiang Kai-shek's commitment, whatever the consequences, to maintaining his claim to be ruler of China.[6]

In light of the likely opposition of both Peking and Taipei, as well as
the entrenched domestic support in the United States for the Chiang
position, it might seem that the diplomatic status quo—letting whatever
dust there is settle or not—may after all be the best alternative. My
advocacy of a new diplomatic posture by the United States takes account of these adverse considerations in the following manner. The
United States relationship to the Peking regime could hardly be worsened in the short run whatever diplomatic steps we took; in an intermediate period the new diplomatic posture would enable a reconciliation between the United States and China that did not necessitate a
simultaneous settlement of Peking's claim to govern the mainland. In
contrast, the dependence of Taiwan upon American military protection

[6] Fairbank, *China—The People's Middle Kingdom*, pp. 49–79.

is so great over any significant period of time that it is unthinkable that Taipei would reject United States support because it resented our dissociation from its internal and external insistence on being "China." After an initial pique it would probably become evident that the real alternatives for Taiwan were either incorporation in mainland China or separate statehood as a small, but viable, entity. Confronted by these alternatives, even a new generation of post-Chiang "realists" could hardly fail to prefer a separate national identity for Taiwan, thereby both maintaining sovereign prerogatives and preserving a higher standard of living and rate of economic growth. Stripped of any external pretension to represent China and to perpetuate the civil struggle for the state, the prospect of an independent Taiwan would probably grow less threatening to Peking over time, and at the same time the difficulties of conquest would keep the prospect of a military solution remote. Thus both Taipei and Peking might be able to pursue converging interests in some sort of *de facto* accommodation without being entrapped in the paralyzing dogma that Taiwan is a part of China.

The most assured result of this separation of Taiwan policy from China policy would be to shift the debate within the United States and in the United Nations to more specific and legitimate issues. It would no longer be necessary for Dean Rusk to respond to a plea for the reorientation of our China policy by indicating that any move in such a direction would be tantamount to surrendering the inhabitants of Taiwan to the mainland.[7] Nor is it entirely appropriate at this point to question the American commitment to defend Taiwan because of the undemocratic character of the Taipei regime.[8] There has been a considerable liberalization of the Taipei regime over the years since 1947.[9] A shift in United States policy toward Taiwan that centered upon a belated insistence on the principle of national self-determination would no longer be very meaningful, nor would it be realistic to insist upon some sort of plebiscite against the will of the constituted government in Taipei. A criticism of the domestic political consequences of regarding Taiwan as a Chinese province is about as far as the United States can reasonably go at this point in reversing its long-term adherence to

[7] *Washington Post,* Feb. 10, 1967.

[8] As was done by Senator Robert F. Kennedy in a major address on China policy. For text see *New York Times,* Feb. 9, 1967.

[9] See, e.g., Michael Lindsay, "Formosa's Future," *New Republic,* October 6, 1958, pp. 8–16.

Chiang's claims. Such criticism is consistent with protecting the *de facto* sovereignty of Taiwan against military attack by mainland China, and it is also consistent with an eventual readjustment of Sino-American relations.

If the United States is to succeed with such a diplomatic initiative, it is essential to make the repudiation of the official declarations of intention during World War II as credible as possible. This repudiation must acknowledge the possible misunderstandings triggered on all sides by the unequivocal and unthinking assignment of Formosa to China.

As has been said, it is difficult to anticipate all of the consequences of taking the action recommended above. At best, it could be the first step in a process that would both safeguard the autonomy of Taiwan and lead to a reconciliation with China. At the very least it would at last end American support for Taipei's claim to serve as a permanent Member of the Security Council. To relinquish support for Chiang's pretensions would certainly permit a fresh reconsideration of American policy toward China, and might lead to a new definition of aims—a reconsideration long overdue.

Morton H. Halperin

6

Chinese Attitudes toward
the Use and Control of
Nuclear Weapons

The development of atomic weapons with their vast destructive power posed a challenge to any individual or group with a view of history and a desire to change the course of civilization. Hiroshima produced the need to examine the extent to which one's plans and aspirations for the postwar world had to be revamped to take account of this new and awesome weapon. Men and institutions reacted in different ways.

The American military tried for a long time to treat the atomic bomb as just another weapon added to their arsenal, a weapon of greater destructive power but one which would not affect the rules of warfare or the requirements for military power. Many in the American government saw the atomic bomb as a threat to their aspirations for a peaceful world under the United Nations. From these concerns there developed the famous Baruch (Acheson-Lilienthal) Plan for the control of atomic weapons. There followed the search for arms control measures to contain the arms race which have characterized American diplomacy throughout the entire postwar period. American officials were basically concerned with finding ways to remove violence from the international sphere and hence the problem for them was either to eliminate nuclear weapons through disarmament measures or to prevent their use through an emphasis in the military sphere on deterrence.

The attitudes of the British government and a small number of people in France stemmed also from an attitude toward the world which sought the end of violence but which perhaps was more conscious of the political and prestige value of nuclear weapons. For Winston Churchill, the atomic bomb posed a threat to Britain's claim to be at the top "table." The status of Britain and France as superpowers had been enshrined in the charter of the United Nations but would this status not be threatened by the development of an atomic capability only in Washington and later in Moscow? The British government, and at a later date the French government, concluded that it might and hence began their quixotic search for participation in the great diplomatic events of the day by the acquisition of a modest nuclear capability.

If the atomic bomb posed serious problems for those in the West who sought an end to the use of force in the world, it posed an even greater challenge to those like Stalin (and Mao) who believed that force and the threat of force was an inevitable part of international politics. Stalin appears to have recognized from the outset that the development of the atomic bomb by the United States threatened his plans for establishing Soviet hegemony in Europe and raised the possibility of an American threat to the existence of the Soviet regime. His reaction was swift and ultimately effective: on the one hand, a public degradation of the role of nuclear weapons; on the other hand, the investment of very substantial resources in developing a Soviet nuclear capability. The Soviet government also paid lip service to the need to control nuclear weapons but mainly, if not entirely, as a part of its propaganda effort, to inhibit the United States from using its nuclear power. Stalin's successors have continued to view a Soviet nuclear capability as necessary to enable the Soviet Union to be sure of survival and to pursue its foreign policy objectives, although they have had to face the increasingly complex question of how much is enough. Their verbal degradation of nuclear weapons has gradually been discarded as Soviet nuclear power has grown and their activities in the arms control field have moved from pure propaganda to interest at least in some limited agreements designed to halt the superpower arms race and, more importantly from the Soviet point of view, to prevent the spread of nuclear weapons to additional countries.

Men everywhere had to ask themselves if their dreams, whether they were for proletarian revolutions or world peace through world law, had been fatally disrupted by the birth of the atomic age, but nowhere was this issue more hotly and seriously debated than in the caves of Yenan. The development of the atomic bomb posed challenges of a fundamental nature to the Chinese Communists, even though their efforts at the time were directed at survival and later victory in a very primitive, conventional war.

This paper is an effort to trace over time Chinese views on a set of related issues which developed from the explosion at Hiroshima and what followed from it. The fundamental question which the Chinese faced and which will be examined here is: "What effect would the development of nuclear weapons have on the doctrines of Marxism-Leninism-Maoism as they had been developed by the Chinese Communist Party (CCP) leadership?" Subsidiary to this, the Chinese have grappled with the questions of what kind of threat of nuclear attack they faced, what role there would be for a Chinese nuclear capability, and finally what functions the proposals to control nuclear weapons should play. The theme that I will try to develop is the essential continuity of the Chinese perception of nuclear weapons from 1945 to the present; changes in tactics and strategy, and to some extent in perception, will also be noted. The attempt will be to portray the world as it looked and looks from Yenan and later Peking, to try to describe as completely and as accurately as possible the Maoist image of the impact of nuclear weapons on the world. Where there are differences among the Maoist leadership that we know about, these will be discussed. However, the focus is on the views espoused by official Chinese Communist media and reflected in China's actions.

The aim here is to explicate, not to evaluate. Only if we have a clear understanding of the Chinese view of nuclear weapons can we hope to come to grips with policy problems posed by the developing Chinese nuclear capability.

The Meaning of the Atomic Bomb

In order to understand the shattering impact that the explosion at Hiroshima had on the Chinese Communist leaders, it is necessary to consider the world as it looked to them in the last days of the pre-atomic age.

During the course of the struggle against the Kuomintang (KMT) and against the Japanese invaders, Mao and his associates had jointly developed a new revolutionary doctrine. This doctrine was stated by Mao in his various writings, by Liu Shao-ch'i in 1949, and then not again in its full and detailed form until its presentation by Lin Piao in his article on people's war in 1965.

The essence of this doctrine was the belief in the development of a new strategy for the seizure of power in a rural society. This doctrine drew on Leninism, emphasizing the importance of a small party with tight central control. But it went beyond Lenin's notions in emphasizing the need for a firm rural base, for a people's army, and for the need to engage in military operations beginning with harassment and sabotage, going through a phase of guerrilla war, and ultimately a conventional attack which defeats either the oppressive ruling class or the invaders.

This doctrine, Mao and his associates believed, could be applied not only in China but throughout the world. They were convinced that the CCP had developed a model for revolution which would be the path to power in the rural, if not the developed, societies of the world. The core of the doctrine was the notion that a people's army, if it developed the proper political attitudes, organized properly, and pursued the proper strategy and tactics, could defeat a much larger and much more powerful conventional military force. Moreover, Mao and his colleagues felt that they had discovered the proper strategy and tactics.

Although they could not anticipate the sudden collapse of Japan, it was clear to Mao and his colleagues that the war against Japan was essentially won. While they must have recognized the contribution of American military power, the CCP probably overestimated the extent to which its own military actions had contributed to the victory. With the defeat of Japan in sight, the Chinese Communists were gearing for the next stage of the operation, the war against the KMT. While confident of the ultimate success of the struggle, Mao and his colleagues do not appear to have had any hope for the quick victory which was in fact to be theirs. Rather they were prepared for a long period of struggle, in which they would attempt to consolidate their rule in parts of the country and perhaps even enter into a superficial coalition with the Chinese Nationalists, but in which ultimately they would engage in people's war and then in conventional war throughout the country. Victory in the long run, they believed, was assured despite the current overwhelming superiority of the Chinese Nationalists and despite the possibility of American intervention. People's war, if carried out long enough, would ultimately triumph. This was the essence of the revolutionary doctrine that Mao and his colleagues brought with them into the Atomic Age.

The atomic bomb intruded into this optimistic view of the long-run future in China and throughout the world. Apparently there was great consternation in the caves of Yenan as the story of the devastation of Hiroshima and then Nagasaki reached these relatively isolated revolutionaries. The bomb became the main topic of conversation and long debates took place. The question which provoked Mao and his colleagues was the simple but fundamental one of whether or not their strategy for revolution remained valid in a world in which the oppressors now had a major new military weapon. In short, they asked themselves whether the thought of Mao would remain valid. Could the weak continue to expect to triumph over the strong if the strong had this new and awesome force at its disposal?

The first effort seems to have been to learn as much as possible about what took place. A Western newspaper reporter visiting Yenan after a stop at Hiroshima was eagerly and widely questioned, not only by Mao but by many of his associates, about what he had seen. The CCP leaders were eager to learn just how destructive this bomb was. There appears to have been no doubt among the Yenan leadership that the atomic bomb represented a major change in the laws of warfare, if not in the laws of history. As far as we know, there was no counterpart to the doubts in the West that anything had changed, no argument that this was simply an increase in destructive power which would have little or no effect on overall military operations or the nature of warfare, much less on the laws of history. Mao and his colleagues recognized the great destructive power of the bomb as they were to continue to do over the years, whatever the Soviets might say about their beliefs and whatever the Chinese themselves might say for propaganda or deterrence purposes. The issue of debate was the much more fundamental question which few were to ask themselves in the West for some time: namely, did this development require a change in one's overall view of history and the nature of political and economic development? Apparently, many in the Maoist leadership feared that it did. They were apprehensive that after all they would not be able to use their revolutionary strategy to capture power in China and to aid a world-wide revolution. They felt, therefore, that victory had been snatched from their grasp by a technological change. Some argued in short that the bomb had repealed the laws of class warfare.

It was this view of the atomic bomb, and not the assertion that it lacked destructive power and was a major advance in weapons technology, that Mao himself sought to counteract in his discussions with his colleagues and in his now famous interview with Anna Louise Strong. At that time Mao declared that the atomic bomb was a paper tiger—a paper tiger in the sense that the KMT was a paper tiger. It was a powerful force, a force of great weight and of great destructive potential, but a force that was not immune to the existing laws of history and could be overcome by the proper application of the strategy and tactics of people's war. Mao addressed himself to his colleagues, more than to anyone else, and asserted that the revolution could still triumph in China. The atomic bomb was not the end of all their plans and all their aspirations, not because it was not an awesome, new weapon, but because in the end revolutionary spirit would triumph over weapons, if one captured the allegiance of the people.

While denying that the atomic bomb repealed the laws of history as he understood them and ultimately rallying his colleagues to this belief, Mao did not in the slightest depreciate in his own mind or even in his early statements the great destructive potential of the atomic bomb or its utility as a weapon in the hands of revolutionaries. The strategy of people's war, while asserting the ultimate importance of the support of the people, does not in any sense denigrate the importance of military power. Rather, it argues that the revolutionaries would be able to seize control of this power as they gain control of the people, and as they captured the weapons of their opponents. Although we lack any specific evidence on the point, it seems probable that in the months following Hiroshima, Mao concluded, at least in the back of his mind, that ultimately China, if she were to play the role of the center of the world revolution, would have to develop its own nuclear capability. In the meantime China would have to seek close alliance with the Soviet Union and rely on whatever nuclear power the Soviets could be expected to produce.[1]

Hiroshima, then, provoked a major intellectual crisis among the Maoist leadership. It led to a new debate on the relevance of people's war in China and throughout the world and of the effect of technology on this strategy. After some debate, Mao issued a new statement which was to guide Chinese thinking on this question to the present time. It was foremost an affirmation of the validity of the strategy of people's war despite the fact that the enemy possessed the atomic bomb. The rules of strategy of warfare might have changed, but the rules of history had not. However, the changes in the rules of warfare required China ultimately to develop a nuclear capability, if she were to take her place as a superpower in the world. These beliefs were to be put to very severe tests over the next twenty years, but the

[1] As far as I am aware, we know nothing about early discussions about nuclear weapons between the Chinese Communists and Moscow. However, given the nature of their overall relationship and the very great sensitivity of this subject, it is doubtful that anything at all was exchanged between the two parties on this subject until at least Mao's trip to Moscow in 1950. Even then it is likely that Stalin did not reveal to the Chinese leader the full extent of his concern or of his nuclear weapons production program. Nevertheless, Mao may well have guessed much more than he was told.

Chinese experience was to lead Peking to a reaffirmation of these views. The atomic bomb did change the rules of warfare and did have its impact on diplomatic and military events, but it did not, in the long run, prevent the triumph of people's revolution, at least not in China.

The Atomic Age, 1946–53

Mao's assertion that American possession of the atomic bomb did not change the laws of historical development was immediately put to the test in the Chinese civil war. As was noted above, the Chinese appear to have been as surprised as everyone else was by the rapid disintegration of the KMT. Moreover, the Chinese were fearful to the end, as apparently was Stalin, that the United States would intervene and attempt to turn the tide of the conflict. This apprehension was reinforced by American possession of the atomic bomb. The Chinese leadership probably was not aware of the very limited nature of the American stockpile of atomic weapons in the period 1946–49, and the CCP may well have overestimated the probability that the United States would intervene and, in doing so, use its atomic weapons. There was of course no such intervention. The Chinese Communists swept to power throughout mainland China and proclaimed the People's Republic in October, 1949, reinforced in their belief that indeed the atomic bomb was simply a paper tiger. In spite of American possession, indeed monopoly, of the bomb, the CCP had been allowed to take power in the largest country in the world comprising one quarter of the world's population.

If the civil war reinforced the confidence of the leadership that revolution was possible despite the bomb, the Korean War was to bring home vividly to the Chinese the difference which the atomic bomb could make in conflicts and the accompanying diplomacy between nations. We still know very little about the Peking-Moscow discussions which must have preceded the North Korean attack on South Korea. However, on the one hand, it appeared doubtful that the attack could have been carried out without Chinese knowledge and tacit approval, and, on the other, it is very unlikely that Peking was itself eager to test the Americans and challenge the nuclear monopoly of the United States once again so soon after seizing power in China and before it had a chance to consolidate its control over the mainland.

Stalin's support for, and indeed probable masterminding of, the attack appeared to have been based on a strongly held belief that the

United States would not intervene. When this proved to be false, Stalin back-pedaled very quickly, fearful of inducing an American nuclear attack on the Soviet Union. This left the Chinese with an American army marching unchallenged toward their border.

The central question which the Chinese asked themselves at this time was what course of action would least jeopardize the continued existence of their regime—standing aside and allowing all of Korea to come under the control of Seoul or intervening with the risk of an American atomic attack on China. The decision seems to have been preceded by a search for data and an intensive debate among the leadership. Peking apparently also attempted, within the limits of its knowledge, to calculate the extent of the American arsenal and the damage that could be done to Chinese military capability and to Chinese cities. It appears to have concluded that there was no doubt that great destruction could be wrought against China by American atomic power. In fact the Chinese calculations appear to have over-estimated the size of the American stockpile and the destructive power of these weapons, as well as the American willingness to use its limited atomic capability on the Chinese mainland. The Chinese appear to have concluded that although an American atomic attack would not destroy China—a theme to be repeated over the years—it would cause such great damage that it would pose a greater threat to Peking's control of China than would American domination of all of Korea. Thus the central question for the regime in making a choice between intervention and non-intervention in the Korean War was whether or not intervention would provoke an American atomic attack against the Chinese mainland. If the answer was yes, then non-intervention would be the safest course. If the answer was no, then intervention, despite its other risks, appeared more satisfactory than remaining aloof. Thus, Peking engaged in its tentative intervention and feints designed to test American reaction, and when it was cofident that there would be no atomic retaliation, Peking intervened in the war in a way that decisively affected the conventional battle.

From this episode Peking probably drew a conclusion which it was later to come to doubt, namely that the United States was unwilling to use its atomic power even when engaged in large-scale military operations. In fact, before the Korean War was to come to an end, Peking was to confront the first of what from its point of view have been several situations in which the United States appeared to be on the verge of using atomic weapons in the pursuit of limited political objectives.[2]

Peking appears to have watched with great concern and interest the Soviet development of nuclear weapons. The Chinese had decided that they could and would rely on the Soviets to give them protection against an American nuclear attack, and they greeted with some relief the first Soviet atomic test and the development of at least some counterbalancing Soviet power. The extent to which they could rely on this power in any situation was a subject of considerable doubt and uncertainty in Peking, as well as in the West.

While facing the threat of American atomic power in Korea and watching the development of Soviet atomic capability, Chinese leaders found themselves drawn into the propaganda battle over the need for nuclear disarmament. As in many other fields of international diplomacy, Peking at this stage in its development hewed closely to the Soviet line. Thus, Peking supported the Soviet campaign to "ban the bomb." Petitions were duly circulated throughout China, calling upon all the world's powers to give up their nuclear capability. This campaign on the part of the Soviet Union as well as China seems to have been designed on the one hand to reduce their own people's fear of the American atomic capability and, on the other, to increase the political cost to the United States of ever using atomic weapons. There seems to be little doubt that neither Peking nor Moscow had any hope or any desire of arriving at disarmament agreements in these years.

Thus, the late forties and the very early fifties confirmed in the eyes of the Peking leadership the essential correctness of Mao's assertion that the atomic bomb was a paper tiger. The bomb, in fact, appeared to be playing only a very small role in international events. Most important, it had not prevented the Communist conquest of China. It appeared to play no role in the revolutions which were launched by various Communist Parties in Asia in 1948, although most of these revolutions failed for other reasons. That revolution was a long hard struggle with its zigs and zags Peking never doubted. That its course was not fundamentally changed by the atomic bomb seemed to be confirmed.

At the same time, Mao did not lose sight of the fact that the bomb did make a qualitative difference in conventional warfare. Concern

[2] This episode will be considered below in examining Peking's reaction to the doctrine of massive retaliation.

about the bomb was at the heart of Peking's hesitation prior to its intervention in Korea and was the basis for the anti-bomb campaign launched under Moscow's leadership. Although American action in the Korean War suggested restraints on American use of atomic power, Peking was probably more aware of her own restraints and of the uncertain nature of Soviet atomic guarantees. Thus, the need for a Chinese atomic capability over the long run was clearly reinforced by the events of the early fifties as was any affirmation of the continued viability of the doctrine of people's war. While the latter belief was not to be questioned by Peking over the next eight years, the coming to power of the Eisenhower administration with a different view of the role of atomic weapons, the death of Stalin, the Sino-Soviet rift, and the growing Chinese industrial and scientific capability all were to combine to lead Peking to a new evaluation of the role of atomic weapons as an instrument of diplomacy and a greater sense of urgency about the need to develop a Chinese nuclear capability.

The Era of Massive Retaliation, 1953–57

In 1953 a new American administration came to power, and shortly thereafter the Stalinist era in the Soviet Union came to an end. The Eisenhower administration was committed to a new look at defense, one of whose explicit objectives was to move away from the notion that nuclear weapons could not be used. In fact, the administration moved quickly to bring the nuclear power of the United States into play. According to President Eisenhower, Peking was warned that unless there was an armistice within a short time in Korea the United States would widen the war with the possibility of the use of nuclear weapons against China. Shortly thereafter, Peking accepted a truce essentially on the terms which the Truman administration had proposed. Much had happened in the meantime, including the death of Stalin and the reorientation of both Peking's and Moscow's policy toward peaceful coexistence. Nevertheless it was clear that the possibility of nuclear retaliation did play some role in influencing Peking's decision to accept an armistice and to give, in effect, Chinese prisoners of war their choice of going to Taiwan or returning to mainland China. It was unmistakably clear to Mao that his new antagonists in Washington were much more likely to use nuclear weapons than was the Truman administration.

The Vietnam crisis in 1954 may well have strengthened Peking in these beliefs. While the American administration in the end did not intervene and permitted an armistice to be concluded, there were many press reports that the administration was leaning toward an intervention which might well involve nuclear attacks against China. In the 1954–55 Taiwan Strait crisis there were again reports of American willingness to use nuclear weapons if necessary to defend its interests.

These specific actions of the Eisenhower administration in critical situations suggesting a willingness to use nuclear weapons if necessary were accompanied by explicit changes in Washington's doctrine. The Peking regime has always followed very closely the published statements, testimony, and press commentaries on American military strategy and has since 1949 tried to define the nature of American military strategy in any given period and its implications for Chinese security. There is no doubt that the "new look" policy of the Eisenhower administration was given such a scrutiny and that it produced great disquiet in Peking.

Many American critics of the policy were pointing out that it was not a credible policy since they assumed that the Soviet Union would inevitably come to the support of China and that any use of nuclear weapons would mean that the United States was prepared to sacrifice Washington and New York for the sake of destroying Moscow. However, from Peking's point of view the situation was very different. The Chinese believed, as may have well been the case, that Dulles in his famous massive retaliation speech was threatening not an all-out attack on the Soviet Union in the event of conventional aggression by China, Russia, or their allies, but rather selected, limited nuclear retaliation, the analogue to the nuclear attacks on Manchuria which had been threatened in the closing days of the Korean War. For the Chinese this threat was very serious, one with a high degree of credibility and one which in their view was very unlikely to bring a Soviet counterattack. Thus, not only at the end of the Korean War but also during the Indochina crisis and the offshore islands crisis some months later Peking saw Washington moving closely toward implementing a strategy of selective nuclear response.

This apparent willingness on the part of Washington to consider the limited use of nuclear weapons—a limited use which Peking had no doubt would devastate China's industrialized sector—coincided with two other disquieting trends in United States policy to suggest to Peking that a nuclear attack on China was more likely than Peking had believed it to be in the later 1940's and first years of the 1950's. One of these was the effort of American Secretary of State John Foster Dulles to conclude mutual security pacts with a number of countries. This effort was to lead ultimately to the SEATO Treaty and to a bilateral pact with the Republic of China on Taiwan. Even more alarming to Peking was the general change in the relationship between Washington and Taipei. Eisenhower had pledged during his campaign to "unleash" Chiang Kai-shek and the formal unleashing took place almost immediately after his inauguration. While in Washington, and even in fact in Taipei, this was clearly understood to be a symbolic gesture and one not implying any short-run plans to move against the mainland, Peking could not be so sure. The mutual security pact between the two countries and Washington's apparent willingness to defend at least some of the offshore islands may well have added to the sense of disquiet on the mainland, by suggesting that in some circumstances the United States might support with its nuclear power an effort of the Nationalists to return to the mainland.

This fear of a greater likelihood of American nuclear attack, particularly if Peking were to attempt to exert its influence and extend its hegemony around its borders, was enhanced by the development of thermonuclear weapons. Just as the Chinese leaders were quick to grasp the significance of the atomic bomb, so were they quick to understand that the hydrogen bomb, because it increased destructive power enormously, represented an even greater revolution in weaponry, one which meant that large segments of China could be destroyed. Peking was greatly concerned about the signs of possible American monopoly in thermonuclear weapons and greatly relieved when the Soviets showed signs of catching up with, and perhaps even moving slghtly ahead of the United States in this new technology.

The events of these years did nothing to shake Mao's belief that nuclear weapons had not changed the laws of history. But they also served to sharpen Mao's perception that unless China developed its own nuclear capability it could be subject to American nuclear pressures which would limit Peking's sphere of action in the Far East and indeed throughout the world. The impression that American nuclear power would not be used, which Peking may have developed as a result of its early Korean War experience, had been undercut by the actions and assertions of the new administration. These feelings were to intensify during the latter years of the 1950's, during which nuclear weapons, their control, and possible use were to come even more centrally into focus as a major element of Peking's policy and as a major issue in the Sino-Soviet dispute.

The East Wind Prevails, 1957–60

It is difficult to overestimate the importance which became attached to various aspects of the nuclear weapons problem during the period 1957–60. These years were crowded by such events as the blossoming of the Sino-Soviet dispute, including a disagreement about the impact of a nuclear war on the nature of the revolutionary process and the role which nuclear disarmament should play; Chinese acceleration of development of their own nuclear weapons with assistance from the Soviet Union; the entrance of both the United States and the Soviet Union into the space age and with it the prospect of intercontinental ballistic missiles; and a major Sino-American clash in the Taiwan Strait, in which the United States again evoked a threat of the use of nuclear weapons. Each of these events had a substantial impact on Chinese doctrine on the use and control of nuclear weapons.

In October, 1957, the Soviet Union tested an intercontinental ballistic missile. Both the Soviet and Chinese leadership viewed this event as one of epic importance. At a minimum, they both agreed that it substantially reduced the possibility of an American nuclear attack on the Soviet Union and by extension on Communist China because it provided, or soon would provide, a Soviet capability to retaliate massively against the United States. Both Khrushchev and Mao also agreed that the Soviet military achievement paved the way for additional political moves on the part of the Sino-Soviet bloc. However, they disagreed on two critical points. The Chinese wished to press the offensive in the Far East and in the underdeveloped world, while Khrushchev wished to concentrate his efforts on Berlin. Moreover, as the Chinese were later to discover, Khrushchev had decided that he could gain the political advantage of a missile program without actually engaging in the production of large numbers of missiles (a mistake Mao would not have made). The reaction of Peking to the Soviet ICBM accomplishment should have destroyed any lingering doubts in the West that Peking understood the effects of nuclear weapons and placed high value on having an adequate nuclear missile capability. In fact, as has been suggested above, the Chinese had been concerned about the nature of the strategic nuclear balance since the opening of the Atomic Age. They were conscious until 1957 of the inferiority of the Sino-Soviet bloc as well as concerned about the possibility that the Soviets would not come to their aid. Sputnik seemed to herald for them as well as for the Russians a new era, an era in which, provided the Soviet Union and China remained united, the possibility of deterring the Americans and hence having greater freedom to pursue the spread of Communism by other means would be substantially increased.

The Chinese pressed this position at the 1957 Moscow Conference of ruling Communist parties. They apparently met some hesitation on the part of Khrushchev in spelling out the doctrine in great detail, but there appeared to be a general agreement between the two countries that a new strategic era had dawned in which the power of the Communist bloc would be greatly increased. There was, however, a clash between the two countries on a number of other issues, including the extent to which a peaceful transition to Communism was possible. These differences of view marked a beginning of the Sino-Soviet dispute.

An attempt to discuss all the causes of the Sino-Soviet dispute, or even those causes which revolve around nuclear weapons, would go far beyond the scope of this essay. But two aspects of the Sino-Soviet dispute are directly relevant to the question of evolving Chinese doctrine on the use and control of nuclear weapons. These need to be mentioned.

The first concerns the fundamental question of the impact of nuclear weapons on the validity of Marxism-Leninism. As early as 1956, Khrushchev began to make clear his belief in the doctrine which had been rejected by Mao in 1946. Khrushchev avowed that the atomic bomb did not respect class laws, that in fact violent revolution was now a dangerous path because it might trigger a nuclear holocaust which would wipe out all the gains of the revolution and destroy the economic and social base for further seizures of power by Marxist-Leninist parties. This was, as we have seen, precisely the position which was taken by some of Mao's comrades in 1946. Far from being slower to understand the implications of the nuclear age than the Russians, the Chinese had in fact discussed and settled at a much earlier time the issues which rocked the Soviet Party in the period following the death of Stalin. What was most threatening and most disturbing about Khrushchev's assertions was that they went precisely to the core of the Maoist position on the atomic bomb. Now Khrushchev was saying that the bomb was not a paper tiger and that it could destroy the laws of Marxism-Leninism and by implication make impossible the violent rural revolution preached by the Chinese Communists. Khrushchev's revisionist position was totally unacceptable to Mao on two counts. Not only would it entail the abandonment of the doctrine which Mao and his colleagues still hoped to implement throughout the Third World, but also, and probably equally important, it represented a challenge to the doctrinal infallibility of Mao.

On a much more practical level, the views of Peking and Moscow also diverged from each other. Because of his ideological position on nuclear weapons, Khrushchev began the search for limited arms control agreements with the United States and the United Kingdom. These initiatives led the Soviets to announce that they were willing to accept a moratorium on nuclear testing. Although the Chinese went along with the Soviet efforts (this cooperation was perhaps the price they had to pay for Soviet nuclear assistance), they were clearly uneasy about the new Soviet position. The measures espoused by Khrushchev would probably mean that it would be impossible for Peking's nuclear program to develop as far as the Chinese desired, even if with Soviet aid they could somehow enter the nuclear club in a token way. Moreover, these measures might serve to freeze the world's balance of power before Peking had obtained her desired place. During the period under consideration in this section Peking continued to hold its peace, partly perhaps because of the aid received from the Soviet Union in the nuclear field and partly because of its general strategy of refraining from public conflict with the Soviet Union.

Chinese support for the Soviet efforts to negotiate a test ban seems to be related to Sino-Soviet discussions about the need for a Chinese nuclear capability.[3] As was suggested above, Mao's aspirations to make China a nuclear power probably went back to the Hiroshima detonation. Concrete planning began almost as soon as Mao seized power and an actual nuclear program was probably launched as early as 1954. However, the program appears to have been vastly accelerated sometime in mid-1958.[4] Prior to this there were extensive discussions between Peking and Moscow about the possibility of the Chinese foregoing a nuclear program in return for increased Soviet support for China as well as about the nature of possible Soviet aid to a Chinese nuclear program. Without necessarily resisting the notion of the Chinese ultimately developing nuclear weapons, Khrushchev appears to have proposed to the Chinese joint defense arrangements, including probably the stationing of Soviet nuclear weapons on Chinese territory.

[3] I have attempted to disentangle these complex relations in some detail in my article "Sino-Soviet Nuclear Relations 1957–1960," in Morton Halperin, ed., *Sino-Soviet Relations and Arms Control* (Cambridge: M.I.T. Press, 1967), pp. 117–43. Only the barest outlines of the argument can be presented here.

[4] After the detonation of a thermonuclear bomb on June 17, 1967, Peking quoted Mao as having said in June, 1958: "I think it is entirely possible for some atomic bombs and hydrogen bombs to be made in ten years' time" (New China News Agency, June 17, 1967).

After some debate this plan was rejected apparently because of the traditional Chinese resistance to foreign bases, as well as the belief of the Maoist leadership that only nuclear weapons in its own hands could serve as a genuine deterrent and provide the basis for a Chinese claim to being a world superpower. Thus, while rejecting Khrushchev's proposals, Mao and his colleagues pressed for aid to the Chinese nuclear program. It is now clear that very substantial aid was in fact given by the Soviet Union in the period 1957–59. How extensive this aid was and Soviet motives for giving it are both matters for conjecture beyond the scope of this analysis. However, it is obvious that the Chinese attached high priority to obtaining this nuclear assistance from the Soviet Union. Despite the debates among the Chinese leadership and between those responsible for control of the party and the government and those responsible for control of the army over a number of issues, including the possibility of accepting Soviet nuclear weapons on Chinese territory under joint control, there appears never to have been any disagreement among the Chinese leadership about the high priority assigned to a Chinese nuclear program. Thus once the industrial and scientific base had been laid in the early fifties and Soviet support attained, a crash nuclear program was launched.

Most of the Chinese concern about nuclear weapons in this period focused on their domestic nuclear program and on Sino-Soviet relations. However, in the summer and the fall of 1958, there was a major clash between Peking and the United States in which the threat of nuclear weapons was evoked. On August 23, 1958, Peking launched a military action against Quemoy, apparently designed to blockade the island and to force it into surrender on the assumption that the United States would not intervene. However, this proved to be a miscalculation, as the United States quickly involved itself in the crisis. Peking spent the next several weeks trying to force the United States off the scene or, at a minimum, to cover its withdrawal while preventing an American nuclear attack against the Chinese mainland. As President Eisenhower makes clear in his memoirs, the United States was ready to defend Quemoy if it came under attack and was prepared to use nuclear weapons in order to do so. Thus Peking again faced a situation in which the United States appeared to be willing to employ new weapons. Although again no nuclear weapons were used, Peking's concerns and fears about the impact of American nuclear capability on China's ability to expand its influence in the Far East were intensified.

What impact then did these traumatic events have on Chinese outlook toward nuclear weapons?

First and most important, Mao's fundamental thesis that the atomic bomb was a paper tiger came under attack, not from other Chinese leaders but from the leader of the Soviet Union. Mao's bitter reaction to this challenge of his doctrine added fuel to the other factors exacerbating the Sino-Soviet relations. It also forced the Chinese into ever more extreme statements about their own attitudes toward nuclear war, leading many in the West to conclude that the Chinese neither understood nor feared a nuclear attack.

At the same time Khrushchev's growing revisionism and search for accommodation with the West, together with his withdrawal of assistance from China at the end of the period, underscored for Mao the correctness of the second basic decision which he had made in 1946, namely that China would have to develop its own nuclear capability. During this period China took in fact the first giant steps toward that capability. The fear of an American nuclear attack, moreover, was heightened by the crisis in the Taiwan Strait. Thus again events forced Peking to reassert its doctrine, and it did so more categorically than it had in the past. Its views, however, remained unchanged: China and the world would survive a nuclear war. Revolution was possible even with nuclear weapons in existence. China needed nuclear weapons to deter the United States and to become a world superpower.

The Challenge of Multiple Options, 1961–67

The 1960's have been marked by three major events which affected the Chinese attitude toward nuclear weapons: the changes in American policy instituted by the Kennedy-Johnson administration, the growing Sino-Soviet rift, and the Chinese nuclear detonations.

The Peking leadership looked with some trepidation upon the changes in military strategy planned by the Kennedy administration. Kennedy and his advisers had campaigned on a platform which suggested that the Eisenhower administration had been unable to use its military power effectively to halt Communist aggression. From Peking's perspectives Kennedy appeared to be committed to finding a way to make credible the threat of the use of American nuclear power. According to analysis published by the Chinese Communists, American doctrine went through three distinct phases in the 1960's. The first phase the Chinese refer to as that of "flexible response." Under this strategy the United States sought to build up its military power across the board in order to prevent successful Communist revolution, particularly in Vietnam, the focus of Peking's analysis of American strategy. The United States aimed at suppressing revolutionary war by conventional means. When it recognized the failure of this strategy, the American government turned to its second strategic innovation, that of "counter-insurgency." With the inevitable failure of this effort from Peking's perspective, American strategy evolved into the third stage which persists until the present time—the strategy of "escalation." In one of its rare references to American strategic analysts Peking attributed this strategy to the writings of Herman Kahn.

Peking describes this strategy as an effort to defeat a revolutionary war by engaging in larger and larger escalations ultimately ending up with the threat of nuclear strikes against the Chinese mainland. The question of whether or not the United States would actually carry the war to China and engage in nuclear attacks on Chinese military and civilian centers has been extensively debated in Peking. In the period 1965–66 most Chinese leaders appeared to have concluded that the United States was on the verge of launching a nuclear attack against China. Peking had no reason to believe that the Soviet Union would assist in its defense and in fact its public statements implied a belief that the Soviet Union might launch a simultaneous attack in the Sino-Soviet border area. Nor at this time had Peking developed its own nuclear capability to the point where China could count on this as a deterrent against an American attack.

This situation brought on another round in the debate over the most effective means to deal with a nuclear attack. The leadership was caught in a dilemma. On the one hand, it desired to underplay the likely effect of a nuclear attack on China in order to contribute to the deterrence of American action. On the other hand, it wanted to arouse the people to take the necessary steps in preparation for an attack. In this situation Peking for the first time appears to have decided to present the Chinese public with a fairly precise estimate of its own internal calculations. The press and radio informed the Chinese people that an American nuclear attack was probable if not inevitable and said that such an attack would do great damage to China. Nevertheless, it asserted that the revolution would go on, that the Chinese leaders would, if necessary, take to the hills and direct the revolution from there, that American nuclear power, even if aided by Soviet nuclear power and followed up by a ground attack by the two countries, could not succeed in destroying the Chinese revolution. While there was agreement on this analysis of the situation, the Chinese leadership was divided on the best way to prepare for American attack. The professional military argument was that if an attack indeed was imminent China should seek to make use of its conventional military forces which had been built up over the years. This force could, of course, not be used in any way to defeat an American missile attack, but it should be the main force to resist the land invasion which the Chinese believe would follow a nuclear attack. Mao, with perhaps a greater sense of the futility of the attempt to engage in conventional warfare against a nuclear power, argued that the People's Liberation Army (PLA) did not have a major role to play in defending China against an American nuclear attack. Rather the only hope lay in a withdrawal from the main centers of population both by the political leadership and by the PLA. The party and the army would return to the hills to preserve themselves intact and to prepare the campaign to ultimately drive the Americans out of China. At the same time the peasants organized in the form of the militia would bear the brunt of attempting to fight off the American invaders and harassing their advance. After some dispute, this line again won out and emphasis was put on preparing the people psychologically for an American attack and training elements of the militia to resist the attack. Mao's attitudes on nuclear war were put to one of their greatest tests during this period, but he and his associates appear to remain firmly convinced that in the end the revolution in China could not be suppressed by an American nuclear attack although such an attack could do great damage to all that had been created in China in the period since 1949.

By the middle of 1966, the Chinese leadership had come to recognize that the United States was not planning to escalate the war indefinitely and launch a nuclear attack against China. At the same time the frenzy of its internal activity was to give the leadership less time to deal with this issue.

The changes in American policy discussed above were paralleled by the rapid deterioration of Sino-Soviet relations to the point where Peking could no longer believe that Soviet nuclear power provided a significant deterrent against an American attack on China. Thus the need for a Chinese nuclear capability increased in Peking's view, at the very time when Soviet aid was cut off and China was forced to go it alone.

The Sino-Soviet rift also caused Peking to discuss in much greater detail than it ever had previously its views on nuclear weapons and to seek to clarify what its differences with the Soviet Union were. Peking faced the problem that all governments face in such a situation, namely the problem of multiple audiences. Peking had to direct its words simultaneously to its potential supporters in the Soviet Union, to other ruling and non-ruling Communist parties, to its own people, and to its potential enemies whose use of nuclear weapons it sought to deter. This problem was complicated by the line that the Soviet Union was taking. Having developed what it considered to be an adequate deterrent, the Soviet leadership was beginning to argue that nuclear weapons had changed the laws of history and that nuclear war had to be avoided at all costs. In order to justify this position, particularly within the international Communist movement, Khrushchev sought to stress the great destruction which would result from a nuclear war and to accuse the Chinese of not understanding the destructive power of nuclear weapons. This charge had the added appeal of painting the Chinese as irrational, thereby demonstrating Khrushchev's real desire for peaceful coexistence with the West and undercutting the Chinese position with other Communist parties and non-Communist nations.

In seeking to answer these charges, Mao faced a dilemma. If he chose to emphasize, as did the Soviet leadership, that nuclear war would be very destructive, he would simply be inviting the West to take advantage of China's weakness to put pressure on Peking. Yet Mao was not prepared to deny the power of nuclear weapons while devoting great resources to their production. Morover, Peking recognized that to deny the destructive power of nuclear weapons was to be branded as irrational and hence to court the danger that China's nuclear capability would be destroyed in a preemptive strike.

In the face of this dilemma, the Peking leadership held to a statement of its own beliefs about nuclear weapons but with a change in nuance as the decade developed. In the late 1950's and into the early 1960's Peking emphasized its belief that socialism, but not capitalism, would survive a nuclear war. Peking discussed the results of a nuclear war in terms which led some critics to believe that China actually desired such a war and underestimated the destruction which would result. This posture had the value of rallying around Peking those who were opposed to Khrushchev's attempts to change Marxist-Leninist doctrine and it also was in line with the Chinese belief that man would ultimately triumph over weapons. However, it served to alienate large parts of the world Communist movement and to produce apprehensions in the West which Peking feared might lead to an attack on China's developing nuclear capability. By 1962 Peking had switched to a new tack in which it emphasized China's understanding of nuclear war and the great destructive power of nuclear weapons. This posture was to reach a crescendo at the time of the Chinese nuclear detonations.

The progress which China has made in developing nuclear weapons makes it unmistakably clear that the Peking leadership has devoted very substantial resources to a Chinese nuclear program, at least since the mid-1950's. In the 1960's China was forced to proceed without Soviet assistance, and this undoubtedly required an even greater domestic effort channeling a large percentage of China's scientific and technical manpower into a nuclear program. Viewed from Peking, this program of developing nuclear weapons was not without its risks. As the time of its first nuclear detonation came near, Peking began to fear that either the United States or the Soviet Union might decide to destroy the embryonic Chinese nuclear capability. This apprehension led Peking to move very cautiously in the period immediately preceding its detonation and to surround the detonation with a series of statements stressing China's reasonableness: that China would never be the first to use nuclear weapons, and that China understood the destructive power of these weapons. Fear of a preemptive nuclear attack not only forced Peking into cautious posture for several years but also gave added emphasis to a desire to get an operational nuclear capability as soon as possible. Only when China had such capability could she hope to deter an American attack, first by threatening to destroy American bases and the Seventh Fleet and ultimately by threatening to destroy American cities.

If Peking was forced to say a great deal more about nuclear weapons in the 1960's, so also was China forced to articulate in much more detail its own position on matters of arms control and disarmament. For one thing, China was no longer prepared simply to give lip service to the Soviet positions. For another, the United States and the Soviet Union were beginning to make progress on disarmament, and Peking was confronted with real measures to which she had to react. Finally, the Chinese sought to use their new disarmament policy as part of their effort to deter the use of nuclear weapons against them.

The Peking leadership viewed with grave misgivings the movement of the Soviet Union, beginning in 1955–56, away from a purely propaganda interest in arms control and disarmament measures toward some interest in actually signing limited nuclear arms control measures with the United States. The signing of the three environment test ban treaty in 1963 was a major turning point in Sino-Soviet relations and produced a series of bitter exchanges between the two governments. Peking viewed Moscow's adherence to the treaty as a logical extension of Khrushchev's belief that a fundamental change had taken place in the world situation, a belief which Peking of course rejected. If there were no fundamental change, then it was impossible to come to serious agreements with capitalist nations on a matter as vital as the most powerful weapons available to each side. Thus Soviet adherence to the treaty was taken as a sell-out, not only of Soviet interests, but those of the world Communist movement.

In responding to the Soviet adherence to the test ban treaty, Peking spelled out in some detail its own position on disarmament. In short, it argued that the only valuable nuclear agreement was one which brought about the total and complete destruction of nuclear weapons. Peking argued that such an agreement would only be possible when "imperialism" had been totally defeated. In other words Peking argued that arms control and disarmament was a sham unless it was an accompaniment of world revolution. To accept arms control agreements in the interim, which affected the capability of Communist nations, was to sell out the revolution because of a misconception of the role of nuclear weapons in world history.

Peking did propose one specific arms control agreement which she was to push vigorously over the next several years. This was an agreement to ban the first use of nuclear weapons. Peking could hardly expect such an agreement to have a real and lasting meaning, nor could she expect that it would be observed at the height of a large-scale military conflict. What Peking did seek by putting forward such an agreement was a propaganda answer to the charge that she was not prepared to sign the test ban treaty. Peking was probably quite prepared to sign a no-first-use agreement. Such an agreement in her eyes would not at all reduce Peking's flexibility, but would perhaps make it somewhat more difficult for the United States to make even the implicit threats of the use of nuclear weapons that Peking had come to fear over the years. Moreover, it would make it less likely that either Russia or the United States would launch a preemptive nuclear attack designed to destroy China's nuclear installations. In short, Peking's support of a no-first-use agreement harked back to the same motivations which guided the Soviets in the late forties and early fifties, namely a desire to reduce the likelihood that the West would use nuclear weapons, while gaining the support of adherents of "peace" and answering the West's disarmament proposals without accepting them.

Peking's disarmament campaign reached a climax at the time of the Chinese first and second nuclear detonations and was clearly designed to reduce the likelihood that the United States or the Soviet Union would attack China's nuclear capability. In 1966 Peking lost interest in its disarmament campaign, as China's interest in the world at large faded.

The Future

Given the uncertain nature of conditions in Peking, it would be hazardous to make any firm predictions about the likely evolution of Chinese attitudes toward the use and control of nuclear weapons. However, it is perhaps worth emphasizing that all of those now competing for power in Peking have been debating the role of nuclear weapons for some time. All of them have understood the great destructive power of nuclear weapons. If there has been any dispute, it has been over how fundamental the change is. There is no doubt that all the leaders in Peking understand that a nuclear war would mean the destruction of all of the modern sectors of society which Peking has built up since 1949. There is perhaps the danger that the Maoist faction, if it comes to believe that it has no alternative between war and capitulation, will decide that the continuation of the ideology in its pure form is worth even the total destruction of the modern sector of China. However, if both the United States and Soviet Union can refrain from confronting Peking with what appears to be an unacceptable ultimatum, we can expect, even from the Mao-Lin leadership, a continuing caution and a desire to avoid a nuclear confrontation.

Comments by Vincent D. Taylor

The major thesis of Mr. Halperin's paper is that immediately after Hiroshima the Communist Chinese intensively debated the implications of atomic weapons for revolutionary warfare and that the debate produced a position on nuclear weapons that has remained essentially unchanged through the present time. The position is that nuclear weapons are a powerful force but a force that is not immune to the existing laws of history and can be overthrown; if one captures the allegiance of the people, one can triumph no matter how strong the weapons of one's opponent. This position was put forth in a statement by Mao Tse-tung in which he affirmed the validity of the strategy of people's war despite the fact that the enemy possessed the atomic bomb. As a separate point, Mr. Halperin surmises that Mao, in the process of analyzing the implications of nuclear weapons, concluded that China would ultimately have to develop its own nuclear capability in order to take its rightful position on the world stage. In short, the beliefs attributed to Mao are (1) revolutionary warfare can still be successful even if the enemy possesses atomic weapons, and (2) the possession of nuclear weapons by the Communist Chinese will facilitate progress toward the goal of socialist world revolution.

What I propose to do in this comment is analyze the Chinese position using general strategic principles and to ask whether the position is logically consistent.

Differences between Conventional and Nuclear Weapons

In order to understand the implications of nuclear weapons for revolutionary warfare, one must first answer the question, "How do nuclear weapons differ from conventional ones?" There are three significant differences. The first and most obvious difference is that the total amount of destruction that can be done by nuclear weapons greatly exceeds the possibilities with conventional weapons. A second difference is the speed with which destruction is wrought. Nuclear weapons make it possible to compress a large amount of destruction in a very short span of time. Although the destructive power of the conventional bombs dropped on Germany during World War II far exceeded the destructive power of the Hiroshima bomb, the destruction in Germany was spread out over years, while the destruction in Hiroshima was practically instantaneous. A third difference between nuclear and conventional weapons is the intensity of destruction. A bombing raid with conventional weapons may do considerable damage within a target area. A raid with nuclear weapons will totally annihilate the same target area.

The vastly different characteristics of conventional and nuclear weapons imply equally profound differences in the character of war. First, nuclear weapons will greatly increase the loss of life and property suffered in a war. Second, the speed and intensity of destruction possible with nuclear weapons means that concentrated targets such as cities, industrial centers, and massed bodies of troops could be totally annihilated. Clearly, a war against an enemy who possesses nuclear weapons must involve different tactics. But, are the principles and strategy contained in Mao's theory of revolutionary war still valid? Further, even if the strategy remains valid, how would one-sided possession of nuclear weapons by the United States affect the Chinese estimate of the likelihood and outcome of a United States–China war?

The Chinese View of a United States–China Nuclear War

To understand the impact of nuclear weapons on warfare, one must trace through the likely course of a war in which nuclear weapons are employed. A classic case, which the Chinese must have considered many times, is a large-scale attack on China by American forces employing nuclear weapons. An assessment of the ability of people's war to deal with such an attack would provide the Chinese with, perhaps, the ultimate test of the validity of Mao's strategy in the nuclear era. If the Chinese could not attach a reasonable probability to the triumph of people's war in such a struggle, it seems difficult to believe that they could continue to accept the unconditional validity of Mao's theories.

Consider, from the Chinese viewpoint, the likely course of a war in which the United States drew freely upon her vast nuclear arsenal of today. First, the Chinese would expect to lose immediately their large cities and industrial areas. Some might fall directly to nuclear attack, others to ground forces employing tactical nuclear weapons. A Chinese would also expect, I imagine, that control of the countryside would remain in Chinese hands and that nuclear tactics would be ineffective against the low-level guerrilla warfare phase of revolutionary war.

But, the theory of people's war states that ultimate victory will come when division-size attacks can be carried out against the enemy. The tactical nuclear weapon capability of the United States would quickly frustrate any attempt to move into this final phase of the war. Thus, there appears to be a fatal weakness in Mao's theory. Although the Chinese could readily imagine preventing a United States takeover of China, it seems unlikely that they could believe it possible to prevent the United States from retaining control over some of the most populous and developed sections of the country.

From a Chinese viewpoint, such an outcome could hardly be considered a victory. Therefore, I find it hard to believe that as the United States nuclear capability has grown, the Chinese have not at least placed some conditions and limitations on the value of people's war. Unconditional faith in people's war may have been logical in the forties when the United States had only a small number of atomic bombs, but it hardly seems logical today when the United States has a vast thermo-nuclear arsenal. Moreover, people's war is not an effective counter against American threats of nuclear strikes on industrial and population targets. Such attacks would inflict huge damage on China with little or no risk to the United States. Such nuclear blackmail greatly restrains China's freedom of action, and people's war is just not an effective counter to it.

This line of reasoning leads to the conclusion that the validity of people's war would be greatly enhanced by Chinese possession of a nuclear capability. It is not at all surprising that the Chinese have made such a major effort to obtain this capability. Even a modest Chinese nuclear capability would raise the costs to the United States of any nuclear war with China. It would first of all reduce the safety of American bases in Asia. Second, it would greatly raise the risk to the United States of undertaking conventional troop actions—perhaps leading to a tacit ban on the tactical use of nuclear weapons. Third, as a counter to nuclear blackmail threats, China could threaten retaliation against allies of the United States in the region.

Summary

To assess the validity of Mao's theory of revolutionary war in the nuclear era, the course of a hypothetical United States–China war was traced. The likely outcome was such that the Chinese could be expected to have reasonable doubts about the ability of the strategy of people's war to triumph in such a struggle. Further, it was noted that the strategy of people's war had little value in countering United States nuclear blackmail. It is, therefore, not surprising that the Chinese have made the effort necessary to obtain a nuclear capability.

Frank E. Armbruster

7

China's Conventional Military Capability

The capability of modern China to wage conventional (classical, standard-formation, non-nuclear) war continues to be a topic of vital interest but one which perhaps still receives inadequate detailed attention. Traditionally, Chinese troops had been thought to suffer by comparison to Western troops and Western-type units. And perhaps the defeat of Chinese armies at the hands of the Japanese in the 1930's tended to confirm this opinion about modern China. The subsequent victories of these same Japanese armies over British and American-Philippine troops in Malaya and the Islands, however, pointed up the exceptional capability of this enemy; and British Field Marshal Viscount Slim said Chinese soldiers under him fought well in Burma.[1] When the Chinese soldier is a member of a good, well-organized, and well-led unit, his record is not one of inevitable failure; seldom in modern times has he had the type of disciplined, centrally controlled organization behind him that he has now. He is basically a hard-working, long-suffering, far from cowardly individual, and today he is said to be "in general . . . loyal to the regime and delighted to be in the army."[2]

The current conventional military capability of the Chinese Communist regime is held in very high esteem—in fact it may now be held in such high esteem that there may be a danger of some error in this direction. There may even be a tendency to overlook some of the distinctions that are essential to assessments of military competence; that

The author wishes to acknowledge the research and editorial assistance of Doris Yokelson Batra.

[1] For Slim's evaluation of Chinese troops see Field Marshal the Viscount Slim, *Defeat into Victory* (New York: David McKay Company, Inc., 1961), pp. 12, 46–47.

[2] Chalmers Johnson, "How Sharp Are the Dragon's Claws?" *New York Times Magazine*, February 28, 1965, p. 22.

is, for example, distinctions between offensive and defensive capability, between different geographic areas in which the power is to be used, between different types of military organizations that might be the opponents, etc. This discussion of Communist China's conventional military capability is an attempt to view the subject in the light of the record of her forces as Peking may see it and in the context of the environment in which these forces may be called into action in the future. It emphasizes factors of geography, logistics, politics, and the required coordinated efforts of the Red Chinese Army, Navy, and Air Force.

Discussions of Red Chinese military power are of course influenced by the number of troops and the troop potential of the vast Chinese population. But emphasis on numbers can be unfortunate.[3] Numbers of troops are best considered only in relation to the factors mentioned above. Rather than "change format" in a discussion of Red China's conventional military power, however, let us cover the question of numbers and proceed to other issues that may be more significant, at least from the point of view of China's neighbors and the United States.

People's Liberation Army

The primary conventional military capability of Red China lies in the People's Liberation Army (PLA). This army is occasionally visualized as consisting of (or potentially consisting of) hordes of fighting men—and to the small nations on her border it may appear so. Such estimates may not appear unfounded when one considers the fact that there are 125 million men of military age in Red China. Furthermore, the Chinese People's Republic has a vast militia which has been said to have had 220 or even 250 million men and women in its ranks (one of every three people) at one time or another. In 1964 the "basic" militia and "general" militia were said to include 200 million people. But these numbers alone are a somewhat shaky basis for estimating Chinese classical, over-all, ground-force capability.

The militia is no military body per se. It appears to be useful primarily as a means of controlling and directing the population in efforts to support the national and local economic plans, etc. About fifteen per cent of the men (and women) in the militia do receive military training,

[3] It may be, however, as one work states, that the size of Red China's large land army, plus its record of successes, makes it appear to its neighbors to be invincible in any of its border areas against any foe (Morton H. Halperin and Dwight H. Perkins, *Communist China and Arms Control* [Cambridge, Mass.: East Asian Research Center, Center for International Affairs, Harvard University, 1965], p. 77).

but the level of training is seldom high. This is not to say that there is no mission for the militia in time of war. First of all, it forms a somewhat "trained" reserve to provide replacements for the regular army (PLA), and indeed the basic militia is made up of army reservists, cadres and party members.[4] Second, in case of an actual invasion of the homeland, the militia may have the mission of defending the communes until overrun,[5] then acting as guerrilla support for the regular army. Under this plan, the militia would be expected to cooperate in the "protracted conflict" role and "bleed" the enemy, through guerrilla action, while the army retreats inland until the invading army is weakened and overextended—at which point the PLA is supposed to turn on the enemy and destroy him.[6] Or, to use Mao's phrase, the militia's job is to "drown" the enemy in "a sea of humanity."[7] This theory of a militia mission does provide a use (defensive only) for large numbers of untrained, quasi-military people. But even it does not provide a use for unarmed people, the category into which the majority of militia men fall.[8]

The 125 million men of military age, therefore, are just that—125 million men of military age. They are not armed, and except for militia and PLA services, they are not trained. They are neither organized nor equipped; in short, they are not an army. Nor does China have the capability to arm a vast army quickly. Even to adequately arm a large ground force at a slower pace would be a terrible drain on her very weak economy. Developing a modern army with high conventional combat capability requires the support of a highly developed economic and industrial base. To date China still has not achieved this goal. Crucial military support industries were hurt by the disorganization of the "Great Leap." With the Russian withdrawal of assistance (including fuel oil),[9] the Chinese experienced a deterioration of their forces in

[4] John Gittings, "China's Militia," *The China Quarterly*, no. 18 (April–June, 1964), pp. 104, 110, 114; Edgar O'Ballance, *The Red Army of China* (London: Faber and Faber, 1962), pp. 204, 205; Johnson, *New York Times Magazine*, February 28, 1965, p. 22.

[5] O'Ballance, *The Red Army of China*, pp. 204, 205.

[6] "China: Dangers of Misunderstanding," *Newsweek*, March 7, 1966, p. 40.

[7] Gittings, *China Quarterly*, no. 18 (April–June, 1964), p. 106; and Johnson, *New York Times Magazine*, February 28, 1965, p. 85.

[8] One of the problems about issuing guns to this vast horde of people may be doubts about the loyalty of some of them. See O'Ballance, *The Red Army of China*, p. 205.

[9] Alice Langley Hsieh, "China's Secret Military Papers: Military Doctrine and Strategy," *China Quarterly*, no. 18 (April–June, 1964), p. 95.

being. They are said to have made considerable efforts to overcome this handicap since 1961, but at least until 1965 without giving the military priority over economic development.[10] Nevertheless, China showed an inability in the early sixties to produce even such basic instruments of war as heavy artillery, although she has produced medium artillery and "some tanks."[11]

China's industrial base is currently expanding somewhat, but it is shaky, and in 1966 output was still placed below that of 1960.[12] China's population is also growing, bringing greater and greater demands on this same industrial base. The result seems to be that China's army has serious deficiencies, e.g., she lacks heavy and self-propelled artillery; her armored forces are far too few in number and they depend on World War II and some fine but not the most modern later Russian tank models.[13]

Radical and large-scale changes in this situation will require considerable time and effort. Furthermore, the "delivery system" of a conventional army is initially the indigenous transport system of the homeland. In China this system is totally inadequate to China's economic and military tasks. The railroad system is not fully developed, and the shortage of motor transport probably still restricts "strategic mobility."[14] Travelers report that the age-old curse of China, lack of transport, is still with her. Demands on the transport system increase daily, and the bottleneck in this area should remain for some time.

The Chinese Army, therefore, is very much smaller than the huge pool of men of military age might lead one to expect. It has 2½ million men grouped primarily into 30 field armies of three divisions each.

[10] Halperin and Perkins, *Communist China and Arms Control,* p. 38.

[11] O'Ballance, *The Red Army of China,* p. 207; *The Military Balance, 1965–1966* (London: Institute of Strategic Studies, 1965), p. 9.

[12] "Since the disasters of the Great Leap, the Peking leaders have not known how to . . . promote sustained economic development. A process of modest growth is under way once again but . . . total agricultural output today is at approximately the level it reached almost a decade ago; in per-capita terms it is even lower. And despite renewed industrial growth in a few key fields, overall industrial production is still below its 1960 peak. There is good reason to believe that . . . Communist China has not really had any effective, long-term national economic plan in operation for over eight years . . ." (A. Doak Barnett, "China After Mao," *Look,* November 15, 1966, p. 33).

[13] O'Ballance, *The Red Army of China,* p. 207; *The Military Balance, 1967–1968* (London: The Institute for Strategic Studies, 1967), p. 10. She has shipped eighty T59 tanks, her version of the Soviet T54/T55 models, to Pakistan.

[14] *The Military Balance, 1965–1966,* p. 9.

There are said to be a total of 120 divisions of about 12,000 men each in the table of organization.[15] But, as in all military tables of organization, even this may not give the real strength of the army. In this army, the divisional "slice" of manpower would amount to about 20,000 men. That could mean a very thin army without sufficient supporting services; it could mean that some of the 120 divisions are not combat-ready and must be filled out in times of crises; or it could even mean that "line of communication troops" are not counted in the numbers one sees.[16] The second explanation may be the best. In any event, the army is known to be primarily made up of light infantry divisions (including two airborne divisions) with little mechanized equipment. There are thought to be only four "full-scale" armored divisions in the whole army, and her airlift capability for her airborne outfits is "probably limited to a few battalions."[17]

The Navy

The navy of Red China consists of a very small, modern surface fleet (4 destroyers, 4–5 destroyer escorts, and 11 frigate escorts); a moderate underseas fleet (31–34 Soviet- and Chinese-built submarines); and a large fleet of small craft (18–19 minesweepers, 60 landing ships, 150 torpedo boats, a conglomeration of new-to-ancient gunboats, etc.). The submarines (21 to 23 of which are post–World War II Soviet "W" class boats assembled in Chinese yards)[18] present the main threat to a modern naval power. The training and competency of the submarine crews are somewhat unknown factors,[19] as is the actual capability of

[15] *The Military Balance, 1967–1968*, p. 10.

[16] See O'Ballance, *The Red Army of China*, p. 200; see also Johnson, *New York Times Magazine*, February 28, 1965, p. 87.

[17] *The Military Balance, 1967–1968*, pp. 10, 11; Halperin and Perkins, p. 36; Raymond L. Garthoff, "Sino-Soviet Military Relations," *Annals of the American Academy of Political and Social Science*, vol. 349 (September, 1963), p. 81.

[18] *Jane's Fighting Ships, 1967–1968* (New York: McGraw-Hill, 1967–1968), pp. 54–58. There have been reports that China has launched one and is building a second "G" class (Soviet-style) submarine that can carry three 400-mile surface-to-surface ballistic missiles. One submarine is now reported to be operational but presumably still lacks her missiles (*The Military Balance, 1967–1968*, p. 11).

[19] In the words of one "naval expert": "The Chinese have absolutely no deep-water submarine experience and their subs are confined mostly to coastal waters. They are not much of a threat and they won't be until they develop some seamanship and some technology in the field" ("China: Dangers of Misunderstanding," *Newsweek*, March 7, 1966, p. 38).

these Chinese-assembled vessels. They are fitted for mine laying and might play a significant defensive role against an invasion fleet as well as cause casualties among the merchant fleet of the attacker, but they present no tool of conquest for the Chinese armed forces. The Red Chinese Navy does not have the capability to carry out and protect a sizable amphibious operation. It cannot support China's primary military force, the PLA, in an offensive across any sizable water barrier in the face of an adequately equipped, determined opponent.

The Air Force

The current Chinese Air Force consists of about 2,500 operable aircraft of which up to 150 are the obsolescent, light, jet bomber, the I128 ("Beagle"), such as the one the Soviets put into Cuba. The fighters are MiG 15's, 17's, and a lesser number of 19's and supersonic MiG 21's. (The Chinese Navy has a land-based air arm of 150 I128 torpedo planes and "substantial numbers" of MiG 15's and MiG 17's.)[20] The Shenyang Aircraft plant builds high-performance aircraft of Russian design, the MiG 17, MiG 15UTI, and "what is thought to be a simplified version of the MiG 21."[21] China is deficient in aviation fuel and in the past was heavily dependent upon the Soviet Union for its supplies. Since the Sino-Soviet split, training programs (at least until the mid-1960's) are said to have suffered from the shortage of fuel and spare parts.[22]

China's Offensive Conventional Military Capability

As indicated earlier, however, merely stating numbers in this fashion does not suffice to indicate China's conventional military power. Certainly it is no indication of the potential threat this power poses to her neighbors. Only by examining her ability to project that power outside her borders can we estimate the threat. Let us therefore examine first the position of the Free World powers that lie on the periphery of China.

South Korea

The first Free World power which comes to mind is a nation that was nearly conquered by a Communist Chinese Army. Korea lives on in the

[20] *The Military Balance, 1967–1968*, pp. 11, 12.

[21] *Jane's All the World's Aircraft, 1967–1968* (New York: McGraw-Hill, 1967–1968), p. 26. China has shipped some MiG 19's to Pakistan (*The Military Balance, 1966–1967*, p. 10).

[22] Johnson, *New York Times Magazine*, February 28, 1965, pp. 85, 86.

minds of Americans as the scene of a bitter, costly, and frustrating war with China. In fact, confrontations with Communists on the periphery of China since that war are almost invariably seen by someone as the threat of "another Korea" (if not a nuclear war). Implicit in such reactions is the suggestion that China has the capability to fight another Korea at the new point of confrontation (which will be discussed later) and second, that (at least in cases such as Vietnam) China would desire to start "another Korea" to retrieve the failure of an undertaking by one of its Communist neighbors.

Before we accept this last premise completely it might be interesting to examine the Korean conflict from the point of view of the Communists. The memory of Korea retained by most Americans is, first, the shock of the Chinese entrance into the war and the precipitous U.N. retreat, and later, the years of frustrating "position" warfare on the 38th parallel during "negotiations," which accounted for so many of the American casualties in that war.[23] But the war may well mean something entirely different to the Chinese Communists. The chronology of events in Korea actually went as we now trace it, and prudent Chinese are not likely to have forgotten it.

In June of 1950, the North Korean Army attacked South Korea and the victim state asked for assistance from the United States. At that point the United States had a 14 billion dollar defense budget and no troops in Korea, and emphasized combat-readiness, primarily in Germany. Congress quickly raised the defense budget to 60 billion dollars—and a race was on between the United States armed forces, which were deployed from their bases in Japan and the United States, and the North Korean Army. The prize was supposed to be South Korea; but within four months of the North Korean invasion, the North Korean Army was in ruins and fleeing through its own country toward the Chinese border.

At this point, fresh Chinese armies, which had been massing in Manchuria, crossed the Yalu in force. The Chinese exploited the opportunity offered by MacArthur's controversial deployment of his forces, and the allied army was soon caught in a precarious position. The U.N. force was driven back into South Korea. But by May, under Generals Ridgeway and Van Fleet, the U.N. forces had turned on the enemy once more. This new textbook counterattack—heavy air attacks along logistic lines and at the front, artillery bombardment, then armored and infantry drives—quickly chewed up the Chinese armies. And they, too, reeled back into North Korea. It was estimated that up to this point—

[23] See note 44.

less than a year after the initial North Korean attack—the Communists had suffered almost 1.2 million casualties,[24] including half a million Chinese lost in the eight months they had been involved.[25] In the last two weeks of May alone, 17,000 Chinese surrendered. Histories of the war talk of the precarious position of the Communist armies at this time. It really appeared that parts of the PLA front were "collapsing."[26]

A contributing factor was that the Chinese had lost control of the air over their own rear areas;[27] and, as the war progressed, it became clear that their air force was simply no match for United States fighters. The North Korean Air Force had been quickly destroyed on the ground and in the air. The Chinese Air Force, even operating from the sanctuary of Manchuria, with all that this meant in ability to choose the time and place of combat (particularly in "MiG Alley")—which in effect also determined the amount of fuel American pilots would have, etc.—suffered losses at the rate of ten-to-one at the hands of the United States airmen. Red Chinese pilots proved absolutely inadequate in combat. Many refused to "break" to maneuver when engaging American fighters (preferring to flee straight away, letting the engine and armor plate behind the seat take the fire) and some even ejected from still operable aircraft when attacked by United States pilots.[28]

Without control of this air space, the Chinese could not support their soldiers with enough supplies to produce sufficient divisional "combat days" to withstand a sustained drive by the high-firepower, high-morale, well-trained Free World-type divisions. Under these conditions, Chinese numerical superiority on the battlefield lost much of its significance.

A gross estimate of the requirement for each American soldier and airman in a theater of operations may be 60 pounds of supplies per day. Using this figure (which is not done in actual planning), 15,000 men—about the man power of one division—would require about 450 tons of supplies per day. Contrary to occasional implications, this tonnage does not appear to consist primarily of nonessential items, such as PX luxuries to maintain "pampered" United States troops, at least not when

[24] Over a million men were captured, killed, or wounded in battle; the rest were non-battle casualties. Robert F. Futrell, *The United States Air Force in Korea 1950–1953* (New York: Duell, Sloan and Pearce, 1961), p. 343.

[25] Robert Leckie, *Conflict* (New York: G. P. Putnam's Sons, 1962), p. 291.

[26] David Rees, *Korea: The Limited War* (New York: St. Martin's Press, 1964), pp. 256–58.

[27] Futrell, *The United States Air Force in Korea,* pp. 344–45.

[28] Futrell, *The United States Air Force in Korea,* pp. 649, 652.

they are in combat. In fact (based on World War II experience), in the attack mode of combat, the United States division with its supporting fire units may expend as much as 800 tons of ammunition alone per day. In the pursuit mode of combat, this figure can go as low as 100 tons per day, but then the gasoline and oil consumption can go to about 200 tons (and even higher for a long road march) for an armored division and support units.[29] This tonnage represents firepower and mobility which in conventional combat can only be countered by heavy logistic support. The stories of the Chinese Army's ability to subsist on a handful of rice brought up to the line by coolies does not refer to this period when U.N. troops could launch unrestricted ground attacks upon them. Under these attacks, when they could not bring up the tonnage, the Chinese had the choice of either "precipitous flight" or destruction.

In the Spring of 1951 many Chinese chose the former.[30] "The Chinese displacement became a rout. U.S. tanks roared past abandoned supplies, pack animals, ammunition. They went by burning villages and dead Chinese lying beside the roads, killed by tank fire or air strafing."[31] General Van Fleet, the field commander, was convinced that ". . . we had the Chinese whipped. They were definitely gone. They were in awful shape."[32] It is probably true that "General Van Fleet's statement about hot pursuit did not mean that he intended another advance to the Yalu,"[33] but he definitely wanted to advance further into North Korea, perhaps to the "waist."[34]

It should be pointed out that in a continuing U.N. offensive, several factors would have changed in favor of the Chinese. The recoiling Chinese armies would have been falling back on their supply bases, short-

[29] *U.S. Army Field Manual FM 101-10, Staff Officers Field Manual Organizational, Technical and Logistical Data,* Part 1, Headquarters, Department of the Army (Washington, D.C.: Government Printing Office, 1961), pp. 217, 250–56, 269; United States field artillery battalions during the 1951 Chinese Spring offensive in Korea were firing the "Van Fleet Load," five times the shell allowance previously used. A battalion in support of the Second Division fired 12,000 rounds in one day (John Miller, Jr., *et al., Korea 1951–1953,* Office of the Chief of Military History, Department of the Army [Washington: U.S. Government Printing Office, 1956], p. 106).

[30] Futrell, *The United States Air Force in Korea,* p. 341.

[31] T. R. Fehrenbach, *This Kind of War* (New York: The Macmillan Company, 1963), pp. 486–87.

[32] Rees, *Korea: The Limited War,* pp. 258–59.

[33] Miller *et al., Korea 1951–1953,* p. 110.

[34] Rees, *Korea: The Limited War,* p. 302.

ening their lines of supply, while U.N. lines would have been extended. Some felt that two or three more divisions would have been needed for a "war of maneuver" in Korea.[35] Van Fleet, however, felt that he had enough troops to carry out his plan for an amphibious landing behind the enemy lines.[36] But the field commander's views were not shared by the United States Joint Chiefs of Staff, who were definitely not in favor of the advance. The theater commander, General Ridgeway, felt that "if we had been ordered to fight our way to the Yalu, we could have done it . . .", but he doubted that further advance to any point on the peninsula would have been worth the cost.[37]

From the Chinese point of view, however, it was not a question of a choice; at this moment all they could do was wait for the U.N. commanders to come to a decision. The Communists were *militarily* unable to prevent the United States Eighth Army from advancing as far north as it was felt safe to go. It certainly appears that the end of the U.N. drive was "dictated not by the Chinese, but by the JCS";[38] and there seems to be evidence to support the claim that in having their spring offensive stopped and their being hit by the U.N. counteroffensive, the Chinese Communist forces may have suffered "a blood-soaked defeat so costly as to approach disaster."[39]

On June 23rd, the Russian U.N. representative Jacob Malik indicated that negotiations were in order. The Chinese may have felt secure in their ability to prevent a renewal of the U.N. offensive and the rout of their forces by negotiating. But it could not have been the most

[35] Rees, *Korea: The Limited War,* p. 25.

[36] "I had the 1st Marine Division and some Korean Marines set for a shore-to-shore operation, leap frogging up the east coast—almost administrative [unopposed] landings. At that time the east coast did not have a big buildup of defensive forces, and we could easily have made landings there. . . . We could have built up faster than the enemy could have managed. With those landings the Chinese couldn't have met it. They're not flexible enough. The Chinese armies had no conception of fast moves; they had no communication system; they had no logistical support" (Leckie, *Conflict,* p. 291).

[37] Leckie, *Conflict,* pp. 292, 293.

[38] Rees, *Korea: The Limited War,* p. 257.

[39] Futrell, *The United States Air Force in Korea,* p. 341; Leckie, *Conflict,* pp. 291, 292. Prisoner of war interrogations seemed to indicate a real danger of a collapse of morale. "Interrogation of prisoners revealed that the Communist Chinese Army facing us had been in a truly desperate condition, undergoing large-scale defections, when a few words by Jacob Malik in the United Nations headquarters in New York caused us to relax our pressure" (Bernard Brodie, *Strategy in the Missile Age,* The RAND Corporation [Princeton: Princeton University Press, 1959], p. 318).

comfortable feeling in Peking to have so much hanging on Malik's offer. The facts, as we may assume prudent Chinese commanders saw them in early June, were that Chinese units were fleeing, pursued by United States armor; even Pyongyang, at the top of the Iron Triangle, was in our hands for a time; and the ROK outfits had swept forty miles north of the 38th parallel to Kaesong on the east coast.[40] The Communists still had a large army in Korea and many units were still fighting stubbornly, but they had neither air force nor navy there. When the weather allowed, the sky was alive with United States planes shooting up everything that moved, even at night.[41]

The Communists had lost the air battle and the logistics race by a wide margin, and now the U.N. forces were pressing their partially routed army. Everything humanly possible had been done on the ground to stem the U.N. drive, but the Chinese situation was precarious. It must have seemed to the Chinese that, should Malik's offer be rejected and a fresh U.N. offensive be mounted, there was a real danger that part of the southern section of the Communist state of North Korea might be lost. Retaking it later would not necessarily be easy either, for the United States had not yet begun to use its capability to bring military power to bear in Korea. For the United States, it was a very limited operation, compared to our wars of the twentieth century. For China it was already a maximum, but obviously inadequate, effort.[42]

The United States military and political leaders decided not to press the offensive;[43] they accepted the offer of negotiation and laid down a policy that, in effect, discouraged any further substantial U.N. drives north of the 38th parallel. The Chinese thus received the respite they

[40] Rees, *Korea: The Limited War,* pp. 256–58.

[41] Futrell, *The United States Air Force in Korea,* pp. 341–42.

[42] "For much of the first year of that war it was the dominant conception in the Pentagon that the Korean aggression was a ruse by the Soviet Union with the sole object of causing us to commit our forces to the wrong theater while they made ready their major attack in Europe. Even when that idea faded, another view prevailed, this time more among the politicians than the military, that the Russians and the Chinese could be all too easily provoked into making total the limited war in which they were engaged. The fact that the Chinese were obviously already committed to the full limits of their capabilities seemed not to affect that anxiety" (Brodie, *Strategy,* pp. 317, 318).

"Had we committed even four more divisions, indeed, even if we had put a time limit on the truce negotiations, we could have achieved a substantial military victory" (Henry Kissinger, *Nuclear Weapons and Foreign Policy,* Council on Foreign Relations [New York: Harper, 1957], p. 152).

[43] See Rees, *Korea: The Limited War,* pp. 302–9 for a discussion of this decision and the possible reasons for having made it.

needed to regroup and dig in. North Korea became, in effect, a sanctuary for the Chinese Army, safe from the U.N. ground forces, as Manchuria was for the Chinese Air Force. Now the Chinese could trickle in supplies for an attack; when the supplies ran low they could retreat to their sanctuary (safe from a counteroffensive of the scope of May, 1951) and trickle in supplies again for another attack. Extremely heavy air attacks on logistic lines, such as those carried out during Operation Strangle, reduced the trickle; but air attacks can never reduce supplies to the zero level. With the Chinese holding the right to choose the pace of the war, they never allowed the supply problem to become so critical that their men starved or ran completely out of ammunition. Two bitter years of "negotiations" and "position warfare" on the 38th parallel, accounting for almost half of the United States casualties in the war, were to follow before the conflict was ended.[44]

It is useless (except for lessons concerning dealings with future crises) to speculate now on what would have happened at the time if Van Fleet's offensive had continued. It is far from useless, however, to realize that when the leaders of the Chinese Peoples Republic think of "another Korea" they may have some tendency to think of it in terms of their military crisis in the dark days of the Spring of 1951.

In North Korea today, the logistic and deployment routes are still the best available for moving Chinese troops outside the homeland against a Free World neighbor. These first-class, Japanese-built road and rail routes connect directly with the Manchurian industrial base supplying those arms and munitions that China can produce.[45] Although the PLA is substantially improved in weapons, organization, and training since 1951, "The Chinese can no longer count on the type of logistic support which the Soviet Union made available to them during the Korean War." In fact there are indications that though

> China's military leaders clearly consider the capability for ground combat as a deterrent to invasion . . . they recognize important limits to offensive use of ground forces. They probably do not see these forces as enabling them to engage in prolonged high level actions that would require extensive logistic support.[46]

[44] Rees, *The Limited War,* p. 303. Some estimates go as high as more than 3/5 of our battle deaths occurring in this "negotiating" period. Leckie states that up to this point we had suffered 12,000 battle deaths (*Conflict,* p. 293) of a total of 33,629 (*The World Almanac* [1963], p. 735).

[45] Mostly small arms, some light and medium artillery, tanks and trucks.

[46] Hsieh, *The China Quarterly,* no. 18, p. 95.

Moreover, the South Korean situation has changed. There is a sizeable, well-trained Republic of Korea Army, plus two United States divisions in South Korea with units on alert near the 38th parallel. These troops are backed up by air bases with high-alert aircraft and crews in Korea and Japan. Also, the United States now has a 60 billion dollar defense budget, and a Strike Command, with ready divisions and tactical air units supported by National Guard and reserve units, which can mobilize and deploy forces at several times the rate possible in the past. Furthermore, with our current 800 billion dollar Gross National Product, we may pour additional money into any new effort there at a rate that would make the logistics race even more one-sided against the Chinese. In short, from a purely conventional military point of view, "another Korea" in Korea could easily end in another crisis for China, similar to (or lacking Soviet support perhaps even greater than) the one she faced in the spring of 1951; and the Chinese are probably not unaware of this possibility.

Taiwan, Quemoy, and Matsu

The next potential region of confrontation between Communists and non-Communists which appears on the periphery of China is in the area of the Taiwan Strait. In the first half of 1950, the United States seemed to impute to the tiny Chinese Communist surface navy and inadequate air force, the capability to launch an amphibious attack across one hundred miles of open sea against Taiwan (though the Pescadores, closer to the mainland, perhaps were of greater concern to us). On June 27, 1950, two days after the start of the Korean War, we placed our Seventh Fleet in the Strait to prevent a move against Taiwan (or the Pescadores if we felt they were to be used as "a stepping-stone" to invade Taiwan) and simultaneously guaranteed the Communist mainland against attack from Taiwan.[47] The second guarantee was meaningful to the Communists. With their feeble navy and air force they were susceptible to, at a minimum, Dieppe-type raids against their coastline. In fact, a large segment of their army has been tied down in Fukien province against such a contingency.[48]

The Chinese have built logistic lines, particularly the Amoy-Shakikow railroad, into the coastal region to support the threatened area. But since October, 1958, they have made no serious attempts to take even Quemoy, an island in the harbor of Amoy only two miles from

[47] Claud A. Buss, *The Arc of Crisis* (Garden City, New York: Doubleday & Co., Inc., 1961), pp. 195, 196.

[48] Johnson, *New York Times Magazine,* February 28, 1965, p. 87.

the mainland.[49] This can be explained in many ways, but it is worth-while to note some essential factors in discussing the issue of Taiwan and the offshore islands.

The first factor is the hundred miles of blue water the Chinese Communist invasion force must traverse to get to Taiwan. Even the twenty miles of the English Channel proved too much of an obstacle to the victorious German armies in World War II when control of the air over it and the surface of it could not be wrested from the British. The Chinese Communists probably can control neither air nor surface in the Taiwan Strait. In 1958, during the so-called Taiwan Strait crisis, the Communists made an attempt to gain control of the air over nearby offshore islands. The result was anything but encouraging to the Red Chinese. The outnumbered Chinese Nationalist aircraft from Taiwan badly mauled the Communist air groups, shooting down main-land aircraft with disturbing consistency, even before Nationalist air-craft began using the Sidewinder air-to-air missile. "The air force's poor initial performance and subsequent inability to take counteraction" pointed out to the Chinese their weakness in this area.[50]

[49] At least no recent serious attempts, although there have been reports of a large-scale Chinese Communist attack on Quemoy in October, 1949. According to these reports they "had used a force of some 40,000 infantrymen in an attempt to take Nationalist-held Chinmen Island (better known as Quemoy), an 'off-shore' island, which ended disastrously. Being influenced by the practi-cally unopposed crossing of the River Yangtse, this mass of infantry had been launched in small boats and on improvised rafts. It ran head-on into strong Nationalist opposition, and over 13,000 Red soldiers were either killed or drowned, and another 7,000 were captured. One or two similar attempts on a smaller scale to take Nationalist-held 'off-shore' islands had also been unsuc-cessful" (O'Ballance, Red Army of China, p. 189).

[50] Alice Langley Hsieh, Communist China's Strategy in the Nuclear Era (Englewood Cliffs, New Jersey: Prentice-Hall, 1962), p. 130. Mende also refers to "the poor performance of the Chinese [Communist] forces during the latest Taiwan Strait crisis . . ." (Tibor Mende, China and Her Shadow [New York: Coward-McCann, Inc., 1962], p. 187). Johnson states that "In every contest with the Nationalist air force on Taiwan, even before the latter was equipped with modern U.S. air-to-air missiles, the Communists were overwhelmingly de-feated" (Johnson, New York Times Magazine, February 28, 1965, p. 85).

The China Yearbook of 1958–59 claims that "in the three-month Taiwan Strait War up to November 22, the Chinese armed forces [Nationalist] ac-quitted themselves admirably. Saberjets of the Chinese air force though out-numbered by the faster MiG 17's completely routed the enemy planes in air encounters over the Taiwan Strait and shot down 31 Russian-made MiGs" (China Yearbook, 1958–59. [Compiled by the China Yearbook Editorial Board.] [New York: Pierce Business Book Co., 1959], p. 3).

On the island of Quemoy itself, Chinese Nationalist troops stand guard in some very well fortified positions.[51] Moreover, elements of the United States Seventh Fleet in the Strait are always an unknown quantity—though after the Nixon-Kennedy debates prior to Kennedy's election, the commitment of the new United States President (as well as Congress) may have appeared somewhat ambiguous.[52] What is not ambiguous, however, is the fact that the Chinese Nationalists on Taiwan do not look on the Chinese mainland as a sanctuary. The Chinese Nationalists are still technically at war with the Communist regime. They very well might strike mainland military targets, including the Amoy-Shakikow railroad, if a crisis should escalate. Communist attempts made against Taiwan, or even the offshore islands, might not be a fishing expedition, with nothing lost except the troops, if the Communists should decide to call it off after it was started. The capture of the tiny island of Quemoy could cost not only many lives among the attacking force and many aircraft (which could also be destroyed on their bases on the mainland under these rules of warfare), but might cost much in other military targets on the mainland.

The Communists may have decided that such an attack just is not worth the possible cost.[53] In any event the "crisis" has dwindled to

[51] *New York Times,* December 9, 1966.

[52] Kennedy, following the wording of Congressional resolution of January 29, 1955 (see Buss, *The Arc of Crisis,* p. 196), stated that he was in favor of defending the offshore islands if their loss was looked on by the Chinese Communists as a first step to the capture of Taiwan.

[53] In the November, 1958 issue of *New Times,* Anna Louise Strong put forward an explanation that Red China did not want Quemoy "without taking Taiwan" because this "would isolate Taiwan and thus assist Dulles in his policy of building 'two Chinas.'" Communist policy therefore was to "strengthen" Quemoy and attach it "firmly to Taiwan" and get them both later in a "package deal." This would prevent the U.N. (under "American pressure") from setting up a trusteeship for Taiwan, for "nobody except an insane person would discuss a trusteeship for [Quemoy and Taiwan]." What comes through is that China did not want to risk a "wider war" and get Quemoy "at a cost," i.e., she would try to get it politically. From Hsieh, *Communist China's Strategy in the Nuclear Era,* p. 128.

But through some violence and a perhaps empty threat of violence (plus a belated Soviet pledge of support and an indication that the USSR would "riposte by the same means" if the United States initiated nuclear warfare), the Chinese gained something which their armed forces could not bring about. Under what appeared to be the urging of John Foster Dulles, the United States and Taiwan declared the Two Chinas policy and formulated a "pledge not to use force for the reconquest of China. . . . Thus, after three years of effort to induce Peking to renounce the use of force to liberate Taiwan, finally exchanging shells loaded with propaganda leaflets every other day.[54] (Incidentally, though it is seldom mentioned, shells have always flown in both directions over this water; it is said that Nationalist counter-battery fire was intense during the height of the crisis.)[55]

Any attempt to gain Taiwan itself would carry the same costs, but in addition would be almost certain to fail utterly. Since Korea, the Communist Chinese have shown a very realistic policy in military matters, despite their bellicose statements. They would undoubtedly like to have Taiwan; but without a surface navy and an adequate air force, it is militarily impossible to take the island. Nor are they so foolish as to give the Nationalists an excuse to strike their airfields and other military targets on the mainland for a hopeless cause. In short, the inadequacy of the Communist navy and air force prevents the projection of large armies to the main target, Taiwan. Stirring up somewhat the same hornets' nest to take Quemoy may be considered extreme "adventurism" with an inadequate reward for the costs.

Southeast Asia

Of course, the greatest interest today is focused on the Chinese capability to escalate in Southeast Asia. The public is frequently quizzed on what they would think if China should "come in" in Vietnam;[56] legislators debate about the consequences of Chinese intervention; and those people who want to "get out of Vietnam," as well as those who wish to guarantee our preparedness, warn of China's "coming in."[57]

There is little doubt that China could get "into" Southeast Asia. But the question is *where* in Southeast Asia and in what size intervention. The easiest place for China to disgorge its army into Southeast Asia is onto the Red River Delta and coastal plain of North Vietnam. There are two main roads from K'unming and Nanning to Hanoi that more

---

the symmetrical commitment was made by Chiang and the State Department, though without any concession on Peking's part" (Mende, *China and Her Shadow*, p. 294). Peking may have considered this prize adequate for the effort.

[54] *New York Times*, December 9, 1966.

[55] Taipei claims that during the 1958 crisis, Nationalist retaliation from Quemoy "destroyed 213 Red field pieces, 86 gun positions, 21 emplacements, 17 ammunition posts, 1 radar station, 96 trucks, 8 ack-ack guns, 4 barracks, 1 weather station . . ." (*China Yearbook*, 1958–59, p. 3).

[56] John F. Kraft, "Survey of American Attitudes toward the War in Vietnam" as reported on the television program *ABC, Scope*, Channel 7, September 24, 1966.

[57] "China: Dangers of Misunderstanding," *Newsweek*, March 7, 1966, p. 35.

or less parallel the two rail routes from China to North Vietnam. There are also several secondary roads which cross the Chinese–North Vietnamese border. South of Hanoi, where the coastal plain is squeezed closer and closer to the sea by the mountains that swing southeast toward the South China Sea, the transportation system is reduced to one main road and one rail line. Thanh Hoa, about one hundred miles south of Hanoi, is the end of the line on this railroad; and it's not much of a line.

The rail system of North Vietnam is a single-track, narrow-gauge [meter] system, and even though it crosses into China at two points, it only connects with the Chinese rail system at Dong Dang on the Nanning route. The line to K'unming does not connect with the Chinese rail system there since K'unming's rail connection with Kweiyang and the rest of the Chinese rail net has never been rebuilt.[58] Thus the Chinese rail connection with K'unming actually goes through Hanoi. But this is not a direct rail connection in the full sense of the word. The Chinese rail system is standard gauge [4 ft. 8½ in.]; so all freight must be trans-shipped from standard-gauge cars to narrow-gauge cars at the border. Furthermore, narrow-gauge rolling stock and motive power lost in air strikes in North Vietnam cannot be replaced by standard-gauge Chinese equipment, as it was in Korea. We need not dwell on the vulnerability of this logistic route—all 500 miles of it, from Litang in China to the 17th parallel—to air attack. Recent events have made this sufficiently clear. Of course, this vulnerability increases as one moves south from Hanoi. The single major road south of Thanh Hoa is often squeezed out almost to the sea coast by the mountains. In this "panhandle" area, the route is not only extremely vulnerable to air attack but, particularly in the southern sector, is literally under the big guns of the United States Seventh Fleet.

The area into which large Chinese ground forces can be introduced—with considerable difficulty, as we have shown—the northern section of Communist North Vietnam, is probably the last place Ho Chi Minh would desire their presence. Any effort to introduce large Chinese conventional ground force capability into *South* Vietnam would be governed by the logistic capability of the trails and secondary roads west across the mountain spine forming the boundary between Laos and North and South Vietnam, and then the series of secondary roads, foot trails, and beast-of-burden tracks, known as the Ho Chi Minh Trail, running south through Laos, Cambodia, and western South Vietnam.

[58] *Bartholomew's World Series—China, Mongolia & Korea P* (Edinburgh, Scotland: John Bartholomew & Son, 1965).

Alien (and traditionally hated) Chinese forces, forced out onto the limb of the Ho Chi Minh Trail, would be incapable of large-scale, sustained conventional combat. If excessive numbers of them were marched down the trail, those who reached eastern Cambodia and western South Vietnam might even starve without local assistance.[59] If lesser numbers of them came down and attempted to fight conventional campaigns without the support of heavy equipment and good logistic capability, they would be in danger of being badly defeated by the high-firepower of the United States land and air forces. Red Chinese intervention with massive land armies in conventional combat in the non-Communist area of Vietnam is at least impracticable and perhaps impossible, particularly in the face of a resolute United States and allied force. There can be no "Korea" here.

The same holds true for Chinese intervention in western Laos,

[59] It should be noted that the capacity of the Ho Chi Minh Trail is very limited, particularly under the bombardment of United States planes from Vietnam and Thailand. Estimates of its capacity ranged from "100 tons per day or less" (*Newsweek*, December 5, 1966, p. 56), to "90 tons a day, or perhaps 75 tons, and there were some indications that during August [1966] this was reduced to 57 tons" (Hanson W. Baldwin, "The Case for Bombing," *New York Times*, October 12, 1966). Intelligence estimates are that North Vietnamese-Vietcong main force units in South Vietnam in early 1966 required 150 tons a day—chiefly in ammunition and weapons. The reduced tonnage is said to have accounted for the "infrequency" of Communist large-scale actions in South Vietnam. (These units seemed to have averaged no more than one or two days' combat a month—see General Maxwell D. Taylor's testimony before the Committee on Foreign Relations, U.S., Congress, Senate, Committee on Foreign Relations, *Hearings on S.2793, to Amend Further the Foreign Assistance Act of 1961, as Amended*, 89th Cong., 2nd Sess., February 17, 1966, p. 495.)

Many troops using the trail arrived in South Vietnam "exhausted, malnourished and somewhat demoralized by the constant bombings" (Baldwin, *New York Times*, October 12, 1966). The trip on the trail used to (and for some groups still may) take months, with some troops having to stop along the way to recuperate from illness (*Aggression from the North*, Department of State Publication 7839 [Washington, D.C.: Government Printing Office, February, 1965], pp. 6–11).

According to a 1966 Pentagon study, the largest North Vietnamese invading army which could be launched into South Vietnam and supported "would be no more than 100,000 men" (Colonel Archie J. Clapp, "Don't Envy the Enemy," *United States Naval Institute Proceedings*, no. 765, vol. 92, no. 11 [November, 1966], p. 56). The Vietcong, North Vietnamese, and Pathet Lao have no doubt spared no effort to increase the capacity of the Ho Chi Minh Trail since 1966. But it is still less than adequate for continued large-scale conventional warfare, for if this army were suddenly forced to depend entirely on this route, rations, ammunition, fuel, etc., might be cut to a few pounds per man, per day.

Burma and northern Thailand. Traditional, high-capacity logistic routes in this area favor the armies from the south. The primary routes follow the great rivers, and their valleys from the Mekong to the Irrawaddy, north from the Gulf of Siam and the South China Sea to the southern slopes of the vast mountain and jungle areas which separate these countries from China proper. Rail lines radiate across Thailand from Bangkok to Vientiane on the Mekong in the north; to Uben in the east with its "arterial route" road net to the Mekong; to Phnom Penh on the Mekong in Cambodia; and up the Suphan Buri Valley to Chiang Mai in northwest Thailand. Thailand's road system supplements the rail system in these same areas. Burma's rail and road system extends from Rangoon up the Irrawaddy through Mandalay to Myitkyina near the Chinese border.

The mountains extending down from the Himalaya massif through South China and Southeast Asia to Saigon generally deny this area to the movement and supply of massed land armies from the north and northeast. The best major road extending westward through the mountains of north and east Laos to Mekong at Savannakhet, comes out of South Vietnam just south of the 17th parallel. Lesser roads cross the mountains out of North Vietnam in the vicinity of Col de Mu Gia and Nong Et; the former reaches the Mekong at Thakhek; the latter crosses the Plain of Jars toward Luang Prabang with a connecting road to Vientiane. Everything else that crosses the mountains falls into the category of "tracks." There is only one "major" road from China proper into Burma and that is the famous Burma Road from K'unming by way of T'engch'ung or Lungling. Another very primitive road may form an alternate to the Burma Road from Hsenwi in Burma to Siangung 150 miles west of K'unming. Another road from K'unming may go as far as the Burmese border at Kenglaw and continue as a track to Kengtung. Nor would one expect the upper reaches of the rivers through the mountains on the Chinese border to be the very good transportation media they are in the valleys to the south.[60]

In brief, as long as the peoples of Southeast Asia have the support of the West and the will to defend their homelands, Southeast Asia is by and large "inaccessible" for the primary conventional military power of Red China—her massed ground forces. Furthermore, China's conventional air power is inadequate to reduce the superior logistic capability of her enemies and probably could not prevent destructive strikes

[60] See *Times* (London) *Atlas of the World*, ed. John Bartholomew (Boston: Houghton Mifflin Co., 1958), vol. 1, plate 24; and *Bartholomew's World Series —China, Mongolia & Korea P.*

against her troops and her own weak, very vulnerable logistic deployment routes.

It must be mentioned here that the Chinese propound a type of *unconventional* warfare which, when practical, is rather cheap and has often been very productive. This form of conflict is the guerrilla war, or the "war of national liberation" which fits in with the historical theories of the Chinese Communists. Although according to their accepted philosophy these wars are supposed to be a sure-fire means of beating "imperialists," exporting Chinese troops to assist in them seems to contradict the theories. Chinese statements indicate that these wars are to be fought by natives.[61]

There is much logic in this point, particularly from the Chinese point of view. One could hardly think of a neighbor of China (Communist or non-Communist) whose citizens would normally welcome China's troops, in regular units or as guerrillas. This does not mean that Chinese guerrillas could not operate in neighboring countries, but that it would be difficult for them to do so. They would be alien troops in an alien land. They would probably be tolerated, if at all, only by a friendly Communist revolutionary movement or in a neighboring Communist country under severe attack. Offensive guerrilla operations by the Chinese outside their border may actually be less effective than those of native Communists, if they could be trained and armed. In fact, Chinese guerrillas may be counterproductive in some areas, at least in the initial phases of the conflict; they may identify the local Communists as a foreign force and solidify the populace against them.

After having shifted from route army formation and tactics to standard triangular Western-type formations at the time of Korea, and then having begun to shift in 1959 to pentomic formation, and then once again seeming to have favored the standard divisional formation,[62] Chinese troops are currently receiving small-unit training for independent operations, particularly at night, which is the basic training needed for guerrillas.[63]

[61] An examination of the declaration of Chinese Communist Defense Minister Lin Piao from Peking on September 3, 1965, urging a "people's war" reaffirms this Chinese theory. In his article, Lin Piao stated that "the countryside, and the countryside alone, can provide the revolutionary bases from which the revolutionaries can go forward to final victory," and for this reason Mao Tsetung's theory of encircling the cities from revolutionary bases in the countryside "is attracting more and more attention among the people in these regions" (*New York Times,* September 4, 1965).

[62] O'Ballance, *The Red Army of China,* pp. 200, 201.

[63] Johnson, *New York Times Magazine,* February 28, 1965, p. 87.

In certain sparsely populated jungle border areas, Chinese guerrillas could perhaps cause great problems. They could infiltrate upper Laos, Burma and Thailand and could wage a low-level, brutal war, perhaps even acting as a screen for larger conventional forces while they built roads and accumulated supplies for a breakout into the river valleys to the south. Yet without the large conventional effort—with all the short-comings of Chinese conventional warfare—the Chinese guerrillas could only hold the less populated jungle areas, unless they could enlist natives into the guerrilla movement. Still, a long, and eventually costly war could result even without native support, unless the constant, low-level infiltration of supplies and small numbers of Chinese replacements could be rooted out and brought to battle by rapid, effective counterinsurgency operations.

The insurgency war is normally fatal to the victim nation only when it causes the government to fall and a native insurgency group takes over. Unless the Chinese were to have some indigenous group in the nation which could remain "native," while importing Chinese forces, and could take the reins of government, Chinese guerrillas alone would be hard put to conquer most neighboring nations, particularly if the victim states had United States or other support. The massed land forces of China normally cannot be used clandestinely in this unconventional mode of operation, so those troops that are engaged may be at a disadvantage numerically as well as linguistically. Without local support, China's troops have no more advantage here than any other high morale, alien insurgency group. Further, they may be much less effective—and because of logistic difficulties normally experienced by alien guerrilla forces—even less numerous than indigenous guerrilla forces.

In the final analysis, China's guerrilla units could best be used in a defensive mode in China itself, where the guerrillas could melt into the population.

India–Pakistan–Afghanistan

With the occupation of Tibet, the PLA manned the country's southern border. Lying on the northern border of India, this area has traditionally formed a defensive rampart against the movements of armies. It consists of a mountain chain over 2,000 miles long and, on an average, about 200 miles broad. It extends from Ladakh in the northwest, contiguous to Sinkiang, to the North East Frontier Agency, contiguous with Burma, and is roughly divided into three sections: the Great Himalayas with an average height of 20,000 feet which extend from Ladakh to Sikkim and include Everest, Kanchenjunga, and Nanga Parbat; the Lesser

Himalayas at an average altitude of 15,000 feet; and the Outer Himalayas from 15,000 feet down to the lesser mountains of southern China
and Southeast Asia.[64] There are very few routes through this barrier;
most are trails which cross through passes at 12,000 feet altitude or
more. Only two "arterial roads" traverse the mountains: one from
Shigatse in Tibet through Gangtok in Sikkim to the Ganges Valley in
India;[65] and another from Katmandu in Nepal south to India, with
an extension being built by the Chinese north to Tibet (though work
may have stopped on this Chinese section now). Obviously this mountain barrier remains a major obstacle to mass attacks southward by
Chinese ground forces. In any direct Chinese attack on India alone,
the two arterial routes are not "available" to the PLA, for they pass
through "neutral" Sikkim and Nepal (though this "neutrality" cannot
be considered as insurance against their being used by the Chinese).

The question that must arise immediately in the reader's mind is
what happened in the Chinese attack on India in 1962? Before this can
be answered one has to look at the probable military objectives (rather
than the pretext) of the Chinese attack. Estimates of political objectives
for China's Tibetan-Indian border incursions range from an attempt to
"blackmail Russia for increased aid in return for greater cooperation
in negotiations with the West" to attempts to "influence India's internal politics." "China," so the argument runs, "is impressed by the unmistakable shifting of Indian internal politics to the right; sees no more
utility in India's neutrality; and by further hastening this shift in
favor of reaction, prepares the ground for the long-range role of India's
Communists as the sole alternative."[66] A bit more plausible is the
theory that China had to confirm its own propaganda that the Tibetan
revolt had been inspired from abroad, i.e., India. China probably was
annoyed by India's granting asylum to the Dalai Lama and allowing
him to indulge in political activities on Indian soil. The Chinese also
may have wanted to close the Himalayan passes against escaping insurgents and infiltrating political agents,[67] and to prevent the flow of information across the border.

This reasoning may be perfectly valid, as is the more obvious motive
that China wished to humiliate India and demonstrate who was the
"Number One" power in East Asia. But a much more explicit military-

[64] George N. Patterson, *Peking Versus Delhi* (London: Faber and Faber, 1963), pp. 166–67.

[65] *The Times* (London) *Atlas of the World,* 1, plate 23.

[66] Mende, *China and Her Shadow,* p. 119.   [67] *Ibid.,* p. 119.

political reason may have carried at least as much weight. The Chinese had laid claim to portions of the border regions in the North East Frontier Agency and Ladakh. The dispute in the former area stemmed from the refusal of the Chinese (Nationalist or Communist) to recognize the "McMahon Line," negotiated between Tibet and Britain in 1914 at the Simla Convention, as the eastern border between Tibet and India. China had attended the convention and even initialled the treaty—which in its original form also recognized Tibet as being under the suzerainty of China—but China later thought better of it and refused to sign the document, from which the suzerainty clause was then removed.[68] But the NEFA appeared really not to be of primary interest to the Chinese.

The dispute over the border in the Ladakh region was something else again. Here the Chinese had laid successive claims to the Aksai Chin northeast "bulge" of the Indian-Tibetan border. "It was obvious that China's primary goal was possession of the vital route between Sinkiang and Tibet across the Aksai Chin."[69] This has been said to be "indisputable Indian territory" (so recognized by the Chinese members of the Boundary Commission of 1847–49), but this road appeared to be part of the Sinkiang-Tibetan highway.[70] The Ladakhi corridor was said to have two roads, one built in 1957, the other in 1960, the latter considerably west of the first, near the Depsang Plains.[71] The Indian government, forced into action by storms of protest over the capture and maltreatment of an Indian border police patrol in the fall of 1959,[72] had begun to reoccupy the region in 1960 and 1961. A game of chess began with border outposts which saw Indian forces re-entering the area, infiltrating between existing Chinese outposts,[73] but this was no region with which the Chinese wished to play chess. The Ladakhi corridor was a deadly serious area to the Chinese. It was the normal route for a road to connect the Tibetan military district with Sinkiang, and the importance of this route was increasing every day.

Very little reliable information comes out of Sinkiang, but what is known about Sino-Soviet competition there in the past, pieced

[68] Patterson, *Peking Versus Delhi*, pp. 170–73.

[69] Margaret W. Fisher, Leo E. Rose, and Robert A. Huttenback, *Himalayan Battleground* (New York: Frederick A. Praeger, 1963), p. 140.

[70] Patterson, *Peking Versus Delhi*, p. 196.

[71] Fisher, Rose, and Huttenback, *Himalayan Battleground*, pp. 2–3.

[72] Patterson, *Peking Versus Delhi*, pp. 197–99.

[73] Fisher, Rose and Huttenback, *Himalayan Battleground*, pp. 130–32.

together with the trickle of more recent reports of unrest, provides a basis for speculation that this corridor, once essential for retaining Tibet, may now be equally essential for retaining Sinkiang.[74]

In any event, even in 1959, Indian offers of a solution which called for both sides to pull back, with the provision that the Chinese could use the Aksai Chin road for civilian purposes, were turned down cold. By accepting this proposition, the Chinese would have accepted, in effect, Indian sovereignty and would have been giving up one of the main purposes for which the road was built.[75] It appeared in the fall of 1962 that the "minimum objective of China's military onslaught . . . presumably was . . . to tighten their grip on the Ladakhi corridor between Tibet and Sinkiang,"[76] and their actions bore this out.

The Indian army under Krishna Menon had been allowed to deteriorate. While it maintained divisions on the Pakistan border but inadequate reinforcement for the Tibetan border, the Chinese Army poured men into Tibet and built roads along the frontier of India. The Chinese became acclimatized to the 12,000-foot Tibetan plateau and maintained the capability to launch effective, if not massive, military operations. When the Indians cut the vital Tibetan-Sinkiang highway, the Chinese reacted—in fact, they "overescalated." They drove in the line held by the Indian forces in the Ladakhi area and retook the Aksai Chin region; and simultaneously, they attacked the Indian forces on the border of the Northeast frontier. The Indian Army was still largely deployed along the Pakistan border, and the three Indian divisions[77] responsible for the defense of the Sino-Indian border proved to be badly deployed and perhaps badly led.

In the North East Frontier Agency, near Tawang, where the pass over the mountain skirts the border of Bhutan, and near Kibithoo, Indian units fared very badly. They seem to have had only one brigade of about 3,000 men on the border north of Tawang, and this unit "was virtually wiped out" while the Chinese troops, according to survivors,

---

[74] *Ibid.*, pp. 145–46.   [75] *Ibid.*, p. 135.

[76] *Ibid.*, p. 145. The North East frontier invasion was "one step in the softening-up process leading up to the offer of settlement after a withdrawal in NEFA, the price of which will be compromise in Ladakh. This still remains the only supreme objective of the entire Chinese strategy." Quoted from N. J. Nanporia, "The Sino-Indian Dispute," *Times of India* (Bombay), 1963, pp. 19–20 in A. M. Halpern *et al.*, *Policies Toward China* (New York: McGraw-Hill Book Co., 1966), p. 220.

[77] Guy Wint, *Communist China's Crusade* (New York: Frederick A. Praeger, 1965), p. 100.

"were like ants. . . . They extended as far as the eye could see." Before two brigades could be brought up from the direction of Tezpur to reinforce Tawang, it had fallen, and the Indian defenders "withdrew according to plan." At Ndhola, the Indians fought until they "ran out of ammunition" and then also retreated.[78] It is not clear how many attempts were made to airlift ammunition to the defenders (ineffective as Indian airdrops were in those days),[79] if a shortage of ammunition was causing their withdrawal. Also, the Indian reserves must have been either too far back or Tawang must have fallen in a hurry. In any event, the usual hordes (100,000) of Chinese were reported to be attacking the Indian force of 20,000 along the border.[80]

The retired Indian Chief of Staff states that according to his "information" three Chinese divisions struck the Indian units in the North East Frontier Agency area, two in the region of Tawang and one near Kibithoo.[81] What followed was a display of the effects of bad judgment and ineptitude on the part of Indian defense leaders and a show of opportunism by the Chinese. It was, in fact, a "rout" of the Indian forces, a "humiliation," and "the prestige of the army as a whole suffered severely."[82] The attack was launched against an "unsuspecting, unprepared Indian Army"[83] by a Chinese force which could hardly have been a "horde," adequate to carry on a sustained campaign against the densely populated Assam plain. But the Indian Army on the border was not up to this challenge despite warnings given by intelligence sources. It appeared to be inferior numerically (at least at the points of contact), badly deployed, and lacking in matériel and perhaps training and leadership:[84] the precise kind of victim to tempt an oppor-

[78] "India," *Time,* November 2, 1962, p. 36.

[79] In some instances . . . "more than 75 per cent" of the air drop material was lost. (Norman C. Walpole *et al., U.S. Army Area Handbook for India,* Department of the Army Pamphlet No. 550–21, Headquarters, Department of the Army [Washington, D.C.: Government Printing Office, 1964], p. 765).

[80] "India," *Time,* November 2, 1962, p. 36.

[81] K. S. Thimayya, "Chinese Aggression and After," *International Studies,* 5, nos. 1–2 (July–October, 1963), p. 51.

[82] Wint, *Communist China's Crusade,* p. 100.

[83] Thimayya, *International Studies,* 5, nos. 1–2, p. 52.

[84] *Ibid.* Thimayya states that "When they attacked us they did it with determination, continued the momentum of their attack, used all their tactics of infiltration, envelopment and subterfuge. . . . [And with even more than a month's warning] . . . it was not possible for us to reinforce, equip and maintain our forces in this most difficult terrain, chiefly due to insufficiency in our

tunistic (but far from rash) aggressor. The Indian force is said to have had 2,500 men killed and given up 5,000 square miles of territory in the short campaign.[85]

The real protector of India's northern frontier in all probability had a major influence on the extent and duration of the Chinese penetration toward the Assam plain. The Himalaya range with its few dirt tracks leading down into the Brahmaputra Valley simply ruled out any rapid, large-scale invasion,[86] and the season of the year may have helped to rule out any deeper penetration or long sojourn of the relatively small Chinese units involved. The snow line begins to move down the mountains in December, and areas above 10,000 feet and sometimes as low as 7,000 feet become covered with snow. Tawang itself (which is in a valley between two mountain ranges over which the road to Tezpur on the Assam plain must pass) has had two feet of snow on the ground in January, and the Sela mountain range south of Tawang has experienced as much as a foot of snow in October with more piling up during the winter. In December, the Sela range can have two feet of snow (three feet by January), and two feet of snow is "normal" even down in Tawang by February.[87] It would have been difficult for the Chinese force to winter over on the barren ridges, and the Chinese leaders may have felt that the small Chinese army could not have afforded to risk

---

logistics." His most significant statement is, however: "The reason why we suffered reverses—the lack of a proper coordinated plan, the lack of control of the battle and our heavy losses in personnel and equipment—is the subject of an investigation, and I am not qualified or sufficiently informed to make any comments. . . ." Rather pathetically he adds: "We have now realized that it is not possible to trust the Chinese anymore." See also Walpole *et al., U.S. Army Area Handbook for India,* p. 765, for further discussion of this. One critical deficiency of the Indian armed forces came out of the inquiry (besides the shortage of modern matériel), namely that Menon's defense plans for India "had been oriented toward its Pakistan borders and not its northern and northeastern borders, beyond which the Chinese had prepared their attack" (Walpole *et al., U.S. Army Area Handbook for India,* p. 767).

85 "A Vast Delusion Shatters India," *Life,* November 9, 1962, p. 53.

86 "Another world whose frightful roads are like paths leading to death" ("India," *Time,* November 2, 1962, p. 36). There was a jeep track to Tawang, but Indian border outposts depended on goat trails or helicopters and airlift (Thimayya, *International Studies,* 5, nos. 1–2, p. 51).

87 Government of India, *India Weather Review, 1953,* Annual Summary, Part B, Snowfall (Delhi: Government of India Press, 1955), p. B3; *India Weather Review, 1954,* Part B, p. B8; *India Weather Review, 1955,* Part B, p. B4.

wintering over further down toward the Assam plain where the weather was milder. In either case the entire force might have had to depend on the route over the mountains near Tawang for reinforcements or logistic support throughout the winter. These passes can be negotiated in winter; in fact, this is the escape route the Dalai Lama and his party took out to Tezpur in March and April, 1959, but it took his party eighteen days to make 220 miles, some of it on foot.[88] Even at the time of the Chinese attack (late October) there were reports of frostbite and snowblindness among Indian troops in the area.[89] Leaving the Chinese further down, near the plain, with its teeming millions of Indians and good logistic routes to bring up overwhelming force as India was mobilized, would have been "overextension" and the wildest of "adventurism." During the first weeks of November, the Indians were in fact bringing troops into the area from the Pakistan border and equipping them with the automatic weapons and suitable aircraft that had been contributed by friendly nations during the emergency.[90]

On November 21, the Chinese ordered a unilateral cease fire along the border, for India refused to negotiate. Chinese forces pulled back from their advanced position in the North East Frontier Agency but *not* from the Aksai Chin region of Ladakh. Here on the desolate, uninhabited Roof of the World, because of the terrain and prior preparations, the Chinese had better access to limited reinforcements and supplies from Tibet than the Indians had from upper Kashmir. Also, this was the region, with its vital link in the Sinkiang-Tibetan highway, which the Indians had partially reoccupied. After the invasion of Assam, however, the Indians did not appear anxious to press the issue of the Aksai Chin—nor have they ever again attempted to reoccupy this region. But this "battle area" also did not support operations that could in any way be considered of a scale to threaten the heavily populated regions of the upper Indus or Ganges Valleys. This is so, particularly in light of the limited ability the Chinese Communists seem to have in maintaining control of the air over their land forces when adequate enemy air forces are brought in.

All along the northern Indian border, the Himalayas stand guard against the large Chinese land armies if India is willing to do the relatively small amount of fighting required to stop the few forces that can

[88] Frank Moraes, *The Revolt in Tibet* (New York: The Macmillan Company, 1960), p. 19.

[89] "India," *Time,* November 2, 1962, p. 36.

[90] Walpole *et al., U.S. Army Area Handbook for India,* p. 765.

be moved through.[91] If unmolested China could, despite the mountain barrier, gradually build up forces on the fringes of one of the populated areas of northern India, and produce enough logistic support to sustain them in low-level combat against a timid foe.

The crisis of 1962 aroused the Indian people, and since then the Indian Government has made a budgetary and organizational effort to develop a competent army to defend the northern border[92] including a move to raise six new divisions. If they are successful in these tasks and in their road building and airlift program,[93] they should be able to thwart the level of conventional attack the Chinese can mount. This does not mean that they could necessarily hold the Chinese at the border, but that they would be capable of the effort required to prevent a significant seizure of Indian territory south of the mountains—or at least delay it until India and the Free World could mobilize for a level of warfare China could not carry on south of the Himalayas. This is the price to the Chinese of their attack in 1962: the new defense effort and the dismissal of Menon and his favorite generals has changed the possible cost of adventures in the area.

Perhaps a measure of Indian success can be gleaned from the Chinese reaction (or lack of it) to the Indian rejection of the Chinese "ultimatum" during the Pakistan-Indian dispute over Kashmir in the autumn of 1965. On the other hand, it may simply underline the fact that the Chinese are not known for their eagerness to risk much in

[91] In discussions with an Indian civil servant after the event, the question was raised why India did not strike the Chinese columns in the mountain passes with her aircraft and he replied, "Then China would have bombed Delhi." This answer is interesting both because of the technical inaccuracy of the description of the threat and the ease with which inaction can be rationalized. The Chinese had only iron bombs at this time, and it is doubtful that they had enough skill or aircraft in Tibet to battle their way through to the target with sufficient tonnage to cripple a large city like Delhi. (As late as 1967 they are said to have had only two airfields which could accommodate even light bombers in Tibet [*The Military Balance, 1966–67*, p. 9].) Furthermore, strikes against targets other than those on the immediate battlefield could have triggered strikes against Chinese airfields in Tibet which might have cost China her air force in Tibet and even raised the prospect of support from the United States Air Force. China now has nuclear devices, so that the threat is physically orders of higher magnitude, and countering arguments for inaction based on the threat depends on less explicit notions of the "nuclear threshold," deterrence, etc.

[92] Thimayya, *International Studies*, 5, nos. 1–2, pp. 52–53.

[93] Walpole *et al., U.S. Army Area Handbook for India*, pp. 767, 768.

furthering aggression, even by a Communist neighbor, to say nothing of entering a dispute between two capitalist powers, regardless of how friendly they are to one or the other of them.

Afghanistan to the Amur-Ussuri Littoral

There is one more Chinese border area which must be discussed with a view to ascertain the ability of China to project its conventional power over its boundary. This is the border with the USSR in Siberia. From the outset, this discussion must have a certain unreal quality about it, for it presumes that the two great Communist powers of the world would throw away the revolution in a "fit of anger" by attacking one another while the capitalist world looked on with glee. This could happen; but relations between the Soviets and the Red Chinese would have to become considerably worse before the Chinese would attack the Soviet Union in any sizable conventional operation. Nor would any of the Siberian territory claimed by China be a sufficient prize to cause a rational Chinese leader to embark on a large-scale conflict with the Soviet Union. At least for the near future, there are also some valid reasons other than political for Chinese caution along this border. Some become obvious from a glance at the map, others do not.

The Sino-Soviet border extends from Afghanistan to Outer Mongolia in the west and from Outer Mongolia to the Pacific Ocean in the east. The barren region of Chinese Sinkiang, bordering Tadzhikistan and Kirgiziya in the USSR, on the western end of the boundary, is so remote from the sources of military power and the populated regions of eastern China that it cannot be considered an area favorable to Chinese aggression. The same is true of the border region of Dzungaria, bordering on Soviet Kazakstan. Even with the Trans-Sinkiang Railroad, which connects Urumchi with Lanchow and China proper, and is said to give access to the Soviet border at the Dzungarian Gates Pass, the inadequacies of transport and the remoteness of these desolate areas just do not give the Chinese any logistic advantage over the Soviets. In fact, if it were not for the Tien Shan range, which forms the border between Sinkiang in the area of Aksu and Soviet Kazakstan in the vicinity of Alma Ata, the Chinese would be hard-pressed to defend Sinkiang, let alone launch an attack from the area. Similar statements can be made about the Dzhungarsk and the Tarbagatay mountains and then the Altai range which form the border to the north. But the area between the Tien Shan and Altai ranges is not nearly as rugged as these high mountain barriers. Hence, the location of the Trans-Sinkiang Railroad, which reaches the USSR there. On the Russian side of the line, the Turkestan-

Siberian Railroad, roughly paralleling the border, the Western Siberian rail net and the great industrial base of the Kuznetz basin, relatively nearby to the north, give a picture of considerably greater strength.

The plateau area of the Soviet buffer satellite of Outer Mongolia is somewhat more vulnerable to Chinese attack. But Soviet logistic capability over the Ulan Ude–Ulan Bator–Erhlien Railroad and the roads into eastern Outer Mongolia are adequate to defend the southern slopes of the Kentai mountains, and Mother Russia lies beyond the mountains to the north. Furthermore, should the Soviets decide to commit their superior armored and air forces, Chinese units would be in grave jeopardy and would probably be unable to defend the plateau areas on the Chinese side of the border in Manchuria and Inner Mongolia.

The region of the great Amur River bend (which, with the Argun River to the west and the Ussuri River to the east, roughly forms the northern and eastern borders between eastern Siberia and the Soviet Maritime Provinces, and Manchuria) is an entirely different matter from a deployment point of view. This is the one area where the Chinese enjoy a distinct logistic advantage. Here they find themselves in somewhat the same situation that favored the Japanese in 1935. At that time the Japanese sat in the central location of Manchuria with a rail net centered on Harbin and Tsitsihar that stretched like the five fingers of a hand toward the perimeter of the Soviet border.[94] They were thus able to strike (or threaten to strike) by an almost direct route from their bases at the center, any spot on the perimeter, while the Soviets were faced with the task of dashing wildly back and forth with their reserves around the circumference to counter any Japanese move. This was for the Soviets a doubly difficult task, because the vulnerable Trans-Siberian Railroad, which is near the border all the way around, was (and still is) the primary, if not the only high-capacity means to move troops and matériel. In the 1930's (after failing to build an alternate rail line to the Trans-Siberian farther north) the Russians were said to have settled for fortifications at key points such as Khabarovsk, at the junction of the Amur and Ussuri Rivers, and Vladivostok. Subterranean tunnels were built and stocked to withstand a siege.[95]

The reason that Red China (with its war industry base here, right in the center of its best transportation system and made-to-order logistic

[94] Major George Fielding Elliot, "Map War in the Orient," *Business*, February 29, 1936, p. 11.

[95] Maurice G. Hindus, *Russia and Japan* (New York: Doubleday, Doran and Co., Inc., 1942), p. 12.

net) does not have the same advantages which the Japanese had in this area in the thirties, is precisely because Red China is not Japan of the thirties. First of all, unless she were lucky and caught all the Soviet aircraft on the ground in a sneak attack, China would doubtlessly lose control of the air early in the battle. Her military columns, transport system, and major industrial base could all be badly damaged or destroyed by conventional air strikes (the Soviets may not be as discriminating as we have been to date in Vietnam). Secondly, the Soviets may not allow China the "fishing expedition" privileges we have allowed her, i.e., if she just goes home no one will follow her across her border. Soviet armored columns may drive into Manchuria, and the Chinese could oppose them with only remnants of four small armored divisions which somehow survived in a milieu of complete Soviet control of the air over the plains of Manchuria.

This is not to say that the Soviet Union's air or ground forces are generally invincible. It merely means that, in conflict with the Chinese Air Force (over Manchuria, or any other border area), the Soviet tactical and long-range air armies in the Far East should be more than adequate. It also means that Soviet ministers of defense are normally not Krishna Menons—the ground forces would probably be ready.[96] This could be a long, hard war for the Chinese against a determined (perhaps ruthless) enemy—a war which China might have to fight alone and without her Manchurian war industry base. China fought this kind of war in the thirties and forties; and without the aid of a massive attack by major outside powers on the overextended Japanese enemy, China would probably have been subjugated.

The danger of the Soviets' wishing to—or perhaps even being able to —take over all of China is quite remote. The sea-lift and Trans-Siberian Railroad capacities place a limit on the size of the army and air force the Soviets can support in the Far East; but taking over much of Manchuria is quite another story. This move would be logical, and perhaps essential, to drive the Chinese forces and their guerrilla demolition teams away from the Amur and Ussuri Valleys which cradle their vulnerable Trans-Siberian lifeline. Nor would the Soviets be at a loss in coping with indigenous or imported Manchurian guerrillas. The Communist (and Soviet) record in counterinsurgency operations—including

[96] Ten of the fifteen Soviet divisions in the Far East are at full strength; the other five can be brought to this level on short notice. The Soviets have about forty-three tank divisions in their inventory (*The Military Balance, 1967–1968*, p. 7) many of which can eventually be brought into combat on the plains of Sinkiang, Mongolia, and Manchuria, unless China can somehow cut Soviet logistic lines in Siberia.

their destruction of the Ukrainian nationalist guerrilla movement after World War II—shows no timidity or lack of knowledge or ruthlessness in insurgency warfare.

The day may come when China's nuclear arsenal may be able, at the last moment, to prevent these extreme circumstances from occurring after an attack on the Soviets; but she would surely suffer great damage in a conventional attack on Siberia with very little chance of gaining much.

China's Defensive Conventional Military Capability

None of the foregoing should be construed to mean that we can dismiss Red China as a "paper tiger" militarily—far from it. Many of the shortcomings of geography and transport which prevent her from projecting her military power outward from her "Zone of Interior," act in her favor when defending the homeland against invasion. Also, her forces— though relatively immobile and lacking in firepower compared with other modern armies—can probably give a good account of themselves in rather static defensive warfare or when falling back on their supply dumps. Furthermore, China can obviously bring many more of her ground forces (including the militia) to bear on her mainland than elsewhere.

On the other hand, because the population and industry of China are crowded into the eastern section of the country, within easy reach of her coastline, she suffers from a unique vulnerability. This coastline is very long, but she has almost no navy to protect it, and her air force probably would not survive in the battle zone after the initial onslaught of a hostile modern air and maritime power with nearby bases. In some respects, in the conventional warfare area, she occupies somewhat the same position she had in the thirties when invaded by Japan. Today China is much better organized to repel an invader, but the power she continually names as the potential invader (the United States) has at least an order of magnitude greater potential to support a massive conventional invasion against her than did Japan in the 1930's.[97] In fact,

[97] One can imagine why Red China points to the greatest capitalist nation as the potential enemy when one considers her campaign to be leader of the Communist world; but it must pose some interesting problems for the military to develop suitable thinking to fit the concept. It is not an urgent matter, for (as Chinese leaders must know) the possibility is infinitely remote; but from the purely technical viewpoint it is difficult to think of ways to cope with an industrial and military giant which, when aroused, has a history of growing stronger as the war goes on, regardless of the remoteness of the battlefield.

some of the more exposed areas, such as Hainan Island, are extremely vulnerable to even a limited amphibious assault. Her poor and vulnerable transport system adds to her embarrassment in meeting the threat of a highly flexible modern air- and sea-borne force which can feint (or strike) at any part of the long coast at will.

There is also the possibility that she may suffer further embarrassment of the type experienced by the Soviets during the German invasion of the Ukraine. There is always the chance that the population of some areas may look on the invaders as liberators.[98] Even without such political upheavals, however, huge sections of China could be occupied by a large, determined adversary willing to expend the great effort this would require.

In areas where the populace is unfriendly or apathetic, or where efforts to root out Communist organizations in the occupied zones has been unsuccessful, the situation may be quite different. Should the Communists be able to mount and maintain it, the invading power may find itself involved in a long, bitter, dirty guerrilla war for actual control of the areas it has occupied. In this phase of the protracted conflict, the United States, despite its power might be found wanting. Furthermore, in this dire emergency, two other options might be open to the Chinese. They could call on the Soviet Union for aid, or consider the use of nuclear weapons. Both options would depend on the resolve of the United States and the USSR.

The Soviets may have no desire to see the United States on its eastern Siberian border, but in that remote region they cannot bring their main conventional power to bear. (Soviet power that would be adequate in defense of this area against current Chinese military power would probably be inadequate to stop an invasion by such a large first-class military power as the United States.) In this region, with the aid of Japanese and Korean bases, the United States may have conventional warfare "escalation dominance" over even the USSR. Whether the United States would make the critical decision to bring its conventional warfare power to bear in this area against either China or Russia (as it did against Japan *without* nearby bases in 1945) is an entirely different matter. One can hardly conceive of the issue over which such a dispute would start and, in any event, any war of this size in the nuclear era would make the crucial decision extremely difficult to make. But (from

---

[98] Indeed one can conceive of situations where one of the dilemmas of an invader of China (particularly if the invasion is to be limited or only a Dieppe-type raid) may be the problem of how to prevent the populace in the area attacked from risking its well-being in a premature acceptance of the invaders.

a purely technical point of view) unless the Soviets could convince the United States (and/or Japan) that the size and ultimate risks of the war were unwarranted for the issue involved, they could lose their Maritime Provinces.

If the Chinese wished to initiate nuclear war on their own in the event of an invasion by the United States, they might (at least currently) have to rely on the Soviet Union to deter a United States retaliatory counterforce strike that would reduce her once more to a nonnuclear power. Voluntary Soviet involvement in such a hair-raising crisis as a massive American invasion of China is quite inconceivable, but United States' involvement in this kind of crisis is even more inconceivable. This speculation therefore is largely academic, as is the theory of a large Sino-Soviet land war. Both practically require a premeditated, extreme act of hostility by China, specifically designed to start a very destructive and costly massive conventional war (which she does not want and probably could not win militarily) with one of the two powers who do not want to fight her (but who probably could not lose militarily).

Conclusions

Chinese conventional warfare capability does not lend itself to large offensive operations outside its borders against a resolute large power. The effort required to radically change this posture is massive, and at least in the near future—except possibly with aid from abroad or at significant cost to her economic well-being—perhaps beyond China's power.

China will, however, experience some increase in her conventional capability, not only because of improvements in her conventional forces, but also as a result of her efforts in the economic area. Her economic plans require an increase in transport capacity which has military significance. Motor transport has the flexibility required for expeditionary forces, and rail transport produces traffic volume to support large-scale logistics at the border. But the roads on and just outside her borders, which are generally not affected by her economic development, in most cases will not support more than a moderate amount of military traffic. Changing that condition is a large-scale program and may even require cooperation from some potential victim states. Increasing rail capacity in many areas, critical from the point of view of possible offensive military operations, also would frequently fail to coincide with China's economic requirements and would sometimes represent expensive, very difficult construction (e.g., in South China).

In addition to the extensive transport equipment and engineering programs required, a major improvement of the air force and perhaps the entire Chinese aircraft industry is necessary to enable China to use her army beyond her borders. This requirement may make the other programs seem simple by comparison. It draws on all the resources that are so scarce in China: highly technical industrial capacity in machine tools, electronics and metallurgy, as well as items in short supply, such as aviation fuels, skilled technicians, qualified training pilots, etc. Yet without this arm of the service, her large land army is severely limited in projecting its power beyond her borders, particularly on the open plains and highlands from Tibet to Manchuria and across open water from her coast.

The same holds true for her navy; although, of course, if her air arm were overwhelming she could do with a less efficient surface fleet (at least for close-in operations). As things now stand, any amphibious force that China might choose to launch would be at the mercy of the air and sea forces awaiting it out on the blue waters off her coast. Increasing her surface navy without increasing her air force would be the height of folly. Without air cover, surface ships can become nothing more than targets. Nor does anti-aircraft missile technology of the level displayed in Vietnam provide an adequate substitute; and China probably has at present inadequate capability to produce even these ground-to-air missile systems in quantity, to say nothing of seaborne systems. She has therefore not made the great sacrifices in her industry which would have been required to increase significantly her surface navy. Her efforts on her submarine force have also been modest, although this primarily defensive force predominates in her navy.

The Red Chinese may well lack more than the equipment required for modern conventional warfare. The good quality of the individual soldiers and at least the junior officers of the light infantry units of the PLA notwithstanding, the Chinese may lack qualified personnel and know-how. Chinese pilots have in the past seemed inadequate to the task of conventional air action, and it appears they could not be counted on to cope with the pilots of a nation with a modern air arm, including Nationalist China. Nor is there any reason to feel that the Chinese naval units would fare any better against modern navies.[99] Further-

[99] The navy did not seem to impede the supplying of Quemoy in 1958, and the Nationalists claim that several Communist surface craft were sunk during the crisis (*China Yearbook,* 1958–59, p. 3). This may, however, have been an unfair test of Communist capability against the Nationalists, because the presence of the United States Seventh Fleet in the Taiwan Strait may have deterred large-scale Communist naval operations.

more, though the PLA is credited with great endurance, "marked stubbornness and persistence" in infantry battles, great bravery and clever tactics and propaganda, the Red Chinese are said to have "little knowledge of combined operations, including navy and air forces,"[100] which are the backbone of modern conventional operations.

The conclusion that one might draw from a study of Chinese conventional military capability is that—because of factors of geography and inadequacy of transportation, mechanized, air and naval forces, and joint operational capability—its role, when confronting large powers, is primarily defensive. Indeed, as indicated earlier, there is evidence that the Chinese leaders do not view large-scale offensive conventional warfare as a practical mission of the armed forces.[101] This is not to say that had she the choice, China would prefer this weak offensive position; but it does provide a logical explanation for Chinese caution in the crises since Korea.

In conventional warfare, therefore, limited wars for limited objectives are the most practical kind of offensive operations for China. Even if some of the physical constraints on her mentioned earlier did not exist, extensive offensive operations might still be considered undesirable because of their great cost and because of China's precarious economic position.

In a defensive mode of conventional warfare, China's land army would have significant capability despite enemy control of the air. The difficulties of terrain which work to her disadvantage in offensive operations would to some degree prove advantageous to China defensively. The invader would now have the logistic problems, while the PLA fell back on its supply dumps. Also, China's militia would have a meaningful role; and, if her government could maintain control of the population, an invader would have to be prepared for a great, hard war if it wished to subjugate China.

[100] Johnson, *New York Times Magazine*, February 28, 1965. See insert on p. 85 of this issue for a Japanese estimate of the Red Chinese military capability.

[101] See p. 172 of this chapter for Hsieh's conclusions drawn from "China's Secret Military Papers: Military Doctrine and Strategy," *The China Quarterly*, no. 18. Meklin cites critics of our training of South Vietnamese troops for conventional war as stating that "floods of intelligence" indicated that the "Communists had concluded after Korea that it was an error to challenge Western industrial power in conventional warfare" (John Meklin, *Mission in Torment* [Garden City, New York: Doubleday & Co., Inc., 1965], p. 11).

Comments by Samuel B. Griffith II

Frank Armbruster's paper provides us with a realistic assessment of Chinese capability to conduct conventional military operations. His major conclusion, with which I agree, is that this capability does not lend itself to extensive offensive operations outside China's borders against a resolute large power.

Further, as he says, the effort required to improve this posture would be massive, and in the near future is beyond China's ability unless it were either to receive very significant aid from abroad, or to sacrifice essential domestic economic programs to give priority to creation of a war industry base.

There may be some differences of opinion in definition of the term "near future." But let us say that we mean roughly a decade. And this would further presume that within the coming year a degree of stability will have been regained within China. At the moment, this seems unlikely.

Even in the context of limited wars for limited objectives, a variety of constraints operate to China's disadvantage. Among the most important are those imposed by terrain and weather. These factors decisively affected the nature and scope of its operations against India in 1962, and they will again be controlling factors in any possible future Sino-Indian confrontation. The Himalayas will no doubt be there for some time.

The prospect of hostilities between the USSR and China is remote. But the seeds of trouble exist. The once fraternal allies continue to quarrel openly, but I would seriously doubt that during the next decade either side would permit relations to deteriorate to the point where one would resort to force against the other.

The Chinese are well aware of the Soviet Union's conventional capabilities. China's two most critical areas—Sinkiang and Manchuria—are vulnerable to Soviet "blitz" attacks. Soviet air power now deployed in the Far East and in Central Asia could destroy a very large proportion of the Chinese industrial plant within twenty-four hours after hostilities began. Certainly, it is not impossible that we will see a war between these Asian powers. But for the immediate future I would agree that the possibility is essentially academic.

Mr. Armbruster's analysis of China's ability to support any sizable number of conventional troops in South Vietnam is realistic, and in my opinion accurate. He considers, as I do, that the danger of effective Chinese intervention in South Vietnam is minimal. He writes:

> Red Chinese intervention with massive land armies in conventional combat in the non-Communist area of Vietnam is at least impracticable and perhaps impossible, particularly in the face of a resolute U.S. and allied force. There can be no "Korea" here.

As to Taiwan, I do not believe the People's Liberation Army (PLA) could take the island even if all direct United States support were withdrawn. The Chinese Communist Air Force could not establish and maintain control of the air over the Taiwan Strait.

As Mr. Armbruster has indicated, Peking's navy has a negligible amphibious capability. This is an expensive weapons system, and I doubt very much that the Chinese Communists are going to devote resources, scarce as they are, to such development.

If money is to be spent on the navy, I would opine that the bulk of it will be spent on submarines and on high-speed patrol boats equipped with relatively short-range (ten to thirty mile) anti-shipping missiles. The Chinese may well opt for a first phase submarine delivery system for missiles of four to five hundred mile range. At night, patrol and motor torpedo boats pose a very real threat, particularly to carrier task forces operating in restricted waters.

High priority might be given to the development of a modern air force and an integrated air warning and missile and gun air defense system. These cost a great deal of money, and require expert design and engineering personnel, skilled labor, modern plant, carefully controlled production processes and so on.

In other words, the Chinese for a long time will have to be really discriminating in resource allocation to improve their defense forces.

I suspect the ground forces now enjoy a relatively low re-equipment priority. This situation cannot change drastically for some time. Perception of a Soviet threat to Manchuria or Sinkiang could change this priority, particularly as far as motor transport, tanks, self-propelled artillery, and anti-tank and anti-aircraft weapons are concerned. At present, I concur with Mr. Armbruster that the possibility of such a threat is remote.

In my opinion, Mr. Armbruster correctly assays Chinese defensive capabilities as of a different order of magnitude. Peking's propaganda is designed to convince the Chinese that the United States "imperialists" and the Soviet "modern revisionists" are colluding in plans to invade China. This line serves the party's purposes. I doubt very much if the Chinese leadership really believes all its own specious propaganda. I agree with General MacArthur's statement to the effect that anyone planning to invade mainland China "should have his head examined." This seems to be Mr. Armbruster's conclusion, also.

One of the many enigmas of the Great Proletarian Cultural Revolution (GPCR) is the role played in it by the PLA. It is clear that the PLA played a significant but discreet role. The PLA organized the Red Defense Guards, provided rail, bus and army transport, instructed the Guards, arranged for feeding and housing them, and stage-managed the demonstrations in Peking and elsewhere. As I say, this was done unobtrusively. But the planning, organization, and management reflects a pretty high level of PLA staff work.

The idea that the Red Guards was some sort of a "grass roots" movement of young middle school and college students is absurd. One doesn't have such a massive movement in a totalitarian country, and certainly not in a society controlled as tightly and pervasively as China's is. On the contrary, the Red Defense Guards are what the Peking press says they are: "an extension of the PLA"; "the reliable reserve of the PLA."

If we can say anything positive about Mao's Cultural Revolution, it would be that the Revolution has pretty thoroughly disrupted the country. The leadership has made efforts to keep the Red Guards from interfering with production and transportation. Apparently, these efforts have not been too successful.

Speculation as to the possibility of PLA regionalism is increasing. One cannot foreclose this possibility, but that regional fragmentation will occur on any dramatic scale seems unlikely to me.

So far, no convincing evidence of PLA disaffection has been produced. Perhaps I should modify this and say that none convincing to me has been produced.

Nevertheless, regionalism is a strong tradition in China, and we have a number of satrapies in China. In at least three of them, incumbent PLA regional commanders also function as commissars. In these special situations, we shall only know in the event of radical change where ultimate PLA loyalties lie.

Apparently, China sees in people's wars a means to redress the global strategic balance which favors the "imperialists," the "modern revisionists," and their assorted "lackeys." She is going to encourage these wars where possible and support them at least vocally. If geography permits more substantive support, I expect that she will offer it.

India's North East Frontier Agency, Burma, Thailand, Laos, and Kashmir are all areas that seem particularly susceptible to generation of this sort of trouble. Already there is a Thai National Liberation Front, with permanent representatives in Peking. Clandestine radios, possibly located in Laos, call upon the Thai to arise, overthrow the incumbent government of American "stooges," and throw the "imperialists" out. The Chinese are committed to support a Thai N.L.F.

The NEFA seems susceptible to Chinese machinations. India has not yet been able to pacify or integrate the hill tribes who live there. There is some doubt that she can do so, at least before the Chinese take advantage of the situation. I imagine they exfiltrated a considerable number of dissidents in 1962 from this area for training in China.

I think we might expect trouble of this sort in Kashmir, as well.

There are reports that the Chinese are training Indonesians on Hainan Island. These reports are from Taipei and Hong Kong, and I consider them credible.

There is cosiderable travel between Peking and various African capitals. An "Afro-Asian Writers Bureau" seems to have become a permanent feature of the Peking scene. This provides a front for seditious and subversive propaganda directed at African states. This Bureau and other so-called "cultural" Afro-Asian agencies are encouraged by the Chinese primarily to lay the groundwork for people's wars.

I anticipate that Chinese policy will continue to be to stir up trouble wherever there is an opportunity to do so.

Finally, I agree in general with Mr. Armbruster's estimates of China's conventional strength and of her low ability to improve her conventional posture. I am also in accord with his conclusion that for a very considerable time limited wars for limited objectives are the only practical conventional offensive operations the PLA will be capable of mounting.

Harold C. Hinton

8

China and Vietnam

Since early 1965 the tide has begun to run, militarily and to a lesser extent politically, against the Communist side in the Vietnamese crisis. Since the People's Republic of China (the CPR) is the only Communist power that might be thought to combine the will and the means to reverse the tide, the actual and potential Chinese role in the crisis, as well as the CPR's relations with Hanoi, is a subject of considerable interest and importance.

General Chinese Interests in Vietnam

As its frequent statements that Vietnam is the lips to China's teeth indicate, the CPR considers Vietnam an area vital to its own security. It is aware of the poorly developed state of the regions of China bordering on Indochina, and it remembers that France penetrated Southwest China from Indochina and made of it a French sphere of influence. The CPR objects to potentially hostile military forces and bases, or the possibility of their introduction, on the Asian continent, including of course Vietnam.

Vietnam is also important to the CPR from the standpoint of expanding Chinese influence. North Vietnam contains valuable minerals, and its rail net in effect constitutes a link in the Chinese rail net. A friendly Communist Vietnam, or North Vietnam, would presumably be able to contribute to the expansion of Communism in Southeast Asia, which the CPR unquestionably regards as its own proper sphere of influence.[1] The CPR would probably prefer, however, not to see Hanoi's ambition for control over Laos and Cambodia, direct or indirect, realized.[2]

In addition to these national interests, the Chinese Communist leadership has long felt a revolutionary interest in the growth and ultimate

[1] Harold C. Hinton, *Communist China in World Politics* (Boston: Houghton Mifflin, 1966), p. 237.

[2] Cf. *ibid.*, pp. 242–43.

201

triumph of the Vietnamese Communist movement. The latter's leaders in turn have studied and made use of the revolutionary strategy and techniques devised by the Chinese Communists and include a strongly pro-Chinese faction thought to be led by Truong Chinh. The mainstream of the Vietnamese Communist movement, however, appears strongly determined to remain independent of Chinese control, despite China's size and proximity, without breaking with the Chinese and to date it has largely succeeded in doing so.[3]

Communist China and the Indochina War

The extension of Communist power down to the Chinese side of the northern borders of Indochina at the end of 1949 transformed the character of the war then in progress between Ho Chi Minh's Democratic Republic of Vietnam (DRV) and the French. The CPR was the first power to recognize the DRV (on January 18, 1950). Limited Chinese military and economic aid to the DRV began in 1950, and Chinese advice is thought to have contributed to the formation of the Vietnam Workers (Communist) Party early in 1951. The Chinese role was nevertheless a highly restricted one, both because further intervention was militarily unnecessary and therefore almost certainly not desired by the DRV, and because the CPR was dangerously embroiled in Korea.[4]

In the spring of 1953, however, the approach of an armistice in Korea created the possibility of a more active Chinese policy toward the struggle in Vietnam, and the increase of French military activity represented by the Navarre Plan provided the rationale. Chinese military aid to the DRV increased sharply and played a critical role in the siege and capture of Dien Bien Phu. In April, 1954, the CPR was implicitly threatened by Secretary of State Dulles with direct retaliation if it intervened in the event of American action in support of the French at Dienbienphu, but no such American action occurred and the CPR was probably planning no intervention of its own in any case.[5]

At the Geneva Conference, the CPR broke the initial deadlock by withdrawing support in mid-June from the DRV's demand for what would have amounted to a package settlement for the three Indochina countries. The CPR was probably influenced by a conditional threat of

[3] Cf. Melvin Gurtov, *The First Vietnam Crisis: Chinese Communist Strategy and United States Involvement, 1953–1954* (New York: Columbia University Press, 1967), pp. 1–17.

[4] Hinton, *Communist China*, pp. 238–41.

[5] *Ibid.*, pp. 241–48.

American military intervention made by Secretary Dulles on June 11. Chou En-lai insisted that the Geneva Agreements must prohibit any American military presence in Indochina, as they did, and that the United States must sign the agreements, as it did not. When it became clear that the United States would under no circumstances sign the agreements, the CPR accepted instead a verbal assurance that the United States would not "disturb" them by force. Throughout the last phase of the negotiations, Chinese concern over the possible American military role in Indochina far outweighed Chinese concern over the political fortunes of the DRV. The latter was offered the consolation prize of all-Vietnamese elections within two years.[6] The joint communiqué issued by Chou En-lai and Pham Van Dong when the former visited Hanoi in November, 1956, suggested that both regimes were angry at the Soviet Union, the Communist co-chairman of the Geneva Conference, for not having made a major issue of the refusal of Ngo Dinh Diem, with American support, to hold the elections specified in the Geneva Agreements.[7]

The Struggle for South Vietnam

Particularly after its failure in 1958 to make a dent in the American and Chinese Nationalist positions in the Taiwan Strait, the CPR turned its attention increasingly to the Indochina area. Beginning at about the time of the Laotian crisis in the spring of 1959, it thought or claimed that it saw an American effort, with the collaboration of the newly installed Sarit government in Thailand, to establish a network of bases in South Vietnam and Laos, with the aim, among others, of ultimately putting military pressure on the CPR.[8] Of these two situations, the CPR clearly regarded Laos as the more urgent, and its public position on South Vietnam went no farther than to demand the "peaceful reunification" of Vietnam through the faithful fulfillment of the Geneva Agreements as the best means of coping with American "aggression" in the area. On this issue Peking therefore appeared to be in line with Hanoi, which was still relying on political approaches to unifica-

[6] *Ibid.*, pp. 248–54.

[7] Text of joint communiqué released by Vietnam News Agency, November 22, 1956.

[8] Cf. documents in *Concerning the Situation in Laos* (Peking: Foreign Languages Press, 1959); also A. M. Halpern and H. B. Fredman, *Communist Strategy in Laos,* The RAND Corporation, RM-2561, June 14, 1960, pp. 91–95.

tion and trying to restrain the Communist cadres in South Vietnam from taking up arms.[9]

By September, 1960, however, Hanoi had decided to support and direct the insurgency.[10] It seems likely that Peking felt some reservations about this shift of strategy. Although politically committed to an ultimate revolutionary victory in Vietnam, it was more immediately concerned with areas farther afield, such as newly decolonized sub-Saharan Africa, where revolutionary prospects seemed better and where American counterinvolvement would be no threat to Chinese security. In Vietnam, on the other hand, a growing American presence would in Peking's eyes create a danger to the CPR as well as to the DRV. The situation in Laos was still causing the Chinese leadership concern. The CPR was in a weak position to make its wishes prevail in Hanoi, however; its economic crisis of 1960 compelled it to cut economic aid to the DRV drastically in 1961.[11]

The increasing American involvement in South Vietnam in 1961, in the form of growing numbers of military and civilian advisers, had the predictable effect of alarming the CPR. A Chinese military mission visited Hanoi at the end of 1961, but Chinese declaratory support for the DRV's announced political objectives, such as neutrality for South Vietnam, the confederation of a neutral South Vietnam with Cambodia and Laos, and the reunification of Vietnam tended to slacken during the next three years.[12] The CPR supported the reconvening of the Geneva Conference until the summer of 1964, however.

The Laotian settlement of 1962 virtually eliminated Peking's fears on that score and apparently moved it to take a more active interest in the Vietnamese situation. The National Liberation Front (NLF) in South Vietnam, although closely linked to Hanoi, retained enough autonomy at that time so that the CPR considered it feasible and useful to conduct a separate diplomacy with each, presumably in order to

[9] George McTurnan Kahin and John W. Lewis, *The United States in Vietnam* (New York: Dial Press, 1967), pp. 108–14.

[10] Cf. *ibid.*, pp. 114–16.

[11] Note that the Chinese delegate to the Third National Congress of the Vietnam Workers Party (September 5–10, 1960), which adopted the policy of supporting armed revolution in South Vietnam (see *ibid.*, pp. 114–15), was Li Fu-ch'un, chairman of the CPR's State Planning Committee; his address to the congress was released by New China News Agency, September 6, 1960.

[12] Cf. Douglas Pike, *Viet Cong: The Organization and Techniques of the National Liberation Front of South Vietnam* (Cambridge, Mass.: The M.I.T. Press, 1966), p. 333.

maximize its influence on both and if possible to gain their support against the Soviet Union in the Sino-Soviet dispute. The NLF for its part probably regarded contacts with Peking as a useful way of balancing Hanoi's influence. A visiting NLF delegation received a huge welcome in Peking in September, 1962, and contacts thereafter were fairly frequent.[13] In September, 1964, several months before the Soviet Union did the same, the CPR received a permanent delegation from the NLF.[14]

By the spring of 1963, the NLF, and apparently Hanoi also, were coming to the conclusion that the old myth of a seizure of power in South Vietnam through a more or less spontaneous "general uprising" was not workable and must be abandoned, and that more intense military pressures, including some exerted directly by the DRV, would be required.[15] Since Chinese semiautomatic weapons began to appear in South Vietnam by July, 1963,[16] and since the DRV in the spring of 1963 began to take an increasingly pro-Chinese line in the Sino-Soviet dispute, it seems to be reasonable to infer that a bargain was struck: the CPR would agree to and support a full-scale military struggle in South Vietnam by both the Vietcong and the DRV, in exchange for Hanoi's support against Khrushchev. The bargain was probably formalized at the time of Liu Shao-ch'i's visit to Hanoi (May 10–16, 1963).[17]

From the spring of 1963, as the gathering Buddhist crisis swept the Diem government toward its fall, the CPR seems to have associated itself with increasing enthusiasm with the cause of Hanoi's and the NLF's armed revolution in South Vietnam. Ho Chi Minh and Mao Tse-tung both issued personal statements (on August 28 and 29, respectively) denouncing Ngo Dinh Nhu's raids on the Buddhist temples and assigning ultimate responsibility for them to the United States.[18]

The collapse of the Diem government was followed by an intensification of Communist military activity in South Vietnam, including a brief series of terrorist attacks on American personnel that terminated at about the time when President Johnson (on February 21, 1964) made a threatening statement on Vietnam.[19] A week later, the New China News Agency reprinted an article from the North Vietnamese periodi-

---

[13] Pike, *Viet Cong*, pp. 311–12.

[14] *Ibid.*, p. 334.

[15] *Ibid.*, p. 160.

[16] *Ibid.*, p. 337.

[17] On the Vietnamese swing to the Chinese side in the Sino-Soviet dispute, and on Liu's visit, see William E. Griffith, *The Sino-Soviet Rift* (Cambridge, Mass.: The M.I.T. Press, 1964), pp. 128–30.

[18] Hinton, *Communist China*, p. 360.

[19] Cf. Pike, *Viet Cong*, p. 252.

cal *Hoc Tap* on the war in South Vietnam, from which it deleted a statement that if the United States attacked the DRV it would have to "cope" with the CPR, "or eventually the socialist camp as a whole."[20] The CPR obviously had no desire to become directly involved in the crisis in Vietnam, especially since it was involved in a major political struggle with Khrushchev.

The possibility of an escalation by the United States seemed to be suggested by the appointment of General Maxwell D. Taylor as Ambassador to Vietnam on June 23, an event that was promptly followed by a series of alarmed statements emanating from both Hanoi and Peking.[21] On July 24, a Chinese official, later identified as Foreign Minister Chen Yi, gave an important unattributed interview to Dr. Hugo Portisch, chief editor of the Vienna *Kurier*, in which he demanded "peace and neutrality" for North Vietnam as well as South Vietnam and Laos and the withdrawal of all foreign troops, denied any aggressive intent on the part of the CPR, but said it would intervene with its own forces if (and apparently only if) the United States invaded North Vietnam or northern Laos.[22] The rather offhand attitude toward North Vietnam, as long as it was not actually invaded, implied in this interview altered after the American air attacks on the DVR on August 5, following the Tonkin Gulf incident. Chinese statements began to imply a promise of "volunteers" if necessary, and the CPR sent a limited number of jet fighters and antiaircraft guns to the DRV.[23]

By the time of the twentieth anniversary of the founding of the "Vietnamese People's Army" (December 22, 1964), the CPR must have been aware that the DRV and the leadership of the NLF, which the DRV increasingly controlled, had decided on a substantial escalation of the military effort in South Vietnam.[24] In an issue of *Hung-ch'i* (Red Flag) published on the anniversary, General Li Tso-p'eng made an important statement obviously aimed at the DRV. Perhaps the most important feature of Li's long summary of the military history of the Chinese Communist movement was his stress on guerrilla warfare as the basic strategy against the Japanese and on mobile warfare as the basic

[20] Hinton, *Communist China*, p. 361.

[21] E.g., Chinese government statement of July 19, 1964 (New China News Agency dispatch, same date).

[22] The interview was published in the *Kurier* on August 1, 1964; English translation in *New York Times*, August 7, 1964.

[23] Hinton, *Communist China*, pp. 365–66; see also *New York Times*, January 17, 1965.

[24] Pike, *Viet Cong*, p. 107.

strategy against the Nationalists, especially after 1946.[25] In view of the fact that the Chinese press was making constant reference to the American military presence in South Vietnam, Li may have been advising the DRV not to escalate prematurely but to wait until an American withdrawal had been achieved before going over to mobile warfare.

Probably because of the outcome of the American election, and despite reports in the American press by the end of 1964 that air attacks on North Vietnam were being contemplated, at least one eminent Chinese seems to have believed at that time that an American withdrawal was not far in the future. On January 9, 1965, Mao Tsetung told Edgar Snow that the United States would not attack the DRV and would withdraw from South Vietnam after a year or two, and that the CPR would not fight the United States unless directly attacked.[26] There seems to be no reason to doubt that this statement represented Mao's actual opinion, and even though it did not necessarily command the agreement of all Chinese leaders concerned with the Vietnamese situation it must have exerted great influence. The Soviet estimate seems to have been far more realistic; when Kosygin went to Hanoi early in February, 1965, his delegation included a high concentration of Air Force generals.

The Impact of the American Escalation

The American escalation, or counterescalation, in Vietnam represented a colossal setback for the CPR. Its neighbor and informal ally, the DRV, was attacked from the air without the CPR being able to do anything effective either to deter the attacks or provide a defense against them. The commitment of American ground forces to South Vietnam threatened to deny both the DRV and the CPR a revolutionary victory there that Peking desired all the more inasmuch as the prospects for revolutionary successes in Africa, notably in the Congo (Léopoldville), seemed increasingly dim. Occasional Chinese statements welcoming the sending of American ground forces to South Vietnam, on the basis of their politically beneficial effect on the cause of revolution, may be dismissed as propaganda; if they were sincere, the CPR would not have insisted ever since on the withdrawal of those forces as

[25] Li Tso-p'eng, "Strategically 'Pit One Against Ten,' Tactically 'Pit Ten Against One,'" *Hung-ch'i* (Red Flag), December 22, 1964 (in American Consulate General, Hong Kong, *Selections from China Mainland Magazines*, no. 453, January 25, 1965).

[26] Edgar Snow, "Interview with Mao," *The New Republic*, February 27, 1965, pp. 17–23.

a precondition for any kind of settlement. The American escalation raised the obvious possibility of a direct military confrontation between the United States and the CPR, never a welcome idea in Peking despite occasional propaganda to the contrary. The inevitable involvement of the Soviet Union in the crisis was unacceptable to the CPR on political grounds.

The escalation sharply intensified the controversy, which was growing keener in any case, between the political ("red") and the professional ("expert") viewpoints in the CPR. With respect to Vietnam, the controversy seems to have related in part to the question of whether the security and viability of North Vietnam as an ally and buffer or the prosecution of the revolutionary struggle in South Vietnam should have the higher priority. The "politicals" appear to have argued that the struggle in the south must be prosecuted regardless of its effects on the north, and the "professionals" have tended to argue that the security of the north must be given priority and must be safeguarded regardless of other considerations. Prior to the escalation, there was no great incompatibility between the two concepts; the war in the south did not jeopardize the north. But now this comfortable situation no longer existed; the more vigorous the struggle in the south, the greater the punishment likely to be inflicted on the north.

The CPR's initial official position, reflecting no doubt the political point of view, was that the United States had "taken the lead in breaking up the line of demarcation" between North and South Vietnam, and by implication that the DRV was now free to invade the south in force.[27] Given this prevailing mood, the Soviet request for the facilitation of Soviet arms shipments to the DRV by rail, which according to a later Chinese statement[28] was first made on February 25, 1965, was most unwelcome. (According to both Chinese and Soviet sources a request was also made for air transit facilities, but it was rejected.) The riots by Chinese and North Vietnamese students outside the American Embassy in Moscow on March 4, 1965, may have been in part an answer to this intrusion by Khrushchev's successors into an area from which he had virtually withdrawn and where the Chinese politicals had no desire to see any Soviet involvement.

The commitment of major American ground forces to South Vietnam in March affected the debate in Peking significantly, since unlike the

[27] Speech by Liu Shao-ch'i (New China News Agency, February 17, 1965).

[28] New China News Agency, December 22, 1965. See also *New York Times,* March 29, 1965; *Christian Science Monitor,* April 2, 1965.

bombing of the north it directly jeopardized the revolutionary struggle in the south. The blow to the interests of the politicals and the professionals was now roughly symmetrical. On March 30, in a substantial concession to the professional viewpoint, the CPR signed a protocol with the Soviet Union for the transit by rail without charge of Soviet military equipment, consisting mainly of antiaircraft artillery and missiles.[29] (The Soviet Union later alleged that the CPR levied freight charges in dollars in violation of the agreement.) By early May, some of the equipment was beginning to move through South China.[30]

If, as seems probable, the forwarding of Soviet arms for the DRV represented a significant triumph for the professionals, something also had to be conceded to the politicals and to their preoccupation with the fate of the NLF and its struggle in the south. Late in March, following the commitment of the first American combat ground units to South Vietnam, two *Jen-min jih-pao* editorials (March 25 and 29) promised that the CPR was "ready" to send its "men" to fight together with the "South Vietnamese people" whenever the latter asked it to do so. The limits to which the professionals were willing to go in this matter was approximately represented by a resolution passed on April 20 by the Standing Committee of the National People's Congress, chaired by Marshal Chu Teh. The resolution called on the Chinese people "to make *full preparations* to send their own people to fight together with the *Vietnamese* people and drive out the U.S. aggressors in the event that U.S. imperialism continues to escalate its war of aggression and the Vietnamese people *need* them."[31] As compared with the earlier editorials in *Jen-min jih-pao*, the resolution stressed caution ("full preparations"), coordination with Hanoi as well as with the NLF (the "Vietnamese people") rather than merely with the NLF (the "South Vietnamese people"), and the decisiveness of objective "need" as determined presumably by the CPR rather than a mere request from the NLF. It may well be significant that at the time (and in fact from mid-April to mid-June) Mao Tse-tung was not mentioned in the Chinese press as having appeared in public or as having made a statement on Vietnam (although a statement was issued in his name in May on the situation in the Dominican Republic) and may have been ill; the

[29] New China News Agency dispatch, December 22, 1965. See also *New York Times*, April 8, 1965.

[30] *New York Times*, May 13, 1965.

[31] New China News Agency dispatch, April 20, 1965. [Italics are the author's.]

American escalation must have been a particular shock to a man who had blithely predicted a month before that the United States would withdraw from Vietnam after a year or two.

A classic statement of a "hawk-like" professional position on Vietnam and on some other strategic questions was put forward by Chief of Staff Lo Jui-ch'ing in an article published on the occasion of the twentieth anniversary of V-E Day (May 8, 1965) and probably intended in part as an answer to Li Tso-p'eng.

Apart from a laudatory survey of the Soviet war effort against Nazi Germany, the first point Lo makes, implicitly rather than directly, is that the Vietnamese crisis demands unity among the Soviet Union, the CPR, North Vietnam, and the Vietcong, and therefore a rapprochement between the CPR and the Soviet Union. He refrains from denouncing the post-Khrushchev Soviet leadership, as some of his colleagues had already begun to do.[32] He opposes appeasement of the United States, the "main enemy." He denounces Chamberlain and Daladier not only for their appeasement of Hitler but for their rejection of a Soviet offer of cooperation against Germany; Lo fails to mention, but was probably aware, that Chamberlain and Daladier were unwilling to agree to the transit of Soviet troops across Poland, a point of definite relevance to the Sino-Soviet discussions on Vietnam. In this, Lo appears to be criticizing any of his colleagues, Mao Tse-tung presumably among others, who in practice favored subordinating the struggle against the United States to the struggle against the Soviet Union. He insists that "the socialist countries should . . . regard it as their bounden duty to support the revolutionary struggles of the oppressed peoples," and that "all revolutionary wars support each other." In short, Lo appears to advocate a joint Sino-Soviet effort to aid and support the "Vietnamese people" so that they can both defend North Vietnam against American air attacks and continue the revolutionary war in South Vietnam in the teeth of the American escalation. It seems probable that he favored using an improved Sino-Soviet relationship established over Vietnam as a means of reviving Soviet aid to and support for the CPR itself.

By implication, Lo addresses some strategic recommendations to the "Vietnamese people." V-E Day is also the approximate anniversary of the fall of Dien Bien Phu in 1954; Lo does not mention Dien Bien Phu, but neither had Li Tso-p'eng alluded in his article to Vietnamese Army Day. Lo's first point is that the American army is overextended and is

---

[32] On this point see Chou En-lai's speech of March 29, 1965, in Albania. Text in *Support the People of Viet Nam, Defeat U.S. Aggressors,* vol. I (Peking: Foreign Languages Press, 1965), p. 25.

basically weaker than Hitler's was. That being so, the Soviet strategy that defeated Nazi Germany is obviously applicable to Vietnam and should be even more effective there: "In any future war against U.S. imperialist aggression, this is the only strategy for the socialist countries to adopt." This strategy Lo defines as one of "active defense" followed by strategic counteroffensive, pursuit, and the promotion of revolutionary regimes in the areas from which the "imperialists" are driven. In contrast to Li Tso-p'eng (and later to Lin Piao), Lo seems to recommend offensive mobile warfare in South Vietnam in spite of American technical superiority: "Without heroic fighting by the ground forces, no new weapons, however powerful, can determine the outcome of battles or achieve the political aim of a war. This is another law governing war. . . . It holds true for oppressed peoples engaged in revolutionary struggle as well as for a powerful socialist country such as the Soviet Union."

As for the Chinese role in the struggle, Lo insists that the CPR "supports" the "Vietnamese people" and will send its own "men" when the Vietnamese "need" them. Again it appears that the decision to send Chinese troops (or "volunteers," or technicians) is to be taken in Peking rather than Hanoi, but unlike the resolution of the Standing Committee of the National People's Congress Lo attaches no cautious qualifications. He adds, "We will go on supporting and aiding the Vietnamese people, whether or not U.S. imperialism bombs our country and whether or not it enlarges the war."

The final section of Lo's argument, then, relates to the implications of the Vietnamese crisis for the CPR, over and above the question of Chinese aid to and support for the "Vietnamese people." Lo insists that there is a danger of an American surprise attack on the CPR with nuclear weapons arising out of the Vietnamese crisis. It is therefore essential that the CPR be prepared: "It makes a world of difference whether or not one is prepared once a war breaks out." Fortunately, he adds, the CPR is prepared: "We are fully prepared for war." The United States will not escape with impunity if it attacks the CPR: "We seriously warn the U.S. imperialists that they must not expect us to refrain from counter-attacking once they have attacked us." It is very likely that one of Lo's purposes in advancing this line of argument was a domestic one—namely, to counter Mao Tse-tung's increasingly politicized program with one in which professional military men and economic planners would have a greater role.[33]

[33] Lo Jui-ch'ing, "Commemorate the Victory over German Fascism! Carry the Struggle against U.S. Imperialism through to the End!" *Hung-ch'i,* May 10, 1965.

In his subsequent public statements during 1965, notably his Army Day (August 1) speech[34] and his V-J Day (September 3) speech,[35] Lo gave some ground, presumably under pressure, but clung to certain of his main points. In the latter statement especially, he thought it best to comment only briefly and innocuously on Vietnam. He attacked the "Khrushchev revisionists" (meaning the current Soviet leadership), referred to the "liberation" of Taiwan, laid considerable stress on the Chinese revolutionary model, and mentioned the possibility of an American invasion (as distinct from an air attack) on China. On the other hand, he continued to insist that the United States was weaker than the Axis in conventional forces, stressed the need for pre-attack mobilization ("A thousand and one things need to be done in preparation") while simultaneously conceding the need to prepare for a "people's war," and made no reference to the favorite Maoist subject of World War III. His last public appearance as chief of staff was made at the end of November, and he was purged and apparently arrested early in 1966 for his wide-ranging disagreements with Mao Tse-tung and Lin Piao.

The first American bombing pause (May 12–18) sharpened the issue between the politicals and the professionals by presenting Peking, as well as Hanoi, with the question of whether a de-escalation of the struggle in the south was an acceptable price to pay for the cessation of American air attacks on the north. The professionals may have answered yes; the politicals unquestionably answered no, and they won. A second Chinese nuclear test, politically timed and propagandistically announced in the manner that is one of the hallmarks of the political approach, was conducted on May 14. The CPR probably hoped in this way to encourage the DRV to ignore American peace overtures and to proclaim its defiance of President Johnson, who had recently stated in a speech that the United States proposed to frustrate an alleged Chinese intent to dominate Southeast Asia. On May 24 Chu Teh's Standing Committee of the National People's Congress authorized, with probable reluctance on his part, the abolition of ranks in the armed forces, effective June 1.[36] Although this measure can be quite properly interpreted as a major step in the general politicization of the armed forces, it also had the specific effect of punishing the more professionally

[34] Excerpts in *Peking Review*, August 6, 1965, p. 6; the full text does not appear to have been published.

[35] New China News Agency dispatch, September 4, 1965.

[36] New China News Agency dispatch, May 24, 1965.

minded officers and of eliminating Chu Teh's military precedence over Defense Minister Lin Piao, whose rise was thereby facilitated.

The classic programmatic statement of the political viewpoint is Lin Piao's famous tract of September 3, 1965, "Long Live the Victory of People's War!" This has been interpreted as an admonition to the DRV and the NLF to adopt a less military and more political strategy for South Vietnam,[37] but its message is in reality much more generalized than that. One of the hallmarks of the political approach is the refusal to take formal account of details, on the ground that Maoist ideology and the Maoist political strategy can overcome all practical obstacles. Lin's tract teems with statements to this effect. His theme is that the peoples of the world, who are threatened by American "imperialism" in much the same way that the Chinese people were threatened by Japanese "imperialism" between 1937 and 1945, can overcome the threat by the same methods with which the Chinese people allegedly defeated Japan: "self-reliant people's wars," or in other words the Maoist politico-military strategy. Unlike Lo Jui-ch'ing in his article of the previous May, and probably in conscious rebuttal of him, Lin attacks the current Soviet leadership, trots out the politicals' hardy perennial that a Third World War would not be a bad thing, demands the "liberation" of Taiwan, makes no reference to American air attacks on North Vietnam, and places much emphasis on the revolutionary struggle in South Vietnam and on the need for the Vietnamese, not the Chinese, to expel American troops. In effect, Lin had reaffirmed Mao's decision of 1958 to subordinate in practice the struggle against American "imperialism" to the struggle against Soviet "revisionism." By implication, he also seems to have recommended to the "Vietnamese people" that they keep their military operations at the guerrilla level.

Politicals in Command

Since Lo Jui-ch'ing was quietly purged in early 1966, probably for his views on Vietnam among other things, and since Lin Piao has become Mao Tse-tung's heir apparent, it would be reasonable to assume that the political viewpoint with respect to Vietnam has prevailed. And so it has, but as with the entire range of issues between the politicals and professionals, not entirely; the politicals, although in the ascendant, have found it advisable or necessary to make certain concessions to the professional viewpoint.

[37] D. P. Mozingo and T. W. Robinson, *Lin Piao on "People's War": China Takes a Second Look at Vietnam*, The RAND Corporation, Memorandum RM-4814-PR, November, 1965.

For more than a year after the spring of 1965, there were no further public statements specifically threatening the commitment of Chinese troops to Vietnam or adjacent areas in retaliation for something that might happen in Vietnam. Instead, there has been an emphasis, characteristic of the political approach, on the idea that if the United States should invade the CPR it would be crushed in a "people's war" that would "have no boundaries"; the classic statement of this theme is in a celebrated press conference given by Foreign Minister Chen Yi on September 29, 1965.[38] A distinguished journalist has interpreted these statements as indicating that the Chinese leadership decided about September, 1965, that war with the United States was "inevitable," although the CPR would not initiate it.[39] This analysis appears oversimplified. The line that the CPR will fight a "people's war" if invaded probably has some use to the politicals in their domestic activities, but it has little value as a deterrent, since the United States has not the slightest intention of invading the CPR. A much more plausible contingency is of course an American air attack on the CPR, but this was not covered specifically in a public Chinese statement until the CPR released, on May 9, 1966, the text of an interview that Premier Chou En-lai had given a month earlier to a Pakistani newspaper, in which he specified American air or sea attack on the CPR as a *casus belli* for a "war without boundaries."[40] Three days later the CPR claimed that American aircraft had shot down a Chinese trainer plane over Chinese soil and used Chou's interview as the text for a warning to the United States not to "trifle" with the "great Chinese people."[41] In reality, Chinese fear of an American attack, at least in the near future, seemed to diminish. The CPR is reported to have told the United States privately in the spring of 1966 that it would not intervene in Vietnam except in case of an American invasion of the DRV or an American attack on the CPR, and to have been assured that the United States intended neither of these things.[42] Indeed, the Soviet Union has been giving signs of genuine concern over some sort of Sino-American deal, probably on the

---

[38] Text in *Vice-Premier Chen Yi Answers Questions Put by Correspondents* (Peking: Foreign Languages Press, 1966), pp. 1–26.

[39] Robert Guillain, "La Chine accepte l'idée du combat," *Le Monde: sélection hebdomadaire*, August 4–10, 1966.

[40] New China News Agency dispatch, May 9, 1966.

[41] Defense Ministry statement, New China News Agency dispatch, May 12, 1966.

[42] *New York Times*, January 17, 1967.

theory that if relieved of its worries over American escalation the CPR might increase its pressures on the Soviet Union.

Furthermore, there is a powerful reason why the politicals would be reluctant to concede, in the course of their private debates with the professionals, the likelihood of such an attack. If it were admitted, then the force of the professionals' demand, voiced more than once by Lo Jui-ch'ing in 1965, for extensive pre-attack mobilization, with great resulting influence for the professionals over the economy and the transportation net, would be considerably enhanced. What has apparently happened instead has been a very modest civil defense program, just enough to enable the politicals to deny that they have done nothing along these lines;[43] a rather modest buildup of Chinese ground forces near the Vietnamese frontier, not enough to impose serious logistical burdens or to excite the DRV or the United States unduly;[44] and a great deal of exhortation to the armed forces to be ready, but politically even more than militarily, for war.[45]

At the end of 1965, Chinese pronouncements on Vietnam occupied themselves mainly with extolling the alleged victories of Communist forces in South Vietnam and excoriating the American bombing pause and "peace offensive" as a fraud. There can be little doubt that the CPR exerted whatever covert pressures it may have thought were necessary to insure that the views of the "hawks" in Hanoi prevailed over those of the "doves," assuming there to be some. The Chinese politicals probably greeted the end of the bombing pause with secret relief, although the Foreign Ministry issued a statement denouncing it.[46]

Whether or not the CPR had reason to be worried at the effect of American peace overtures on Hanoi, it definitely had reason to be irritated at the attractiveness for the DRV of the Soviet advocacy of "united action" on its behalf, if only the CPR would cooperate. Peking must have been angered by the decision of the Vietnam Dang Lao Dong and the NLF to send delegations to the Soviet party's Twenty-third Congress in late March and to congresses of various pro-Soviet parties during the spring, all of which the Chinese boycotted. Certainly the DRV was in no position or mood to go too far in antagonizing the CPR; there were a number of statements from Hanoi in the spring of

[43] Cf. *Washington Post,* September 3 and November 24, 1965.

[44] Cf. *New York Times,* January 29, 1966.

[45] E.g., "The Most Important Fundamental War Preparation," *Liberation Army Daily,* February 14, 1966.

[46] Text released by New China News Agency, February 2, 1966.

1966, perhaps made under Chinese pressure, denying that the CPR had obstructed the flow of Soviet military matériel to the DRV.[47]

In the spring of 1966, a North Vietnamese general, Nguyen Van Vinh, made a secret speech, whose text has recently become available, to some of his colleagues in South Vietnam, in the course of which he commented on the CPR's attitude toward the struggle. These comments are interesting because they tend to confirm the CPR's concern for the DRV's security, its basic preference for a prolonged guerrilla war in South Vietnam, its strong tendency to oppose any sort of negotiations unless and until a victory has been won sufficient to humiliate the United States and regenerate the lagging momentum of "people's war" in the developing areas, and its willingness to resort to some extraordinary arguments in pressing its case on Hanoi:

> If the war is expanded to North Vietnam, . . . the enemy will have to fight not only the Vietnamese people, but also the Chinese people. . . .
>
> China holds the view that conditions for negotiations are not yet ripe, not until a few years from now, and, even worse, seven years from now. In the meantime, we should continue fighting to bog down the enemy, and should wait until a number of socialist countries acquire adequate conditions for strengthening their main force troops to launch a strong, all-out, and rapid offensive, using all types of weapons and heeding no borders. What we should do in the South today is to try to restrain the enemy and get him bogged down, waiting until China has built strong forces to launch an all-out offensive.[48]

The American bombing of oil dumps and other targets near Hanoi and Haiphong on June 29 evoked a stern governmental statement from the CPR on July 3:

[47] Cf. Premier Pham Van Dong's thanks to the CPR for its "devoted help in the transit of aid from the Soviet Union and other fraternal Eastern European countries in accordance with schedule" (report to National Assembly, April 16, 1966; text released by Vietnam News Agency, April 28, 1966). See also Vietnam News Agency dispatch, June 19, 1966.

[48] The writer has seen a copy of the speech in translation. This speech and some related documents are analyzed, interestingly and accurately except for a tendency to overstate Hanoi's independence of Peking, in four columns by Joseph Alsop, "Now We Really Know," *Washington Post*, April 24, April 26, April 28, May 1, 1967.

> The development by United States imperialism of its war of aggression to a new and still graver stage has now further freed us from any bounds or restrictions in rendering . . . support and aid. In accordance with the interest and demands of the Vietnamese people, we will at any time take such actions as we deem necessary. . . . China is prepared and . . . once the war breaks out, it will have no boundaries. . . . we will unswervingly support the fraternal Vietnamese people in fighting through to the end, till *they* thoroughly and completely drive the United States aggressors out of Vietnam and win final victory.[49]

On July 22, after the proclamation of a partial mobilization by Ho Chi Minh on July 17, a huge rally was held in Peking at which leading politicals (T'ao Chu, Li Hsueh-feng) and professionals (Liu Shao-ch'i, Chu Teh) joined in proclaiming support for the "Vietnamese people" and condemnation of the United States. In keeping with the increasingly sharp distinction between the public images of the two groups projected from Peking, Liu and Chu in their governmental capacities prepared formal statements that were read, apparently not by them, whereas T'ao and Li as party figures made live speeches. In any case, the substance of the two most important messages, those of Liu and T'ao, was identical, except that Liu refrained from denouncing the Soviet Union: apart from repeating propositions already enunciated, they insisted that "The vast expanse of China's territory is the reliable rear area of the Vietnamese people."[50] Presumably this remark was intended to convey a promise of increased Chinese aid and logistical support for the DRV and the NLF, including perhaps the construction of North Vietnamese bases on Chinese soil.

Ten days later there convened the crucial Eleventh Plenary Session of the Chinese Communist Central Committee, at which the politicals prevailed over the professionals on a number of issues, although not quite completely. The final communiqué of the session dealt with Vietnam:

> The Plenary Session most strongly condemns U.S. imperialism for its crime of widening its war of aggression against Vietnam. The Session most warmly and most resolutely supports the Appeal to the People of the Whole Country issued by Comrade Ho Chi Minh, President of the Democratic Republic of Vietnam, and

[49] New China News Agency dispatch, July 3, 1966 (text in *New York Times,* July 4, 1966). [Italics are the author's.]

[50] See *Peking Review,* July 29, 1966, pp. 9–16.

firmly supports the Vietnamese people in fighting to the end until final victory is achieved in their war against U.S. aggression and for national salvation. The Plenary Session fully agrees to all the measures already taken and all actions to be taken as decided upon by the Central Committee of the party and the government in consultation with the Vietnamese side concerning aid to Vietnam for resisting U.S. aggression.[51]

The last sentence quoted, which is a highly unusual one, seems to hand a blank check for dealing with Vietnam to Mao, Lin Piao (the sole vice chairman of the Central Committee since the Eleventh Plenary Session), and Premier Chou En-lai (who frequently appears with Mao and Lin in photographs and ranks immediately behind them in party standing).

While debating and deciding its policy toward the Vietnamese crisis, the CPR has continued its substantial military aid to the DRV and the NLF, mainly in the form of infantry weapons. It has also sent at least 50,000 "technicians" to North Vietnam. They appear to be involved mainly in trying to keep the rail lines to China open under American bombing and in constructing airstrips near the Chinese border.[52]

According to a series of Soviet charges,[53] the Chinese replies to which do not appear convincing,[54] the CPR continued, or more probably resumed in late 1965, the obstruction of Soviet equipment destined for the DRV,[55] or possibly in some cases for relatively pro-Soviet Chinese commanders.[56] The obstruction seems to have taken the form, on occasion, of diverting or copying sophisticated equipment. Soviet overflights have been restricted to the point where the Soviet Union is reported to be seeking a new air route to the DRV, via Laos.[57] Taking advantage of the issue of Chinese obstructionism, the Soviet Union has accused the CPR with great political effect of preventing "united action" on behalf

[51] Text in *Peking Review,* August 19, 1966, pp. 4–8.

[52] *New York Times,* January 24 and July 2, 1966; *Washington Post,* November 19, 1966.

[53] *Pravda,* December 25, 1965; secret Soviet letter of January or February, 1966, to other parties (text in "Geheime Anklageschrift Moskaus gegen Peking," *Ost-Probleme,* vol. 18, no. 8 [April 22, 1966], pp. 228–37; statement by Marshal Malinovsky (Budapest radio, April 21, 1966).

[54] New China News Agency dispatch, December 22, 1965; Chinese Foreign Ministry statement, May 3, 1966; "Who Is the Inventor of the Rumor?" *Jenmin jih-pao* [People's Daily], July 7, 1966.

[55] See *New York Times,* March 20, 1966; February 10, 1967.

[56] *Christian Science Monitor,* January 26, 1967.

[57] *New York Times,* February 3, 1967; *Washington Post,* February 24, 1967.

of the "Vietnamese people,"[58] a charge to which the Chinese have showed themselves extremely sensitive.[59]

As for the fighting in South Vietnam, the CPR has made it reasonably clear that it favors keeping the struggle at the guerrilla level, rather than escalating it as Hanoi has tried to do.[60] The article by Li Tso-p'eng referred to above was reissued in 1965 and 1966 in revised form; several passages in the original referring to mobile warfare in the last years of the struggle against the Nationalists were deleted, so that the emphasis fell even more heavily than before on the guerrilla stage.[61]

Whatever doubts the CPR may have had about North Vietnamese military strategy, there can be no doubt of the seriousness with which the struggle in Vietnam has continued to be viewed from Peking. On December 18, 1966, after the alleged American bombing of the Chinese embassy in Hanoi, a huge rally was held in Peking as part of a propaganda campaign whose purpose seemed at least as much domestic as external. In mid-January, 1967, most of the conditions under which Chinese intervention in the struggle had been threatened up to that time were drawn together by former Marshal Yeh Chien-ying in a speech welcoming an Albanian military delegation:

> The Chinese people have no hesitation in making the greatest national sacrifices to support the Vietnamese people to the end in their resistance to U.S. aggression. The Chinese People's Liberation Army has made every preparation. We will go to the forefront to aid Vietnam and resist U.S. aggression, fight shoulder to shoulder with the Vietnamese people, and completely wipe out the U.S. aggressors as soon as the situation requires, the Vietnamese people require, and Chairman Mao, our great supreme commander, gives the order.[62]

The domestic implications of this rather absurd statement are evident in the references to Chairman Mao and to the proposition that the Chinese army has already "made every preparation," so that nothing

[58] E.g., "Unity of Action Is an Imperative Demand of the Anti-Imperialist Struggle," *Pravda*, June 19, 1965; the secret letter cited in note 53.

[59] E.g., "Refutation of the New Leaders of the C.P.S.U. on 'United Action,' " *Jen-min jih-pao* and *Hung-ch'i*, November 11, 1965 (in *Peking Review*, November 12, 1965, pp. 10–21).

[60] Cf. *New York Times*, January 4, 1967.

[61] Li Tso-peng, *Strategy: One against Ten, Tactics: Ten against One* (Peking: Foreign Languages Press, 1966).

[62] New China News Agency dispatch, January 14, 1967.

military remains to be done. The threat to intervene is made character-istically ambiguous by the play (in this official translation by the New China News Agency) on the word "require" ("need" as against "re-quest") and in the use of the more ambiguous word "forefront" rather than "front."

At about the same time, the Chinese leadership was embarrassed by publication of reports, which it denied, of the tacit understanding with the United States of the previous spring already mentioned. A much more serious problem, not necessarily appreciated as such at first in the feverish atmosphere of Peking although it was mentioned in the Chinese press, was the impending stationing of American B-52s in Thailand.[63] This action, representing the first occasion on which major strategic weapons systems have been based in continental Asia by the United States since World War II, threatened the DRV. The threat to the CPR was also obvious enough, but Peking presumably felt that the risk was a tolerable one in view of the slight probability, in spite of all the bellicose talk, of a Sino-American clash over Vietnam, at least in the near future.

The obscure but important sequence of events that ensued may per-haps be most plausibly interpreted by supposing that it began with a North Vietnamese request for increased Soviet military aid of many kinds, including of course antiaircraft guns and missiles, both to pro-tect the North and to escalate in the South despite the B-52s and the worst the American "imperialists" could do, at any rate short of using nuclear weapons. It may be further supposed that the Soviet Union agreed, but that due to the sensitive nature of the equipment it would have to be moved across China rather than by sea, where it would be exposed to the attentions of the Seventh Fleet. Obviously such an arrangement would be dependent on Chinese cooperation, which was known to be an uncertain quantity.

On January 25, 1967, as the most important of a series of similar demonstrations in other capitals, Red Guards and other militant Chi-nese besieged the Soviet embassy in Peking. This action brought two strong Soviet public protests (on February 4 and February 9), in the second of which it was pointed out that one of the effects of the siege was to prevent Soviet officials on the embassy staff from supervising and expediting the flow of military equipment to North Vietnam. Assuming this to be true, as seems likely, it also appears probable that such ob-struction was one of the purposes of the siege. On February 10, the CPR announced the suspension of an agreement that had previously

[63] New China News Agency dispatch, January 15, 1967.

permitted such movements by Soviet officials.[64] The CPR was undoubtedly angry at Premier Kosygin's mission to the United Kingdom in mid-February, and Chou En-lai is reported to have stated in late March that Peking had urged Hanoi at that time not to listen to peace proposals from any source.[65] At the same time, the DRV was making a series of vague and ambiguous statements, which without really committing it to anything seemed to suggest that it might be willing to settle for something less than its maximum demands if the United States stopped bombing the North permanently and unconditionally. Both the Soviet and the North Vietnamese initiatives, which were probably supplemented by pressures applied secretly, may well have been intended mainly as a form of pressure on the Chinese, who of course regarded a cessation of American bombing as an entirely inadequate basis for negotiations and reiterated their view on this point in a statement on February 20.[66]

The pressure on the CPR to be more cooperative must have been considerable. The anniversary (February 14) of the signing of the Sino-Soviet alliance of 1950 passed without notice in either capital. On February 16, *Pravda* published a strongly anti-Chinese editorial in which it again raised the issue of Chinese obstruction of Soviet aid bound for North Vietnam and the siege of the Soviet embassy. Occasional Soviet references to these issues, especially the former, were made during the succeeding weeks, and the Chinese continued to denounce the Russians for revisionism and collusion with the United States and to repudiate the idea of "joint action" with the Soviet Union over Vietnam. It appears, nevertheless, that possibly owing to the influence of Chou En-lai some sort of agreement was reached between Peking and Hanoi (not Moscow) under which Soviet aid would be more promptly forwarded, perhaps under the supervision of North Vietnamese personnel.[67] Certainly increased quantities of Soviet equipment soon began to arrive in North Vietnam, and perhaps as a *quid pro quo* Hanoi published a secret letter from President Johnson on March 21, thereby

[64] *New York Times,* February 12, 1967.

[65] Simon Malley in Washington *Evening Star,* May 15, 1967. It is questionable whether this celebrated series of articles represents authentic statements made by Chinese leaders; subsequently the CPR, probably for reasons of domestic policy as well as diplomacy, saw fit to deny that Malley had interviewed the leaders in question (see *New York Times,* May 17, 1967).

[66] "Smash the Major Plot of the United States and the Soviet Union," *People's Daily,* February 20, 1967.

[67] Cf. *New York Times,* April 12, 1967.

seeming to demonstrate its own lack of interest in negotiations under existing conditions.

At the end of March, Chou En-lai reportedly gave a foreign journalist the impression that the CPR would intervene in the Vietnamese struggle with its own forces if the DRV so requested, if American escalation threatened the CPR, and especially if American troops invaded the DRV and approached the Chinese border—or with or without Hanoi's consent if the United States and the Soviet Union tried to arrange a "sellout peace" at Hanoi's expense.[68] The credibility of these threats will be considered shortly.

Strategic Problems of Protracted People's War

One of the main reasons why the CPR is so insistent on the continuation of the struggle in Vietnam is domestic. Militancy of this kind is officially, and to some extent popularly, regarded as a necessary concomitant of "the thought of Mao Tse-tung" and the Great Proletarian Cultural Revolution. The latter's imminent spread to other countries is one of the current items in the Maoist credo, and there have been some recent hints in the Chinese press that the North Vietnamese "people" support the Cultural Revolution and might even be disposed to imitate it.[69]

Of greater practical importance is the fact that the Chinese leadership regards the Vietnamese struggle as a test case in its struggle (largely by proxy, to be sure) against the United States by means of "people's war," and one success in this struggle might unhinge the whole American position in Asia and even in the entire Third World. Vietnam is especially important in this respect because of the recent Chinese revolutionary setbacks elsewhere, of which those in Indonesia and the Congo (Léopoldville) seem to be taken the most seriously in Peking.

The Chinese leadership also regards Vietnam as a test case in its struggle against the Soviet Union. Since the current Soviet leadership's domestic policy is alleged to be intrinsically bad because of its revisionist character, and since its foreign policy is alleged to be intrinsically bad because of its "collusion" with the United States, it follows that there can be no "joint action" with it over Vietnam.

Much as the CPR made opposition to the nuclear test ban treaty a crucial test of the acceptability to itself of other parties and states in the 1963–64 period, so it is making support for its Vietnamese policy, including the crucial component of denunciation of "joint action" with

---

[68] Simon Malley in Washington *Sunday Star*, May 14, 1967.

[69] E.g., New China News Agency dispatch, April 21, 1967.

the Soviet Union, a test case now. In Peking's eyes, the struggle in Vietnam must go on until the United States withdraws or is forced out under appropriately humiliating conditions and the NLF is left in control of South Vietnam, so that reunification is achieved *de facto* even if not *de jure*. So strongly does Peking feel about this that in the event Hanoi should decide to seek a "sellout peace," which contrary to Chinese charges the Soviet Union has apparently not been pressing it to do since the Shelepin mission at the beginning of 1966, the CPR might, in spite of the obvious military risks and political costs, conduct a Hungarian-style intervention in North Vietnam in order to bring to power a regime willing to carry on the struggle.

Short of such a contingency or of the direct intervention of Chinese ground forces, there are a number of steps the CPR might take if it felt that American escalation were moving to unacceptable levels. These would include increased Chinese military aid to the DRV, the basing of Vietnamese aircraft on Chinese soil, and the use of Chinese aircraft (whether with Chinese or Vietnamese markings) flying from Chinese or possibly Vietnamese bases in the air war over North Vietnam. Any of these steps, except probably the first, would be risky for the CPR, but presumably less so than the direct commitment of Chinese ground forces and would be much less objectionable to Hanoi, which would be reluctant to invite Chinese ground forces in except under the most extreme circumstances.

Under what conditions, if at all, might Chinese intervention on the ground occur? American invasion of the CPR need not be considered as a practical possibility. American air attacks against Chinese bases that were being used by aircraft engaged in the air war over North Vietnam would probably not produce a Chinese intervention in Vietnam on the ground unless Peking felt reasonably sure that the United States would not escalate further in retaliation. The pertinent considerations are not only those of felt need and risk but of feasibility. The logistics of a Chinese ground intervention in Vietnam would be horrendous, far worse than was the case in Korea, and furthermore Southwest China has been one of the least responsive regions in the country to Peking's direction during the Great Proletarian Cultural Revolution. The Korean analogy, which if imperfect is at least suggestive, would indicate that if the United States invaded North Vietnam, presumably at first the area near the 17th parallel, the CPR would send troops into the northern part of the DRV, Hanoi's probable objections notwithstanding, to establish a buffer zone along the Chinese border. It would presumably be hoped that this step would not only deter the United States from further escalation of the conflict but also help to invigorate the revolutionary struggle in South Vietnam. Under these assumptions, the Chinese troops, whether called "volunteers" or not, would actually fight on a large scale only if the United States insisted on denying the CPR its buffer and advanced close to the Chinese border.

In the absence of such direct Chinese intervention, which would obviously create "an entirely new war" as it did in Korea, and barring an American withdrawal, it appears probable that the struggle must go on until Hanoi becomes convinced that it cannot win and that it need not fear coercion by Peking. Such a development would probably require a major prior change of leadership in the CPR, and perhaps in the DRV as well.

Comments by David Mozingo

Professor Hinton's paper is a useful summary of the major issues which have confronted Peking in developing a policy toward Vietnam. I find myself in general agreement with many of his specific points and conclusions, notably those which demonstrate that Peking and Hanoi have rather consistently followed different policies toward South Vietnam, including a veiled competition for influence on the National Liberation Front (NLF) and differing attitudes toward Soviet involvement in the Vietnam conflict. In the space of a few pages, it is impossible to take up all the themes developed in this paper, and therefore the present comments will be confined to discussing only certain general features of Hinton's analysis.

The principal difficulty I have with Hinton's study stems from his basic characterization of the Peking-Hanoi relationship. Evidently, China's Vietnam policies are to be understood, essentially, as a series of opportunistic maneuvers designed to manipulate the Vietnamese situation in ways which conform to Peking's national and revolutionary interests. According to Hinton, these basic interests are China's security objectives and her desire to direct the advance of Communist movements in Southeast Asia. No one will question the assertion that China's policy must serve, and at the same time adjust, both of these interests. But this does not tell us much, in concrete terms, about the specific aims, content and direction of her policy. Nowhere in Hinton's paper do I find a central thesis or theses concerning Peking's major and specific aims in Vietnam or how she has attempted to reconcile the frequently conflicting demands of her national and ideological interests. For example, in Hinton's view, the Chinese have regarded North Vietnam as being able "to contribute to the expansion of Communism in Southeast Asia, . . ." but he thinks China probably does not want "to see Hanoi's ambition for control over Laos and Cambodia, direct or indirect, realized." The logical conclusion to be drawn from this distinction is that Peking has been prepared to support Hanoi's objectives in South Vietnam, but no further, since he thinks China covets the rest of Southeast Asia as her own "sphere of influence." But Hinton's own subsequent data and analysis clearly reveal that Peking and Hanoi have rather consistently pursued different, often conflicting, policies toward South Vietnam. Therefore, if one of China's basic interests has been to support North Vietnam as a vehicle for the expansion of Communism it becomes necessary to explain why the two powers have often worked at cross-purposes.

Hinton correctly points out that after the 1954 Geneva Conference settlement Peking was not advocating a revolutionary line in South Vietnam. When the insurgency became more fully organized in 1960, with Hanoi's support, she initially felt some reservations about it and in 1961 sharply reduced economic aid to North Vietnam. Obviously, there are important implications to be drawn from these facts but Hinton avoids analyzing them. Instead, he asserts that around 1960 China was more interested in promoting revolutionary prospects in Africa which, in fact, was not a major area of interest to China until 1963–64. It is China's alleged satisfaction with the 1962 Geneva Accords on Laos, so we are told, which rekindled her interest in the Vietnamese revolution. However, since the Accords were at no time really honored by Hanoi, the Pathet Lao or the United States, and since a Laotian coalition government did not materialize, it is difficult to see Laotian developments as somehow freeing Peking to intensify her involvement in Vietnam. Clearly, the more significant developments were that the Vietcong insurgents were becoming an effective revolutionary force and that the United States was enlarging its commitments to Saigon. Hinton is correct in noting that the NLF was sufficiently independent of Hanoi to enable Peking "to conduct a separate diplomacy with each." Surely, this important conclusion suggests a great deal more about Peking's relations with Hanoi and the NLF than a general desire "to maximize its influence on both and if possible to gain their support against the Soviet Union in the Sino-Soviet dispute." If, as Hinton says, "the NLF probably regarded contacts with Peking as a useful way of balancing Hanoi's influence," how was this regarded in Hanoi and what does it suggest about China's aims in dealing separately with North Vietnam and the NLF? Down to 1963, Hinton's own data do not sustain his argument that the People's Republic of China (CPR) supported Hanoi's aspirations to reunify and dominate the country.

Nor do Hinton's data support the vaguely defined contention that after 1963, "the CPR seems to have associated itself with increasing enthusiasm with the cause of Hanoi's and the NLF's armed revolution in South Vietnam." By this time some Chinese weapons were in the Vietcong's possession but, on the other hand, Hinton shows that Peking was reluctant to publicly commit herself to intervene in defense of North Vietnam when the latter was attacked by the United States. Moreover, he demonstrates that as of 1964, Chinese articles on revolutionary strategy strongly emphasized guerrilla warfare at the very time Vietcong units began employing mobile warefare tactics which virtually destroyed the South Vietnamese army. This evidence and Hinton's earlier conclusion that Peking "may have been advising the DRV (Democratic Republic of Vietnam) not to escalate prematurely but to wait until an American withdrawal had been achieved before going over to mobile warfare" suggest that in late 1964 Hanoi and the Vietcong moved to a phase of mobile warfare over the contrary advice of the Chinese. But in describing the American escalation in Vietnam as "a colossal setback for the CPR," Hinton seems to imply that Chinese policy and influence on Hanoi and the Vietcong were in some way directly responsible for this setback. This may not be his view, but since he does not develop the basic conclusion his own data suggest—that Peking probably opposed the decision to move to mobile warfare as dangerous and premature—the reader is, regrettably, obliged to draw his own inferences.

Similarly, the reader is left in doubt as to the conclusions he should draw from Hinton's description of an alleged controversy between the views of Peking's "politicals" and "professionals" which he says resulted from the escalation of the Vietnam conflict after 1965. According to Hinton, the essence of the controversy has been whether the security of North Vietnam should have higher priority than the prosecution of the revolutionary struggle in South Vietnam. The "politicals" want the Southern struggle to go on "regardless of its effect on the North," whereas the "professionals" want to safeguard North Vietnam's security, "regardless of other considerations." This distinction clearly implies that the "professionals" would favor sacrificing the Southern insurgency, including even the abandonment of the guerrilla warfare tactics Peking advocated earlier, if that became necessary to safeguard the North. I find no indication in the articles written by the "professionals" that any group in Peking has suggested, as Hinton implies, that the Southern revolution in general, or guerrilla warfare tactics, might have to be abandoned to safeguard North Vietnam. And since the Chinese were not very successful in getting Hanoi to follow their advice on strategy in the past, what reasons are there to believe that a split in the Chinese Communist Party would develop principally over the issue of whether or not to emphasize the Southern insurgency? There is precious little evidence to show that any Peking leadership could turn the war in the South on or off. On the contrary, the available evidence suggests that China wants the Southern insurgency to continue, though probably with less emphasis than Hanoi and the NLF attach to larger-scale battles with United States forces. Since the most likely form of direct Chinese intervention to safeguard the North would occur probably only in the event of an American invasion of North Vietnam—which Hinton argues the Chinese do not believe will happen—it seems most unlikely that an important "professional" faction has emerged in Peking to champion the cause of defending Hanoi in the event of an unlikely contingency. The essential weakness in Hinton's "professionals" vs. "politicals" drama is that China actually cannot take either of the courses of action he thinks the two factions have been debating. She may be able to influence, but she cannot force Hanoi to abandon or intensify the Southern insurgency; and, short of an unlikely American invasion of the North, to effectively safeguard North Vietnam from the real threat to her security—United States air power—would require a level of strategic power China does not possess.

No doubt the Chinese are divided over certain issues related to Vietnam. But the content of the speeches and articles Hinton has analyzed in terms of a "professionals"-versus-"politicals" split suggests that the internal Chinese debate primarily concerns policy toward the Soviet Union rather than whether to give priority to the struggle in North or South Vietnam. At issue is whether it is necessary to accept some form of temporary "united action" with the Soviet Union on Vietnam or go-it-alone at the cost of alienating Hanoi and possibly facing a future confrontation with the United States, alone. Whereas "politicals" or "professionals" in Peking could agree on the need to emphasize guerrilla warfare in the South, it has evidently been more difficult for them to resolve differences over the Soviet role in the conflict. I would tend to argue that those who oppose "united action" have more concrete objections than Hinton indicates when he says simply that Moscow's involvement is "unacceptable to the CPR on political grounds." Soviet aid which was actually intended to help defeat the United States and "win" the struggle in the South is one thing; Soviet aid in a form which increases Hanoi's dependence on Moscow to the point that the latter might eventually arrange a United States–Soviet "deal," Koreanizing Vietnam, is something else. It seems probable that certain Chinese leaders, possibly those who were never as anti-Soviet as Mao, thought that Kosygin's opposition to United States policy in Vietnam was more genuine than Khrushchev's, and consequently that it was now possible to take some form of "united action." If there was a group of "professionals" in Peking, their argument, presumably, was not that the Southern revolutionaries be abandoned, but that the risk of a possible future Soviet betrayal of "united action" had to be accepted since the alternative course of action was more dangerous.

The preceding comments, if valid, suggest that Hinton's characterization of China's policy toward Vietnam does not satisfactorily answer certain fundamental questions. Having liberally sprinkled criticism, the critic is obliged to develop a general thesis explaining those points which, in his opinion, have been neglected in the analysis.

Since 1954, China has attempted to use her limited influence to create a belt of weak and disunited Southeast Asian states. Ideally, this configuration would have included an independent South Vietnam, the existence of which would have acted to "contain" Communist North Vietnam as a small Chinese dependency. This objective conformed to Peking's general strategy after the Korean War which sought to remove American presence from Asia primarily by political means, and to conciliate the non-aligned Asian states. It was also intended to create the political conditions for local Communist parties to acquire the appeals of nationalism which, as the Maoist revolutionary doctrine insisted, was the indispensable prerequisite a Communist movement must have to capture leadership of a revolution. To further these aims, at the 1954 Geneva Conference China was prepared, together with the Soviet Union, to sacrifice the Vietminh's aspirations to "liberate" South Vietnam. Down to 1963, China hoped that a settlement along the lines of Laos, Cambodia, and Burma could be applied to South Vietnam; that is, a weak, non-aligned Saigon regime, vulnerable over the long-run to an indigenous Southern national Communist movement more vigorous than its non-Communist opponent. Her broader interests in attempting to forge an anti-American coalition with Asian nationalism required that Peking refrain from sponsoring or inciting Communist uprisings in Indochina because that was the surest way to drive the very nations she was wooing directly into the American embrace. In view of Hanoi's consistent policy of steering a middle course between Moscow and Peking, a posture which stemmed from Vietnam's traditional desire to escape Chinese domination, Peking had little reason to encourage Vietnamese reunification. That eventuality could only result in increasing Hanoi's independence from China and, consequently, Ho Chi Minh's ability to pursue policies within the Communist bloc and toward other Southeast Asian states that might further depart from those of Peking. Mao's problem with Ho Chi Minh was similar to the one Stalin had with Tito; he did not want to encourage Hanoi's aspirations for a little "Balkan" sphere of influence on the Indochina peninsula.

But the record is quite clear that the Chinese have not been very successful stage managers of events in Vietnam. The internal policies of the United States–supported Diem regime quickly generated a revolt in South Vietnam composed of Communist and non-Communist elements. Prior to 1959, this revolt did not, in fact, conform to either Peking's or Hanoi's preferred solution; the former wanted a weak, neutral South Vietnam and the latter still hoped for a peaceful reunification of both zones, as envisioned in the 1954 Geneva Conference agreements. Indeed, there is a case to be made that since the outset of the Southern insurgency, the leadership of the NLF, Hanoi, and Peking has each been guided by distinctly different aims and policies. The very fact that Peking and Hanoi subsequently became engaged in veiled competition for influence over the Southern revolution, as Professor Hinton's analysis correctly demonstrates, suggests that the NLF, especially in the earlier stages of the conflict, was not simply a manipulated agent but possessed a degree of autonomy that enabled it to do some manipulating of its own vis-à-vis the Chinese and the North Vietnamese. In the second Indochina war there is much truth in the saying, "the weak lead the strong."

I would further contend that these three Communist actors in the Vietnam drama have been drawn closer together, reluctantly, by the policies of the United States. Beginning in 1955, the United States decided to oppose the emergence of a belt of non-aligned Southeast Asian states governed by regimes that might be friendly to China and, owing to the gross incompetence of their nationalist leaders, potentially vulnerable to both political and revolutionary pressure from their indigenous Communist parties. Such a belt of weak, neutral states was the pattern of development implied in the Geneva Conference settlement and the Bandung Conference—a pattern thoroughly unacceptable to the United States. Thus, from 1955 on, Washington attempted by overt and covert means to facilitate the ascendance to power of elites in South Vietnam and Laos (not to mention Thailand, Indonesia, and Cambodia) who would be staunchly anti-Communist in foreign and domestic policy. It was not until the 1962 Geneva Accords on Laos that the United States formally recognized the failure and dangers of this policy and, all too belatedly, came to appreciate that neutralism might not be such a bad thing.

By this time, unfortunately, the issue raised in South Vietnam had acquired a central importance not only to Saigon and Hanoi, but also to Peking and Washington. The United States was by 1963 deeply committed to the propositions that the Koreanization of Vietnam must be established; that an effective "counterinsurgency" capacity must be developed; and, that American power must demonstrate, if necessary acting alone, that it could create a state, a government and a nationalist following in South Vietnam, despite the inability of an amply armed and financed Saigon regime to accomplish these ends on its own. Peking was equally committed to the proposition that the United States must not be allowed to determine, unilaterally, the question of which elites would hold power in neighboring Southeast Asian countries where China possessed any means to oppose her. By 1963, this issue had become critical to Peking given the growing evidence that the Soviet Union wanted to negotiate certain agreements with the "imperialists" that were contrary to China's interests, and because a chain of American interventions in Southeast Asia after 1955 looked quite threatening to the Chinese. In my opinion, Professor Hinton's paper has not adequately stressed the effects of a long series of American-initiated actions on the policies of the several Communist actors in Vietnam.

The weight of the evidence will not, I believe, sustain the view that Peking was anxious to encourage a unified Vietnam under Hanoi's control. Actually, the record shows that down to 1964, Peking favored a neutral, independent South Vietnam. She rarely commented on reunification with the North, nor did she call for a Communist take-over by means of "people's war." Until late 1964, as Professor Hinton acknowledges, she still supported a negotiated solution arranged by the Geneva Conference powers. Though influenced by Chinese writings and experience, the Vietnamese Communists have developed and applied their own doctrine on revolutionary war. They have not been stage-managed by either Moscow or Peking. If anything, the Vietnamese—North and South—appear to have held their own with the Chinese and the Russians so far as manipulations within the Communist bloc are concerned.

To make a long story short, originally neither Hanoi nor Peking wanted, or saw the need for, a dramatic revolutionary struggle in South Vietnam. But the outbreak of Southern Communist resistance to Diem's suppression, coupled with the policies of the United States, confronted both of them with an unavoidable revolutionary issue. Whereas Hanoi's direct involvement in the Southern insurgency began early (at least by 1959–60), it was not until 1963, after the United States had become deeply committed to Saigon, that the war in Vietnam became a principal concern of Peking. And until large United States forces arrived in the South, China still hoped to salvage the diminishing prospects for some kind of independent, neutral South Vietnam; that is, some settlement short of United States or North Vietnamese domination. The Americanization of the conflict in the South had the effect of drawing Hanoi and Peking together but it has also exposed their differences on the correct strategy to follow in defeating the United States.

Against this background, I draw certain conclusions that depart from those advanced in Hinton's article: (1) Peking did not want to see a unified Vietnam under Hanoi's direction; (2) she would have preferred a South Vietnamese solution modeled on Cambodian or pre-1964 Laotian lines; (3) in the face of American efforts to Koreanize Vietnam, Peking supported the Southern revolt and the NLF's original line of independence and non-alignment; (4) as a result of Hanoi's and Washington's decisions to escalate the conflict, Peking reluctantly came to the direct aid of the NLF and North Vietnam; (5) the insurgency in South Vietnam has been organized and fought along Hanoi's rather than Peking's revolutionary line; (6) as Soviet and American roles in the conflict have become more dominant, China's capacity to influence events has been reduced, while the threat of a confrontation with the United States has become greater.

Notwithstanding the setbacks China has encountered, it does not appear that she is pessimistic about the ultimate outcome of the Vietnam conflict. Hanoi's deep involvement in the war may preclude the prospect of a separate Communist South Vietnam, even if the struggle is won. But there was never much doubt that China preferred Hanoi's hegemony to that of the United States. Even if the United States succeeds in frustrating Hanoi's hopes for reunification, the Chinese are entitled to doubt how successful the Americans will be in creating a South Vietnamese state that will indefinitely refuse to come to terms with Peking.

Comments by George McT. Kahin

I find myself largely in accord with Harold Hinton's paper. However, there are some points which I feel are important enough to warrant comment. I shall confine myself largely to the Vietnamese side of the matters which are discussed, so as to complement David Mozingo's comments on the more specifically Chinese aspects.

It is, I think, appropriate at the outset to register my disagreement with regard to Professor Hinton's introductory premise that "Since early 1965 the tide has begun to run, militarily and to a lesser extent politically, against the Communist side in the Vietnamese crisis." This assumption provides the backdrop for his discussion of both Peking's and Hanoi's reactions to developments in South Vietnam and makes a number of his arguments concerning both Chinese and North Vietnamese policies appear more plausible, in particular his assertions concerning Hanoi's dependence upon China and willingness to submit to Chinese pressure.

It is not simply that in these arguments he gives too little weight to the persisting strength of a traditionally anti-Chinese nationalism in Vietnam, which continues to be acutely sensitive to any intimation of outside efforts to control Vietnam's political destiny. But the actual nature of political and military circumstances in Vietnam is, I submit, considerably more favorable to the National Liberation Front (NLF) than he suggests. (Here, it seems to me that Mr. Hinton has all too unquestioningly accepted the Administration's assertions at face value.) There has been operative in Vietnam since early 1965 no such adverse military and political tide as to induce the NLF and/or Hanoi to accept the extent of policy subordination to Peking that Mr. Hinton suggests.

This is not the place to dwell in detail on this matter, but I feel that brief comments on a few key aspects of the situation will suggest that Mr. Hinton's operative premise may not be correct. A capacity to mass and project superior American firepower in ways that are usually successful against major concentrations of Vietcong and North Vietnamese

232

troops does not add up to a military tide against the Vietcong. Application of this power appears usually to oblige their forces to pull back and often to divide up into smaller military groupings. But the subsequent operations against these smaller units have entailed an appreciably higher United States casualty rate. For this massed, superior firepower is often a clumsy and ineffective instrument when applied against a widely dispersed enemy that resorts to intense guerrilla activity in a situation where it is much more difficult to differentiate Vietcong from civilians.[1]

Moreover, it is generally agreed that no matter how militarily successful these "search-and-destroy" operations may be, they cannot have any lasting result unless the South Vietnamese Army's follow-up "clear-and-hold" operations are effective. Agreement is widespread among American officers in the field that the South Vietnamese Army has failed miserably in this role. Although the Vietcong desertion rate is reported to be increasing, its recruiting capacity in the South remains high (well above combined desertion and combat losses), while that of the South Vietnamese Army is insufficient, and its desertion rate continues to be much higher—so high as to cripple many of its fighting units.[2]

American action has undoubtedly halted the course of military victory which the Vietcong appeared to be in the process of consummating in December, 1964. But although the tide is not running militarily in favor of the Vietcong in the sense that it was then, that tide can hardly be said to be running against it. For the forces of the Vietcong are much stronger today than they were two years ago, both in an absolute sense and vis-à-vis Saigon's army. Without the shield provided by the American armed forces, the South Vietnamese Army could be overrun by the Vietcong (irrespective of any northern support) even more rapidly than seemed in prospect at the beginning of 1965. Both the Vietcong and Hanoi know this, and this realization constitutes a political factor of enormous importance, and one which must be weighed against their concern over the magnitude of American support to Saigon.

The same is true with respect to the political tide. The American and Korean "search-and-destroy" operations constitute a major cause for a

[1] Thus in the last months of 1966 and first months of 1967 enemy sniper fire and land mines accounted for approximately 52 per cent of United States Marine casualties in Vietnam.

[2] As of January 1967, when I was in the area of responsibility assigned to the South Vietnamese 25th Division (Long An Province, just to the south of Saigon), its desertion rate was running at more than 1,000 per month.

political deterioration which is as ominous in the long term as in the present. For these operations tear down the structure of rural Vietnamese society infinitely more rapidly than the pacification effort—even according to the most glowing official reports—is building it up. It is not merely that these operations kill and maim many more civilians than they do Vietcong and that whole villages are destroyed and crops ruined, but also that a tremendous and steadily mounting number of refugees are thereby generated. By the end of 1966 this uprooted group amounted to approximately 2 million out of a total rural population of around 12 million.[3] It was generally understood that the mounting of American search-and-destroy operations which got under way at the end of 1966 in the heavily populated delta areas will bring about a rapid acceleration in the growth of this refugee population.[4]

Another important reason why the political tide has in fact continued to run against Saigon was Premier Ky's suppression of the Buddhists and their adherents in the spring of 1966. This resulted in the destruction of a large part of the non-Communist administrative infrastructure in the northern provinces of South Vietnam. Because of this, U.S. Marines have suffered a major handicap in their pacification efforts there. In those areas thus lost to Vietcong control the Marines have won back only a very small part.[5]

Finally, the base of public support for Premier Ky's government remains appallingly slender. It is as true today as it was two years ago when Marshal Ky and General Thieu first took over effective power, that the Saigon government could not possibly stand on its own and would quickly fall were it not for massive American backing. Despite the Administration's efforts to hold up the Constituent Assembly as proof of major progress toward broadening the base of government, that body is much less representative and has proved much more subservient to the military junta than the Administration has indicated.

[3] The extent of this disruption of rural society varies from province to province, and tends to be highest where search-and-destroy activity is heaviest. Thus, in Binh Dinh Province where this action was especially heavy during 1966, the Refugee Office reported a total of over 275,000 refugees out of a population of 784,000 (or 36 per cent) by the end of November, 1966. That office's Director General describes this province as "one great refugee camp."

[4] The director general of the Refugee Office stated that he expected these operations alone would increase the number by at least 400,000.

[5] As of mid-January, 1967, when I visited Quang Nam Province (the principal locus of U.S. Marine activity) only 18 out of 549 hamlets were classified as having been "secured."

It is against factors such as these that one must measure North Vietnamese and Chinese Communist policies, for they are factors of which Peking as well as Hanoi must surely be aware.

In parts of his paper Dr. Hinton, I believe, tends to exaggerate the importance of China in the Vietnamese context. The amount of Chinese arms made available to the Vietminh prior to the end of the Korean War was minor in comparison to those captured from the French and their Vietnamese auxiliaries, and it is misleading to state that the arrival of Chinese Communist power at the northern border of Vietnam "transformed the character of the war then in progress between Ho Chi Minh's Democratic Republic of Vietnam (DRV) and the French." It is quite true that at the battle of Dien Bien Phu in 1954 heavy artillery pieces sent from China (American equipment originally given to Chiang Kai-shek) played a critical role. But it is important to point out that while that particular battle was politically of great importance (especially because it took place during the Geneva negotiations), it was not the military turning point. Well before the French lost that battle, and before the Geneva Conference had even begun, the French position in Tonkin had become so desperate that they had already set in train their evacuation of most of the Red River delta not already taken over by the Vietminh. And in this really critical area—the rice bowl of North Vietnam—the Vietminh victories were won without any critical degree of dependence upon Chinese arms.

In addition, available evidence suggests that the Chinese role in the air defense of North Vietnam is not only minor in comparison with that of Soviet Russia, but that it is largely restricted to defending rail communications, in particular that major North Vietnamese rail line which is important to China in that it links up Yunnan and Kwangsi provinces.

Much more serious than this, I think, is Mr. Hinton's assumption pertaining to China's ability to pressure the Hanoi government: specifically that China has the capacity to bend the will of North Vietnam's leaders so as to insure that they retain a more militant stance than they might elect on their own. It is not merely the intensity of nationalist feeling and traditionally strong anti-Chinese bias in Hanoi that makes it unlikely that its leaders would yield to such pressure. With respect to critically important pragmatic considerations, North Vietnamese needs with regard to heavy military equipment and defenses against American bombardment can and are being met substantially more by Soviet Russia than by China. As Mr. Hinton himself suggests, whatever ideological influence China may have had must have been seriously undermined by the internal schism and political turmoil which has gripped China during the past year.

Let me be more specific. Hinton states that at the end of 1965, "There can be little doubt that the People's Republic of China exerted whatever covert pressures it may have thought were necessary to insure that the views of the 'hawks' in Hanoi prevailed over those of the 'doves,' assuming there to be some." He appears, then, to assume that Peking has the capacity to effect basic changes in the political orientation of Hanoi's leaders, and that it can accomplish this simply by exerting whatever pressures it deems necessary. Available evidence just does not indicate that this would be possible. Indeed, if in their dealings with Hanoi's leaders, the Chinese were politically so gauche as to try to prod the Vietnamese into a policy they did not wish to follow, the effort would almost certainly backfire. The Vietnamese leaders would be unlikely to acquiesce, and their traditional distrust of the Chinese would receive further nourishment.

More perplexing is his speculation that the Chinese might resort to an intervention of "the Hungarian type" in North Vietnam with the purpose of overthrowing any leadership prepared to compromise with the United States. To suggest that considerable military risks and political complications would be involved in such a course of action is clearly an understatement, and it is hard to understand why he persists in offering the hypothesis, one which he says is possible "in spite of the obvious military risks and political costs." First of all, such a course of action would be likely to bring China into a direct confrontation with the United States, involving at least aerial bombardment, something Dr. Hinton has correctly insisted Peking is trying to avoid. Secondly, if Hanoi did indeed show signs of giving up the war in the South the Chinese would surely prefer a settlement that would at least preserve the DRV intact as a friendly buffer on their southern flank. A Hungarian-type intervention by China would almost certainly be politically counterproductive, mortally alienating the North Vietnamese. Consequences adverse to China would not be confined to North Vietnam, and anti-Peking sentiment would grow in both NLF and Saigon-controlled areas of South Vietnam as well as in other areas of Asia.

Donald Zagoria

9

The Strategic Debate
in Peking

Introduction

There have been several views advanced about the issues involved in
the power struggle in Peking. One view, which need not detain us long,
contends that it is a "pure" power struggle as though power were a
disembodied substance without relation to issue. This view seems to me
profoundly unpolitical.

A second view holds that domestic issues are at the forefront of the
struggle and a third that foreign policy, particularly the war in Vietnam, is the key. Within the third school there seem to be three different
groups: one that argues that the hard-liners have emerged on top, a
second that believes the soft-liners have won, and a third that contends
the centrists have been victorious.[1]

The thesis I want to advance is one that is in some respects closest to
Schurmann's view that the "centrists" have won, but which diverges
from his interpretation at several points. First, it seems to me that both
domestic and foreign policy issues have been involved in the struggle.

Second, it is my view that the victorious centrist group has defeated
both a hard-line group among the professional military which wanted
a tougher line on Vietnam and a "rationalist" group within the party
and government which wanted to turn inward and concentrate on
building China's economy rather than expend China's energies in an
ultra-revolutionary line that has proved to be a failure—most recently
in Indonesia. Common to both groups of oppositionists—hard-liners and
soft-liners alike—was a desire for reconciliation with Moscow. It is here
that I differ with Schurmann, who contends that it was only the mod-

[1] For the first, see Victor Zorza, *Look Magazine*, August 24, 1966; for the
second, see Christian Duevel, "China's Yezhovshchina," *Radio Liberty Research Paper*, no. 10 (1966); for the third, see Franz Schurmann, *New York
Review of Books*, October 20, 1966.

erates who wanted such a reconciliation, and with Duevel, who argues that it was only the "hawks" who wanted it. Both the "hawks" and the moderates desired reconciliation with Moscow, but for different reasons.

The hard-liners in the military—led by former Chief of Staff Lo Jui-ch'ing—wanted such a reconciliation because they felt "united action" with Russia was essential both for deterring either American escalation of the war in Vietnam or an attack on China, and for fighting the U.S. if deterrence failed. The professional military has long been the principal interest group in China advocating a strong tie to the Russians, as the *Chieh-fang-chün pao* (Liberation Army Daily) has recently confirmed.[2] From 1953 to 1958, the military wanted to maintain the Russian tie in order to "regularize" and "modernize" the Chinese army, and particularly in order to obtain a nuclear capability. In 1959, it was the Chinese Minister of Defense, Marshal P'eng Te-huai, who sought to prevent the widening split with Moscow and was purged as a result.[3] In 1965, it was Lo Jui-ch'ing, the chief of staff, who advocated a reconciliation with Moscow and was subsequently purged, a point I intend to develop here.

The army's[3a] persistent interest in maintaining close relations with Moscow is not difficult to understand. It has sought such ties for both strategic reasons and because of its interest in obtaining modern weapons. Only the timing of its recent struggle with the party requires some brief explanation at this point. It was the ouster of Khrushchev in October, 1964, and the American escalation of the war to North Vietnam in March, 1965, that together gave some army leaders an opportunity to press their case for reestablishing the Russian connection. Their leaders argued, as I will try to show, that such rapprochement was both possible and necessary. It was possible because the new Soviet leaders were not revisionists like Khrushchev, had shown good will by not resuming open polemics against China, and had offered a program of united action to defend both China and North Vietnam from American attack—a program that promised to bolster the defense of China and to prevent an American victory in Vietnam.[4]

[2] *Peking Review,* August 5, 1966, pp. 8–10.

[3] P'eng has been in disgrace ever since.

[3a] I am aware that the "army" is not a monolith in China any more than it is elsewhere.

[4] According to secret exchanges between Moscow and Peking subsequently revealed by Edward Crankshaw in *The Observer* on November 14, 1965, never

The interest of the Chinese "rationalists" in rapprochement with Moscow stemmed from entirely different perspectives. From charges made against them it can be inferred that they wanted to normalize relations with Russia, to reduce assistance to foreign revolutionaries, which only led to China's isolation and "making enemies everywhere," and to concentrate on industrializing China. One of their slogans, said their accusers, was "construction before destruction."

The accusations against this faction indicate that they put their main stress on domestic issues. They advocated a variety of revisionist measures to pump new life into the economy, including expanding private plots and free markets for the peasantry and using profitability as a criterion for small enterprises. They were also opposed to mass mobilization, to a frenetic pace of economic development, and to radical social and economic experiments such as the ones adopted during the Great Leap in 1959, on the grounds that such frenzy could only impede China's industrialization. Their watchword was economic rationality—a policy that could best be promoted by a moderate foreign policy.

This group, in short, was evidently prepared to make considerable concessions to both foreign and domestic class enemies for the sake of industrialization. While the professional military saw reconciliation with Moscow as a necessary prelude to tougher measures against the Americans, this rationalist group saw it as a means to more leisurely industrialization.

In both cases, evidently, the oppositionists were prepared to make substantial concessions to Moscow. They were prepared, among other things, to give up the challenge to Soviet hegemony in the international Communist movement, to stop open polemics against Moscow, and to refrain from undermining Soviet authority in the Third World.

---

denied by either party, and publicized by several European Communist parties, the Russians in mid-1965 asked Peking to grant them an air corridor and the use of air fields in southern China to help Hanoi. Peking reportedly rejected the proposal. (See *L'Humanité,* November 16, 1965, *L'Unità,* November 17, 1965, and *Neues Deutschland* editorial November 20, 1965, cited in Kevin Devlin, "Which Side Are You On?" in *Problems of Communism,* January–February, 1967.) Several times in 1965 and 1966, Moscow also called for summit meetings and international committees to help coordinate aid to Vietnam, but Peking rejected them all. (See, for example, *Trybuna Ludu* editorial of December 3, 1965, which reveals that one united action proposal rejected by Peking advocated a meeting of party and government leaders of the Communist states.) The Chinese even rejected a compromise proposal for united action that was sponsored by the Japanese Communists and the North Koreans, with the apparent approval of North Vietnam itself.

The victorious Maoist faction, led by Mao, Lin Piao, and Chou En-lai, can best be viewed as anti-Soviet above all else. It regards the Russians and Russian revisionism as an even greater enemy in some respects than the Americans. It rejected the army's demand for a hard-line policy on Vietnam both because it would have greatly increased risks of war with the United States and because it would have meant reconciliation with Russia on Russia's terms. This faction believed that the struggle with revisionism both at home and abroad should take priority over everything else, including both the war in Vietnam and the struggle against the United States.

As far as Vietnam is concerned, this now dominant Maoist faction has rejected Moscow's persistent offers of "united action." It discredits all offers of Soviet aid to North Vietnam as a trick designed to establish Soviet influence in Hanoi in order to pave the way for a sellout to the Americans. Moreover, it has rejected an effort made by the Japanese Communists, with the approval of North Korea and North Vietnam, to arrange a compromise solution on the details of "united action" in order to present a united Communist front on Vietnam—an intransigent posture that has greatly strained Peking's relations with all Asian Communists, including the North Vietnamese.

As far as the United States is concerned, this Maoist faction continues to regard "American imperialism" as its main enemy, but it increasingly sees the Soviet Union as a Trojan horse within international Communist ranks whose revisionist virus must first be rooted out if United States imperialism is eventually to be defeated. Otherwise revisionism, which has already led to a "restoration of capitalism" in Russia and has seriously infected the Chinese party, will spread.

Unlike the military "hawks," this Maoist faction rejects any actions in Vietnam that will increase the risks of war with the United States. It has, for example, specifically indicated that it will fight only if the United States attacks China first. It has also advised North Vietnam and the Vietcong—since the massive American intervention began—to prepare for a long war of attrition in which substantial help from other Communist states, including China, should not be expected, and in which the Vietcong should assume the defensive until the balance of forces changes in the future. But unlike the moderates, this Maoist faction rejects compromise in Vietnam. It warns North Vietnam against negotiations. Believing as it does that China must dig in for a long Cold War with both Russia and the United States—that might at some point lead to a hot war—this faction urges ideological preparation for protracted struggle on two fronts. This seems to be one of the purposes of the Great Proletarian Cultural Revolution.

That the victorious Maoist faction in Peking is anti-Soviet as well as anti-American has been the cause of considerable concern to the Russians. After a two-year hiatus in their polemics against Peking, the Rusians resumed their attacks on China beginning in October, 1966. This followed the August 1966 Chinese party plenum when the pro-Soviet factions in China were routed. The Russians' recent actions indicate they are digging in and preparing for long struggle with China.

Moscow is particularly alarmed at the possibility of improved Sino-American relations in the context of deteriorating Sino-Soviet relations. Moscow is concerned that the United States might seek to fish in troubled waters by opening up relations with China and thus facilitate China's ability to concentrate its fire on its Russian flanks. I want to examine the implications of this development after first presenting the evidence to support the interpretations that I have just sketched. Let me turn first to the views of the military "hawks."

The Military "Hawks"—Demand for Rapprochement with Russia and Hard Line on Vietnam

The struggle between the professional military "hawks" and the Maoists over what to do about Vietnam reached its peak sometime between February, 1965, when the Americans began bombing North Vietnam, and November, 1965, when Lo Jui-ch'ing, at that time still chief of staff, was last seen in public. The scope and intensity of this struggle were suggested by the army newspaper, *Chieh-fang-chün pao,* when it observed in August, 1966,[5] that there had been since 1949 "three big struggles against representatives of the bourgeois military line who wormed their way into the Party and the Army." The third "big struggle," the editorial said, "took place not long ago." Exposed in this struggle were representatives of the bourgeoisie who had "usurped important posts in the army." Lo Jui-ch'ing was not mentioned by name, but since he has been purged as chief of staff, along with other high-ranking army officers, he doubtless is one of the usurpers.

The best outline of Lo Jui-ch'ing's views is provided in an article he wrote in May, 1965, soon after the American bombing of North Vietnam began and half a year before he disappeared from public notice in November, 1965. Lo's views were advanced in the esoteric form used

[5] *Peking Review,* August 5, 1966, pp. 8–10.

by Communists to engage in polemical discussion with their comrades; but their meaning is clear enough.

Lo's article ostensibly concerned the lessons that might be drawn from World War II on the 20th anniversary of its conclusion. As is well known by students of current Communist politics, however, such articles are not written for the sake of history; they almost always have contemporary relevance. The political relevance of Lo's article on this occasion is brought out by another article written for the same occasion by the editorial staff of the party paper, *Jen-min jih-pao* (People's Daily). The two articles appeared side by side in *Peking Review*. The differences between them are thus all the more striking.[6]

By a variety of devices, Lo called for unity with Russia and a hard line on Vietnam. Using the Munich analogy, he inveighed against appeasement. *Jen-min jih-pao,* on the other hand, rejected unity with the Soviet Union, took a softer line on Vietnam, and expressed less fear of the dangers of appeasement.

The difference is evident in a number of ways. First, it is apparent on a quantitative level. While *Jen-min jih-pao* put even emphasis on the alleged perfidious role of both United States imperialism and Soviet revisionism, Lo placed much greater stress on the evils of the former. Approximately 21 paragraphs in Lo's article warned about the dangers of United States imperialism, while only about three denounced modern revisionism. In *Jen-min jih-pao,* the emphasis by paragraph was about 14–12. Similarly, in *Jen-min jih-pao* there were 27 specific references to "Khrushchev revisionism" or "Khrushchev's successors," as opposed to 33 references to United States imperialism. In Lo's article, there were only four specific references to Khrushchev revisionism and 41 to United States imperialism.

Substantively, too, the entire thrust of Lo's article was a call for rapprochement with Russia aimed at deterring both an American attack on China and United States escalation of the Vietnam War. *Jen-min jih-pao,* however, argued that such a rapprochement was neither possible nor necessary. The difference in emphasis between the two articles is so great that it could not conceivably be accidental.

On the Need for and Possibility of Rapprochement with Russia

1. While Lo warned that the actions of the modern revisionists helped United States imperialism and that China must relentlessly oppose such actions, he did not specifically condemn the principle of

[6] *Peking Review,* May 14, 1965, pp. 7–15, 15–22.

"united action," which *Jen-min jih-pao* called a "swindle" designed to realize Soviet-American world hegemony.

2. Lo specifically argued that a vitally important factor in the World War II victory was the rallying of a "united front with the Soviet Union and the world proletariat as its main force." The clear implication is that victory in the next world war—if it comes—will also require a united front. *Jen-min jih-pao*, on the other hand, stressed the tremendous vitality of the socialist system and Stalin's wise leadership as the main factors in Russia's ability to defeat Hitler. It implied that China's social system and Mao's leadership can do the same for China if a Sino-American war develops.

3. Lo consistently avoided use of the phrase "Khrushchev's successors" in the few attacks he made on Soviet policy. He criticized only "modern revisionists such as Khrushchev," thus leaving open the possibility that not all present Soviet leaders are revisionists. *Jen-min jih-pao*, on the other hand, at several points lumped "Khrushchev's successors" together with Khrushchev. While they are "more cunning," said the party paper, they cling to Khrushchev's revisionist line.

4. Both Lo and *Jen-min jih-pao* made many favorable references to Stalin, but they utilized the Stalin symbol for quite different purposes. If one substitutes "Mao" for Stalin, the significance of these differences becomes apparent. Lo said that one of Stalin's major contributions was that he "correctly" analyzed the then current situation, identified the principal contradictions in the world arena and was "therefore able to advance the correct slogan of an anti-fascist united front . . . with the Soviet Union and the world proletariat as its main force." In short, if Mao could only correctly analyze the present world situation, he would recognize the need for a united front with Moscow. *Jen-min jih-pao*, on the other hand, used Stalin to demonstrate that his infallible leadership before and after the outbreak of war made possible the Russian victory. Moreover, said *Jen-min jih-pao*, it was only the revisionists who sought to besmirch Stalin's great deeds by arguing, as did Khrushchev, that he "was not a great commander but an 'idiot.'" Only the revisionists tried to belittle or obliterate Stalin's role in the war. The implication seems clear that anyone in China today who doubts Mao's rejection of a united front policy is a revisionist like Khrushchev.

5. Lo came close to saying that a United States attack on China could be deterred only by Chinese rapprochement with Moscow, while *Jen-min jih-pao* pointed to a variety of other factors deterring the Americans. Thus, Lo said that United States plans for war and aggression could be frustrated, "provided that we are good at uniting the socialist

camp and the people's anti-imperialist forces in all countries as well as at making use of the contradictions within the imperialist camp." [Note the sequence.] *Jen-min jih-pao,* on the other hand, concluded that the United States "is in a much worse strategic position than was Hitler in his day" and that "it is much more difficult for the U.S. to unleash a world war." It emphasized the struggle of the "revolutionary peoples and the peace-loving countries" as the main deterrent forces and said nothing about the need for uniting the socialist camp except to argue that such unity is impossible so long as the Soviet Union continues to align itself with United States imperialism.

On the Proper Policy in Vietnam

Both Lo and *Jen-min jih-pao* warned against pinning hopes for peace on negotiations and agreements which the imperialists may tear up at any time. But Lo gave much greater weight to this lesson than did *Jen-min jih-pao.* He warned that firm opposition to any "Munich policy" is one of the principal lessons (he lists seven) of the Anti-Fascist War, and he devoted five paragraphs to pinpointing the dangers of appeasement, of cherishing illusions about pledges or "fine words," of pinning hopes for preventing war by signing treaties and agreements, etc. Moreover, he warned of this danger not in the context of an attack on revisionism but in that of "our dealings with the imperialists and reactionaries." *Jen-min jih-pao,* on the other hand, did not consider the danger of appeasement as one of the four principal lessons it drew from reviewing the experience of the Anti-Fascist War. It mentioned in passing the danger of trying to prevent war by relying excessively on negotiations, but it quickly pointed out that only the Khrushchev revisionists might succumb to this dangerous policy. Lo, in short, was evidently warning that not only the Russians but certain leaders in China and North Vietnam as well might commit the error of appeasing the imperialists. His warning against appeasement was probably directed against those Chinese, North Vietnamese, and Russian leaders who were then thinking about the possibility of negotiating a Laos-type solution of the Vietnam war at a new Geneva conference. It seems probable that some of the Chinese "rationalists"—like the Russians—were then endorsing a Lao-type settlement in Vietnam. (For the Soviet position, see my book, *Vietnam Triangle* [New York: Pegasus, 1968].)

Lo was probably also warning against any Chinese steps away from a confrontation with the United States over Vietnam. It is interesting in this respect to note that Lo specifically promised that "we will go on supporting and aiding the Vietnamese people, whether or not U.S.

imperialism bombs our country and whether or not it enlarges the war." *Jen-min jih-pao,* on the other hand, made only the very general statement that "it is the bounden (sic) international duty of all revolutionary forces . . . to support and aid the Vietnamese people in their struggle." Lo also promised to help the Vietnamese people "materially to the limit of our capabilities" and to "send our men to fight. . . ." *Jen-min jih-pao* said relatively little about what China was prepared to do to help the Vietnamese people but spoke of what "all revolutionary forces" throughout the world could do to help. This was later to be one of the principal themes in Marshal Lin Piao's famous speech of September, 1965, a speech that—as I shall try to show—was intended as the response of the Mao–Lin Piao group to the "hawk" challenge posed by Lo Jui-ch'ing and his allies.

On Preparations for a War with the United States

Lo's image of a future war with the United States was quite different from that of *Jen-min jih-pao.* Lo devoted one entire section to "active defense" as "the only correct strategy for socialist countries in fighting against imperialist wars of aggression." This means "strategic pursuit to destroy the enemy, . . . energetically wiping out the enemy's effectives, . . . defending cities and other places, . . . actively supporting the anti-fascist armed uprisings of the peoples of other . . . countries, . . . close cooperation among the different armed services, of which the ground forces, and particularly the infantry, are primary." This, he said, was the historical lesson of World War II.

Jen-min jih-pao, on the other hand, argued that World War II was won by means of a "people's war." "It was the people and not the fascists with their military superiority who proved really powerful." Elsewhere it wrote: "Given correct leadership in accordance with a correct line, the people will gradually grow stronger and become powerful in struggle, gradually change the balance of forces, and in the end they will defeat the fascist aggressors. The just people's war is bound to triumph." In short, while Lo was urging preparations for repelling an American attack by a variety of conventional means, *Jen-min jih-pao* was stressing the efficacy of guerrilla warfare.

Maoist Response to the Hawks

Although the regime decided against a rapprochement with Moscow the question was still alive in June. This is made clear by a broadside against revisionism fired in mid-month by the Chinese leadership which argued against any compromise with Moscow.[7] Significantly, the article was entitled "Carry the Struggle against Khrushchev Revisionism through to the End." Lo Jui-ch'ing's article in May had been subtitled "Carry the Struggle against U.S. Imperialism through to the End." There could be no better symbolic indication of the differences in the two viewpoints. The army leaders saw the United States as the main enemy, against whom it was necessary to unite with Russia, while the Maoist group in the party saw Russia as the main enemy.

To combat further Lo's views, the party warned against being "taken in" by Russia's "honeyed words." "The question confronting the Chinese Communists today," the article said, "is whether to carry the struggle against Khrushchev revisionism through to the end or whether to stop halfway." It went on to say how "of late, the new leaders of CPSU have been loud in chanting honeyed words such as 'unity.'" Marxist-Leninists, however, must not be taken in by such words. "In our struggle against the revisionists, we must be able to deal both with their tough and with their soft tactics, we must dare to resist all their pressure and must refuse to be *misled by any of their fine words.*" [Italics are the author's.] Continuing in this defensive tone, the article asserted that flexibility was important; but "it would be wrong to exercise unprincipled flexibility, to create ambiguity and confusion on questions of principle on the pretext of flexibility." To "abandon our principled stand and accommodate ourselves or yield to the Khrushchev revisionists" would be a "grave historical mistake." Clearly, some Chinese leaders were urging greater "flexibility" in dealing with the Russians.

Further evidence to support this interpretation can be found in a joint article by the editorial departments of *Jen-min jih-pao* and *Hung-ch'i* (Red Flag) which appeared in mid-November, 1965, or about the time when Lo was last seen in public.[8] The entire article was devoted to defense of an uncompromising stand against Moscow. First, it argued that there could be no "solid unity" without struggle against revisionism. It denied that China, by struggling against revisionism, was destroying unity—as some had apparently charged. Mao was merely seeking unity on a higher plane—without the Russians. Second, the article sought to demolish the idea, apparently held by some, that the Rus-

[7] *Peking Review,* June 18, 1965, pp. 5–10.

[8] See "Refutation of the New Leaders of the CPSU on 'United Action,'" *Peking Review,* November 12, 1965.

sians were in fact sincere in their offers of united action in Vietnam. It went into considerable detail to argue that the Russians were merely using "united action" slogans to increase their influence in Hanoi and thus to help the United States find a way out of Vietnam and to regain their influence generally in the international Communist movement. Third, the article explained in considerable detail why it was impossible to stop open polemics. It was necessary to carry the debate "to the finish," first because "the more the polemics, the higher the level of revolutionary consciousness." But the most important reason was that if China stopped open polemics or equivocated in the struggle with Moscow, this would be tantamount to giving up the long-standing efforts to establish a new coalition of anti-Soviet but "pure"—i.e., pro-Chinese—Communist parties throughout the world. As the article put it, adoption of a middle course would mean that the Chinese party would no longer be free to support or to rebuild genuine revolutionary forces throughout the world, in effect to challenge Soviet hegemony in the revolutionary world. The article went on to reject the view—clearly held by some—that limited forms of united action might be taken against the imperialists in Vietnam and elsewhere. (After all, the Chinese party often cooperated for limited purposes with bourgeois nationalists whose ideological perspectives it does not share. Why then could it not cooperate for limited purposes with Moscow?)

> Some people ask, why is it that the Marxist-Leninists and the revolutionary people cannot take united action with the new leaders of the CPSU, yet can unite with personages from the upper strata in the nationalist countries, and strive for united action with them in the anti-imperialist struggle, and can even exploit the contradictions among the imperialist countries in the struggle against the U.S.?[9]

The Maoists answered that the main criterion for deciding whether it was possible to engage in united action with others was whether they opposed United States imperialism and Russia flunked the test.

Russia, said the party paper, continued to make "deals" with the United States on nuclear proliferation, to aid the Indian reactionaries, and to use the United Nations as a "stock exchange" to dominate the world with the United States. In short, it was possible from time to time and "in varying degrees" to unite with Morocco, the UAR, or France, in order to weaken the United States, but it was never possible to unite

9 *Ibid.*

with the Russians. Doubtless many Chinese oppositionists found the argument wanting. While it is true that Moscow and Washington share some overlapping interests, it is also true Mao has consistently overstated the degree and purposes of cooperation between Russia and the United States for his own polemical purposes. The argument prevailed nonetheless.

With the danger of a Sino-American confrontation over Vietnam growing daily in the summer and fall of 1965, it was increasingly clear that powerful groups within the professional military were calling not only for a rapprochement with the Soviet Union but also for reducing party control within the army.

The extent of party control in the Chinese army had been a chronic problem since the Communist take-over. But with the growing danger of war and differences of view over how best to meet the American threat, the problem became more acute than ever.

On August 1, the 38th anniversary of the founding of the People's Liberation Army (PLA), Ho Lung, a marshal before the abolition of ranks, took as his theme the "democratic tradition of the Chinese People's Liberation Army." What Ho Lung meant by "democracy" was the subordination of military professionalism to party leadership. He suggested this when he said:

> ... The army's history over the decades proves that whenever any unit undermined or weakened the Party committee system, it inevitably developed a trend of warlordism characterized by individual arbitrariness and undermined ... the Party's leadership over the army....[10]

Ho pointedly warned against the danger of "left opportunism"—the call for abolition of the party committee system in the army. Moreover, he insisted, "democracy" was "entirely feasible under conditions of modern equipment and modern war." It was not true, as those with "bourgeois views on military affairs" insisted, that in conditions of modern warfare "only those commanders and technical experts who had undergone strict professional training were to be depended on."

Throughout the late summer and early fall of 1965, Washington and Peking were exchanging ominous threats. Washington was intent on warning Peking that if the war in Vietnam turned into another Korean-type situation, China would be attacked and there would be no sanctu-

[10] *Peking Review*, August 6, 1965, pp. 6–16.

ary. Peking, for its part, was trying to convince Washington that it would not be intimidated by such threats. Thus, on August 7, 1965, a Chinese Government statement said:

> We, the 650 million Chinese people, have repeatedly pledged to the Vietnamese people our all-out support and assistance, up to and including the sending, according to their need, of our men to fight shoulder to shoulder with them to drive out the U.S. aggressors. We warn the U.S. aggressors once more: We Chinese people mean what we say![11]

A week earlier, Lo Jui-ch'ing specifically referred to United States warnings that it would permit no sanctuary this time, as it had in Korea, and said the United States was mistaken if it misjudged the strength and determination of the Chinese. On the next to the last public appearance he made before he was purged, he warned that if the United States imposed a war on China, the PLA "would not only take them on till the very end but would invite them to come in large numbers. And the more the better. . . ."[12] He also warned threateningly that "in the past year, too, we have successfully mastered the material [as opposed to the spiritual] atom bomb which we did not possess in the past."

It was in this context—a debate among the top leaders within China as to how best to meet an American attack on China if it came, and how hard a line to pursue on Vietnam—that the famous article by Lin Piao appeared on September 3, 1965. There are two popular interpretations of this article. The first is that the article was mere Fourth of July rhetoric.[13] The second is that the article was intended to serve notice on the West of China's expanionist ambitions and can therefore be reasonably compared with Hitler's *Mein Kampf.*[14]

Let us briefly examine the first explanation. It has long been apparent to students of contemporary Communist affairs that major pronouncements by Communist leaders provide important clues to the outlook and assumptions of those leaders as well as to political differences

[11] *Peking Review,* August 13, 1965, p. 8.

[12] *Peking Review,* August 6, 1965, p. 5.

[13] See, for example, the testimony of Professor John K. Fairbank, to the Senate Foreign Relations Committee, March 10, 1966 (*U.S. Policy with Respect to Mainland China,* pp. 97–178).

[14] Such a view has been stated on several occasions by Secretary of State Dean Rusk.

within the leadership. Evidence to support this belief comes from numerous ex-Communists. It is also supported by many scholars of Communist politics who, by using the speeches and documents of Communist leaders, have been able to suggest interpretations that later were validated. To regard Lin Piao's article—and articles by other Chinese leaders of his stature—as mere rhetoric, is moreover, to ignore why the "rhetoric" changes over time, why it often is a matter of dispute between top leaders, and why Communist leaders are often accused of having violated the current "rhetorical" line.

Statements such as Lin Piao's, in fact, provide the very stuff of politics in any Communist state. To dismiss such statements is to deprive oneself of one of the few means available to us for studying contemporary politics in Communist China and to reduce all explanations of political phenomena to "deep" historical and cultural factors. While such historical and cultural factors are unquestionably necessary to a full understanding of politics in contemporary China, they are by themselves inadequate to explain specific political developments, as Benjamin Schwartz has so well brought out.[15]

The second explanation, which equates Lin Piao's statement with *Mein Kampf*, is misleading for several reasons. First, Lin Piao's article was in many respects a rehash of what Chinese Communist leaders have been saying on and off since 1949.The analogy with *Mein Kampf* comes, therefore, a little late, to say the least. Secondly, such an analogy is misleading because it equates Maoist and Nazi ideology in such a way as to evoke the specter of overt Chinese Communist military and territorial expansion in Asia. While few students of contemporary China would deny that Communist China is a dissatisfied and expansionist power, equally few would assert that China regards direct military expansion as a major instrumentality of its foreign policy. Neither in the Lin Piao statement nor in the multitude of similar statements made in the past is there any suggestion of Chinese Communist intentions to engage in direct, military expansion. Nor, with the possible exception of its invasion of Tibet, has China been guilty of military expansion in the past 15 years. The attack on India in 1962 was made for limited political objectives in disputed territory. Shelling of the offshore islands was aimed at forcing Nationalist withdrawal from them. The Chinese

[15] See the excellent article by Professor Benjamin Schwartz on the inadequacy of "deep" cultural and historical explanations of the Sino-Soviet dispute in "Communist China and the Soviet Bloc" in *The Annals of the American Academy of Political and Social Science,* September, 1963, pp. 38–49.

have never made any serious attempt to invade the islands—much less to move against Taiwan, mindful that such action would lead to confrontation with the United States. The intervention in Korea was defensive. China intervened only reluctantly after General MacArthur crossed the 38th parallel and moved toward her Manchurian border. Indeed, any careful study of Chinese foreign policy during the past 15 years would have to conclude that China's main concern has been defensive.[16]

Third, the equation with *Mein Kampf* ignores one of the key messages in Lin Piao's article and one of the basic principles of "liberation wars"—that Communist revolutionaries throughout the world must make their revolutions on their own. Far from giving notice of any intention to intervene aggressively in Vietnam or in other "people's wars," Lin Piao was rationalizing Peking's unwillingness to intervene directly and massively in such wars. He was reiterating what is essentially a "do-it-yourself" model of revolution for foreign Communists. Lin Piao's article was—far from a sign of Chinese belligerence—an answer to the military "hawks" like Lo Jui-ch'ing, who were clamoring for a tough line on Vietnam.

There are two more plausible and not incompatible interpretations of Lin Piao's article. The first, initially suggested by David Mozingo and T. Robinson, argues that Lin Piao was addressing Hanoi and the Vietcong.[17] The second interpretation is that he was reporting the position of the "professional" military on how to defend China against a possible American invasion.

According to the Mozingo-Robinson interpretation, Lin Piao was urging on Hanoi and the Vietcong a strategic retreat in the face of the massive introduction of American troops and firepower in mid-1965, which had completely changed the military and political situation in Vietnam. This American intervention may well have given rise to two extreme points of view in North Vietnam, defeatism on the one hand and pressures for a quick victory on the other. These two extremes were in fact specifically condemned by Lin Piao under the labels of "defeatism" and "blind optimism." In response to such pressures, the Chinese may have been arguing that the Vietcong should prepare for a

[16] See Harold Hinton, *Communist China in World Politics* (New York: Houghton Mifflin, 1966).

[17] See their RAND analysis, Lin Piao on "People's War," "China Takes a Second Look at Vietnam" (RM–4814–PR, November, 1965, Rand Corporation, Santa Monica, California).

protracted struggle and for shifting to the defensive. This meant avoiding regular warfare with the better-armed American units, consolidating their political grip on the base areas in the countryside, and seeking to build a broad anti-American united front to include the Buddhists, the various sects, and such other groups and strata as could be won over. Such a strategy of temporary retreat and digging in for protracted war would be the only alternative for the Vietcong to costly military setbacks at the hands of the larger and better-equipped American forces.

There are a number of points in the article to substantiate such an interpretation. First, there is the obvious parallel between the situation then confronting the Vietcong and the situation which Lin Piao was discussing—the dilemma of the Chinese Communists in 1937, in the face of the Japanese invasion of a China rent by civil war. Much of Lin's article is an effort to show—by using the war against Japan as an example—"how it was possible for a weak country finally to defeat a strong country" and how it was possible "for a seemingly weak army to become the main force of the war." Second, Lin Piao expends much effort explaining how the Chinese Communist party "made a series of adjustments in its policies" after the Japanese invasion to unite all anti-Japanese parties and groups, including the Kuomintang (KMT). Many of these "adjustments" are relevant for the Vietcong: e.g., conciliating the rural rich and making political concessions to non-Communists in Communist-held base areas.

Third, there is a clear warning that "people's wars" should be carried out primarily by the efforts of the indigenous guerrillas without reliance on foreign assistance—even from countries which "persist in revolution," i.e., China.

Fourth, Lin Piao places very heavy emphasis on the virtues of guerrilla as opposed to conventional or mobile warfare in a situation where the enemy is still stronger than the insurgents. Thus he says:

> . . . [Mao] raised guerrilla warfare to the level of strategy because, if they are to defeat a formidable enemy, revolutionary armed forces should not fight with reckless disregard for the consequences when there is a great disparity between their own strength and the enemy's. If they do, they will suffer serious losses and bring heavy setbacks to the revolution. Guerrilla warfare is the *only way* to mobilize and apply the whole strength of the people against the enemy, the only way to expand our forces in the course of the war, deplete and weaken the enemy, gradually

> change the balance of forces between the enemy and ourselves, switch from guerrilla to mobile warfare, and finally defeat the enemy. [Italics are the author's.]

It is true that Lin Piao by no means ruled out mobile, or conventional, warfare. "Guerrilla warfare is basic, but lose no chance for mobile warfare under favorable conditions." Lin's major stress, however, was on guerrilla warfare as the main tactic during the initial stages of the war. Mobile warfare should be relied upon only at a later stage of the war, *after* the balance of forces has changed in favor of the insurgents and the cities are ripe for storming.

> In the later period of the war of resistance against Japan and during the third revolutionary civil war [i.e., 1945–49], we switched our strategy from that of guerrilla warfare as the primary form of fighting to that of mobile warfare in the light of the changes in the balance of forces between the enemy and ourselves. By the middle, and especially the later period of the third revolutionary civil war, our operations had developed into large-scale mobile warfare, including the storming of the cities.

Lin thus seemed to be recalling to the Vietcong the experience of the Chinese Communists in their victory over Chiang Kai-shek between 1945 and 1949. It was only in 1948, at a time when the Chinese Communists had forced the KMT forces to retreat into the cities from the countryside, and when large-scale unit defections from the KMT army had begun, that the Chinese Communists began to launch frontal, conventional attacks on the cities. Only at that time did they consider the balance of forces to have changed sufficiently in their favor to risk such attacks. The implication for the Vietnamese seemed clear: at a time when American ground troops were arriving in South Vietnam in large numbers to help defend the cities and to attack Vietcong base areas, the balance of forces was hardly propitious for a Vietcong offensive.

Moreover, argued Lin Piao, whether fighting guerrilla or mobile warfare, the guiding principle should be to take whatever action is best suited to waging "battles of annihilation."

> A battle in which the enemy is routed is not basically decisive in a contest with a foe of great strength. A battle of annihilation, on the other hand, produces a great and immediate impact on any enemy. Injuring all of a man's 10 fingers is not as effective as chopping off one, and routing ten enemy divisions is not as effective as annihilating one of them.

In order to annihilate the enemy, it was necessary "in every battle" to concentrate an absolutely superior force (two, three, four, and sometimes five or six times the enemy's strength); to avoid battles of attrition; to concentrate first on dispersed or isolated enemy forces and only later on strong enemy troops, to fight no battle "we are not sure of winning." Moreover, it was advisable to give up certain indefensible positions: "We are firmly against dividing up our forces to defend all positions and putting up resistance at every place for fear that our territory might be lost . . ."—a suggestion perhaps that the Vietcong should not try to defend the heavily populated Delta but retreat to the more difficult terrain of the Central Highlands.

Fifth, and perhaps most important, Lin said that successful revolutionaries had to be adept at assessing the balance of forces properly and careful not to yield either to defeatism or blind optimism. Pursuing the example of the Chinese war against Japan, Lin Piao said:

> The defeatists came forward with the assertion that China was no match for Japan and that the nation was bound to be subjugated. The blind optimists came forward with the assertion that China could win very quickly, without much effort.

While advising against negotiations—presumably favored by the defeatists—Lin was also advising against continuing on the offensive in light of the massive American intervention. His advice to Hanoi evidently was to retreat to the strategic defensive, concentrate on guerrilla warfare and united front tactics, and avoid any premature actions that could spell disaster. Thus he repeatedly attacked "left-wing opportunist" views during China's own civil war. These leftists thought they could win the war quickly by attacking the cities; they moved too quickly to mobile warfare; they neglected painstaking work among the peasants; they failed to build rural revolutionary base areas; they neglected united front tactics—they thus courted disaster.[18]

In sum, then, there were a number of points in Lin Piao's article that were pertinent to the situation facing the North Vietnamese and Vietcong forces in late 1965—particularly the crucial question of what to do in the face of a vastly superior enemy—whether to negotiate, continue to take the military offensive, or dig in for a long, hard war by retreating back to the strategic defensive and concentrating on guerrilla warfare. Lin seemed to be advocating the last course of action that—if adopted—would serve two important Chinese strategic goals: First, it would reduce the dangers of escalation that might eventually result in

[18] For full text of Lin Piao, see *Peking Review,* September 3, 1965.

an American attack on China; second, it would tie down United States forces in Vietnam indefinitely in a long war of attrition with minimum Chinese involvement and risk.

Lin's Audience in Hanoi

Perhaps the best indication that Hanoi and the Vietcong were among the audiences Lin Piao addressed himself to is the fact that Hanoi subsequently criticized him in indirect but unmistakable fashion. There is no indication that Hanoi's newspapers or journals ever republished the text or even portions of Lin Piao's programmatic analysis or that North Vietnamese leaders even referred to it in passing. By contrast, there has been persistent reference to General Giap's writings on guerrilla warfare and to North Vietnam's own rich revolutionary experience against the Japanese and French. For a document so broadly disseminated by the Chinese themselves, this slight on the part of the North Vietnamese was remarkable and was prima facie evidence of their disapproval of its contents.

But Hanoi then went on to reject Lin Piao's advice in several speeches delivered by top North Vietnamese leaders at an army conference in May, 1966—speeches which were not releasd until July. Other replies to Lin Piao appeared in the July issue of *Hoc Tap,* North Vietnam's party journal. The burden of these speeches was that Hanoi and the Vietcong could defeat the Americans by taking the offensive, and that no foreign revolutionary experience was valid for conditions that the Hanoi leaders knew best.[19]

Le Duan, Secretary-General of the Lao Dong party, pointedly remarked at the conference that "We cannot automatically apply the revolutionary experiences of other countries in our country." Since no country other than China was offering to apply its own experience, the implication of that remark was plain. Duan stressed the need for "creativity," for keeping the realities of the Vietnamese situation in mind when planning revolutionary strategy, and for not "mechanically" following "the experiences of the fraternal parties."

> Creativity is a very important problem. Without a spirit of creativity, we cannot successfully carry out the revolution. We cannot automatically apply the revolutionary experiences of other countries in our country. Our party line is correct, because it was conceived in a creative manner. It has cleverly associated Marxism-Leninism with the revolutionary realities in Vietnam. Our party

[19] Victor Zorza first pinpointed the significance of these articles in *The Guardian* on September 1 and 2, 1966.

has paid special attention to studying the experiences of the fraternal parties, but it has not studied them mechanically. We must
have the requirements of the Vietnamese revolution in mind
while studying these experiences. We must also know how to
apply these experiences to the concrete conditions of Vietnam.
Creativity is a manifestation of the spirit of independence and
autonomy, patriotism, and a high revolutionary spirit. If we are
obsessed with an inferiority complex and with a desire to rely on
others, we cannot have a spirit of creativity. We are not genuine
revolutionaries. We do not understand Marxism-Leninism.

Then Le Duan replied to Lin Piao's argument for a strategic retreat,
saying:

It is not fortuitous that in the history of our country, each time we
rose up to oppose foreign aggression, we took the offensive and not
the defensive. . . . Taking the offensive is a strategy, while taking
the defensive is only a stratagem. Since the day the South Vietnamese people rose up, they have continually taken the offensive.

Even during the recent dry season, he continued, when the United
States imperialists introduced 200,000 troops into South Vietnam, the
southern troops "unhesitantly and resolutely took the offensive," repeatedly attacked the enemy, and achieved great victories. Pointedly he
noted that "without understanding the Vietnamese people and Vietnamese history, one cannot understand the strategy and tactics of the
Vietnamese revolution, nor can one lead the Vietnamese people in
fighting the enemy."
   Evidently countering Lin Piao's argument that a basic principle of
Maoist strategy was to make sure that the enemy was always outnumbered, Le Duan stated that:

. . . our troops and people have invented unique tactical methods
which enable a lesser force to attack a larger force. . . . In combat,
there are times when we concentrate quite a strong force and firepower to outnumber the enemy by two or three to one, but there
are also times when our ratios are one to one, one to ten, or even
more, and we still won. Thus, our army and people have the
methods, tactics and techniques which are suitable to the Vietnamese battlefields and to the Vietnamese themselves.

China, Le Duan hinted, had better limit itself to supplying weapons
and leave the strategy to Hanoi:

We do not disregard foreign countries' weaponry and technology, but we have to know how to apply the . . . techniques which are suitable to *our* country's situation and characteristics and to *our* combat methods. [Italics are the author's.]

About the same time that Le Duan's speech was published, another strong, if still indirect, attack on Peking came from Nguyen Chi Thanh, a powerful Politburo member, member of the National Defense Council, and widely rumored to be Hanoi's man in charge of the war in the south. Writing in the July issue of *Hoc Tap*, Thanh warned against the man who "would cite profuse experiences from here and there to demonstrate vaguely that 'we can be successful,' but would accompany all this with a lot of 'buts'—thus making it impossible to understand what he meant and what his purpose was in speaking this way." With Lin Piao clearly in mind, he warned that some people pointed to enemy strength not to cope with it "but to threaten others, thus intentionally or unintentionally spreading pessimism. . . ." Of course, he went on, the Americans were stronger in certain respects, "but they absolutely do not have any peerless strength. . . ."

Thanh then turned to assess the balance of forces on the ground in South Vietnam and rejected the conclusion that the balance favored the enemy since the introduction of United States ground troops. Such a conclusion was "formalistic" and not dialectical, he declared. Although the enemy had increased its forces, "our strategic position has been much better than before. . . ."

> If we only looked at the quantity of the enemy's strength . . . indeed the comparative balance of forces has clearly changed in favor of the enemy. Yet that was an evaluation made according to formalistic logic. . . . It is a fact that the enemy has considerably increased his troop strength, but our strategic position has been much better than before, the initiative on the battlefield is already ours. . . .[20]

Thanh branded as adventurists those who repeat obsolete experiences from textbooks and invoke magic formulae instead of examining the realities. Criticizing those who copied the "experience of foreign countries," he said that people who talked of necessary superiority of at least seven to one or nine to one, and so forth, were "diviners" and not scientists. And those who "repeat exactly in a new reality what belongs to history" are committing "adventurous" acts.

[20] *Hoc Tap,* July, 1966.

Thanh also said one could not settle "in an old-fashioned manner the question of relations between the delta and the mountainous region and between the rural areas and the cities in the southern revolutionary war." This reference, in this particular context, would seem to suggest—as indicated earlier—that the Chinese not only advised the Vietcong to postpone attacks on the cities and to concentrate on rural areas, but also that they suggested less attention be given to fighting in the heavily populated delta and more to the relatively inaccessible mountainous regions.

The Vietnamese launched other attacks on Lin Piao's thesis. Writing in the June issue of the military journal *Quan Doi Nhan Dan*, Truong Sen, a pseudonym, asserted that the Vietcong attacked not only the places where the enemy was weak but those which were vital. Moreover, he argued that during the past dry season, "had we retreated to the strategic defensive position," this would have led to serious consequences. With apparent reference to Lin Piao's thesis that main blows should now be directed against the Americans—not against the Saigon military—in order to maximize the united front appeal, Truong Sen said "we aimed our blows at both the Americans and [their] puppets." His conclusion, like that of the other North Vietnamese leaders, was that, despite the American intervention, the Communist troops maintained the initiative.

Such Vietnamese arguments support the idea that one of Lin Piao's target audiences was Hanoi and that the Hanoi leaders did not take kindly to a lecture from Peking on how to fight revolutionary wars, particularly at a time when the Chinese were hampering North Vietnam's war effort by refusing to engage in united action with the Russians to deter American escalation. Hanoi's leaders must also have had occasion to reflect on the fact that they had been the first Communists outside Russia to conduct a successful revolution—a feat they accomplished in 1945, four years before the Chinese Communists seized power. It does not require too much imagination to guess that China's heavy-handed approach must have deeply embittered Hanoi.

But if Hanoi and the Vietcong constituted one audience for Lin Piao, there was another audience as well—namely, the Chinese military. As we have seen, one question that had been debated between the military and the Chinese Communist Party concerned the best way to meet an American attack—by launching guerrilla warfare, retreating to mountain and rural bases and sacrificing Chinese cities or by fighting a conventional war. Lin's analysis seems directed at certain points to

Chinese generals who wanted to fight the United States by conventional means. Thus, at one point, he says:

> In order to annihilate the enemy, we must adopt the policy of luring him in deep and abandon some cities and districts of our own accord in a planned way, so as to let him in. It is only after letting the enemy in that the people can take part in the war in various ways and that the power of a people's war can be fully exerted. It is only after letting the enemy in that he can be compelled to divide up hs forces, take on heavy burdens and commit mistakes. In other words, we must let the enemy become elated, stretch out all his ten fingers and become hopelessly bogged down.

Lin continues:

> We are firmly against dividing up our forces to defend all positions and putting up resistance at every place for fear that our territory might be lost and our pots and pans smashed, since this can neither wipe out the enemy forces nor hold cities or localities.

Elsewhere, the defense minister says:

> The Chinese people definitely have ways of their own for coping with a U.S. imperialist war of aggression. Our methods are no secret. The most important one is still mobilization of the people, reliance on the people, making everyone a soldier and waging a people's war. We want to tell the U.S. imperialists once again that the vast ocean of several hundred million Chinese people in arms will be more than enough to submerge your few million aggressor troops.

Such a strategy of "letting the enemy in" and drowning him in people's war clearly is different from that outlined by Lo Jui-ch'ing, which advocated fighting the Americans with the Chinese infantry and "close cooperation among the different armed services, of which the ground forces, and particularly the infantry, are primary."

Lin Piao's article can be understood in part as a rejection of this hard line advance by Lo Jui-ch'ing and the military professionals—rapprochement with Russia, a get-tough policy in Vietnam, and preparation for conventional war with the United States. Lin was rejecting cooperation with Moscow, advising the Vietcong that they could win only by preparing for a protracted war which they would wage themselves, and arguing that an American attack on China could be absorbed by guerrilla war.

Perhaps the most striking difference between Lin Piao's formulations and the much tougher ones of Lo in May was that Lin minimized the danger of Chinese-American confrontation in Vietnam and insisted that the United States would be defeated not by China but by a number of people's wars throughout the underdeveloped areas:

> The more successful the development of people's war in a given region, the larger the number of U.S. imperialist forces that can be pinned down and depleted there. When the U.S. aggressors are hard pressed in one place, they have no alternative but to loosen their grip on others. . . . Everything is divisible. And so is this colossus of U.S. imperialism. It can be split up and defeated. The peoples of Asia, Africa, and Latin America and other regions can destroy it piece by piece, some striking at its head and others at its feet. That is why the greatest fear of U.S. imperialism is that people's wars will be launched in different parts of the world. . . .

Whereas Lo had suggested that the Chinese army would defeat the United States, Lin was saying that Vietnamese, Peruvian, and Angolan peasants would do the job.

Although Lo Jui-ch'ing and his followers had apparently backtracked on the question of "united action" with Russia by September, 1965, when Sino-Soviet relations had reached a new low, they were evidently continuing to take a harder line than Mao and Lin Piao on Vietnam. This is suggested in the last public statement made by Lo, on the very same occasion that Lin Piao spoke on "people's war."

Although stepping up his attack on Soviet revisionism, Lo in this statement particularly stressed the threat of United States imperialism and the urgent need to take preparatory steps to meet a likely attack. The United States, he warned, "will not reconcile itself to defeat, still less give up altogether." It is bent on accelerating the war in Vietnam, recklessly shouting about spreading the war to China. He continued:

> It is possible that U.S. imperialism may go mad in trying to save itself from its doom; we must take this into full account and make preparations against its expansion of the war of aggression in Vietnam and against any war it may impose on us. A thousand and one things need to be done. . . .[21]

While Lin and other regime spokesmen were making it clear—as we shall see in a moment—that China would not intervene in the war un-

[21] *Peking Review*, September 3, 1965, p. 3.

less the United States attacked the mainland, Lo was calling for unspecified preparations not only against an attack on China, but even against American "expansion of the war of aggression in Vietnam." Apparently he was still intent on lowering the threshold at which China should intervene. This interpretation is supported by his injunction—quite contrary to Lin Piao's "do-it-yourself" approach—that China must "give still more effective support to the Vietnamese . . . in their struggles against U.S. imperialism."

Lo dismissed Lin's article on people's war as a good textbook which "there is . . . no need for me to dwell on. . . ." He also paid the proper obeisance to Mao by arguing that the most important of the thousand and one things to be done was to hold high the great red banner of Mao's thought. It was undoubtedly tactics such as this which prompted the Army paper a year later to observe that the military-firsters in the army "had waved 'red flags' to oppose the red flag" and had overtly agreed with Mao's thought while "covertly opposing" it and putting military affairs and techniques first.[22]

By the winter of 1966, however, it was apparent that the regime had decided against Lo and was intent on limiting support to the Vietnamese and reducing risks of war with the United States. There were several indications of this. First of all, China's warnings against American military provocations—over 400 of which have been issued since 1958— reached a high point in October, 1964, after the Gulf of Tonkin incident, then again in April, 1965, after the American bombing of North Vietnam began; but dropped off sharply beginning in the summer of 1965.[23] While these warnings bear some relation to reality, inasmuch as United States ships and planes unquestionably violate Chinese boundaries as these boundaries are conceived by Peking, it is also clear that the Chinese manipulate such warnings for political purposes. Perhaps the best implicit proof of this fact is, as Mr. Tretiak observes, there is no necessary relationship between China's serious warnings and American violations as listed by the Chinese elsewhere. For example, during the period June 29, 1964, to April 5, 1966, according to a Chinese statement on the latter date, there were 241 intrusions of Chinese territory. Yet in this period only 100 serious warnings were issued. The fact that such warnings sharply declined during the summer of 1965 and have re-

[22] *Ibid.*, August 5, 1966, p. 9.

[23] See Daniel Tretiak, "Challenge and Control," in *Far Eastern Economic Review*, October 27, 1966, pp. 216–21.

mained low since thus seems to reflect a desire on the part of Peking to reduce Sino-American tensions.

Further signs of such a desire can be found in Chinese statements since the winter of 1966, which make it clear that Peking will not intervene in the Vietnam war unless China itself is attacked. For example, in October, 1965, Foreign Minister Ch'en Yi declared: "Should the U.S. imperialists *invade* China's mainland, we will take all necessary measures to defeat them. By then, the war will have no boundaries."[24] Premier Chou En-lai, in a December 20 speech at a reception for an NLF delegation, listed a number of actions that the U.S. might take in Vietnam, including: the bombing of Haiphong and Hanoi, blockading the Bao Bo (Tonkin) Gulf, bombing the central and southern parts of Laos held by the Pathet Lao, invading the southern portion of Laos bordering on Vietnam, and intensifying attacks against Cambodia in order to seal off the borders between Cambodia and South Vietnam. He said nothing about Chinese counteractions in the event of such actions. He went on to say that if the United States failed to achieve its purposes by such means—and it certainly would fail—it might then "go a step further and extend its war of aggression to the whole of Indochina and to China. And indeed U.S. imperialism is now making preparations for this eventuality." Chou strongly implied that only at that point would China fight. Again, on New Year's Day, 1966, *Jen-min jih-pao* said editorially that it was necessary to plan for a large-scale war that the U.S. might launch; but it again implied that China would fight only if invaded: "If the U.S. aggressors should dare to invade our country, we shall wipe them out resolutely, thoroughly, wholly, and completely."[25] In April, 1966, an editorial in *Jen-min jih-pao* amplified the threat somewhat by warning: "Should the U.S. imperialism dare to attack China, either on a limited scale or in full strength, the only result will be the total annihilation of the U.S. invaders."[26] The threat of Chinese action was still conditional on United States invasion, however.

Finally, on May 13, 1966, Chou said explicitly that "China will not take the initiative to provoke a war with the U.S."; but that if the Americans started such a war, "once in China" the United States would not be able to pull out. Chou also warned that, once the war breaks out, it will have no boundaries. "If you can come from the sky, why can't we fight back on the ground?"[27]

[24] *Peking Review,* October 8, 1965, p. 14.   [26] *Ibid.,* April 8, 1966, p. 8.

[25] *Ibid.,* January 1, 1966, p. 8.   [27] *Ibid.,* May 13, 1966, p. 5.

It may therefore be conjectured that by the winter of 1966 the Chinese "hawks" had been defeated and a policy of restraint in Vietnam decided upon. A decision had been made not to intervene directly in the Vietnamese war unless the Americans actually attacked China. The Chinese had probably also decided not to give the United States any pretext for attacking the mainland. That would explain why they have not used Chinese airplanes or bases in southern China to help North Vietnam shoot down American bombers. Such action, the United States has warned, would lead to retaliation against the bases themselves in line with the doctrine of "hot pursuit."

The Foreign Policy Views of the
Party Opposition

The foreign policy positions of party opposition leaders like Liu Shao-chi, Teng Hsiao-ping, and P'eng Chen—all of whom were demoted during the Cultural Revolution—have been discussed elsewhere in this volume by Uri Ra'anan.[28] Suffice it to note that the Maoists clearly intended to establish a link between some of the party oppositionists and the pro-Soviet army group. Thus, in May, 1966, the following charges were leveled against Wu Han, former deputy mayor of Peking, and Teng To and Liao Mo'sha, two of P'eng's senior aides on the municipal committee. Their writings, the article charged, had been directed "against the Lushan meeting" of 1959, at which Peng Te-huai had been purged. They sought to "reverse the decisions of that meeting." The message of Wu Han's drama, *Hai Jui Dismissed from Office,* published in 1961, was that the "Right opportunists" should come back to "administer 'court affairs.' " The attack also criticized one of Teng To's essays for advocating "learning from" and "uniting with" countries "stronger than our own," and for arguing that "we should be pleased if a friend is stronger than we are." In one essay, the attack continued, Teng To had said, "If a man with a swelled head thinks he can learn a subject with ease and kicks his teacher out, he will never learn anything." This, said the article, was a "vicious attack on our struggle against modern revisionism and a demand that we ask the revisionists in and let the wolves into the house."[29]

The Chinese "rationalists" wanted a reconciliation with Moscow for reasons quite different from the army's. They seemed to desire a

[28] See Uri Ra'anan, "Peking's Foreign Policy 'Debate,' 1965–66," in this volume, pp. 23–71.

[29] See *Peking Review,* May 27, 1966, pp. 5–18.

reconciliation with Moscow not to get tough on Vietnam—as the military faction did—but to reduce the danger to China from both Russia and the United States. Such a policy would have enabled China to concentrate on its main task of internal economic development.

And, in fact, it is clear that the burden of their attack was on Mao's frenetic economic policies. The "rationalists" were accused specifically of opposing the Great Leap Forward, wishing to extend private plots and free markets, and of wanting to use profitability as a criterion for small enterprises.[30] Their talismans included "construction before destruction." The charges against them suggest that some of them were even inclined to modify drastically the collective farm system.

Implications for International Relations

Having put forward the evidence to support the contention that the Chinese power struggle has in part concerned vital foreign policy issues —particularly Vietnam—I would now like to raise some questions and offer some conjectures about recent events in China and their implications for international relations.

First, there seems little doubt that a major dispute developed in the past two years between army professionals and party leaders over *how* to fight a war with the United States if such a war occurred. As Morton Halperin and John Lewis have indicated, it seems likely that the party and army agreed that the first stage of an American attack would involve the nuclear bombing of China's main centers.[31] Disagreement centered largely on how to meet the second stage, namely, an American ground invasion. As the two analysts point out: "Basically, the Party proposes reliance on a strategy of people's war—the strategy which the Party pursued in the Japanese war—while the PLA proposes to rely on the modernized military forces to fight a positional war against the American ground forces." While the army wanted to fight a more conventional, offensive war, the party argued the need for a defensive war in which China would take whatever punishment the United States could mete out in air attacks and then force American troops to fight against Chinese guerrillas on Chinese soil.

The reasons why the army objected to such a strategy are many. First, it meant upgrading the role of the people's militia and downgrading that of the professional army. This fact was underlined by the Chinese

[30] See *ibid.*, June 17, 1966, pp. 7–13.

[31] See their article in *China Quarterly*, April–June, 1966, "New Tensions in Army–Party Relations in China, 1965–66."

decision in May, 1965, after the American escalation in Vietnam, to abolish ranks in the PLA.[32]

Second, it meant withstanding a United States invasion without support from the Soviet Union, which Mao continued to alienate for what many army professionals must have thought were foolish reasons.

Third, it meant reconciling the army to a passive rather than active strategy, and few armies appreciate such roles.

Fourth, it meant sacrificing China's cities and urban population and retreating to rural bases.

Fifth, it envisaged a defense of China by "amateurs" such as the people's militia, on whom the professional army leaders must have looked with contempt.

Another point which merits further discussion is the fact that it was both the "hawks" in the Chinese army and the "rationalists" in the party who called for a rapprochement with Moscow. What were the perspectives of each group? More particularly, why did the "hawks" believe they could persuade Moscow to support them in a tougher policy on Vietnam, and what price were they willing to pay for such support?

There are several possible explanations of the military perspective. First, as we have seen, sometime in mid-1965 Moscow did in fact put forward a proposal for sending Soviet airplanes to southern China and troops to North Vietnam as part of its offer of "united action" with China to defend Vietnam. Mao and the party leaders rejected this proposal on the grounds that Moscow was interested only in laying the groundwork for a Cuban-type deal with the Americans that would sell out Hanoi and the NLF. The military, on the other hand, may well have argued—like the Japanese, North Korean, and North Vietnamese Communists—that this was an unjust interpretation of Soviet purposes, or that even if it was a correct interpretation, the Soviets could not back out once having made such a commitment. Furthermore, in military eyes, such a deployment of Soviet forces in China and Vietnam— regardless of Soviet motives—would give the Americans pause about further escalation of the war. The military may also have believed that not all the Soviet leaders were "revisionists" and that some might be willing—given the proper inducements from China—to stand up to the United States in Vietnam. They may have argued that the Chinese party should make concessions to the Soviet Union within the international Communist movement in order to obtain Soviet support in Vietnam.

[32] Chieh–fang–chün pao [Liberation army daily], May 25, 1965.

Such concessions might have included an offer to tone down, if not eliminate, the Chinese challenge to Soviet authority in the Communist world and in the Third World generally.

What, then, were the perspectives of the Chinese moderates who desired a normalization of relations with Moscow? Perhaps they believed that such normalization might eventually lead to a restoration of Soviet economic aid. Or that a reduction of tension with both Moscow and Washington would give Peking a much-needed breathing spell to concentrate on economic development and reduce defense spending. While there is nothing to indicate that the Chinese "rationalists" were aiming at a rapprochement with the United States, a curtailment of aid to foreign revolutionaries, a Laos-type solution in Vietnam, and a "turning-in" towards domestic problems—all of which this group favored—would almost certainly have resulted in an easing of tension with the United States.

Clearly, it is this particular school of thought in China that the Johnson Administration has hoped to encourage. The vigor with which this faction challenged Mao is ample testimony to its strength. It will undoubtedly be heard from again, particularly once Mao dies or the present transient coalition dissolves. Nor is it impossible that Lin Piao, Mao's heir apparent, could become Mao's "Khrushchev" and steal the revisionist thunder once Mao is off the scene.

What is particularly interesting to note about this faction is that it wants to opt out of the international chess game temporarily while it concentrates on modernization at home. This should give hope both to Washington, which fears a Sino-Soviet reconciliation at its expense, and to Moscow, which dreads a Sino-American rapprochement.

The future relationship among the three great powers is, however, one that could evolve in a variety of ways. Much will depend on both Soviet and American policies and how these policies are perceived in Peking. The possibility that clearly most worries Moscow is a Peking-Washington understanding, however unlikely that may seem at present. Such an understanding would expose the Russians to powerful enemies on two fronts. While this is to some extent the case now, the Soviets can take some comfort from the fact that its two potential foes are at one another's throats. Any Sino-American understanding, no matter how slight, could change that situation and enable either of the two—or both—to exert greater leverage on Russia.

There are some indications that such thoughts have occurred to certain leaders in Peking. Thus, a recent French emissary to the Chinese capital was told that the Americans, although enemies, were to be respected, while the Russians were "traitors" who could never be forgiven.[33] A delegation of Japanese parliamentarians who talked with Ch'en Yi on September 6, 1966, were told by the Chinese Foreign Minister:

> We shall not attack the United States. As a matter of fact, China is not strong enough to attack America. To tell the truth, America is afraid of China and China is somewhat afraid of America. I do not believe that the United States would invade present-day China. . . . I do not take a particularly pessimistic view of relations between the United States and China.[34]

Commenting on these remarks, the Polish party newspaper, *Trybuna Ludu*, pointed out that

> The calm, business-like tone of this statement would arouse no objections were the PRC to pursue a policy of unity and cooperation with the Soviet Union and the entire socialist camp. However, in the light of the disruptive policy of the CPC, this statement acquires a somewhat different complexion. Commenting on Chen Yi's statement, *France Presse* observed that "it undoubtedly confirms the opinion held by many observers that China is sharpening its conflict with the Soviet Union in order to prepare the ground for direct negotiations with the U.S. government."[35]

Obviously the Russians and some of their East European allies portray the Chinese as interested in making a deal with the American imperialists in order to discredit Peking. The Chinese have, of course, used the same argument to try to discredit Moscow. But there is sufficient evidence to suggest that this is not mere polemics, that Moscow is frankly alarmed at the possibility of improved Sino-American relations in the context of deteriorating Sino-Soviet relations. The Russians have not been slow to observe that recent Chinese statements have tended to concentrate their attack on the dangers of revisionism, while mentioning imperialism "only in passing."[36] Nor are the Russians unaware of a strong school of thought in Europe, particularly in West

[33] See *Le Monde*.

[34] These remarks were cited by the Polish party newspaper *Trybuna Ludu*. See Information Bulletin, issued by *World Marxist Review* Publishers, no. 83, p. 60.

[35] *Ibid*.

[36] *New York Times*, November 28, 1966, p. 1.

Germany, that the United States should ease relations with China in order to compel concessions from Russia.

For Peking to ease tensions with the United States at this time, however, it would be necessary for it to make a major and far-reaching change in the strategy it has been pursuing without letup since 1958. This strategy has identified United States imperialism as the main enemy of all peace-loving peoples and has involved Peking's active encouragement of all anti-American groups and countries throughout the world. Any substantial adjustments in Peking's relations with the United States would alienate it from the most extreme anti-American forces in the Third World, which it has most assiduously cultivated in recent years. Moreover, it is unlikely that the United States would make any major concessions to Peking, and perhaps not even any minor ones. Given the present intransigence of the American administration, any such adjustment would have to be made on the basis of the present status quo in the Far East, which Peking finds intolerable.

Finally, it is apparent that Washington is more interested at the moment and for the foreseeable future in reaching an accommodation with the Soviet Union than in reaching one with Peking. Indeed, Washington recently suggested that one of its major reasons for continuing to oppose Chinese admission to the United Nations was its fear of disturbing its relationship with the Soviet Union.[37]

Under these circumstances, Peking's room for maneuver is limited. Nevertheless, the future shape of relations among the three powers is fluid. The present realities of the international situation are more conducive to a Soviet-American understanding than to either a Sino-Soviet or Sino-American accommodation, but this situation could change under circumstances that are not foreseeable.

[37] *Ibid.*

Roger Hilsman

10

Two American Counterstrategies to Guerrilla Warfare: The Case of Vietnam

So-called "wars of national liberation," which is the Communist euphemism for guerrilla insurgency, have been encouraged and supported by both Moscow and Peking. In his speech of January 6, 1961, for example, Khrushchev made what amounted to a declaration of war by such means. And in his meeting that same year with President Kennedy at Vienna, it was on Soviet encouragement and support for "wars of national liberation" that Khrushchev was harshest and most intransigent, even more so than on the question of Berlin and Germany. But the principal impetus for "wars of national liberation" and the major effort in developing the doctrine have been Chinese. By the 1960's, in fact, the concept of "wars of national liberation" had become a central theme in Chinese Communist global strategy.

The failure of their attempt to seize power in 1927 drove the Chinese Communists into the mountains and later to undertake the Long March to Shensi, and eventually to Yenan. More importantly, it forced them to base themselves on the peasants and the countryside rather than on the workers and the cities, and so to turn Marx and Lenin upside down. It was these experiences that focused Mao's thought on guerrilla warfare and led the Chinese Communists to develop the doctrine and strategy of "people's" or "revolutionary" warfare.

In 1948, local Communist parties launched revolts throughout Southeast Asia—in the Philippines, Malaya, Indochina, Indonesia, and Burma. Initially, the techniques were unsophisticated, little more than campaigns of indiscriminate terrorism. But after the Chinese Communist victory on the mainland in 1949, the influence of Chinese doctrine on both tactics and strategy began to be felt. As it happened, it was only the Vietminh revolt against the French in Vietnam that achieved any real success, but it could be argued that in the Philippines and Malaya, at least, the indiscriminate use of terror had already alienated so many of the peasantry that it was too late for a change in strategy to do much good.

The North Korean attack on South Korea in 1950 was an experiment in large-scale, conventional war, and the United States' decision to intervene and the resulting stalemate carried a clear lesson. In 1957, when Mao Tse-tung declared the end of the "Bandung" period of relatively peaceful coexistence with his Moscow statement that the "East Wind prevails over the West Wind," it was a signal not for conventional war but for the re-opening of guerrilla warfare in both Laos and Vietnam. Not long afterwards, the doctrine of "revolutionary" warfare began to take its central place in Chinese global strategy. Lin Piao, in his major policy statement of September 3, 1965, said that the main battlefield of the future was the "vast area of Asia, Africa, and Latin America" and that it was an "urgent necessity" for the people of these countries "to master and use people's war" as a weapon. "The contradiction between the revolutionary peoples of Asia, Africa, and Latin America and the imperialists headed by the United States," he wrote, "is the principal contradiction in the contemporary world." The strategy of "revolutionary" warfare, Lin Piao seemed convinced, would not only win victory for the Communists within each country but also in the struggle between East and West:

> Taking the entire globe, if North America and Western Europe can be called the "cities of the world," then Asia, Africa, and Latin America constitute the "rural areas of the world." . . . In a sense, the contemporary world revolution also presents a picture of the encirclement of cities by the rural areas.

The Chinese Communist doctrine of revolutionary warfare is laid out in Mao's various works.[1] There are also the analyses and comments

[1] Mao Tse-tung, *Strategic Problems of China's Revolutionary War* (Peking: Foreign Language Press, 1954), *Strategic Problems in the Anti-Japanese Guerrilla War* (Peking: Foreign Language Press, 1954), and *On the Protracted War* (Peking: Foreign Language Press, 1960) are the principal ones. See also Mao Tse-tung, *On Guerrilla Warfare,* trans. Samuel B. Griffith (New York: Praeger, 1961). Also of interest are North Vietnamese Defense Minister Vo Nguyen Giap, *People's War, People's Army; the Viet-Cong Insurrection Manual for Underdeveloped Countries* (New York: Praeger, 1962), and Ernesto Guevara, *Guerrilla Warfare* (New York: Monthly Review Press, 1961).

of western observers.[2] The combination of what Mao was saying and what the Chinese and the various guerrilla movements actually did added up to more than a call from the Chinese to other peoples to follow their revolutionary example. It was this, of course, but also more. What it ultimately amounted to was a new and more subtle way of using force for national purposes than orthodox warfare. It slipped past the ancient definitions of aggression that were embodied in international law. It was a way of using military force not across national boundaries, but inside them—a new kind of "internal" war.[3]

Mao's first principle was the famous phrase that guerrillas were fish swimming in the sea of the people: "Guerrillas are fish, and the people are the water in which they swim. If the temperature of the water is right, the fish will thrive and multiply." One familiar comment is that revolutionary warfare is guerrilla tactics plus political action.

[2] See Edward L. Katzenbach, Jr., and Gene Z. Hanrahan, "The Revolutionary Strategy of Mao Tse-tung," *Political Science Quarterly,* vol. 70, no. 3 (September, 1955); Mao Tse-tung, "Chinese Communist Revolutionary Strategy, 1945–49," ed. Sin-ming Chiu, Princeton University, Center for International Studies, Research Monograph no. 13, 1961; Ralph L. Powell, *Politico-Military Relationships in Communist China* (Washington, D.C.: External Research, Bureau of Intelligence and Research, U.S. Department of State, 1963); Harold Hinton, "Political Aspects of Military Power and Policy in Communist China," in Harry L. Coles, ed., *Total War and Cold War* (Columbus: Ohio State University Press, 1962); Tang Tsou and Morton H. Halperin, "Mao Tse-tung's Revolutionary Strategy and Peking's International Behavior," *American Political Science Review,* vol. 59, no. 1 (March, 1965); and Howard L. Boorman and Scott A. Boorman, "Chinese Communist Insurgent Warfare, 1935–49," *Political Science Quarterly,* vol. 81, no. 2 (June, 1966). Also of interest are Lucian W. Pye, *Guerrilla Communism in Malaya, Its Social and Political Meaning* (Princeton: Princeton University Press, 1956); Sir Robert K. G. Thompson, *Defeating Communist Insurgency: Experiences from Malaya and Vietnam* (London: Chatto & Windus, 1966); Bernard Fall, *Street Without Joy; Insurgency in Indochina, 1946–63* (Harrisburg, Pa.: Stackpole, 1963); and George K. Tanham, *Communist Revolutionary Warfare: The Vietminh in Indochina* (New York: Praeger, 1962). On guerrilla warfare in general, see Peter Paret and John W. Shy, *Guerrillas in the 1960's* (New York: Praeger, 1962); Otto Heilbrunn, *Partisan Warfare* (New York: Praeger, 1962); and two collections of readings: Col. T. N. Greene, ed., *The Guerrilla and How to Fight Him* (New York: Praeger, 1962); and Franklin Mark Osanka, ed., *Modern Guerrilla Warfare: Fighting Communist Guerrilla Movements, 1941–1961* (New York: Free Press of Glencoe, 1962).

[3] For a full historical treatment of the growth of the "internal war" threat and the developing American response during the Kennedy administration, see Roger Hilsman, *To Move a Nation, the Politics of Foreign Policy in the Administration of John F. Kennedy* (New York: Doubleday, 1967), from which this analysis has been adapted.

Mao has a great deal to say about tactics, but the gist of the difference between mere tactics and "revolutionary warfare" itself is contained in his description of a "revolutionary" war's three phases. The first stage is almost purely political, with the activist cadres building support among the people, propagandizing, and recruiting. The second stage is active guerrilla warfare, with bands of guerrillas ambushing government forces, raiding and harassing, but avoiding pitched battles. All this is combined with highly discriminating terrorism, assassination of government officials, especially unpopular government officials, and sabotage. The second stage is a systematic effort to destroy the people's confidence in the government's ability to function and to protect them. Its purpose is to make the government suspicious of the people and the people distrustful of the government—turning government and people against each other. It may be that power can be seized in the turmoil that follows this second stage, especially if the government leaders lose their nerve. If not, the third and final stage is to establish "liberated areas." These are base areas, in which not only can supplies and recruits be obtained but in which the efforts of the people can be directed to the support of the war. In these base areas, the guerrillas can be transformed into regular forces and so turn guerrilla terrorism and harassment into a civil war in which the government troops can be engaged directly in conventional combat and destroyed.

In the first stage—if the temperature of the people is right—all that is needed are trained and dedicated cadres and a doctrine to guide their efforts. Food, money, and supplies can be obtained from the people, and the fact of their making the contribution commits them to the cause. Even in the second stage, outside help is not really essential. Money and supplies come from the people; weapons and ammunition can be taken from the government forces through ambush or surprise attack. Building the political base is still the first priority, and too many arms too soon from outside might actually interfere with that task. In most guerrilla movements the most useful outside help at this stage has been in highly specialized equipment—radios, codes, and medical supplies. It is only in the third and final stage that outside help might make a decisive difference, after the struggle has been transformed into a regular civil war. At that time, two conventional armies are locked in sustained combat, and the need for ammunition, weapons, and supplies assumes really large-scale proportions. But even at this stage, the need for outside help might not be great if the "liberated areas" are large enough and if there is no large-scale outside assistance going to the government side.

The American Response[4]

This, in brief, was the nature of the threat. The American response was slow in coming, principally because of a failure to recognize that there was a true threat. The United States military aid mission to Vietnam, for example, believed that their task was to help the South Vietnamese build a conventional army that could fight a Korea-type war, and they resisted any change toward developing counter-guerrilla forces. Even as late as April, 1961, for example, after President Kennedy had moved to upgrade the Special Forces and to emphasize the need for new approaches to the guerrilla problem, General Lyman L. Lemnitzer, then Chairman of the Joint Chiefs of Staff, was quoted in the newspapers as saying privately on his return from a visit to Vietnam that the new administration was "oversold" on the importance of guerrilla warfare and that too much emphasis on counter-guerrilla measures would impair the ability of the South Vietnamese army to meet a conventional assault by the ten or more regular North Vietnamese divisions.

It was not Mao's words that finally evoked an American response but events in South Vietnam. After Mao's "East Wind prevails over West Wind" speech in November, 1957, following the Soviet sputnik success, the North Vietnamese reactivated the Communist cadres who had remained in South Vietnam after the 1954 Geneva agreements, and began to use the old Ho Chi Minh trails through Laos to send down new cadres, selected from among the 90,000 southerners who had gone north in 1954. By mid-1961, the Vietcong were estimated to have about 12,000 regular guerrilla troops, and they more or less controlled as much as a third of the countryside. Over 1,400 civilians, mainly village officials, had been assassinated in the previous twelve months, and over 2,000 kidnapped.

---

[4] No matter how hard the participants in historical decisions may try to be fair to all sides of the policy debates in which they took part, they cannot avoid being somewhat more eloquent in describing the arguments their own side espoused than in their attempt to describe the arguments of their opponents. This paper also has this failing.

As a consequence, two things need to be said: The first is that, in the debate described here, there were reasonable arguments on both sides, and anyone's ultimate judgment, no matter which side it comes down on, must rest on a fine balancing of pros and cons. The second is that, although the debates were sometimes heated, it would be wrong to deduce from the high level of passion a doubt as to anyone's motive. The participants were high-minded, patriotic, and intelligent men, wrestling manfully with stubbornly intransigent problems that were awesome in their complexity.

In the late spring of 1961, Vice President Lyndon B. Johnson visited Vietnam, and he returned to recommend a fundamental decision to "move forward with a major effort to help these countries defend themselves." He stated the choice in dramatic terms: the United States had to pull its defenses back to San Francisco or go ahead with a full, "forward strategy," implying that what was needed was a major American commitment in military terms.

By the fall of 1961, the situation in Vietnam had worsened, and President Ngo Dinh Diem and the Vietnamese government were calling for help. On October 11, 1961, President Kennedy announced that he was sending General Maxwell D. Taylor and Walt W. Rostow to Vietnam to investigate and make recommendations.

The final report of the Taylor-Rostow mission contained three sets of recommendations. The first was in effect a series of demands for political, governmental, and administrative reforms on the part of the government of President Diem. The second set of recommendations was that the United States should provide material aid and the technical advisers required for a broad-gauge counter-guerrilla program—economic measures; village-level civic, social, and political action; arms and equipment for a self-defense corps; and the specialized equipment, helicopters, and so on, to free the Vietnamese military from static defense and to give them the mobility to seek out the guerrillas in their own territory. The program would include helicopter pilots, mechanics, and other highly trained technicians who would operate the equipment while training Vietnamese to take over. In addition, the report also recommended the sending of two special Air Force squadrons—with the code name "Farmgate"—of slow-flying, propellor-driven B-26's and T-28's. These were Air Force units specially designed and put together for the purposes of small-scale, guerrilla warfare. They were to be operated on a semi-covert basis—although Americans would do the actual flying, each would always be accompanied by a Vietnamese "observer" and the markings on the planes would also be Vietnamese.

With the exception of the semi-covert "Farmgate" squadrons, all this was merely more of the same kind of assistance that had been given in the past. The third set of recommendations was for a qualitative change in the nature of the United States commitment in the direction that Vice President Johnson had recommended. For the Taylor-Rostow report also proposed that 10,000 American ground troops be introduced into Vietnam immediately and that the possibility be accepted that as many as six full divisions might eventually be required. The mission of the American troops would be to hold the ring against infiltrators or an attack by regular North Vietnamese divisions while the South Vietnamese forces dealt with the guerrillas.

President Kennedy approved the recommendations designed to bring about reforms in the Diem government and the step-up in military and economic aid with an increase of American advisers, technicians, and helicopter pilots, including the introduction of the "Farmgate" B-26's and T-28's with their pilots and mechanics. But he did not approve the commitment of American troops.

The Search for a Strategic Concept

From the beginning of his administration, President Kennedy was convinced that the techniques of "revolutionary" warfare constituted a special kind of threat. As early as May, 1961, he broke tradition by delivering in person a "Special Message to the Congress on Urgent National Needs" in which he described the threat as an aggression more often concealed than open. "They have fired no missiles; and their troops are seldom seen. They send arms, agitators, aid, technicians and propaganda to every troubled area. But where fighting is required, it is usually done by others—by guerrillas striking at night, by assassins striking alone, . . . by subversives and saboteurs and insurrectionists, who in some cases control whole areas inside of independent nations." And he continued to hammer on the point that guerrilla warfare was different from any other kind and that it required new tactics and doctrines. "This is another type of war," he told the graduating class of West Point in 1962,

> new in its intensity, ancient in its origin—war by guerrillas, subversives, insurgents, assassins; war by ambush instead of by combat; by infiltration, instead of aggression, seeking victory by eroding and exhausting the enemy instead of engaging him. . . . It requires in those situations where we must counter it, and these are the kinds of challenges that will be before us in the next decade if freedom is to be saved, a whole new kind of strategy, a wholly different kind of force, and therefore, a new and wholly different kind of military training.

In spite of resistance from the Joint Chiefs of Staff and the top level of the Pentagon, President Kennedy elevated the status of the Special Forces and their school at Fort Bragg. He created an inter-departmental committee on counter-insurgency problems, in which his brother, Robert F. Kennedy, played a prominent role, and he directed the Foreign Service Institute of the State Department to set up a special course of instruction on counter-insurgency that men from all departments, military and civilian, could attend. To the pressure from the President was added the pressure from events, and much of Washington became engaged in searching for a strategic concept for dealing with "revolutionary" warfare.

As it turned out, the search resulted not in one, but two strategic concepts. One was the descendant of the thinking embodied in Vice President Johnson's recommendations calling for a "forward strategy," in the Taylor-Rostow report, and in the thinking of the Joint Chiefs of Staff and the top levels of the Pentagon, including Secretary of Defense Robert S. McNamara.

The other strategic concept had a more diverse ancestry. Some of the ideas came from the American OSS experiences with guerrilla operations in World War II; some from the Special Forces effort at Fort Bragg; some from work in the universities on Chinese military thought and the guerrilla struggles in Greece, the Philippines, Malaya, and Algeria; and some from similar work on the problems of political development in the emerging countries. The main support for this second strategic concept came from the Special Forces and their supporters just below the top levels in the Pentagon, from the State Department, and from the White House, including Robert F. Kennedy.

The Johnson-Taylor-Rostow-JCS view tended to see the main source of revolutionary warfare as aggression from outside the country and in general believed that the principal means for dealing with it must be military. The White House–State Department view tended to see the principal source as internal to the country afflicted with insurgency and in general believed that the principal means for dealing with it must be political. In reality, of course, the two strategic concepts were neither so clear-cut nor so mutually exclusive as they seemed to be—or as it is necessary in this paper to make them appear to be for the purposes of analysis. In addition, there were people in the Pentagon who adhered to the "political" approach and people in the White House and the State Department who adhered to the "military" approach. And even the people clearly associated with one or the other view were not always convinced that the position with which they were associated was completely right. The adherents to the "military" concept understood that the conditions for insurgency had to exist inside a country if the outside stimulus was to work, and they were also convinced that military measures had to be supplemented by political measures. The adherents to the "political" concept recognized that there was a very large military component in dealing with insurgency and that military measures were necessary. They also recognized that the insurgency probably would not have started without the aggressive stimulus from outside and that the measures for dealing with insurgency had to be placed in an international framework that included a policy toward the source of the outside stimulus.

But in spite of all these qualifications, there was a fundamental difference between the two positions, as well as a serious political struggle between their adherents. McGeorge Bundy once said that Vietnam was the most divisive issue in the Kennedy administration. Indeed, it was, and the split came over these two essentially rival strategic concepts. The fundamental difference between them is whether revolutionary warfare should be met with a military program to which political measures are subordinate or with a political program to which military measures are subordinate.

The "Military" Approach

Among intellectuals, Walt W. Rostow was the main spokesman for the "military" approach in both the Kennedy and Johnson administrations. In 1961, at the very beginning of the Kennedy administration, he delivered a major speech analyzing the Communist use of guerrilla warfare and its relationship to the modernization process in developing countries.[5] Rostow saw the modernization process as true revolution, containing its own dynamics. Like all revolutions, modernization was disruptive, upsetting the old ways and producing extreme vulnerabilities in the transition on which the Communists could prey. The Communists, Rostow said, were the "scavengers of the modernization process."

Rostow's conclusion was that the best way to fight guerrilla warfare was to prevent it from happening, and his analysis of the strains of modernization led to valuable insights on how this could be done in the villages and countryside of the emerging nations. He saw the task for the United States as twofold—first, to hasten the modernization process past the vulnerable period of transition, and, second, to protect the country and preserve its independence during that vulnerable period. And it was because the vulnerabilities of transition were so awesomely great that Rostow was led in the end to put his emphasis on military means for dealing with a guerrilla war that had already begun. In the same speech he called the "sending of men and arms across in-

[5] The speech is reprinted in Osanka, *Modern Guerrilla Warfare,* and in Greene, *The Guerrilla.*

ternational boundaries and the direction of guerrilla war from outside a sovereign nation" a new form of aggression. He also warned that

> this is a fact which the whole international community must confront and whose consequent responsibilities it must accept. Without such international action those against whom aggression is mounted will be driven inevitably to seek out and engage the ultimate source of the aggression they confront.

And applied to Vietnam, of course, this was an argument for attacking the North.

A high enough level of punishment on the state that was the ultimate source of a guerrilla attack could, of course, eventually make it cease its support and exercise whatever control it had over the guerrillas to make them stop fighting. If the level of punishment were high enough the only alternative to ceasing its support to the guerrilla would be complete destruction.

International political considerations, on the other hand, might make it desirable to limit the punishment. Although many people argued that neither the Chinese nor the Soviets would intervene if the United States carried its punishment of North Vietnam through to complete destruction, if necessary by actual invasion, the advocates of the "military" approach in general agreed that political considerations made it desirable to keep the attack on the source of aggression limited. Even so, in the case of North Vietnam the lower levels of punishment to be inflicted by the proposed limited bombing program were severe, designed to destroy the transportation system and a significant proportion of the industry on which the North Vietnamese had based their hopes for economic development. There seemed to be a good possibility that at some point the North would prefer to call off the guerrilla warfare rather than face continued punishment. If not, the argument for the "military" approach concluded, the punishment would at least impose a substantial cost on the country that was continuing to support the guerrilla warfare, and cut down on the flow of infiltrating men and supplies.

As it was developed in the Pentagon, however, the strategy of the "military" approach was twofold—not only to punish and wear down the source of the aggression outside the country under attack, but to seek out and destroy the guerrilla units inside. The idea was to make maximum use of superior American technology and of American abundance. American wealth was sufficient to meet the supply needs not only of the government forces but of the civilian population, too, if that became necessary. Superior American equipment could give the counter-guerrilla forces incredible mobility and overwhelming fire-power. In the case of Vietnam, there was a lack of manpower and especially of combat units with the necessary training and aggressive-ness, but if no other way could be found this lack could be made up by using troops from the United States itself.

With complete and total command of the air and with vast fleets of helicopters, the government forces and their allies could maintain the offensive and could seek out the guerrilla in his own jungle and moun-tain terrain. If mobility and aggressiveness were maintained, the argu-ment continued, the kill-rate on the guerrillas could be kept at a level that would become unbearable. Casualties, difficulties of supply, and continued harassment from both ground and air would collapse the morale of many guerrilla units and simply destroy the others.

Inevitably, this "military" strategic concept had corollary implica-tions for the United States attitude toward the internal politics of the country under attack. Although everyone concerned recognized the importance of winning the people, of political, economic, and govern-mental reform, the success of a "military" approach depended on in-ternal political stability and a single-minded determination on the part of both the government and the armed services. The government and the armed forces had to concentrate on maintaining a highly aggressive offensive against the guerrilla units and not be distracted by political or social unrest. Inevitably, as a consequence, and for perfectly sound reasons, the result was a bias toward somewhat authoritarian rulers and military juntas and toward postponement of political and social meas-ures that might create social and political instability in the short run even though they would develop popular support in the long run.

The "Political" Approach

President Kennedy himself was a principal spokesman for the "polit-ical" approach. Much work had been done on guerrilla warfare at Fort Bragg and in the universities, and President Kennedy was familiar with all of it. As related above, much of the impetus toward developing a "political" strategic concept came from the President himself.

In the State Department, work on guerrilla warfare had been cen-tered in the Bureau of Intelligence and Research as well as in the Policy Planning Staff, and this work, too, resulted in a speech.[6] The State Department view agreed that the "United States must be pre-pared to become deeply involved," but differed about the methods.

---

[6] See Roger Hilsman, "Internal War: The New Communist Tactic," re-printed in Osanka, *Modern Guerrilla Warfare*, and in Greene, *The Guerrilla*.

The basic premise was that a successful counter-insurgency program depended on winning popular support. This meant that military measures had to be very carefully circumscribed. The danger of large-scale military operations was that their very destructiveness would alienate the people. What is more, the argument ran, regular forces—although essential for the task of deterring conventional aggression—were unsuited by both training and equipment for the task of fighting guerrillas. Regular forces were road-bound, unwieldy, and cumbersome, inevitably telegraphing their movements to the elusive guerrilla. Drawing on our historical experience as a young nation in Indian fighting, on the jungle experience during the Philippine Insurrection at the turn of the century, and on OSS experience in World War II, the speech argued that the way to fight the guerrilla was to adopt the tactics of the guerrilla. Small bands should be spotted at intervals throughout the area to be pacified. Using guerrilla tactics they would harass and ambush, while central reserves would be used to reinforce and themselves to ambush on escape trails leading from the point of contact. As the guerrillas in an area were slowly worn down, government control could be extended and the people given the means to protect themselves. And when the area was cleared and secured, the security forces could move on to the next.

On the political side of the equation the bias in the speech was toward rapid change.

> We may find ourselves encouraging reformers to organize mass parties. . . . We are seriously interested in broadening the will and capacity of friendly governments to augment social and political reform programs as a basis for modernization. . . . We must foster the growth and use of international organizations as sources of help . . . —help that can be on the scene and in action before the crisis reaches its peak.

But having stressed the vital importance of gaining popular support, the speech went on to argue that "it would be mistaken to think that guerrillas cannot thrive where governments are popular and where modernization, economic development, and reform are going forward." The point of the argument was that the existence of a guerrilla movement did not mean that a government was either popular or unpopular, and that modernization, reform, and measures to make the government popular could not alone defeat an established guerrilla movement, but had to be combined with military and police measures to give the people physical security.

R. K. G. Thompson

It turned out that parallel work of a more detailed and specific kind was well advanced in Saigon itself, carried on principally by the head of the British Advisory Mission, Robert K. G. Thompson. Thompson was a career officer of the British colonial service who had spent most of his life in Malaya. He had played an important role in the defeat of the Communist guerrilla terrorism in Malaya, where he had served as deputy secretary and then secretary for defence. At first, the British had dealt with the guerrilla terrorism in Malaya as if it were a purely military problem, relying on large-scale military operations, bombing jungle hideouts, and so on, but after two years they were worse off than when they started. It was then that they developed the "new village" program that finally defeated the Communist guerrillas. Applying this experience to Vietnam, Thompson had come up with what he called the "strategic hamlet" plan.

Thompson pointed out that the Vietcong's main effort was not in fighting the government's regular troops—they could have done more of that than they were actually doing at the time—but in attempting to gain *administrative* control over the 16,000 hamlets in South Vietnam. Winning battles against regular Vietcong units in the field would not really affect the struggle for the villages either way. It was exactly the technique the Communists had used against the French.[7] The French forces established an "iron triangle" of forts around the Red River delta and Hanoi and won every engagement along the battle line. But in the villages *inside* the triangle, Communist agents were at the same time extending and consolidating their administrative control over more and more villages by alternating propaganda and political persuasion with assassination and terror. Some villages had two "governments"—a French colonial government by day and a Communist one by night. But it made no difference even if French troops occupied a village for a time. Everyone in the village knew the French would leave sooner or later and whoever had given them information on Communist agents would be executed in the most dramatic fashion. In one case, for example, the Communists woke a whole village in the middle of the night and forced them to watch while three offending youths had their heads hacked off—and the heads were then nailed on the bridge leading to the village as a reminder. In any case, administrative control of the villages gave the guerrillas a base for both taxation and recruitment.

[7] See Bernard B. Fall, *Street Without Joy* and *The Two Vietnams: A Political and Military Analysis* (New York: Praeger, 1967).

Thompson argued that it was a classic axiom that guerrillas could maintain themselves indefinitely so long as they had support from the population in the area where they operated. The support could be voluntary, motivated by, say, patriotism, as was the support given the French *maquis* effort against the German occupation in World War II. Or it could be given reluctantly, because the guerrillas so ruthlessly dominate the population that the forces of law and order cannot give the people protection from terroristic retaliation on those who help the government. More often, support is mixed, some from loyalty and some from terror. Where a guerrilla force enjoys support from the people, whether willing, forced, or mixed, it can never be defeated by military means. However much it is harassed and attacked, shelled, mortared, and bombed by superior forces of infantry and artillery, air and sea power, Thompson argued, it is the essence of the guerrilla force that it avoids combat except in conditions of its own choosing. It retains the initiative and selects its own targets. It pursues this policy through all the stages of Mao's "people's revolutionary war."

The only way to defeat a guerrilla force operating in this way, Thompson believed, was systematically to cut it off from its true base of support—the people. For this, obviously, the first step had to be to find a way to give the people physical security. For if they were not protected from the marauding bands of guerrillas and from their retaliation, they could not exercise a free choice between supporting the guerrillas and supporting the government. And what he proposed as the instrument to provide this physical security was the "strategic hamlet."

Strategic Hamlets

The strategic hamlet program was, simply, a way of arming the villagers of Vietnam so that they could defend themselves if they were attacked by a small band of marauding guerrillas and at least hold out until reinforcements came if they were attacked by a large band. Setting up a strategic hamlet, however, would require political skill, care, and time. Civic action teams would have to be trained to go into each village, to provide simple government services, agricultural extension loans, a school and a teacher, wells, good village and district administration, and effective police protection, as well as training in the use of weapons for self-defense. The role of the police, of course, would be vital—for they would have to win enough people over to the government side to identify the Communist agents before it would be safe to distribute arms to a village militia. And during the weeks and months that all this was going on, regular military forces would have to be stationed in the region to protect both the civic action teams and the villagers until the hamlet was ready to defend itself.

A task that would require especially delicate handling would be con solidating the inhabitants into a compact, defensible unit which could be surrounded by a moat and barbed wire. Most hamlets in Vietnam are a cluster of huts, with a few more scattered out from the main cluster at distances of anywhere from a hundred yards to a mile or so. The outlying houses would have to be dismantled and moved inside the hamlet defenses—and there would be opposition to being moved from the traditional homesite, away from family graves, away from family fields, even if it were only a few hundred yards. Later on in the program, as the area covered by strategic hamlets increased, in some cases whole villages would have to be moved, as had happened in Malaya, if they were isolated or particularly accessible to a nearby guerrilla unit, and in those circumstances, the opposition would be even greater.

The essence of the program, however, was that it had to be a program —one lone strategic hamlet could not effectively defend itself. There had to be a hedgehog of hamlets, spreading out like an oil blot from the sea toward the mountains and jungle. Plastic identity cards had to be issued, curfews established, and provincial forces trained to set up checkpoints and ambushes during curfew hours—an iron grid of security had to be established to control the movement of both goods and people, of rice and recruits. A solid bloc of these strategic hamlets, firmly established and consolidated, extending outward to make a zone of security, armed for their own protection and supported by military and paramilitary forces serving as reinforcements and ensuring the security of their rear areas and their lateral communications with each other, Thompson argued, could create the physical security the villager must have before he could make a free choice between the Vietcong and the government. The primary role of the strategic hamlet was to provide that free choice.

But even though security is the first requirement in an effective counter-insurgency program, it would not be enough by itself to make the villager choose the government side. He could only be brought to choose the government side if the government could show him that what it had to offer him was something better than the enemy could offer him.

And this, Thompson said, was the second role of the strategic hamlet. He saw the hamlet scheme and the bureaucratic apparatus that would be created to run it as the means for bringing about a revolutionary change in the peasant's lot—economically, politically, socially, and culturally. The election of village officials, which President Diem had abolished, should be reinstituted. Land reform should be pushed forward, better medical services should be provided, and so should schools, teachers, agricultural credit, and extension work. A governmental structure should be set up in which information about villagers' needs would go up the ladder, and simple government services would go down for the first time in the history of Vietnam.

All this, Thompson argued, should be looked upon as a war measure more important than defeating the Vietcong in actual battle. If the program was successful, if the peasant in the strategic hamlet really did come to see that he was better off than under the Vietcong or than his counterpart was in North Vietnam, and if he was also free of the fear of retaliation, then he would finally commit himself to the government's side. He would give the government forces information about the location and movement of Vietcong units and individuals; he would deny the Vietcong the food and funds and supplies they needed; he would fight against their raids on his village and deny them the opportunity to acquire recruits, whether by persuasion or impressment. The peasant, in effect, would be the one who defeated the Vietcong, not by killing them but by reducing them to hungry, marauding bands of outlaws devoting all their energies to remaining alive. It would take years of slow, painstaking work, but once this turning point was reached, as Thompson saw it, once the majority of the population had taken the vital decision to throw in their lot with the government, the struggle against the guerrillas would be won. From then on only mopping up operations would remain.

Reaction in Washington

Thompson's ideas were well received in the State Department and the White House, as well as at the Special Forces school in Fort Bragg. In the State Department's Bureau of Intelligence and Research, an analysis of past guerrilla wars seemed to indicate that guerrilla techniques were successful in only two sets of circumstances. One was when the main body of the enemy was fully engaged. The French *maquis*, for example, enjoyed the support of virtually the entire population, they were well supplied by air drops from the United Kingdom, and they were well organized. Yet they were not successful until after D-day, when the main body of the enemy was tied down in Normandy. The other set of circumstances was that to be found in Southeast Asia, as well as parts of Africa and Latin America. In Southeast Asia most peasants lived in villages, in a village culture that turns each village inward on itself.

The people have little or no identification with the national government. The government is remote and little felt, except at tax collection time, and it is in any case incapable of giving the villagers day-by-day protection. The villagers are politically and psychologically isolated, by distance and lack of modern transportation systems. In such circumstances, it is not difficult for a trained and organized cadre to recruit an effective guerrilla force. In Burma in World War II, for example, several hundred officers and non-commissioned officers of the American OSS succeeded in building a guerrilla force of 30,000 men behind the Japanese lines—and they did it with white faces.

The State Department analysis also argued that the idea that government existed for the benefit of the people, that a government could really *care,* was as revolutionary in most of Asia as anything the Communists had to offer. The program had at least a chance to win over the allegiance of the people—if they could be given physical security for a long enough period of time for the appeal to begin to work.

There were also advantages in this "political" strategy to the military side of the equation. Two axioms of war are to cut the enemy's supply lines and to destroy the main body of his strength. But it was a mistake, in the State Department view, to conceive of the infiltration routes as the enemy's main supply line and the regular Vietcong guerrilla units as the main body of his strength. In a guerrilla war, the true supply lines were the thousands of roads and trails radiating out like spokes of a wheel from each of the 16,000 hamlets of South Vietnam. And the main body of the enemy's strength was the people of South Vietnam—at least potentially. What the strategic hamlet program was designed to do was to cut these true lines of supply and destroy the guerrilla's access to the main source of strength, the food and potential recruits in the villages.

And the concept had one other strategic advantage of especial moment—it would force the guerrilla to fight on the government's terms rather than the guerrilla's. Cut off from their normal flow of supplies from the villages, the guerrillas would have to come out from their mountain and jungle fastnesses to find food and recruits. If a guerrilla band ventured into an established zone of strategic hamlets, it would be entering a meat grinder. Sooner or later it would run into a patrol or ambush of the provincial civil guards, which would trigger the dispatch of reinforcements and further ambushes on the escape routes. If the group went deeper into the zone, it would get hungrier, starved by the controls on the movement of food and people. Eventually, the guerrilla group would be forced to attack a strategic hamlet, announcing its presence and triggering more reinforcements and more ambushes. In other words, once solid blocs of strategic hamlets were established the whole war could be turned around. Instead of the government forces seeking out the guerrillas and being ambushed, the guerrillas would be forced to come to the government forces and themselves be ambushed.

It seemed more and more possible that an effective strategic concept could be developed by combining Thompson's strategic hamlet plan with the work in Washington and Fort Bragg on both the military tactics to be pursued and the measures to combat the strains of modernization with which Rostow was concerned.

What was clear above all else was that the single most important principle of all—as the British had discovered in Malaya—was that civic, police, social, and military measures had to be combined and carefully coordinated to an overall counter-guerrilla program and that there had to be a unified civilian, police, and military system of command and control.

The political and civic action effort at the village level had to be given central emphasis, as in Thompson's plan, and so did police work. If military measures were effectively meshed in, the orthodox military priorities would have to be turned around—a change which would be difficult for the top levels of the Pentagon to accept. Orthodox military doctrine, as mentioned above, demands that a commander seek out the main body of the enemy and destroy him. The emphasis is on mobility, for in conventional war there is great danger in tying forces down in static defense where they can be defeated piecemeal. For the purposes of conventional war all this is sound doctrine, forged in the fire of combat through many wars. But if the analysis of the nature and requirements of guerrilla warfare was correct, the military priorities would have to be quite different.

The Military Tasks in a Political Approach

In a political approach to revolutionary war, there would be five separate military tasks. The first would be static defense, an unattractive but unavoidable task. Forces would have to guard bridges, power plants, communication centers, and other installations needed to keep the economy functioning.

The second task would also tie forces down in static defense—but it was the guts of the strategic hamlet program. This was the "clear-and-hold" task of pushing the regular guerrilla units out of a district and holding them at bay so the civic action teams could go to work in the hamlets for the weeks or months it took to turn the area into a solid bloc of loyal strategic hamlets capable of defending themselves.

The third task would be only partly mobile—to send in reinforcements for strategic hamlets under attack and to set up ambushes on escape routes.

Only the fourth and fifth tasks would resemble conventional tactics, emphasizing true mobility to seek out the enemy, but even these would require a guerrilla rather than a conventional approach. For the fourth task would be to keep jabbing at the regular guerrilla forces to keep them off balance so they could not concentrate in large enough force to move into a zone of strategic hamlets and destroy enough to discredit the program. But even this would not conform to the "seek-and-destroy" idea, for the bulk of the government forces would have to be used to concentrate on the first three tasks, and for a long time there simply would not be enough troops available to do any more than jab at the regular guerrilla forces. It would be only in the last stages of the struggle, when the remaining hard core of guerrillas was isolated in the mountains, the rural population protected by strategic hamlets, and the regular forces freed from the first three tasks that it would be possible to shift to a "seek-and-destroy" strategy.

The fifth task—even more particular—would be purely guerrilla itself. "Sealing off" the borders of South Vietnam and cutting the infiltration routes in any absolute sense would take a million men, at least. But pro-government guerrilla forces operating in South Vietnam—and possibly in Laos as well—could chew up the infiltration. Laying ambushes, raiding, and patrolling as guerrillas themselves, these units could make it much more difficult for the infiltrators to get through, forcing them to fight their way, to carry more food, and supplies. Pro-government guerrillas could not "cut" the Ho Chi Minh network of trails, but they could choke down the flow over it.

Summation of the Two Approaches

The "military" approach, in sum, saw "revolutionary warfare" as essentially war in its classic terms. A static defense attempting to protect the mass of the people from the guerrillas seemed hopeless, requiring an impossibly large number of troops. The strategy for dealing with guerrillas must therefore be that of orthodox warfare. First, the main body of the enemy troops had to be sought out and destroyed. This meant aggressive offensive operations against the guerrillas, with the emphasis on mobility and firepower—helicopters, artillery, and air bombardment. Tight rules to avoid injuring the friendly population and damaging their property would be established, but the troops could not be denied whatever firepower they needed. In areas controlled by the enemy, the rules could also be drawn to minimize the damage to civilians, but since the population in those areas supported the guerrillas there was no choice but to treat them as hostile. Second, the lines of infiltration for cadre and supplies coming from the outside had to be interdicted by whatever means were available, which meant in practice principally by air bombardment. Although there were some air enthusiasts who thought bombing could actually cut off the flow of supplies entirely, most advocates of the "military" approach felt that the maximum that interdiction could accomplish was to cut down the rate of flow and make the effort more costly. But they still regarded it as an essential element of the strategy. Third, the outside source of the aggression, the source of overall direction, of the trained cadres, and of key supplies, which in this particular case meant North Vietnam, itself had to be attacked—by air bombardment as a minimum and if necessary by invasion. If the punishment were severe enough, the outside source would inevitably choose to call off the war. If political considerations made it desirable to limit the level of punishment, attrition might still wear the enemy down enough to cause him to quit, and at the very least the level of outside support to the guerrillas would be curtailed and the cost increased.

Success would depend on maintaining a steady aggressiveness in the offensive and a high kill-rate among the guerrillas. It was recognized that doing this required highly motivated, highly skilled, and well-equipped troops, and that this was a point of weakness. It was also recognized that the "military" approach required single-minded devotion to the war effort on the part of the government, that such devotion would be impossible without political stability, and that this was another point of weakness. And the need for political stability, in turn, meant that American pressure on the government of the country for political reforms away from authoritarianism and toward democracy had to be exercised with restraint and that social and economic change had to proceed slowly and deliberately lest they create additional instability. Success also depended on maintaining a high level of military pressure on the outside source of aggression, and it was recognized that this would entail considerable international political cost. This political cost, in the view of the advocates of the "military" approach, simply had to be borne. It could be mitigated by making an all-out effort and ending the struggle as quickly and cleanly as possible. But it was a recognized weakness.

The "political" approach was the opposite in all of its essentials. It saw "revolutionary warfare" as mainly political. It saw the main source of both recruits and supplies as being within the country and the main lines of supply and communications as the dozens of roads and trails leading, like spokes of a wheel, into each of thousands of villages. The strategy for dealing with the guerrillas was to cut them off from the villages—to protect the people, to win their allegiance, and to arm them so they could defend themselves. This meant that, in President Kennedy's words, it was "their war"—the South Vietnamese themselves had to win the war or lose it. American military power could be used to deter the outside source from escalating the war, and the United States could furnish military and economic aid and advisers. It might even be possible for American combat forces to be used in certain circumstances to help protect vital installations, such as ports and airfields. But if this viewpoint was upheld, it would be contradictory and politically self-defeating to attempt to use American troops as the principal force to protect the Vietnamese people and to win their allegiance to a Vietnamese government.

For the "political" approach, success required more or less rapid social and political change and at the same time a careful coordination of economic, military, and police efforts to insure that they were meshed into an overall political program. It was recognized that doing this required honest and dedicated leaders at the local level and an enlightened and reasonably efficient national administration, and that both of these were weaknesses. It was also recognized that the "political" approach required a broadly based political leadership, incorporating as many as possible of the country's different political groupings, and that this was also a weakness. For in the case of South Vietnam, this meant bringing together the Buddhists, the Catholics, the Army, the nationalists among the intellectuals and students, some of the sects such as the Cao Dai, and representatives of the old political parties, which had been exiled by President Diem, including those with neutralist sentiments—and the mutual hostility among some of these diverse groupings was high.

Practice: 1962 to 1965

Although the initial policy decision, first made following the return of the Taylor-Rostow mission in 1961 and reiterated early in 1962, favored the "political" approach, it is a comment on the pluralism of the American government that the implementation was never clear-cut. In general, the military representatives in Saigon continued to recommend the essentially "military" approach to the Vietnamese; the representatives of the State Department and the Agency for International Development (AID) continued to press for the "political" approach;

and the American mission lacked any clear line of authority and command that could control and coordinate the representatives of the often rival American departments and agencies. Partly for this reason and partly because of forces and rivalries that were purely Vietnamese, the result was frustration for the advocates of both the "military" and the "political" approaches.

The advocates of the "military" point of view felt that the "shooting war," as they called the military side of the effort, was hampered by lack of aggressiveness among the commanding officers of the Vietnamese forces, by the inefficiencies of the highly centralized Diem regime, and by the regime's tendency to appoint officers for reasons of political loyalty rather than military efficiency. They found it particularly irksome to try to insure the vigorous implementation of military operations while playing the role of advisers, with no direct control or command. In general, however, the two greatest frustrations, from the viewpoint of the advocates of the "military" approach, were, first, the limitations on the war, both the strict rules about bombing in the South and the immunity enjoyed by the North, and, second, the political instability and disunity, which in their view kept the Vietnamese from devoting their full attention to the military effort. They tended to sympathize with President Diem's policy of dealing ruthlessly with the Buddhists in the crisis of 1963 and were increasingly unhappy as the schism between the United States government and Diem widened. For a short period following the overthrow of Diem, hopes ran a little higher. But when the Vietnamese military junta failed to produce a unified government and a natural leader, and coup began to follow coup in rapid succession, the advocates of the "military" approach regretted the fall of Diem more and more and were confirmed in their conviction that the best hope for the vigorous military effort they desired lay not in broadening the government but in a single strong man, even though his government was authoritarian.

The advocates of the "political" approach were equally frustrated. They felt that a sound strategic doctrine had been developed around the strategic hamlet program, but that it was simply not being carried out. President Diem stubbornly refused to broaden his political base or institute the necessary social and political reforms rapidly and decisively. The failure to provide overall coordination at the center left huge gaps—for example, in police work, which was as important to the "political" approach as social, economic, and political reform. Most importantly, the military effort was not coordinated with the strategic hamlet, "pacification" effort. Military operations proceeded independently, emphasizing "search-and-destroy" missions, although the very heart of the "political" approach was to concentrate the military effort on "clear-and-hold" missions that would provide both physical security and time for the political and social effort required to win the people's allegiance. For this failure, many of the advocates of the "political" approach blamed the American military as much as they did the Vietnamese. The culminating frustration, however, was the growing conviction, which was confirmed following the coup against Diem in November of 1963, that Ngo Dinh Nhu, Diem's brother, had corrupted the strategic hamlet program to his own neo-Fascist purposes. Rather than following a carefully phased, oil-blot plan of priorities, in which the loyalties of each area were assured and all Vietcong agents eliminated before the troops and civic action teams moved on to the next, Nhu had thrown up so-called "strategic hamlets" all over Vietnam. Most of them were a sham, nothing more than a string of barbed wire around a village and a blast of propaganda, while the Vietcong agents remained in place and the village continued to be under their control.

Following the coup against Diem, the advocates of the "political" approach were also frustrated by the failure of the military junta to produce a unified government. But they were even more frustrated by the failure to make the most of this "second chance" to adopt a "political" strategic concept. They were dismayed both by the fact that American advice, following the death of President Kennedy, turned increasingly toward the "military" approach and by the fact that the Vietnamese military junta seemed to be receptive to no other.

The Crisis of 1964–65

It was in late 1964 and early 1965 that the fundamental incompatibility between the two approaches was most starkly revealed. For what was a crisis by the criteria set up by one strategic concept was not necessarily a crisis when measured by the criteria set up by the other. In 1964, the Vietcong shifted the focus of their military operations to the central and northern highlands, seizing outlying strategic hamlets and military outposts. From the set of assumptions held by the advocates of the "military" approach, this produced a crisis. The Vietcong were very close to controlling Route 19 from Pleiku to the sea, and Vietcong control of Route 19 would "cut the country in half." Hanoi could increase the flow of men and supplies over the infiltration routes, and the infiltrating guerrillas would meet no line of defense to the south until they reached the provinces bordering Saigon and the delta itself.

But from the set of assumptions held by the advocates of the "political" approach this was not necessarily a crisis. The strategic element in their view was not territory, especially not the mountainous, sparsely populated territory of the highlands. The strategic element was the people, who were concentrated in the delta. The infiltration could not be stopped in any case, and it did not matter too much whether the infiltrators traveled a little less easily by jungle trails or a little more easily by Route 19. If the population centers around Hué in the north and especially in the delta could be protected, if the guerrillas' access to the people could be cut, if the people could be won to the government's side and then armed—if all this could be done, it would not matter who controlled the sparsely populated highlands, nor would the level of infiltration be overly important. Although the infiltrators were the essential cadres for the Vietcong and the supplies coming over the trails were key items, the bulk of the recruits and supplies came from the villages of South Vietnam. Really large-scale guerrilla operations could not be supported and supplied over the infiltration routes, and without the support of the population, the guerrillas would be forced to spend more and more of their time and strength in merely staying alive. In the opinion of the advocates of the "political" approach, the question of who controlled the sparsely populated jungles and mountains was not crucial. In Burma during the post-war years, they argued as an example, Communist and other guerrillas controlled the mountains but since the basic population in the country was unsympathetic to their cause the guerrillas were not successful in the end. Once the loyalty of the population was assured, the advocates of a "political" approach argued, even an increasing flow of infiltrators could be dealt with at the government's leisure. The only crisis in the view of the advocates of a "political" approach, was the long-standing failure to concentrate on protecting the population and winning their allegiance.

Escalation, 1965

The recommendation made by the advocates of the "military" approach was for a bombing program by American forces in both South Vietnam and North Vietnam. The bombing program for the South was to be simply an increase in the firepower available to support the troops fighting the Vietcong by the use of regular American Air Force units, and it would be subject to the same tight rules of engagement already in effect, rules designed to minimize civilian casualties. The program for bombing the North would begin on a small scale and gradually increase in intensity, in an attempt to convince Hanoi to call off the guerrilla war. The arguments adduced in support of these recommendations were those already described.

Under the pressure of a "crisis" and the specific set of recommendations, the advocates of a "political" approach added somewhat to their previous arguments against a bombing program.

In the first place, a program for bombing in the South using American planes and pilots openly, in their view, violated the most fundamental principle of a strategic concept that was based on the idea of winning the allegiance of the people. If Americans did the bombing it would give powerful support to the Vietcong charge that the United States purpose in Vietnam was a new form of colonialist-imperialism, and it would help them enlist the forces of nationalism on their side. Beyond this, bombing in the South would greatly increase the obstacles already in the way of the attempt to win the allegiance of the people. Air power and artillery were essential for close-in support for a unit locked in combat with a guerrilla unit. In very special circumstances, when the intelligence was beyond question, artillery and bombers might also be used to good effect against Vietcong hideouts and base areas. But what was bound to be bad was *preparatory* bombing of villages or areas contiguous to villages prior to helicopter landings or *interdiction* bombing of "suspected" Vietcong areas—more Vietcong would be recruited, the advocates of a "political" approach warned, than would be killed.

A program for bombing North Vietnam raised even thornier questions and introduced all the interrelated complications of international politics. North Vietnam had only 35 or so industrial plants and power installations, which they had acquired through much sacrifice, and it was probably the risk of losing these that had deterred Hanoi from infiltrating any of their 250,000 regular North Vietnamese troops into South Vietnam. But once these factories and power plants were destroyed, they would have nothing left to lose. If North Vietnam retaliated in this way, the outcome would be a conventional war of the type and scale of the Korean War.

Then there was the question of Communist China and its response. The closer that American power got to the borders of China, the greater was the possibility of a massive intervention by "Chinese People's Army Volunteers," as had happened in the Korean War. Vietnam was not a peninsula like Korea, and if there was a Chinese intervention the possibility of the war spreading to the whole of Southeast Asia would obviously be high.

A more limited program for bombing North Vietnam, one which

attacked only military installations and communications routes in the North, ran much less risk of causing Chinese Communist intervention. Both the Soviets and the Chinese could be expected to step up their aid and might even bring in volunteers to man anti-aircraft units and to pilot fighter planes, but probably not much more.[8] The full strength of the North Vietnamese would probably not be infiltrated to the South in response to limited bombing. But as a way of matching the escalation initiated by the United States and in retaliation for it, they might well begin to introduce battalions of North Vietnamese regulars into the South.[9]

[8] As it turned out, Soviet aid was in fact increased after the bombing from what had been only a token level to approximately one billion dollars per year.

[9] When President Johnson decided to bomb North Vietnam in February, 1965, those officials who favored the decision did so for different reasons. Some thought it would so punish North Vietnam as to cause Hanoi to end the struggle. Others doubted this, but favored the bombing on the grounds that it would cut off the flow of supplies and infiltrators or severely reduce it. Still others favored bombing the North on the grounds that it would make the whole North Vietnamese effort more costly and painful, even if it did not stop the flow of supplies and men, and that this would improve morale in South Vietnam. The public position at the time, however, tended to justify the bombing as a retaliation for attacks on American installations in South Vietnam, such as the attack on the American barracks at Pleiku, or as a retaliation for an increased use of the infiltration routes or a change in the type of infiltrators to include North Vietnamese as well as ex-Southerners. Many outside observers felt that all this was merely a rationalization and excuse—that the decision was made on the grounds described above and then delayed until a suitable incident provided the justification. In any event, the public case was weak. First, there had been attacks on Americans and American installations all along—a grenade was thrown at the American ambassador as early as 1961, for example; there was an attack on the American Special Forces camp at Plei Mrong in early 1962, and so on. Second, the number of people coming over the infiltration routes remained fairly steady, ranging from 5,400 to 12,400 per year from 1961 until after the bombing of North Vietnam in 1965. When all the intelligence was in, in fact, it turned out that fewer infiltrators had come over the trails in 1964 than in 1962. Third, the evidence available at the time that there had been such a significant introduction of North Vietnamese during 1964 as to justify retaliation was unconvincing. The evidence was assembled in the Department of State's white paper, *Aggression from the North, The Record of North Vietnam's Campaign to Conquer South Vietnam*, which was issued in 1965 to support the case for bombing. No captured documents, equipment, or materials were presented that indicate either the presence of North Vietnamese regular units or of individual North Vietnamese in significant numbers. The white paper was able to present the case studies of only

There were also the political drawbacks. Any bombing of North Vietnam would be an escalation at American initiative and a violation of the Geneva accords at a time when the more desirable political posture would be one of restraint. Escalation would raise questions among both neutrals and allies about the sense of responsibility of America's leadership. A posture of restraint was also essential to preserve as much as possible of the 1954 Geneva accords. For the 1954 Geneva accords would become, as they had in Laos in 1962, the basis for any negotiated

---

four captured infiltrators who were ethnic North Vietnamese. No evidence was presented of the presence of regular North Vietnamese units except the allegations of two of these and two other captured Vietcong of southern origin.

Later evidence permits two conclusions: First, that at least one battalion of North Vietnamese regulars had already entered South Vietnam at the time the bombing began in February, 1965; and, second, that the United States did not know of this fact at that time. In December, 1964, and January, 1965, the first of a new family of Soviet small arms were recovered after clashes with disciplined and uniformed enemy units—which aroused suspicion. But it was not until the Highway 19 campaign in February and March of 1965 captured significant numbers of North Vietnamese members of a march unit, that hard evidence began to accumulate that regular North Vietnamese units had definitely appeared inside South Vietnam and not until the enemy summer monsoon campaign in the central highlands that it was definitely established that the infiltration of North Vietnamese regulars had begun in late 1964 and was of substantial size.

One final comment can be made. William P. Bundy, the Assistant Secretary of State for East Asian and Pacific Affairs, in a speech on August 15, 1967, described the 1964–65 infiltration of North Vietnamese regulars as "moving in for the kill." Agreed that we now know they were beginning to move in, the question is why for the kill? What is puzzling is why the North Vietnamese would take the chance of provoking an American retaliation if they were winning, as the Administration believed and as the Administration believes the North Vietnamese and the Vietcong believed.

Since there is no doubt that the North Vietnamese had assembled forces along the border and in Laos, the counterargument would presumably be that since the Vietcong were winning anyway, Hanoi had no interest in escalating the struggle. The North Vietnamese were well aware of the debate in the United States about bombing the north, according to the counterargument, and their real intent in assembling the troops on the border and in Laos was to try to deter the United States from escalating the struggle by threatening to retaliate for any bombing of the North by introducing regular forces into the South in large numbers. The purpose of the one battalion already in the South, if this view is correct, would have been a preliminary and secret reconnaissance.

For my own part, I find both arguments unconvincing, but I must also confess that I cannot think of a third explanation that would be any more persuasive.

settlement—and a negotiated settlement was probably the most likely outcome even if the effort in Vietnam were successful.

Another result of bombing North Vietnam that was predicted at the time was that it would create formidable pressure from our allies and from a significant segment of domestic opinion pushing the United States toward offering to negotiate *prematurely*. Although the advocates of a "political" approach tended to see negotiations as probably the most likely outcome of the situation even in reasonably favorable circumstances, many of them felt that if negotiations took place before there had been progress in winning the allegiance of the peasants, especially in the delta, the result would be the neutralization of Vietnam, which in those circumstances would be tantamount to the Vietcong taking over completely.

The advocates of a "political" approach felt that bombing the North would also put an obstacle in the way of furthering the détente with the Soviet Union, which had been begun with the limited nuclear test ban treaty, and make it difficult for the Soviets to follow their own national interest regarding Southeast Asia—which was to press Hanoi to keep the struggle damped down. And bombing the North would add credibility to the Chinese argument for more belligerent Communist policies, and strengthen their hand in the Sino-Soviet dispute.

But above and beyond all these unwelcome consequences, bombing the North, in the opinion of the advocates of a "political" approach, would be a mistake for the fundamental reason that it would probably not work. Many advocates of bombing believed that it would force North Vietnam to order the Vietcong to quit or that it would cut the flow of supplies to the South and make it impossible for the Vietcong to continue. All-out bombing might accomplish that objective, the counterargument went, but all-out bombing would run too great a risk of massive Chinese intervention. Limited, measured bombing, on the other hand, could not hurt the North Vietnamese economy enough to matter. Nor could any bombing, no matter how heavy, the advocates of a "political" approach believed, succeed in "cutting" the flow of supplies. They contended that most of the supplies for the Vietcong, like the recruits, came from the villages of the *South*. The Vietcong required only five or six tons of supplies a day from the outside world. This amounted to three or four truckloads—which could easily be transported by a few dozen coolies or one big sampan. Of course bombing the supply routes would hurt the Communists. They would have to travel at night. They would have to spend time and energy filling in bomb holes in the roads, putting their supply dumps in camouflaged underground warehouses, and repairing bridges. But bombing, the advocates of a "political" approach argued, does not "destroy" an underdeveloped economy, in which trade is often conducted by barter, nor does bombing "destroy" communications lines that are really dirt roads and jungle trails with timber bridges that are usually placed where there was once a ford anyway. In a country like North Vietnam, bombing communications routes would do little more than make the enemy put more effort into maintaining the flow of supplies, an effort mainly requiring manpower. And manpower was the one thing that North Vietnam and their Chinese allies had plenty of.

In the minds of the advocates of a "political" approach, in other words, there was a real question whether the results of bombing would be substantial enough to justify the loss of the expensive American airplanes that would inevitably be shot down and the lives of the pilots that would be lost along with them.

To the advocates of a "political" approach, the proper role for American military power was not to use it to try to defeat the Vietcong or to force the North to order them to quit—both of which seemed to be self-defeating in the senses that they would not lead to a politically stable result. The proper role for American military power was to deter North Vietnam and Communist China from escalating the struggle. But even for this more limited goal of deterring the North from stepping up the war by introducing regular North Vietnamese units or Chinese volunteers in massive numbers, it seemed more likely that it would not be American air power alone that would be the effective deterrent, but the totality of American military power, including especially ground power.

The fact of the matter in the view of the advocates of the "political" approach was that Asians tended to interpret the use of air power *alone* as a weak response, even though they feared air power. The United States had so often flirted with the idea of "immaculate" war in Asia, war fought in the clean, blue sky above the muck and blood of the jungle, that Asians had begun to think of air power alone as an attempt to bluff. In the circumstances, it seemed that the only thing the United States could be sure would impress either Communist or non-Communist Asians was ground forces.

But the purpose would not be to use American ground forces to take over the war effort, for that again, in the view of the advocates of the "political" approach, would be politically self-defeating. The purpose in using American ground forces, if it came to that, would not be for the United States to escalate, to repeat, but to deter the other side from escalating. For example, if the North Vietnamese began to escalate the struggle by infiltrating regular North Vietnamese combat units into Vietnam or Chinese People's Army Volunteers—neither of which they had yet done according to the intelligence available—the response, from the viewpoint of a "political" approach, would have been to put a division of American ground forces not into Vietnam but into Thailand as a warning and to couple it with private communications to North Vietnamese representatives in the various Communist and neutral capitals. If the warning was not heeded, that division could be moved right up to the Laos border, and a second division introduced into Thailand. If that set of warnings was also ignored a division could be introduced into Vietnam, and so on—not to fight the Vietcong, which should, in the view of the advocates of a "political" approach, remain the task of the South Vietnamese, but to deter the North from further escalation.

Practice: 1965–66

President Johnson's decision, however, went the other way. The bombing program for North Vietnam was begun on February 7, 1965, and the bombing program for South Vietnam on February 24. Political pressures from our allies, from the neutrals, and from domestic public opinion was high, and by April, 1965, President Johnson felt obliged to put forward his offer to negotiate in his speech at Baltimore. Even though it seemed obvious that the political situation in South Vietnam favored the Communist side, Hanoi unaccountably did not take up the offer, and the large-scale introduction of American ground forces in July, 1965, gave the non-Communist side bargaining counters to offset those which the political situation conferred on the Vietcong.

By January, 1966, after a year of the bombing program during which American combat forces had also taken over a significant portion of the ground fighting, the situation was worse than it had been before. During the year, the guerrilla forces had actually doubled in size from about 124,000 to something between 215,000 and 245,000.

During the year 1965, infiltration had increased from 7,400 for the year before to 26,000 (the following year, 1966, it ran to something like 60,000). Much more significantly, however, the infiltrators included significant numbers of regular North Vietnamese units, bringing the total North Vietnamese regiments in South Vietnam to 10. In a short time the military side of the struggle became not one war, but two. One was the old guerrilla struggle against the Vietcong, now continued mainly in the delta. The other was a limited conventional war similar in many of its aspects to the Korean War. The opponents in this second war were regular North Vietnamese units on one side and American troops on the other, and it was being fought mainly in the highlands in the northern half of South Vietnam, whose sparse population had largely fled to escape both American bombing and Communist terrorism and impressment.

Most significantly of all, however, during the year following the bombing decisions the recruitment of Vietcong guerrillas from among the villagers of *South Vietnam* increased almost threefold—from 40,800, according to official United States estimates, to something between 105,900 and 135,900, as illustrated in the following table.

VIETCONG STATISTICS
(From Official United States Government Sources)

Year	Strength as of January 1st	Killed	Captured	Infiltrated	Recruited in South Vietnam
1960.......	Unknown	6,000	Unknown	4,500 ('59–'60)	Unknown
1961.......	5,000 reg. 30,000 irreg.				
	35,000 Total	12,000	Unknown	5,400	34,600
1962.......	23,000 reg. 40,000 irreg.				
	63,000 Total	21,000	5,500	12,400	31,100
1963.......	30,000 reg. 50,000 irreg.				
	80,000 Total	21,000	4,000	7,400	29,600
1964.......	32,000 reg. 60,000 irreg.				
	92,000 Total	17,000	4,200	7,400	45,800
1965*......	34,000 reg. 90,000 irreg.				
	124,000 Total	35,000	5,900	26,000†	105,900– 135,900
1966.......	75,000– 85,000 regulars 100,000–120,000 irregulars 40,000 political cadres				
	215,000–245,000 Total				

* Bombing program began February, 1965.
† Includes 10 regular North Vietnamese regiments.

This massive recruitment within South Vietnam dramatically illustrated the importance of Vietcong access to the villages as contrasted with the infiltration routes. The response was a decision, publicized at the February, 1966, Honolulu Conference between President Johnson and General Ky, Prime Minister of Vietnam, to launch a major "pacification" effort along the lines of the "strategic hamlet" program that would combine village defenses and police action against Vietcong agents with social and political reform and simple economic development at the village level. In effect, the United States strategy became an attempt to pursue both the "military" and the "political" approaches to "revolutionary" warfare at one and the same time.

Interim Results

By late 1967 the United States bombing program had been enlarged to include military targets near and within Hanoi and Haiphong, such as petroleum storage and distribution facilities and the Longbien bridge, which crosses the Red River at Hanoi. The total tonnage of bombs dropped in North Vietnam began to rival the totals dropped on Nazi Germany, with essentially only three target systems still excluded—the dikes and irrigations system, the ships and docks in the Haiphong harbor, and the civilian population. The American forces in Vietnam increased to approximately 500,000 men, with further increases of a few thousand already planned.

Although the bombing program against the North had obviously made the effort of infiltration more costly during 1966, it had not prevented the North from increasing the number infiltrated eightfold, from the 7,400 infiltrated the year before the bombing began to approximately 60,000 in 1966. Nor had the bombing prevented the infiltration of arms and ammunition. As Secretary McNamara pointed out, "the quantity of externally supplied material, other than food, required to support the VC-NVN forces in South Vietnam at about their current level of combat activity is very, very small—significantly under 100 tons a day—a quantity that could be transported by only a few trucks."

Neither had the bombing hurt the North Vietnamese economy or morale sufficiently to cause any visible lessening of their will and determination to continue. There is reason to believe, in fact, that the North Vietnamese may consider that at this stage, when most of the possible damage to their industry has already been done, the cost of the bombing to the Americans in lives and treasure is greater than the damage they inflict. In an interview with David Schoenbrun on September 3, 1967, the prime minister of North Vietnam, Pham Van Dong, said categorically that the North Vietnamese would offer no *quid pro quo* whatsoever for cessation of the bombing.

Inside South Vietnam, it was clear that the North Vietnamese regular divisions and the main force Vietcong divisions had been severely mauled by the superior firepower of the American forces, who had a monopoly of armor, helicopters, the heavier types of artillery, and air power.

The Vietcong irregular forces, on the other hand, who were concentrated mainly in the delta, continued to rely principally on guerrilla tactics and, from all the evidence available, they had not yet suffered militarily to anywhere near the same degree. In fact, certain evidence emanating from the Socialist countries that had been active in trying to bring about negotiations indicated that among the guerrillas confidence and determination may have actually grown.

In the "pacification" effort, there were considerable improvements in the organization of the American side of the effort, but the results continued to be disappointing, due partly to the continued emphasis on General Westmoreland's "search-and-destroy" strategy, but mainly to the continued lack of improvement in the effort of the South Vietnamese. The success of the "Tet" offensive in February, 1968, confirmed that the Communists continued to be as strong as ever.

Conclusion

For the moment, at least, the Chinese Communist concept of "revolutionary" warfare and the American response to it appear to be at a stalemate. It is difficult to believe that the Communist side can push the United States into the sea, now that its power and prestige are so heavily committed. At the same time, it is equally difficult to believe that the Americans can now defeat the Vietcong in the political sense of bringing about an independent, politically stable, and loyally non-Communist South Vietnam.

From the American point of view, what is even more frustrating is that all the basic questions about the rival strategic concepts for dealing with "revolutionary" warfare still remain:

Given the instabilities and vulnerabilities of the transition period in modernization and the cheapness of destruction, terror, and the techniques of "revolutionary" warfare, will there ever be time enough for the "political" approach to work in a country in which even the beginnings of insurgency exist?

Given the need to work with the existing government and social system, rather than sweep them away as the insurgents do, and given the inadequacies of the leadership in most underdeveloped countries, the lack of skills, training, and more often than not the lack of dedication and even integrity in the national cadres of a country whose development is still at the village level, can the fundamental principle of the "political" approach that the people of the country must do the job themselves ever be fulfilled?

Given the forces of nationalism and anti-colonialism in most countries vulnerable to "revolutionary" warfare, is it really possible to defeat insurgency by the massive application of military force—especially outside force, which means American—without so alienating the people as to make a political victory impossible, leaving no alternative but continued military occupation?

Can the "military" and "political" approaches actually be combined into a single strategy without nullifying each other, with political strictures hobbling the military effort and military measures canceling out the social and political effort to win the people's allegiance?

Even if the combined strategy does somehow succeed in Vietnam, in how many other places can the United States afford, in terms of both blood and treasure, to make such a stupendous, costly effort?

One thing only seems certain. No matter what the outcome in Vietnam, the experience has been ambiguous. Even if the result is something the United States can claim is a success, there will remain doubt that the United States has developed a response to "revolutionary" warfare that is reasonable enough in terms of cost, acceptable enough in terms of international risk, and effective enough in terms of political results to be worthy of universal application.

Throughout the rest of Southeast Asia, the "revolutionary potential" seems small at the present time. In Indonesia the Communist party has been decimated. In Burma the Communists are indentified with Peking and alienated from the forces of nationalism. The same is true in Cambodia. Even in Thailand, at a time when the presence of the American air force operating against North Vietnam from Thai bases gives the Communist side the highest of incentives to ignite guerrilla warfare, the result of their attempt is so far unimpressive. Much the same can be said both of Africa, where the heavy-handed Chinese methods have largely backfired, and of South America, where Che Guevara's death has dramatized the failure of "revolutionary" warfare in Bolivia. The suspicion arises, in a word, that "revolutionary" warfare is not the wave of the future and that Vietnam may be unique in Southeast Asia, and perhaps even in Africa and Latin America—that it may be the last country in which Communism will succeed in capturing the deep though inchoate forces of nationalism.

The fact that the experience in Vietnam has been ambiguous, however, will be noted throughout the world, even if the ultimate result permits the United States to claim something that can be called success. If and when political and social conditions in other developing countries make them vulnerable again, ambitious men in those countries will be encouraged to try the techniques of "revolutionary" warfare for themselves, and ambitious men in Peking and elsewhere will be encouraged to give them support.

Comments by Morton A. Kaplan

I welcome the opportunity to appear before this conference and to comment briefly and extemporaneously on my friend Roger Hilsman's paper. Roger is, of course, an expert on guerrilla warfare. He engaged in it himself during the Second World War, and served as assistant secretary of state during the Kennedy administration with many specific responsibilities for the problem of Vietnam. His paper is, as one would expect, sharp, perceptive, and informative. The substantial contributions he has made to our understanding of the Vietnam problem are on the record and require no praise from me. My function, if I understand it properly, is to worry Roger, as a dog worries a bone in the effort to illuminate some of the obscurities that even his distinguished analysis has failed to dispel.

Roger Hilsman is too decent a man and too distinguished a scholar to write a party history. He indeed refrained from stating that Johnson's Vietnam policies contrast poorly with those of Kennedy, although he obviously sincerely believes that to be the case. However, it will be argued here that Johnson is primarily continuing policies that Kennedy initiated and with less freedom of choice than Kennedy had. This is said neither in condemnation of Kennedy, who voiced the best ideals of many Americans, nor in praise of Lyndon Johnson, whose policies in some areas this speaker vigorously disagrees with. But, and Roger would surely agree, as a matter of record these matters deserve to be clarified.

According to Hilsman, two schools of thought can be distinguished in the Kennedy administration with respect to Vietnam: the political school and the military school. As he points out, these labels oversimplify the complexities of the positions taken, including the fact that some advocates of the military solution held positions in the Department of State while some advocates of the political solution held positions in the Department of Defense. The political team which was led by Robert F. Kennedy has since, for the most part, left the government while the so-called military team led by W. W. Rostow and General Maxwell Taylor now reflects dominant sentiment within the Johnson administration. The Rostow-Taylor point of view, according to Hilsman, portrays the Vietnam war primarily as a matter of external aggression and places the main emphasis on defeating the aggression by military means, although, as Hilsman himself points out, the Rostow-Taylor mission to Vietnam in 1961 came back with a recommendation for political reforms. The team led by Robert F. Kennedy believed that the problem in Vietnam was primarily political, that classical military measures should be eschewed, and that the primary task was to win the population over. As part of this strategy, there was to be a strategic hamlet program, as in Malaya, with the Vietnamese population in the built-up and heavily-populated regions concentrated behind barbed wire in militarily-controlled hamlets. Political reforms would occur within these strategic hamlets, militia would be used within them to control the situation, and counter-guerrilla forces would sortie out from them in order to maintain security. The only thing wrong with this strategy, according to Hilsman, was that it was not possible to carry it out because of President Diem's sabotage.

It is very curious to label a strategy a political strategy when it leaves out of account one of the primary political factors: the willingness of the local regime to cooperate with it. For an administration and a team supposedly attuned to political considerations, the Kennedy administration—despite Hilsman's statement that Kennedy approved Rostow's 1961 recommendations for political reforms in Vietnam—put to use none of the opportunities available to it in 1961 to force President Diem during his period of weakness to agree to substantial political reforms. Now this speaker was not a particular believer in the strategic hamlets program, at least in Vietnam, although Hilsman's great expertise gives

his opinion more weight. In the Vietnamese context, the strategic hamlets would likely have become enlarged prison camps that would have
lowered morale within the country and increased the disaffection of the
population from the administration in Saigon, even in the absence of
interference from Saigon. But regardless of whether the strategic hamlet
idea was this bad or was as good as Hilsman believes, one of the greatest
weaknesses in the Diem regime stemmed from its replacement of elected
hamlet and village leaders by Diem appointees. The rigid, bureaucratic, Mandarin character of the regime, which was well known to
American officials, was as thoroughly inconsistent with success for this
so-called political approach as anything could have been. Yet it was
pursued under circumstances that could only have worsened the situation in Vietnam.

Hilsman refers to the fact that in no American administration is any
program carried out in clear-cut fashion. This is an unfortunate truth
about the administration of foreign policy in the United States. A politically necessary consensus-building runs counter to the prospects for
coherency in foreign policy. Therefore, it is merely facile to criticize
an administration for discrepancies between an ideal policy and the
policy it carries out in practice. Nonetheless, it is difficult to deny that
the policy initiated under the Kennedy administration was self-defeating and without any substantial prospect for gain for the United States
or Vietnam.

There is a temptation for any of us who have disagreed with the
course of policy to read into the failures of policy vindications of our
own proposals to the contrary. This applies also to the present speaker
who no doubt overvalues the advice that he offered on Vietnam during
the Kennedy administration. But there is a painful memory of running
down to Washington several times to argue that we were losing the
guerrilla war, a conclusion that at least one official in the Department
of State, who was not opposed to the political approach, found simply
incompetent. There were several officials in the Kennedy administration, although they were not in the Department of State, who were
willing to listen past that unhappy assumption. However, when they
heard the only possible conclusion—either to get out of Vietnam while
our investments and commitment were small or to insist upon a major
overhaul of the government, that might mean the elimination of Diem,
and to combine it with a major military escalation—the atmosphere
grew so tense that the conclusion seemed mandatory that such advice
would not be welcomed at the top. Of course, one cannot be sure what
the North Vietnamese might have done in the event of such major

escalation in those days, but it is not an unreasonable assumption that it is far easier to respond in kind to small escalations than to a single major escalation that makes the costs loom much larger and the choices seem much more difficult. Perhaps the speaker can be forgiven for repeating his prediction that the course followed at that time would only lead to a sequence of small escalations that would not solve the problem but would increase the costs tremendously.

It is generally argued by the Kennedy people that the real commitment to Vietnam occurred under Lyndon Johnson. It is difficult to accept this conclusion. Eisenhower most likely should be exculpated. There is nothing in the record of the Eisenhower administration that compelled us militarily or politically to remain in Vietnam. Even though we called them only military advisors, however, the military commitment occurred under Kennedy. Nonetheless, this commitment as late as 1962 or early 1963 was sufficiently small so that the United States could have withdrawn (an alternative this speaker would not have preferred) without major political costs, at least in the immediate term. The binding political commitment to Vietnam occurred with the overthrow of President Diem. Roger—as well as others in the Kennedy and Johnson administrations—asserts elsewhere that the United States did not overthrow or participate in the assassination of President Diem. It is plausible, even convincing, that no such direct orders were given; and there is no reason to suspect a CIA plot in this case. It is, however, not subject to serious argument that the Kennedy administration deliberately took those measures which it knew would be interpreted in Vietnam as the withdrawal of American support from Diem and which it knew would lead to his forcible overthrow. Whether it is true or not, as some claim, that President Diem tearfully went to the American Embassy the night before his overthrow and said he would do whatever we asked if only we would save him, the American role was so important that the insistence upon our technical noninvolvement in the decisions that led to his overthrow is an exercise in scholasticism.[1]

[1] Supporters of the Kennedy position claim that the United States could not have prevented the overthrow of President Diem except by active intervention in Vietnamese politics, in particular, by actively preventing the military from carrying out the coup. Whether this is accurate, I am not competent to say, although surely part of the military willingness to stage the coup stemmed from recognition of an American desire to dispense with President Diem. Nonetheless, this decision by the American administration to withhold support from Diem did not occur in isolation. There were several instances in the past when the United States government had intervened to maintain President Diem in office. The failure to intervene in late 1963 must be placed within that con-

Just imagine the discussions in the presidential palaces and chancelleries in Southeast Asia after that event. There is little doubt what the political leadership in Southeast Asia thought of Diem's overthrow: it was part of an American plan. Each leader must have asked himself, "If I remain an ally of the United States, will they dispense with me in that way also?" Bad as this reaction must have been, imagine what the reaction would have been if, after "cooperating" in the overthrow of Diem, we had withdrawn from South Vietnam. The reverberations would have been felt throughout South Asia and Japan; they also would have been felt in Europe, even in those capitals where there was a preference that the United States not be involved in Asia. The real commitment of the United States to South Vietnam occurred with that event. Although it is true that Lyndon Johnson could have withdrawn with less difficulty in 1964 or even in 1965 than he could today, his options nonetheless were so narrowly constrained by the actions of the Kennedy administration that disengagement was not seen as a feasible option.

The reforms that could perhaps have been forced upon Diem in 1961 were much harder to impose with the overthrow of Diem because the situation had already deteriorated so much. The difficulty confronting the United States was magnified because the intelligence network that informed American officials of guerrilla activities dissolved with the procession of transitory governments. Informers do not inform unless there is protection for them. The United States was pressed into a situation in which it was committed and in which sheer survival of the South Vietnamese regime was difficult to manage. Whatever mistakes Johnson has made, and he has made several, he did not create this mess; he inherited it.

------

text. Moreover, the reason for the withdrawal of support from President Diem involved a basic appraisal by the United States government that the war could not be won while Diem was in office and an intention to foster changes consistent with winning. Thus the purpose of the decision, the degree of involvement in the past, and the context within which the American actions occurred seem fully to justify the interpretation that was placed on Diem's overthrow by most informed observers both in the United States and in Southeast Asia. The attempted exculpation of the Kennedy commitment resembles a lawyer's ploy. It is technically correct; of course, the government of the United States would not issue a direct order to overthrow a foreign president, except under the most desperate circumstances, including the unavailability of some alternative course of action. But the conclusion is inescapable that the leaders of the Kennedy administration knew exactly what they were doing, intended the actual result, and merit the judgment that history will likely place upon their actions.

The classical military approach is subject to criticism although a purely counter-guerrilla war would not be likely to succeed either. A combination of wide sweeps and point defense permits the guerrillas to reinfiltrate. It is much more likely that more limited sweeps, much greater emphasis upon militia and home-force activities, and constant fluid patrolling within the swept area, would improve the limited prospects for success.

A policy of unlimited bombings does not seem unrebuttable as a policy. Initially the bombings probably had a very important role to play in restoring the morale in the South. Within a limited area near the Demilitarized Zone, bombing serves definite military functions in reducing the amount of supplies to the guerrillas and imposing important costs upon North Vietnam. However, its cost to us may outweigh the gains from it, although this is subject to legitimate debate, and it is likely at least partly counterproductive in some of the ways that Hilsman states. On the other hand, there is an argument to be made for a strictly limited occupation of North Vietnam up to the 18th Parallel. This would help to effectively seal the border, would form a much more defensible position, would serve as a warning to North Vietnam that it was not immune to possible ground attack, and would probably not be sufficiently threatening to call in either the Russians or the Chinese. It would be a mistake to do this, however, until such time as it was combined with a more effective military strategy in the South and with a more effective political implementation.

As to whether the war is a war of aggression or a civil war, the clichés on both sides of this argument could well be dispensed with. It is sheer naïveté to argue that the Vietcong is not part of one Lao Dong apparatus directed from Hanoi. This does not mean, however, that the apparatus is directed as smoothly as the operations of the pistons in a well-oiled engine. Even during the height of Stalin's power in Russia, things never went that smoothly. Undoubtedly there are conflicts both within the Hanoi regime and between those in North Vietnam and South Vietnam. Perhaps these conflicts can be worked upon, although none of the evidence that proponents of this view have presented seems substantial. Still, it would be silly to deny that the Diem regime ran into trouble because it created sufficient disaffection within the South for the Communist apparatus to make use of legitimate grievances. Since the overthrow of Diem, however, the more important non-Communist organized forces in South Vietnam that at one time cooperated with the National Liberation Front have ceased to do so. Its main base of power is still in those areas over which the old Vietminh never lost control, even after the 1954 agreements. At the risk of appearing moderate, therefore, let me say that South Vietnam is subjected to external aggression and at the same time is undergoing rebellion at home. This is a complicated phenomenon and will not be dealt with here.

Although Roger did not refer to it in his paper, many in the so-called political faction now refer to the Trollope ploy as the device that solved the Cuban missile crisis and as the kind of device that could be used to solve the Vietnamese problem. According to this viewpoint, the Trollope ploy involves acceptance by re-interpretation of an offer that is not really being made; this action forces the other party to accept the acceptance. Whatever may be true of Trollope's ladies and gentlemen, the world of international politics operates differently. The so-called Trollope ploy worked in Cuba because Khrushchev desperately needed some way out of a situation that he could no longer control, not because social pressures left him no choice. He lacked the means of coping with American power either in the Cuban area or elsewhere in the world, given the great American strategic advantage. Unfortunately for us, it is the North Vietnamese who hold the advantage at the present time in Vietnam. It is Ho Chi Minh who could employ the Trollope ploy; all he has to do is to accept one of Johnson's offers for negotiation and Johnson will be forced into a conference for which the United States is not yet prepared. It is precisely because the situation is so advantageous to him, given at least the not unfounded North Vietnamese belief that the United States cannot indefinitely maintain its effort in Vietnam for political and economic rather than for military reasons, that Ho Chi Minh is unlikely to force the United States into negotiations, at least until after the 1968 elections, which he probably hopes will provide him with even better alternatives than he has at present. At the risk of appearing silly by the time these comments appear in print, let me state that the Trollope ploy, so-called, merely substitutes a slogan for analysis. It also probably overestimates the pressure that Russia either could or would desire to place upon the North Vietnamese. Any time, however, that we desire to surrender, with perhaps a modest face-saving, then perhaps we can propose to accept Ho Chi Minh's supposed overtures. In these circumstances he might, although not surely would, accept our Trollope ploy. Short of that only a major improvement in our situation, perhaps a South Vietnamese government with reasonable legitimacy supplemented by an improved military strategy, seems to offer a hope of a way out.

Davis B. Bobrow

11

Liberation Wars,
National Environments, and
American Decision-Making

American responses to "wars of national liberation" can involve the direct and indirect manipulation of three major classes of factors: Communist intentions, capabilities, and action; characteristics of the national environments in which liberation wars may occur or are in progress; and American intentions, capabilities, and actions. This paper discusses only the last two types of manipulations.

Since the topic of Vietnam has been and will be treated more adequately by individuals with better data than I, the following comments do not involve diagnoses of, predictions about, or even value analyses of the Vietnamese conflict. They are directed at the American responses to national liberation wars, which present problems far broader than their specific Vietnamese instance, and at Vietnam as an *historical analogy* affecting future American responses to this type (perhaps to other types) of war. I think many of us anticipate that for those who will make and advise on future American responses, the Vietnamese experience (no matter how "ambiguous" its outcome) will probably assume the import of the Munich and Spain models. Accordingly, this commentary raises a number of considerations about, first, the national environments on which liberation war may impinge and their similarities to the Vietnam case; and, second, the implications of a few attributes of American decision-making for our responses to national liberation wars.

I   National Environments

Within the scope of this paper we obviously cannot originally or comprehensively describe the patterns and variations in the national environments which may host liberation wars. What we can do is to use data originally compiled and analyzed by others to clarify the proba-

311

bilities of relationships between a variety of national environment characteristics and revolution and guerrilla war. Like all data, these data are only suggestive, and, like all aggregate data, they do not necessarily inform us about a specific case which may confront policy-makers. However, they do suggest general perspectives. Since everything we know about human thinking under conditions of uncertainty indicates the crucial role of general perspectives as parameters on the information and options which are considered in the decision, it might be fruitful to look at these as competitive perspectives.

The parameters to be discussed are: (1) the extent to which revolutions and guerrilla wars are positively associated, i.e., the extent to which one accompanies the other, and American policy toward one is accordingly a policy toward the other; (2) the extent to which other kinds of violent domestic political instability co-occur with national liberation wars (in their subversive or more advanced stage), i.e., the extent to which you have one if you have the other, and accordingly, the extent to which American policies that affect the probability of one affect the probability of the other; (3) the extent to which domestic socioeconomic and political characteristics are in a strongly patterned relationship to national liberation war, implying that American success in affecting these characteristics will affect the challenges of a national liberation war; and (4) the extent to which Vietnamese political and socioeconomic attributes characterize many other states, implying that the United States will encounter in other nations a similar combination of non-military circumstances. Relative to the data for investigating these first four questions, the data for looking at the next two are fragmentary. However, it might be useful to include the last two questions—they are sufficiently important and the data sufficiently unfamiliar: (5) the extent to which Asian populations have political beliefs that dispose them toward some, rather than other, political options, implying that Americans can differentially marshal popular indigenous support depending on which indigenous political options they support; and (6) the extent to which American-supported Asian elites perceive the relationship as rewarding and as one of co-operation or followership rather than leverage.

Revolution and Guerrilla Warfare

The extent to which the problems presented by national liberation war are the same as those presented by revolutions and guerrilla wars determines the extent to which an American response optimal for one type of war is optimal for all three. Although these definitions are not necessarily the most useful, the ones we are using for "revolution," "guerrilla warfare," and "national liberation war" are as follows:

> Revolution: ". . . an illegal or forced change in the top government elite, any attempt at such a change, or any successful or unsuccessful armed rebellion whose aim is independence from the central government."[1]

> Guerrilla warfare: ". . . any armed activity, sabotage, or bombings carried on by independent bands of citizens or irregular forces and aimed at the overthrow of the present regime."[2]

> National liberation war: revolution, pursued initially through the means of guerrilla war and directed by Communist groups.

On the basis of our definitions, national liberation wars require the presence of both revolutionary attempts and guerrilla actions. If the positive association between these phenomena is reliably high, we have fairly good reason to believe that an American response which is optimal for national liberation wars will also be optimal for guerrilla wars and revolutions. If the association is not positive, or if it is only weakly positive, we seem to be dealing with three, in some respects dissimilar, contingencies, which suggests that an American response useful for one type is not necessarily useful for another.

Three studies[3] are directly relevant for testing the sign and degree of association between revolutions and guerrilla wars. The results are given in table 1, which follows. As we read from left to right across the table, each row presents the time period covered, the number of nations included, and the strength of the correlations. The correlations

[1] Raymond Tanter, "Dimensions of Conflict Behavior within and between Nations, 1958–1960," *Journal of Conflict Resolution,* vol. 10, no. 1 (March, 1966), p. 62.

[2] *Ibid.*

[3] For a complex comparison of the three relevant studies, see: Raymond Tanter, "Dimensions of Conflict Behavior within Nations, 1955–1960: Turmoil and Internal War," *Peace Research Society (International) Papers,* 3 (1965): 159–84. For documentation on the studies other than Tanter's, see: Francis Hoole, "Stability and Instability within Nations: A Cross National Study," M.A. thesis, San Diego State College (1964); and two articles by R. J. Rummel, "Dimensions of Conflict Behavior within and between Nations," *General Systems Yearbook,* 8 (1963): 1–50, and "Testing Some Possible Predictors of Conflict within and between Nations," *Peace Research Society (International) Papers,* 1 (1964): 79–112.

are positive in all three studies, squared to express the percentage of association greater than chance.

The data clearly show an increasing, positive correlation between guerrilla warfare and revolutions as we move forward in time. However, they do not warrant the assumption that, in our historical period, revolutions and guerrilla warfare are powerfully linked events. Accordingly, it would seem that American policy responses should be adjusted to three different contingencies: national liberation wars, revolutions without guerrilla warfare, and guerrilla warfare without revolutionary objectives.

TABLE 1

CORRELATION BETWEEN REVOLUTIONS
AND GUERRILLA WAR

Time Period	No. of Countries Coded	Correlation Squared
1948–62..........	66	.27
1955–57..........	77	.11
1958–60..........	83	.42

Source: Constructed from data reported in Raymond Tanter, "Dimensions of Conflict Behavior Within Nations, 1955–60: Turmoil and Internal War." *Peace Research Society (International) Papers*, 3 (1965): 169.

Domestic Turmoil and National Liberation War

It has been argued that when the United States is trying to deal with unstable and internally violent polities, any policy which increases conflict of any kind increases the possibility of national liberation conflicts. If this argument is correct, we would expect to find a positive association or co-variance between (1) forms of domestic violence such as riots and demonstrations, and (2) guerrilla war and revolutions. A reverse argument is that American policies which encourage relatively spontaneous and temporary forms of domestic conflict will decrease the possibility of national liberation wars. If this argument is correct, we would expect to find a strong negative association between (1) riots and demonstrations and (2) guerrilla war and revolutions. Each of the two arguments shares the assumption of association between what we can call spontaneous and temporary as opposed to premeditated and prolonged domestic violence. In factor analytic terms, these different kinds of violence should load heavily on the same dimension if either argument is correct, although the signs of association between the two kinds will differ, according to which argument is correct.

Three studies in comparable form are relevant here: table 2 presents Rummel's manipulation of data from Eckstein's study of 113 countries for the period 1946–59 (the "E" columns); Rummel's study of 77 nations for 1955–57 (the "R" columns) and Tanter's analysis of 83 nations for 1958–60 (the "T" columns).[4]

The data in table 2 support neither of the two arguments stated above. (The matrix is particularly convincing because the technique used, oblique rotation, allows interdependence as well as independence to emerge.) As the bottom rows of the table indicate ("factor [cosines] correlations"), those factors on which relatively spontaneous forms of violence load heavily (E1, R1, and T1) are highly independent of those on which guerrilla war and revolution load heavily (E2, R2, E3, R3, and T3). In other words, these data show that temporary, spontaneous forms of domestic violence don't have any patterns of association with prolonged, premeditated forms of violence. Accordingly, American policies which are supposed to affect the incidence of one form of violence should not be expected to affect the incidence of the other form.

The Domestic System and National Liberation War

Roger Hilsman[5] has distinguished very nicely what we can inexactly but meaningfully call the "military" and "non-military" perspectives in American responses to national liberation wars. In other words, some American officials regard policies that affect non-military variables as crucial to the solution of national liberation wars. Others regard military variables as central. It may be useful to distinguish several reasons officials give publicly for the second position: (1) domestic social, economic and political factors defy the kind of untangling conducive to focused policy planning ("key variables") and even moderately reliable effectiveness estimates; (2) we can "win" more economically and

---

[4] The studies under discussion are those of Rummel, "Dimensions of Conflict Behavior," and "Testing Some Possible Predictors"; Tanter, "Dimensions of Conflict Behavior, 1955–1960" and "Dimensions of Conflict Behavior, 1958–1960"; and Harry Eckstein, "The Incidence of Internal War, 1946–59," Appendix I of *Internal War: The Problem of Anticipation* (report submitted to the Research Group in Psychology and the Social Sciences, Smithsonian Institution, Washington, D.C., January 15, 1962).

[5] Roger Hilsman, "Two American Counterstrategies to Guerrilla Warfare: The Case of Vietnam," in this volume, pp. 269–303.

TABLE 2—THE STRUCTURE OF DOMESTIC CONFLICT

ECKSTEIN VARIABLES	RUMMEL-TANTER VARIABLES	OBLIQUE P FACTOR MATRICES								
		E1	R1	T1	E2	R2	T2	E3	R3	T3
1. UE	9. Killed	(76)	32		(52)	(80)			43	(72)
13. UE+E		(75)			(57)					
2. Warfare 12. External Violence 5. Large-scale terrorism	3. Guerrilla War	47				35		(77) (84) 45	(91)	(91)
6. Small-scale terrorism	1. Assassinations	(66)	(63)	(52)	37				(65)	32
3. Riots	6. Riots	(74)	(82)	(87)	41	36				
4. Turmoil		(55)								
7. Mutinies 8. Coups 9. Plots	7. Revolution				(72) (85) (83)	(87)	32			(82)
10. Admin. actions 11. Quasi-private	5. Purges .... 2. Gen. strikes 4. Major govt. crises 8. Demonstrations	30 (58)	38 (57) (62) (88)	 (70) 32 (90)	(57)	(73) (63)	(87) −31			(60)
100×(sum of squares/number of variables):		24.0	31.0	27.8	25.6	29.7	12.2	13.4	16.5	28.2

Factor (cosines) Correlations: E_{12} = .05 R_{12} = −.12 T_{13} = .03
E_{13} = −.05 R_{13} = −.03 T_{12} = .35
E_{23} = .10 R_{23} = −.09 T_{23} = .17

Only loadings ≥ |.30| are given. Those ≥ |.50| are shown in parentheses.

Column abbreviations:
E   signifies an Eckstein factor.
R   signifies a Rummel factor.
T   signifies a Tanter factor.

Row abbreviations:
UE   signifies incidents of unequivocal violence ("clear-cut internal wars").
E   signifies incidents of equivocal violence (unclear whether or not internal war).

Source: R. J. Rummel, "Dimensions of Conflict Behavior Within Nations, 1946–59." Journal of Conflict Resolution, vol. 10, no. 1 (March, 1966), p. 69.

certainly if military factors are treated as central, because the problem is a "military" one; and (3) we do not have time to achieve the necessary social, economic, and political changes. My comments are directed principally to the first rationale.

A number of scholars have located the following relationships between a variety of national liberation war indices and domestic system characteristics (other than the forms of conflict manipulated in tables 1 and 2). This review does not pretend to be comprehensive.

1. The existence of an organized opposition party is in a moderately inverse relationship to the incidence of guerrilla war (data base: 84 nations, 1948–62).[6]
2. Deaths from domestic group violence (of which national liberation war can be one cause) peak when GNP per capita is between $100 and $200 and decline as the economy crosses that upper limit (data base: 74 nations; GNP data, 1957; violence data, 1950–62).[7]
3. Russett and his associates have fruitfully explored the interaction between the dependent variable of deaths from domestic violence (germane to national liberation war at least in its latter stages) and the independent variables of GNP per capita, annual rate of change in GNP per capita, votes as a percentage of voting-age population (turnout), life expectancy ("distribution of welfare within a society"), inequality in agricultural land-holding, and the percentage of the labor force employed in agriculture.[8] The results are given in table 3.

Each row of the table has somewhat different implications. The first (b-Coefficients) indicates, crudely, how much of a change in any one independent variable from its mean will change the dependent variable. (If you change X, how much will Y change?) Thus, in the first row of table 3 we see the proportionate changes in violent domestic deaths which result from a proportionate change in GNP per capita and from unit changes in other independent variables. Distributing agricultural land more equally reduces the level of fratricide most powerfully, and the rate of growth of and proportionate increase in the GNP are significantly effective. Increased life expectancy contributes modestly to

[6] Ivo K. and Rosalind L. Fierabend, "Aggressive Behaviors within Polities, 1948–1962: A Cross-National Study," *Journal of Conflict Resolution,* vol. 10, no. 3 (September, 1966), p. 225.

[7] Bruce M. Russett *et al., World Handbook of Political and Social Indicators* (New Haven: Yale University Press, 1964), p. 307.

[8] *Ibid.,* pp. 311–13, 319–21.

pacification; increased voting and urbanization do not seem to affect pacification (either because they have no relationship to it or have mixed effects).

The second row in the table (B-Coefficients) shows us the relative "weight" and "theoretical importance" of each independent variable in explaining the level of fratricide. (Why do you have Y?) The data suggest that lack of economic improvement (annual rate of change in GNP per capita), welfare measures (life expectancy), voting turnout, land reform, and relative urbanization account primarily for domestic violence, and that proportionate economic growth contributes most weakly.

TABLE 3

EXPLAINING DEATHS FROM DOMESTIC GROUP VIOLENCE

(33 Nations)

	Log₂GNPC	GPCH	VOTE	LIFE	LFAG	LNDG
b-Coefficients of the column variables for log VIOL.	$-.10$	$-.16$	.01	$-.03$	.01	1.34
B-Coefficients of the column variables for log VIOL.	$-.13$	$-.34$	.27	$-.32$	.20	.22

KEY

GNPC   signifies gross national product per capita.
GPCH   signifies annual rate of change in gross national product per capita.
VOTE   signifies votes as a percentage of voting-age population.
LIFE   signifies life expectancy.
LFAG   signifies percentage of the labor force employed in agriculture.
LNDG   signifies distribution of agricultural land by the Gini index of inequality.

Source: Bruce M. Russett *et al.*, *World Handbook of Political and Social Indicators* (New Haven: Yale University Press, 1964), pp. 320–21.

In sum, if it is well-implemented, an American response to national liberation war will tend to be successful if it is structured in terms of land reform, relative economic improvement, welfare measures, and an organized opposition party. To the extent that our policies are not organized in these terms or if they are not successfully implemented, the data imply that, *ceteribus paribus*, violent domestic deaths will not decrease.

In effect, it has been argued that all of this is beside the point in the "real world" because successful implementation is assumed and because the nature of the national liberation war environment with which American policy must cope is omitted. Whether or not this critique is valid for the range of liberation war challenges likely to evolve I do not know, and I suspect that no one else does, either. However, three points are relevant here. The first is that the geographical proximity of support and the history of liberation war in Vietnam contaminate that case so that, if we tried to test the data conclusions more systematically than we do now, it cannot demonstrate or fail to demonstrate the policy implications of the data. Second, we have no adequate empirical basis for saying whether the domestic changes implied by the data are or are not feasible in the many national environments which may host national liberation wars. *The attempt which has been made for military policies, either in terms of monetary investment or priority in talent allocation, has not been made for non-military policies.* One very crude indicator of the scale of our effort is the total amount of non-military foreign aid appropriations, exclusive of the Marshall Plan, since World War II—$73.1 billion in economic obligations for fiscal years 1946 through 1966, including $10 billion for Taiwan, South Korea, and Vietnam. Whether an *annual* foreign aid budget of $20–25 billion, *allocated to one country,* would be more effective in curtailing national liberation wars than a military expenditure of that order, I do not know. However, even though dollar cost and effectiveness are by no means necessarily commensurate across a range of policies, the fact remains that the discrepancy in resource allocation between the "military" and "non-military" options is so enormous that we cannot even begin to talk about competitive effectiveness. Third, the time for American policies to take effect is that which remains between adoption and the national liberation war situation we want to prevent. Accordingly, we lessen time binds when we increase our ability, first, to diagnose possible host environments, and, second, to act on our diagnosis rather than wait for crises. Only when we have seen evidence of reasonable efforts on all these counts can we conclude that non-military measures require too much time for them to alter the course of national liberation wars.

South Vietnam as a Typical Case

The previous section presented data designed to clarify relationships between the non-military characteristics of national environments and national liberation wars. This section deals not with the importance of political and socioeconomic variables, but with the similarity between those aspects of South Vietnam and other national environments. To the extent we think these variables matter for the American response, it seems helpful to estimate the extent to which we will face national environments in other states like that of South Vietnam. The relative similarity of national environments to South Vietnam's de-limits our ability to extrapolate confidently from the Vietnamese case. We explore degrees of similarity first in political and second in socio-economic terms. In both cases we are concerned with which nations, relative to the universe of nations, are most similar to South Vietnam.

Political Similarity. We have data on political system similarity from an analysis of the relationships of 68 political characteristics for 115 independent nations.[9] In this analysis, nations are given "scores" on five political system dimensions. These dimensions are named and de-fined as follows: (1) "polyarchic"—relatively democratic; (2) "elitist"—"small 'modernizing elites' . . . attempting to bring about rapid radical social change in the face of impressive cultural resistance of an essen-tially 'parochial' character that remains as a carry-over from the colo-nial period"; (3) "centrist"—"totalitarian, semi-totalitarian and authoritarian"; (4) "personalist"—"sporadically authoritarian," with emphasis on a small ruling clique; and (5) "traditional"—forms of and relationships between the patterns of power, deference, and organiza-tion we associate with a traditional way of life. South Vietnam scores significantly on the Elitist, Centrist, and Personalist dimensions. We care here not about the wisdom of the dimension descriptions but about the empirical question of what nations are like South Vietnam in that they also score significantly on these three dimensions. Nations which do so may then differ from South Vietnam only in that they may score significantly on the Traditional or Democratic dimensions. To the extent that the indigenous population or foreign intervening actors act to alter the Traditional or Democratic patterns toward that which characterizes South Vietnam, i.e., to change the scores of these nations on these two dimensions, we have reason to conclude that the affected polities become more like South Vietnam, *qua* political system.

Table 4 states which of the 115 independent nations scored re-sembles South Vietnam and groups them according to the nature of the similarity.

Of the 16 polities which can be characterized as Elitist, Centrist, and Personalist, only three have significant scores on those dimensions

[9] Arthur S. Banks and Phillip M. Gregg, "Grouping Political Systems: Q-Fac-tor Analysis of *A Cross-Polity Survey*," *American Behavioral Scientist*, vol. 9, no. 3 (November, 1965), pp. 3–6. For perspective on their data, see: Arthur S. Banks and Robert E. Textor, *A Cross-Polity Survey* (Cambridge: M.I.T. Press, 1963).

alone (Group 1). Eleven also have significant scores on the Traditional dimension (Group 2), and two also have significant scores on the Polyarchy (roughly democratic dimension) (Group 3). In other words, most of the entries differ from South Vietnam in the greater extent to which their political systems contain traditional elements. Accordingly, if we use responses which disturb the traditional political fabric of the states in Group 2, we can expect to increase their political

TABLE 4

SIMILARITY OF POLITICAL SYSTEMS TO THE
REPUBLIC OF VIETNAM

Group 1	Group 2	Group 3
Similar Important Factors (Elitist, Centrist, Personalist)	Elitist, Centrist, Personalist, and Traditional	Elitist, Centrist, Personalist, and Polyarchic
Indonesia Republic of Korea Haiti	Burma Sudan Pakistan Jordan Nepal Ethiopia Syria Iraq Thailand Laos Iran	Lebanon Cyprus

Source: Constructed from data in Arthur S. Banks and Phillip M. Gregg, "Grouping Political Systems: Q-Factor Analysis of *A Cross-Polity Survey*," *American Behavioral Scientist*, vol. 9, no. 3 (November, 1965), p. 5.

Procedure: Country scores were examined for loadings greater than or equal to .30. Group 1 contains nations which had such significant loadings (a) on, and (b) only on, those factors on which South Vietnam had significant loadings. Group 2 contains nations which meet the previous criterion and also had a significant loading on the one additional factor labeled "Traditional." Group 3 consists of those nations which meet the first criterion for inclusion in Group 1, do not meet that for inclusion in Group 2, and, finally, have a significant loading on the factor labeled "Polyarchy."

similarity to South Vietnam unless our policies simultaneously increase the "democratic" elements in their political life. The regional characteristics of the states entered in table 4 imply a second, much stronger inference. None of the newly independent sub-Saharan states, the former French colonies in North Africa, or the "Latin" nations of Central and South America are in the table. Their absence suggests that we cannot extrapolate the national liberation war implications of the South Vietnamese political system *qua* system to possible national liberation war environments in North or sub-Sahara–Africa and Central or South America.

Socioeconomic Similarity. Here we explore the similarity of nations to South Vietnam on a number of socioeconomic indices. The extensive discussions of the relationships between socioeconomic traits, national liberation wars, and modernization suggest these as appropriate bases for comparison: (1) resource allocation to the armed forces; (2) mass communication; (3) mass welfare; (4) education; (5) economic development; (6) equality in the agricultural system; and (7) population. We have used several measures of each of these seven dimensions because there is little agreement on their relative advantage and degree of duplication (i.e., power and independence) as national indicators and because data are not present for each nation for each measure in the source available. The measures and number of nations for which data are given are: (1) for military allocations—(a) military personnel as percentage of the working-age population, i.e., 15–64 years (N=88), and (b) defense expenditures as percentage of the GNP (N=82); (2) for mass communication—(a) daily newspaper circulation per 1,000 population (N=125), and (b) radios per 1,000 population (N=118); (3) for welfare—(a) inhabitants per physician (N=126), and (b) inhabitants per hospital bed, annual percentage rate of change (N=90); (4) for education—(a) students enrolled in higher education per 100,000 population (N=105), and (b) percentage literate of population aged 15 or over (N=118); (5) for economic development—(a) gross national product (N=122), and (b) gross national product per capita (N=122); (6) for agricultural system—(a) distribution of agricultural land: Gini index of inequality (N=50), and (b) farms on rented land as total percentage of farms (N=55); and (7) for population—(a) annual percentage rate of increase in population for 1958–61 (N=111), (b) population per square kilometer (N=133), and (c) population per 1,000 hectares of agricultural land (N=115). Obviously, the fluctuations in the countries for which data were reported inject error, but the data should provide a first order clarification.

Table 5 reports on the nineteen nations which were similar as defined at the bottom of the table) to South Vietnam on at least three of our seven dimensions and four of our fifteen measures. The nations are grouped by region, and the particular forms of similarity are indicated in the row for each country. The higher the number associated with a country, the more similar it appears to be to South Vietnam in terms of these socioeconomic indices. The degree of similarity is summarized in the two final columns.

Not surprisingly, table 5 shows that few nations have the same socioeconomic profile as South Vietnam, and that even these differ along

TABLE 5

SOCIOECONOMIC SIMILARITY TO THE REPUBLIC OF VIETNAM

Region	Country	Military Resources (Max of Measures = 2)	Mass Communications (Max = 2)	Welfare (Max = 2)	Education (Max = 2)	Economic Development (Max = 2)	Agricultural System (Max = 2)	Population (Max = 3)	Dimensional Similarity (Max = 100%)	Measures Similarity (Max = 100%)
Asia:	Indonesia	1	1	2	1	1		2	71	47
	Burma	1	1	2	1	1			71	40
	Cambodia	1	1			1		2	57	33
	Taiwan	1		1		1	1	1	57	27
	Sarawak		1	1		1	1		57	27
	Laos	2	1	2					43	27
	Afghanistan					1		1	43	27
	Pakistan				1	1		2	43	27
Latin America:	Guatemala		1	1	2	1	1	1	86	47
	Dominican Rep.		1		1	1	1	3	71	47
	Bolivia		1		1	1	1		57	27
	El Salvador		1		2			2	43	33
Africa:	Ghana		2	1	1	1			57	33
	Kenya		2	1		1		1	57	33
	Uganda		1	2	1	1			57	33
	Angola		1	1		1	1		57	27
Middle East:	Syria	1	1		1	1		1	71	33
	Iraq	2	1			1		1	57	33
	Iran	2			1				43	27

Source: Bruce M. Russett et al., *World Handbook of Political and Social Indicators* (New Haven: Yale University Press, 1964).
Procedure: Tables for key variables on which South Vietnam appeared were scanned and the 20% of the table countries ranked closest to South Vietnam were identified. The tabulation reported omits NATO, Communist-party, "Old Commonwealth," and European neutral identifications, in addition to exclusions according to the rule given in the text.

what may be important variables. Second, although Southeast Asian and Central American nations are over-represented relative to their numbers and Africa and South America under-represented, the contents of the table recommend extrapolation judgments on a country, not a regional basis.

Treating national "political systems" as independent from national "socioeconomic" profiles is obviously artificial, and we can now ask the extent to which the same nations appear in both tables 4 and 5. Seven of the sixteen states which seem to be similar politically appear similar socioeconomically: Indonesia and six similar, but also significantly traditional polities—Burma, Pakistan, Syria, Iraq, Iran, and Laos. In sum, to the extent that we think the political and socioeconomic attributes of South Vietnam have important implications for "wars of national liberation" and for American responses to these wars, these implications are most relevant to: Indonesia, Burma, Pakistan, Syria, Iraq, Iran, and Laos.

The data discussed up to this point have been relatively clear and objective indices of the nature of national environments, even though all the original sources stress the important problems of these data. The remainder of part I of this paper relies on data about indigenous cultural beliefs and problem-conceiving styles which might be relevant to the American response. The data here are fragmentary, and the import of the class of variables involved in these data for national liberation wars is not known. However, indigenous cultural beliefs and problem-conceiving styles obviously affect indigenous behavior, and presumably the interaction between these and American responses can as easily be counter-productive as productive.[10]

Asian Political Beliefs

It is often argued that popular and effective political systems in the developing countries greatly reduce the probabilities of national liberation wars and, when these wars do occur, powerfully increase the chances that the challenged system will survive without massive social destruction. It is also usually agreed that even in the advanced stages of liberation war an indigenous government that is popular with the indigenous population—though not necessarily with Americans—is valuable. Accordingly, the political development aspects of an American

[10] The case for this rests largely on the "action" component of beliefs. For a sophisticated and short discussion, see Milton Rokeach, "Attitudes, Values and Political Behavior." (Paper presented at the annual meetings of the American Political Science Association, New York, September 9, 1966.)

response should help the "legitimate" government compete with the insurgents for the political loyalties of the population, i.e., it should be compatible with indigenous political preferences. If the national environment is not conducive to this type of political development, estimates of our policy effectiveness should include this fact.

Although all of this reasoning is common, we have few significant chunks of data about Asian political beliefs and priorities. Thus, it

TABLE 6

POLITICAL BELIEFS OF URBAN ASIANS

		Manila	Bang-kok	Singa-pore	Bom-bay	Tokyo
Question: "Do you think that graft and corruption are serious problems in this country or not?"	Yes	93%	94%	80%	91%	94%
Question: "Do you think it would be a good thing or a bad thing for this country if the national government turned over its powers for a while to one strong leader?"	Good	16	34	24	*	14
	Bad	83	*	50	53	59
Question: "When people vote, which of these considerations affects their choice the most, in your opinion: the character of the candidate; the party he belongs to; his stand on political issues; or what he can do for the voter?"	Candidate	43	39	19	27	25
	Party	4	4	27	29	40
	Stand on issues	20	19	13	19	10
	What do for voter	28	16	29	22	21

* Signifies data not reported in source.

Source: Constructed from data reported in "Five Key Cities Answer Questions on War, Children, and Censorship," *The Asia Magazine*, Oct. 31, 1965, pp. 7–8.

might be helpful to consider the results of an ASIAPOLL conducted in the second half of 1965. The field staff of International Research Associates interviewed 2,000 adults distributed over five major Asian cities: Manila, Bangkok, Singapore, Bombay, and Tokyo. Obviously, a few survey questions do not a belief system make, and urban Asians do not necessarily reflect the views of their rural countrymen. If we treat these data skeptically, the answers to three questions are still suggestive.

Table 6 shows the answers to questions about graft, strong-man government, and respondent voting considerations. First, the overwhelming percentage of respondents stated that graft is a "serious" problem, implying that the urban Asian publics in these cities are neither indifferent to nor disposed toward corrupt governments. Second, the political option of delegating powers to a strong man was not selected by even a majority in any city. Third, political support is accorded less on the basis of broad policy positions (issue stand) than on the basis of candidate and personal reward expectations. The data have these implications for our initial reasoning about Asian political development and liberation wars. First, an American response is dysfunctional to the extent that the indigenous population associates it with a corrupt counter-insurgent government. Second, an American response will not encourage majority support for the counter-insurgent government if it allows a strong man to absorb the powers of government or maintains that situation. An American response tends to capture indigenous political loyalties to the extent that it supports a popular candidate or visible benefits to the citizen. If the United States is unable to support and associate itself with an indigenous political group which does not combine at least some of these images with other policies we find congenial, that group will probably not be able to engender popular support for itself.

Cultural Precedents and American Intervention

In this final section on the attributes of national environments which could affect the "happiness" of our liberation war responses, we look at examples of less specific, more latent cultural ideas. Here our data are confined to interviews with four Vietnamese, conducted by the psychiatrist, Walter Slote.[11] The subjects were a student demonstration leader, an activist Buddhist monk, an imprisoned Vietcong terrorist, and a "leading intellectual and writer." Obviously, Slote's material cannot be extrapolated in its present state to any segment, let alone all, of Vietnamese society, and certainly not to populations outside of Vietnam. At this time, we do not know to what extent his findings do or do not apply to a larger population. However, again, it seems useful to comment on several of his conclusions, if only to suggest examples of ways in which basic cultural dispositions might affect the consequences of American policy. Slote reports that:

—Younger siblings exploit the cultural fact that their older siblings are responsible for the behavior of the younger ones and punished for the misbehavior of the younger ones.

[11] Walter H. Slote, "Observations on Psychodynamic Structures in Vietnamese Personality: Initial Report on Psychological Study—Vietnam, 1966" (The Simulmatics Corporation, New York, September 29, 1966).

—Blame for an event is assigned without taking into account "precipitating antecedent events."

—Failure of an all-powerful substitute father to be all-powerful or all-loving creates feelings of rejection and "hate."

The implications of the foregoing are these. First, weak American allies in national environments that host national liberation war will perceive our commitment to them as a leverage opportunity, not as a co-operative or dependent relationship. Second, host populations will not evaluate our actions, e.g., ones which inflict social and physical damage on civilians, on the basis of a "just cause." Third, American intervention will have an initial "honeymoon" period. However, if we cannot curtail the war quickly and drastically, and if our commitment becomes primarily associated with one group in the non-insurgent population, we can expect a "backlash" of hostility from other groups of non-insurgents.

II   American Decision-Making

How we Americans make our decisions crucially affects our responses to "wars of national liberation"—our goals, our conceptions of the problem which we are trying to solve, our selection of information in estimating the costs and effectiveness of alternative responses, our flexibility in reacting to feedback from our efforts to implement our policies, and the distribution of political power and access among those American officials who have different estimates and recommendations. These factors are in our power to control and change; our learning from their operation in the Vietnamese case need not be "ambiguous," even if the ultimate results in Vietnam should be.

To explore the models which American officials might be using in policy-making, we selected the results of 89 interviews conducted during the spring and summer of 1965.[12] The affiliations and numbers of respondents are (1) Department of State: Bureau of Intelligence and Research and the European Bureau (N=48); and (2) Department of

[12] The principal investigator for this study was Lloyd Jensen. See his "United States Elites and Their Perceptions of the Determinants of Foreign Policy Behavior." (Paper presented at the Midwest Political Science Association Meeting, Chicago, April 28–30, 1966.) For two very different approaches to the relationship between national liberation wars and American decision-making, see Ralph K. White, "Misperception and the Vietnam War," *Journal of Social Issues,* vol. 22, no. 3 (July, 1966), pp. 1–164; and Robin M. Williams, Jr., "Are Americans and Their Cultural Values Adaptable to the Concept and Techniques of Unconventional Warfare?" *Annals of the American Academy for Political and Social Science,* 341 (May, 1962): 82–92.

Defense: military officers and civilians from International Security Affairs (N=41). For us, the relevant questions are about how important these officials thought seven factors were in United States and USSR decision-making. The seven factors are: "national power capabilities"; "internal economic and political situation"; "behavior of other states"; "ideology"; "personality of leadership of the state"; "structure of the decision-making process"; and "historical tradition."

Obviously, we cannot necessarily say that these data "explain" American policy in Vietnam or will affect future American responses to liberation wars. We can say they suggest *hypotheses* about what factors and policy options American decision-makers will consider in a situation of liberation war. These hypotheses can be partly tested by accounts of American decision-making on Vietnam, for example, by Hilsman's suggestive account.[13] To the extent that they are confirmed, we have reason to expect that: (1) future American responses will conform to the same decision-making tendencies unless something *basic* occurs to change these tendencies; and (2) the general models which officials use are more responsible for our responses to a specific national liberation war than are the specifics of the challenge. These points say nothing about the utility or disutility of the policies which these models generate.

Our data let us talk about three aspects of American official beliefs which seem particularly relevant to liberation wars: (1) images of the factors responsible for American and allied decisions; (2) images of the factors responsible for enemy decisions; and (3) the primacy of "national power capabilities," a primacy which approaches the status of a "law" in international politics.

America and Our Allies

For purposes of discussion, let us make an assumption which may be incorrect—that American officials tend to believe that what matters in our decisions matters in those of our allies, i.e., our allies are "like us." Table 7, which follows, summarizes what our sample thought to be important in *American* decision-making.

Although most of the respondents thought all seven factors mattered, they clearly thought they mattered differentially. More officials think that national power capabilities, the internal political and economic situation, and the behavior of other states are more important than ideology, structure of the decision-making process, and historical tradi-

[13] Hilsman, "Two American Counterstrategies," in this volume, pp. 269–303.

tion, and that the personality factor is intermediate between the two groups. These data suggest the following hypotheses:

1. American officials will expect our indigenous allies to be primarily responsive to their capabilities, internal situation, and the behavior of other independent actors. Their anticipations of how our allies will behave will be based more on these factors than on those of their belief system, decision-making structure, and historical tradition.

2. American policies designed to alter the behavior of our indigenous allies will be expected to succeed primarily on the basis of their impact on the first group of factors.

TABLE 7

AMERICAN OFFICIALS ON THE DETERMINANTS OF
AMERICAN FOREIGN POLICY

(Entries Represent Number of Respondents)

Determinant	Very or Relatively Important	Relatively Unimportant or Unimportant
National power capabilities...............	85	4
Behavior of other states..................	80	9
Internal economic and political situation...	76	12
Personality of leadership of state..........	67	21
Ideology..............................	60	27
Structure of decision-making process......	60	27
Historical tradition......................	60	28

Source: Constructed from data reported in Lloyd Jensen, "United States Elites and Their Perceptions of the Determinants of Foreign Policy Behavior" (Paper presented at the Midwest Political Science Association Meeting, Chicago, April 28–30, 1966).

3. To the extent that our allies do not operate the way we anticipate they will, American officials will be more likely to see the personality of the indigenous leadership as the problem, rather than their belief system, decision-making structure, or historical tradition. Accordingly, changes in the indigenous leadership will lead officials to expect the originally predicted behavior.

The Sources of Enemy Decisions

When the American officials estimated the import of these variables for Soviet decisions, their answers revealed two particularly interesting things. First, the only case in which a majority of even one group of respondents ranked any of the factors as unimportant (to some degree or other) was the Soviet case, and the two factors so rated were: "behavior of other states" and "historical tradition." Second, the distribution of these responses differs according to organization.

In table 8, which follows, we see that the Department of State respondents see the role of historical tradition in Soviet foreign policy very differently from the Department of Defense respondents. In the former, about two-thirds of the officials interviewed place it in the important half of an important-unimportant scale; in Defense, two-thirds place it in the unimportant section of the scale. In part B of the table, we see that only in the Bureau of Intelligence and Research of the Department of State is there nearly consensus that the behavior of other states significantly influences Soviet foreign policy decisions. Again, for the purposes of discussion, let us assume that American official thinking has been sufficiently conditioned by the focus on the Soviets as the Communist "enemy" for us to assimilate other Communist actors to that model. To the extent that this is the case, we can generate hypotheses about tendencies in American estimates and selection of policy in a national liberation war situation.

1. Estimates which stress the enemy's historical experience and memory will be seen as legitimate and important in the Department of State, but will be given only marginal consideration in the Department of Defense.

2. With the possible exception of Department of State Bureau of Intelligence and Research, there will be no strong tendency to see enemy actions as in large part responses or reactions to our policies (except indirectly as these impinge on enemy national power capabilities or internal political and economic situation).

National Power Capabilities

In the preceding parts of this section, data and hypotheses have dealt with American images of either ourselves or the Soviet Union. In the final section, it seems useful to deal with an image which the respondents have of both countries. The image is that of the primacy of "national power capabilities," as distinct from our other six determinants of policy decisions. In essence, this amounts to the primacy of military equipment and forces and those facilities directly relevant to a military effort. For both the Soviet Union and the United States, more American officials saw this "military" factor as important than did so for any other factor. The agreement approaches 100 per cent. This finding suggests that we have encountered a "consensus" in the official culture on what "really" determines what governments do in international politics. If this is the case, and this is only an assumption for heuristic purposes, we would expect the following hypotheses to be valid for the American response to national liberation war:

1. American officials who assert that variables other than "national power capabilities" principally determine the behavior of actors in a national liberation war are bucking a cultural consensus.

TABLE 8

A. PERCEIVED IMPORTANCE OF HISTORICAL TRADI-
TION IN SOVIET FOREIGN POLICY-MAKING

	Very or Relatively Important	Relatively Unimportant or Unimportant
State:		
Intelligence and Research (N = 23)	65.2%	34.7%
European Bureau (N = 23)	73.9	26.1
Defense:		
I.S.A. Civilians (N = 16) . .	31.3	68.8
I.S.A. Military (N = 19) . .	31.6	68.5

B. PERCEIVED IMPORTANCE OF THE BEHAVIOR OF
OTHER STATES IN SOVIET FOREIGN POLICY-MAKING

	Very or Relatively Important	Relatively Unimportant or Unimportant
State:		
Intelligence and Research (N = 21)	81.0%	19.0%
European Bureau (N = 23)	52.2	47.8
Defense:		
I.S.A. Civilians (N = 17) . .	47.0	52.9
I.S.A. Military (N = 20) . .	65.0	35.0

Source: Constructed from data reported in Lloyd Jensen, "United States Elites and Their Perceptions of the Determinants of Foreign Policy Behavior" (Paper presented at the Midwest Political Science Association Meeting, Chicago, April 28–30, 1966).

2. American response alternatives which are designed to affect "national power capabilities" seem obviously "valid" because of the previous cultural commitment about what matters.

3. It follows from these two hypotheses that predictions which rest on great Communist responsiveness to changes in "national power capabilities" will have high credibility in Washington; predictions which rest on a contrary assumption will have low credibility.

4. It follows from these three hypotheses that it will take unusual

power to get American alternatives adopted which do not impact visibly and dramatically on enemy "power capabilities"; that once adopted, many will not commit themselves to these alternatives because they believe they will not work; and that in the absence of rapid results, the cultural consensus will reassert itself in favor of measures which directly hit the enemy's military capability.

III   Summary

This paper has drawn on data gathered for other purposes to clarify important patterns which relate national liberation war to other national traits, to clarify the extent to which other possible host environments are similar to South Vietnam as political and socioeconomic systems, to locate cultural characteristics which indigenous populations will use in responding to the American response and, finally, to locate some dispositions in American decision-making. These avenues to policy analysis can be usefully integrated with other types of analyses, including ones of the Vietnamese experience such as Hilsman's,[14] to work toward a more evidence-oriented perspective on the problems and constraints that impinge on the American response to national liberation wars. Learning why we thought what we did about Vietnam may suggest particularly accessible ways to improve our responses to liberation wars. This sort of learning does not need to wait until the end of the conflict.

[14] *Ibid.*

12

China's Policy
toward Indonesia

Indonesia's Position in China's Foreign Policy

Since the establishment of the regime in 1949, Communist China's foreign policy has had as one of its paramount objectives the removal of Western presence and the establishment of a China-centered political order in the Far East. Achieving this objective has proven to be quite difficult. China's power is limited and the major Western states, including Russia, remain determined to exert their influence on Asian affairs. But in a more basic sense, China's attempt to become the preeminent power in the area has been frustrated by an emerging Asian nation-state system dominated by forces of nationalism which have proven to be highly resistant to the hegemonial ambitions of all the great powers.

In the mid-1950's, the Chinese leaders came to the conclusion that their aspiration for preeminence in Asia could be best advanced by exploiting existing and potential conflicts between the Western powers and independent Asian states. In effect, they believed it was possible to create a broad "anti-imperialist" united front between various currents of Asian nationalism and Chinese Communism. Peking's attempt to organize an Asian united front served a two-part political strategy: first, it was designed to promote China's power interests by undermining the American effort to organize Asia against her; second, it served Peking's broader ideological goals to assist other Asian Communist parties in coming to power. By drawing non-Communist Asian states into her anti-Western orbit, China hoped to promote their eventual transition to Communism. Peking believed that various local Communist parties would benefit from the anti-imperialist orientation of their country if these parties developed strong organizations and became the most vigorous exponents of anti-Western nationalism. Communization of these states was, however, more a long-range than an immediate objective—and in any event depended on local conditions—with the result

333

that China attached first priority to courting the non-Communist governments of Burma, Pakistan, Cambodia, Laos, and Indonesia. Prior to 1959 this approach also applied to India. But, as Nehru abandoned an "anti-imperialist" foreign policy and the Sino-Indian boundary dispute erupted, any basis for New Delhi's participation in the Chinese-led united front was shattered. The same hostile attitude also applied to those Asian nations which were militarily aligned with the United States.

The strategic aim of securing the withdrawal of unwelcome Western presence in Asia obliged Peking to de-emphasize revolutionary objectives in nonaligned neighboring states. Essentially, China's position on the issue of supporting revolutions has been that in countries which adopt conciliatory policies toward Peking, *when* the proletariat takes power is a riddle the local Communists must solve on their own. The "hard line," supporting or calling for armed Communist revolutions, applies to those countries China regards as hostile to Peking and tied to, or dominated by, United States "imperialism."

It was not until 1955 that Peking began to apply the policy of alignment with "anti-imperialist" nationalism to Indonesia. In that year, China departed from a long-standing position on relations with Southeast Asian countries by concluding a treaty with Indonesia that renounced China's jurisdiction over foreign-born ethnic Chinese who desired voluntarily to be considered Indonesian nationals.[1] The Dual Nationality Treaty was an important first step forward since Djakarta was keenly suspicious of Peking's ties to the overseas Chinese minority. By agreeing to sharply reduce her overt influence on the Chinese community, Peking hoped to normalize the position of this minority and remove a basic source of friction with Djakarta. The treaty was not implemented until 1960[2] and various Indonesian political groups remained suspicious of China's motives. Nevertheless, in 1955, this agreement signified that Peking had made a major concession designed to foster future political cooperation with Indonesia.

Opportunities to lay the basis for more concrete "anti-imperialist" alignment began to unfold after 1956 when Indonesia's brief experiment in parliamentary democracy collapsed, giving rise to President Sukarno's political dominance. From this time on a basic objective of China's Indonesian policy was to cultivate ties with Sukarno. More

[1] Sino-Indonesian Treaty on Dual Nationality, April 22, 1965, *People's China* (supplement), no. 10, 1955.

[2] The instruments of ratification bringing the treaty into force were exchanged on January 20, 1960.

forcefully than other non-Communist Indonesian leaders, Sukarno favored closer contacts with China and he wanted to place Indonesia in the forefront of Afro-Asian opposition to Western "imperialism." Anti-imperialism was an especially deep current in Sukarno's political thought, and it was linked to his feeling that the Western powers would have to be forced to recognize Indonesian claims to the disputed West Irian territory and her rights, as the largest nation in Southeast Asia, to a commensurate voice and influence in world affairs. To a greater extent than the other major powers, China understood the political significance of Sukarno's demand to be recognized as an important world figure and his opposition to those manifestations of Western presence in Asia which frustrated his conception of Indonesia's destiny and interests. Moreover, Sukarno's opposition to the anti-Communist and anti-Chinese voices in Indonesia inclined Peking to regard him as a reliable ally. Opportunities to cultivate Sukarno's friendship began to appear in 1958 when a serious rebellion occurred in Sumatra. This rebellion, which initially received the tacit support of the United States, had the effect of driving Sukarno more closely toward the Communist powers. During this crisis, China extended Sukarno's government an $11 million credit and strong political support.[3] Sukarno's subsequent views of both China and the United States were powerfully affected by the 1958 rebellion, a fact that is frequently forgotten or underemphasized.

China's efforts to cultivate Sukarno were, however, suddenly impaired in 1959 by a serious dispute over the status of the Indonesian Chinese minority. This issue arose over two Indonesian government regulations; one banning aliens from engaging in retail trade in rural areas and the other prohibiting Chinese from maintaining residence in West Java. Peking considered both provisions, especially the latter which stemmed from Indonesian Army demands, to be clear violations of the 1955 Dual Nationality Treaty, under which Djakarta agreed to "protect the proper rights and interests" of Chinese nationals. More alarming to Peking was the fact that the discriminatory economic measures were being used by the Indonesian Army to exploit everpresent anti-Chinese sentiments for the purpose of discrediting the Indonesian Communist Party [PKI]. A serious dilemma thus confronted the Chinese leaders: to vigorously defend her nationals meant risking a conflict with Indonesian nationalism which Peking wanted to

[3] New China News Agency (Peking) (hereafter cited as NCNA), March 25, 1958, and *Peking Review*, May 20, 1958.

direct against the West; to accept the decrees involved acknowledging that China was unable to protect the overseas Chinese. Moreover, a passive response probably would have encouraged the Indonesian anti-Communist elements to attempt still bolder measures.

On the apparent assumption that vigorous resistance would force Sukarno to curb the army—for the sake of his own interest in preserving the existing political balance—Peking attempted to interfere in the execution of the two decrees and to inflict punitive damage on the Indonesian economy by encouraging her nationals to repatriate to China. This proved to be a serious miscalculation. Sukarno refused to be coerced and so many overseas Chinese answered the call to repatriate that Peking was obliged to reverse her position and accept the discriminating regulations. Only then did Sukarno curb the growing anti-Chinese campaign. Accepting Djakarta's discriminatory measures was distasteful, but in doing so Peking once again revealed the extent of her willingness to make concessions in order to protect the possibility of drawing Indonesia into a Chinese-led anti-imperialist coalition.

Peking-Djakarta Relations and the Sino-Soviet Split

Peking's retreat during the overseas Chinese dispute was undoubtedly influenced by the extension of Sino-Soviet rivalry to Indonesia. Moscow's influence in Djakarta began to rise after 1960 as a result of large Soviet military credits to Indonesia in support of the campaign to acquire the disputed West Irian territory. Although this aid enabled Indonesia to play an active anti-imperialist role, many other implications of Soviet assistance to Djakarta no doubt disturbed Peking. Moscow's aid strengthened the hand of the decidedly anti-Chinese, anti-Communist Indonesian Army at a time when Peking and Djakarta were engaged in a serious dispute. Nor could Peking overlook the fact that arming Indonesia ran parallel to Moscow's policy of aiding India when a border dispute existed with China. To Peking, Moscow's chief aim in assisting Indonesia, as well as India, appeared to be less designed to oppose "imperialism" and more intended to strengthen these powers as counterweights to China in Asia. Ending the overseas Chinese dispute was therefore essential if Peking was to avoid an estrangement with Indonesia from which Moscow and Washington would derive the major benefits. The fact that Sukarno, unlike Nehru, continued to adhere to an active anti-imperialist policy enabled China to absorb her defeat in the overseas Chinese dispute without abandoning her more important quest for an alignment with Indonesia against the Western powers. Moreover, the Chinese leaders appeared to have confidence that Sukarno's friendship for Peking was durable and that he would not be a party to any anti-China schemes. Sukarno's June, 1961, visit to China restored good relations between the two countries[4] and later resulted in a Chinese credit to Indonesia of U.S. $30 million.[5]

China's assessment of Sukarno was vindicated once again when in 1963 Indonesia launched the "confrontation" policy against the newly created Federation of Malaysia. The "confrontaton" policy had the effect of drawing Peking and Djakarta closer together and isolating Indonesia from the Western powers, especially Britain and the United States, who moved to back Malaysia. It also tended to undermine Soviet relations with Indonesia. In view of the emerging Sino-Indonesian rapprochement, Moscow was reluctant to extend further major economic and military assistance to Djakarta for the purpose of crushing Malaysia. To do so would also have threatened the Soviet's new interest in a détente with the United States. After the Geneva Accords on Laos (July, 1962), the Cuban missile crisis (October, 1962) and the Nuclear Test Ban Treaty (July, 1963), Soviet policy in the Far East underwent a significant retrenchment. Moscow's decision to refrain from fully backing Djakarta's "confrontation" policy cost her the loss of considerable influence with Sukarno and the Indonesian Communist Party whose interests were closely tied to the campaign against Malaysia. As the Chinese had correctly argued, the Soviet Union was prepared to abandon the struggle against "imperialism" whenever this interfered with her own state interests in reaching accommodations with the Western powers.

The Indonesian Communist Party's own interest in encouraging Sukarno's "confrontation" policy caused it to come out openly in support of the basic Chinese Communist position in the Sino-Soviet ideological conflict. Until the "confrontation" with Malaysia, the PKI refrained from siding with either the CPSU or the CCP and, instead, capitalized on the split to stress its own independence.[6] The Indonesian Communists felt secure enough to criticize Soviet "modern revisionism" and Chinese "classic and modern dogmatism." Much of Aidit's analysis

[4] *Ta-kung pao* (Peking), June 13, 1961.

[5] NCNA (Peking), October 11, 1961.

[6] For an analysis of the PKI's position in the dispute prior to 1963, see Donald Hindley, "The Indonesian Communists and the CPSU Twenty-Second Congress," *Asian Survey*, March, 1962, pp. 20–27.

of the Indonesian revolution was taken directly from Mao Tse-tung,[7] but for more than a decade the PKI leadership had insisted on its right to creatively develop and "Indonesianize" Marxism-Leninism in conformity with its own revolutionary conditions. Under Aidit the PKI rejected the Maoist concept of an armed struggle path to power and instead adopted a policy of building a massive political organization potentially capable of taking power "democratically" if elections were held, or if President Sukarno's efforts to include the Communists in the government (i.e., the NASAKOM formula) materialized.

It was, therefore, the dispute over what policies the world Communist movement should adopt toward "imperialism" (i.e., Malaysia), rather than what path local Communist parties should take in coming to power, which prompted the PKI to align with the CCP. The PKI's united front strategy was dependent on Indonesia's continuing a militantly "anti-imperialist" foreign policy. Moscow's failure to give full support to Sukarno's "confrontation" campaign thus had the effect of also undermining the PKI's strategy for taking power. From February, 1963 on, it was clear that Moscow's failure to actively support Indonesia's "confrontation" policy caused the PKI to reappraise its previous ideological neutrality.[8]

Soviet policy was, therefore, a major factor which promoted an ever-closer cooperation between the CCP and the PKI, as well as between Peking and Djakarta. By 1965, Sino-Indonesian foreign policy objectives appeared to be sufficiently congruent to sustain a two-power political axis, provided Sukarno's position remained unimpaired. The maintenance of Sukarno's authority also appeared to be a decisive factor in the PKI's bid to build up sufficient organizational strength and monopoly of nationalist appeals to make its gradual domination of the government acceptable to Indonesia's non-Communist elite, including the army. It became increasingly clear that Sukarno, although he was not a Communist, viewed the Indonesian radical Left, including the PKI, as the preferred successors to his leadership of the Indonesian revolution. Although the anti-Communist forces were stronger, they

[7] Compare, for example, D. N. Aidit, *Indonesian Society and the Indonesian Revolution* (Djakarta: Jajasan Pembaruan, 1958), pp. 38–69, with Mao Tsetung, "The Chinese Revolution and the Chinese Communist Party," in *Selected Works*, vol. 3 (London: Lawrence & Wishart, 1954), pp. 72–101.

[8] For the first major statement indicating the PKI's shift, see D. N. Aidit, *Dare, Dare and Dare Again,* Political Report to the First Plenary Session of the Seventh Central Committee of the Communist Party of Indonesia (Peking: Foreign Language Press, 1963), p. 66.

were divided and, moreover, bore a heavy responsibility for Indonesia's political, economic, and moral breakdown on the basis of which PKI programs had become increasingly acceptable to many as an alternative to the demonstrable immobilism of the nation's non-Communists.

China and the Indonesian Coup

In the five years preceding the so-called October 1, 1965 coup attempt, China could look with satisfaction on her efforts to secure an "anti-imperialist" alignment with Indonesia. She had strongly supported the policies of President Sukarno and worked to diminish any potential areas of friction with Djakarta. In 1965, Peking strengthened Sukarno's government by the extension of a new $50 million credit. She gave enthusiastic support to Indonesia's decision to leave the United Nations. The two countries had concluded a battery of agreements on economic, technical, military, and cultural cooperation. Earlier, in March, 1964, Peking voluntarily turned over to Djakarta the assets of The Bank of China in Indonesia, an act of major political significance since the bank was widely regarded by Indonesians as a main source of financial support for the PKI. In her relations with the Indonesian Communists, Peking was careful to avoid any actions that could be cited as subversive. Similarly, China was careful to avoid provoking any dispute with Djakarta arising from the occasional mistreatment of her nationals, a matter which had been a constant strain on relations between the two countries in the past. By 1965, it appeared that Peking might eventually be prepared to render some aid to Indonesia in the field of nuclear development, if political alignment between the two states became more complete.

All this seemed designed not only to enhance Sukarno's policies and standing, but also to favorably influence other political forces in Indonesia, including the military, long suspicious of China but also very much interested in developing ties with foreign powers capable of helping their country become the major indigenous power in Southeast Asia. The extent to which the CCP deferred to the PKI's policies strongly suggests that Peking had been brought around to accept, willingly or otherwise, that it would be possible, eventually, to modify the Indonesian military's suspicions of China and to promote instead a growing sense of the two nations' common interests and objectives in opposing the Western position in Southeast Asia. It was in Peking's strongest interests that the political situation existing in Indonesia in late 1965 be preserved rather than endangered by any adventurist action from the Left directed against a much stronger and already apprehensive anti-Communist army leadership.

If Communist China played a part in the October 1 coup attempt,[9] it has not been established to date on the basis of reliable evidence. Some reported confessions of imprisoned and dead Communist leaders, together with statements made by the Indonesian army, suggest that Peking had foreknowledge of the coup, participated in planning it, and secretly smuggled weapons into the country to support it. These allegations may be well-founded, but the subsequent trials conducted and controlled by the Indonesian military have produced such contradictory testimony that uncertainty exists as to who and what was actually involved in this incident. Consequently, the army's charges cannot be taken entirely at face value. Moreover, the Indonesian army itself has the strongest interest in establishing a case of exclusive Communist responsibility for an incident which, it is clear, could not have been launched without the close cooperation of a considerable number of military officers who played the vital roles at most of the key points during the events: in the Palace Guard, in the Air Force Headquarters, in the Diponegoro Division, in Jogjakarta, and at Halim Air Force Base. No doubt, the army's attempt to build a case of exclusive PKI-Peking guilt has been politically necessary to legitimize its own subsequent takeover of the government and its massive extermination of the Communist and other suspected elements. Similarly, the wholly different interests of Sukarno (whose own role remains the key mystery in the events surrounding October 1, 1965) no doubt influenced him in portraying the attempted coup in terms which contradicted the army's version. Sukarno condemned the incident as "stupid" and a "disease" of the revolution but he refused to charge the Communists with exclusive responsibility for it. He has not suggested China was involved, and from the beginning he opposed the army's post-October attempts to destroy the alignment with Peking.

If the coup was designed to take power from Sukarno, it seems most unlikely that Peking was involved in it. So long as Sukarno was guiding Indonesia in an anti-imperialist direction while restraining the army from suppressing the PKI, China had a strong interest, as did the PKI,

[9] Various hypotheses have been advanced to explain the events surrounding the Indonesia coup. See, for example, Arthur J. Dommen, "The Attempted Coup in Indonesia," *China Quarterly*, January–March, 1966, pp. 144–70; Daniel S. Lev, "Indonesia 1965: The Year of the Coup," *Asian Survey*, February, 1966, pp. 103–10; John O. Sutter, "Two Faces of 'Konfrontasi': 'Crush Malaysia' and 'Gestapu,'" *Asian Survey*, October, 1966, pp. 523–46.

in preserving his authority, not overthrowing it. No evidence has come to light suggesting that Peking urged the PKI to seize power by violent means. Actually, two years earlier the CCP had already publicly endorsed Aidit's non-violent policy of building a mass political following under PKI hegemony capable of taking power, ultimately, through a united front composed of the "progressive" forces.[10] For years the PKI's policy had evidenced "capitulationist" tendencies and an apparent belief in "structural reform" notions similar to the errors Peking accused the French and Italian parties of committing. Yet the Indonesian party was hailed by Peking as a "great Marxist-Leninist party" and Aidit himself was described as a "brilliant Marxist-Leninist theoretician."[11] The Chinese leaders may have doubted the wisdom of the PKI's line, but they were certainly not prepared to undo their relationship with Sukarno by urging a revolt against him. Certainly no foreign Communist party was capable of dictating to the PKI. The interests of both Communist parties lay in supporting Sukarno and strengthening his ability to restrain the much stronger anti-Communist forces in Indonesia.

China's interest in protecting the favorable relationship that existed with Djakarta prior to October 1, 1965, strongly suggests she was engaged in various overt and covert actions designed to assist Sukarno and the PKI. As a result of the latter's efforts in 1965 to secure Sukarno's endorsement of proposals to arm elements of the citizenry (the "fifth force" concept) and to establish a political commissar system in the armed forces, greater than usual tension existed between the army and the PKI. Implementation of such proposals would presumably have enabled Communist elements to acquire arms and training, developments the army would not accept. The conflict over the "fifth force" and commissar system thus brought to a head the growing army-PKI rivalry which had developed steadily ever since the military lost much of its control over Communist organizational activities when the army's martial law powers were revoked by Sukarno in 1963. Whether or not it is true—as the coup group charged—that a "Council of Generals" existed and planned to overthrow the government (and suppress the PKI), it seems reasonable to assume that the anti-Communist generals were not wholly unprepared for certain contingencies, and that Sukarno's serious illness in early August, 1965, brought them to a higher stage of readiness.

[10] Hsiung Fu, "Yin-tu-ni-hsi-ya jen-min ti ko-ming tou-cheng ho Yin-tu-ni-hsi-ya kung-ch'an-tang" ["The Indonesian People's Revolutionary Struggle and the Indonesian Communist Party"], *Hung-ch'i* [Red Flag], May 20, 1963.

[11] See speeches by CCP leaders P'eng Chen and Kang Sheng, as reported in NCNA (Peking), September 2 and September 4, 1963.

Assuming there were strong suspicions of a possible military coup from the Right, China would most probably have used whatever resources she possessed to assist any forces thought to be loyal to Sukarno.

Evidently a limited number of Chinese-made weapons were in the hands of certain Indonesian armed forces well before the October 1 coup.[12] Possibly these weapons came into Indonesia as a result of arrangements between the two governments implementing the January 28, 1965, Sino-Indonesian joint statement calling for further political-military contacts.[13] They may also have been in the possession of only certain reliable military units (i.e., loyal to Sukarno) as a result of high-level secret agreements. This hypothesis is implicitly suggested by the subsequent testimony of former foreign minister Subandrio. If this was the case, then the probability is strong that Peking's intention was to assist those elements, including certain military officers, who could act to defend Sukarno's government in a showdown instigated by the anti-Communist generals. It does not seem likely that Sukarno would have continued to insist so strongly on China's friendship and the need to preserve the alignment with her—which he did—if he really knew that Peking had run guns to the PKI and worked with the Communists to overthrow his government.

China's willingness to assist in the defense of Sukarno against a possible coup attempt initiated by his generals would probably have extended to supporting a PKI, or loyalist army faction's preventative strike against the anti-Communist command structure of the army. Her readiness to do this would have been especially strong if she feared an impending army attempt to suppress the PKI. But a critical factor determining Peking's action under these circumstances would certainly have been her concern not to antagonize Sukarno. To participate in a plot against the anti-Communist generals contrary to Sukarno's wishes ran the severe risk of destroying China's entire position in Indonesia. Unless he was also a target, which seems most unlikely, the coup group would have confronted a leader still capable of rousing the nation to exterminate the Communist movement, a deed he had performed once before with a single speech in 1948—the annihilation of the PKI at Madiun was the well-remembered result.

A final possibility exists that Peking was involved in the attempted coup as the result of her convictions that Sukarno's death was imminent and that the succession to power of an anti-Communist army junta was

[12] As reported in *New York Times,* October 19, 1965.

[13] Text in *Peking Review,* February 5, 1965.

unacceptable. The difficulty in constructing a plausible case of Chinese interference in this instance is that a sudden deterioration of Sukarno's health apparently took place in early August, shortly before the coup—hardly enough time for Peking to arrange all the details involved in a clandestine weapons shipment for a coup. On the other hand, if she succeeded in doing this, and had in fact been shipping arms to Indonesia for some time, then it is surprising that the subsequently suppressed Communist elements had so few weapons to defend themselves or to organize a resistance. And if the PKI and China planned only a small-scale action requiring limited arms, then it was surely an incredible blunder to have pressed demands for arming a "fifth force" which could only heighten the army's sense of impending danger, thus depriving the conspirators of the elements of secrecy and surprise. In the absence of more reliable evidence, especially concerning Sukarno's attitude and role in the coup, it would seem that if China was involved at all—and this is doubtful—her aim was probably limited to protecting the position of Sukarno and the PKI. For no evidence has appeared suggesting that Peking wanted to undermine Sukarno or that she considered the situation in Indonesia ripe for a PKI takeover.

The Collapse of the Peking-Djakarta Axis

The political balance of forces in Indonesia which supported the alignment with Peking rapidly disintegrated as a result of the army's post-October 1 suppression of the PKI. Sukarno's ability to play the balance between Communist and anti-Communist forces was greatly weakened when the enraged generals who survived the coup overrode his attempt to provide a "political solution" for the crisis and, instead, seized the moment to forcibly settle matters with the PKI once and for all. Sukarno's inability to curb the army's anti-Communist suppression meant that a serious rupture of relations with Peking was virtually inevitable. For the generals had long regarded the PKI, Peking and the overseas Chinese as essentially interdependent parts of the same Communist security problem. Consequently, while crushing the PKI, the army was also bent on proving Chinese Communist involvement in the coup in order to undo Sukarno's alignment with Peking.

Within two weeks of the coup's suppression a rash of anti-Chinese and anti-China incidents broke out, sparked by the army's search and detention of a number of suspected Chinese nationals and the appearance of newspaper articles implying Peking's involvement in the coup. The impending conflict between Peking and the Indonesian military came into the open on October 16 when the army forcibly entered and searched the offices of the Chinese Commercial Counselor in Djakarta. On the same day, an article in the army's newspaper, *Angkatan Bersendjata,* alleged that the Indonesian Foreign Ministry had lodged a protest with the CPR over the latter's refusal to fly its Embassy's flag at half-mast in honor of the Indonesian generals killed during the attempted coup. On October 18, Peking formally protested the army's search of her Counselor's offices, warning that "an anti-Chinese wave is starting in Indonesia and if it is not checked the consequences will be serious."[14] She dismissed the army's alleged flag issues as "sheer fabrication."[15]

Prior to these events, China's only official comment on post-coup developments was a personal message from Liu Shao-ch'i and Chou En-lai to Sukarno extending "cordial regards and heartfelt wishes" on hearing he was safe and expressing the hope that under his leadership, Indonesia would "develop still further the spirit of opposing imperialism and Malaysia."[16] But the army-inspired incidents of mid-October apparently convinced Peking that the Indonesian generals had decided to provoke a full-fledged dispute with China as part of their plans to destroy Communist influence in the country. On October 19, Communist China broke the silence she had maintained, publishing a long and curious compilation of various foreign news reports clearly designed to show: (1) that the PKI was being victimized; (2) that the army was launching an unrestrained suppression against all "progressive forces"; (3) that President Sukarno was in favor of a political settlement; (4) that the United States "imperialists" were overjoyed by the turn of events in Indonesia.[17] This action was certain to further antagonize the Indonesian army and play directly into the hands of all those elements hostile to China. Nevertheless, the Chinese leaders evidently again calculated, as they had during the initial phase of the 1959–60 dispute, that the Indonesian "reactionaries" could only be curbed if Peking pressured Sukarno to restrain the army.

The attempted coup and its aftermath, however, had greatly weakened Sukarno's ability to bridle the army command. This time he was unable to intercede on Peking's behalf as he had done in 1960. Consequently, during the months following the coup numerous Chinese nationals were searched, detained or arrested. Others were injured in clashes with anti-Communist demonstrators. Peking, appealing to Sukarno, vainly protested these incidents and the series of violent mob

[14] Text of Chinese Protest Note in NCNA (Peking), October 18, 1965.

[15] NCNA (Peking), October 20, 1965.

[16] Text of the letter in NCNA (Peking), October 4, 1965.

[17] *Jen-min jih-pao* [People's Daily], October 19, 1965.

attacks on her Embassy and consulates in Djakarta, Medan, and Makassar.[18] In retaliation, China withdrew her technical advisers and cut off aid to Indonesia. On numerous occasions after the anti Chinese campaign began, Sukarno called for an end to the incidents which were damaging relations with China. He also insisted there should be no change in Indonesia's "anti-imperialist" policy.[19] On February 21, 1966, in an attempt to restore his authority, he removed Defense Minister, General Nasution. This political comeback proved to be short lived. In March, he was obliged to empower General Suharto with sweeping authority which the latter promptly used to ban the PKI (March 12, 1966) and to instal a new cabinet representing the army's views. Following this turn of events, Peking concluded that "the Indonesian right-wing generals' clique" had "coerced" Sukarno and "seized state power by staging a coup d'état."[20]

By April, 1966, the only effective brake against a massive anti-Chinese campaign was the army's interest in pursuing its anti-Communist objectives without inflicting a threatening level of damage on the economy, which was dependent on the skills and enterprise of the local Chinese. As in the 1959–60 dispute, the real violence fell on this community of helpless individuals (many of whom were Indonesian citizens) whose human dignity and welfare were matters of relative indifference to both Peking and Djakarta. Nor, indeed, did any other major government show concern for the suffering of this minority when to do so might entail the risk of sacrificing some temporary tactical gain in this round of maneuvers in the cold war. The plight of the overseas Chinese was most acute in Atjeh and other parts of North Sumatra, but there were also numerous anti-Chinese incidents in East and Central Java and in Sulawesi. Except for brief intervals, such incidents have erupted almost continuously since October, 1965, including the killing of apparently several hundred Chinese in Atjeh, the closing of all overseas Chinese schools (April and May, 1966), acts of extortion and intimidation, the boycotting of Chinese shops, suppression of Chinese organizations, and innumerable acts of vandalism.

On May 18, 1966, the CPR announced that ships would be sent to repatriate those Chinese wishing to leave Indonesia.[21] But unlike 1959,

[18] Text of CPR Protest Notes in NCNA (Peking) reports for November 3, 1965; November 5, 1965; May 7, 1966; August 22, 1966.

[19] See, for example, Sukarno's speeches of October 23 and 26, November 6 and 20, and December 18, 1965.

[20] NCNA (Peking), April 4 and 6, 1966.

[21] Text of CPR Foreign Ministry note in NCNA (Peking), May 18, 1966.

this time Peking Radio beamed no broadcasts to Indonesia urging a mass exodus. Exact figures on the number of departing overseas Chinese are unavailable. However, scattered reports indicate that as of May, 1967, no more than 4,000 had repatriated to mainland China, while perhaps twice this number were waiting or making preparations to leave Indonesia. A few Chinese managed to find shelter on Taiwan.

In contrast to the 120,000 Chinese who left Indonesia between 1959 and 1961, the recent far more violent Indonesian anti-Chinese current demonstrates that both Peking and the overseas Chinese have had some sobering second thoughts about the effectiveness of repatriation as a solution to Indonesia's periodic outbursts of anti-Chinese sentiments. As a result of that earlier experience Peking discovered that the number of repatriates was too large to handle and that it was wise to discourage others from coming. The overseas Chinese soon learned that remaining in Indonesia involved less severe adjustments than adapting to "socialism" in China. Djakarta learned a few lessons too. Indonesia's economy can ill-afford the loss of the large numbers of Chinese who presently constitute an irreplaceable skill group. And finally, the 1959–60 experience taught Peking that her ability to coerce Djakarta by withdrawing the Chinese was not only quite limited, but also politically counterproductive. Peking's desire to inflict punitive damage on the present Indonesian regime is surely greater than before but she is also facing a leadership which would be even less coercible than Sukarno was. Consequently, although a massive suppression of the overseas Chinese could force Peking to take radical actions, her interest continues to dictate a policy which seeks to keep the Chinese community in Indonesia, however difficult that objective is to achieve under present circumstances.

Peking's most serious setback in Indonesia has been the reorientation in Djakarta's foreign policy. After the army took over the government, Indonesia terminated the "confrontation" with Malaysia (June 1, 1966), secured assurances of forthcoming United States economic aid (September 19, 1966), recalled her ambassador to Peking (February 19, 1966), reclaimed her seat in the United Nations (September 27, 1966), obtained a rescheduling of her payments on the extensive debt owed to the Western powers (September 29, 1966), and to the Soviet Union (November 24, 1966), and drastically curtailed her trade with Communist China. These reversals in policy were carried out over Sukarno's strong objections and, predictably, earned Peking's harsh criticism. After the army-Sukarno showdown in March, 1966, China began to charge that "state power" in Indonesia had been seized by a "rightist military regime" working in collusion with the United States and the USSR.[22] The extent of Peking's hostility toward the Indonesian Army has been stated quite openly:

> The underlying spirit of the Bandung principles is for the Asian and African countries to unite in order to oppose imperialism and old and new colonialism. You are, however, the loyal agents of U.S. imperialism and diehard reactionaries. You have hired your-selves out to U.S. imperialism, and you are exerting your utmost in opposing China and wrecking the Afro-Asian cause of sol-idarity against imperialism. Is it not you who have shamelessly trampled underfoot the Bandung principles and soiled the glori-ous name of Bandung? We would advise you, the rightwing chief-tains in Indonesia, to drop all this clumsy performance of yours.[23]

As ideological hostility intensified, diplomatic relations strained to the breaking point. On March 26, 1966, Peking closed "temporarily" her consulates in Medan, Bandjermasin, and Makassar. The following month the CPR granted political asylum to Sukarno's former ambas-sador to China, Djawoto, and called home her ambassador to Indone-sia, Yao Chung-ming. In July, 1966, Indonesia closed her consulate in Peking. These actions were followed by the closing of the respective offices of the New China News Agency in Djakarta and the Antara News Agency in Peking, the suspension of Indonesian airline flights to Canton, and the abrogation of a previous agreement to establish a Sino-Indonesian shipping line. On April 24, 1967, the Indonesian gov-ernment expelled CPR Chargé d'Affaires ad interim, Yao Teng-shan, and Consul General Hsu Jen, following a mass demonstration by over-seas Chinese in Djakarta. On April 25, following demonstrations in Peking, Indonesian Chargé d'Affaires ad interim, Baron Sutadisastra, was recalled.

Despite a steady deterioration in diplomatic relations and Djakarta's mistreatment of the Chinese minority, Peking did not adopt a com-pletely hard line toward Indonesia, advocating revolutionary armed struggle, until July, 1967.[24] In taking this step, China placed the pres-

[22] NCNA (Peking), May 27, 1966. See also, NCNA (Peking), June 12, 1966, and *Peking Review,* October 14, 1966.

[23] Article by Commentator, *Jen-min jih-pao,* April 27, 1966. See also, CPR protest note to the Indonesian Foreign Ministry, June 9, 1966; full text in *Peking Review,* June 17, 1966.

[24] "People of Indonesia, Unite and Fight to Overthrow the Fascist Regime," *Hung-ch'i,* no. 11, 1967. English translation in *Peking Review,* July 14, 1967, pp. 15–17.

ent Indonesian government in the category of other hostile Southeast Asian countries (Laos, South Vietnam, and Thailand) where "reactionary" military elites dominate governments clearly aligned with the United States. Prior to mid-1967 Peking's revolutionary activity had been limited to providing a political sanctuary for PKI Politburo member Jusuf Adjitorop, former ambassador to China, Djawoto, and other Indonesian "progressives" who appear to have fled to China after the coup. In the event of a future Indonesian political upheaval, or civil war, these elements were evidently regarded as the potential nucleus of a Peking-sponsored "government in exile" or a reconstituted Communist Party.[25]

Given the severity of the dispute, from the outset a strong possibility existed that Peking might break diplomatic relations with Djakarta and encourage the Indonesian Communists to adopt a new policy of armed struggle. The Albanian Communists, who frequently reflect Chinese views, were the first to argue that the PKI's downfall stemmed from its overestimation of both Sukarno's political strength and the potentialities of a peaceful transition to power. They concluded that, henceforth, the Indonesian Communists would have only one alternative: "the armed struggle of workers and peasants to preserve freedom and democracy and to counter fascism and terror."[26]

Jusuf Adjitorop reached the same conclusions when he presented his first major PKI policy statement since the party's suppression. In November, 1966, he confessed to the Fifth Congress of the Albanian Workers' Party that the Indonesian Communists had made serious mistakes in "assessing the class character of state power in Indonesia." These mistakes, he declared, deprived the proletariat of its independence and subordinated it to the national bourgeoisie. Adjitorop also argued that henceforth the party must discard Aidit's erroneous theory that the "pro-popular forces" could take power from the "anti-popular forces" by peaceful means. He called for re-establishing "the correct Marxist-Leninist principles on state and revolution," namely that "the people can take power only by means of armed revolution under the leadership of the working class."[27] Asserting that the path of Mao Tse-tung was

[25] Evidently, Peking now publishes a periodical, *Suara Pemuda Indonesia* (*The Voice of Indonesian Youth*), on behalf of the Indonesian Communists in China.

[26] "The Fascist Coup d'État in Indonesia and Its Lessons for Communists," translated from *Zeri I Popullit*, May 12, 1966.

[27] Text of Greetings to the Fifth Congress of the Albanian Workers' Party from the Central Committee of the Indonesian Communist Party, November 4, 1966.

the only one for the Indonesian revolution, Adjitorop summed up the PKI's urgent tasks in a characteristically Maoist formula: (1) reconstruction of the PKI "on a Marxist-Leninist basis"; (2) preparation "to lead a long, armed struggle integrated with the agrarian revolution of the peasants in rural areas"; (3) formation of a "united front" of all forces opposed to "the dictatorship of the right-wing generals" and based on an "alliance of the working class and the peasants under the leadership of the proletariat." In conclusion, the PKI leader declared that, "armed with Marxism-Leninism and with the ideas of Mao Tse-tung, the Indonesian Communist Party will certainly . . . lead the revolutionary struggle . . . to inflict a defeat on the military dictatorship of . . . Suharto and Nasution and to instal popular power."[28]

Future Prospects

China's reluctance to openly advocate an armed struggle in Indonesia before July, 1967, may, in part, have reflected simply her continuing appreciation that the geographical centers of Communist support (Central and East Java) are ill-suited for the development of "liberated base areas" necessary to sustain guerrilla warfare. In Sumatra, Kalimantan (Borneo) and Sulawesi (Celebes), geography favors guerrilla warfare techniques. Down to the present these areas have not been effectively penetrated, politically, by the Indonesian Communists to the point where "revolutionary war" could be successfully carried out, a fact the CCP and the PKI long recognized as a serious barrier to a strategy based on armed struggle. However, since the Communists once again find the parliamentary road closed to them, the validity and wisdom of accepting a non-violent revolutionary line, on account of the special characteristics of Communist strength in Indonesia, now appear to be under reexamination.[29]

The duration and intensity of Peking's recently declared ideological war on Indonesia may be heavily influenced, if past history is any guide, by the future course of political rivalry in Djakarta. Despite the ideological hostility conveyed in editorials, China seems to doubt that the present ascendancy of the Indonesian "reactionaries" will be

[28] *Ibid.*

[29] In reporting Adjitorop's speech at the Fifth Albanian Party Congress, Peking did not reprint the full text but only brief excerpts which, significantly, did not include any of the passages admitting past PKI errors, or Adjitorop's main point that, henceforth, the Indonesian Communists must rely on the armed struggle path developed by the Chinese. *Peking Review*, November 25, 1966.

permanent. The army dealt the PKI a crippling organizational and psychological blow. But no more than a fraction of the Communists' three million members, and sixteen million other followers, were eliminated. It is impossible to say how many Indonesians still support, however quietly, Communist goals and programs. Of more importance, the PKI's setback has yet to be accompanied by convincing evidence that the Indonesian non-Communist forces are using their new lease on life to effectively cooperate on behalf of national construction and political stability. It was the destructive character of the endless rivalry among the Indonesian non-Communists after 1949[30] which, more than anything else, energized and aided the growth of that country's Communist movement. Actually, the PKI's suppression has set the stage for the reemergence of the older, fundamental friction between Indonesia's Islamic, nationalist, and regionalist elements. Basic rivalries among these groups were only temporarily submerged, not resolved, by the intense struggle between the army and the PKI since 1957. The Islamic and the nationalist elements have little enthusiasm for military rule or pronounced army interference in Indonesian politics. But they have never been able to develop institutional means for composing their fundamental differences over religious and political ideology. Indeed, since the latter half of 1966, reports coming from Indonesia suggest that political conflict between various Moslem and nationalist groups is on the rise again, especially in heavily populated East and Central Java.[31] The military's unchallenged authority during the "New Order" period has created an artificial image of political stability. How stable it really is can only be judged when and if openly contested national elections, scheduled for 1968, are actually held and if a full range of political choice is permitted. Only then will it be known whether Indonesia's basic political ills have been corrected by the removal of Sukarno and the suppression of the PKI.

President Sukarno, whose political demise now seems complete, would probably be the principal beneficiary from any recurrence of the apparent "Iron Law" of Indonesian political anarchy. He is still the major focus of loyalty for many in the Indonesian Nationalist Party (PNI), in Central and East Java, and indeed, for many officers in the

[30] For the definitive analysis of this period, see Herbert Feith, *The Decline of Constitutional Democracy in Indonesia* (Ithaca, N.Y.: Cornell University Press, 1962).

[31] See, for example, Donald Kirk, "Sukarno's Holdouts in Central Java," *The Reporter,* September 8, 1966.

armed forces which are by no means politically monolithic organizations. Should the more conservative, anti-Communist forces once again fail to develop programs which effectively respond to Indonesia's often tragic expressions of diversity, Sukarno (his health permitting) might recapture much of his former role. While he remains president and physically active, Sukarno is unlikely to just fade away. After his capitulation to the army in 1966, China recognized that under the new power balance Sukarno no longer possessed any real authority. But her reluctance to push the dispute with the present army-controled government to an open diplomatic break evidently reflects Peking's desire to avoid undermining whatever future opportunity Sukarno or other "progressive" Indonesian leaders may have to overturn the present regime in Djakarta.

Several considerations suggest that even a consolidation of power by an Indonesian anti-Communist military regime would not necessarily result in China's permanent support for revolutionary war. The cardinal act of hostility toward China on the part of the government of an independent Asian nation is its *de facto* participation in the United States-led anti-China bloc, not its suppression of Chinese nationals or a local Communist party. On the basis of past history and experience, Peking may fairly doubt that future Djakarta governments will indefinitely subordinate Indonesian interests and aspirations to American policy. The dramatic defeat of the PKI has tended to obscure the fact that Sukarno's hopes to project Indonesia's power and influence in the Third World, and especially in Southeast Asia, were enthusiastically shared by a broad spectrum of the Indonesian elite, including top members of the present military command. It was not the legitimacy of these aspirations that Indonesian anti-Communists questioned, but rather Sukarno's attempt to pursue them by a policy of alignment with China against the Western powers. The Indonesian military also wanted to "crush Malaysia," but they viewed the internal Communist problem as more urgent. Once the PKI was crushed and the new government embarked on an economic stabilization program, ending the confrontation with Malaysia (already made less urgent by Singapore's departure), was essential to secure assistance from the West. One can scarcely imagine an act more likely to turn on the flow of American largess than Djakarta's hasty termination of the alignment with Peking. It nevertheless remains to be seen whether Djakarta's termination of the confrontation policy and other aspects of her former "Manifest Destiny" complex reflect a permanent change of goals or a reassessment of priorities and timing. Hence, the character of China's future policy toward Indonesia may be strongly influenced by the role Djakarta chooses to play in Southeast Asia and the extent to which that role complements, or is independent of, American policy.

Having terminated the Peking-Djakarta axis, the present Indonesian government has, thus far, avoided rushing into an embrace with Peking's enemies. Djakarta now advocates restoring Indonesia's traditional "active and independent" foreign policy. Past suspicions of certain Western powers, notably the United States and Britain, have not been entirely discarded. Nor has the defeat of the PKI resulted in an Indonesian decision to support United States policy in Vietnam. Whether in relation to Peking, Moscow, or Washington, Djakarta has once again served notice that the force of Indonesian nationalism cannot be easily, or reliably, manipulated by any foreign power.

In the decade after the Bandung Conference, China accepted the necessity of working with, not against, this force of Indonesian nationalism. The alternative policy of emphasizing a revolutionary line was not only unfeasible and rejected by the Indonesian Communist leadership, it was also contrary to China's interests since to do so was certain to play into the hands of her adversaries, Russia and America. Moreover, Peking's policy was fundamentally shaped by her leaders' ideological assumptions that the inherent "contradictions" between Indonesia and "imperialism" would propel Indonesia toward China's anti-Western orbit and, in this process, aid the PKI in coming to power as the most vigorous exponent of nationalism. Her attempt to forge an alignment with Djakarta was, however, vulnerable to changing political developments in Indonesia which China could not control.

With the drastic alteration of the political balance of forces after the 1965 attempted coup, the Chinese leaders stood at a crossroad in their relations with Indonesia. They presently regard the Indonesian government as an enemy and they have declared ideological war on it. But it is uncertain whether Peking will indefinitely continue this stance or, when the present upheaval in China has subsided, once again compose her differences with an anti-Communist but non-aligned Indonesia. Provided Djakarta does not align herself with America's Asia policy, the main trend of China's diplomacy over the last decade argues against Peking's pursuing a permanent revolutionary line. And over the long range, the actions of the Indonesian leaders themselves will undoubtedly exert a major influence on whether Peking will attempt to reach a conciliatory settlement with Indonesian nationalism, or emphasize ideological antagonism between the two powers.

Comments by George McT. Kahin

My comments on Professor Mozingo's paper are made largely in the interest of clarification rather than by way of criticism. The first relates to his discussion of the degree of compatibility between Chinese and Indonesian interests—or what they have perceived to be their interests—in the area of Southeast Asia. The Indonesian confrontation with Malaysia and Sukarno's flirtation with the Maphilindo formula should, I believe, be viewed as having an anti-Chinese character as well as standing in opposition to Britain and Kuala Lumpur. Apprehensiveness over the political potential of the local Chinese in Malaysia—and the nature of their relationship with Peking—was undoubtedly of central importance in securing the Indonesian Army's backing of confrontation and was a factor that also weighed with many non-communist Indonesian civilian leaders.[1] It is important, I think, to recognize that at least through most of 1964 the Indonesian army and not merely Sukarno and the Indonesian Communist Party (PKI) strongly supported confrontation.[2]

Thus, I would question whether it is appropriate to speak of "China's unqualified support for the 'confrontation' policy." For regardless of Peking's public statements in support of Djakarta's policy, I think it unlikely that China's leaders did not appreciate the significantly anti-Peking and anti-overseas Chinese thrust of confrontation.

Moreover, it is difficult for me to accept the thesis that China's support of Indonesia's confrontation policy "caused the PKI to shift to the

[1] If this did not actually constitute an important reason for Sukarno's support of the Maphilindo formula, he was at least very much aware that it was a basic consideration for Manila and Kuala Lumpur—and in 1963 Malayan and Philippine leaders certainly were given the impression that Djakarta's support for Maphilindo was primarily in terms of containing the political influence of the overseas Chinese.

[2] The army's desire to disengage from confrontation was to a considerable degree brought about by its worry over the PKI's increasing power and a desire not to denude Java of army strength in the face of this.

basic Chinese Communist position in the Sino-Soviet ideological conflict." The PKI's backing of the Chinese Communist position on international issues should, I believe, be attributed primarily to considerations broader than and transcending the Malaysia issue. Peking's endorsement of the PKI position on confrontation came at least a year after the PKI declared its own opposition to Malaysia and well after it had become clear that on other international issues the PKI stood much closer to Peking than to Moscow. Communist China's public support for Indonesian confrontation against Malaysia, it seems to me, was at best a subordinate, contributory factor in determining the PKI's attitude in the Sino-Soviet dispute.

"By drawing non-Communist Asian states within her anti-Western orbit," Mr. Mozingo states, "China hoped to promote their eventual transition to communism." Peking undoubtedly desired this. But I think it should be observed that China, like the Soviet Union, has generally been more concerned with insuring that these countries pursue foreign policies unaligned with the United States and on balance favorable to her own interests, than with promoting the welfare of local communist parties. China's good relations with the strongly anticommunist Pakistan government, for example, stand in marked contrast to her relations with India, a state which does permit the legal existence of a communist party.

Professor Mozingo states that following Djakarta's discriminatory measures against local Chinese, Peking was prepared to make concessions "in order to protect the possibility of developing an 'anti-imperialist' alignment." Despite the importance of this consideration, I think it is misleading to imply that Peking had the capability of taking retaliatory measures that could have been effective in curbing the anti-Chinese actions of the Indonesian government.

Also I find it hard to agree that the extension of large-scale Soviet aid to Indonesia and India after 1959 "strongly suggested that Moscow's chief aim was to strengthen these two powers in the hope of undermining China's position." This may well have been an important calculation, but I would wonder whether, with respect to Indonesia at least, it could have been Moscow's "chief aim" as early as the period 1959–60. Such a consideration would have to be weighed against the Soviet Union's desire at that time to undermine the American position. Nor is it clear to me how Moscow could have hoped that its provision of arms to Indonesia in Sukarno's campaign to take West Irian "would help to turn Djakarta against Peking."

With reference to my earlier point, I would dispute the argument that the Soviet Union's reluctance to extend further major economic and military assistance to Djakarta in its anti-Malaysia campaign was because this campaign was "evidently seen as likely to advance the growth of China's influence in Southeast Asia." Could one not conclude that in addition to its desire not to prejudice the growth of better relations with the United States, Moscow was reluctant to extend further substantial economic and military assistance to Djakarta at the time of its anti-Malaysia campaign primarily because, despite the magnitude of the existing Soviet outlay, there had been precious little Indonesian repayment—either financially or politically. Already, beginning at Belgrade in 1961, Sukarno was displaying a policy which was contrary to Soviet international interests (and which was also at odds with the positions of Cairo, Belgrade, and New Delhi).

With respect to the abortive coup of September 30, 1965, one should note, I believe, that whether or not the PKI was the principal instigator, it is no longer seriously argued that this move was aimed at the overthrow of Sukarno. More germane to Mr. Mozingo's speculations is the still open question of whether Sukarno himself might have taken an initiative in the coup attempt. Major involvement by Sukarno would not necessarily mean Chinese involvement, but if established would argue for a wider canvassing of possibilties than Mr. Mozingo has undertaken.

Mr. Mozingo states that the continuing strength of Indonesian nationalism is sufficient to insure that, notwithstanding the defeat of the local communists, there will be no abandonment of Indonesia's opposition to American policy in Vietnam. Indonesian leaders, whether of the extreme left or the extreme right, have certainly been strongly opposed to the American intervention in Vietnam; but I think one must recognize that Indonesia's current desperate need for American economic assistance leaves her leaders vulnerable to possible American pressure that they soft pedal their opposition to United States Vietnam policy.

Professor Mozingo makes an important point when he concludes that

> the character of China's future policy toward Indonesia may be strongly influenced by the role Djakarta chooses to play in Southeast Asia and the extent to which that role complements or is independent of American policy.

Perhaps it would be reasonable to suggest that with China currently, and presumably for some years to come, too weak to be a major force in Southeast Asia, and with the massive growth of the American presence there, Peking might be inclined to encourage Indonesia to assume a greater role in continental (as well as insular) Southeast Asia if this reflected a policy that was truly non-aligned and independent.

Mr. Mozingo notes that the Indonesian army leadership has long regarded the Indonesian Communist Party, Peking, and the overseas Chinese as essentially interdependent parts of the same communist security problem, while Sukarno viewed the three elements more as separate entities and undertook to protect the overseas Chinese from the extremes of repression which some army leaders urged. It might be worth adding that with Sukarno's influence no longer operative in this respect, the now politically dominant army is under greater pressure from Indonesian commercial groups who, out of self-interest, have long advocated repression of Chinese businessmen—those who are Indonesian citizens as well as the resident Chinese nationals. Moreover, it is likely that the local Chinese will be made the scapegoat if the army fails in its governmental tasks, particularly if it does not sufficiently eliminate smuggling and other corrupt practices within its own ranks. Most American policy-makers appear to recognize quite as clearly as do the able young Indonesian economists on whom General Suharto relies for advice that Indonesia's economic recovery is not compatible with precipitate destruction of the entrepreneurial position of Indonesia's Chinese. But clearly much of the Indonesian army leadership has not yet become disabused of its erroneous conclusion that a corollary of Washington's anti-Peking policy is its encouragement of, or at least acquiescence in, discriminatory measures against overseas Chinese.

Ruth T. McVey

13

Indonesian Communism
and China

China has been not one thing to the Indonesians but three: a state, a revolution, and an ethnic minority. As a revolutionary symbol it became visible to the Indonesians in about 1923, a time when Sun Yatsen's radical nationalism, the armed struggle of the Kuomintang for dominion over a united China, and the Kuomintang alliance with Soviet Russia against the forces of "imperialism and feudalism" found considerable response among the intransigent leftists of the first generation of the Indonesian independence movement and the rising new wave of radical secular nationalists. This leftist and revolutionary image of China remained, for the post-1927 period of Communist eclipse in China was also one in which Indonesian interest in foreign Asian examples was centered on Japan, now appearing as a symbol of anti-Western, militant nationalism. Insofar as China presented an image to Indonesian political leaders of the 1930's, it was as a participant in the international struggle against fascism, a theme which was utilized by the moderate and radical left partly from real concern and partly to justify its decision to abandon an unsuccessful policy of refusing to cooperate with the colonial authorities. Moreover, radically-inclined Indonesian-language journals published by members of the local Chinese minority exhibited an interest in the Chinese Communist movement; these newspapers were also read by the Indonesian anti-colonial opposition (some of whose principal leaders published articles, pseudonymously or otherwise, in them), so that the radical nationalists were thus provided with a continuing source of sympathetic information on the Communist effort in China.[1] The result was that China's image was

[1] These journals were principally *Sin Tit Po* of Surabaja and *Matahari* of Semarang. *Sin Tit Po* published the first Indonesian translation of Edgar Snow's *Red Star over China,* which appeared in serial form during 1938 until the Indies government banned it as dangerous. The book had considerable

preponderantly a leftist one, and so it remained until Communist victory in that country made it unambiguously a symbol of social revolution.

The contrast between the social radicalism of China as a revolutionary symbol and the popular Indonesian image of the overseas Chinese as clever and merciless exploiters of the Indonesian masses (a picture based on the prominent role of the local minority in commerce and lending) has meant that any Indonesian political movement that wished to utilize the first had somehow to separate it from the second. Furthermore, any revolutionary group wishing to gain the support of the local Chinese had somehow to persuade them that its aims were not in conflict with their entrepreneurial or communal interests. Neither was at all easy to do, though the Indonesian Communists in the end came perhaps as close to accomplishing this as one could imagine possible.

The third element in the Indonesians' image of China, their view of it as a state, remained fairly ephemeral until after the achievement of Indonesian independence and the founding of the People's Republic of China (CPR). When this did become an issue it intensified the contradictions in the Indonesian impression, for China almost immediately made claims to be not only a state entering into relations with the Indonesian republic but also a revolutionary model and the protector of Indonesia's Chinese population. Though by the mid-1950's the CPR had begun to give strong preference to the advancing of diplomatic relations above the protection of the overseas Chinese and the furtherance of revoluton, it has not been possible to separate completely these aspects from each other, either in practice or in the Indonesian mind. It has been very hard for any Indonesian group or government to find a satisfactory formula for confronting China's multiple presence; neither the enthusiasm of the later years of Guided Democracy nor the intense strain that has followed the October, 1965, coup has represented a course held entirely without misgivings or internal contradictions.

The problem of the Chinese image has posed the Indonesian Communist Party (PKI) some difficult questions of strategy. The most persistent and delicate aspect of the Chinese question, so far as the Indonesian Communists have been concerned, has been that of relations

---

effect on Indonesian revolutionary thinking, affecting particularly A. H. Nasution's ideas on guerrilla warfare. For a discussion of the Chinese minority and Indonesian radical politics in the period before World War II, see Mary Somers Heidhues, "Peranakan Chinese Politics in Indonesia" (unpublished diss., Cornell University, 1965), pp. 95–100.

with the overseas Chinese minority. The PKI's refusal to attack that group in the 1950's and 1960's was commonly charged by Indonesian anti-Communists to lie, if not in outright servitude to Peking, at least in an opportunistic acceptance of money from the local Chinese and favor from the CPR. Whatever the influence of such motives, it should be noted that throughout its history Indonesian Communism has exhibited a notable tolerance of the Chinese minority, even at times when the advantages of taking an anti-Chinese position far outweighed the benefits that might conceivably be gained from defending that minority. A principal factor in this abstention seems to have been the internationalist, anti-racist character of Marxist ideology; another, the fact that anti-Chinese sentiment has always been strongest on the right —on the part of the Indonesians competing with or aspiring to replace the Chinese shopkeepers, merchants, and moneylenders—and there has thus been a natural tendency for the left to become involved in such defense as the Chinese minority enjoys.

Direct participation of members of the Chinese minority in the Indonesian Communist movement has been very small. Early efforts of the Indonesian Communists to attract the support of the Chinese population were aimed at working-class Chinese and were apparently inspired by internationalist and anti-racist considerations.[2] They were, however, quite unsuccessful, for although the number of Chinese who belonged to the urban proletariat was not small, it was largely composed of relatively recent immigrants, who made up part of the "totok" Chinese community, a grouping which was China-oriented, Chinese-speaking, and usually China-born. The new immigrants among the totok working class had frequently absorbed revolutionary ideas—Kuomintang and, in the 1920's, Communist—in their South China homeland, but this was not sufficient to orient them on arrival in Indonesia to what was, in spite of its internationalist ideology and European beginnings, a very Indonesia-oriented movement.

PKI organization in the labor field expanded rapidly in the post-colonial period, but largely in European-owned industries and planta-

[2] The first attempt to attract Chinese support that I have discovered is the attendance by leaders of the nascent Communist movement at the 1918 May Day celebration of the Chinese union Kung Tan Hwee Koan in Surabaja. They explained the aims of their group to the audience and invited cooperation, but the language barrier prevented much comprehension of their appeal (H. Sneevliet, "Onze eerste 1-Mei viering," *Het Vrije Woord,* May 10, 1918, p. 197). The principal effort to arouse interest in China and to attract local Chinese support was made in 1924–26. See Ruth T. McVey, *The Rise of Indonesian Communism* (Ithaca: Cornell University Press, 1965), pp. 223–30.

tions, where labor was almost exclusively Indonesian. The party and union leadership seems to have made no particular effort since independence to recruit among the working-class Chinese, even those of the Indonesia-born and Indonesia-oriented (peranakan) community, and the Chinese poor in turn seem to have been equally indifferent to the PKI. Those Indonesian Chinese whom the Communists did attract tended in both the colonial and post-colonial periods to be radical peranakan intellectuals, who were drawn to the movement across rather than along class lines. These have been quite few and far between—the only Indonesian political party with Chinese participation of any importance is the Catholic party—though individually several Indonesian Chinese leaders have played important roles.

The most important PKI leader of Chinese extraction was Tan Ling Djie, who was one of the few top members of the party to survive the Madiun Affair, a clash between government and Communist forces in September, 1948, which ended the second period of the PKI's development.[3] In January, 1951, D. N. Aidit and his allies of the younger generation seized control of the party organization from Tan and his associates, and at the October, 1953, Central Committee meeting that consolidated Aidit's command the older leadership group was denounced for the sin of "Tan Ling Djie-ism." Shortly thereafter Siauw Giok Tjan, co-editor and founder of the party paper *Harian Rakjat*, resigned from that journal along with the only other Chinese member of its editorial staff.[4]

Siauw was a friend of Tan Ling Djie, and it is not clear whether his departure was a matter of association with Tan or of a party decision

[3] Before the war Tan Ling Djie had been editor and also correspondent in Holland for *Sin Tit Po*. He became a leader of the Socialist party during the revolution; in August, 1948, he announced, along with other major leftist leaders, that he also belonged to the PKI. Arrested at the time of the Madiun Affair, he became secretary of the standing committee of the Politburo in 1949 following his release.

[4] It is not clear whether Siauw was formally a PKI member in spite of the fact that he edited the party paper. He served in the Indonesian parliament at the time as a member of the Indonesian Popular Union (SKI), a minor party of no clear ideology (cf. *Antara News Bulletin*, Amsterdam, March 7, 1954). He had edited the Semarang daily *Matahari* in the colonial period; at that time he had belonged to the Indonesian Chinese Party (PTI), the major peranakan political group. See Mary Somers, *Peranakan Chinese Politics in Indonesia* (Ithaca: Cornell Modern Indonesia Project, 1964), p. 11; Parlaungan, *Hasil Rakjat Memilih Tokoh2 Parlemen* (Djakarta: C. V. Gita, 1956), pp. 321–22.

to minimize the number of Indonesian Chinese holding leading public positions in the Communist movement. That the latter was possible is indicated by the fact that the new party leadership was intensely nationalistic: the charges laid at the feet of Tan Ling Djie and his associates were, in fact, that they had paid too much attention to foreign opinion and had too little appreciation of Indonesian Communism's historic role in the national awakening and of the leading part the PKI should rightfully play in the further development of the Indonesian revolutionary process. Once in power in the party, Aidit and his colleagues placed strong emphasis on the Indonesianness of the PKI and, as they gained in ideological self-confidence, on efforts to "Indonesianize" Marxism-Leninism.[5] It is not surprising that a leadership of this temperament might, even though it did not itself entertain anti-Sinic feelings, find it embarrassing to have Indonesians of Chinese extraction occupying leading positions in the party. Though the presence of a member of that population group might demonstrate the PKI's desire for the integration of the Chinese into the mainstream of society, it would very likely find objections from the lower ranks of the party; even as it was, the lower cadres objected in later years that the Chinese minority should be held more responsible by the party for Indonesia's lack of prosperity.[6] Nor would the inclusion of Indonesian Chinese leaders have been likely to improve the party's chances of gaining acceptance in the eyes of the authorities; the government made this clear at the outset of Aidit's stewardship when, in razzias aimed, as it claimed, against Communism, it detained not only a good part of the PKI leadership but also a number of Indonesian Chinese who had nothing to do with the party. The point was made even more strongly by the anti-Chinese measures of 1959–60 and riots against the Chinese in May, 1963, which were largely army-instigated and aimed as much at

[5] Although the "Indonesianization" of Marxism-Leninism was an ongoing process in the Aidit era, it received its greatest impetus and conscious expression in the 1963–65 period. Aidit's major statement on the subject appeared in *Harian Rakjat*, February 24 and 25, 1964, and was also published as a pamphlet: D. N. Aidit, *Marxisme-Leninisme dan Peng-Indonesianja* (Djakarta: Pembaruan, 1964).

[6] D. N. Aidit, interview March, 1965; Njoto, interview February, 1965. It is not clear to me whether these objections were strong before the removal of most European and American presence had made the Chinese the obvious target for resentment at continued economic deterioration; I should imagine, however, that the complaints would have become stronger and harder to handle in the latter period.

the embarrassment of the PKI and the exacerbation of relations with China as at the harassment of the local Chinese.[7]

Whether or not such considerations influenced the jettisoning of the Chinese editors of the party journal, it would seem likely they figured to some degree in determining the fact that the PKI had no really important officers of Chinese extraction during the Aidit period, and that the party did not itself publicly promote activities within the Indonesian Chinese minority until after the anti-Chinese riots of May, 1963. Even then, having come to the conclusion that the non-involvement of the Indonesian Chinese in public affairs was doing the minority more harm than good,[8] the PKI did not encourage members of the Chinese minority to become Communists but to join the left nationalist Partindo or other parties. Indonesian Chinese did come in the 1963–65 period to sit in the executives of a number of PKI-sponsored organizations, but these were almost exclusively associations of intellectuals, thus involving a social group with relatively little anti-Sinicism and with little visibility as far as mass politics was concerned.

In March, 1954, after having left his post on the PKI newspaper, Siauw Giok Tjan had involved himself in the establishment of the Baperki (Citizens' Consultative Council). The association was designed to defend the interests of Indonesian citizens of Chinese extraction, and since its members were overwhelmingly from the independent middle class a great part of its activity was devoted to the defense of private enterprise. Siauw, who became its chairman, acquitted himself admirably in his new cause, building the Baperki into a surprisingly effective machine and winning the firm loyalty of a great part of the peranakan population. The Baperki leadership, particularly in the provinces, was not overwhelmingly sympathetic to the left, and in the 1955 general elections the association followed a pragmatic strategy which resulted

[7] For an account of the 1959 anti-Chinese campaign, see Somers, *Peranakan Chinese Politics in Indonesia*, pp. 24–29. The 1963 riots took place in West Java, where they were widespread in principal cities. For a PKI view of them, see *Harian Rakjat*, May 31 and June 1, 1963. It was widely said at the time (though denied by the Communists) that Communist youth in several areas had joined in the anti-Chinese demonstrations; if true, this may have given impetus to the party decision to take a more active role in achieving the integration of the local Chinese.

[8] D. N. Aidit, interview, February, 1965. The party urged a policy of "revolutionary integration," which meant that the Chinese should be allowed to preserve their character as one of Indonesia's many ethnic divisions (suku) while striving to eliminate their social and economic apartness from the indigenous population.

in its endorsing as many alliances with the Catholic party as it did with the PKI.[9] Siauw himself was elected to parliament on the Baperki ticket and there joined the National Progressive Fraction, a minor and highly heterogenous coalition which included the civilian prominent in the post-coup New Order, Adam Malik. Nonetheless, Siauw's continuing personal association with the far left, coupled with the fact that the PKI was the only major party to take a firm stand against anti-Chinese discrimination, tended to identify the Baperki in the popular mind as leftist; this apprehension received not a little encouragement from the leaders of the Indonesian right, who sought thereby to arouse mistrust of both the Baperki and the PKI. In the end, a *de facto* alliance did spring up between the two, largely because, with the growing social and economic tensions and the polarization of political power under Guided Democracy, the Chinese minority came into an increasingly exposed position in which it needed the support of the only major force that was willing to defend it, which was the Communist party.

Baperki's promotion of the interests of the independent middle class, the asli (indigenous) Indonesians' inclinations toward statism, and the PKI's defense of the Indonesian Chinese against racial discrimination led sometimes to curious combinations of strategies and alliances. For example, the controversy over the Assaat movement, an anti-Chinese effort of 1956–57, found the principal association of asli businessmen, representing a force of the anti-Communist right, arguing for state assumption of control over an important economic sector—the bus and trucking industry, which was very largely in Indonesian Chinese hands —whose right to remain under private ownership was defended vigorously and in the end effectively by Baperki and the Communists.[10] The PKI drew a sharp distinction in both principle and practice between "national" and "compradore" or "bureaucratic" capital. The former— which for the PKI included non-asli capital domiciled in Indonesia— was to be encouraged as a positive contribution to the development of

[9] For a discussion of the electoral alliances of the Baperki, see Heidhues, "Peranakan Chinese Politics," p. 159.

[10] For the position of the Indonesian businessmen's association, see *Kensi Berdjuang* (Djakarta: Djambatan, 1957), especially the report by Assaat. For the political course of the Assaat movement, see Herbert Feith, *The Decline of Constitutional Democracy in Indonesia* (Ithaca: Cornell University Press, 1962), pp. 481–87; Somers, *Peranakan Chinese Politics in Indonesia*, pp. 16–18. Possibly in order to redress any "pro-Chinese" impression left by its opposition to the Assaat movement, the PKI endorsed with especial vigor the measures against pro-Kuomintang Chinese taken as a result of Taiwan's support for the Indonesian rebellion in 1958.

the economy. The compradores were condemned for being allied to foreign capital, while the bureaucratic capitalists—a phenomenon of sharply increasing concern for the PKI in the Guided Democracy period—utilized positions gained in the management of state enterprises or connections in the bureaucracy to fatten themselves without concern for the development of the enterprise or the economy as a whole.[11]

The PKI's attitude toward the national entrepreneurs was similar to that expressed by the Chinese Communists, and inasmuch as Indonesian Chinese businessmen of the 1950's were aware that the fate of cooperating "national capitalists" in the CPR was not unfavorable compared to their own politically and economically precarious position in Indonesia, the incompatibility of PKI and peranakan economic interests was not felt so strongly as one might otherwise suppose. This being the case, we might ask ourselves whether, as the PKI's enemies were wont to claim, the party's funds were drawn substantially from the local Chinese. No real information is available on this, and so we can only proceed by asking what is likely to have been the case given the logic of the circumstances and consider whether this explains the more effective PKI organizational financing as compared to the other major Indonesian parties.

It is probably quite safe to assume that by no means all the PKI's funds were internally derived; the party probably could have mounted fairly considerable activity without recourse to outside financing but it is unlikely it felt constrained to do so.[12] The question, then, is on what

[11] For an exposition of this position, see M. H. Lukman, *Adjakan PKI kepada Kaum Pengusaha Nasional* (Djakarta: Pembaruan, 1963).

[12] Most of the party's members were quite poor and could pay at best the minimum in dues, which were scaled according to income. There were, of course, very many party and mass organization members, and a considerable effort was made to get them to contribute regularly, this as much by way of encouraging a feeling of active participation as for the satisfaction of the PKI's own financial needs. Moreover, the PKI had a highly developed system of volunteer work, donations in kind, and so on, which increased the resources available to it without placing too much of a burden in direct money payment on its following. For a general discussion of PKI financing, see Donald Hindley, *The Communist Party of Indonesia 1951–1963* (Berkeley: University of California Press, 1964), pp. 110–18. The methods of collection and control of funds seem to have improved generally between the time of Hindley's observations (1959–60) and mine in 1964–65. However, rapidly advancing inflation and the demands of an expanding apparatus may have offset much if not all of the gain. Publication, cadre training programs, and educational projects were frequently well behind schedule in the latter period; on inquiry, lack of funds was almost always given as a principal explanation.

basis the PKI could have obtained money from the local Chinese. Gratefulness for Communist support for their minority may well have inspired some to supply extramural funds; it would be surprising if this were not so. However, gratitude is notoriously poor as a source of steady income, and the PKI was not in a good position to extract money on a less voluntary basis from the Indonesian Chinese. The individual Chinese businessman might appreciate the PKI's over-all defense of his group, but he was likely to see his immediate physical security lying in contributions to the welfare of army officers and civilian officials who might otherwise see to his harassment. His economic security was best attended to by bribes, kickbacks, and informal profit-sharing arrangements with those who held the rights to give licenses, permissions, exceptions, and the other economic keys of Guided Democracy; and these were almost never Communists.[13]

As the PKI's strength grew under Guided Democracy, it became possible for it to secure financial support from wealthy individuals who donated lest the party otherwise be inspired to promote denunciations of them for corruption and mismanagement of office. Hints of such action would doubtless have been effective among the vulnerable Indonesian Chinese, and certainly they would have gained a wide response among the party following. The problem was that such a response would quite likely have been too enthusiastic for the well-being of the China alliance and for the PKI's general policy of racial pacification, for the party's enemies would surely have turned such attacks to their own profit. Consequently, the PKI was limited in the amount of public pressure it could bring to bear on individual Chinese businessmen, and this absence of effective leverage probably affected adversely the amount of funds received from members of the Chinese community.[14]

[13] It has sometimes been suggested that threats of strikes by Communist unions and other labor pressure were used by the PKI to extract money from Chinese businessmen. See George McT. Kahin, "Indonesia," in Kahin, ed., *Major Governments of Asia* (Ithaca, N.Y.: Cornell University Press, 1963), p. 618; Hindley, *The Communist Party of Indonesia,* pp. 117–18. No direct evidence for this has been produced, however; and it does not seem likely it could have been employed effectively to any significant extent, in the first place because most Chinese enterprises were commercial rather than industrial, in the second place because Chinese-run industries tended to be very poorly unionized, and in the third place because after 1957 strikes were generally illegal.

[14] I am indebted to Mary Somers Heidhues for conversations which led me to a consideration of these aspects. Dr. Heidhues informed me, from her knowledge of the peranakan Chinese community and its Communist relations, that it was her impression the PKI was able to obtain from the Chinese minor-

So far as the receipt of money from or by courtesy of the CPR is concerned, we again have no information on the subject save the anti-Communists' firm claim that this was so and the Communists' firm claim that it was not. It is safest to assume that considerable funds were supplied, for there was probably no major power interested in Indonesia which did not find it worthwhile to make available, by one means or another, funds for the support of the sympathetic, the neutralization of the hostile, and the persuasion of the vacillating. It seems unlikely on the face of it, however, that more Chinese than American (or, given the importance of Indonesia to the Sino-Soviet dispute, Russian) money was available for influencing Indonesians. Moreover, although foreign donations can result in the acquisition of a powerful and more or less reliable clientele among individual members of the elite, they are notoriously ineffective in giving substance to mass movements which do not possess vigor and popularity of their own.

In terms of quantity alone, the money from foreign or Indonesian Chinese sources available to the PKI may well have been considerably less than that going to members of the army, the palace, and the principal non-Communist parties. The explanation for the PKI's relative organizational effectiveness lay, most likely, not in its superior access to funds but in its superior ability to mobilize and channel the resources on which it could call. Because Indonesian Communism represented a movement as well as an organization, the party was able to appeal beyond the immediate self-interest of its members. Consequently, it did not find itself in the situation, common to the other groupings, in which funds received had to be at least equally repaid in favors, with the result that the party concerned became a sort of self-perpetuating patronage machine, incapable of the rational accumulation and allocation of funds. Secondly, because the PKI was an apparatus rather than a collection of leaders and their followings, donations received were generally given to it as an organization and utilized for organizational ends, rather than, as was usually the case with the other power groupings, accruing to an individual member for a favor he himself dispensed, and being disbursed by him in the service of his own needs or ambitions.

---

ity much less than it sought, being most able to obtain donations for its educational projects, inasmuch as this was something the Chinese felt was worthwhile. Perhaps, if this was so, it was a reason why the PKI frequently placed Chinese as executives of the scholarly and educational groups it promoted in 1963–65.

In spite of the relative proximity of Indonesia and China, the Indonesian consciousness of China as a revolutionary symbol, and the long existence of both Communist movements,[15] there has historically been remarkably little direct exchange between Indonesian and Chinese Communism. Substantial communications between the Chinese and Indonesian Communist movements were never direct before 1950. Except for the heretic Tan Malaka, only one Indonesian Communist leader of stature can be said to have been "trained in China" in the sense of having spent much time there. This was Alimin Prawirodirdjo, who had been prominent in the first period of PKI development and had spent long years in Soviet exile following the 1926–27 Indonesian Communist rebellion. Sent back to Indonesia as the war began, he found himself stranded in China by the Japanese advance; he spent the war years with Mao's troops in Yenan, returning in mid-1946 to find his homeland in revolution against the Dutch. Far from advocating guerrilla warfare or an all-out national liberation struggle, however, Alimin directed the party towards self-effacement in domestic politics and advocacy of compromise with the Dutch, which policy he continued to defend long after the party as a whole had renounced it. Commentators have occasionally labeled Alimin a "Maoist," discerning this or that evidence of his Yenan years, but on the whole it appears that the experience really passed him by.[16]

Alimin was among the leaders ousted in 1951 by D. N. Aidit, who had himself gone to China in early 1949 following the disastrous Madiun Affair. Aidit and his close ally M. H. Lukman stayed for a little over a year with the Communist forces in China and (briefly) in Vietnam, returning to Indonesia in mid-1950. Like Alimin, however, Aidit seems to have been largely unaffected by his Chinese experience; by his own claim, he and Lukman did not learn much. They were too

[15] The Indonesian Communist movement had its origin in 1914 with the founding of the Indies Social Democratic Association (ISDV), which was reduced to its Leninist component in 1917. In May, 1920, it took the name PKI; in December it voted to join the Comintern.

[16] For Alimin's views on returning from China—which were notable for their lack of reference to that country's experience—see his *Sepatah Kata dari Djaoeh* (Jogjakarta: Bintang Merah, 1947). He defended his stand on compromising with the Dutch, to the great annoyance of the Aidit leadership, in his autobiography, *Riwajat Hidup* (Djakarta: Kesedjahteraan N.V., [1955?]). Interviewed in June, 1959, Alimin recounted his China experience as an interesting if time-consuming episode on his way from the Soviet Union to Indonesia.

young and insignificant—they had no posts in the reconstituted leadership of what was, following the Madiun debacle, an insignificant party —to excite the attention of the Chinese or Vietnamese Communists, who were at that time fully occupied with more important affairs. Consequently, the two Indonesian refugees were largely left, according to Aidit, to their own devices.[17]

Aside from the frustration attendant on being ignored, Aidit seems to have been put off by the thought that the sort of struggle carried on by the Chinese and Vietnamese movements was inappropriate to the Indonesian situation at that stage. The Chinese and Vietnamese had achieved hegemony over the national liberation forces in their countries and led them towards triumph against foreign and discredited domestic enemies. The Indonesian Communists were faced, in contrast, with a popular and legitimate non-Communist leadership, and they themselves had been discredited for having challenged it. Aidit was convinced—or became so soon after his return to Indonesia—that the only practical way for the Communists to regain their lost influence was by developing as a peaceful and loyal force; consequently, the strategy on which he based his leadership was fundamentally different from that pursued by either the Chinese or the Vietnamese Communist movements at the time. Some party members apparently wished to carry out a protracted armed struggle à la China, or else to remain passive until a third world war brought new revolutionary opportunities, but the new leadership denounced them as unrealistic.[18]

Until the Central Committee meeting of October, 1953, Aidit claimed to base his policy on Marxism-Leninism-Stalinism, the New Road policy laid down in 1948 by the slain party leader Musso, and the Thought of Mao Tse-tung—the last being, we will remember, then still part of the internationally recognized formula for Asian Communist success. After that session, however, it seemed no longer necessary to call on Musso's memory; and the Thought of Mao began to be replaced in PKI invocations by that of D. N. Aidit. The pantheon of international Communist heroes customarily displayed on the walls of party offices consisted

[17] D. N. Aidit, interview, October, 1964. Aidit's trip was rarely mentioned in party biographical sketches or other occasions where reference might have been made; perhaps this was the reason.

[18] Cf. D. N. Aidit, "Djalan ke Demokrasi Rakjat bagi Indonesia," *Bintang Merah*, vol. 9, no. 9–10 (October–November, 1953), p. 454. This speech to the October 1953 Central Committee plenum was the major statement of early PKI policy under Aidit.

of Marx, Engels, Lenin, Stalin (with a brief interlude of de-emphasis in the latter 1950's), and (increasingly) Aidit. In the heyday of the Sino-Indonesian alliance of 1963–65, the PKI quoted Lenin frequently as a Communist authority, Stalin often, Aidit always, and Mao almost never. Much was done throughout the Aidit period to make Indonesian translations of Chinese Communist writings and statements available to the PKI following, but in commenting on them it was stressed that the Chinese experience, if important and useful for the Indonesian Communists, was not to be accepted unquestioningly.[19]

The PKI did borrow much from the Chinese in terms of mass organizational techniques, particularly when, after 1959, it threw its energies heavily into developing its strength among the peasantry. The decision for a major shift of cadres, funds, and attention from the labor movement to the rural areas may itself have been inspired ultimately by the lessons of the Chinese revolution, but its actual implementation appears to have resulted from the realization by party leaders that, with labor organization and agitation sharply curtailed and most major enterprises in army hands following the ousting of the Dutch, they would be well advised to turn their attention to areas of activity where they were less likely to run afoul of the military. In developing a wide-ranging role in the countryside, the Communists used traditional appeals and activities, their own innovations, and ideas borrowed from Chinese practice. The last were almost never credited to their original inventor, and often took quite different shape in their Indonesian guise, if only by virtue of the fact that they were not being applied by a government in power or a force with effective territorial control but by a movement which, even in areas where it enjoyed great popularity, never had real command of the means of coercion.

The Aidit leadership established its claims to an independent line in the international Communist movement at a very early date, having proclaimed in 1953, at a time when America was still doctrinally held to be Imperialist Enemy No. 1, that for Indonesia the Dutch filled that role. The Soviets endorsed this, after the fact, for their own strategic reconsiderations were leading them to increased tolerance for Asian

[19] Thus when the PKI provided a translation of Mao's "On Coalition Government" in its theoretical journal, it cautioned that "There are similarities between the Indonesian and Chinese revolutions, but there are also many differences. If this fact is always kept in mind, the study of 'On Coalition Government' will be very useful." (Editorial note, *Bintang Merah*, vol. 11, no. 9–10 [September–October, 1955], inside front cover.)

nationalism.[20] However, in 1956 a second difference between Soviet and Indonesian Communist opinion arose, and this time, being part of the developing Sino-Soviet dispute, it marked the beginning of a permanent schism. Khrushchev's denunciation of Stalin at the Twentieth CPSU Congress came as a considerable shock to a party leadership that had known Stalin at best as a distant demigod—Aidit, who attended the meeting, had himself only been to the USSR once previously, in 1953, when he arrived just in time to witness Stalin's funeral. Moreover, the PKI leaders were disturbed that, without warning, the Soviets had taken it upon themselves to deal a considerable blow to other Communist parties' pretensions to unity and infallibility by disowning what had been a towering figure in the international movement. Consequently, when the Chinese declared their criticism of the Soviets' handling of the matter following the congress, the PKI endorsed their stand. What the Russians wished to do with a national issue was their own concern, the Indonesians maintained, but on matters which affected the international movement no action should be taken without prior discussion with its other components.[21]

This marked the beginning of a long history of friction between the Soviet and Indonesian parties over the matter of authority within the international movement. It was in the PKI's interest to have a maximum degree of outward unanimity and a minimum amount of actual control; hence the party argued against the exclusion of maverick members like the Albanians, against the acknowledgment of any au-

[20] For the PKI's declaration, see Aidit, "Djalan ke Demokrasi Rakjat bagi Indonesia," p. 455. For the Soviet endorsement, see *Pravda*, November 14, 1953, which referred to the PKI position without disfavor. The Netherlands Communist Party gave the Indonesians' position unqualified acceptance: see H. de Vries, "Nieuw beginselprogram van de P.K.I.," *Politiek en Cultuur*, vol. 8, no. 12, p. 548. After the takeover of Dutch enterprises at the end of 1957, emphasis on the Netherlands as Indonesia's principal imperialist enemy gradually declined in favor of the stress on the American role. It was not, however, until after the Irian accession in 1963 that the United States was officially declared Indonesia's immediate enemy (cf. *Harian Rakjat*, May 29, 1963).

[21] Cf. D. N. Aidit, "Tentang Perlawatan ke Empat Negeri," *Bintang Merah* vol. 12, no. 6 (June, 1956), pp. 216–18 (report of Aidit's trip to the twentieth CPSU congress delivered June 27, 1956). The Indonesian Communists did, however, join in the condemnation of the cult of personality and generally avoided mention of Stalin until 1959, when they issued an evaluation of his accomplishments (*Stalin dan Karjanja* [Djakarta: Pembaruan, 1959]) and commenced his rehabilitation. The Stalin issue formed part of Aidit's critical report on the twenty-second CPSU congress, issued after his return to Indonesia (*Harian Rakjat*, December 15, 1961).

thority other than that of the sense of the movement as a whole, and for the settlement of all questions affecting international Communist affairs by consultation and consensus among the parties concerned.[22] This was an extreme nationalist view, typified by the insistence that the true wording of the slogan was not "Proletarians of the world unite!" but "Proletarians of all nations unite!"[23]

The Indonesian Communists did not include the Yugoslav Communist League among those within the pale, for Tito's connections with the West made difficult the PKI's task of persuading Indonesia's leaders that to achieve true national independence it was necessary for them to break political, economic, and cultural ties with the West—the source of support for the PKI's enemies—and to replace them with ties to the Communist bloc. Moreover, the Yugoslavs at an early stage entered into close relationships with the Indonesian army, which was to be the PKI's principal enemy in the Guided Democracy period. The Indonesian Communists tended to view this as one more sign that the Yugoslavs, while still claiming the Communist label, were actually serving the other side.

It was not the Yugoslavs' domestic revisionism that really disturbed the Indonesian Communists, for the PKI was, so far as its internal policies were concerned, among the most moderate of Communist parties. It sought to come to power not by overthrowing the national

[22] The PKI began to devote favorable attention to Albania in its publications in 1959. The Soviet handling of the Albanian issue became a major target of PKI criticism of the twenty-second CPSU congress—see Aidit's speech on "It is Not a Question of Who Will Leave But Who Will Enter the Socialist Bloc," *Harian Rakjat,* December 15, 1961. According to Aidit (interview, February, 1965), he had been particularly irked at the congress by the fact that the Soviets had neglected to inform the other parties there would be an attack on the Albanian issue, much less that such a harsh stand would be taken toward a small party.

[23] For PKI treatments of the relationship between nationalism and internationalism, see M. H. Lukman, *Mengamalkan Tjinta Tanahair* (Djakarta: Bintang Merah, 1957); and *Patriotisme dan Internationalisme* (Djakarta: Depagitprop CC PKI, 1962). When the PKI's stand in the Sino-Soviet dispute turned toward the Chinese side the Soviets were able to arouse the PKI's defensive indignation by hinting the party was "unfree" (see, for example, Njoto's arguments on the subject in *Harian Rakjat,* February 10, 1964). Aidit (interview, February 1965) evinced considerable indignation that the CPSU would not credit the Indonesian Communists with various anti-Soviet theoretical innovations, but insisted on attacking the Chinese for them. The PKI, he said, had written the CPSU formally demanding the Indonesians be attacked directly for their assertions, but the Soviets had not answered the letter.

elite but by persuading it that no other group could do the job of governing so well, that no other had the necessary ability to mobilize and control the masses, to organize, and to deal with the world at large. Hence, when Khrushchev proclaimed the possibility of a peaceful transition to socialism at the Twentieth CPSU Congress, the Indonesian party endorsed this road, on which it was already embarked, as suitable for Indonesia.[24]

The Indonesian party had, in fact, very little choice in electing to travel the peaceful road. When Aidit had assumed command of the party it was a disgraced and divided group consisting of under ten thousand souls. It hardly seemed possible that it would so rapidly extend its strength that in general elections held four years later it would emerge as Indonesia's fourth strongest party, much less that regional elections in 1957–58 would indicate it was close to surpassing all its rivals. As a minor party it constituted a nuisance but not a menace. It might suffer harassment should the authorities decide to clamp down on it, but the advantages legality offered it for spreading the word and for forming protective alliances were far greater than those obtainable from trying to build an underground in a society not overly conducive to clandestine operations or from carrying on an insurrection in a country not graced with geography favorable to a guerrilla campaign. Emerging as Indonesia's major party, the PKI found itself with a huge but exposed apparatus, with a following oriented toward legality and hence of uncertain quality should the party go underground, and with no real purchase on the bureaucratic structure or the military.

In the decade following the elections, the PKI represented the forces of social transformation against an elite which became increasingly united against change. Still committed to the ideology of revolution, that elite sought to substitute revolutionary rhetoric and the ceremonial mobilization of the masses for the closing avenues of social transformation. The military, moving into the economic and political arena with the institution of martial law and the takeover of Dutch enterprises in 1957, soon lost what hope it had proffered of becoming a force for social change, for, uncertain and divided on most issues, its confidence soon dissolved into a concern for the securing and expanding of the advantages it had acquired for itself within the framework of a postparliamentary order. In the process, the civilian and military bureaucratic elites became closely intertwined, particularly at the central level, confronting any force seeking amelioration with a lack of

[24] D. N. Aidit, "Tentang Perlawatan ke Empat Negeri," *Bintang Merah,* pp. 214–16.

institutional channels for securing change and a very powerful array of forces wedded to the status quo.

Left as the only major organized force whose hierarchy had not been drawn significantly into the Guided Democracy system, the PKI sought the protection of the President, who used it as a counterweight to the military and supported its inclusion in the establishment under the Nasakom formula—the union of nationalist, religious, and Communist elements. It is an open question whether, had it been so absorbed through the implementation of Nasakom, the PKI would have maintained the élan and relative freedom from corruption that so marked it off from the other major political elements under Guided Democracy. However, there was a successful resistance on the part of the governing elite to more than token representation for the Communists. The PKI's cohesion, its exclusive faith, the strength of its organization, and above all its claim to speak for the myriad poor made its inclusion appear a risky business to those who, while none too confident of their own abilities to solve Indonesia's problems, were quite certain they did not wish to abandon the position of rulers for that of the ruled.

To counter objections to its acceptance and to prevent itself from being placed in an impossible position either by pressure from the elite above or its following below, the PKI pursued two main lines. One was to show that it was so well qualified to handle the country's affairs that its inclusion in their management would result not in lessening the space at the top but in broadening the opportunities open to both the elite and the masses. Hence the PKI pursued a domestic policy under Guided Democracy which strongly emphasized demonstrations of responsibility, expertise, civic virtue, and the ability to do much on very few resources. Though it did not abandon social protest, the party presented the complaints of the poor in so cautious a manner that "economism" appeared as a sin of the left rather than the right. In short, the PKI attempted to prove the Soviet assumption that Communism could be sold to the emerging countries as a managerial weapon.[25]

[25] Cf. *Harian Rakjat,* May 4, 1965, reporting a speech by Aidit of May 2, 1965. The PKI endorsed the concept of national democracy, advanced by the Soviets as the form of the transitional state. For an exegesis on its application to Indonesia, see Aidit, "Programma KPSS i bor'ba narodov za pol'noe natsional'noe osvobozhdenie," *Kommunist,* vol. 39, no. 1 (1962), pp. 92–95. The PKI maintained Indonesia was in the process of its national-democratic revolution; something of a problem for this analysis was created when in April, 1965, Sukarno declared that Indonesia was now entering the socialist stage. Much disturbed that it should be claimed the country's condition was that advanced, the PKI protested, and the President eventually backed down (cf. *Harian Rakjat,* April 29, 1965, and May 6, 1965).

The second line of PKI approach was to stress that what confronted the Indonesian nation was not a class struggle between elite and masses but a struggle of both of these against the forces of Western imperialism. In this the party echoed and reinforced a theme which Sukarno himself had been energetically developing for the sake of preserving national unity and achieving recognition of Indonesia as a major world power; it is difficult in many cases to say when it was the President and when the Communists who had introduced a particular theme along this line.[26]

The idea of a worldwide struggle of the oppressed and backward countries of the East against the wealthy and arrogant West is a theme which, so far as Indonesian nationalism is concerned, had far older roots than Guided Democracy and the Sino-Soviet dispute.[27] It assumed its most militant form, however, in 1963 when, the campaign for West Irian successfully concluded and an attempt at dealing with economic problems having proved politically too costly, energies were turned instead to the struggle to liberate the world outside. There were direct and practical calculations as well. For Indonesian diplomacy a principal motive was the desire to secure what Indonesia felt to be its rightful role as paramount power in that area by combining forces with China, the other major nation interested in blocking the replacement of fading European influence in the area by that of the United States. From the point of view of the PKI, there was the desire to cut its opponents

[26] Thus Aidit's reply to the invitation to attend the Moscow peace congress of July, 1962—"We love peace but we love freedom more" (*Harian Rakjat,* April 7, 1962)—was also the title of the message Sukarno sent to the congress with the Indonesian delegation; and this in turn echoed a slogan that had been used by the Republic during the revolution against the Dutch.

[27] Thus Mohammad Hatta, later the Indonesian Vice President, predicted in 1926 that there would be a war between the colored races and the whites, centering in the Pacific area, and opined that the more civilized and peaceable character of the colored peoples made an armed crusade against the whites both necessary and beneficial (Moh. Hatta, "Economische wereldbouw en machtstegenstellingen," in Hatta, *Verspreide geschriften* (Djakarta/Amsterdam/Surabaja: Van der Peet, 1952), pp. 65–67. One finds the concept of East-West struggle endorsed by anti-Western groups of both right and left before World War II; but the greatest impetus came during the Japanese occupation, when the powerful and decadent West, in the persons of Britain and the United States, was portrayed as the principal enemy. The late period of Guided Democracy, during the anti-Malaysia campaign, saw the revival of many of the slogans and much of the style of the Japanese period, employed by both right and left. I am indebted to Benedict R. O'G. Anderson and Harry J. Benda for pointing out the significance of this development to me.

off from their sources of moral and material support and to make it hard for them to turn their attention from the international struggle to the contemplation of measures against the Communist enemy at home. From the point of view of the army, however, the China alliance deprived it of the two sources, the United States and the USSR, which could provide it with the amount and type of aid it needed—for the Indonesian military possessed a major, highly equipped force with virtually no industrial base to back it. The China relationship could not match the emoluments to the elite attendant on relations with the United States, and it was advantageous to the army's arch-enemy, the PKI. It is hardly surprising that as soon as it came into power the army moved to break the tie.

Partly because the idea of a struggle of the "New Emerging Forces against the Old Established Forces" had a moral life of its own, and partly because the China alliance was important to the PKI's efforts to weaken the army's hostility and strength, it was a bitter disappointment to the party when the Soviet Union showed itself inclined not to compromise with China but to seek a détente with America instead. Moreover the USSR, having given a great deal of aid to the Indonesian military, showed itself little inclined to use such influence as it thereby acquired for the sake of the Indonesian Communists, who, particularly prior to the lifting of martial law in 1963, had endured considerable harassment at the hands of the army. It became apparent that the Soviets were placing their bets on the army and not the PKI. Moreover, the mutual interest of the United States and USSR in preventing the extension of Chinese influence in Southeast Asia brought Soviet and American policies into close congruence in Indonesia, thus deepening PKI suspicions as to the nature and extent of Soviet revisionist leanings. Inasmuch as many of the Sino-Soviet battles of 1963–65 were fought in the conferences and councils of the Asian-African solidarity associations, in which Indonesian representation was governmental and multi-party rather than exclusively Communist, Indonesian domestic politics soon became entangled in the meshes of the Sino-Soviet dispute, further exacerbating PKI-Soviet relations.[28]

[28] Of the various consequences of the penetration of international politics onto the national political scene, the most notable was the alliance between the Soviet Union and the Murba party, a minor grouping which had been founded by the Indonesian Communist heresiarch Tan Malaka. In 1959, Murba leaders maintained that they regarded China the most highly of the Communist states (Sukarni Kartodiwirjo and Maruto Nitimihardjo, interviews, May, 1959), but by 1963, with the development of the PKI alliance with

Although relations between the PKI and the Soviet Union deteriorated almost steadily during the 1960's, a critical point appears to have been reached in 1963 when Aidit, attempting a mediatory trip to the major Communist capitals, was thoroughly snubbed by the Soviets (and well praised by the Chinese); in something of a fury he returned home and, to the accompaniment of descriptions of reviving capitalism in the USSR, he proclaimed a theory on degrees of revisionist infection within the world Communist movement, declared that Communism could not be built until the last remnant of imperialism was wiped from the face of the earth, and argued that the present struggle was one of the villages of the world against the cities of the world, with Southeast Asia as its center.[29] At the same time, Aidit announced his discovery of North Korea as the model Asian Communist state: for if he was going at last to abandon any effective neutrality in the Sino-Soviet dispute, he did not deem it advantageous to appear to be sailing in China's wake either. North Vietnam was not selected, though it was in Southeast Asia and seen as engaged in a challenge to American imperialism; the principal reason for this appears to be that, just as Indonesian diplomacy

the CCP, opportunity arose to profit from alignment with the Soviet Union, a relationship facilitated by the fact that from 1960 to 1963 the Murba leader Adam Malik had been Indonesia's ambassador to the USSR and consequently had the opportunity to establish good contacts with the Russians. By 1964 negotiations were taking place between Murba and the Soviets for the replacement of PKI mass organizations with their own in the eventuality of a split in such international groups as the WFTU; in return for this consideration Murba supported Soviet inclusion in the Asian-African fraternity (conversations with Murba leaders, October and November, 1964).

[29] For Aidit's report on returning from his trip, see *Harian Rakjat,* October 4 and 5, 1963; also Sudisman's report in *Harian Rakjat,* September 29, 1963. The speeches made by Aidit in China have been published in English as D. N. Aidit, *The Indonesian Revolution and the Immediate Tasks of the Communist Party of Indonesia* (Peking: Foreign Languages Press, 1964). Following this end of hope for an early resolution of differences, Aidit's major statements on the Sino-Soviet dispute were published under the reassuring title "The Sky Won't Fall Down" (D. N. Aidit, *Langgit Takkan Runtuh* [Djakarta: Pembaruan, 1963]). According to Aidit (interview, February, 1965), he had prepared four or five speeches which he expected, following usual practice, to be asked to deliver in the USSR; but he was not invited to do so, and in general was kept out of the public view. Quite different his reception by the Chinese, who, he remarked, "were a lot smarter about handling it": they gave him much attention and even made him the first foreign member of the Academica Sinica. Afterwards, he claimed, the Soviets had decided they had made a mistake and issued him an invitation to come to the USSR and speak; but he replied that he was too busy.

had laid tacit claim to representing the major state power in Southeast Asia, so the PKI came to view itself as the premier Communist party in the region. The PKI did not itself enter into the Sino-Soviet polemics with anything like the vehemence of the Chinese, and it never publicly broke with the Soviets; for the most part it limited itself to publishing the major exchanges and the commentary of other parties in its news-paper. But it was easy to see where its heart lay, and indeed, in the heated atmosphere of late Guided Democracy, the Soviet arguments appeared singularly alien to the Indonesian experience.

For all its hectic activity, its tensions and its millenarian slogans, Guided Democracy as a system represented essentially a stalemate of political forces which slowly coagulated about two poles, the army and the PKI. Far above these contenders was President Sukarno, whose au-thority had grown to the point where he assumed many of the attributes of the traditional sacral king. It appeared by 1965 that Sukarno, faced with the choice of a future falling in the end either to the PKI or to the army—with its backing among conservative trading and landholding Islamic elements and its probable international preference for the United States—had decided to work for a post-Sukarno regime which would lead, eventually, to the Communists. As he made his preference increasingly apparent, the army leadership not unnaturally grew con-cerned. Hitherto it could wait for the President's demise to insure its domination; but if he were to survive much longer it now appeared he might succeed, through the appointment and "retooling" of high officers and officials and by his own indications of preference, in causing so many to identify their interests with those of the left that they would resist any serious effort to reduce the PKI once Sukarno was gone. The military was under severe and mounting pressure from within, as economic deterioration and the frustrations posed by a congealed revo-lution intensified service and territorial rivalries, the impatience of younger officers at their less highly qualified superiors, and the suspi-cions of the radical nationalists among the military that the army high command was too cosmopolitan, too high-living, and too inclined to look to the West rather than to its President. In the civilian elite, there were analogous pressures and confusions. It became less and less pos-sible to avoid declaring for either right or left, and the probable penalty of making a wrong choice grew higher. Alliances and alle-giances changed rapidly as people attempted to hedge their political bets. The Communists were enthused but nervous. The land reform laws for whose implementation they had agitated had run into impres-sively strong opposition in the countryside, particularly in East Java, where landowners, with the quiet cooperation of the military, had raised armed bands of Muslim youths to hold back by force the tide of peasant unrest. In the cities, generalized denunciations of corruption and bureaucratic capitalism found a surprisingly vehement response, both from a populace rendered desperate by mounting inflation and from the military hierarchy, which seemed convinced (not wrongly) that the accusations were aimed at it. All groups endured great pressure and uncertainty, and the result was an extreme political tension.

On the morning of October 1, 1965, the commander of Battalion 1 of the Tjakrabirawa presidential guard regiment, Lt. Col. Untung, broadcast that he had rescued Sukarno from a coup by a CIA-supported cabal of his generals. The army leadership declared Untung's action to have been the product of a China-backed Communist plot; and since it was the army and not Untung that won out it is the army's version that has stuck. There is still a very great deal that remains to be discovered about the affair, and the reconstruction of its events will doubtless engage historians for some time to come. On the basis of the evidence so far proffered, however, it seems doubtful that either Untung's or the army's version of the affair quite reflected the truth.[30]

It appears that the army leadership—and in particular the group of seven generals attacked by Untung's "September 30 Movement," which constituted what amounted to the army's politburo—had come to debate whether, given the perversity of the President's leanings, his increasing ability to tinker in military affairs, the dislocation of Indonesia's economy, and the seriousness of the Malaysia entanglement, it might not be necessary to act before Sukarno's natural passing from the scene. Similarly, the PKI contemplated the need for reducing the anti-Communist military leadership, a project which must have seemed urgent if reports—correct or incorrect—were received concerning army plans for a coup. It is most unlikely, however, that the PKI considered acting without Sukarno, its benefactor, sole effective protector, and ally

[30] Most reconstructions of the affair thus far published present variations of the army view; see Justus M. van der Kroef, " 'Gestapu' in Indonesia," *Orbis,* vol. 9, no. 2 (summer, 1966), pp. 458–87; John O. Sutter, "Two Faces of Konfrontasi: 'Crush Malaysia' and the Gestapu," *Asian Survey,* vol. 6, no. 10 (October, 1966), pp. 534–46; Arthur Dommen, "The Attempted Coup in Indonesia," *China Quarterly,* no. 25 (January–March, 1966), pp. 144–67; Tarzie Vittachie, *The Fall of Sukarno* (New York: Praeger, 1967), pp. 75–115. For reconstuctions which argue that the affair was primarily a military one, see J. van Tijn, "De coup in Indonesië: 1 Jaar geleden," *Vrij Nederland,* September 10, 17, 24, 1966; and Lucien Rey, "Dossier of the Indonesian Drama," *New Left Review,* no. 36 (March–April, 1966), pp. 26–40.

against the military, unless it had become panicked by the thought that he was dying; and the September 30 Movement was not the product of such a reaction.[31]

No credible evidence has yet been presented for China's role in inspiring the affair, and indeed this has not been a point which has been stressed by the army except for the purpose of breaking the axis with Peking.[32] The September 30 Movement, which called for an "inde-

[31] The military maneuver was to all appearances based on the assumption of a presidential public endorsement which would legitimize the action against the army leadership and prevent a rallying of its supporters for a counterblow; and this could hardly have been forthcoming if Sukarno were in a dying condition. Moreover, it is apparent that meetings concerning the contemplated action had been held at least since August and that, while the President's health and the generals' plans were important areas of concern, the actual timing of the blow was dictated not by either consideration but by the arrival in Djakarta of units that had previously served with Untung. These were components of Brigade III (Airborne): Battalions 454 (Diponegoro Division, Central Java), 530 (Brawidjaja Division, East Java), and 328 (Siliwangi Division, West Java). They were "Green Berets" who had received paratroop training and had played a prominent role in the campaign to secure West Irian (Netherlands New Guinea) from the Dutch. Untung, who had commanded Battalion 454 before his appointment to the presidential guard in February, 1965, had headed the contingent of Irian "guerrillas" on their triumphal return to Djakarta at the beginning of 1963 (see *Nasional,* February 16 and 20, 1963). As heroes of the Irian campaign, the components of the brigade participated in the 1963 Armed Forces Day (October 5) celebration in Djakarta, and were also called there for the 1965 celebration, which, marking the armed forces' twentieth anniversary, was intended as a major demonstration of Indonesian military glory and might. The units began to arrive in Djakarta on September 26; the move was originally planned for September 30 (hence the name assumed by the group) but was postponed for a day because a cavalry battalion whose assistance the conspirators hoped to acquire had not yet arrived.

[32] The principal evidence for this was the initial claim that the "volunteers" at the air base which the September 30 Movement made its headquarters (see below) were armed with Chinese weapons smuggled in crates sent under diplomatic privilege and supposedly containing equipment for the Conefo building, a new show-piece project of Sukarno's. See *Api Pantjasila,* October 20, 1965. Apparently as a result of presidential protest, an official denial was issued (*Sinar Harapan,* October 22, 1965), though army spokesmen continued to maintain it informally. It later appeared that the volunteers were armed with weapons taken on air force orders from the Fifth Regional Air Command dump at Mampang/Prapatan (*Berita Yudha,* July 15, 1966). The protocol for the Conefo project was signed only on September 14 (*Berita Yudha,* September 16, 1965). In any event, given the amount of pilferage of privileged goods at the army-controlled port of Tandjong Priok, it is very unlikely the CPR would have risked sending weapons by that means, especially when the well-

pendent and active foreign policy"—thus reviving a slogan officially
abandoned by Sukarno in favor of the "era of confrontation" and the
Djakarta-Peking axis—gave no overt sign that its denunciation of the
generals' ties with the West was accompanied by a preference of its own
for Peking.[33] Peking was not able to influence the Indonesian president
or the PKI to the extent that it could have urged them to a course they
would not themselves have wished to take, particularly one in which
their survival was involved. The promotion of a Kong Le type coup
would have had its advantages to China (whatever it might imply for
the fortunes of the local Communists) if it were a question of weakening or replacing a regime whose foreign policy was unfavorable to the
CPR. However, Indonesia was at the time playing a role entirely satisfactory to Peking. Particularly given the mounting intensity of the Sino-
Soviet dispute, which left Indonesia as China's only ally of major international stature, it is hard to see why China would have chosen to do
anything but play out the Sukarno string for as long as it lasted. Indeed, after the coup Peking's reactions to the Indonesian anti-Communist campaign were relatively restrained as long as there seemed
some hope that Sukarno would regain power.

In the maneuverings that preceded the September 30 Affair, several
political elements in addition to the PKI were concerned to prevent a
move by the army—most importantly Sukarno, the air force (which had
long carried on a bitter rivalry with its fellow service), and the strongly
pro-Sukarno leadership of the Nationalist Party (PNI). Three major
paths of action were open to them. One was to encourage rivalry at the

---

established commercial smuggling network was largely in Chinese hands.
Later, the army pressed the accusation that Sukarno and the air force had
been negotiating with China for small arms for the militia without the permission of Gen. Nasution. This seems likely from the evidence so far adduced,
but the arrangements were just being made at the time of the coup. Air Force
Commander Dhani undertook the negotiations in his capacity as head of the
Mandala Siaga (Malaysia Confrontation) command, and the weapons were to
be divided among the services, with the bulk accruing to the army. The Indonesian armed forces already used Chinese arms; possibly the army's indignation
at this initiative stemmed from the fact that it meant the army leadership was
no longer able to control the allocation of all military supplies.

[33] Antara *Warta Berita*, October 1, 1965 (afternoon). For various declarations issued at the time of the coup, see "Selected Documents Relating to
the 'September 30 Movement' and its Epilogue," *Indonesia*, 1 (April, 1966):
131–204; and for a selection of newspaper reportage from the same period,
see Eric Schmeits, " 'The September 30 Affair' in Indonesia," *France-Asie,* no.
184 (winter 1965–1966), pp. 204–38.

top of the army leadership, and Sukarno had long attempted this by seeking the cooperation of army commander Lieutenant General Yani for the ouster of armed forces chief of staff General Nasution. A bolder course, essential perhaps in the face of an impending coup, would have been for Sukarno to call his opponents' bluff by summoning the top army leadership and arresting those he wished removed on charges of conspiring with foreign interests against the state. Done with the full demonstration of presidential authority and followed by party-backed displays of public outrage this, given the leftward momentum of the day and the reputation of the political generals for Western contacts, might well have settled the matter, though unless the charges could be documented it would probably have raised considerable and possibly dangerous resentment among important segments of the officer corps.

A less compromising possibility was to play a waiting game, allowing either the cabal to make a misstep and expose itself to reprisal, or pressures within the army to bring results of their own. There were good precedents for such a development. The previous major military attempt to alter radically the course of state had been the affair of October 17, 1952, in which the Nasution-led army command attempted to force Sukarno to dissolve parliament. On being confronted with the coup, Sukarno adopted a stance that was officially mediatory but also very visibly cool. This indication of his displeasure, accompanied by the quiet encouragement of action by subordinate officers, led army men in the provincial commands to "coup" or refuse obedience to pro-Nasution superiors. Nasution was soon forced to resign, not to be brought back to active duty for three years, and the army underwent a period of internal confusion and vulnerability to civilian political penetration. Three of the seven generals forming the army "politburo" in 1965 had been ringleaders of the 1952 affair, and Sukarno and his allies were doubtless mindful of this in estimating the chances of a coup and the best method of preparing to face it. Moreover, during the regional crisis of the late 1950's it had been common for Djakarta to encourage subordinate officers in unreliable commands to move against their superiors in the name of the President and the nation.[34] And during

[34] These affairs could also have provided reminders that it was very easy for the Communists' large and easily tapped following to become involved in actions not of their own doing or interest. During the regional crisis, PKI-affiliated plantation workers and laborers were armed and employed by the military in the course of the struggle for control of the North Sumatra command between Lt. Col. Wahab Makmur and Lt. Col. Djamin Gintings (see John Smail, "The Military Politics of North Sumatra, December 1956–October 1957," *Indonesia*, no. 6, October, 1968). The promoters of the October 1952

1965 the affair of the Progressive Revolutionary Officers' Movement in the navy, which resulted in the considerable improvement of Sukarno's position vis-à-vis the commander of that service,[35] gave added reason to encourage intra-military developments whereby the President, while playing the role of impartial mediator, could effectively rid the army high command of the elements he found most distasteful and supplant them with military leaders of more pliant fiber.

None of these earlier affairs had involved physical violence against officers on either side. The same elite solidarity that made it so difficult for the PKI to penetrate the bureaucratic hierarchy dictated an absence of bloodshed and—particularly striking considering the proportion of guidance to democracy in the system—a minimum of force in settling intra-elite disputes. In the maneuverings of 1965, it was particularly important for Sukarno and the PKI to avoid violence, for they lacked immediate control of arms and had to allay elite nervousness at rising

----

affair rounded up Communist-affiliated workers to demonstrate in front of the palace while they were placing their demands before the President. This gave an opportunity for the PKI's enemies to claim the attempted coup was really a Communist plot, to the intense embarrassment of the PKI union leaders (see *Disekitar Peristiwa 17 Oktober 1952* [Djakarta: Kementerian Penerangan R.I., 1952]).

[35] The Progressive Revolutionary Officers' Movement (GPPR) was formed of middle-rank naval officers who sought, among other things, the ouster of naval chief Admiral Eddy Martadinata. Its leaders appealed to Sukarno; and he, while initially declaring his firm intention to keep out of an internal service affair, ended in fact by heavily influencing the course of the settlement. The PKI, while making similar avowals, urged a reconciliation with the younger officers' demands. In the end the navy commander was not ousted, and a purge of the dissidents took place; but Martadinata's position was so shaken that, from having been known as something of a Nasution ally, he endorsed Sukarno's controversial proposal for a fifth armed service (militia) and became the first service head to call on Aidit at PKI headquarters. For the official navy statement following the confrontation of Sukarno by the Progressive Revolutionary Officers' Movement, see *Suluh Indonesia,* March 5, 1965. The text of the statement, representing Martadinata's attempt to restore order more or less on his own terms, charged that the rebellious officers were "managed" by civilians and that foreigners were involved. It appears possible—no further evidence for this claim having been produced—that this was an attempt to weaken the position of the mutineers by identifying them as tools of outsiders and foreigners, a maneuver thus perhaps analogous to the army leadership's response to the September 30 Movement. The GPPR affair was still being "settled" by the navy, with the active participation of Sukarno and other political leaders, several months after its occurrence (see *Suluh Indonesia,* May 17, 1965; *Warta Bhakti,* June 10, 1965).

Communist prominence and recent signs of popular unrest. Any move on their side had to be fully "respectable": if it appeared to threaten the general position of the elite, Guided Democracy's supersaturated political atmosphere might well condense into violent reaction. If it constituted a blow of proportions unacceptable to the officers' corps, it would unite rather than divide the military; and it had been demonstrated all too recently in Algeria that the most popular revolutionary leader has little chance against an army united to oppose him.

So far it is impossible to discern whether and how much Sukarno, the PKI, the air force leadership, and perhaps other parties knew of the cabal, consisting largely of middle-rank Javanese officers, to which Untung belonged. Broad hints but little evidence as to the President's role were provided in the post-coup anti-Sukarno campaign. The air force leadership, it seems, had been discussing the matter of dealing with a generals' coup for some weeks and, when informed on the night the coup took place that the September 30 group was establishing itself at Djakarta's major air base for a move against the army high command, it assumed a cooperative attitude. The PKI appears to have undertaken the encouragement of "progressive-revolutionary" officers who wished to prevent a move by the generals, and from the beginning of September it prepared its local cadres to meet an expected situation of emergency in the capital. But Untung and his colleagues were not the only officers opposed to the army general staff group, particularly on a matter of loyalty to Sukarno.[36] One suspects that if the major political actors had previous knowledge of the September 30 grouping, it was as one of a number of officer cliques of widely varying potential which had indicated an intention to stand by the President in his hour of need, that they did not know it would seize the initiative itself, and that they were not aware of its plan of action, which envisaged a maneuver fatal to their interests.

On the apparent assumption that presidential endorsement of their deed would be promptly forthcoming, confirming them as saviors of the revolution, the conspirators kidnapped and assassinated the political generals, confronting Sukarno with six members of his general staff

[36] The army leadership later declared it had been concerned before the coup that there might be a move against it but could not take preventive measures because it did not know where the blow would come from (Brig. Gen. Ibnu Subroto, spokesman for the army commander, in *Pikiran Rakjat*, November 10, 1965). This multiplicity of enemies is perhaps the reason for the very extensive series of purges and shifts of command that took place in the army following the coup.

dead and his archenemy, Nasution, escaped but wounded and out of action. Untung's blow was one the army hierarchy could scarcely afford to take lightly; at the same time it did not constitute an effective seizure of power, for no attempt was made to seize military installations other than the air base, to remove from action officers immediately controlling troops in the area, to interfere with the military communications system, or to establish control over any areas in the capital save that around the central square. In itself, the move had the illegitimacy of a coup and the lack of supportive action of an arrest. In effect, it rested on the presumption that there was no conflict of interest between Sukarno and the man to whom military control would automatically fall with the removal of Generals Nasution and Yani—the head of the Army Strategic Command (Kostrad), Major General Suharto.[37] Conse-

[37] As the senior general on active military duty, Suharto customarily replaced Yani when he was out of the country. Moreover, there were standing orders that in case of emergency Suharto would act in place of Yani. This must have been known to the conspirators, especially as one of them, Col. A. Latief, headed the mobile force of the Djaya (Djakarta) Division and had commanded a series of interservice capital defense maneuvers; he must have known the basic provisions for an emergency in the capital. Moreover, as commander of the Kostrad, Suharto could call directly on the RPKAD (paracommando regiment), which was a major force for controlling the capital area, and he had prior claims on the services of all units assigned to the Kostrad, which included the best troops in the Java divisions. After the coup various stories circulated of Suharto's miraculous escape from attackers, but it is apparent he was not considered part of the generals' conspiracy and was not a target of attack (see "Speech by Major-General Suharto on October 15, 1965, to Central and Regional Leaders of the National Front," *Indonesia*, no. 1 [April, 1966], pp. 160–61; Brig. Gen. Ibnu Subroto, statement in *Pikiran Rakjat*, November 10, 1965). The September 30 Movement leaders may have reckoned at least in part on past bonds with Suharto, who had made considerable effort to cultivate the elite troops assigned to the Kostrad and to the Mandala (Irian liberation) Command, which he had headed. He displayed a high enough regard for Untung, presumably in this connection, to attend his wedding in Central Java in 1964 (see *Kedaulatan Rakjat*, April 29, 1964). Latief, also a Diponegoro Division officer, had fought under Suharto during the revolution; at the time of the Irian campaign he was at Mandala Command headquarters in Ambon, where he seems to have commended himself. He was assigned to the Kostrad; his command at the time of the coup, Brigade I, was one of three Kostrad infantry brigades. Its headquarters had been in Ungaran, Central Java, just down the road from Srondol, the base of Untung's Battalion 454. In late 1963 brigade headquarters were transferred to Djakarta and were put in charge of the Djaya Division's mobile forces (*Kedaulatan Rakjat*, November 8, 1963; *Merdeka*, December 28, 1963). Brig. Gen. Supardjo, the only officer of general rank to take part in the September 30 affair, had also served under Suharto, but only since late 1964, when he had been assigned to the emergent Mandala

quently, no attempt was made by the conspirators to interfere with Suharto and his activities; the General, declaring himself emergency commander of the armed forces, established his base of command at Kostrad headquarters, just off the occupied central square, where he swiftly gathered all the military cards into his hand. It happened, however, that the ambitions of the President and the General did not coincide, for both Suharto's personality and his claims to power within the military were such that neither Sukarno nor the PKI, desirous of a weak and flexible army leadership, would have wanted to see him in control.[38]

Faced with the *fait accompli* of the generals' deaths, the President appears to have played for time, negotiating with the leaders of the conspiracy and trying to obtain the best possible advantage from the situation without committing himself either to them or to Suharto. He attempted to reject Suharto's claim by placing himself in charge of the

Siaga (Malaysia confrontation) Command, whose army units Suharto headed; in 1965 he was placed in charge of the Kostrad combat brigade in West Kalimantan, in which capacity Suharto spent some days with him a month before the coup (*Berita Yudha*, August 21, 23, 1965). It is not necessary to assume Untung's move aimed specifically at putting Suharto in power; it would seem more likely on the basis of present evidence that the conspirators assumed that, as an officer not identified with the Nasution-Yani grouping and a good field commander of strongly Javanese cultural orientation, he would share their general viewpoint and would not think of defying any decisions the President might make. In any event, the usual explanation given for the failure of the September 30 Movement to put Suharto out of action—that he was forgotten or thought insignificant—seems quite unlikely. The second major officer controlling troops in the capital area, Maj. Gen. Umar Wirahadikusumah, commander of the Djaya Division, was similarly ignored by the September 30 Movement. Possibly the conspirators reckoned on the fact that Supardjo had been his chief of staff and successor in regimental command.

[38] Sukarno is said to have declared, on being confronted with the question on the day of the coup, that Suharto was "too stubborn" to be acceptable as commander of the army. The President's opinion may have arisen from an incident during the revolution, following the affair of July 3, 1946, when Suharto successfully led a group of officers who forced the appointment of General Susalit as commander of the Third Division over the objections of both Sukarno and the army high command. During the revolution Suharto commanded key units around the republican capital of Jogjakarta, and there seems to have been some friction between him and the government leadership over the sending of men and material from that area to more distant fronts. However, in the postrevolutionary period there was no indication of disagreement between the government leaders and Suharto, who, while working himself into a position of prime importance within the military, kept entirely out of the limelight as far as civilian politics was concerned and did not have the reputation of being one of the military opponents of Sukarno's rule.

armed forces and putting the army under the caretaker command of the less senior but more pliable Major General Pranoto. At the same time he refused to lend his name to Untung's action, but seems instead to have eventually promised his protection to the September 30 Movement leaders in return for their orderly withdrawal. To the end he seems to have been of two minds as to whether he should cast his lot with Untung's forces, if necessary maneuvering from their and his base of strength in Central Java, or whether he should stay in the capital area and attempt to resolve matters by negotiations at the top. He finally chose the latter, a fatal mistake, as he had by then lost the initiative to Suharto, who never allowed him to regain it.

The Seventh (Diponegoro) Division of Central Java, in which Untung had served until early in the year of the coup, had also involved itself heavily in the affair, and portions of that territory were taken over by military elements in support of the Djakarta action.[39] Suharto now

[39] The Diponegoro Division's involvement may have stemmed from a trip Untung took to Central Java in August 1965, during which he visited former military associates. Officers playing a major role included a good part of the divisional staff, led by Col. Sahirman, head of army intelligence for Central Java. Sahirman was a former commander of Untung's battalion, 454, and Untung had fought under him in the campaign against the regional rebellion in West Sumatra. Reportedly, they were good friends (*Berita Yudha*, October 23, 1965). On October 1, temporarily successful seizures of power from commanding officers were made by subordinates in the provincial capital of Semarang and in the other major towns along the Semarang-Jogja road: Salatiga, Surakarta, and Jogjakarta; unsuccessful attempts were made in Magelang, Tegal, and elsewhere. In many places no overt action took place, but there appears to have been a great division of sympathies regarding a proper response to the affair. After the coup the army endeavored to show that PKI agents had sparked these individual revolts. While the Communists were doubtless endeavoring, along with other pro-Sukarno elements, to sow distrust of the army leadership among the military and to prepare for a move to counter the generals, the lack of overt action outside the Diponegoro Division —in spite of the fact that PKI influence and pro-Sukarno feelings were as strong in the neighboring Brawidjaja (East Java) Division and were not absent elsewhere—makes this claim somewhat questionable. It has been suggested that Col. Sahirman and his associates played a major role in initiating the September 30 Movement (see Daniel Lev, "Indonesia: The Year of the Coup," *Asian Survey*, vol. 1, no. 2 (February, 1966, pp. 105–6). This seems possible, given the magnitude of the division's involvement and the fact that the first order by Suharto discharging leaders of the September 30 Movement, issued on October 1, lists the culprits as Untung, Supardjo, and Sahirman (*Tjatatan Kronologis Disekitar Peristiwa G30S* [Djakarta: Seksi Penerangan KOTI, mimeo., 1965], Surat Keputusan 100/Sem/10/1965). Unlike the Djakarta leaders, those from the Diponegoro divisional staff were shot summarily shortly after their arrest.

faced the problem of regaining control of Central Java, of defusing the generally tense situation within the military, and of preventing any political challenge to his position. The army could hardly have accepted the standpoint that the affair had been essentially one within the military, for the consequences to army morale and unity would be unforeseeable; moreover, past experience had shown it was highly unlikely either Sukarno or his principal allies would refrain from attempting to meddle in the affair once their own position was safe. On the other hand, the slain generals were cardinal enemies of the PKI; the Communists (as well as the PNI) had exposed themselves by declaring for Untung late on the day of the coup[40] and by the September 30 group's use of youths, most of them PKI-affiliated, who were receiving militia training at Halim air base, to cover their retreat from the city. This, coupled with reference to the Madiun Affair and combined with the extreme tension and confusion of the moment, could be used to

[40] The chief PKI newspaper, *Harian Rakjat,* published an editorial on October 2, 1965, which declared that the party disapproved of coups and that if that was what the generals were attempting, it sympathized with Untung's action. This issue of the party paper went to press late in the afternoon of October 1. The *Harian Rakjat* issue which appeared on the morning of October 1 said nothing; two other PKI-sponsored newspapers in the capital, *Kebudajaan Baru,* which went to press about noon, and *Gelora Indonesia,* which went to press in the early afternoon, carried no editorial comment on the September 30 Movement announcements, though the former inserted a rather nervous little note about "The Situation in the Capital": "The situation in the Capital today remains calm. Life continues as usual. The streets remain crowded with traffic, offices continue work as usual. So also street vendors, shops, schools, and so on."

The PNI also seems to have made the decision in the late afternoon of October 1 to come out with an indication of support for Untung. It appears that the PNI leadership, gathering that morning, drew up a statement asserting the party's loyalty to Sukarno and its approval of those who had rescued him. They decided to hold this until they had further information regarding the nature of events. Late in the afternoon they released it, together with a supporting statement signed by ten leaders of PNI mass organizations. They were able to suppress the declaration in its original form in Djakarta that evening, but copies which had been sent to some of the provincial PNI newspapers were published.

Inasmuch as Untung's effort was fast failing from the military point of view by late afternoon, it is curious that the Nationalists and Communists elected then to declare for it. It seems possible their move was the result of Sukarno's announcement that he had taken personal command of the armed forces and placed General Pranoto in charge of the army. The statement, made public about 3:30 in the afternoon, may have persuaded them that Sukarno had decided to endorse the action against the generals and that therefore they also should make public their support.

unite the anti-Communist forces with the cry that the PKI had again betrayed the nation. Quite aside from the value this would have for eliminating the army's principal opponent and in the process reducing Sukarno's power and reversing the China alliance, it would make infinitely easier the process of restoring central control over the dissident army elements, who would be much less likely to resist if they thought they had been duped by the PKI. It would have been unwise for the army to do other than blame the PKI; and Suharto soon showed himself to be far from foolish.

There followed a period of extreme tension, in which a mounting anti-Communist campaign was combined with delicate maneuverings to disarm and transfer dissident or dubious units and officers, in which Sukarno struggled vainly to regain the initiative and in which the PKI endeavored fruitlessly to protest its noninvolvement in the September 30 Movement and to demonstrate its lack of rebellious intent. Once the military situation was in hand, the army proceeded to a violent solution of the Communist problem, securing, where possible, the participation of civilian groups hostile to those identified with the Communists; in some areas communal tensions were so high that the slaughter soon threatened all semblance of social order. Estimates of the dead vary greatly—from a hundred thousand to a million—and it is likely that none of them represents much more than a guess.

How much was destroyed of the Indonesian party cadre is difficult to say. The PKI did its bit toward facilitating its own elimination by attempting to the very end to placate the army by remaining above ground and docile; when the extent of its disaster became apparent its followers seem, with minor exceptions, to have succumbed with the passivity of complete demoralization. The party's rapid disintegration meant, however, that no unity was forged through a struggle against it and that the rightist energies aroused by the campaign were not consumed in the elimination of the PKI but went on to destroy the whole structure of Guided Democracy. While initially the Indonesian Communists were blamed for attempting to overthrow Sukarno, within the year Sukarno was being blamed for attempting to overthrow the generals, who had become the new symbol of legitimacy.

The ultimate results of the self-fulfillment of Untung's charges are difficult to foresee. While the New Order's lumping together of Sukarno and the PKI was effective during the period of post-Guided Democracy hangover, it is historically perilous, since it would be easy for a future dissident military or political challenger to claim that it was after all the generals and not the founder of the Republic who had betrayed the nation. The army leadership has had to take the reins of public power more openly than it desired, and it has set up economic performance as the criterion by which it should be judged—a standard excellent for arousing immediate popular sympathy but most demanding given the extent of economic chaos and the impossibility of improving living standards on short notice. Similarly the massacres, though they were more than effective in the short run, also served to intensify hatreds, increase tensions along communal and economic lines, and make less possible any nonviolent social reform.[41]

The most visible activity of the PKI in the post-Sukarno era has been that of its leadership in exile; this has been centered in China, which has given shelter not only to resident Indonesian Communists but also to leftists expelled by a Soviet Union anxious to rid itself of an ideological nuisance and to smooth relations with Suharto's New Order.[42] However, it was not China but Albania which became the

[41] For an interesting discussion of some of the social aspects of the massacres, in particular their relation to the land problem, see the comments of Professors W. F. Wertheim and E. Utrecht in *De Groene Amsterdammer*, October 8 and 15, 1966, and January 7 and 14, 1967; and Wertheim, "Indonesia Before and After the Untung Coup," *Pacific Affairs*, vol. 39, no. 1/2 (Spring/Summer, 1967), pp. 120–27. That the agrarian question played a fundamental role in the reaction seems borne out by the underground PKI's assessment that its rural organization had suffered the most from the killings. See "Build the PKI along Marxist-Leninist Lines . . . ," *Indonesian Tribune*, January, 1967, p. 27.

[42] Most prominent of these was the Moscow *Harian Rakjat* correspondent, Anwar Dharma. The latter, arriving in Peking in September, 1966, issued a scathing denunciation of the Soviets, who were profiting from the PKI's disaster, he charged, by accompanying their official silence on the September 30 affair with informal assurances that the PKI had attempted a coup on orders from Peking (see *Peking Review*, vol. 9, no. 42 [October 14, 1966], pp. 30–32). Soviet policy after the coup was aimed principally at attempting to profit from previous cultivation of the army and to secure the repayment of Indonesia's very large debt, which precluded strong criticism of the New Order regime and particularly of the military; instead, Suharto was pictured as a moderate whose position must be defended against the "ultra's" on the pro-Western right. See for example Ivan Antonov, "After Sukarno—What," *New Times*, no. 17 (April 26, 1967), pp. 17–18. This approach was received coldly by Indonesian leftist exiles, including those in eastern Europe, who presumably were under the greatest pressure to accede to such a view. See Pamudji, "Sedjumlah Pertanjaan atas Kesimpangsiuran," *Bulletin Badan Pekerdja Badan Koordinasi PPI se-Eropah*, December, 1966, pp. 26–28. In early 1967 the Soviets promoted a "Marxist-Leninist Group of the Communist Party of Indonesia," which was apparently aimed at splitting the underground movement and preventing the unquestioned dominance of a militant, pro-Peking viewpoint; the splinter-

official seat of PKI activity in the diaspora, probably because neither the PKI exiles nor the Chinese government found it convenient to have publicly close relations.[43] In addition to party professionals, a considerable number of pro-Communist and left nationalist Indonesians, chiefly students in Europe, formed centers of activity against the Suharto regime. Initially, it would appear, the principal cleavage within such opposition groups was that between PKI and PNI sympathizers; later, with the New Order's drive against Sukarno and the center-left, the PKI's isolation was reduced in a general militant rejection of the "military fascist" government. The principal conflict became instead one between those who formulated their position in terms of the Sukarno revolutionary tradition and the Nasakom concept of anti-imperialism and social peace, and those who declared that Indonesia's salva-

---

group title given it indicates there was little hope that it would become the PKI's major voice. A statement of the Marxist-Leninist Group was published in the pro-Soviet Indian Communist journal *Mainstream* (March 11, 1967, pp. 35–36; March 18, 1967, pp. 26–30); it blamed the October 1965 affair on the "Leftist 'revolutionary' demagogues" who had headed the party, urged concentration on the proletariat rather than the peasantry, and called on the Indonesian Communists to "forge a united Left-wing front, progressive, democratic and patriotic in nature, a front able to carry on a consistent struggle against pro-imperialist and anti-democratic reaction and thus to deal it a crushing blow, as before [the decision to side with Peking in the Sino-Soviet dispute] to concern itself with keeping Indonesia in the camp of anti-imperialism and peace and preserve the good relations of the Republic of Indonesia with the Socialist-bloc countries" (March 18, 1967, p. 30).

[43] The Albanian arrangement was apparently made when Jusuf Adjitorop, a Politburo candidate member resident in the CPR since before the coup, attended the Albanian Labor party congress in November, 1966. A monthly English-language journal, the *Indonesian Tribune*, was instituted then in Tirana, its publishing house called "Indonesia Progresif." An Indonesian-language student organ, *Api*, was also published in Tirana. It was announced that in March, 1967, the international service of Radio Tirana would begin a program of twice-daily Indonesian-language broadcasts. See *Indonesian Tribune*, vol. 1, no. 3 (February, 1967), p. 67. The Albanian connection may also have been sought because, in spite of the post-coup PKI emphasis on rejecting Soviet revisionism, it offered an opportunity for contact with the movement in eastern Europe. Such cooperation existed at least on the student level: the Indonesian Students Association (PPI) in Albania was represented, together with the anti-Suharto PPI organizations of all eastern European countries save Yugoslavia, in the Coordinating Body of the Indonesian Students Associations in Europe; the second vice-chairmanship was allotted to the Albanian PPI, and it was announced the 1968 congress of the association would be held in Albania. *Bulletin Badan Pekerdja Badan Koordinasi PPI se-Eropah*, no. 1 (Jan.–Feb., 1967), pp. 13, 14.

tion lay in social revolution and that all political energies must be devoted to an armed agrarian struggle.[44]

Much the same development seems to have taken place in Indonesia itself. The political destruction of the non-Communist left and most of the center meant that the PKI was less isolated in its opposition to the authorities than it had been in the wake of its 1948 defeat. There seems, however, to have been a severe dispute within the party as to whether it should cultivate this support in the same manner as the Aidit leadership had; increasingly, those supporting such a course lost out in favor of the proponents of armed agrarian struggle. The progress of the latter viewpoint is measurable in the three major statements issued by the underground PKI between May and September, 1966. These—possibly representing the viewpoint of different and successively dominant factions—reflected stages in the repudiation of the Aidit approach and range from an initial call for unity, rethinking, and resurgence[45] through a general criticism of the Indonesian peaceful road[46] to a full-scale denunciation.[47] The battle was by no means over even with the last, the "self-criticism" of September, 1966, for it was admitted then that the achievement of "unanimity of mind" concerning the mistakes of the past still required first priority; and the new leadership proceeded to demonstrate its interest in this by violently denouncing the personal

[44] The latter viewpoint appears to have won out with the conference of European PPI leaderships held at the end of December, 1966, which issued a joint declaration calling for agrarian revolution (text in *Ibid.*, pp. 5–6).

[45] "Hold Aloft the Good Name and Honour of the Communist!" *Indonesian Tribune,* vol. 1, no. 1 (November, 1966), pp. 17–20. This was declared to be a statement of the PKI Politburo dated Jogjakarta, May 23, 1966. The three statements have circulated in Indonesia and have been accepted by the authorities there as genuine; it does not seem likely they were produced abroad, though we cannot be completely certain of this as yet. Nor can one judge with certainty whether they represent the opinion of the leadership of an effective portion of the former PKI following, though this also seems accepted by both the international movement and the Indonesian military. Presumably, the post-coup party leadership has been affected by the continuing capture of Communists, including most of the surviving former party chiefs.

[46] "Take the Road of Revolution to Realize the Tasks Which Should Have Been Accomplished by the 1945 August Revolution," *Indonesian Tribune,* vol. 1, no. 1 (November, 1966), pp. 6–20. It is stated to have been a declaration of the PKI Politburo dated Central Java, August 17, 1966.

[47] "Build the PKI Along the Marxist-Leninist Line to Lead the People's Democratic Revolution in Indonesia," *Indonesian Tribune,* vol. 1, no. 3 (January, 1967), pp. 6–29. This is declared to be a self-criticism of the Politburo put forth in September, 1966.

behavior as well as the policies of the former party heads and assigning to them full responsibility for the disaster of 1965.

The underground party's self-criticism labeled the former course revisionist and compared Aidit's concepts to those of the Italian Communist Party and the "distortions" of Karl Kautsky. The former leadership had "failed in totally discharging its task to expose the bankruptcy of bourgeois democracy. Worse still, the PKI, instead of using the general elections and parliamentary struggle to accelerate the political obsolescence of parliamentarianism, had even strengthened the system of parliamentarianism."[48] When parliament became obsolete anyway, the PKI had sold itself to the national bourgeoisie and to Sukarno; it had not prepared itself for counter-revolution, but had continued to trust in legality and the peaceful road:

> The legality of the Party was not considered as one method of struggle at a given time and under certain conditions, but was rather regarded as a principle, while other forms of struggle should serve this principle. Even when counterrevolution not only has trampled under foot the legality of the Party, but has violated the basic human rights of the Communists as well, the Party leadership still tried to defend this "legality" with all their might.[49]

The party had avoided rather than promoted the class struggle and had substituted the international struggle against imperialism for the class conflict at home, although the latter had been the central question since the ending of the war with the Dutch. It had rejected the Chinese revolutionary example, whereas in fact that was the one true road. It had adulterated Marxism-Leninism by "Indonesianizing" it, when it should have been steeling its cadres with the Thought of Mao Tse-tung.[50]

[48] *Ibid.*, p. 14.

[49] *Ibid.*, p. 11. It appears that there was some problem with securing general acceptance of armed struggle in spite of the disastrous ending of the peaceful road under Aidit, for the first party statement remarked that "Such tendencies [to seek power peacefully] may also arise from among those comrades who cannot bear the extremely difficult situation in which the Party and the people's revolutionary movement are finding themselves. For this reason we must continue to raise high the banners of anti-revisionism" ("Hold Aloft the Good Name," p. 20).

[50] "The experience of the struggle waged by the Party in the past has shown how indispensable it is for the Indonesian Marxist-Leninists, who are resolved to defend Marxism-Leninism and to combat modern revisionism, to study not only the teachings of Marx, Engels, Lenin, and Stalin, but also to

Therefore, it was abjured, the PKI must rebuild its shattered rural cadre and prepare to lead an agrarian revolution aimed at the establishment of a people's democracy. It must attempt to establish a "revolutionary united front" with the urban petty bourgeoisie and the national bourgeoisie, but it must remember that the Communists and no other force should lead that front. Internationally, the party must struggle more vigorously against Soviet-led revisionism, for though the PKI's former leadership had declared itself opposed to revisionist doctrine it had attempted to maintain friendly relations with the apostates and had cherished their cardinal errors as regards the class struggle.[51]

There was apparently some hesitation at publicly identifying the new PKI road as Maoist, for the moves in this direction were gradual if cumulative. The first of the three party statements referred only to opposition to "Khrushchevite modern revisionism" and not at all to China. The second reiterated the rejection of the "Khrushchevites," adding that they were helping United States imperialism in Vietnam. It also referred to the "great Chinese revolution" but only in a context which placed it on the same level as others, including the Indonesian. Although the program of protracted armed agrarian struggle was already elaborated here, at all points where Mao or the Chinese road could have been cited, Lenin's authority was invoked instead. It was only with the final, full rejection of the past that Mao and China were called upon as pointing the party's way.

It seems likely that the authority of the Chinese example was being used, as it had been by Aidit fifteen years before, to give doctrinal legitimacy to a still uncertain leadership. In the same manner, Musso and his "Great Correction" of the party line were used by the post-coup leadership against Aidit as he once had employed them against Alimin and Tan Ling Djie.[52] In any event, the reliance on Maoist authority seemed not to be coupled with hopes of Chinese intervention, for it was stressed that the Indonesian agrarian revolution "cannot be enforced from without. It will break out on the basis of the high consciousness and conviction of the peasants themselves obtained through their own experience in the struggle and through the education by the working class."[53]

What happened to the PKI in attempting to live under Guided

devote special attention to studying the Thought of Mao Tse-tung, who has succeeded in inheriting, defending, and developing Marxism-Leninism to its peak in the present era" ("Build the PKI," p. 26).

[51] *Ibid.*, pp. 9, 26.   [52] *Ibid.*, pp. 6–7.   [53] *Ibid.*, p. 11.

Democracy was, essentially, what happened to the Chinese Communists in attempting to come to power in the 1920's under the wing of the Kuomintang. The Nasakom formula gave no greater protection in the end than the formula of the bloc of four classes; what mattered ultimately was who possessed the apparatus of the state and the means of violence. Possibly the PKI could have succeeded in walking the tightrope to a peaceful assumption of office—though office is not quite the same thing as power, and true power would be needed by any group attempting the radical reversal of Indonesia's social and economic fortunes. As it happened, it did not; but the party did have fifteen years in which to build up an enormous organization, become the sole effective representative of a modernizing left, and establish itself deeply in the countryside. This was no small accomplishment even in view of the price that was ultimately paid; for, much as it is easier to restore an advanced economic structure shattered by war than to develop one in the first place, so it is easier to resurrect a smashed social revolutionary movement than to create one from a politically inert base. The society has been made familiar with the movement, with its techniques of organization and its ideological message, and this gives no small advantage to those who would revive it illegally. The Communists' opponents, for their part, have inherited an economy suffering the consequences of grave structural defects as well as mismanagement, an enormous pool of rural and urban discontent, and an elite which has little to unite it beyond the determination to hold on to what remains of a rapidly vanishing national wealth. Inasmuch as this is what would have faced the PKI had it come peacefully into office, the trade may not, from the point of view of the ultimate real power of the two contenders, have been a bad one. The proof will lie in whether, in the long run, the PKI's opponents can create a viable system from their inheritance, and, if they fail, in whether the Communists unite the people in revolution.

Wayne Wilcox   14

China's
Strategic Alternatives in
South Asia

This paper seeks to set forth the several special qualities of regional international politics in South Asia, to relate discrete aspects of this regional subsystem to the world powers and their conceptions of strategic interests, and to analyze within this context China's diplomatic opportunities, capacities, and constraints in South Asia. The analysis attempts to minimize the problems inherent in gauging national interests and goals by emphasizing, instead, the manifest saliency of the region as measured by the intensity and scale of contact between the five principal states active within it. These five states—China, India, Pakistan, the Soviet Union, and the United States—are the five most populous countries in the world. Four of them occupy contiguous and contested central Asian territory, and all of the "legs" of the pentagonal relationships among them are marked by high levels of rivalry or distrust. A regional analysis promises an amplified if narrow definition of the relationships between the world powers and a more detailed assessment of the roles of smaller states, historical change, and "positional" variables in those relationships.

South Asian Regional Relationships:
India and Pakistan

The group hostilities that lay at the root of the undeclared civil war in British India and led to its partition at independence in 1947 stemmed from many sources. Political, religious, economic, and psychological tensions divided large segments of articulate Hindu and Mus-

The author wishes to thank the late Mr. M. J. Desai and Professor Michael Brecher as well as all of the participants of the Chicago conference on China, the United States, and Asia for their critical and hence useful remarks, some of which have been incorporated in this paper.

lim political leadership in the last three decades of British rule. Group security relationships between these two large communities were in essence managed by British colonial authority. The processes of social mobilization and political democratization accompanying the growth of nationalism heightened social tension as the ability of the British to guarantee communal peace decreased. Many Muslims expected the British to "hold the balance" and insure minority rights on the basis of communal group *parity;* many Hindus expected the British to honor the mandate of a large *majority* and cease to "divide and rule." The patchwork pattern of constitutional reform limited the institutional alternatives available to resolve this fundamental problem and the exigencies of nationalist politics tended to complicate it.[1] As independence approached at war's end, the Muslim League party demanded structural safeguards, either in a highly decentralized federal system or in an independent Muslim nation. The leaders of the Indian National Congress, especially Jawaharlal Nehru and Sardar Vallabhai Patel, were unwilling to sacrifice future policy alternatives on the altar of constitutional compromise. Accompanied by widespread internal confusion and violence throughout north India, Pakistan emerged as an independent state in 1947, the product of an unexpectedly successful secessionist elite.

The creation of the divided state with its two wings separated by a thousand miles of Indian territory testifies to the potent quality of "religious" symbols and group insecurities in the subcontinent at mid-century.[2] Partition did not "settle" group security relationships, however, because large religious minorities continued to reside in each state. Subsequent irredentist claims in both countries were championed by political groups sensitized to religious difference, and the "nationalization" of internal group rivalries, once confined within British India, produced after 1947 "international" rivalries in which the Muslims re-

[1] The Muslim League was on record as late as 1946 as favoring a united, federal India but the division between provincial Muslim political elites and the "national" leadership of the Muslim League was a principal factor in the commitment of the latter to an independent state, and in the tactics that they followed which led to higher levels of local violence.

[2] This is a central problem in the analysis of the nature of Indo-Pakistan enmity. If, for example, the implications of alternative religious *weltanschuungen* lead to policy conflicts, peaceful relationships between neighboring states might be inhibited. Muslim political theory makes clear that the security of the faith and the faithful presupposes a Muslim government. For an elaboration of these complex themes, see the contributions in Donald E. Smith, ed., *South Asian Politics and Religion* (Princeton: N.J.: Princeton University Press, 1966).

mained a one-to-four minority still the close neighbor of the Hindu nation. Yet, independence for Pakistan provided a psychological boost for Muslim political elites because it restored autonomy to Muslim leadership in its search for external support to counter Hindu superiority. In short, it restored a group security position in the subcontinent comparable to the early 20th century.

Their acute weakness was demonstrated to leaders of the new Pakistani government in the 1948 war for the princely state of Jammu and Kashmir.[3] The British plan for partition was internally inconsistent and ambiguous. The ruler of the state of Jammu and Kashmir eschewed the accession policy guideline of "religious majority" in favor of that of "princely autonomy" and attempted to assert his independence. Both Muslim League and Congress leaders attempted to secure his accession before independence; after independence, Kashmir was swept into the civil disorder convulsing much of northern India. The Kashmir war thus began as part of a wider civil war that witnessed spiraling intervention, first from tribal insurgents from northwestern Pakistan followed by Indian regular troops in support of the maharaja's accession to India, and finally involving troops from both countries in a struggle for the state in a limited war.[4] The United Nations-arranged truce of 1949 confirmed the obvious; India was the paramount power in South Asia. And more significantly, Pakistan's national independence was a function of India's intentions tempered by British guarantees.[5]

[3] The war led to heavy internal political costs: an abortive *coup d'état*, wide-spread popular distrust of political leadership, the politicization of the army, and the crystallization of a set of political attitudes toward India that made accommodation based on trust almost impossible.

[4] The dispute is inordinately complex, and there is little agreement on many of its most crucial aspects. The latest major study, Sisir Gupta, *Kashmir: A Study in India-Pakistan Relations* (Bombay: Asia Publishing House for the Indian Council on World Affairs, 1966), lists 365 English language books and pamphlets on the problem. Soviet views are very briefly stated in V. V. Balabushevich and A. M. D'Yakov, eds., *A Contemporary History of India* (New Delhi: Peoples Publishing House, 1964), pp. 489–91, and Yuri Gankovsky and L. R. Gordon-Polonskaya, *Istoriya Pakistana* (Moscow: State Publishing House for Eastern Literature, 1961), pp. 132–34. In brief, the Russians argue that the dispute is the product of American and British interest in a strategic base area on the Sino-Soviet frontier, not the product of conflicting national and indigenous forces in South Asia.

[5] Thus, Nirad Chaudhuri, a close student of Indian military affairs, has written: "India held the pistol at the head of Pakistan, until, in 1954, the American alliance delivered the country from that nightmare. . . . I think I am right in saying that at least twice, if not three times, between 1947 and

From this realization and a realistic appreciation of their own tenuous domestic political position, Pakistan's leaders fashioned from very limited resources a "garrison state" primarily concerned with deterring India from establishing a hegemonic relationship that would nullify Pakistan's *raison d'être* and with maintaining a semblance of national unity.

Kashmir has since 1949 been both a symbol and an active agent of the bitter conflicts between India and Pakistan because it represents to Pakistan both a denial of a complete national personality, and Indian superiority in the subcontinent. India sees Kashmir as both an example of denied Pakistani *irredenta* and a demonstration of the new India's regional position but more especially as a testament to its religious pluralism. Despite world concern, two costly and inconclusive wars, and over 1,600 reported incidents between the countries in Kashmir, no solution or compromise has emerged. Kashmir is an intractable problem because it is part of a continuing civil war; contemporary boundaries give it the appearance of being an international dispute. As long as India controls Kashmir, it demonstrates its superiority to Pakistan, and this superiority threatens Pakistan's identity and security because in civil wars, the victor takes all.[6]

Since its independence, Pakistan's resources have been heavily committed in "state building" with the purpose, minimally, of deterring India from a major attack.[6a] Given the disparities of resources, diplomatic support, and armed forces, this has meant that Pakistan has been forced to heavily mortgage its international position and autonomy to serve its national need for security. This explains Pakistan's active alli-

---

1954, India intended to invade Pakistan and was deterred only by American and British remonstrances." *The Continent of Circe* (New York: Oxford University Press, 1966), p. 244. (1950 and 1953 were probably the years of greatest tension.) For similar arguments, see Aslam Siddiqi, *Pakistan Seeks Security* (Lahore: Longmans, Green, 1960) and Latif Ahmed Sherwani, *India, China and Pakistan* (Karachi: Council for Pakistan Studies, 1967).

[6] I have only been able to find one close parallel in European history for the Kashmir dispute: the Vilnius dispute between Lithuania and Poland in the inter-war period. The parallels are almost identical, even to the extent that Nehru and Pilsudski each considered the respective disputed territory his ancestral home.

[6a] This perspective is spelled out in considerable detail in Mohammad Ayub Khan, *Friends Not Masters: A Political Autobiography*, New York, Oxford University Press, 1967, pp. 47, 62, 65 and 114–85.

ance policy, whether with the Baghdad Pact, later CENTO and Regional Cooperation for Development (RCD), a phantom Pan-Islamic bloc,
an anti-Communist (American) bloc or with the Communist states. Once
involved in alliances, Pakistan has attempted to turn its allies toward
regional policies that increase the cost to India of maintaining regional
hegemony and continued domination of Kashmir. The optimum Pakistani goal seems to be a parity on the subcontinent that would both insure the permanence of Pakistan's secession from greater India, and
produce conditions in which India would have to negotiate Kashmir's
future with Pakistan on the basis of parity of bargaining position. It
seems clear that these conditions can be realized only under two circumstances: a binding international or Great Power mandate equating the
claims of India and Pakistan, or a radical decay in India's political unity
and military capacity. Neither of these circumstances is very likely but
one or both are necessary goals of Pakistan's policies.

India's security position is complex and difficult, in large measure because of Pakistan but also because of other splintering effects of the end
of British rule in southern Asia.[7] India inherited the principal responsibilities for, and problems of, defense but it did not inherit the industrial might, the secure flanks, the weak northern neighbors and the
command and control positions developed by the British in a century
and a half of rule. The continuation of Muslim-Hindu rivalry as Paki-
stan-India rivalry after 1947 forced India to permanently commit a large
portion of its diplomatic and military effort to offset the single-minded
Pakistan foreign policy of Kashmir *irredenta*. When, in 1953, Pakistan
moved outside an Indian-imposed diplomatic isolation to secure American support despite proffered Kashmir concessions by India, Indian
foreign policy autonomy was further reduced. The subsequent arrival
in the subcontinent of both world powers as patrons of domestic clients
in the regional civil war further reduced alternatives. Countering
United States support for Pakistan meant developing support for Delhi
from the USSR and a neutralist "third bloc"; now, countering Chinese
support for Pakistan means alignment with both the United States and
USSR. All such arrangements reduce India's freedom of action and do
not necessarily enhance its regional security.

The acceptance of Pakistan as an equal or near-equal on the subcontinent, clearly unjustified on objective "power" grounds, is even more
objectionable to India since it would complicate Indian minority

---

[7] I have spelled these out in some detail in *India, Pakistan and the Rise of
China* (New York: Walker and Co., 1964).

policy,[8] lead to the forfeiting of at least part of Kashmir and still not bring an inexpensive "settlement" between the communities. Parity with Pakistan would confirm a system on the subcontinent not unlike that of British colonial rule in which the Hindu majority's interests were compromised or deflected by a potent coalition of Muslims and their external allies. This pattern would obviously increase the cost of maintaining India's inherited position and limit Delhi's future alternatives. India must therefore foreclose the Kashmir issue, increase the cost to Pakistan of its hostility, and use its diplomacy to consolidate its regional position. Some Indians believe that with the passage of time, their countrymen and Pakistanis will no longer think of themselves as "cousins," Pakistan will become more conservative and secure and more normal relations will evolve. In the meantime, most Indian leaders expect Pakistan to continue to pressure its allies and muster its own resources against India, and India must therefore be prepared to resist a broad range of persistent challenges. As long as this pattern of regional politics continues, India must realistically designate Pakistan its most salient enemy.

It is clear that Pakistan's leaders see their national security as a function inversely proportional to India's strength. Pakistan's foreign policy is consequently extremely sensitive to any increase in India's capabilities, and to some degree is keyed on variations from what Rawalpindi considers a minimum acceptable position; a stable deterrent relationship and the retention of some options in Kashmir.[9] India, on the other

    [8] This is the problem to which the Indian domestic principle of the "secular state" is addressed. If India could eliminate the religious or communal forum in which the civil war is being fought, it could normalize relations with Pakistan on the basis of national interest. This would, of course, destroy the legitimacy of Pakistan's claim in Kashmir which is based on the "right" of Kashmir Muslims to opt for Pakistan.

    [9] Pakistan's defense position, 1953–63, was to accept a 2.5 to 1 troop disparity ratio, but to maintain with American support strike forces capable of doing considerable damage to Bombay (from Karachi), and Delhi (from Lahore and Sialkot). The bulk of the army was deployed around Rawalpindi from where it could go north into Kashmir, or east with the support of armor on the Indian plains. Frontiers, especially in the west, between the two countries minimize static defense possibilities. India's remarkable build-up in the aftermath of the Chinese border war of 1962 raised the troop ratio to more than 4 to 1, provided India with potent static defense resources including air defense systems for the Indian cities threatened by Pakistan's air force, and led to a five year, $1 billion Indian capital investment plan in defense production plants. Coincident to these developments, India moved to legally integrate Kashmir into the Indian Union and American military assistance to Pakistan

hand, sees its security as a function of South Asian *regional* security, and regional security requires Indian leadership and strength. This is the meaning of India's often repeated plea for some form of Indo-Pakistan confederation, and explains the vehemence of Pakistan's negative reply. Pakistan would not have been created had Muslim political leadership trusted or shared common goals with the leadership of the Indian National Congress. Nothing that has happened in the 20 years of national independence of the two countries has eroded suspicion or laid the basis for mutual trust. The Kashmir dispute, symbolizing Pakistan's weakness and its incomplete identity (the *k* in the acronym Pakistan stands for Kashmir), is probably farther from settlement than at any time in the past. Therefore, just as India must look for regional unity and strength to solve its security problem and consolidate its modern national experience, Pakistan must look outside the subcontinent to serve its security, national identity, and development interests. This relationship negates all of the British-developed strategies for the defense of the subcontinent, and allows foreign powers alternatives for local presence under concessional conditions.

South Asian Regional Relationships: The Himalayas and Tibet

The British in India followed a strategic frontier-zone policy based on the control of the "reverse slope" of the mountainous northern frontiers.[10] The configuration of the strategic frontier zone was dominated by buffer states on the periphery and military-administered regions at their rear. Outposts were linked to major fortifications along transport lines backed by strategic railways connecting securely administered areas with the defense zone. The most vulnerable areas, notably the northwest, were most heavily fortified while the north central Himalayan area was least defended. As long as there was no prospect of a Chinese Hannibal able to cross Asia's Alps, the British were content to maintain a presence in Tibet, classified as an "outer buffer," while en-

---

was not increased. It seems reasonable to infer from this set of circumstances that Pakistan's adventurism in the September, 1965, Indo-Pakistan war was triggered by a calculation that India was militarily foreclosing the Kashmir dispute permanently.

[10] For a classic statement on the importance of the problem, see Lord Curzon's *Frontiers, The 1907 Romanes Lecture* (London, 1907). The subject will be comprehensively treated in a forthcoming study by Ainslee Embree. See also Bisheshwar Prasad, *Our Foreign Policy Legacy, a Study of British Indian Foreign Policy* (New Delhi: Peoples Publishing House, 1965).

couraging independent political forces and maintaining a residual Chinese suzerainty there. It was in the British interest to facilitate Tibeto-Indian trade, to maintain intelligence about developments in inner Asia, and to deny Tibet to Russia. Domestic political autonomy in Tibet served the first two interests, and support for Chinese suzerainty served the latter.

Closer to British vital interests, "the inner buffer," was Nepal which was allowed internal autonomy as long as Gurkha troops fought for the British and Nepal's external relations were managed by the British. Sikkim and Bhutan, small and isolated kingdoms, were linked to Nepal by traditional and dynastic politics, and to British India by indirect supervision and external control.[11] The North-east Frontier Agency (NEFA), was analogous to the North-west Frontier province, a region populated by scattered and often hostile tribes in difficult terrain. The administration was one of tenuous management rather than firm control.

In the west, behind the western Himalayas and the Pamirs, lay Russia, the principal threat to Britain's empire in India. While Kashmir was legally a princely state, its strategic northern frontiers of Gilgit, Baltistan, and Chitral were under the direct administration of British "politicals," military officers seconded to "civil" frontier administration. Farther west, the British cast Afghanistan in a role that they hoped would be similar to Nepal. The Afghans were not accommodating; the British were denied the reverse slope and consequently were forced to make heavy expenditures on the fortifications of the Khyber and Bolan Passes and the extraordinary defense infrastructure of northwestern India, all of which Pakistan inherited.

While Japanese successes in World War II dramatized the inadequate defense infrastructure of eastern India, the Himalayan zone seemed secure, even tranquil. Tibet proclaimed itself neutral in the war and used China's involvement to further extend its autonomy. After the war ended and the British withdrew, however, the Peking government began the process of the reimposition of Chinese rule in inner Asia. Ambiguous zonal frontiers were inherently unstable, the product of another era, and both China and India understood the need for boundary demarcation. But the Himalayan frontier was not a two-party

---

[11] The precise terms of the treaties may be found in C. U. Aitchison, *Collection of Treaties, Engagements and Sanads Relating to India and Neighboring Countries*, 5th ed. (Calcutta, 1931). In general, the Indian government claimed the exclusive right to manage the external relations of the states, allowing them considerable internal autonomy.

region. Kashmir was contested by Pakistan and large areas were claimed by China. Chinese maps indicated a massive historical claim in Nepal, Bhutan, and North-east Frontier Agency. What seemed to be at stake for India was not border "adjustments" but an entire frontier system, the eastern and western portions of which had already collapsed with the creation of Pakistan.

The Indian predicament was apparent. The British imperial inheritance was fully claimed by the successor states but the legacy of rights won by British strength was supported by very little indigenous capacity or structure to service them. Where they had the power, the governments of India and Pakistan moved to secure their frontier interests. For India, the problem was posed in Kashmir, Nepal, Sikkim, and Bhutan when restive leaders tried to move their states outside historic client relationships as "states which are attached to India by special treaties."[12] For Pakistan, the tribal zones presented analogous problems.[13]

Nepal was much larger and more assertive than the small princely states, its legal independence had been accepted by the British, and its leaders were interested in removing external controls on their freedom of action.[14] Within Nepal modern democratic forces and a large segment of the civil service were not unfavorable to Indian influence. Yet notwithstanding the fact that the kingdom is the only one in the world that has adopted Hinduism as the state religion, the ruling house and many Nepali politicians viewed Indian hegemony as onerous. Nepal's

[12] We are ill-served by the standard authorities on the problem of "lapse" when the British left. They are briefly treated in V. P. Menon, *The Integration of the Indian States* (New York, 1956), but by E. W. R. Lumby and Alan Campbell-Johnson not at all. For a detailed treatment of the areas, see Pradyuma P. Karen and William Jenkins, *Himalayan Kingdoms, Bhutan, Sikkim, and Nepal* (Princeton, N.J.: Van Nostrand, 1963), and Leo Rose and Margaret Fisher, *The North-east Frontier Agency of India* (Washington: Department of State, Bureau of External Research, 1967).

[13] See my *Pakistan: The Consolidation of a Nation* (New York: Columbia University Press, 1963), especially pp. 142–64, 203–7, and Fazal Muqeem Khan, *The Story of the Pakistan Army* (Karachi: Oxford University Press, 1963), pp. 123–36.

[14] See among others, Bhuwant Joshi Lal and Leo Rose, *Democratic Innovations in Nepal* (Berkeley and Los Angeles: University of California Press, 1966), and Leo Rose, "The Role of Nepal and Tibet in Sino-Soviet Relations" (Ph.D. dissertation, University of California, Berkeley, 1960). We await Mira Sinha's parallel study based on the Chinese materials, but an official Chinese statement can be found in *New Developments in Friendly Relations between China and Nepal* (Peking: Foreign Languages Press, 1960).

position in the traditional Himalayan subsystem of princes, families, and tribes is central; even "Chinese" Tibet sent an annual tribute to Kathmandu. The British exercised some of their influence in Lhasa because of their special relationships in Nepal, and this influence was as important for Indian diplomacy and defense as it had been for the British, perhaps more so.

Nepal is central to India's northern defenses and its government has sought a neutralist position between India and China. Thus China offered an available local counterforce for Nepali leaders, especially King Mahendra, to balance pro-Indian forces within the kingdom. Lacking recent success in sponsoring its proxies in Kathmandu, Delhi has had to devalue some of its Nepali allies to maintain a voice in the king's policies toward China. India is almost forced to assist Nepal to keep it from "falling to China" regardless of Nepal's policies toward India and toward domestic factions favorable to India. The Chinese, on the other hand, brought resources and policies to bear to make inroads in Indian influence and weaken Kathmandu's role in the Indian defense system.[15]

While it does violence to the extraordinarily complex policy problems faced by India in 1949, a gross summary of the alternatives in the Himalayas suggests two choices; India could cling to its inherited, potentially costly and ambiguous role as a third party in Tibet's future or it could attempt to exchange a withdrawal from "the reverse slope" for a favorable Himalayan border settlement "closer in." It is difficult, from the evidence available, to measure the Indian capacity to maintain its Tibetan trade and communication facilities either directly or by attempting to use Nepal as a political proxy, but it seems reasonably clear that the Indians did not think they could support an advanced commitment, especially after Peking forced the issue of its *de facto* control of Tibet on the eve of the Korean War.[16] Even so, the Chinese

15 One student argues that "Chinese aid to Nepal had one overriding purpose: to encourage those elements in Nepal which saw China as a counterweight to India." Eugene B. Mihaly, *Foreign Aid and Politics in Nepal* (London: Oxford University Press for the Royal Institute of International Affairs, 1965), pp. 152–53. It is equally likely that the Chinese saw the Nepali government in need of a Chinese counterweight, and extracted a strategic price, such as the Kathmandu-Kodari-Tibet road, for providing it. This pattern, of course, was responsible for the American, British, and Soviet aid strategies designed to offset Chinese successes.

16 The few scraps of evidence on these events from the Indian side may be found in K. M. Panikkar, *In Two Chinas, Memoirs of a Diplomat* (London, 1955). He describes himself as shocked on arrival in Peking in May, 1950, by

were very proper in continuing to honor Tibet's tribute to Nepal, and to respect India's rights for trading and communication facilities until the 1954 treaty that legitimized exclusive Chinese control of Tibet.

The Chinese did not force India's hand further as they extended political and military control, even though the actions precipitated the internal violence that has characterized Tibet since 1952–53. In the winter and early spring of 1954, India and China discussed the future of Tibet and their relations. On April 29, the governments signed an "Agreement on Trade and Intercourse between the Tibet Region of China and India" that included the famous declaration of Panch Shila (five principles of peaceful coexistence). This agreement laid the basis for Chinese participation in the Bandung Conference, for enhanced trade and for an exchange of state visits. In a sense, it was a normalization of Sino-Indian relations without a demarcation of frontiers; general interests were served, but specific boundary claims were deferred. Objectively analyzed, this appears to have been a statesmanlike settlement. India and China were pursuing parallel courses of action, the Korean and Vietnamese wars were over, China's economic progress had been considerable in the first five year plan, and Bandung lay ahead holding the promise of China's acceptance into the comity of new nations. Only the United States continued to bedevil China and, by extending its military aid to Pakistan, India as well. The Chinese showed some sensitivity to India's interests in the Himalayas, and India appeared to have liquidated worthless "rights" for the real advantages of a major *détente* with China. It must have been clear to both parties that India's position was weak, but so was China's and India and China had little genuine cause for mutual hostility.

South Asian Regional Relationships: Burma and the Northeast

India also inherited security problems in the northeast. Events in World War II had demonstrated the vulnerability of India's industrial complex along the Hooghly River to attack from Burma. After the British withdrew, Burma became an independent state although it had been administered as part of the British Indian empire until 1935. The partition settlement, in a typically perverse strategic fashion, divided Bengal with its eastern portion going to Pakistan. The northwestern tip of East

---

posters demanding the "liberation" of Tibet (p. 79) and was struck by the Chinese concern over Nepali troops in Tibet (p. 105) and the charge that India's Tibet policy was "influenced by the imperialists" (p. 113).

Pakistan comes within some 30 miles of pinching Assam off from the rest of India, and leaves Assam, Tripura, Manipur, and NEFA connected with the rest of India only by air and a tortuous meter gauge railway. The broad gauge strategic railways system of eastern India, and its important river transportation system, were severed with the creation of Pakistan.[17] The Indo-Burmese frontier, more than 800 miles long, is a turbulent one for both countries; it includes the Naga and Mizo Hills in India where a tribal insurrection of major proportions is entering a sixth year. It fronts on Burma's northern frontier with China and the Chindwin Valley. In access, moreover, India's more serviceable frontier with Burma is the 780 mile nautical route between Calcutta and Rangoon. East of Burma, the Indians have a historic interest but have lacked the independent national capacity to support regional goals,[18] especially in light of the stakes in Southeast Asia since 1950.

Indo-Burmese relations began in a felicitous way after World War II. The Chinese civil war had spilled over into northern Burma where Kuomintang guerrillas battled both Communist Chinese and Burmese troops in irregular battle, the KMT irregulars being supplied in part by United States-aided airdrops. As the Burmese recruited a large army to restore order in the historically turbulent northern districts, they asked for but were denied arms from the United States and Britain. India, however, responded and earned the gratitude of U Nu's government. For a decade, the Burmese army was committed to battle in the north, finally encountering major Chinese Communist forces in Wa State and taking sizeable losses.[19]

Burma has the longest frontier with China of any southern Asian state, and it was increasingly clear to its leaders that India's resources were spread too thin, that American and British assistance, assuming it could be forthcoming, would exacerbate rather than mollify relations with the Chinese, and that the only practical alternative was to con-

[17] Assam is still served by river transport through Pakistan but its vulnerability was shown when, during the Sino-Indian war of 1962, the inland waterways labor unions struck in Pakistan, leaving Assam dependent on over-clogged railways and nearly nonexistent air transport capacity.

[18] See Ton That Thien, *India and South-East Asia, 1947–1960* (Geneva: Droz, 1963).

[19] For a chronology, see Daphne E. Whittam, "The Sino-Burmese Boundary Treaty," *Pacific Affairs*, 34, no. 2 (summer, 1961): 174–83. A full but controversial interpretation is William Johnstone, *Burma's Foreign Policy: A Study of Neutralism* (Cambridge, Mass: Harvard University Press for the RAND Corporation, 1963).

clude an agreement largely on Chinese terms. Three Burmese governments made such an effort, but the frontier agreement was not reached
until 1961, when China's South Asian policy had crystallized into a
policy of isolating India. Burma's subsequent policy of nationalization
resulted in a mass exodus of the Indian commercial minority, but in
general Indo-Burmese relations have been correct, and frequently
cordial. Insurrectionist forces continue to trouble Rangoon's leaders,
however, and the diplomatic consequences of the July, 1967, Burman-
Chinese riots show how tenuous are Sino-Burmese relations.

The Thin Indian Line

It should be remembered that India did not inherit British India. It
inherited 9,425 miles of linear, not zonal, frontiers that the British had
not been forced to defend. This line was drawn in a fashion that defied
defense and pitted the peoples of the subcontinent against one another
over the nature of those frontiers. Independence meant removal from
the British Indian army of the arsenals that produced sophisticated
weapons and the graving yards that produced and serviced the fleet
charged with defending 3,535 miles of coastline. Even the strongest
viceroys had not had to deal with a united and well-organized China,
or a militant Communist party within India backed by superpowers
across the Himalayas and Pamirs.

It is also well to remember that the government of India pursued
policies of *realpolitik* where its vital interests were concerned, and
where it had the strength to insure success—Kashmir, Bhutan, Sikkim,
Goa, periodically in Nepal, and at least once in Burma. The Indian role
in the various Tibetan rebellions has not been documented but was
probably important, especially in conjunction with that of the United
States. Where India did not have the capacity to serve its own interests,
it imaginatively mobilized international resources for its policies in the
United Nations and in Moscow, London, and Washington.

It is true that the Indian Defense Ministry rarely had men of great
political stature,[20] that the military establishment was not raised much
above half a million men organized along British colonial lines and
that foreign intelligence was collected by a civilian agency. Defense
support industry was developed, but it had to compete with the other
priorities of developing India—steel production, transport facilities,

[20] This seems to have been the product of Nehru's concern for civil supremacy. All Defense and Home Ministers were his political appointees, not men
strong in the party or the country, until Y. B. Chavan's appointment in the
1962 crisis.

agricultural investment, and social overhead facilities. India's economic underdevelopment had obvious implications for its military forces, but this is a far cry from charges that "pacifist leadership," "political colonels" and "naïve leftists" led India down the garden path of military unpreparedness. Quite the contrary is true.[21] K. M. Panikkar's concept of Indian Ocean regional security, the Indian-inspired Colombo Plan, Nehru's architectonic role in the creation of the Nasser-Nehru-Tito neutralist axis and the Bandung gambit of legitimizing China's entry into the constraints of the comity of nations were efforts to parlay general Indian weakness into strength, its positions of regional strength into hegemony, and resultant regional hegemony into parity with China in a peace of peers. What undercut the Indian policy was the conflicting role of the Great Powers and China, and their policies in South Asia.

South Asia and the World Powers

By most criteria, South Asia is a relatively unimportant area to the world powers. It has no major resources central to Soviet or American industry; it lies half way around the world from the United States and thousands of miles from the population centers of the Soviet Union and China. Its large populations are the world's poorest; its regional literacy, productivity, and energy utilization levels are near the bottom of world statistics. Foreign private investments are largely British, and only about a third of Indian exports are to the United States and United Kingdom. While nearly half of India's imports are from America and Britain, this reflects the availability of foreign assistance tied to donor-state purchases since the balance of trade is adverse. In 1963–64, for example, India's imbalance of trade was over $700 million.[22] The pattern in Pakistan is similar and its much less developed economy is even more dependent upon the services of the sterling area for facilitating external trade.[23]

Traditional American interests in southern Asia have been more

[21] Skeptics might consult the record of an exchange between Senator Stuart Symington and Mr. Samuel Cummings in "Arms Sales to Near East and South Asia," *Hearings* before the Subcommittee on Near Eastern and South Asian Affairs of the Committee on Foreign Relations, United States Senate, 90th Congress, 1st session (Washington: Government Printing Office, 1967), p. 38.

[22] These and subsequent figures are computed from *India, 1965* (Delhi: Government of India, 1965), pp. 322–29.

[23] A good survey of Pakistan's trade patterns and problems is J. Russell Andrus and Azizali F. Mohammed, *Trade, Finance and Development in Pakistan* (Stanford, Calif.: Stanford University Press, 1966), pp. 24–81.

philanthropic than commercial or strategic, and Russian and Chinese contact has been less extensive. Moreover, the governments in the region have been relatively competent, stable, and effective in maintaining order, and there has been little of the fluidity that allows and provokes foreign involvement in search of control. One can, of course, invent for any place the notion of strategic importance. For example, Sir Olaf Caroe, in *Wells of Power*,[24] argues Pakistan's strategic importance on the basis of its location on the Persian Gulf oil basin but Karachi is 1,160 miles from Kuwait and Abadan and its propinquity to the mouth of the Gulf of Oman is not inherently important, especially to the Great Powers, since it lacks naval and air power.

In short, shorn of its crude mercator bulk and its large but unmobilized population, South Asia weighs lightly in the contemporary strategic balance. It is something of a paradox that South Asia has emerged as a region of central importance to the world powers, and that its saliency is so high when measured by indices of foreign assistance, military assistance, intensity of diplomatic competition, and polemical exchange. As a prize in global competition, as a potentially important region, and as a major segment of humanity—one in every six human beings—the region is politically important.

United States Policies toward South Asia

The competitive quality of United States–USSR post-war policies helps explain the sequential quality of policy initiation and response. The American involvement in South Asia dates from the first Eisenhower administration. In the five years after Indian and Pakistani independence, the Truman administration was primarily concerned with the Marshall Plan, Truman Doctrine, and problems of the Middle East. Asian policy was dominated by the Korean conflict and the China question.[25] The Dulles-Eisenhower policy of regional alliances stemmed from what were considered to be the lessons of the Huk rebellion, the Malayan insurgency, the Korean War, and the Indochinese War; namely that the Communists were pursuing their aims in limited, local wars,

[24] (London, 1951).

[25] Russian observers of American South Asian policy do not agree with this generalization. They argue that United States Cold War strategy favored the creation of Pakistan, played on the Kashmir dispute to get strategic rights on the Sino-Soviet frontier, subverted Pakistan to American strategic aims in Asia and the Middle East, and frustrated more progressive Indian diplomacy. See Yuri Gankovsky and L. R. Gordon-Polonskaya, *Istoriya Pakistana,* and V. Kumar, *Anglo-Amerikansky Zagovor Protiv Kashmira* (Moscow, 1954).

and could be stopped only by resolute collective action. This was congruent to the imagery of "containment" as practiced in the Truman Doctrine and it tended to justify the increasing involvement of America in Asian international politics in the wake of the withdrawal of the French, British, and Dutch.

Pakistan and America

Pakistan, desperately in search of military, economic, and diplomatic support, was eager to conclude agreements with the United States. The price was low—condemnation of Communism, public support for U.S. postures in international politics, some property "rental" in the north useful for aircraft and electronic intercept facilities. The benefits were remarkably high—first claim as an ally on grant aid,[26] a completely re-equipped military striking force built around Pakistan's regional defense needs[27] and opportunities to build support for Pakistan's Kashmir case in the United States. As time passed, the Pakistan government came to realize that it was frustrated in the Kashmir dispute, in part because the Soviet Union had been mobilized by India to frustrate the potent United States-Pakistan alliance, and in part because the United States was unwilling to sacrifice general interests in India for special ones in Pakistan. During the second Eisenhower administration, Pakistan, after 1958 led by General Mohammad Ayub Khan, pushed for force levels and weapons systems capable of asserting local parity in Kashmir and re-opening the dispute militarily with at least United States forebearance.

It became increasingly clear to Ayub Khan that the general American aim underlying involvement in Asia was the stabilization of a region on the fringe of the Communist countries, not their destabilization with arms races stimulated and financed by the United States.[28] Ayub Khan

[26] Totaling by 1966 about $3 billion in grants, loans, and commodities, much of it grant aid.

[27] In 1965 the Institute of Strategic Studies publication, *The Military Balance, 1965* (London, 1966), estimated that the army was 8 divisions (230,000 men) equipped with M-47 (Patton) tanks, an air force of about 25,000 men with 200 aircraft (including 20 B-57 bombers, a squadron of F-104A and 4 squadrons of F-86F together with 4 C-130 transports and other auxiliary equipment). It seems reasonably clear that the roles and missions assigned to Pakistan as a Cold War ally did not require M-47 tanks or B-57 bombers, yet both of these weapons systems constituted a direct threat to India and were part of a "deterrent defense" against India.

[28] This critique of past policy was convincingly presented in a series of three articles by Selig S. Harrison in *New Republic*, August-September, 1959,

was denied the weapons and force levels he sought, but the Tibet insurrection of 1959 offered him an opportunity to initiate talks with India for a joint subcontinent defense alliance. Pakistan's expectation was that India might be willing to negotiate on Kashmir in exchange for Pakistan's commitment to face its armies north to meet an expansionist China in a joint defense arrangement. Pakistan's offer, twice made, was twice rejected by New Delhi which saw in both United States and Soviet policy new sources for military support that were not contingent upon a *détente* with Pakistan.

Ayub Khan saw the same developments shaping, and following the Indian rejection of his regional plan, began searching for alternatives to a policy of exclusive reliance upon decreasing American support. The May, 1960, U-2 affair[29] offered him an excuse to assert his independence, and in the same year Pakistan's vote on the seating of Communist China in the United Nations returned to its 1950 position in favor of Peking. After an arduous pursuit, Pakistan was able to pry out of Moscow a loan for oil exploration signed in 1961.

These actions were also keyed to the election of John F. Kennedy. Many Pakistanis tend to associate all Laborites and Democrats with India, and assume that all Conservatives and Republicans are with them; from the new administration in Washington, Pakistan expected the worst and soon received it. The new administration was unsympathetic to increased military aid although economic assistance would remain at high levels. Washington was much more attentive to the heightening tension between India and China than it was to the Cold War, and Professor Kissinger's speeches and Ambassador Galbraith's cables, diplomatic and otherwise, underscored the new concerns. The Sino-Indian border war of October–November, 1962, the subsequent U.S. military assistance to India, and Pakistan's new-found friendship with Peking completed the break in close relations that had begun early in 1959.

---

on the eve of President Eisenhower's state visit to India. The United States had already begun to draw back from its special relationship with Pakistan, and the first hard evidence of the Sino-Soviet split seemed to justify reduced costs in securing the containment of the Communist "bloc" threat in Asia.

[29] The Russians had frequently referred to the United States military installations in Pakistan but both Washington and Karachi denied their existence. The Powers' flight and the dispute arising from it made such denials impossible. Khrushchev's threats were prominently displayed in the Pakistani press once Ayub Khan had decided to use the bases as a "visible" bargaining point, not only with Washington but with Moscow as well.

American, British, and Russian responses to the Sino-Indian War and the Indian Five Year Defense Plan led to dramatically increased Indian force levels in a period in which the United States was unwilling to match increased Indian strength for Pakistan. Sino-Pakistani relations had shown some increase in cordiality and breadth from 1961, and thereafter the United States faced unhappy alternatives; continued military assistance to India, either from the United States or the Soviet Union, would have the effect of compromising Pakistan's sense of military security and forcing it closer to Peking; but not to arm India was to leave it open to Chinese pressure or greater dependence upon Soviet assistance. In this situation, both India and Pakistan, claiming weakness, were able to make maximum claims on American resources with a minimum commitment to American goals.

India and America

American policy toward India has followed a pattern corresponding in general to Indo-Pakistan relations and problems. For the first five years of independence, India remained closely tied to the British strategic posture, an arrangement valued by London no less than Delhi.[30] The Indian army used British equipment and doctrine, its officers were posted to the Imperial Defence College and large numbers of British officers continued to serve free India. In any case, India was busy consolidating its domestic unity, drafting a constitution and priming for the first general elections in 1952. Prime Minister Nehru was ready to talk about foreign policy on his first visit to the United States in October, 1949,[31] but Washington was not as attentive as New York.

Nehru's neutralist message had special appeal when the Cold War was fully joined and decolonization was the first order of international business. It was precisely then, however, that the United States was responding to local wars in Asia by constructing a forward policy of containment. To some, India's neutralism appeared to be without scruple. Certainly the response of India's leaders to the announcement of U.S. military assistance to Pakistan made it appear that India claimed the prerogatives of managing Asia, and that neutralism was a guise for the Indian national interest. The polemical exchanges of the period mark the breakdown of India's ability to convert its superiority in the subcontinent's politics to hegemony. India's *apertura a sinistre*, marked in the 1957 elections, in the new shape of India's second five year plan, but

[30] This very important point is underscored in the comments of M. J. Desai in this volume (*infra*).

[31] At Columbia University, October 17, 1949.

more importantly in Indo-Soviet relations after the death of Stalin, was in part a response to U.S. policy. The symbol of the period was V. K. Krishna Menon, charged by many casual observers as being the force behind a socialist India acting as a Trojan Horse for Russia's subversion of the new countries of Afro-Asia. Indo-American relations were at their worst from 1956 to 1958, but the enormous financial crisis in India in 1958 and President Eisenhower's state visit in December, 1959, symbolized both India's need for American assistance on a very large scale, and America's willingness to accept India's foreign policy independence, nominally by emphasizing the struggle between China and India in Asia and de-emphasizing the Soviet-American rivalry.

The period between Eisenhower's visit and the Sino-Indian border war witnessed a major struggle for influence in India between the United States and the Soviet Union, culminating in the Russian agreements to finance heavy industrial development on a wide scale and to build in India an aircraft plant to manufacture MiG-21 aircraft and weapon systems.[32] American support for Indian economic development, both bilaterally and through the "Aid India" consortium was similarly on a large scale. It is from 1959 that the Chinese charge India with expansionism aided by China's rivals.[33]

Soviet Policies and South Asia

Russia's policies in South Asia are extremely difficult to unravel. After the initial militancy of the Zhdanov line,[34] Moscow became very inter-

[32] The unprecedented Soviet decision to give India the capacity to produce high performance aircraft is a sharp break from Soviet and American military assistance which emphasizes "controls" on armaments. This decision was later criticized in Soviet academic circles as an example of Khrushchev's "adventurism." But the record of negotiations and delays suggests, rather, a tortuous policy in response to heavy Western counter-pressures and considerable Indian leverage. See I. C. C. Graham, "The Indo-Soviet MiG Deal and its International Repercussions," *Asian Survey,* vol. 4, no. 5 (May, 1964), pp. 823-32.

[33] The most concise Chinese statement is the February 17, 1963, interview of Foreign Minister Ch'en Yi with a correspondent of the Swedish Broadcasting Corporation, reprinted in *The Sino-Indian Boundary Question* (Peking: Foreign Languages Press), 2: 1–12.

[34] The changing nature of early Soviet perceptions of independent India is traced in detail in Gene Overstreet and Marshall Windmiller, *Communism in India* (Berkeley, Calif.: University of California Press, 1959), especially pp. 252–75. There is no serviceable study for the contemporary period of India's policy toward the Soviet Union, although Richard Siegel's forthcoming Columbia doctoral dissertation and Stephen Clarkson's "L'Analyse Soviétique des Problèmes Indiens du Sous-Développement, 1955–1963," Sorbonne, 1964, partially meet the problem.

ested in India, and its South Asian policy was a pro-Indian policy until the Tashkent Conference in early 1966. Initially the Russians appear to have believed that New Delhi's policy was in fact made in Whitehall. As British power declined and American influence grew, the calculations behind Soviet actions appear to have been aimed at forestalling an "Eisenhower Doctrine" applicable to the subcontinent. Pakistan's agreement with the United States in 1953 was coincident to an Indo-Soviet trade agreement. Two years later India as leader of the neutralist bloc, sponsor of Bandung, friend of progressive China and foe of American pacts, rated a visit by Bulganin and Khrushchev. By this period, Soviet doctrine appears to have evolved into a global "united front" strategy made possible in the Middle East and South Asia by the regional rivalries crystallized and polarized by the regional security pacts underwritten by the United States and Great Britain. By 1959, Soviet doctrine appeared to have changed the priorities of its competition in Asia from the West to China, and India appeared to the Soviet Union as an alternative alliance partner in Central Asian politics, a perspective that illuminated the importance of Pakistan and seems to have led to a new conciliatory spirit of the USSR toward Pakistan after 1962. Contemporary Soviet policy toward India and Pakistan, therefore, appears to be based on a short-range calculation, the isolation of Maoist China, and a longer-range calculation, the detachment of the societies of the subcontinent from integration into the international system of the West. The subcontinent is the most costly investment of Soviet assistance policy, with India having received more than a billion dollars in economic assistance and an undisclosed amount in loans for large numbers of aircraft and other high-cost military equipment. Soviet assistance to Pakistan is just beginning at a relatively low scale.

In retrospect, 1957 seems to have been the crucial year in Soviet-Indian relations. As a low point in relations of the United States with India, it was an ideal time for the Soviet Union to detach India from its previous course, both in planning goals and international posture. It is clear that Soviet leadership did not think foreign assistance would buy a "socialist" state, but pro-Soviet foreign policy would be a helpful short-term adjunct to India's long-term slide into problems, the only solution of which would be "Leninist." With this perspective, Moscow could counsel popular front moderacy to the Communist Party of India and increase government-to-government assistance. The 1957 Sino-Soviet confrontation in Moscow on aid policy is also clear in retrospect, the Soviet argument favoring widely distributed aid to eliminate American influence and the Chinese favoring socialist unity, (all aid to the socialist bloc) and party militancy in the new states. Chinese acquiescence to the Soviet line was apparently purchased by the secret nuclear weapons agreement of October, 1957. Two years later, the strident Soviet-American competition in aid to India was at its zenith; the Chinese were unwilling to continue to accept a relatively lower position in Soviet assistance than India and, according to the Chinese, "the Soviet government unilaterally tore up (in June, 1959) the agreement on new technology for national defense concluded between China and the Soviet Union in October, 1957, and refused to provide the Chinese with a sample of an atomic bomb and data concerning its manufacturer."[35]

From 1959 to the present, Soviet policy toward South Asia has continued to fall in the category of highest priorities. While the border war of 1962 produced embarrassed Soviet references to the unnecessary struggle on frontier questions, the USSR shipped several MiG-21's by slow boat to Bombay and offered the Indians every private assurance of their support. In the years since, the Soviets have told Indian officials that they mobilized on the Sinkiang frontier to save India a border war in 1959 after the Tibetan insurrection.[36] Although the war in 1962 marked a low point in Soviet influence (Defense Minister Y. B. Chavan, in his first public speech, said that India had been the victim of Communist aggression), both because of its ambiguous policy statements and because the Indians were obviously counting on the Soviet Union to act as a restraint on Peking, Soviet prestige was restored as the Sino-Soviet rift became more visible and bitter, and as Soviet assistance continued to arrive, in ever increasing amounts in India. And in both the Rann of Kutch and September, 1965, Indo-Pakistan wars, the Soviet Union was constant in its supplies for India while the United States and Britain were embarrassed into pleas for peace and a cessation of assistance to both sides.

Pakistan attempted to "unfreeze" relations with the USSR from 1960 to 1962 but was unable to do so until the Breznev-Kosygin government came to power. For some time the Russians must have viewed Pakistan's good relations with China as an annoyance to their South Asian diplomacy. In the aftermath of the September, 1965, war, the Kremlin offered its good offices to the disputants. The Russians may have

[35] "The Polemic on the General Line of the International Communist Movement" (Peking: Foreign Languages Press, 1965), p. 77.

[36] The official Soviet statement on contemporary China's political goals argues that it seeks "hegemony . . . in countries of Asia, Africa, and Latin America," *Pravda,* Nov. 27, 1966, as translated and distributed as Soviet Mission to the United Nations Information Service #47, Nov. 28, 1966, p. 8.

doubted that Pakistan would accept the offer since Russia was India's most constant patron. Much to their surprise, probably, Pakistan accepted *before* India, and there is much reason to believe that both the Russians and the Indians looked for ways to avoid the consequent embarrassment, especially since the proferred good offices would be based on the United Nations Security Council mandate of September 20, 1965.[37] The resolution called for a cease fire, a rollback of forces, and a political settlement of the dispute between India and Pakistan. When India reluctantly accepted, it was forced to accept the Soviet Union's support of the United Nations' language concerning the dispute in which the USSR had previously (1957 and 1962) cast two vetoes in support of India.

The events at the Tashkent conference are not fully known, but it is clear that President Ayub Khan publicly threatened to leave without signing any final communiqué as late as twenty-four hours before the conference was due to end, and that considerable intervention and action by the Russians was noted in the last day of the conference. Pakistan was able to use the conference to elicit from Moscow a declaration they sought. Whether Ayub Khan was bluffing, and Moscow was maneuvered into this position, or whether the Russians were seeking a chance to reduce their total commitment to India in favor of regional influence is difficult to determine; perhaps all factors were operative.[38] Since Tashkent, a Pakistan air force mission has been to Moscow, a $200 million loan has been announced, a few "non-lethal" military items have been shipped, and more cordial relations have been marked by Ayub Khan's state visit in October, 1967, but the shape of Russo-Pakistani relations is still indistinct.

The World Powers: Parallel Policies in South Asia?

The outcome of the various foreign policies of the Soviet Union and the United States have been similar. Both states have moved to positions of friendship with both major subcontinent powers; both have declared an interest in seeing them avoid conflict; both seek to reduce the

[37] United Nations Security Council, Resolution 211 (1965), September 20, 1965. The Russians voted in favor of the resolution.

[38] For a thoughtful general statement, see Aswini K. Ray, "Pakistan as a Factor in Indo-Soviet Relations," *Economic and Political Weekly*, 1, no. 12 (November 5, 1966): 503–7. It seems clear that President Ayub Khan, who had seen President Lyndon Johnson before Tashkent, had been unable to get American support, and had little choice but agreement.

costs of maintaining influential relationships. Similarity has emerged because Soviet and American assistance policies have in mode and in scale become similar and potentially parallel even if their ultimate goals are divergent.

Both world powers share a concern with economic viability in the subcontinent because failure would threaten their future relations. The United States has made a large investment in pluralist free economies which, if they can sustain growth, will provide both examples and partners in a world economy in which the United States can feel comfortable; India's long-term failure would threaten present international economic arrangements. The Soviet Union would find massive economic failure in India destructive of the groups that could lead its underdeveloped society into the Socialist system, and would lead to unwelcome massive debt default. A threatened dictatorship and a disorganized society would be more in Russia's interest than a truly widespread and indigenous social revolution, a preference reflected in the program of the pro-Moscow faction of the Communist Party of India. For different reasons, both world powers seek at least a minimum level of economic success in South Asia and both seek to avoid convulsive social revolution there. In short, both favor the status quo.

The second shared goal of the United States and the Soviet Union is the stabilization of the strategic environment in South Asia. A strong India and a friendly Pakistan at peace offers a minimally fluid international environment and the fewest opportunities for other external powers. A strong India is something of a counterweight to China, and entails the commitment of some Chinese resources in the Tibet-Sinkiang area that otherwise might be employed elsewhere. These diplomatic goals shared by Moscow and Washington counsel Indo-Pakistan peace and relatively high Indian conventional military force levels.

The third shared goal of United States and Soviet policy toward South Asia is the prevention of an Indian nuclear weapons program. An Indian nuclear weapon would not threaten either state but the demonstration effect it would have might end chances for the nonproliferation treaty that is in the declared Soviet and American interest. If India can be persuaded that nuclear weapons should not be developed, the world powers have more options and more time to work out their mutual goals in arms control.[39] This interest, too, presupposes

---

[39] A useful survey of the debate and the stakes is Robert L. Rothstein, "On Nuclear Proliferation," in Occasional Papers of the School of International Affairs (New York: Columbia University, 1966).

peace in the subcontinent and an enhanced sense of national security in India and Pakistan.

There seems to be every indication that both the Soviet and American governments are willing to accept these goals as mutual interests and, to a degree, coordinate their policies. The handling of the Indian food grains crisis of December, 1966, suggests that President Johnson almost explicitly committed the Soviet Union to a joint food shipment program. It is much less clear that either world power has as clear a notion of parallel interests in Pakistan as in India, and Pakistan has every reason to continue to follow policies that destabilize the region since its goals can only be reached by a major transformation of the strategic environment in the subcontinent. Therefore, to find China's likely role in South Asia and the opportunities Peking has to avoid "foreclosure," one must look first to Pakistan, and then to the smaller Himalayan states of Nepal, Sikkim, and Bhutan.

Chinese Policies toward South Asia

Chinese relations with the South Asian states have been relatively complex because of the many levels of policy being served and the highly differentiated way in which the various countries have been seen by Peking. The region as a whole has been less important to the CPR than some other frontier areas, in part because its problems were less pressing and more manageable, in part because the region itself is barren and inhospitable, and in part because the frontier did not directly concern the world powers until 1959. There was little diplomatic contact between India and China until the Korean War, and Sino-Indian relations were not thought to be central problems in either country's foreign security policy in the period. Since 1959, however, India's frontier has become an internationalized concern of the Western powers and the Soviet Union as well as China.

Peking's policies toward the other states in the Himalayas have fluctuated in response to domestic, regional, and international developments. Toward several of the principalities the Chinese have advanced irredentist claims associated with Tibetan policy. Burma, Pakistan, and, to a lesser extent, Nepal have enjoyed the fruits of "Bandung moderacy" tempered by frontier claims. Chinese policy toward India has been consistently competitive,[40] becoming stridently hostile as India

[40] As early as 1948 in Nanking, India's ambassador to Nationalist China noted that the Chinese considered themselves "the recognized Great Power in the East after the war and expected India to know its place." K. M. Panikkar, *In Two Chinas*, pp. 26–27. The Chinese invasion of Tibet in 1950 on the eve

took advantage, first, of Soviet-American rivalry and, later, Sino-Soviet and Sino-American differences to build its own regional power. This pattern corresponds to the analysis of China's Asian strategy suggesting that India, Japan, and Indonesia are principal rivals with China for leadership in Asia and that China seeks Asian preeminence in order to assert its parity with the established Western world powers.[41]

Contact between the new Chinese government at Peking and the Himalayan states stemmed in the first instance from the extension of Chinese public authority. All of the South Asian states except Sikkim had contested or ambiguous frontiers with Tibet and China. Frontier consolidation in China was the responsibility of the army, and it implied battles with Kuomintang (KMT) guerrillas and hostile local leaders together with the sealing of thousands of miles of ill-defined frontiers. The inherited Chinese maps of the frontier were as ambitiously expansionist as the British maps inherited by the South Asian governments, and some conflict was inevitable in the conversion of zonal frontiers to demarcated boundaries. The Burmese and Indian governments sought an early general frontier declaration and settlement but Peking was engrossed in the problems of establishing a government, restoring order in the wake of civil war and organizing the country for the sacrifices of the Korean War.[42] In any case, Peking shared the political doctrines associated with the militancy of Zhdanov, and had

---

of Korean War intervention was a clear challenge to India's strength and even in the heyday of Sino-Indian friendship at the Bandung Conference of 1955, A. Doak Barnett remembers that Chou En-lai and the Chinese delegation made no secret of their disparagement of India's "position" in the world and took every opportunity to "up-stage" Nehru. See *Jen-min jih-pao* [People's Daily], October 27, 1962, for the last major statement on Indian policy. The subsequent statements on Sino-Indian relations charge deception and trickery to the Indians. See Anna Louise Strong, *Letters from China* (Peking: New World Press, 1963), nos. 1–10, pp. 1–77, *The Sino-Indian Boundary Question* 2 (Peking: Foreign Languages Press, 1965), *A Mirror For Revisionists* (Peking: Foreign Languages Press, 1963), and *Vice-Premier Chen Yi Answers Questions Put by Correspondents* (Peking: Foreign Languages Press, 1966), pp. 1–3.

[41] This has been well summarized by David Mozingo, "China's Relations with Asian Neighbors" (The RAND Corporation, personal paper P-2947, July, 1964, mimeographed.)

[42] Burma had been notified by Nationalist officials in 1948 that the frontier arrangements were unsatisfactory. When Rangoon asked Peking to consider the matter, it was at Chinese insistence deferred "to a more appropriate time." See Daphne E. Whittam, "The Sino-Burmese Boundary Treaty," *Pacific Affairs*, 39, no. 2 (summer, 1961): 175.

little interest in normalizing relations with bourgeois nationalist governments even if it had had the necessary resources.

On October 25, 1950, as part of the process of consolidation, the Chinese army was ordered into Tibet "to free three million Tibetans from Western imperialist oppression and to consolidate national defenses on China's western borders." India considered this both a slur on its independence and an attack on an outer point of its inherited Himalayan defense system. To Delhi's restrained note calling for Tibetan autonomy within a system of Chinese suzerainty (the 1914 Simla formula), the Chinese intimated that India's concern was motivated by external powers hostile to China, that India had no right to challenge Chinese sovereignty in Tibet, and that legitimate Indian diplomatic, commercial, and cultural interests in Tibet would be accommodated "through normal diplomatic channels," that is, through Peking. The Dalai Lama's plea to the United Nations, sponsored by El Salvador, was lost in the confusion attendant on Chinese intervention in Korea, and the resolution was disavowed by the government of India after Peking's assurances that local autonomy in some measure would be assured.

While it has been argued that "India wrote off Tibet in her defense calculations, and decided to lean on Sino-Indian friendship for the security of her northern frontier,"[43] the case is not altogether clear. India was not ready to contest tenuous Tibetan rights that would have been expensive to service, that had lost some of their strategic importance, and that were unimportant in commerce. On the other hand, Delhi wanted to demonstrate determination and strength "closer in" along the Himalayan line. To this end it negotiated a defense treaty with Nepal in 1950 calling for joint consultation in time of attack and providing for Indian military and economic assistance for Nepal. India also hardened its commitment to the defense of Bhutan and Sikkim. The Chinese response to India's regional demonstration of resolve accompanied by support for Peking in the world was conciliatory;[44]

[43] P. C. Chakravarti, *India's China Policy* (Bloomington, Ind.: Indiana University Press, 1962), p. 38.

[44] Ch'en Yi's statement on the dispute is relevant. "India already occupied, around 1950, more than 90,000 square kilometers of Chinese territory in the eastern sector of the Sino-Indian boundary, south of the illegal McMahon Line. The occupied area was three times the size of Belgium. The Chinese government did not accept this encroachment, but in order to seek a peaceful settlement of the question, it restrained its frontier guards from crossing the illegal McMahon Line." *The Sino-Indian Boundary Question 2*, p. 2.

the 1951 Sino-Tibetan agreement both guaranteed Tibetan "autonomy" and Indian trade. Tibet continued to send symbolic tribute to Nepal until 1953, and Peking spared Tibet the "reforms" of the "Great Leap Forward" and the communes. Official Chinese pronouncements about India lost their abrasive quality by 1952 and despite the *contretemps* on Korean prisoner exchange and other issues, the Chinese were not unresponsive to Indian interests in the Himalayas. There is evidence of a reduction in advance patrolling along contested regions of the frontier.

From 1954 to 1956 India and China pursued closely parallel policies. China had emerged from the Korean War seasoned and more prudent; it was accepted at the Geneva Conference of 1954 as an Asian great power; its economy was prospering and the country was at peace for the first time in several decades. India's general conciliatory posture toward China on world issues was reinforced by its growing opposition to American intervention in Asia, especially in Pakistan. In the 1954 Tibet treaty both governments subscribed to a new charter of five principles of peaceful coexistence, for Peking an international version of the united front strategy, and state visits were exchanged before the year passed. The agreement paved the way for a step-down from the postures of confrontation along the Himalayan frontier even in the absence of a precise border settlement. This was symbolized by Chinese willingness to "do nothing" in Tibet, and India's willingness to accept direct Chinese representation in Nepal.[45]

By 1956, China had been given clear title to Tibet and Nepal had been detached from an exclusively Indian orientation. The Chinese were developing roads and defense facilities in Tibet along the Indian border, in part as a response to uprisings from Kham and Amdo tribesmen in Tsinghai and Szechuan. During this period the Aksai Chin road between Sinkiang and Tibet was developed, in large part because land access to Tibet from the northeast was difficult and control in Lhasa

[45] Tibet ended its tributary payment to Nepal in 1953, and in 1954 the CPR opened discussions with the Nepalese government aimed at establishing diplomatic relations which were consummated in 1955. In 1956 Sino-Nepalese relations were regularized in a general treaty ending Nepal's rights in Tibet in exchange for Chinese economic assistance, and in 1957 Nepal's foreign exchange was held independent of the Reserve Bank of India. See *New Development in Friendly Relations between China and Nepal* (Peking: Foreign Languages Press, 1960) for the texts of agreements and treaties as well as an interview with Chou En-lai on Sino-Nepalese relations.

was uncertain.[46] China controlled almost all of the principal passes as part of a "sealed frontier" policy aimed at minimizing the effect of insurrections in Tibet. In short, the Chinese tenuously occupied a strategically superior position in Tibet and were improving it in the period of good relations with India.

In 1957, Chinese policy underwent major changes. China's economic development under the first five year plan had not been impressive enough for its leaders, the internal dialogue in the Hundred Flowers period had produced dissension and required embarrassing suppression, moderation in foreign policy had neither brought Peking international acceptance nor mollified the United States; the Taiwan problem had become more intractable and the new Soviet leadership was adopting a foreign policy of peaceful coexistence with the United States and the sacrifice of China's needs for large-scale assistance in favor of a strategy emphasizing an anti-imperialist bloc of new bourgeois governments.

Faced with such problems and unenviable prospects, the Maoist leadership of the Chinese government adopted radical policies at home in the Great Leap Forward and "communes" and hardened its foreign policy. As noted above, China agreed to support Soviet foreign policy toward the new states only at the price of the secret nuclear weapons assistance agreement of October, 1957, and in the next year with Marshal Ch'en Yi as Foreign Minister pursued the adventurous Quemoy-Matsu confrontation. Harsh internal policies provoked dissension and in March, 1959, a major Tibetan rebellion broke out, its leaders demanding Tibetan independence. The Chinese saw India's hand in the rebellion, just as they had seen it in Tibet's claim to special status in 1950, in the 1951 agreement, in the 1954 trade and *panch shila* accord, in the Dalai Lama's temporary asylum in India in 1956, in Nehru's attempted visit to Lhasa in 1958, and in the asylum granted to the Dalai Lama and the several thousand Tibetan refugees who fled into India to escape Chinese troops in 1959. In the resulting recriminations, the Soviet Union in the Tass statement of September 9 took an equivocal position between India and China that was unprecedented, and all Soviet technicians had been withdrawn in July.[47]

[46] The Chinese themselves first publicized the road in a pictorial magazine and the Indian government confirmed its existence by sending several patrols, that were captured, to its site. See *The Sino-Indian Boundary Question*, enlarged ed. (Peking: Foreign Languages Press, 1962), pp. 14–15 and M. W. Fisher, L. E. Rose, and R. A. Huttenbach, *Himalayan Battleground, Sino-Indian Rivalry in Ladakh* (New York: Praeger, 1963).

[47] Donald Zagoria, *The Sino-Soviet Conflict, 1956–61* (Princeton, N.J.: Princeton University Press, 1962), p. 283.

Sino-Indian relations had never been "good" as the Indian public was to learn from the first in a series of white papers on the frontier problem, and China charged that "there has been a dark side to the Sino-Indian relations from the very beginning."[48] Nehru admitted in parliament in 1959 that India had been aware of the great dangers on the frontier but saw no point in making them public; indeed, he saw considerable advantage in publicly denying that there was a dispute.

On March 22, 1959, Nehru sent a short, general letter to Chou En-lai setting forth the Indian claims in summary, offering to discuss several areas where the demarcation line was unsettled and brusquely noting that

> It was in the confidence that the general question of our common frontier was settled to the satisfaction of both sides that I declared publicly and in Parliament on several occasions that there is no room for doubt about our frontiers as shown in the published maps.[49]

The Chinese reply was not received until September 8, 1959, three months after the suspension of Soviet nuclear aid and nearly six months after Nehru's letter, and it noted "a fundamental difference between the positions of our two Governments on the Sino-Indian boundary question."[50] From this period until October–November, 1962, relations between the two countries rapidly deteriorated, reports of armed clashes multiplied and defense preparations were hurried.[51] This was probably also related to internal Chinese factional politics, and seems to have been part of Lin Piao's claim, in 1962, to be a national hero in a period of harsh policy review.

China's Regional Constraints

Although the Indo-Pakistan rivalry offered China a potential ally in its struggle with India, the United States had very great influence on Pakistan's foreign policy postures from 1953 to 1960. Pakistan was a mem-

---

[48] *The Sino-Indian Boundary Question,* enlarged ed., p. 12.

[49] *Notes, Memoranda and Letters Exchanged and Agreements Signed between the Governments of India and China, 1954–1959, White Paper,* Ministry of External Affairs, Delhi, India, 1963, p. 57.

[50] *White Paper 2* (India), p. 27. That the significance of China's reply was not missed in Delhi is shown by the inclusion, in the second white paper, of "A Note on the Historical Background of the Himalayan Frontier of India."

[51] For a chronology of events and maps giving the contested areas of the frontier, see my *India, Pakistan and the Rise of China,* pp. 107–9; 121–23.

ber of SEATO, although hardly an enthusiastic one, and Peking found Pakistan more difficult to swallow than India during the Bandung period. Nonetheless, the Pakistanis went to some length to explain to China that their alliances were in no way a reflection of hostility toward the CPR, and the Chinese were willing to accept such assurances, especially since the United States presence in Pakistan was directed against the USSR in the main, not against Communist China. In 1956 a trade agreement was signed[52] and a China-Pakistan Friendship Society was organized. Pakistan's largest capitalist families played a conspicuous, almost exclusive, role in the organization for its first six years, and Peking lionized its leaders almost as if they were a shadow cabinet.[53]

Shortly after General Mohammad Ayub Khan seized power in Pakistan, the Chinese committee for Afro-Asian Solidarity protested his arrest of the Marxists Maulana A.H.K. Bhashani and Faiz Ahmed Faiz, and when Ayub offered India a joint defense agreement after the Tibetan rebellion in 1959, the Chinese pressed Pakistan on the question as to what threat such an arrangement would respond. The Chinese press, however, gave little coverage to the matter and indicated more concern about Pakistan's support for the American inspired "two Chinas scheme." Throughout the period of increasing tension on the Indian frontier, Chinese contact in Pakistan was relatively restricted; its impressive expansion follows rather than precedes the 1962 border war. It is equally clear that the Chinese interest in Pakistan is dictated as much by its own interests in transportation and communication facilities as by political tactics in isolating India.[54]

[52] Early Sino-Pakistani contracts are described in S. M. Burke, "Sino-Pakistan Relations," *Orbis* (summer, 1964): 391–92. The article is a preliminary sketch of a forthcoming major study of the subject.

[53] See, for example, *Survey of China Mainland Press (SCMP)*, September 27, 1959, for coverage of the arrival of M. A. H. Ispahani and his wife.

[54] In 1962, both agreements reached by the two countries concerned their willingness to demarcate the Sinkiang-Azad Kashmir frontier. In 1963, the boundary agreement "in principle" was signed, and other agreements concerned trade, a short-term barter agreement, an air transport agreement, and direct radiophoto and photographic service between Karachi and Peking. In 1964 New China News Agency (NCNA) and Associated Press of Pakistan negotiated an agreement, the air protocol was signed, and Chou En-lai and Ch'en Yi paid a state visit. In 1965 Ayub Khan returned the state visit, the border protocol and a cultural agreement were signed, Pakistan received a $60 million interest-free credit. In 1966 China agreed to supply Pakistan electrical equipment; a scientific and educational exchange agreement was negotiated; a July

CHINESE MISSIONS TO PAKISTAN

	1960	1961	1962	1963	1964	1965
Cultural	2	1	3	4	4	4
Trade	0	0	0	2	0	2
Diplomatic	0	0	0	0	4	11*
Political	0	0	0	0	0	0
Military	0	0	0	0	1	0

* Includes all Karachi airport conversations attended by other than protocol officers.

PAKISTAN MISSIONS TO CHINA

	1960	1961	1962	1963	1964	1965
Cultural	2	0	1	2	2	1
Trade	0	0	0	2	5	7
Diplomatic	0	0	0	1	1	1
Political	0	0	0	3	1	1
Military	0	0	0	0	1	0

As compiled by Martin Bresnick, Columbia University, from reports in *Survey of the China Mainland Press.*

Pakistan's rapport with China began improving in August, 1962, with the reposting in Peking of Major-General N.A.M. Raza as ambassador.[55] Two weeks later the Chinese Red Cross had given relief assistance to East Pakistan flood victims and within two months the Indian border war began. On December 10, General Raza entertained Chou En-lai at dinner, and in a major speech made six points while enunciating a careful new Pakistani policy: Pakistan was pleased with the progress being made in the Sino-Pakistan frontier demarcation, Pakistan was concerned with peace with India and justice in Kashmir, China had used admirable restraint in unilaterally proclaiming a cease fire on the

---

trade protocol was signed changing Pakistani textiles and light manufactured goods for tools, chemicals, and structural steel. China agreed to supply the $9 million foreign exchange component for an industrial center near Taxila (from the previous credit) and to supply 100,000 tons of rice to East Pakistan. The military assistance agreements have not been made public, but Chinese T-34 and T-59 tanks and MiG-19 aircraft made their first appearance on March 23, 1966. Supplies probably started arriving via ship, and perhaps via air from Sinkiang, in October, 1965.

55 General N. A. M. Raza is a career diplomat but entered the foreign service after being commissioned in the army, and hence has a military rank. His plucky behavior in several tours in Peking has earned him a wide reputation as an able if unorthodox advocate.

Indian frontier, Pakistan was intent upon friendship with all states, Pakistan's membership in defense pacts was not aggressive, and President Ayub Khan was a great statesman. These were cautious words as Pakistan tested the American tolerance for a Sino-Pakistani relationship that would go beyond pious words and UN votes.

Throughout 1964 Pakistan and China developed joint communication facilities; the air route (April 28) and more general communications apparently including roads (October 12). On February 13, 1965, direct radio and telephone communications were opened. In March, 1965, Ch'en Yi noted that the efforts of some countries to isolate China had been unsuccessful because China's peaceful relations with Pakistan made it possible for the world, through Pakistan, to know of China's peaceful intentions and efforts at national reconstruction.

The greater test of the Sino-Pakistani relationship was posed by the September, 1965, war between India and Pakistan. The war was initiated by Pakistan to offset recent Indian advances in military strength, diplomacy, and political consolidation in Kashmir. The Chinese made well-timed threats against India,[56] and some observers saw an incipient two front war. But Pakistan appears to have been cautious in utilizing Chinese assistance (if it was in fact proferred) and India did not have to meet a joint challenge. After American military and economic assistance was cut off, sizable amounts of Chinese equipment arrived in Pakistan and diplomatic contact increased appreciably. While China was being isolated in northeast Asia by the Soviet Union's Siberian development agreement with Japan and North Korea's statement of neutrality in the socialist world, its allies were also being crushed in Indonesia and East Africa. One of the few countries in which the Chinese have managed to do everything right is Pakistan, but the nature of Pakistan's need for American economic assistance sets fairly narrow limits on the relationship.[57]

[56] The threats were oblique. The Peking government "demanded that India dismantle the 56 aggressive military works she had built within Chinese territory on the China-Sikkim border and withdraw the intruding Indian troops. The China-Sikkim boundary is the boundary between China and Sikkim and does not fall within the scope of the Sino-Indian boundary." Ch'en Yi's statement on September 29, 1965, in *Vice-Premier Ch'en Yi Answers Questions*, Peking: Foreign Languages Press, 1966, p. 1.

[57] This may help explain the comradely quality of such statements as "Pakistan and China will continue to be friends even after you get Kashmir and we take Taiwan." Quoted in *India, 1965*, a reference annual (Delhi, 1965), p. 480, or President Ayub's wry characterization of his foreign policy as rather like walking a "triangular tightrope." *Friends Not Masters*, p. 119.

The Tashkent Conference offered the Soviet Union an opportunity to play a greater role in Sino-Pakistan relations than it had in the past, in part by making assistance available to Pakistan to pre-empt further Chinese influence. This has provoked even greater amounts of Chinese support for Pakistan. On balance, it seems clear that China's position in Pakistan is very much the creature of President Ayub Khan's policy; it is not a "natural" reflection of Chinese capacities. It is, therefore, an external factor keyed to Pakistan's needs and policies rather than to China's South Asian capacities as an independent power in regional politics. As such, Chinese policy suffers great constraints in affecting the Indian security position in the absence of Pakistan's initiatives.

The Range of China's Capacities
in Southern Asia

The region in which China has the greatest capacity for decisive, low-risk action is in the Himalayan states. China occupies contiguous high ground; its forces are acclimatized and familiar with the terrain; India's legal position is weak under the "protectorate" arrangement and local political factions are split on issues involving Delhi's control. Sikkim's position is crucial to the support of Bhutan; Bhutan would be difficult to defend against any form of irregular warfare organized by the Chinese. If Sikkim were lost to India, the northern defense system would be greatly weakened and a credible Indian effort in the eastern Himalayan area would be even more difficult to sustain.[58]

Following the lead of Nepal, the leaders of Sikkim and Bhutan have begun demanding revisions of the treaties linking them to India. On February 8, 1966, the Chogyal of Sikkim called for treaty revision while noting that "We fully appreciate India's vital interest in Sikkim. The security of the Indian border and the defense of Sikkim are essential."[59] Movements for Sikkimese autonomy are interesting because the statements followed by only two months a border skirmish in which six Indian solders were killed and two captured on the Sikkim-Tibet frontier, and because the annual subsidy from India to Sikkim is almost $4 million. The border skirmishes of September, 1967, seem representative of a persistent pressure by China in Sikkim.

[58] See Brigadier D. Som Dutt, "The Defense of India's Northern Frontier," London, Adelphi Paper 25 (November, 1965). The Chinese have made it plain that they consider Sikkim an independent unit regardless of Indian statements that it is a protectorate. See Ch'en Yi's statement of September 29, 1965, p. 1.

[59] Quoted in *Hindustan Times*, February 8, 1966.

The Indian position in Bhutan is even more complex because the state is larger, more isolated, and more vulnerable. The king of Bhutan paid a "state visit" to New Delhi in April, 1966, the press noting that the visit was

> of special significance because only recently he assumed direct responsibility of running the administration of his kingdom . . . following a series of unhappy incidents in which the dynamic Prime Minister of Bhutan, Mr. Jigme Dorji, was assassinated.[60]

On the final day of the visit, the king raised the question of Bhutan's eventual membership in the United Nations,[61] and it was announced that India's subsidy to Bhutan was $6.28 million in 1966.

These reports might have been ignored as part of the bargaining process by which the principalities attempt to increase their benefits by asserting their autonomy in foreign policy but for a steady Chinese concern in the outcome of their factional politics. On October 11, 1966, Peking radio reported that Indian troops had begun to enter Bhutan to suppress its demands for independence while India charged that Chinese troops were massing on Bhutan's frontiers.[62] From "somewhere in NEFA" Prime Minister Indira Gandhi announced that India was pledged to the defense of Bhutan if it was attacked. These verbal skirmishes testify to an exposed Indian position in important zones of its frontier buffers which presumably China could contest if and when it would serve Peking's interests.

In Nepal, King Mahendra has proven adroit in maintaining his independence, suppressing his local rivals, and winning increased latitude for policy in the last ten years. The Indian government has been unable to meet the Nepalese demands for equipment and assistance and both the United States and the Soviet Union have played a major part in the confused foreign assistance programs. The Chinese have signed a border protocol with Nepal and their position toward the kingdom seems to be analogous to that toward Burma. So long as Nepal is neutral,

[60] *Hindustan Times,* April 27 and May 1, 1966.

[61] Mr. M. J. Desai's comments on the Bhutan-Indian relationship are most valuable. He characterizes Indian policy toward Bhutan as permissive of, indeed championing, Bhutanese membership in the United Nations. It would appear from the public record that this policy was articulated reluctantly in 1965.

[62] Most observers see the conflict arising from the domestic rivalries between the king and a displaced prime minister, Lhendup Dorji, exiled in Nepal, whose sister has traveled to London, Kathmandu, Dacca, and Peking.

weak and disorganized, China may be willing to remember the Bandung spirit. Nonetheless, it uses its assistance to strengthen its strategic position in the Sino-Nepalese region. Nepal's contemporary position is not unlike that of Tibet in the inter-war period, a buffer state in which all parties are *engagé* but in which goals are not decisive and are hence unlikely to be forced. In the unlikely event that India (and its allies) should be excluded from Nepal and be forced to accept pro-Chinese factions in Sikkim and Bhutan, India's conventional defense posture would be greatly compromised.

If China's low risk options are confined to direct action in the Himalayan states in support of indigenous factions favorable to Peking, if Sino-Pakistan relations are in the main dictated by Rawalpindi subject to immense restrictions from Washington, and if China's conventional military capabilities in southern Asia are weak compared to growing Indian strength,[63] only two independent Chinese strategies would seem to hold promise in forcing developments in South Asia: nuclear "blackmail" diplomacy, and guerrilla warfare in aid of radicals in the Communist Party of India.[64]

The question of nuclear weapons strategy in Sino-Indian affairs has never been mooted by Peking. The Chinese posture on the Indian frontier is one of a satisfied power; it controls the Aksai Chin salient and almost all of the strategic positions that were in contest. Chinese claims and actions in Sikkim, Bhutan, and Nepal have been carefully stated by Peking as being independent of India. Even the Sino-Pakistan and Sino-Burmese boundary agreements were circumspect in their statements relating to the Indian frontier. It is difficult to imagine precisely what goals short of conquest of the subcontinent the Chinese might seek to serve by a nuclear threat against India.

Moreover, India is if anything over-insured on the possibility of a Chinese nuclear threat. Both of the superpowers are semi-allied with India; both have made a major investment in India's military and economic development and both are concerned about China's growing nuclear might. No single act would carry more disabilities to China than an explicit nuclear threat; it would offer the United States and the Soviet Union ample "peacekeeping" legitimacy for a pre-emptive destruction of the Sinkiang Chinese nuclear establishment at very little risk for either nation, all in the name of protecting the non-nuclear

[63] As is argued in Armbruster's paper, this volume, chapter 7.

[64] An option that seems increasingly possible to the Chinese. See "Spring Thunder Over India," *Peking Review,* July 14, 1967, pp. 22–26.

world. One Indian proposed a "division of labor in nuclear deterrence" which is based on the assumption "that the West, including Russia, provides strategic, long-range cover which it alone can do, and we provide tactical, short-range capability which we can and must have to match similar capability on the Chinese side."[65] This choice, besides having dire consequences on the restriction of nuclear proliferation,[66] would present extremely difficult problems to India. Would "tactical" nuclear weapons supported by a "strategic" nuclear guarantee embolden the large conventional army of India to undertake a revision of present frontiers? The range of similar questions is apparent.

The second Chinese strategy for influence in India would imply an active policy to capture and radicalize the Communist Party of India. The Chinese press has noted the factional disputes within that party and the last major doctrinal statement seems to have been "A Mirror for Revisionists," March, 1963, which is a polemical denunciation of pro-Moscow S. A. Dange. Most students of the Communist Party of India would not believe that the highly decentralized and small left wing of the Indian Communist Party had the potential to become a major threat to the government of India in pursuit of "Chinese" goals, although tribal insurrections and urban despair in economic distress might provide new opportunities. In short, China suffers under great constraints should it seek to produce a major revision of the strategic environment in southern Asia.

[65] Raj Krishna, "India and the Bomb," *India Quarterly*, 21, no. 2 (April–June, 1965): 127. This argument, of course, might be likened to buying the trigger on someone else's gun and would not be unfamiliar to General Pierre Gallois.

[66] India's national security policy and the problem of the nuclear option is an exceptionally broad and complex subject; the dialogue on choices is equally comprehensive. It ought not to be forgotten that India has played an important role in the international dialogue on atomic energy. It was the *first* non-nuclear state to sign the test ban treaty in 1963; its 1962–63 predicament prompted the first hard discussions of a "nuclear shield" and it moved the 1965 United Nations General Assembly resolution keyed on the "mutual obligations" of nuclear and non-nuclear powers. In October, 1966, Lord Chalfont, British Minister for Disarmament, went to New Delhi to explore India's willingness to accept a United States–USSR joint guarantee in exchange for support of a "horizontal" non-proliferation treaty. The credibility of such a guarantee lies at the heart of the problem. An index to the intensity of the Indian debate can be judged from the fact that since the Chinese nuclear explosion of 1964, at least 10 books and 108 articles have been published in English on the subject.

Optimum Chinese Policies toward
South Asia

Lacking the independent capacity to produce favorable results, Chinese policy toward South Asia has as a principal goal keeping the region and its leading state, India, weak. China can serve this interest either by exploiting divisiveness within the region, and hence encouraging the diversion of resources from the Chinese challenge, or by taxing the region by increasing the cost of competition with China through the device of keeping constant pressure on would-be rivals.[67] A third tactic to keep the area weak is to develop friends in it, apparently the strategy in Pakistan, perhaps Nepal and perhaps Ceylon.

India is not a latent ally of China because of its de facto alliances with the USSR and the United States, its regional posture of strength in Asia, and the bad blood of the frontier struggles. It seems inconceivable that any Indian government would be willing to forego the benefits of double alignment with the superpowers, and China is therefore forced to consider India a rival so long as the superpowers are its rival. It must attempt therefore to isolate India, to encourage national disunity to weaken its government, but not to allow the Indian government to commit its patrons to a war against China. The confrontation must not be direct because the risks are too high.[68]

Until China's nuclear deterrent force attains credibility in Moscow and Washington and probably thereafter, Peking's diplomatic alternatives in Southern Asia will be defined, in the main, by regional rivalries. In both the Himalayan region and between India and Pakistan there are opportunities for profitable Chinese diplomacy. A weak India presents few problems to China, it poses no threat and policies weakening it are consonant with the general aim of establishing good relations with the smaller states of South Asia. For the foreseeable future, therefore, China's diplomacy in southern Asia will lay special stress on the role of Pakistan and the Himalayan states, and will continue, indirectly, to press its advantage against India.

[67] This may be the rationale of both the Himalayan border state struggles and China's goading on nuclear weapons development, the latter discussed in this light by Morton Halperin, China and Nuclear Proliferation (Chicago: Center for Policy Study, 1966), pp. 39–41.

[68] Adequate indication of China's conservatism can be found in The Sino-Indian Boundary Question 2 (Peking: Foreign Languages Press, 1965), which summarizes Chinese statements on the subject, 1963–64.

Comments by Michael Brecher

A regional framework for the analysis of China's foreign policy—or the policy of any other Asian state—is rarely found in the literature on Asian studies and International Relations. Professor Wilcox is to be commended for adopting this macro approach. There are some real insights into specific aspects of this region's international politics; for example, the observation that Kashmir is so intractable because it is really part of an unresolved civil war, with only the appearance of an international dispute, and the penetrating comment on the root of India's security problem—it inherited the principal responsibility and the problems of frontier defense, without the industrial strength, secure flanks, weak neighbors, and control positions developed by the British *Raj*. There are also controversial interpretations and speculations which are bold if not always accurate. Some are specific in content, while others flow from the general construct of the paper. The latter is more important and may be treated first.

The stated aim of Professor Wilcox's paper is to relate aspects of what he calls "the regional subsystem" to the "world powers" and, within that context, to analyze China's diplomatic opportunities, capacities, and constraints. His method, however, is conventional and compartmentalized; almost half of the paper takes the form of a unilinear survey of the attitudes and policies of the three extra-area actors, the United States, the USSR, and China, towards India and Pakistan. What is missing, and what would have conformed to the stated aim, as well as being challenging and novel, is a three-stage construct: the subordinate system of South Asia, its structural and textural features in 1948, and the changes that occurred in these salient characteristics at certain nodal points in time; a parallel analysis of the dominant system of global politics, focused on inter-bloc relations since 1948; and, most important, the linkages between the two systems. These are revealed not only in the policies of the three outside actors towards South Asia but also in three other dimensions of analysis: the relationship between those policies and the broader objectives of the United States, the Soviet Union, and China within the dominant system; the reverse flow of Indian and Pakistani policies towards those states, and their links to Indian and Pakistani general policies and to patterns of conflict and accommodation among those key actors. Thus, if periodization is undertaken, it should involve a dual flow of policy between the dominant and subordinate systems, noting the turning points. Unless one uses a framework of the two systems and their interaction—the declared aim of Professor Wilcox—a major dimension is lost and errors will occur.

Some of these may be noted briefly. There is an exaggerated stress on the place of Pakistan in India's foreign policy. It is true, as Wilcox suggests, that Pakistan has been dominated by a security complex vis-à-vis India and by a parochial or sub-continental focus for policy. But this is not true of India, certainly not in the Nehru era. India *assumed* her hegemony in the sub-continent and reacted against challenges such as American arms aid to Pakistan from 1953 onwards—but India, many think unwisely, devoted the bulk of her energies to the dominant system, not to her principal neighbor. Similarly, it is incorrect to ascribe to India preoccupation with the region of South Asia; on the contrary the region or subordinate system was utterly neglected; there is abundant evidence of this indifference, which need not be detailed here. Nor is it correct, in my judgment, to interpret India's China policy as aiming at parity with China in Asia. What we are offered in Wilcox's paper is a rationalizing reconstruction by an able student of what India's policy *should* have been; the tragedy is that India's China policy for a decade was dictated by ideological rather than strategic considerations; here too the evidence would take us too far from our principal concern. In this connection, one would have welcomed some reference to the images or perceptions of China held by India's decision-makers; it would have cast much light on this point. There is only a bare mention of elite images—and that regarding Soviet attitudes toward South Asia. Another *lacuna*, due to the absence of systemic analysis, is the failure to explain China's South Asia policy as a function, in part, of her goals in the dominant system, with respect to the inter-bloc rivalry that shaped the system until recently and the struggle for leadership within the Communist bloc. In the same vein, American and Soviet policies in South Asia are not related to their general strategies and goals.

One other illustration of the value of a two-system framework may be mentioned. To say that the Soviet Union was constant in her support of India during the 1965 War seems a misreading of events; rather, the Soviets changed sharply, though quietly, to the position of "broker" and mediator, both in the discussions leading to the September 20 resolution and at Tashkent; this represented a real break in Moscow's posture in South Asia. Moreover, Wilcox's reading of the Tashkent episode seems very doubtful—the thesis that the Soviets offered their good offices but did not want or expect the Pakistanis to accept. On the contrary, this was a conscious Soviet effort to disengage from an unqualified pro-India policy during the previous decade. And the reason is to be found in the profound changes in the dominant system, still the primary focus for the Soviets: the increasingly intense Sino-Soviet conflict and the moves toward a Soviet-American *détente* made stability in the subcontinent a Soviet, as well as an American, foreign policy aim; secondly, Moscow was keen on weaning Pakistan from its China flirtation. In short, Soviet interests within the dominant system dictated a shift from a pro-India stance to equal friendship with India and Pakistan—to the extent the Pakistanis would permit. It is only through an integrated analysis of interests and interaction within each system and between them that the policies of the three outside actors in South Asia can be illuminated. Wilcox himself alludes to this in a passing reference. Moreover, he offers a very good analysis of Soviet-American shared goals in South Asia—economic viability, strategic stability, and nuclear nonproliferation; a pity that he does not link this to changing Soviet policy from 1964 to 1966, culminating in Tashkent.

Professor Wilcox has traversed a very substantial terrain, the South Asia region, and a period of almost twenty years. Inevitably, perhaps, he has made some sweeping statements. Some of these are thoughtful and persuasive, others less so. Given the scope and aim of his paper, and the limited space, this manner of presentation is justified. At the same time, some of his observations and interpretations require comment. Primarily, those relating to China's policy will be presented.

To suggest that Pakistan created a "garrison state" in the early 1950's is to misuse Lasswell's concept. The Pakistani polity was so disintegrative and the society was so fractured that such an ordered system of authority was impossible. The term is applicable only in the sense of a very high proportion of the budget allocated to defense. It is not only Pakistan that has to look outside the subcontinent for her security; India is in the same position; and it is precisely that power weakness which enabled the superpowers and China to penetrate the subordinate system of South Asia.

India should not be grouped with Burma as eager for a formal general frontier settlement. On the contrary, Sir Girja Bajpai, then Secretary-General for External Affairs, and others in Delhi pressed for a settlement as part of the 1954 treaty over Tibet, but their plea and advice were rejected by the Government of India. India merely assumed that the frontiers had been settled.

To assert that China's policy toward India has been "consistently competitive" seems to me incorrect on two counts: as Wilcox himself indicates in a footnote quotation, China always thought of herself as superior to India, and one doesn't compete with an inferior; secondly, China's policy toward India has not been static since 1949; there have been well-delineated stages. The notion that India, Japan, and Indonesia are China's principal rivals for Asian leadership seems fanciful and wishful thinking. In any event, it is not part of China's elite perception of their external environment and therefore cannot be a guide to China's policy toward India.

The nub of the paper is contained in the concluding sections on China's regional constraints and capacities in South Asia. Wilcox sets out a provocative thesis that China's position in Pakistan, really in Indo-Pakistani relations, is dependent on Ayub's policy, that it is not a reflection of China's natural capabilities, and that China therefore suffers great constraints in affecting India's security. This interpretation is sound and important, with multiple policy implications—which are regrettably not explored. Wilcox also notes that China's greatest capability in South Asia is in the Himalayan border states, but here too he is unfortunately brief, without any discussion of China's techniques of penetration of these weak polities.

Looking to the future, Wilcox anticipates the continuation of recent and current Chinese policy in South Asia: stress on friendly ties with Pakistan, efforts to dislodge the Himalayan border states from India's control, and pressure on India, weakening her government, causing disunity, and isolating her—but without a direct military confrontation, lest the superpowers come to her assistance. This is certainly plausible, but it would have enhanced the paper's value to add some thoughts on prospects for success and some discussion about the techniques used by China in penetrating India's political system and the Hill States.

Throughout the paper there is an implicit assumption, namely that of a stable Chinese capability to project her influence and interests in South Asia, an unchanging military, political, diplomatic, technological, and communications capability to exploit the diplomatic opportunities. Yet the current convulsion suggests that, even if the objective opportunities postulated by Professor Wilcox are valid, the capability of Peking to utilize them may be severely curtailed. The author cannot have fully anticipated this in his analysis, but it does raise some basic questions about China and South Asia. It may well be that the Great Proletarian Cultural Revolution will give rise to speculation and analysis about the balance of forces in the Himalayan borderland, with suggestions about India's diplomatic opportunities in the Aksai Chin and NEFA. Certainly no analysis of future Chinese relations with South Asia can ignore the potentially profound effect of China's internal schism on China's nuclear capability, on her pace of industrialization and the development of her conventional military power, on China's image in the rimland of Asia, and on her ability to act on the periphery of her Central Asian borderlands.

Professor Wilcox set an admirable goal in his paper, an exploration of the links between two systems of state interaction and their consequences for China's opportunities in South Asia. His surveys of the policies of three major extra-area powers are succinct and highly informative, though the historical background left him little room to elaborate a few provocative hypotheses. Leaving the Great Proletarian Cultural Revoluton aside, his prediction of future Chinese behavior and opportunities was convincing. But can those concerned with this problem in 1967 ignore the impact of political trauma within China on her foreign policy objectives and capabilities?

Professor Wilcox seems to imply that an analysis of the historical flow enables one to project probable future behavior in response to opportunities. There is a large element of historical continuity in the external behavior of states. Yet phenomena of the order of magnitude of the current struggle for control of the Chinese revolution may delay and significantly alter both opportunities and prospects. There was, it seems to me, too much historical data and not enough examination in depth of the current opportunity-capability nexus between China and South Asia. But more important was the theoretical *lacuna,* the failure to achieve the goal set out at the beginning of this paper. Yet Professor Wilcox has brought to bear his very considerable talents and knowledge to provoke discussion and comment; in this he has performed an important service.

Comments by M. J. Desai

When one looks at South Asia from a distance, one naturally misses quite a few of the varying shades and sub-shades. If one is dealing with the global strategy of the United States in Asia in the context of China and other powers operating in the area, one may assume that it is the broad picture that counts. But this broad picture is not easy to paint. The shades and sub-shades which one misses sometimes have special relevance to the broad picture. I will mention a few of these sub-shades insofar as they concern China's policy, not by way of criticism but to make the broad picture a little fuller:

1. Mr. Wilcox writes: "India's role in the various Tibetan rebellions has not been documented but was probably important. . . ." This is not only factually incorrect but, if I may say so, unnecessarily anti-Indian because both Burma and India as well as China know very well where the support came from. Had India really been taking an active interest in the fashion indicated, either in Tibet or in Nepal, the results in both places would have been different. This is where the conflict between philosophy and *realpolitik* was definitely resolved in favor of philosophy despite odd local officials or minority political groups airing views to the contrary. There was a certain humanism and predilection for democratic patterns in the thinking of the government of India which led to general statements of interest or sympathy, but there was no support for any faction either in Tibet or Nepal. If anything, both in Nepal and Tibet, the government of India bent over backward to keep a clear position, much to the disgust of Nepali Congress political refugees in India and the Dalai Lama and his advisers. As a matter of fact, it was other governments' representatives who were taking an interest, and it was the unpleasant role of the representatives of the government of India to restrain them. Ever since 1947, Western powers on the one hand and the USSR and China on the other have shown fairly intense interest in this area, particularly in Nepal. The foreign offices concerned know what developments occurred.

437

2. It is not for me as an Indian to contest Wilcox's statement: "The Indians have a historic interest [in Southeast Asia] but have lacked the independent national capacity to support regional goals." This would, however, be factually correct if "in the context of Big Power politics in the area" were added. The history of developments from 1947 up to date will support this addition. Professor Wilcox says as much elsewhere in his paper but gives it a different relevance.

3. Professor Wilcox asserts that the Sino-Burmese and Sino-Nepalese boundary settlements were made by China to isolate India. But India had not only informed both to go ahead and to get the best settlements they could, but had assisted them with expert advice based on old treaties, maps, etc. In the case of Burma, Nehru even wrote to Chou En-lai asking the latter to deal with the question in a generous spirit. Perhaps this annoyed China, but it benefited India's smaller neighbors.

4. The reference to Pakistan's offer to conclude a joint defense alliance with India and India's rejection is too brief. If Pakistan's offer had been made in good faith, the first step in her move would have been the end of mutual hostility without conditions, and she would have approached India through the normal diplomatic channel. But she did neither. Public offer of an alliance on condition of surrender in a given dispute can hardly be considered genuine. The offer was made for only one purpose, i.e., to prepare the ground for switching from a policy of exclusive reliance on American support to a policy of actively cultivating the friendship of the Soviet Union and China. By 1959, Chinese manipulations had gone very far. From March, 1956 to 1959, Keng Piao was the Chinese ambassador in Pakistan, and in 1960 he became the vice-minister for Asian Department in the Ministry of Foreign Affairs at Peking. A senior official of this stature was not sent to Pakistan for nothing. In September, 1960, Pakistan decided to reach a boundary settlement with China on the terms announced nearly three years later for the Pakistan-Kashmir China boundary. Professor Wilcox himself gives some instances of Pakistan-China relationships from 1956 onward.

5. Professor Wilcox's comments on the Tashkent Agreement require a little elaboration. President Ayub Khan visited Washington before Tashkent and after the end of the three-week Indo-Pakistan War. If, as alleged, Ayub threatened to leave Tashkent without any agreement, this could have been only due to India's hard attitude. In this context, Russian intercession with the late Indian Prime Minister Shastri must be mentioned. It was the Washington discussions of Ayub

that made the Tashkent Agreement possible, and the Russians knew what they were doing and acted with Washington's blessings.

6. According to Mr. Wilcox, "the Soviets have told Indian officials that they mobilized on the Sinkiang frontier to save India a border war in 1959 after the Tibetan insurrection." If this was mentioned privately to an Indian diplomat, it must have been after 1964. In any case, it has been known that there were internal troubles in Sinkiang in 1959. Whether the statement was made or whether Russia did mobilize on the Sinkiang border is not quite relevant in the Indo-Soviet context, as such Soviet precaution would be natural in the light of troubles in the Sinkiang border region.

7. The references to India's implicit strategy, "division of labor in nuclear deterrence," and the reference to Raj Krishna's article, "India and the Bomb," do not, I hope, pertain to India's strategy. These are Raj Krishna's personal views, not shared either by any major group or by the government of India. If Indian strategy as such is referred to, it has to be ascertained from governmental pronouncements.

Professor Wilcox states: "What undercut Indian policy was the conflicting role of the great powers and China and their policies in South Asia." While I will refrain from commenting on the alleged *realpolitik* character of Indian policy, I would say that a lot of South Asia's problems of today arise from manipulations of historical hangovers or differences inherent in traditional societies by outside powers—Great Britain, the United States, the USSR, and China. This has been a fact of history since 1945 and more so since 1949 when the Communists took over at Peking. Neither the Americans nor the Russians nor the Chinese considered the transfer of power by the British in South Asia of any consequence in global policies until 1952. That is why the Russians showed interest in the Kashmir problem in the U.N. for the first time in January, 1952, four years after the problem came to the U.N. That is why the United States from 1952 onward began to take an interest in Pakistan in the context of its global containment policies. Similarly, the Soviet interest in India, beginning with the Steel Project in 1955 and the commitment of 130 million dollars, aroused Chinese suspicion and Chinese interest in Pakistan, which grew with Khrushchev's policies and actions such as: the dismissal of Zhukov in October, 1957; Khrushchev's five-power summit proposal during the Lebanese crisis on July 19, 1958, excluding China but including India; Khrushchev's Camp David meeting with Eisenhower and attempts at rapprochement, September, 1959; and the mid-1961 Indo-Soviet Agreement for the manufacture of MiG 21's in India. It was these developments rather than the Tibet revolt of

1959 and Dalai Lama's flight to India which led inevitably to the Sino-Indian crisis of 1962, simultaneously with the Cuban crisis, the border dispute being just a handy excuse. Subsequent developments in 1963 and 1964, the Indo-Pakistan clash of 1965 and the Chinese ultimatum, the Tashkent Agreement, and the position today illustrate the significance of global power policies in the area. One could illustrate this with reference to Nepal, Afghanistan, even Burma and Ceylon.

The important thing when making an assessment of China's diplomatic initiatives in the area is to appraise the results of similar initiatives by other global powers in the area in the past and to make certain, at least for the future, that none of the other global powers, consciously or unconsciously, allows themselves to be manipulated into positions which would serve China's interests in the area. The Chinese have an infinite capacity for manipulating their friends as well as their enemies to their advantage. This is a most vital matter requiring constant and continuous attention.

A. M. Halpern

15

China and Japan

Any analysis of Communist China's foreign policy made at the close of the year 1966 is of necessity conducted in the shadows; specifically, in the shadow of the Great Proletarian Cultural Revolution in China, with its attendant political turmoil and uncertainty, and in the equally dense shadow of the war in Vietnam. Both situations forced the Chinese leaders (at least that faction of them which has been in control of their communications) to maintain in public certain rigid postures to which not all of them were genuinely committed in their private thinking. Foreign policy issues, it seems clear, were not the major source and doubtless not the directly precipitating cause of the tensions which have developed in relations within the Chinese elite. Nevertheless, differences on many aspects of foreign policy obviously existed and were utilized in the domestic political struggle. Under these circumstances it must be taken for granted that any declaration on a foreign policy issue had a polemical function in internal politics besides its other purposes. Such declarations would have constituted demands for universal assent to propositions which were in fact highly controversial.

Throughout 1966 the regime insisted that there was a great new revolutionary upsurge among the oppressed nations and that this movement was capable of sapping the foundations of imperialism. Concurrently, official Chinese commentary continued to emphasize the validity of Mao's description of the United States as a "paper tiger." The "paper tiger" theme was more prominent after May 1 and especially in the period following the eleventh plenary session of the Central Committee of the Chinese Communist Party (CCP), which took place in August. In the autumn months all Third World guests in China were offered the opportunity to pay tribute to the thought of Mao Tse-tung in most extravagant terms as the acme of Marxism-Leninism in the modern age, as the "red sun in the hearts of the world's peoples," and as pointing out the path that revolutionists all over the world should follow. The majority of such visitors accepted the opportunity, though a significant few declined it. The domestic political reason for procuring such statements seems clear. They provided refutation of the criticism that the regime's foreign policy had led to China's being isolated and proof of a sort that it still had "friends all over the world." Similar purposes no doubt underlay the emphasis given to the "paper tiger" and other themes.

To characterize all such expressions as rhetoric solves no problems. Certainly they are heavily loaded with rhetoric, and one can recognize the tactical necessities which doubtless account for much of the exaggeration and overstatement they contain. Still, they are issued with every sign that much attention has been given to their timing, and this alone indicates that they are a form of political currency. Many of the themes stressed during 1966 were not new but were repetitions of points frequently made in the past. The Mao-Lin faction, then, was not so much engaged in reappraising the world situation as in insisting that its past analysis was still basically valid.

Communist China's problem with the United States, whether one analyzes it in terms of broad principles or of immediate tactics, is defined by the continued opposition of the power interests of the two countries in almost all parts of the globe and by an absolutely minimum level of direct contacts. Whatever results the cultural revolution may bring, it is likely that the Chinese will want to see some changes in the power relationship—whether from their side, the United States side, or both sides simultaneously—before they are willing to address themselves to increasing direct contacts. The United States remains for the People's Republic of China (PRC) the great ultimate enemy as well as a most serious menace in the short term. In their dealings with third countries, the Chinese of necessity take account of the relations those countries maintain with the United States. This factor does not dominate all others in the Chinese approach to such countries, but it is always present.

The major unknown factor, which could influence China's approach to all countries, including the United States, is the overall final impact on China of the Great Proletarian Cultural Revolution. One possibility for the future is that a number of new top-echelon leadership figures will emerge and that they will recognize the need for a domestic program of economic and political reconstruction. They will then need to buy time, and if this need leads them to put a high value on a stable, peaceful international environment, their approach to the United States and to other countries would necessarily change.

A change in the Chinese perspective such as is suggested here would not necessarily lead to a high priority being placed on rapprochement with the United States, but it would bring about a difference in the quality of Sino-American relations. There would then be some reflex effect on the relations between the PRC and prudent third parties to whom their own relations with the United States are of great importance. Japan is obviously one such prudent third party.

The pattern of Sino-Japanese relations shows a considerable contrast with the pattern of Sino-American relations, despite the virtual partnership which exists between Japan and the United States. While there are differences in power interests between Japan and China, there are no critical issues or confrontations which require immediate decisions. In the field of direct relations, the Chinese over the past five years have actively promoted contacts with a variety of elements of the Japanese body politic. The latter, in turn, have shown a distinct interest in dealing with China on several levels, an interest which produces Japanese concern with and occasional pressures on Japan's overall China policy as well as attention to trends in United States policy toward China.

The growth of Sino-Japanese trade since late 1962 has been conspicuous. It was especially rapid in 1964 and 1965 and showed signs of continuing to grow through the first half of 1966. Total trade volume rose from $137 million in 1963 to $310 million in 1964 and $470 million in 1965.[1] In 1965 the PRC became Japan's fifth largest trade partner,[2] and Sino-Japanese trade outgrew Japan's trade with the USSR. Sino-Japanese trade in that year, however, accounted for only 2.8 percent of Japan's total world trade. Trade figures for January–May 1966 were $266 million total, and at midyear it was expected that the annual volume would exceed $650 million.[3] Prospects for reaching this level were somewhat affected in the second half of the year by the impact of the Cultural Revolution on the efficiency of the personnel of Chinese trading organizations, port operation, etc., but the basic picture was not altered. The total volume for the year worked out to approximately $625 million, enough to exceed the total volume of Sino-Soviet trade and to establish Japan as the PRC's largest single trading partner.

[1] These figures, based on customs clearance statistics, are those usually cited in the Japanese press. Until 1965, Japanese imports normally exceeded exports, but in 1965 Japan's exports to mainland China were $245 million against $225 million in imports.

[2] After the United States, Australia, Canada, and the Philippines.

[3] The January–May totals included $138 million in Japanese exports to $128 million in imports, and the PRC became Japan's second biggest export market for the period. Japan's trade with Southeast Asia as a region still exceeds by a good deal its trade with mainland China.

The expansion of Sino-Japanese trade occurred as part of the general substitution by the PRC of non-Communist countries for Soviet bloc countries as major trading partners. Foodstuffs (rice, soybeans, seafood, etc.) account for some two-thirds of PRC sales to Japan. The market for these is not infinitely expandable, and some Japanese businessmen feel that such purchases are in part a gesture of accommodation. Major growth in imports from China is to some degree dependent on the availability of coking coal and iron ore of suitable quality and price and in reliable amounts. Japan's capacity to export is limited partly by Western European competition, joined to the Chinese desire to avoid again becoming dependent on a single supplier, and to the restrictions placed by the Japanese government on the export of industrial plants under deferred-payment agreements. Still, mainland China supplies not only a sizable market for Japanese exports but one which at times can rescue enterprises which would otherwise be in difficulty. Fertilizer is one such industry, and machinery and machine tools are potentially another.

The political condition for the growth in Sino-Japanese trade was a decision by the Chinese in 1960–61 to accept the realities of the distribution of power in Japan by, for example, tacitly consenting to tolerate the Japanese government's established principle of "separating economics from politics." Rapid growth of trade followed the Liao-Takasaki agreement of 1962, which made it feasible for major Japanese firms to enter the China trade actively without creating political complications and more or less secure against the risk of arbitrary, politically motivated reprisals by the Chinese. The agreement also opened the way for comparatively large-scale transactions. Up to the end of 1964, under the Ikeda premiership, the Japanese government's attitude toward the PRC was "forward-looking," tending to go as far as circumstances allowed in moving towards normal relations. With the accession of Satô Eisaku to the prime ministership, the Japanese attitude became somewhat sterner. Satô's government has been less willing than Ikeda's to facilitate exports of plants and equipment on a scale that would require semi-official underwriting of deferred-payment agreements, and it has shown a definite disposition to control the exchange of persons in sensitive cases by withholding passports and visas.[4]

4 In 1964, before becoming prime minister, Satô made some gestures which were generally regarded as the equivalent of a promise to be as forward-looking as Ikeda. The Chinese now justify their open dislike of him by saying he has proved himself to be untrustworthy. This accusation finds a response among some Japanese, to whom Satô's ways appear mysterious.

The volume of Sino-Japanese trade has not been seriously affected by the Satô stance, but there has been a certain political reaction on the part of the PRC. The Japanese establishment has always hoped that trade with China would be handled through a single channel, expecting to benefit by limiting competition. The Chinese have been able to maintain several Japanese channels in existence by making choices on particular deals between different Japanese organizations. Several such organizations exist, differing in part in the size of their constituent companies and in part in their members' prior experience with and attachment to trade with China. The volume of L T trade[5] has increased year by year, but the proportion of China trade handled through the L-T channel declined from some 47 percent in 1963 to 37 percent in 1964 and 39 percent in 1965.[6] The L-T memorandum also provided for annual negotiations to take place alternately in Peking and Tokyo, and this practice was followed until 1966. In that year the Chinese refused to send representatives to Tokyo for a scheduled meeting in midsummer, thus forcing the L-T organization to send its representatives to Peking in November. These representatives were handled quite coldly, and the negotiations had only moderate success. Throughout the year, the Chinese showed an intention of favoring "friendly firms," who were willing to give verbal endorsement to the principles, some of them political,[7] which the Chinese would like to see govern their trade relations with Japan.

The Chinese choice of trading channels had only a negligible effect on total trade volume. It was taken in Japan as an expression of displeasure with Satô and, to a degree, as an effort to bring pressure on

[5] So called because it is conducted according to the terms of the L[iao]-T[akasaki] memorandum of 1962, through an organization formed for that purpose.

[6] Percentages of Japanese exports to and imports from China through the L-T channel for these years were (in round figures):

	1963	1964	1965
Exports.........	59	45	37
Imports.........	37	29	41

Source: *Nihon Keizai*, Sept. 14, 1966.

[7] Especially important is agreement to the inseparability of trade and politics. See, e.g., minutes of talks between the China Council for Promoting International Trade and the delegation of the Japanese International Trade Promotion Association, in *Kwang-ming jih-pao*, September 19, 1966, text in *Survey of China Mainland Press* (hereafter cited as *SCMP*), no. 3798.

him from within Japanese conservative ranks. On the other hand the
Chinese at the end of the year took real punitive action against the
Japan-China Trade Promotion Association (JCTPA). This organization speaks for a large number of friendly firms, but some of its leading
officials are affiliated with the Japan Communist Party (JCP). The Chinese decided that because of the hostile attitude of that party the
JCTPA was no longer qualified to guide the development of trade relations.[8]

The JCTPA was replaced by the Japanese International Trade Association, a group which, ironically enough, is heavily engaged in trade
with the Soviet Union and Eastern Europe.

The PRC's motives for maintaining separate trade channels are thus
in part political. According to their analysis of Japanese society, there
are "contradictions" between small and medium enterprises on one side
and large enterprises on the other. By holding out to the small and
medium enterprises the prospect that trade with China is one available
route of escape from domination by the large, the PRC can hope to
create a certain amount of pressure on the political establishment to be
more forward-looking. This, however, points up one characteristic of
the PRC's policy toward Japan over the last five years—that it has
apparently aimed at small payoffs in the short run while deferring the
prospect of large payoffs (e.g., the neutralization of Japan or bringing
Japan into the Chinese orbit) to a rather remote and uncontrollable
future. Up to 1960, the Chinese seemed to place great value on constructing in Japan a united front of forces which might compel the government to change its China policy radically. The support they gave to
the anti-Security Treaty struggle of 1960 seems best explained on the
assumption that the Chinese had a good deal of confidence in the
effectiveness of mass movements in Japanese politics. The anti-treaty
struggle resulted in the overthrow of Prime Minister Kishi, who was a
prime target of Chinese Communist hostility, but produced no change
in the balance of power between political parties in Japan.[9] Almost
immediately thereafter, the PRC moved to rehabilitate trade with
Japan, which they had reduced almost to the vanishing point. Initially
they reopened trade through selected firms designated as "friendly," but

[8] The blow fell especially heavily on three trading firms—Sanshin, Haga, and
Mutsumi—whose transactions had reached an annual value of some $21 mil-
lion, according to *Nihon Keizai*, December 30, 1966.

[9] Kishi was succeeded as Prime Minister by Ikeda Hayato, whose initial
popularity was as spectacularly high as Kishi's had become low.

it was obvious that they would also have to trade with major firms, who could not accept any political conditions, if trade were to reach the composition and volume that the PRC needed.

By 1962 the PRC had apparently concluded that the anti-government united front in Japan could be neither as cohesive nor as powerful as would be necessary to achieve the results the Chinese wanted, and their own circumstances dictated that they take a more pragmatic approach. A *modus operandi* in trade with Japanese conservatives was achieved through unofficial negotiations, in which major roles were played on the Japanese side by Matsumura Kenzô and Takasaki Tatsunosuke and on the Chinese side by Chou En-lai and Liao Ch'eng-chih. The Japanese became satisfied that the PRC genuinely recognized the necessity of dealing with Japanese conservatives and on the whole remain satisfied that subsequent Chinese behavior has been in accord with this recognition.

At the same time, the Chinese committed themselves to a militant JCP in lieu of a broad united front as the primary vehicle for accomplishing their ultimate political objectives in Japan. Within the JCP, power gravitated toward the hands of men who had spent time in China and received training there. The party aligned itself closely, both in ideology and policy, with the Chinese Communist line, especially on all issues related to the Sino-Soviet dispute. Much of the management of exchange of persons between Japan and China came under the control of the JCP. Party membership grew and the Party achieved some gains in representation in the Diet. In terms of real political effectiveness, however, too close an identification with Communist China tended to isolate the JCP from other left-wing forces and made it appear both sectarian and dependent on foreign support.

In February and March 1966, a delegation of the JCP headed by Miyamoto Kenji carried out a visit to China, North Vietnam, and North Korea. The separation of the JCP from its close ties with the Chinese followed this trip. The issues over which the break took place were doubtless several. They evidently included Vietnam policy and the attempted Communist coup in Indonesia in September–October 1965. Miyamoto has stated that the break came over a demand by Mao that the text of a proposed joint communiqué contain a strong condemnation of Soviet revisionism. To Miyamoto this was the last of a long series of attempts at dictation by the Chinese to the JCP. His refusal, which resulted in no communiqué being issued, was partly a reaction to Mao's dictatorial attitude, partly a judgment that Mao's demand was bad politics—though not necessarily bad ideology. The

Japanese press, however, has tended to identify the critical issue as a Chinese demand that the JCP be more militant in its anti-imperialist, anti-American stance, even at the expense of alienating the Japanese public and non-Communist left more than it already had.[10]

One side effect of the Cultural Revolution has been to further the disintegration of the institutions for promoting Sino-Japanese contact which were left over from the earlier period. A series of such institutions, through which recurrent contacts and exchanges of personnel were carried out involving youth, labor unions, academics, participants in the peace movement, women, religionists, etc., still exist, but several of the key organizations have been split by the demands the Chinese made on them. The JCP's stand of independence has proceeded to the point of being, if not anti-Chinese, definitely opposed to the leaders of the Cultural Revolution. The JCP in 1966 prevented its youth organizations from responding to an invitation to send a delegation to visit China, an invitation which in earlier years was always automatically accepted. The JCP's attitude was also responsible for the severe loss of Chinese influence on the Council for the Prohibition of Atomic and Hydrogen Bombs.[11] A few important members of the JCP, who remained faithful to Peking, were expelled from the party and formed a splinter group.

In the field of cultural exchange, the Chinese relied on a civil organization, the Japan-China Friendship Association (JCFA) to assist in two-way exchanges. The membership of this organization comes from many different areas of society and represents many different social and political stands. 1966 was the tenth year of the JCFA's existence. Strains on

[10] P'eng Chen was host to the Miyamoto delegation and disappeared from public view after the delegation's departure. There has been some speculation in the Japanese press that this visit precipitated P'eng Chen's degradation, either because he was not able to persuade the JCP to follow the Chinese line, or more probably, because he was willing to accede to their position. In the conversations between the two parties, however, Liu Shao-ch'i played a more important role than P'eng Chen.

[11] It is instructive to compare the Chinese Communist Party's greetings to the recent Tenth Congress of the JCP with those it had sent to the Ninth Congress. The greetings to the Ninth Congress were the acme of fraternal affection and approbation. Those to the Tenth Congress said, in effect, that the CCP expected every true Marxist-Leninist to do his duty. The message did not carry the authority of its Nelsonian prototype. See *Peking Review*, no. 44 (October 28, 1966).

the relations of the Chinese with this organization developed in June, 1966,[12] after which time, as one Chinese source puts it,

> . . . false friends, who have honey on their lips and murder in their hearts, have pursued an anti-China policy within the Japan-China friendship movement; and they have shamelessly opposed Mao's thought. They have colluded with U.S. imperialism, the Soviet modern revisionists and the Japanese reactionaries. . . .[13]

On September 26, a group of 32 pro-Peking figures issued an "appeal to nationals to promote Japan-China friendship in this period of internal and external crises." Some of the group then proceeded to Peking, where they signed a joint statement with the China-Japan Friendship Association condemning both United States imperialism and "modern revisionism, at the core of which is the Soviet leading clique," and thoroughly endorsing the Cultural Revolution. Of the last, the statement said:

> . . . it is a guarantee for the Chinese people that their revolution will advance along the correct road, it is an inevitable step on the long journey of the revolution, and it is producing very clear results.[14]

The statement was debated at a meeting of the permanent council of the JCFA. On October 25, several members of the council seceded from the association and announced on the next day the formation of a new organization called Headquarters of the Japan-China Friendship Association (Orthodox). Concurrently the Japan-China Trade Promotion Association was dissolved and pro-Peking members of the Japan Congress of Journalists seceded from that organization. The solid pro-Peking front in Japan had thus been reduced to remnants of these organizations, expelled members of the JCP, some leftists in the Japa-

[12] A delegation of the Japan-China Cultural Exchange Association was in China in that month. On July 5, a joint statement on cultural exchange was signed with the Chinese People's Association for Cultural Relations and Friendship with Foreign Countries. The statement seemed innocuous, except for a reference to "intrigues and tricks . . . played by forces which are hostile to Sino-Japanese friendship, persist in the 'two Chinas' plot and obstruct the normalization of Sino-Japanese diplomatic relations." See *SCMP*, no. 3735.

[13] New China News Agency Dispatch, Peking. (Hereafter cited as NCNA, Peking.) December 12, 1966, in *SCMP*, no. 3842.

[14] NCNA, Peking, October 20, 1966, in *SCMP*, no. 3802. The statement appears to have been signed on October 12.

nese Socialist Party, and the Japanese Committee for Afro-Asian Solidarity, which has not wavered.[15] This series of developments was approved by the Chinese, who seem to wish to demand the same radical orthodoxy of their foreign friends as of the Chinese cadres and masses. Clearly the price of success is a definite weakening of the base of support in Japan for the PRC's short-term objectives. To the outside observer, such obviously fruitless gestures, which try to force people to declare themselves on propositions which they cannot accept, are one symptom of the abnormal stresses generated by the political struggle in China.

Since the middle of 1966, the JCP has moved steadily away from its identification with the Chinese line and toward a position of independence in Communist affairs. It has not actively sought to transfer its loyalties to the Soviet side, but it has been able to resume contact with the Soviet party. Restoration of a rudimentary JCP-Soviet dialogue may have contributed to a decision by the Chinese to permit Miyamoto to be attacked by name in wall posters which appeared in Peking in January and February 1967. At the end of February, antagonism between pro- and anti-Peking groups in Tokyo flared up in a series of physical clashes over the use of a building called the Zenrin Kaikan.[16] The Chinese press and radio blew the affair up into a matter of principle, and the Japanese Communist press retorted in kind. It became evident that the Chinese preferred to alienate the mainstream JCP leadership completely rather than relax their demand for absolute loyalty and obedience from their supporters. In July the JCP felt itself forced to recall from Peking its last two official representatives, Sunama Ichiryô (an alternate member of the JCP Presidium) and Konno Junichi (special correspondent of *Akahata*), both of whom had been harassed by Red Guards.

Any issue which involves China produces reactions in Japan's internal politics. The important ones are not necessarily those directly connected with the Cultural Revolution, but are of longer standing. The one safe generalization one can make about Japanese attitudes toward China is that they are heterogeneous. On one end of the spectrum is the attitude of those, including many younger intellectuals, who fail to

[15] See *Peking Review*, nos. 46 and 51 (November 11 and December 16, 1966), and the joint statement of the Chinese and Japanese Committees for Afro-Asian Solidarity, NCNA, Peking, October 9, 1966, in *SCMP*, no. 3800.

[16] Literally, "Good Neighbor Hall." The building, whose ownership is legally obscure, houses student activities and the offices of various organizations which seek to promote friendly relations with China.

be inspired by the political program of the establishment and who regard China as the wave of the future. Whatever disillusionment or embarrassment the Cultural Revolution causes them, many of them react according to their established preconceptions and tend to accept it as a necessary step to preserve the purity of the thought of Mao against revisionist erosion. On the other extreme are those who ridicule the whole thing and find in it renewed reason for being proud of themselves as Japanese and of Japan as a society where such irrationalities do not occur.

Since early 1962, China has been a divisive issue in the Japanese Socialist Party (JSP) because of the efforts the Chinese have made to drive that party in a radical direction. The left wing of the party, which welcomes this influence, tends to justify the Cultural Revolution. The right wing of the party cannot justify it but equally does not wish to be equated with those conservatives who are antagonistic to Communist China. It therefore takes the stand of refraining from making premature judgments and of waiting for the facts to be verified before determining their significance.[17] In the eyes of the Japanese public, the JSP is still regarded as pro-Chinese, and this view evidently damaged—it certainly did not help—the JSP in the lower House election of January, 1967. The left wing of the party, under the leadership of Sasaki Kôzô, continued to be sympathetic to the PRC. In mid-1967 this faction proposed that the party support the position of the pro-Chinese Japan-China Friendship Association (Orthodox). Intra-party controversy again flared, and Sasaki lost the chairmanship of the party in August, 1967, to Katsumata Seiichi of the right wing of the party.

The positions taken by the broad middle range of Japanese interested in the China problem do not derive from or depend on any one incident, even such an obviously convulsive one as the Cultural Revolution. They are related rather to concepts of Japan's place in the world, preferences concerning Japan's overall foreign policy, and increasingly in the past two or three years to the emerging concept of national interests.[18] Within the political and economic establishment, there is a small but powerful group sometimes referred to as the "Taiwan lobby"

[17] See Eda Saburô, "Hope for Peaceful Co-existence between Japan and China," *Sekai*, November, 1966.

[18] This is a novel term in Japanese discussion, and it translates into Japanese only awkwardly. Several attempts have been made recently to define its content, without satisfactory results. It is also difficult to define clearly another phrase, "autonomous foreign policy," which has been advocated almost universally and has been current longer than "national interest."

which tends to see Japan's relations with China in the context of conflict between capitalism and Communism. This group favors close Japanese-American cooperation. Some of its members are concerned about Japan's ocean lifeline and see Communist China as a military threat as well as an undesirable psychological influence on Japanese society. This general view is represented in the Liberal-Democratic Party (LDP) by the Asian Problems Research Group (A-group), whose typical members are sometimes referred to as the "old right." On the opposite extreme in the Liberal-Democratic Party is the Asian-African Research Group (A-A group), whose members are sometimes said to represent the "new right" and which believes in a Sino-Japanese rapprochement.[19]

China policy is a political issue in the Liberal-Democratic Party, but it is not a vote-getting issue among the public. There is thus a considerable segment of the party for which China policy is not an urgent question, but which finds itself involved in controversy because the extreme factions raise the question. In May, 1966, Matsumura Kenzô, the doyen of the A-A group, made a trip to China for consultations with Chinese leaders, primarily about trade matters. On his return he announced that the step-by-step approach to improving Sino-Japanese relations[20] was no longer sufficient, but that a major new step forward toward normalizing relations was needed. He was even prepared, if necessary, to resume a position he had taken in the past and to propose that he and his followers break away from the party on this issue and form a second conservative party.

Matsumura to some extent reflected the growing vested interest in good relations with the mainland which is bound to result from the increase in Sino-Japanese trade. His major purpose, however, was probably to raise an issue around which several elements of the party could be united to counteract the influence which the "old right" was believed to exert on the Prime Minister. In this he had some success. He enlisted the cooperation of Fujiyama Aiichirô, one of the few LDP figures capable of offering himself as an alternative to Satô as party president, and he facilitated the September visit to China (which had been in the planning stage for several months) of the group of younger

[19] The "new right" is less easy to identify than the "old right." The A-A group clearly does not contain all LDP members who belong to the "new right," but it reflects an orientation towards Asia which is one of the things that helps distinguish the "new right" in contrast to the pro-Western orientation of the "old right." It is probably useful to think of "new right" not as referring to specific individuals but to an attitude favoring flexibility and innovation in the LDP's thinking and organization.

[20] Also called the accumulation formula.

LDP members headed by Kosaka Zentarô. Largely on the score of party unity, Matsumura was unable to carry with him his close colleague in party affairs, Miki Takeo.[21] Matsumura could raise the issue of China policy and compel attention to it, but he could not mobilize a large, unified base of support.

Underlying the urge toward a more positive approach to relations with the PRC are some conceptions of China which are rather widespread in conservative circles. One is that the Chinese are reasonable and realistic in dealing with practical problems. This is not a mere preconception, but a point which a number of Japanese feel they can prove by their own experience in dealing with the Chinese. Another is that the Chinese are all nationalists and that productive dealings with them have been possible when they have been approached on this basis by equally nationalistic Japanese. Some who hold this position argue that there is a national character which transcends or overcomes ideology, and that the Chinese character is basically reasonable. The Cultural Revolution, in this view, may interrupt or interfere with the improvement of economic and political relations but will not prevent it forever. Nevertheless, even before the Cultural Revolution, there was a majority view among responsible businessmen that while the Chinese character would eventually override the influence of ideology on policy, that point had not yet been reached.[22] Such people looked forward to the future with real hope, but for the present saw no realistic approach except to "wait and see" when and how the Chinese would change.

Some Japanese of this school see the role of China in broader world-political terms. They tend to see the real threat to world stability in the Soviet Union and to see China as an offset to Soviet influence. To some extent optimism about China's future contribution to Asian stability is a reflex of anti-Soviet feeling. To some extent it rests on the belief that the Chinese will see Asian stability as being in their own interest, if they do not already see it that way. To people who reason this way, the U.S. policy of containment as hitherto practiced seems a historic error. Some such people emphasize, for example, that the Sino-American relationship is free from one great historic source of wars—border conflicts. Lacking that cause of mutual antagonism, the natural relationship of China and the United States ought to be based on the dis-

---

[21] Miki became foreign minister in the cabinet reshuffle of December, 1966. He has advocated a restudy of China policy based on long-range analysis but for the present seems to aim more at achieving flexibility than at any specific new departures.

[22] My impression, at least, is that this was a majority view.

covery and cultivation of common interests. This line of thought leads
to the conclusion that a real basis exists not just for a Sino-American
détente but for a good Sino-American understanding and collaboration,
and that the U.S. would serve its own interests best by permitting Asian
affairs to develop along natural lines rather than by trying to force
them.

How much of this outlook rests on hope, how much on a Pan-Asian
approach whose roots are fifty years old or more, and how much on
direct exploration of the thoughts of Chinese policy makers, is difficult
to say. The idea that Japan can be a bridge to promote Sino-American
understanding springs in part from these considerations—the belief in
Chinese nationalism, in Chinese realism, in the special ability of Asians
(at least of Chinese and Japanese) to communicate with each other—or
simply from the observation that dealings with Orientals can be ex-
pedited by using go-betweens. The bridge theory has recently lost some
of its former appeal. Very few Japanese have been able to get a hearing
from those Chinese whom they have tried to persuade that a Sino-
American rapprochement is possible, and they have not had much better
success with the Americans. Further, some of the younger academic
China specialists now raise doubts about the existence of a special
Japanese understanding of the Chinese. They would prefer to see Japan's approach based on intensive analysis of the present realities of
China rather than on past connections, and they are not convinced that
Japan's capability in this field is as yet equal to the world's best. There
are also those, among them some younger scholars who definitely do
not identify themselves with the establishment but who proceed from
the standpoint of *realpolitik*, who favor an American-Japanese-Soviet
understanding directed toward containing China.[23] The Japanese government, however, has made few political overtures to the Soviet Union,
and these have achieved little by way of response.[24]

The role that Japan might have in an Asia from which Sino-American confrontation had been removed remains unclear. It can be argued,
as Foreign Minister Shiina Etsusaburô is reported to have done to
Secretary Dean Rusk when Rusk visited Japan in July, 1966, that Japan
and the United States have a common interest in promoting the PRC's
involvement in normal peaceful relations with the outside world, and

[23] Nagai Yônosuke, for instance, argues that a country insures its future best
by cultivating most intensively the friendship of those most able to do it
damage. In Japan's case, they would be the United States and the USSR rather
than China.

[24] See Mushakôji Kinhide, "Sino-U.S. Confrontation and Japan's Independent Diplomacy," *Ushio*, December, 1966.

that the expansion of Sino-Japanese trade can help draw China out of its isolation. Some Japanese emphasize that a suspicious approach to China impedes this process, whereas some definite manifestation of a trustful attitude would hasten it. Progress along these lines would be convenient for Japan and would create room for movement in Japan's China policy. On the other hand, it is theoretically conceivable that a Sino-American rapprochement could go so far that it would produce, if not condominium over Asia, some stable agreement on mutually respected spheres of influence. What Japan's role in such a future would be is debatable, unless Japan were intimately involved in all stages of the process. The Japanese government evidently does not envisage such a development in the foreseeable future.

Japan's official China policy seems to satisfy no one in the country. It is not even unanimously endorsed within the Foreign Ministry, which has so large a hand in making it. Yet it displays a remarkable degree of what some might call stability and others inertia, perhaps just because there are so many conflicting influences which bear on it. Communist China's protests against Japan's position on the question of China's representation in the United Nations, conclusion of a treaty with the Republic of Korea, permission for American nuclear-powered submarines to visit Japanese ports, participation in the Asian-Pacific Council (ASPAC), and alleged collusion with the United States and the USSR in a plot to contain China, etc., seem to have little effect on the Japanese government, if only because there is little prospect that the Chinese will take any action to back them up. There is no atmosphere of crisis surrounding the conduct of China policy, which therefore proceeds by dealing with those decisions which have to be made at the moment. Two factors play an important part in planning. One is that the temporizing approach for which the Foreign Ministry is often criticized is producing satisfactory results. The other is that the Ministry enters calculation of Japan's resources early in the planning process and is much aware of how limited they are.

One trend which can be observed in official policy-making is the trend toward regarding China policy less in bilateral terms and more in the context of Asia policy as a whole. Japan's Asia policy is coming to be defined as one of building on the status quo. As this principle is more clearly recognized, it will provide a basic common factor with U.S. policy toward Asia but produce certain differences in emphasis between the two. The Japanese government does not take it for granted that America's quarrel with the PRC is a necessary one or that the methods by which America's containment of China is being carried out are always correct. Thus the Japanese government avoids opposing

U.S. actions in Vietnam but does not endorse them without qualification. The Japanese also do not see a need to force other Asian countries to align themselves with the Free World against China. They tend rather to work toward providing the various Asian countries, aligned or non-aligned, with enhanced conditions for behaving as independent national entities and with greater freedom of maneuver in their relations with the larger powers. While this approach may produce some differences of interest between Japan and the United States in specific cases, it is also likely to develop long-term differences between Japan and the PRC, so long as the PRC pursues a strategy aimed at altering the status quo.

For the present, the making of China policy in Japan is of necessity more or less in abeyance. Its future evolution must wait on two things. First, it must await the outcome of the Cultural Revolution. Depending on which faction triumphs in the power struggle, the PRC's foreign policy is capable of developing in the future in quite different directions.[25] Depending on how much economic and political damage the cultural revolution does, the resources which the PRC will have available to devote to foreign affairs may be considerable or may be comparatively insignificant. Second, China's nuclear capability poses some unavoidable problems. This matter receives close attention and analysis in Japan, with the usual diversity of views, but on the whole not surrounded by an atmosphere of crisis. A point on which there seems to be general agreement is that the Chinese did not acquire nuclear weapons primarily for the purpose of using them in its relations with Japan. It is also quite widely recognized that having acquired such weapons, the Chinese may find ways of using them in dealing with Japan, and that there now exists a potential threat to Japan from the direction of the mainland, a situation which few Japanese have been disposed to worry about in the past. But it is difficult to determine how this threat may materialize concretely, and in just what foreseeable circumstances. The matter, therefore, must be kept under study but does not strike the Japanese as requiring immediate actions or decisions of them.[26]

[25] Japanese commentators refrain from committing themselves to firm predictions but enjoy their latitude for speculation. Some see the possibility that the Cultural Revolution may end in a process of de-Maoization comparable to de-Stalinization in the USSR.

[26] Compare, for example, a comment by Miyazawa Kiichi, who can be described as a prudent "new rightist," on the problem of security: "I consider this question by first affirming the fact that Japan is under America's nuclear deterrent. Therefore, I think the good way for Japan is to stay under the

The Cultural Revolution and China's nuclear capability have had a tremendous impact on Japan, at least in attracting the attention of the press and the public, modifying the Japanese image of China, and stimulating a certain complacent pride in Japan over its own freedom from comparable political perturbations. Some Japanese react to the Cultural Revolution with sarcastic glee, some with sympathy, some with studious attention.[27] All of them, however, agree on the need for more intensive study of the realities of China and for improved Sino-Japanese communication. I would hazard the guess that Japanese reaction to the stimuli provided by current events is not likely to have a decisive influence on Japan's China policy in the longer run. Rather, the emerging concepts of Japan's role in Asia and the world, definition of Japan's national interests and of the content of an autonomous foreign policy based on them, and views of China's role in world politics, which I have tried to describe above, will serve as the basis for major decisions when the time comes for making them. The shape of Japanese-American and Sino-American relations of course continues to affect these decisions. Recently, however, the Japanese sense of the situation emphasizes the necessity of adjusting to the realities of these relationships rather than the existence of pressure to acquiesce in American desires.

For reasons of proximity and history, most Japanese are more aware of China than most Americans and more inclined to believe that, whatever may happen in the short run, China is always going to be a very significant power and their country's relations with it are always going to be a central factor in their own role in the world. No observer of the Japanese dialogue on China can fail to be struck by the rise in the level of its professional competence in recent years. This applies to the Japanese analysis of all Chinese affairs, including the PRC's nuclear capability. It helps account for the fact that, while Japan's relations with China are not as between powers with equal ability to affect their common environment and symmetrical interest in doing so, nevertheless the Japanese dialogue on China addresses itself to major strategic questions as much as to subsidiary ones.

---

present set-up, especially when Communist China comes to have nuclear weapons. I say so in particular because, although I do not think Communist China's nuclear weapons are being manufactured with offensive intentions, they could become that way at any time through misunderstanding." See *Sankei Shinbun,* June 20, 1966.

[27] On its visit to China in September 1966, the Kosaka group showed less interest in interviewing Red Guards than in gathering information on the PRC's agricultural policy and defense structure or in probing Chinese attitudes toward the Satô government and the United States.

Comments by Marius B. Jansen

Mr. Halpern's paper points up important changes in the relations between Japan and China in recent years. No part of these changes is more striking than the images which the Japanese hold of China. This is an area of subjective impressions into which one enters warily, but it is also an area of great interest.

A decade ago most Japanese writing about contemporary China tended to use the vocabulary of the post-surrender and occupation era. There was great economic uncertainty, great doubt that Japan would be able to satisfy its needs for raw materials and markets without close ties with China. There was a lively fear of isolation from Asia, and a suspicion that the Chinese path of revolution and reform was likely to become normative for Asia. In committing herself to the West, Japan seemed somehow to be making a historic mistake for which future generations would have to pay. Periodicals and newspapers were also conspicuous for talk of the culture that Japan shared with China, and wrote of the debts of conscience and experience that Japan owed to China.

Japanese writing today is very different. War guilt has little meaning to younger Japanese, and even for the middle and older generations the violence that has broken out throughout the world since 1945 has had the effect of watering down the sense of Japan's unique criminality. The theme of "common culture" also loses more of its meaning with every year. The Chinese generation that was educated in Japan or through Japanese books is passing, as is the Japanese generation that was steeped in classical Chinese civilization and that struggled to find meaning and mission for its country in ties with modern China. The two cultures grow constantly farther apart. Japanese travelers are often incredulous at Chinese ignorance of Japan, and astonished to find Chinese convinced that they have direct leverage in Japanese politics. Chinese is less important to the Japanese curriculum, and Japanese culture scarcely treated in Chinese universities. Although the wallposter era gave Japanese reporters in China a temporary advantage over their Western competitors, Chinese alterations of the written language even throw doubt on the old and favorite arguments about a common writing system. The area of shared experience between the two countries is diminishing; for the younger generation coming into positions of authority it is virtually nonexistent. Japanese travelers today seem more impressed by the contrasts which the contrasting rates of modernization create between Japan and China than they are by comparisons. It becomes recognized that proximity makes the two countries important to each other, but has little effect upon the warmth or understanding between them.

Nor is there nearly as much talk today about the abnormality and impermanence of the state of official relations between China and Japan. "Normal" is in any case increasingly difficult to define in a relationship that has been so consistently difficult. The century of modern diplomatic relationships between China and Japan that followed those of mutual isolation was remarkable for a series of acrimonious disputes over Okinawa, Formosa, Korea, Shantung, and Manchuria as a result of which Japan bore the chief brunt of modern Chinese nationalism. This was not the whole of Sino-Japanese relations by any means, but it tended to dominate the rest. Actually, it could be argued that the present "abnormality" constitutes one of the longest periods of peace between the two countries since the mid-nineteenth century.

Perhaps one can conclude that no easy relationship is possible, given the differences in size, wealth, and industrial power, between the two countries. In modern times neither has been able or willing to think of the other as its leader, or even, in fact, as a full equal. Instead there have been successive attempts, and so far failures, to "lead" the other or to "liberate" it from Western dominance.

The discovery by the Japanese that prosperity is possible without a close China tie is central to the change from the nervous view of the 1950's to the more relaxed posture of the 1960's. Japan's policies and alignments have not only brought it prosperity and security within the Western circle but, as the Halpern paper shows, a very strategic place at the bargaining table with China. As the businessman's monthly *Diamond* put it in December, 1966, it has been proved that "economic interchange is not being interrupted by Japan's affiliation with the West and China's with the East." China, the analysis continued, cannot carry out its goals without approaching the capitalist camp more closely, and Japan has an excellent chance of dealing with China from within that camp.

The story of Sino-Japanese economic relations is fully of irony. Economics and ideology are inseparable, according to Chairman Mao, but in fact the Chinese have been willing to separate them, while the Japanese government, whose official standpoint has been to separate them, has in fact preferred steps (like the Liao-Takasaki formula of 1962) which lessen the "private" role of "friendly firms" and thereby the Chinese ability to manipulate prices through competition and politics through favoritism. Japanese governmental efforts to achieve this never proved successful, but the Chinese Communists have now assisted Tokyo by punitive measures against the "friendly" firms that were tied in with the Japanese Communist Party.

China's resolute repudiation of East European trade has deprived it temporarily, at least, of the opportunity to work seriously at influencing Japanese politics through trade agreements. In 1965 and 1966 trade prospered beyond even the anticipations of Japanese government planners of a half decade ago. For a time in 1966 China became Japan's second most important export market (although figures for trade with the United States, more than ten times larger, have been more stable, and show faster growth), while Japan was temporarily first (after Hong Kong) for China. Of course Japanese will always wish for more of China's trade, and Mr. Halpern points out the particular importance of that trade for several more or less marginal industries in Japan. But the limitations on that trade do not lie with Peking's policies alone. They are to be found in China's inability to pay for more imports, Japanese governmental refusal to grant long-term credits, and Japanese industrialists' hesitation to jeopardize far larger and more important accounts with the United States. Political considerations like the importance of Taiwan, the late Premier Yoshida's reassurances (by letter of May, 1964) to Chiang Kai-shek about deferred credits to the mainland, and American and Soviet policies, all come in to complicate the scene further. And as could be expected, the confusion of the Cultural Revolution seems to have affected trade totals also. The point to make, however, is that it is no longer easy for Japanese to assign praise or blame in simple, one-dimensional terms in the way that was common a decade ago. As a result the Japanese government has more maneuverability than it has enjoyed since the war, and the consequences of this are greater confidence and security within Japan.

1967 also found the Japanese a good deal less worried about being "isolated" from Asia than they professed to be a decade ago. Instead it is the Chinese government that seems to have isolated itself by its policies. Japan, for all its American ties, is in as good a position for contacts with China as any other country. China itself seems less of a closed book for Japan than it is for other countries. Japanese visitors far outnumber other foreigners in China, and in the past few years their number has gone up from around two thousand to over five thousand. (In contrast, there were only about five hundred mainland Chinese among the more than four hundred thousand foreigners who visited Japan in 1966.) The increased scale of travel from Japan has resulted in far more varied verdicts on China. The earlier visits tended to be made by groups of invited guests, who responded to what they were shown with courtesy and praise. But more recent traffic has included people who are more independent and vastly more critical.

The Cultural Revolution as reported through these eyes was significant chiefly for the way it served to highlight changes in attitude that were already in progress in Japan. It was the first of the mass movements in China to be fully reported to Japanese by their own writers. It dominated the newspapers and magazines for months, and it seems to have had great effect on many Japanese liberals.

Particularly striking evidence of this came from the numerous reports published by a group of intellectuals led by Oya Soichi who visited China in the fall of 1966. These men paid their own way, and felt free to refuse invitations and reject insults. They taped their impressions every evening, and for several months upon their return the press and periodicals were full of their observations and reflections. Of course no group is "typical," but Oya and his friends popularized a kind of cynical, acerbic, and often derisive comment that would have been quite unthinkable in Japan ten years ago. A few examples will illustrate.

The Peoples Liberation Army, instead of impressing the group, struck them as remarkably similar, in its amuletic use of the phrases of Mao Tse-tung, to what the Japanese Imperial Army used to do with Imperial Rescripts. They told their hosts the Imperial Army probably had better discipline and spirit, however, and reminded them of its fate when it met superior technology. The Chinese people's daily life, they suggested, was rather like the wartime life of the Japanese; as the latter bowed before the imperial palace, the Chinese would soon bow before the Tienanmen. They were revolted by the personality cult of Mao, and lost no opportunity to lampoon it. The Cultural Revolution they described as uncultured, as a paint revolution (for the plethora of signs and slogans), and as a duck revolution (because everyone they met quacked the same way). And, in what is perhaps the ultimate in disrespect for Japanese intellectuals, they suggested at one point that Soka Gakkai members be recruited to compete with Red Guards in street

corner evangelizing. Even the memory of the Pacific War could backfire; when Chao An-po, of the China-Japan Friendship Association,
made his usual statement of sympathy for Japanese bondage to the
United States, Oya and his friends professed insult and refused to
attend a dinner arranged for them. They reflected caustically that Chao
used to brainwash Japanese prisoners at Yenan, and suspected that he
still thought of all Japanese as captives.

The Cultural Revolution has thus served to remind Japanese that,
in the words of the *Mainichi*, "China is not a free nation like Japan."
Of course it finds defenders and apologists in Tokyo also. But the
principal response has been one of astonishment. The romantic image
of a heroic, dynamic, and progressive China is not dead, but it is badly
tarnished. One wonders, at times, whether some old Japanese attitudes
toward China as unorganized and unorganizable, may not find new life
again. The distinguished Sinologist Yoshikawa Kōjirō raised a voice of
warning in the *Asahi* of January 6, 1967, to suggest to his countrymen
that they adopt a more modest tone and stop talking about a "China
problem." Japanese never, he pointed out, talk about an "America
problem" or a "Russia problem"; how would they like to find "Japan
Problem Study Center" signs everywhere in America?

In the final analysis, however, most of this comment can be traced to
a new-found sense of self-confidence and national consciousness in
Japan. Professor Yoshikawa himself adds a cultural dimension in re-
gretting that, of all major peoples, the Chinese have expressed perhaps
the least interest in Japanese civilization. Some twenty universities in
Japan teach Chinese literature, he suggests, but he has yet to hear of
one in China that teaches Japanese literature.

There can thus be little argument with Mr. Halpern's reminder that
the basic determinants of Japanese attitudes toward China lie within
Japan. China is not a vote-getting issue, as Mr. Halpern says and as the
socialists have just found out again. (It may, however, have been a vote-
losing issue.) Surely the most important development, then, is the fact
that the Japanese once again think it no shame to be pro-Japanese. A
new practicality has come into discussions of Japan's place in the world
and Japan's needs for defense; and there is new readiness to treat with
logic issues that until very recently were seen chiefly in emotional terms.
Undoubtedly the Chinese bombs have contributed to this trend. If the
development of a nuclear threat was meant partly to convince the Japanese that the American alliance was dangerous, for many it has had
exactly the opposite effect. An important group of "new realists" now

present the public with long discussions of defense alternatives and needs.

Although these developments have been long in coming, they are still affected by many variables that lie outside Japan. The world economy, the political stability of Southeast Asia, and Sino-American relations all bear directly on what has been said. A strong and successful China could undo much of the harm that a hysterical and divided China has done. But it seems reasonable to predict that whatever commitments the Japanese people and government make in the future will be entered into with more reflection and more dispassion because of the events of the mid-1960's. And for the present, one may say that the China-Japan relationship has more in it to please Tokyo than it does to please Peking. China's convulsive efforts have for the moment reduced its freedom of action, while Japan's caution and restraint have brought it more maneuverability than it has enjoyed since the end of the Pacific War.

Contributors

Frank E. Armbruster, director of the Guerrilla Warfare Studies and co-director of European Security Studies at the Hudson Institute, is a specialist in political and military operations analysis. Mr. Armbruster works on area studies of a political-military nature on China, Southeast Asia, and Europe, as well as on the analysis of present and future weapon systems and force postures of the United States and Soviet Union strategic forces.

Davis B. Bobrow, senior social scientist, Director's Division, Oak Ridge National Laboratory, has written numerous articles on Communist China and edited and contributed to *Components of Defense Policy.*

Michael Brecher, professor of political science and head, South Asia Programme, Centre for Developing-Area Studies, McGill University, has written *The Struggle for Kashmir; Nehru: A Political Biography; The New States of Asia; Succession in India: A Study in Decision-Making;* and (forthcoming) *Krishna Menon, India and World Politics.*

The late *M. J. Desai* was Commonwealth Secretary to the government of India in 1954 and again from 1955 to 1960. He served as chairman of the International Commission for Supervision and Control in Vietnam from September, 1954, to December, 1955. Mr. Desai was Foreign Secretary from 1961 to 1963, and Secretary-General in the Ministry of External Affairs in 1963 and 1964.

Richard A. Falk, the Albert G. Milbank Professor of International Law and Practice at Princeton University, coeditor of *World Politics,* an editor of the *American Journal of International Law,* and associate editor of *The Journal of Conflict Resolution,* has written *Law, Morality, and War in the Contemporary World; The Role of Domestic Courts in the International Legal Order;* and *Legal Order in a Violent World.* He is editor of *Security in Disarmament* (with R. J. Barnet) and *The Strategy of World Order* (with S. H. Mendlovita).

465

Norton Ginsburg, professor of geography at the University of Chicago, is the author of *Atlas of Economic Development* and (with C. F. Roberts, Jr.) *Malaya.* He edited *The Pattern of Asia* and *Essays on Geography and Economic Development* and was general editor of *An Historical Atlas of China.*

Samuel B. Griffith II, Brigadier General, USMC (ret.), of the Hoover Institution, Stanford University, has written *Sun Tzu: The Art of War; Mao Tse-tung: On Guerrilla Warfare; Peking and People's Wars; The Battle for Guadalcanal;* and *The Chinese People's Liberation Army.* He has contributed articles to *Foreign Affairs, Diplomat, Réalités, Saturday Evening Post, Town and Country,* and *The New Yorker.*

Morton H. Halperin, Deputy Assistant Secretary of Defense (ISA) for Policy Planning and Arms Control, is the author of *China and the Bomb, Communist China and Arms Control* (with Dwight H. Perkins), and *Contemporary Military Strategy* and is the editor of *Sino-Soviet Relations and Arms Control.*

Abraham M. Halpern, research associate at the Center for International Affairs at Harvard University, is the editor of *Policies Toward China: Views from Six Continents* and has written numerous articles on China. He is at present completing a book-length study of the foreign policy of the People's Republic of China and is working on a study of Japan's national security policy.

Roger Hilsman is professor of government at Columbia University. His most recent book is *To Move a Nation: The Politics of Foreign Policy in the Administration of John F. Kennedy.* He was Assistant Secretary of State for Far Eastern Affairs during the administration of John F. Kennedy.

Harold C. Hinton, professor of international affairs at the George Washington University and staff member of the Institute for Defense Analyses, is the author of *Communist China in World Politics* and has contributed to the volumes *Major Governments of Asia* and *Total War and Cold War.*

Marius B. Jansen, professor of history and director of the East Asian Studies Program at Princeton University, is the author of *The Japanese and Sun Yat-sen* and *Sakamoto Ryōma and the Meiji Restoration* and is the editor of *Changing Japanese Attitudes toward Modernization.*

George McT. Kahin, professor of government, director of the Southeast Asia Program at Cornell University, and director of the Cornell Modern Indonesia Project, has written *Nationalism and Revolution in Indonesia, The Asian-African Conference,* and (with John W. Lewis) *The United States in Vietnam.* He is the editor of *Major Governments of Asia* and *Governments and Politics of Southeast Asia.*

Morton A. Kaplan, professor of political science and chairman of the Committee on International Relations at the University of Chicago, has written *United States Foreign Policy, 1945–1955* (with William Reitzel and Constance G. Coblenz), *System and Process in International Politics,* and *Political Foundations of International Law* (with Nicholas Katzenbach).

Richard Lowenthal, professor of international relations at the Otto Suhr Institute (of political science) at the Free University of Berlin, has written *World Communism, the Disintegration of a Secular Faith* and (with Willy Brandt) *Ernst Reuter: Ein Leben für die Freiheit, eine Politische Biographie.*

Roderick MacFarquhar, editor of *The China Quarterly,* and associate fellow of St. Antony's College, Oxford, is the author of *The Hundred Flowers Campaign and the Chinese Intellectuals* and coauthor of *The Sino-Soviet Dispute.*

Ruth T. McVey, research associate of the Cornell Modern Indonesia Project at Cornell University, has written *The Rise of Indonesian Communism* and articles on Asian affairs. She also edited *Indonesia.*

Hans J. Morgenthau, the Albert A. Michelson Distinguished Service Professor of Political Science and History and director of the Center for Study of American Foreign and Military Policy at the University of Chicago, has written *Scientific Man vs. Power Politics, Politics Among Nations, In Defense of the National Interest, Dilemmas of Politics, The Purpose of American Politics, Politics in the Twentieth Century,* and *Vietnam and the United States.*

David Mozingo, assistant professor of government at Cornell University, has written *Sino-Indonesian Relations: An Overview, 1955–1965; Lin Piao On "People's War": China Takes a Second Look at Vietnam* (with T. W. Robinson); and "Containment in Asia Reconsidered," in *World Politics.* Forthcoming publications include "Communist China and her Southern Border Lands," in *Perspectives on Communist China.*

Uri Ra'anan is professor of international politics, the Fletcher School of Law and Diplomacy, Tufts University; visiting professor of political science and research associate at the Center for International Studies, Massachusetts Institute of Technology; and associate, the Russian Research Center, Harvard University.

Robert A. Scalapino, professor of political science at the University of California, Berkeley, and editor of *Asian Survey,* is the author of *The Chinese Anarchist Movement* (with George T. Yu), *Parties and Politics in Contemporary Japan* (with Junnosuke Masumi), and *The Japanese Communist Movement, 1920–1966.* He is the editor of *The Communist Revolution in Asia* and *North Korea Today.*

George E. Taylor, chairman of the Department of Far Eastern and Slavic Languages and Literature and director of the Far Eastern and Russian Institute at the University of Washington, has written *The Struggle for North China, The Far East in the Modern World* (with Franz Michael), *The Philippines and the United States: Problems of Partnership,* and *The New United Nations: A Reappraisal of United States Policies* (with Ben Cashman).

Vincent D. Taylor, RAND Corporation economist, is a specialist in the field of nuclear strategy and weapon-system choice.

Paul A. Varg, dean of the College of Arts and Letters, Michigan State University, has written *Open Door Diplomat: The Life of W. W. Rockhill; Missionaries, Chinese, and Diplomats: The American Protestant Missionary Movement in China, 1890–1952;* and *Foreign Policies of the Founding Fathers.*

Wayne Wilcox, associate professor of government and research member of the Institute of War and Peace Studies at Columbia University, is the author of *Pakistan: The Consolidation of a Nation; India, Pakistan and the Rise of China;* and *Asia and United States Policy.*

Donald Zagoria is an associate professor of government and director of the Research Institute on Modern Asia at Hunter College, the City University of New York. His publications include *Sino-Soviet Conflict,* and he is currently working on a book on Indian Communism.

Index

U